The
AMERICAN HERITAGE®

Dictionary *of* Phrasal Verbs

HOUGHTON MIFFLIN COMPANY
Boston • New York

Visit our website: www.houghtonmifflinbooks.com

Library of Congress Cataloging-in-Publication Data

The American heritage dictionary of phrasal verbs.
p. cm.
ISBN-13: 978-0-618-59260-9
ISBN-10: 0-618-59260-1
1. English language--Verb phrase--Dictionaries. I. Houghton Mifflin Company.
PE1319.A57 2005
423'.1--dc22

2005012835

Manufactured in the United States of America

ABCDEFGH-MP-098765

Table of Contents

Editorial & Production Staff

Vice President, Publisher of Dictionaries
Margery S. Berube

Vice President, Executive Editor
Joseph S. Pickett

Senior Editor
Steven R. Kleinedler

Editors
Susan I. Spitz
Catherine Pratt

Associate Editors
Erich M. Groat
Uchenna C. Ikonné
Patrick Taylor

Editorial Assistant
Nicholas A. Durlacher

Vice President, Managing Editor
Christopher Leonesio

Database Production Supervisor
Christopher Granniss

Art and Production Supervisor
Margaret Anne Miles

Editorial Production Assistant
Katherine M. Getz

Production Assistance
Tracy Duff

Proofreader
Diane Fredrick

Text Design
Catherine Hawkes, Cat & Mouse

Guide to the Dictionary of Phrasal Verbs

The American Heritage® Dictionary of Phrasal Verbs defines thousands of phrasal verbs. This guide explains how to use the information presented in this Dictionary.

A phrasal verb is a combination of an ordinary verb and a preposition or an adverbial particle that has at least one particular meaning that is not predictable from the combined literal meanings of the verb and the preposition or particle. Prepositions and particles include words like *back*, *in*, *off*, *on*, and *up*.

For example, the basic meaning of *make* is roughly "to create, to do." *Off* is both a preposition, as in *I took the books off the table*, and an adverbial particle, as in *I took my shoes off. Off* imparts a sense of removal or of motion away from a place. The phrasal verb *make off* has the sense "to depart in haste; run away," as in *I quietly left the room and made off as fast as I could*. Knowing the meanings of both *make* and *off* is not enough to be able to understand this special sense of *make off*. This Dictionary defines thousands of phrasal verbs like *make off*.

This Dictionary does not include entries whose sole meanings are a combination of the literal meaning of the verb and the literal meaning of preposition or particle. Such literal combinations are included for phrasal verbs that also have nonliteral meanings. The senses at **back down** are an example of this. There, the literal senses are given first, followed by nonliteral ones.

Guidewords

A boldface guideword at the top of each even-numbered page shows the first main entry or phrasal verb on that page, and a boldface guideword at the top of each odd-numbered page shows the last entry on that page. For example, on pages 16 and 17 **bask** and **be behind** are guidewords. They and all of the entries that fall alphabetically between them appear on these two pages.

Main Entries

The symbol ◆ is placed before the main verb that is associated with a phrasal verb or set of phrasal verbs. Each main verb is listed in alphabetical order. The phrasal verb or set of phrasal verbs associated with that main verb then follow alphabetically: ◆ **stir, stir in, stir up,** ◆ **stitch, stitch up,** ◆ **stock, stock up**.

Variant Forms

If a verb has two or more different spellings, the most common spelling is presented first in boldface type as the entry word, followed by less common variant spellings, which are also in boldface and are separated from the main form by the word *or*. An example of this is at **sync:**

◆ **sync** *or* **synch** (sĭngk)

If all of the meanings of two phrasal verbs are shared, these phrasal verbs are shown together at an entry, separated by *or*. An example of this is at **pivot on:**

pivot on *or* **pivot around**

The more common form is listed first; however, both forms are equally acceptable.

For information about variants in inflections, see "Inflected Forms" below.

Pronunciations

Pronunciations appear in parentheses after boldface entry words and inflections.

◆ **pave** (pāv)

If a word has more than one pronunciation, the first pronunciation given is usually more common than the other pronounciations, but often they occur with equal frequency. The pronunciation symbols used in this Dictionary are shown on page xii.

Inflected Forms

Following each entry word are the inflected forms—the past tense, past participle, present participle, and present tense, third-person singular—entered in boldface type. The pronunciation of each inflected form is shown.

Three Forms: If the past tense and past participle of a verb have the same form, three inflected forms are shown in this order: past tense, present participle, present tense of the third person singular. An example of this is **bounce,** which has the past tense form and the past participle form **bounced,** the present participle form **bouncing,** and the third person singular present tense form **bounces.**

◆ **bounce** (bouns)
bounced (bounst), **bouncing**
(boun′sĭng), **bounces** (boun′sĭz)

Four forms: If the past tense is different from the past participle, four inflected forms are shown in this order: past tense, past participle, present participle, present tense of the third person singular. An example of this is **blow,** which has the past tense form **blew,** the past participle form **blown,** the present participle form **blowing,** and the third person singular present tense form **blows.**

> ◆ **blow** (blō)
> **blew** (blo͞o), **blown** (blōn), **blowing**
> (blō′ĭng), **blows** (blōz)

Variants: Sometimes an inflection has a variant, and this is indicated by the word *or,* as at **bid.** In this example, the past tense form can be **bade** or **bid,** the past participle form can be **bidden** or **bid,** the present participle form is **bidding,** and the third person singular present tense form is **bids.**

> ◆ **bid** (bĭd)
> **bade** (băd, bād) *or* **bid** (bĭd), **bidden**
> (bĭd′n) *or* **bid** (bĭd), **bidding**
> (bĭd′ĭng), **bids** (bĭdz)

Be: All of the forms of *be* are shown because that verb is completely irregular.

Definitions and Examples

This Dictionary uses example sentences to show how each phrasal verb is used. These example sentences have been carefully designed to convey the meaning, tone, and grammatical structure of each definition.

The definitions of phrasal verbs that are associated with one or more objects are defined by using words such as *some, someone, something,* and *somewhere.* These words indicate the kind of object or objects typically required by the verb.

Phrasal Verbs Associated with One Object

Many phrasal verbs take only one object. This object can usually be placed either before or after the preposition or particle. This variable word order is shown with two example sentences, one for each possibility, as at the second sense of **billow out:**

> To cause something to stretch or puff out: *The wind billowed the sails out. The breeze billowed out the sheets that were hung up on the clothesline.*

In the first example, the noun phrase *the sails* comes between *billowed* and *out*. In the second example, the noun phrase *the sheets* follows *billowed out*. (When the object is a pronoun, the particle almost always follows the object. Thus, *The wind billowed them out* is acceptable, while *The wind billowed out them* is not.)

If an object is given in all of the examples, an object is always required. In some contexts, the object of a phrasal verb can be dropped entirely. In this case, at least two example sentences will be shown: one with the object, and one without. An example of this is at the first sense of **log in:**

> To provide the necessary information to a computer for someone to be allowed to access computer resources; log on: *I'll log you in so that you can access the library's resources. I sat at the terminal and logged in using my student account.*

In the first example sentence, the object *you* is explicitly stated. In the second sentence, there is no object, indicating that with this phrasal verb, the object does not need to be explicitly stated.

Some phrasal verbs require that the object follow the preposition or particle. An example of this is at **grow on:**

> **1.** To be nourished by something and develop in size or quality: *Wheat does not grow on sandy soil. Baby mice grow on only a few drops of milk every hour.*
> **2.** To become gradually more evident to someone: *A feeling of distrust grew on me.*

In these cases, the absence of an example in which the object comes between the verb and the preposition or particle implies that this word order is not customary.

Rarely, some phrasal verbs require that the object must come between the verb and the preposition or particle.

Phrasal Verbs Associated with Two Objects

If a phrasal verb takes more than one object, expressions using *some*, *something*, *someone*, etc. will be found in the definition more than once, and the position of these *some*-words in the definition will indicate the position in which the objects occur with the phrasal verb. An example of this can be found at the first definition of **pepper with:**

To intersperse something with something else, especially to make it more exciting, interesting, or colorful: *She peppers her stories with interesting details. Our vacation consisted of long days at the beach peppered with exciting trips to the city.*

Thus, the two objects in the definition correspond with two objects used with the verb, the first an object of the verb itself, and the second the object of the preposition *with*.

Three-word phrasal verbs

Most phrasal verbs are used with optional prepositional phrases, and some prepositions are especially common in association with a particular phrasal verb. The example sentences show the kinds of prepositional phrases typically associated with the phrasal verb. Sometimes, a phrasal verb may have an additional sense when a certain preposition is used with it. If the preposition is necessary for a given meaning, all three words are shown in boldface type before the definition. For example, the phrasal verbs **get in on** and **get in with** are listed under **get in,** which has other senses as well:

get in

1. To enter something...
8. get in on To gain access to or knowledge of something: *At the dance club, we got in on the latest dance moves. Everybody wanted to get in on the secret.*
9. get in with To become involved with something, especially with some group: *She got in with a bad group of people.*

If the phrasal verb occurs only as a three-word combination, it will appear as a headword:

nose in on

To listen in on or get involved in something where one's presence is not wanted: *You're always nosing in on my conversations, and I wish you'd stop.*

Phrasal Verbs Associated with No Objects

Some phrasal verbs never occur with objects. In these cases, the definitions do not include words like *someone* and *something,* and their example sentences do not have any objects, as at **black out:**

> To stop emitting light; go out: *The traffic lights blacked out when the storm knocked down power lines.*

Often, only one example sentence is shown at these kinds of phrasal verbs.

Passive Constructions

Some phrasal verbs commonly occur in passive constructions in which the subject of the verb is the object of the action. A passive form of *She ate the pear,* for example, is *The pear was eaten*, in which the object *the pear* now acts as the subject of the sentence. These passive constructons are illustrated in the example sentences.

If the definition includes the phrase *Used in the passive*, this means that the *only* way the phrasal verb can be used is in the passive. The definition is therefore written as if there were no active form of the phrasal verb at all, and the subject of the definition corresponds to the subject of the phrasal verb in the example sentences. An example of this is the second sense of **root in:**

> To have something as a primary source or origin. Used in the passive: *The cause of much homelessness is rooted in poverty. The word "tantalize" is rooted in Greek mythology.*

If the definition includes the phrase *Used chiefly in the passive*, then the definition will be given for the active voice, but the examples will likely be in the passive. If examples in the active are shown, this is to suggest that the active use is possible but less common; if none are shown, then they are relatively uncommon. An example of this is the second sense of **face with:**

> To force someone to confront or deal with something or someone. Used chiefly in the passive: *When I'm faced with a problem, I ask my parents for advice.*

The definition includes the word *someone* as the direct object of the verb, and the words *something* or *someone* as the objects of the preposition *with*. But in the example sentence, we see only one object, *a problem* (the object of *with*). Here, the example sentence is passive. The person being forced to confront something—the verb's object in the definition—is the subject in the example sentence. Sentences such as *His new job faced him with a problem* are rare if not unidiomatic.

Labels

Slang words are used chiefly in informal or casual speech, and are used in place of standard terms for added humor, irreverence, or some other effect. If all the senses of a phrasal verb are slang, this is indicated by the label Slang at the beginning of the entry. If only some of the senses of a phrasal verb are slang, that label appears at the beginning of each of those senses.

Most phrasal verbs are somewhat informal, although the degree of informality often depends on the context. When the use of a phrasal verb in a particular sense is informal, the tone of the example sentences and the situations they describe suggest the level of the phrasal verb's informality.

Vulgar senses are indicated with the label Vulgar Slang.

Pronunciation Key

ă	pat
ā	pay
âr	care
ä	father
är	car
b	bib
ch	church
d	deed, milled
ĕ	pet
ē	be, bee
f	fife, phase, rough
g	gag
h	hat
hw	which
ĭ	pit
ī	pie, by
îr	dear, deer, pier
j	judge
k	kick, cat, pique
l	lid, needle
m	mum
n	no, sudden
ng	thing
ŏ	pot
ō	toe
ô	caught, paw
ôr	core
oi	noise, boy
o͝o	took
o͝or	lure
o͞o	boot
ou	out
p	pop
r	roar
s	sauce
sh	ship, dish
t	tight, stopped
th	thin
th	this
ŭ	cut
ûr	urge, term, firm, word, heard
v	valve
w	with
y	yes
z	zebra, xylem
zh	vision, pleasure, garage
ə	about, item, edible, gallon, circus

Foreign

œ	French	feu
	German	schön
ü	French	tu
KH	German	ich
	Scottish	loch
N	French	bon

The symbol (ə) is called *schwa*. It represents a vowel with the weakest level of stress in a word. The schwa sound varies slightly according to the vowel it represents or the sounds around it.

Stress is the relative degree of emphasis with which a word's syllables are spoken. An unmarked syllable has the weakest stress in the word. The strongest, or primary, stress is indicated with a bold mark (**′**). A lighter mark (′) indicates a secondary level of stress. The stress mark follows the syllable it applies to. Words of one syllable have no stress mark, because there is no other stress level that the syllable is compared to.

A

◆ **abandon** (ə-băn**′**dən)

abandoned (ə-băn**′**dənd), **abandoning** (ə-băn**′**də-nĭng), **abandons** (ə-băn**′**dənz)

abandon to

1. To desert someone or something in some situation: *Because it was too dangerous for us to save our sinking boat, we had to abandon it to the storm's waves.*
2. To allow someone to accept or enjoy something without resisting it. Used reflexively: *At the amusement park I abandoned myself to the excitement of the roller coaster rides.*

◆ **abound** (ə-bound**′**)

abounded (ə-boun**′**dĭd), **abounding** (ə-boun**′**dĭng), **abounds** (ə-boundz**′**)

abound with *or* **abound in**

To be brimming with something plentiful: *The lake by the cabin abounds with fish. The quaint villa abounded in charm.*

◆ **abstain** (ăb-stān**′**)

abstained (ăb-stānd**′**), **abstaining** (ăb-stā**′**nĭng), **abstains** (ăb-stānz**′**)

abstain from

To have made a deliberate choice not to do something: *I abstained from eating fatty foods when I was on my diet. The minister abstained from drinking alcohol.*

◆ **account** (ə-kount**′**)

accounted (ə-kount**′**ĭd), **accounting** (ə-koun**′**tĭng), **accounts** (ə-kounts**′**)

account for

1. To keep a record of how money has been spent: *The job of the treasurer is to account for every penny that is earned or spent.*
2. To know or find out where something or someone is: *She has accounted for every item that was missing.*
3. To explain or justify something: *This is a good theory, and it accounts for all the data that the scientists collected. How do you account for their strange behavior?*
4. To form some proportion or amount of a larger whole or group: *These useless catalogs account for at least half the mail we get every day.*
5. To be the reason or explanation for something: *His good manners account for his popularity.*

◆ **accustom** (ə-kŭs**′**təm)

accustomed (ə-kŭs**′**təmd), **accustoming** (ə-kŭs**′**tə-mĭng), **accustoms** (ə-kŭs**′**təmz)

ă	pat	är	car	ī	bite	ô	paw	ŏŏ	took	ûr	urge
ā	pay	ĕ	pet	îr	pier	ôr	core	ŏŏr	lure	zh	vision
âr	care	ē	be	ŏ	pot	oi	boy	ōō	boot	ə	about,
ä	father	ĭ	pit	ō	toe	ou	out	ŭ	cut		item

accustom to

To bring someone or something into a condition that is harmonious with something else, especially through repeated experience: *I have accustomed myself to waking up when the sun rises. They are not accustomed to such formal clothing.*

◆ **acquaint** (ə-kwānt′)

acquainted (ə-kwān′tĭd), **acquainting** (ə-kwān′tĭng), **acquaints** (ə-kwānts′)

acquaint with

To make someone familiar with something or someone: *The next chapter of the textbook acquaints the student with several new concepts. I am not acquainted with the mayor of this town, although I would like to meet her.*

◆ **act** (ăkt)

acted (ăk′tĭd), **acting** (ăk′tĭng), **acts** (ăkts)

act out

1. To communicate something through actions rather than words: *In a game of charades, you describe words by acting them out. One comedian acted out simple phrases, and the other one tried to guess what they were.*
2. To play some role: *The first graders acted out the roles of the villagers in the school play.*
3. To fulfill some role: *Though they no longer trusted him, they continued to act out their parts as good wife and daughter.*
4. To express some feeling or emotion behaviorally, especially unconsciously: *I understand why you're angry, but I don't like the way you're acting out your aggression toward me.*
5. To demonstrate bad behavior or negative feelings: *The student was upset after losing the game and began to act out in class.*

act up

1. To misbehave: *The driver stopped the school bus because the kids were acting up. When my children act up, I send them to their rooms for an hour.*
2. To cause problems by operating strangely or unexpectedly: *The thermostat suddenly started acting up, and now it's always too hot or too cold in here.*
3. To become active or troublesome after a period of operating normally: *My knee starts acting up when the weather is cold.*

◆ **adapt** (ə-dăpt′)

adapted (ə-dăp′tĭd), **adapting** (ə-dăp′tĭng), **adapts** (ə-dăpts′)

adapt to

1. To alter something so that it is better suited to something else: *The immigrants adapted their cooking recipes to the ingredients that were available in their new country.*
2. To change in order to be better suited to something: *At first, I didn't like the new school, but I quickly adapted to the way things were done there and was soon very happy.*

◆ **add** (ăd)

added (ăd′ĭd), **adding** (ăd′ĭng), **adds** (ădz)

add on

1. To increase, by some additional amount, a quantity that is associated with something: *The waiter added $5 on the bill for the extra pretzels we ordered. That tip is too low for the good service we had, so let's add on another dollar. Last night, the storm added on more than twenty inches to the record snowfall.*
2. To attach something in order to extend or enlarge something else: *We're adding another room on the back of the house. The guest list is full, so we can't add anybody else on. If there aren't enough logs in the fire, add another one on.*

add to

To increase the amount or intensity of something: *The increase in fuel prices will add to the cost of living in the city. After I broke my arm, I added to my misery by chipping a tooth.*

add up

1. To calculate a sum by adding some set of numbers: *The students added up the numbers they had copied from the blackboard. If you add all the scores up, we'll find out who won.*
2. To calculate something, especially by addition: *The shopkeeper added up the day's profits.*
3. To amount to an expected total: *Unfortunately, when we put the numbers into the equation, they did not add up.*
4. To be reasonable, plausible, or consistent; make sense: *The jury did not believe the witness's testimony because it simply did not add up.*

◆ **address** (ə-drĕs′)

addressed (ə-drĕst′), **addressing** (ə-drĕs′ĭng), **addresses** (ə-drĕs′ĭz)

address to

1. To indicate that something is to be sent to someone or some place by writing an address on it: *She addressed the letter to her brother.*
2. To say something directly to some specific person or group: *The school president addressed the speech to everyone who plans to graduate this year.*
3. To focus someone on a problem in order to find a solution. Used reflexively: *In the next meeting, the town officials will address themselves to the issue of privacy.*

◆ **adhere** (ăd-hîr′)

adhered (ăd-hîrd′), **adhering** (ăd-hîr′ĭng), **adheres** (ăd-hîrz′)

adhere to

1. To stick or cling to the surface of something: *After the fire, soot and smoke adhered to the walls.*
2. To follow some law, set of beliefs, or course of action: *Let's adhere to the plan we already discussed. You need to adhere to our rules very strictly if you want to join our organization.*
3. To believe that some idea is true or right: *Although some people are*

ă	pat	är	car	ī	bite	ô	paw	o͝o	took	ûr	urge
ā	pay	ĕ	pet	îr	pier	ôr	core	o͝or	lure	zh	vision
âr	care	ē	be	ŏ	pot	oi	boy	o͞o	boot	ə	about, item
ä	father	ĭ	pit	ō	toe	ou	out	ŭ	cut		

skeptical, most people adhere to the notion that our changing climate is a serious problem.

◆ **adjust** (ə-jŭst′)

adjusted (ə-jŭs′tĭd), **adjusting** (ə-jŭs′tĭng), **adjusts** (ə-jŭsts′)

adjust to

1. To alter something to make it fit, accommodate, or match something else: *We adjusted the radio to the frequency of the radio transmission.*
2. To get used to something or someone: *It took many years for me to adjust to the cold winters in Vermont.*

◆ **admit** (ăd-mĭt′)

admitted (ăd-mĭt′ĭd), **admitting** (ăd-mĭt′ĭng), **admits** (ăd-mĭts′)

admit into

To allow someone or something to enter or be a part of something: *This school does not admit students into a degree program without a high school diploma. The judge admitted the documents into evidence. We were admitted into the theater even though we were very late.*

admit of

To allow the possibility of something: *This problem admits of two very different solutions.*

admit to

1. To confess something to someone: *I didn't want to admit my crimes to them. At first they lied, but later they admitted to the police that they had stolen the bicycle.*
2. To confess something: *He will never admit to feeling jealous. She admitted to her lies.*

◆ **advance** (ăd-văns′)

advanced (ăd-vănst′), **advancing** (ăd-văn′sĭng), **advances** (ăd-văn′sĭz)

advance on *or* **advance upon**

To move increasingly closer to someone or something: *On the last lap of the race, I looked back and saw the other runners advancing on me. The army advanced upon the enemy's position.*

◆ **affiliate** (ə-fĭl′ē-āt′)

affiliated (ə-fĭl′ē-ā′tĭd), **affiliating** (ə-fĭl′ē-ā′tĭng), **affiliates** (ə-fĭl′ē-āts′)

affiliate with

1. To cause someone or something to associate or cooperate with someone or something: *The badges that the scouts wear affiliate them with different troops. The medical school is affiliated with the university.*
2. To associate or cooperate with someone or something: *This medical school affiliates with the large university.*
3. To associate someone with something or someone as a subordinate, employee, or member. Used reflexively: *After she finished law school, she affiliated herself with a good law firm.*

◆ **age** (āj)

aged (ājd, ā′jĭd), **aging** (ā′jĭng), **ages** (ā′jĭz)

age out

To reach an age at which one is no longer eligible for certain special services, such as education or protection, from an authority: *Unfortunately I have aged out of the special student scholarship program, so I have to pay full price for these classes.*

◆ **agitate** (ăj′ĭ-tāt′)

agitated (ăj′ĭ-tā′tĭd), **agitating** (ăj′ĭ-tā′tĭng), **agitates** (ăj′ĭ-tāts′)

agitate against

To stir up public opposition to some cause or issue: *The students in front of the administration building were agitating against the increase in tuition.*

agitate for

To stir up public support for some cause or issue: *The union decided to agitate for better health insurance.*

◆ **agree** (ə-grē′)

agreed (ə-grēd′), **agreeing** (ə-grē′ĭng), **agrees** (ə-grēz′)

agree to

To consent to something; accede to something: *The store owner agreed to the supplier's new proposal for a weekly shipment. I cannot agree to going with you on such a dangerous adventure!*

agree with

1. To be in accord with someone or something: *I agree with Mary that we should sell the car. Since we agree with each other, the matter is settled.*
2. To be well suited to someone: *The excitement of the big city certainly agrees with you!*
3. To approve of something: *The protesters don't agree with capital punishment.*
4. To be easily digestible. Used in the negative: *I didn't eat the crab cakes, since shellfish don't agree with me.*

◆ **aim** (ām)

aimed (āmd), **aiming** (ā′mĭng), **aims** (āmz)

aim at

1. To point or direct something at someone or something: *The archers drew back their arrows and aimed at the target.*
2. To intend something for some purpose. Often used in the passive: *We aimed our discussion at a solution to the financial problems. The new computer classes are aimed at teaching how computers work.*
3. To be intended to achieve something: *This new program aims at raising awareness about privacy issues.*
4. To do or say something intended to affect someone or something. Used chiefly in the passive: *Their sarcasm was aimed directly at me. The antismoking campaign was aimed at teenagers.*

◆ **alight** (ə-līt′)

alighted (ə-lī′tĭd) *or* **alit** (ə-lĭt′), **alighting** (ə-lī′tĭng), **alights** (ə-līts′)

ă	pat	är	car	ī	bite	ô	paw	ŏŏ	took	ûr	urge
ā	pay	ĕ	pet	îr	pier	ôr	core	ŏŏr	lure	zh	vision
âr	care	ē	be	ŏ	pot	oi	boy	ōō	boot	ə	about,
ä	father	ĭ	pit	ō	toe	ou	out	ŭ	cut		item

alight on

1. To come down and settle on something; land on something: *I watch the birds alight on the branches outside my window.*
2. To discover or arrive at something by chance: *The workers alighted on a simple solution to the problem.*

◆ **allow** (ə-lou′)

allowed (ə-loud′), **allowing** (ə-lou′ĭng), **allows** (ə-louz′)

allow for

1. To make some provision for something: *The schedule allows time for a coffee break. The design of the building allows for an addition to be built at a later time.*
2. To take some possibility into account: *I allowed for the possibility of rain by setting up a big tent at the picnic. The shipping company has to allow for some breakage of the products it ships to the stores.*

allow of

To offer or permit something as a possibility: *The poem allows of several interpretations.*

◆ **amount** (ə-mount′)

amounted (ə-moun′tĭd), **amounting** (ə-moun′tĭng), **amounts** (ə-mounts′)

amount to

1. To add up to some number or quantity: *I forgot to return the DVD on time, and the late charges amounted to almost $25.*
2. To be understood as something: *Your behavior amounts to an insult.*
3. To be as important or valuable as some level of quality: *They never thought I'd amount to anything, but look at me now! The facts I have so far don't amount to much. My parents never thought I'd amount to as much as my sister.*

◆ **answer** (ăn′sər)

answered (ăn′sərd), **answering** (ăn′sə-rĭng), **answers** (ăn′sərz)

answer back

1. To respond to a question or request; reply: *After I requested a catalog from the clothing company many times, they finally answered back, saying they didn't have any catalogs left. We leave message after message with them, but they never answer us back.*
2. To respond rudely or inappropriately: *Don't answer back to your mother like that!*

answer for

1. To speak on behalf of someone else: *I think my friend would agree to your offer, but I must speak with him first, since I can't answer for him.*
2. To accept responsibility or blame for something: *When your parents come back, you'll have to answer for the mess you made.*

answer to

1. To be called some name: *His real name is Edward, but he usually answers to Ted.*
2. To be liable or accountable to someone or something: *The treasurer answers directly to the vice president.*

◆ **ante** (ăn′tē)

anted *or* **anteed** (ăn′tēd), **anteing** (ăn′tē-ĭng), **antes** (ăn′tēz)

ante up

1. To put some amount into the pool at the beginning of a round in poker or a similar card game: *Everyone should ante up $1 to start the game. It may be your last dollar, but you'll have to ante it up! We must ante up before the cards are dealt.*
2. To provide some funds or capital: *The fundraisers anted up $10,000 for the charity.*
3. To pay some amount of money, often reluctantly: *Travelers are forced to ante up $5 for a candy bar at the airport. Can you imagine having to ante money up to use the restroom?*

◆ **appeal** (ə-pēl′)

appealed (ə-pēld′), **appealing** (ə-pē′lĭng), **appeals** (ə-pēlz′)

appeal to

1. To make an earnest or urgent request to someone or something: *The citizens appealed to their mayor to try to find a solution to the housing crisis.*
2. To be interesting or attractive to someone: *This new style of clothing doesn't appeal to me; I prefer the older fashion.*

◆ **apply** (ə-plī′)

applied (ə-plīd′), **applying** (ə-plī′ĭng), **applies** (ə-plīz′)

apply for

To request or seek some assistance, admission, or employment: *At least fifty people applied for the job. I might have to apply for unemployment benefits.*

apply to

1. To attach something to the surface of something: *You must apply the glue to the paper sparingly, or else the paper will wrinkle.*
2. To put something to some special use: *She applied all her income to the mortgage.*
3. To be pertinent or relevant to someone or something: *This rule applies to everyone; there are no exceptions.*
4. To request or seek assistance, admission, or employment from some organization: *I will apply to college next year.*
5. To devote someone or someone's efforts to something. Used reflexively: *In the summer I relaxed, but in the fall I applied myself to my studies.*

◆ **approve** (ə-pro͞ov′)

approved (ə-pro͞ovd′), **approving** (ə-pro͞o′vĭng), **approves** (ə-pro͞ovz′)

approve of

To consider someone or something right, good, or appropriate: *My voice teacher does not approve of eating ice cream before singing. My parents need to know exactly where I plan to go before they can approve of my trip.*

ă	pat	är	car	ī	bite	ô	paw	o͝o	took	ûr	urge
ā	pay	ĕ	pet	îr	pier	ôr	core	o͝or	lure	zh	vision
âr	care	ē	be	ŏ	pot	oi	boy	o͞o	boot	ə	about,
ä	father	ĭ	pit	ō	toe	ou	out	ŭ	cut		item

◆ **argue** (är′gyo͞o)
argued (är′gyo͞od), **arguing** (är′gyo͞o-ĭng), **argues** (är′gyo͞oz)

argue against
1. To present reasons opposing something; make a case against something: *In my history paper, I argued against the idea that we could have won the war.*
2. To act as evidence against something: *There are some new scientific discoveries that argue against earlier ideas about the growth of cells.*

argue down
1. To end the opposition of someone or something by arguing strongly: *He tried to object, but I argued him down. Our tax reform proposal was argued down by the committee.*
2. To negotiate some lower price: *The buyer argued me down to such a low price that I made no profit from the sale. If you want to buy that washing machine, I'm sure you can argue down the owner to half the price.*

argue for
1. To put forth reasons supporting something; make a case for something: *The students argued for a new gymnasium, but the administration did not want to spend the money needed to build it.*
2. To act as evidence or support for something: *These new facts argue for a different analysis. The fact that your route to work is so slow argues for giving my suggestion a try.*
3. To speak on behalf of someone in an argument: *Lawyers are supposed to argue for their clients.*

argue with
1. To engage in an argument or quarrel with someone: *I argue with my brothers and sisters all the time about who should wash the dishes.*
2. To challenge or dispute something: *It is difficult to argue with your conclusions, but I still feel that you are not taking all of the facts into account.*

◆ **arise** (ə-rīz′)
arose (ə-rōz′), **arisen** (ə-rĭz′ən), **arising** (ə-rī′zĭng), **arises** (ə-rī′zĭz)

arise from
1. To result, issue, or proceed from something: *Many mistakes in mathematics arise from a misunderstanding of the basic concepts.*
2. To move upward from something; ascend from something: *The hot air balloons slowly arose from the ground.*

◆ **arrive** (ə-rīv′)
arrived (ə-rīvd′), **arriving** (ə-rī′vĭng), **arrives** (ə-rīvz′)

arrive at
1. To reach or come to some place: *Because of the snowstorm, we arrived at the airport three hours late.*
2. To come to some conclusion or decision: *I think you're right, but how did you arrive at that answer?*

◆ **ask** (ăsk)
asked (ăskt), **asking** (ăs′kĭng), **asks** (ăsks)

ask for

1. To make a request for something: *I can't solve the problem alone, so I'm asking for help.*
2. To request someone's presence: *I called the front desk and asked for Chris Smith.*
3. To behave in a way that is viewed as provoking or inviting some outcome, usually one that is negative: *You are asking for an accident by driving so fast!*

ask out

To invite someone to a social engagement: *I am so happy that Pat finally asked me out to a movie.*

◆ **assent** (ə-sĕnt′)

assented (ə-sĕn′tĭd), **assenting** (ə-sĕn′tĭng), **assents** (ə-sĕnts′)

assent to

To agree to something: *The committee assented to the proposal that they had been discussing.*

◆ **associate** (ə-sō′shē-āt′)

associated (ə-sō′shē-ā′tĭd), **associating** (ə-sō′shē-ā′tĭng), **associates** (ə-sō′shē-āts′)

associate with

1. To keep company with someone or some group: *They are very snobbish and don't associate with people from our side of town.*
2. To link something in the mind with something else: *People often associate sunny weather with happiness.*

◆ **attach** (ə-tăch′)

attached (ə-tăcht′), **attaching** (ə-tăch′ĭng), **attaches** (ə-tăch′ĭz)

attach to

1. To fasten or secure something to something: *The electrician attached the wires to the socket. The carpenter attached the knobs to the cabinet doors.*
2. To adhere, belong, or relate to something: *It is not a very difficult job, and not much responsibility attaches to it.*
3. To affix or append something to something: *I attached all of my receipts to my spending report.*
4. To ascribe or assign some quality to something: *Several ambassadors said they would walk out of the meeting, but our officials attached no significance to the threat.*
5. To associate closely with someone or something: *I quickly attached myself to the chess club when I started school.*
6. To be bound emotionally to someone or something: *I'm still attached to that old sweater I used to wear in high school.*

◆ **attend** (ə-tĕnd′)

attended (ə-tĕn′dĭd), **attending** (ə-tĕn′dĭng), **attends** (ə-tĕndz′)

attend to

1. To deal with some business: *I can't talk now as I have some urgent affairs to attend to.*

ă	pat	är	car	ī	bite	ô	paw	o͝o	took	ûr	urge
ā	pay	ĕ	pet	îr	pier	ôr	core	o͝or	lure	zh	vision
âr	care	ē	be	ŏ	pot	oi	boy	o͞o	boot	ə	about,
ä	father	ĭ	pit	ō	toe	ou	out	ŭ	cut		item

2. To help or look after someone or something: *A good host attends to the needs of every guest. After the accident, the paramedics came quickly to attend to my injuries.*
3. To listen or pay attention to someone or something: *Be sure to attend to everything they say at the meeting.*

◆ **attract** (ə-trăkt′)

attracted (ə-trăk′tĭd), **attracting** (ə-trăk′tĭng), **attracts** (ə-trăkts′)

attract to

1. To exert a force or influence on something that tends to draw it toward something else: *Bright colors attract insects to flowers. Many different kinds of metal are attracted to magnets.*
2. To arouse in someone or something an interest or desire for something else: *I've always been attracted to movies from the 1960s.*

◆ **attune** (ə-to͞on′)

attuned (ə-to͞ond′), **attuning** (ə-to͞o′nĭng), **attunes** (ə-to͞onz′)

attune to

To bring something or someone into some harmonious or responsive relationship with something else: *Proper training will attune you to the fine details of a classical symphony. This industry is not attuned to the needs of the people who buy its products.*

◆ **auction** (ôk′shən)

auctioned (ôk′shənd), **auctioning** (ôk′shə-nĭng), **auctions** (ôk′shənz)

auction off

To sell something to the person who offers the highest amount of money, at or as at an auction: *We don't need this table anymore, so we should auction it off. To clear out the warehouse, the company auctioned off the old inventory.*

◆ **average** (ăv′ər-ĭj)

averaged (ăv′ər-ĭjd), **averaging** (ăv′ə-rĭ-jĭng), **averages** (ăv′ə-rĭ-jĭz)

average out

1. To calculate the average of something: *Let's average out the students' scores to see how well the class did overall. We took the rainfall figures for every summer since 1950 and averaged them out.*
2. To have some amount as an average: *The time you spend on the phone averages out to three hours each day. Though there are some very high prices here, there are some low ones, too, and they average out.*

B

◆ **back** (băk)

backed (băkt), **backing** (băk′ĭng), **backs** (băks)

back away

1. To move backward away from something or someone; retreat: *The dog backed away from the hissing cat. I told the kids to keep their distance from the burning fire, but they wouldn't back away.*
2. To move something backward away from something or someone; retreat: *I backed the car away from the oncoming traffic.*
3. To withdraw one's interest or support from something or someone: *The candidate backed away from his previous controversial views.*

back down

1. To move backward through some region, especially in a vehicle: *We backed down the driveway.*
2. To cause something, especially a vehicle, to move backward through some region or space: *I slowly backed the truck down the hill.*
3. To withdraw from a position or confrontation, especially due to intimidation: *The smaller bear kept growling so loudly that the larger bear backed down and walked away. Even though they appeared to have a very strong argument against me, I wouldn't back down, and I eventually showed them their conclusions were wrong.*

back off

1. To move backward so that one is farther away from someone or something: *Back off the car ahead of you: you're driving too close to it. The dog growled at me when I approached, so I backed off.*
2. To move something backward beyond the edge of something: *He accidentally backed the truck off the ledge and broke an axle.*
3. To decrease the intensity or amount of something: *I think I should back off the desserts for a little while so I can lose some weight.*
4. To decide not to continue doing something or supporting an idea: *You've made up your mind, so don't back off your idea now! Just before they were about to sign the papers to buy the new house, they got nervous and backed off.*
5. To stop intimidating, threatening, or pressuring someone: *Even as I left the store, the salesman wouldn't back off me. Whenever anyone bothers me, I just tell them to back off.*
6. To cause someone or something to stop intimidating, threatening or

ă	pat	är	car	ī	bite	ô	paw	o͝o	took	ûr	urge
ā	pay	ĕ	pet	îr	pier	ôr	core	o͝or	lure	zh	vision
âr	care	ē	be	ŏ	pot	oi	boy	o͞o	boot	ə	about,
ä	father	ĭ	pit	ō	toe	ou	out	ŭ	cut		item

pressuring: *The angry dogs were barking at the poor kid, so I waved a stick and backed them off.*

back out

1. To move backward out of some region: *The bear backed out of the cave.*
2. To move or drive something backward out of some region: *The sergeant backed the tank out of the trench. We picked up the heavy sofa and slowly backed it out of the living room and onto the porch.*
3. To decide not to keep a commitment or promise: *They backed out of the deal at the last minute. We had a plan to finish the work together, but they backed out.*

back up

1. To move backward: *We passed the house we were looking for, so we had to back up a little bit.*
2. To move something or someone backward: *I backed the car up against the garage wall. Let's back up the car to the curb.*
3. To prove something to be true: *There was not enough evidence to back up the theory. What I told you is true, and now I have even more evidence to back it up.*
4. To support someone by confirming that they are telling the truth: *We told our version of the events, certain that the witnesses would back us up. They won't back up anyone who is known for lying.*
5. To provide help or support for someone or something: *If I decide to take on the job, can I count on you to back me up? The political party backs up any candidate who follows its basic principles.*
6. To cause to accumulate, especially due to an obstruction: *The accident backed the traffic up for blocks. Something got stuck in the drain, and now the kitchen sink is backed up.*
7. To make a copy of a computer program or file for use if the original is lost or damaged: *I backed up the disk so that I wouldn't lose any data. Be sure to back your files up before you turn off the computer.*

◆ **bail** (bāl)

bailed (bāld), **bailing** (bā′lĭng), **bails** (bālz)

bail out

1. To jump out of a plane, especially one that is going to crash: *I grabbed my parachute and bailed out at the last possible minute.*
2. To stop doing or taking part in something because of difficulties or unpleasantness: *The actor bailed out on the play after a fight with the director. Our investors bailed out when it looked like the project might not be profitable.*
3. To free someone who has been arrested and would otherwise remain in jail until the trial by providing an amount of money: *I had to spend the weekend in jail because I had nobody to bail me out. Do you know who bailed out the accused thief last night?*
4. To rescue someone or something from a difficult situation, especially by providing financial assistance; extricate: *Just when we thought we might have to close the business, my uncle bailed us out with a loan. The government tried to*

bail out the struggling airline industry.

◆ **balance** (băl′əns)

balanced (băl′ənst), **balancing** (băl′ən-sĭng), **balances** (băl′ən-sĭz)

balance against

To consider the value of something in relation to another thing: *To be fair, we must balance the problems in this plan against its possible benefits.*

balance out

1. To be or become equal in amount, value, or effect: *I had to spend more money this year, but my higher income and my increased spending balanced out.*
2. To cause to be equal in amount, value, or effect; equalize: *Unfortunately, my loan payments balance out my new income, so I don't have any more money to spend now than I did before.*

◆ **balk** (bôk)

balked (bôkt), **balking** (bô′kĭng), **balks** (bôks)

balk at

1. To stop short and refuse to go on to do something: *The horse balked at jumping over the fence.*
2. To refuse something obstinately or abruptly: *The politician balked at the compromise suggested by the opposing party.*

◆ **ball** (bôl)

balled (bôld), **balling** (bôl′ĭng), **balls** (bôlz)

ball up

1. To roll something into a ball: *I balled up the lump of clay. I balled the rest of the yarn up when I finished knitting.*
2. To make a mess of something: *I think you balled your assignment up. I'm afraid someone will ball up the arrangement.*

◆ **band** (bănd)

banded (băn′dĭd), **banding** (băn′dĭng), **bands** (băndz)

band together

1. To form a cohesive and cooperative group; unite: *The people who opposed the new policy banded together to fight it.*
2. To cause some things or people to form into a cohesive or cooperative group; unite things or people: *The fact that we all had gone to the same school banded us together, and we became good friends.*

◆ **bandy** (băn′dē)

bandied (băn′dēd), **bandying** (băn′dē-ĭng), **bandies** (băn′dēz)

bandy about

To make frequent and casual or frivolous use of a name, word, or idea: *The word "genius" is bandied about too much when new authors are discussed. It made me*

ă	pat	är	car	ī	bite	ô	paw	o͝o	took	ûr	urge
ā	pay	ĕ	pet	îr	pier	ôr	core	o͝or	lure	zh	vision
âr	care	ē	be	ŏ	pot	oi	boy	o͞o	boot	ə	about,
ä	father	ĭ	pit	ō	toe	ou	out	ŭ	cut		item

angry that gossipy neighbors were bandying my name about.

◆ **bang** (băng)

banged (băngd), **banging** (băng′ĭng), **bangs** (băngz)

bang away

1. To hit something repeatedly, especially loudly or forcefully: *He kept banging away on the door even though nobody answered.*
2. To play a musical instrument with the hands, often loudly and with little skill: *I couldn't get any sleep because my neighbor was banging away on the piano all night.*
3. To work diligently and often at length at something: *She banged away at the project until she finished it.*

bang into

1. To bump loudly or squarely into someone or something, usually by accident: *When the lights went out, I banged into the wall when I was looking for the door.*
2. To hit or strike someone or something loudly or squarely with something: *I banged my foot into the wall.*

bang out

1. To write something very quickly, especially using a keyboard: *Facing a deadline, the writer banged out an editorial for the paper. I need to reply to the bank right away; could you bang a letter out for me?*
2. To play a piece of music very loudly, especially on a piano: *I sat down and banged out some funny songs to entertain my friends. I think of this waltz as a quiet piece of music, but some players really bang it out.*

bang up

To injure or damage someone or something, especially by hitting: *The truck banged up my car in the accident. I banged myself up when I fell down the stairs.*

◆ **bank** (băngk)

banked (băngkt), **banking** (băng′kĭng), **banks** (băngks)

bank on

To rely on someone or something: *You can bank on her to get the job done when it has to be done quickly. I wouldn't bank on the bus arriving on time.*

◆ **barf** (bärf)

barfed (bärft), **barfing** (bär′fĭng), **barfs** (bärfs)

barf up

SLANG

To eject some contents of the stomach by vomiting: *He barfed up his dinner because the food was spoiled. She was so sick she was even barfing soup up.*

◆ **bargain** (bär′gĭn)

bargained (bär′gĭnd), **bargaining** (bär′gĭ-nĭng), **bargains** (bär′gĭnz)

bargain down

1. To negotiate some lower price: *I bargained the price down by $200. They want $30, but if you try, you can bargain it down to $20. If that offer is too expensive, bargain it down some more.*
2. To negotiate with someone to pay a lower price: *If I can't bargain him*

down to $20 dollars, I won't buy the coat. The savvy shopper bargained the clerk down.

bargain for

1. To negotiate with someone about obtaining something: *I had to bargain for the car with the sales person, who finally lowered the price by $250.*
2. To expect or be prepared for something: *She got more than she had bargained for when the little puppy she bought grew into a very big dog with a large appetite.*

bargain on

To expect or be prepared for something: *He thought he was on time, but hadn't bargained on waiting 30 minutes for the bus.*

◆ **barge** (bärj)

barged (bärjd), **barging** (bär′jĭng), **barges** (bär′jĭz)

barge in

1. To intrude and disrupt: *The party was going fine until some uninvited guests barged in.*
2. **barge in on** To intrude on and disrupt some activity or group: *I wish you hadn't barged in on the meeting—that was very rude. We were playing cards when my brother barged in on us and told us the news.*

◆ **base** (bās)

based (bāst), **basing** (bā′sĭng), **bases** (bā′sĭz)

base in

1. To operate from some location. Used chiefly in the passive: *Our company is based in Fresno.*
2. To establish or found something in some location: *We based our organization in the heart of the city.*
3. To have something as a foundation or origin: *The linguist based the analysis of the sentence structure in a standard framework.*

base on

To form, develop, or found something on the basis of something else: *I based my decision on the information you gave me. The film was based on a popular book.*

◆ **bash** (băsh)

bashed (băsht), **bashing** (băsh′ĭng), **bashes** (băsh′ĭz)

bash in

1. To break or smash a hole in something: *The robber bashed in the window with a crowbar. When I slipped, I fell against the door and bashed it in.*
2. To strike a strong blow to something, causing it to penetrate a hard substance or surface: *I didn't have a hammer, so I placed the nail over the wood and bashed it in with a wrench.*
3. To make some indentation or hole in something by hitting it suddenly: *I was so angry that I kicked the car and bashed a dent in it.*

ă	pat	är	car	ī	bite	ô	paw	o͝o	took	ûr	urge
ā	pay	ĕ	pet	îr	pier	ôr	core	o͝or	lure	zh	vision
âr	care	ē	be	ŏ	pot	oi	boy	o͞o	boot	ə	about,
ä	father	ĭ	pit	ō	toe	ou	out	ŭ	cut		item

◆ **bask** (băsk)

basked (băskt), **basking** (băs′kĭng), **basks** (băsks)

bask in

1. To expose oneself to pleasant warmth: *We basked in the afternoon sun at the beach.*
2. To take great pleasure or pride in something; revel in something: *For a long time, I basked in the success of my first book.*

◆ **bat** (băt)

batted (băt′ĭd), **batting** (băt′ĭng), **bats** (băts)

bat around

1. To knock something around with or as if with a bat, hand, or similar object: *We batted around some baseballs at the park. The cat batted the squeaky toy around the entire afternoon.*
2. To discuss something back and forth in order to come to a decision: *They batted around ideas all night before they made up their minds. We batted a few names around when thinking about nominees.*

bat out

To produce something in a hurried or informal manner: *The new store owner batted out thank-you notes to his first customers all morning. I don't have time before the big party to bake hundreds of cookies, but I think I can bat a few dozen out.*

◆ **bawl** (bôl)

bawled (bôld), **bawling** (bô′lĭng), **bawls** (bôlz)

bawl out

To scold someone loudly or harshly: *My boss bawled me out for coming to work late. I am going to bawl out my students if they don't prepare for the next test.*

◆ **be** (bē)

Past tense, first person singular *(I)* and third person singular *(he, she, it)* **was** (wŭz)

Past tense, second person singular and plural *(you)*, first person plural *(we)*, and third person plural *(they)* **were** (wûr)

Past participle **been** (bĭn)

Present participle **being** (bē′ĭng)

Present tense, first person singular *(I)* **am** (ăm)

Present tense, third person singular *(he, she, it)* **is** (ĭz)

Present tense, second person singular and plural *(you)*, first person plural *(we)*, third person plural *(they)* **are** (är)

be about

1. To be present and active in a place or region: *Are there any bees about? I'd like to take a walk in the woods, and I hope there are no bears about.*
2. To be actively engaged in something, especially a regular activity: *I was about my usual shopping that morning when a mysterious aircraft appeared in the sky.*
3. To be at the point of doing something. Used with the infinitive: *That book is about to fall off the shelf. I was just about to leave when they told me to stop.*
4. To be willing or prepared to do something. Used negatively: *I'm*

not about to tell anyone the secret and ruin the surprise!

be after

1. To follow or be later than something: *Who is in line after me? The meeting is after lunch.*
2. To pursue, seek, or desire someone or something: *That hawk is after the rabbit. What sort of answers are you after?*
3. **be after for** To pursue someone or something in order to obtain something else: *You are only after me for my money.*

be against

To be opposed to something or someone: *I'm against that kind of severe punishment. All those who are against this proposal should raise their hands.*

be ahead

1. To be in a position in front of something or someone along some path being followed: *The tour guide was ahead of us as we walked through the museum.*
2. To be more advanced in the pursuit or study of something: *I have always liked science and am ahead of my classmates in biology.*
3. To have accomplished more of some activity than is immediately necessary: *I'm ahead in my work, so I have time to take a short break.*

be at

1. To be located somewhere: *The hotel is at the center of town. I am at the corner of 11th Street and Third Avenue.*
2. To take place at some given time: *Our meeting is at noon. The movie is at 8:00, so we've got plenty of time for dinner.*
3. To be busy trying to accomplish something; keep at. Often used with *it: I have been at this interminable project for weeks now.*
4. To remind someone regularly about something or to do something: *He's been at me about the book he lent to me.*

be behind

1. To be located to the rear of something: *The stables are behind the barn. I couldn't see the whole stage because my seat was behind a pillar.*
2. To be late or slow in something: *We are all behind in our work. She was ahead of the other bicyclists for a while, but now she's behind. He spends too much money and is always behind on his bills.*
3. To perform less well or advance more slowly than others: *Your child is behind in math skills and will need extra lessons.*
4. To offer support or assistance to somebody or something, especially when one does not directly take part in the activities supported or is unknown: *Don't worry; I'm behind you completely in your endeavors. Who was really behind the assassination attempt?*

ă	pat	är	car	ī	bite	ô	paw	ŏŏ	took	ûr	urge
ā	pay	ĕ	pet	îr	pier	ôr	core	ŏŏr	lure	zh	vision
âr	care	ē	be	ŏ	pot	oi	boy	ōō	boot	ə	about,
ä	father	ĭ	pit	ō	toe	ou	out	ŭ	cut		item

be down

1. To be located or to take place at a location lower than where one currently is: *The party is down in the basement.*
2. To be located at some distance, following some path: *The grocery store is three miles down this road. Her house is down that driveway. There is a gas station two miles down.*
3. To be temporarily out of service or nonoperational: *I tried to call you, but the circuits were down. The computer will be down for repairs until this afternoon.*
4. To be at a low level or have a low quantity: *Our fuel is down; we need to go to the gas station. The price of carrots is down from last year.*
5. To be generally unhappy, in bad spirits, or depressed: *Your jokes always make me feel better when I'm down.*
6. **be down on** To disapprove of something or the behavior of someone: *I thought we should sell off the unused land, but the committee was down on the idea. They are down on you for your silly remarks.*
7. **be down to** To be reduced or lowered to some quantity or amount: *Because of the big sale, the price of these shirts is now down to four dollars.*
8. **be down to** To have available a lower quantity of something, especially due to gradual use or loss: *I've spent most of my money; now I'm down to $3. The airplane was down to only three gallons of fuel when it landed.*
9. SLANG **be down with** To be in agreement or to cooperate with someone or something; to find something acceptable: *That sounds like a good idea; I'm down with that. I need a partner; are you down with me?*

be for

To be in favor of something or someone: *I'm definitely not for cutting down the trees; we need the shade. Are you for these candidates, or against them?*

be in

1. To be located inside something: *The spare keys are in the glove compartment.*
2. To have been put or have come inside: *You can close the door now; the cat is in.*
3. To have successfully become a part or participant: *The baseball team struggled to make the playoffs, but now they are in.*
4. To have been elected or appointed to a political office: *The current administration is in for at least one more term.*
5. To be a consenting participant: *The old bank robbers showed the young thief their plans and asked whether he was in.*
6. To be fashionable or trendy: *Narrow ties were in during the early 1960s and early 1980s.*
7. **be in for** To be subject to something imminently: *If you haven't read her books before, then you are in for a great surprise. Those dark clouds make me think that we are in for some wet weather.*
8. **be in for** To participate in an activity, offering or risking something on its behalf. *As far as painting the house goes, we are in for a day's*

work, but no more. We all placed our bets, and I was in for $10.

9. **be in on** To be aware of or to participate in some information shared with others or some group activity: *I am not in on their plans, so I don't know what they are going to do. Are you in on our secret?*
10. **be in with** To be on good terms with someone, especially with a group, to one's potential advantage: *Although he is poor, he is in with the rich crowd and always goes on expensive trips with them.*

be into

1. To be interested in or enthusiastic about something: *I am into reading nonfiction these days. Are you into rock music?*
2. To have reached some point in an ongoing process or measure of time: *I was halfway into this book when I lost interest in it. We were well into April before the snow stopped falling.*

be off

1. To have left or been removed from a surface: *The crows have flown away; they're all off the roof now. The snow is off the roads, and it should be safe to drive now.*
2. To leave or have left: *I was already off to the airport when you called.*
3. To be disengaged, not currently functioning, especially through lack of power supply. Used mostly of machines: *It's dark now that the lights are off. Before I leave the house I always checks to see if the stove is off.*
4. To be no longer connected to or broadcast by some communication system: *How long have you been off the phone? The television program is now off the air.*
5. To be inexact, imprecise, or not meeting expectations: *Something is wrong with this calculation; these figures are definitely off. My golf playing was really off last weekend.*
6. To be spoiled: *Don't use this milk in your tea; it's off.*
7. To be no longer dependent on, addicted to, or desirous of something: *I'm finally off caffeine. He's been off of drugs for a long time now.*

be on

1. To be in contact with the upper or outer surface of something: *There are toys on the rug. Frost is on the windowpane. Your glasses are on the kitchen table.*
2. To be engaged or functioning. Used mostly of machines: *When the spotlights are on, it gets very hot. Is the car engine still on?*
3. To be connected with or broadcast by some communication system: *You have been on the computer for three hours. Come listen; my favorite radio show is on.*
4. To be precise, in good form, or well executed: *My dart throwing was definitely on, and that night I got four bull's-eyes. The remarks you made were right on, and everyone understood immediately.*

ă	pat	är	car	ī	bite	ô	paw	o͝o	took	ûr	urge
ā	pay	ĕ	pet	îr	pier	ôr	core	o͝or	lure	zh	vision
âr	care	ē	be	ŏ	pot	oi	boy	o͞o	boot	ə	about,
ä	father	ĭ	pit	ō	toe	ou	out	ŭ	cut		item

5. To be dependent on or desirous of something: *I am on medication to lower my cholesterol. They suspect that their child is on drugs.*
6. **be on about** To talk excitedly about something, especially to others who are not interested or do not understand: *They are always on about the prizes their children keep winning. I don't know what he is on about, but he is giving me a headache.*

be onto

To be in the process of finding or understanding something: *I'm not sure, but I may be onto a solution to this math problem. The gang was afraid that the police were onto them.*

be out

1. To be at the exterior of some space, such as a building: *I won't close the window if the cat is still out.*
2. To be away from home or other central location: *Your brother was out when I came by to see him.*
3. To be no longer in prison: *I've been out for five years, and I don't want to end up behind bars ever again.*
4. To be unobstructed by clouds. Used of the sun, moon, and stars: *It's quite light outside now that the moon is out.*
5. To be in some weather condition. Used with *it: Is it nice out? It was rainy out, so we stayed inside.*
6. To be extinguished. Used of sources of light: *The lamps are out and I can't see a thing.*
7. To be nonfunctional due to disconnection: *We can't take that road because the bridge is out. All of the phone lines were out for three days after the storm.*
8. To be asleep or unconscious: *I drank some soothing tea before I went to bed, and I was out in three minutes.*
9. To be no longer in fashion: *Wide ties and thick socks are out this year.*
10. To be excluded as a possibility: *We have to pick them up; driving home without them is out. I would like to meet you today, but this afternoon is out; how about this evening?*
11. To be determined to do something. Used with an infinitive clause: *Watch out: they are out to steal your wallet!*
12. To be open and honest about something that one might hide: *He was completely out about his past as a jewel thief.*
13. To be open about being a gay man, a lesbian, or a bisexual: *Most of her friends were out, but she was still shy about it.*
14. Baseball To have lost a position as a batter or runner: *If someone catches the ball you hit before it reaches the ground, you're out. The player was out at third base.*
15. **be out for** To have left a central location in order to fetch or do something: *John's not here; he's out for a walk. They were out for more supplies when we arrived at their camp.*
16. **be out of** To no longer have something that has been used up; have run out of something: *We're out of pickles; could you go to the store and buy some? The car wouldn't start; it was out of gas.*

be over

1. To be located above something: *The lamp is over the desk.*
2. To be on the other side of something: *My grandparents' house is over the river.*
3. To have come to an end; be finished: *When the movie was over, we went to bed.*
4. To have recovered emotionally from something: *It was a terrible year, but I am finally over it.*
5. **be over with** To have finished doing or experiencing something, especially something unpleasant: *I'm not over with my homework yet.*
6. **be over with** To be finished; have passed or been experienced. Used especially of unpleasant things: *Now that my dental surgery is over with, I can stop worrying and get some rest.*

be past

1. To be later than some time: *It's already past noon and I still haven't eaten breakfast.*
2. To be located at a greater distance than something: *The graveyard is past the school.*
3. To have overcome some experience or no longer believe it to be important: *It used to annoy me when they called me "four-eyes," but I'm past that now.*
4. To have given up on something: *I believe my cat has run away, and I am past hoping for his return.*
5. To be too old or feeble to accomplish something: *That football player is clearly past it and should give up the sport.*

be through

1. To have penetrated or crossed to the other side of something: *Once you've pushed on it, the tack should be through the cloth, and it will stay attached.*
2. To have finished something: *You started that book yesterday; are you through yet? I was through with my homework, so I went out and played.*
3. To be finished: *Once this ironing is through, I'll be able to join you for coffee.*
4. To have ended a romantic relationship, especially on a bad note: *I hate to say it, but Chris and I are through.*
5. **be through with** To have ended, or to desire to end, a relationship or engagement with someone or something: *She said she was through with me and walked out the door. I am through with this awful job.*

be up

1. To have reached some high position: *Now that all the sails are up, the boat will move pretty quickly. The cat is up the tree again.*
2. To be awake: *Although it was two o'clock in the morning, I was still up because I had drunk so much coffee.*
3. To be in an energetic or positive mood: *I was really up about the*

ă	pat	är	car	ī	bite	ô	paw	o͝o	took	ûr	urge
ā	pay	ĕ	pet	îr	pier	ôr	core	o͝or	lure	zh	vision
âr	care	ē	be	ŏ	pot	oi	boy	o͞o	boot	ə	about,
ä	father	ĭ	pit	ō	toe	ou	out	ŭ	cut		item

painting I had finished; it was one of my better efforts. She was tired and worried and wasn't feeling very up that day.

4. To have been used to completion. Used especially of time: *Please get off the computer; your time is up. My luck has gone, and all of my chances are up.*
5. To be put to an end, especially by being revealed: *Your schemes are up; you should just admit what you did.*
6. To be next in line for something: *I've been waiting to buy tickets for hours, and I am finally up next.*
7. To be occurring. Used especially of noteworthy or unusual events: *The noises from the cellar are strange; I'll go down and see what is up.*
8. **be up against** To have someone or something as an adversary or challenge: *This year our team will be up against yours for the first time. The shopkeepers were up against some serious difficulties when the tax laws changed.*
9. **be up before** To appear in some court of law: *Their case is up before the Supreme Court. I was up before the local courthouse for failure to pay my liquor license.*
10. **be up for** To be visiting a place for some purpose: *My roommate from college is up for a visit.*
11. **be up for** To be positive about or capable of doing something: *Are you up for another coffee before we go home? Don't make them try to walk such a distance; they are not up for it.*
12. **be up to** To have reached some quantity: *The temperature is now up to forty degrees. We are now up to four weeks without rain.*
13. **be up to** To have something as a possible upper limit: *The prices can be up to three times higher in the big cities.*
14. **be up to** To be doing something: *I don't want to know what he is up to in the kitchen. What are you up to this afternoon?*

be upon

To be imminent or just beginning to have an effect on someone or something: *Winter is upon us, so we'd better be ready to shovel lots of snow.*

◆ **bead** (bēd)

beaded (bē′dĭd), **beading** (bē′dĭng), **beads** (bēdz)

bead up

To form into the shape of a bead; come together in droplets: *Because I just waxed my car, the rain beaded up its surface as it fell. Sweat started to bead up on my forehead.*

◆ **bear** (bâr)

bore (bôr), **borne** (bôrn) *or* **born** (bôrn), **bearing** (bâr′ĭng), **bears** (bârz)

bear down

1. To press or push down heavily on someone or something: *To knead this dough you have to bear down on it with both hands. I grabbed the corners of the blanket and bore down hard to stop the wind from blowing it away.*
2. To apply maximum effort and concentration: *Now that the games are over, I can really bear down on my studies. To finish this job*

you'll need to bear down and work very hard.

3. To advance upon someone or something in a threatening manner: *As soon as I had control of the soccer ball, I saw the tackle bearing down on me. The storm bore down and ravaged the island.*

bear out

To be evidence that something is true or that what someone says is true; support something or someone: *The test results bear out our claims. I told them my side of the story and the evidence bore me out.*

bear up

To withstand stress, difficulty, or attrition: *The patient bore up well during the long illness. The president had a hard time bearing up against his critics.*

bear with

To be patient with someone or something: *The explanation I will give is complicated, so please bear with me.*

◆ **beat** (bēt)

beat (bēt), **beaten** (bēt′n) *or* **beat** (bēt), **beating** (bē′tĭng), **beats** (bēts)

beat down

1. To hit something until it falls down: *The police beat down the door of the suspect's house. They approached the crumbling wall and beat it down with their bare hands.*
2. To defeat or demoralize someone: *The constant criticism beat me down, and it was hard for me to try again. The invaders beat down every village they passed through.*
3. To fall down steadily and heavily: *The rain beat down on the roof.*
4. To persuade someone to reduce the price of something: *The clerk wanted $40 for the shoes but I beat him down to $30.*

beat into

1. To mix something with something else with a vigorous stirring motion: *I beat the eggs into the milk and flour gently, so that the batter didn't get too stiff.*
2. To batter someone or something into some state or condition: *The robbers beat their victim into submission.*
3. To force someone to do something, especially through the use of physical violence: *I didn't want to cooperate with those crooks, but they beat me into being the driver of the getaway car.*

beat off

1. To drive someone or something away, especially by fighting or hitting: *Two robbers attacked me on the subway, but I beat them off with my bag. After a long battle, the soldiers beat off the invaders.*
2. To defeat someone or something in a competition: *Our company intends to beat off our rivals for the*

contract. The visiting team was behind us for most of the game, but beat us off squarely in the end.

3. VULGAR SLANG To masturbate. Used of males.

beat out

1. To defeat someone or something in a competition: *I won a lot of games, but the top athlete beat out everyone. You're ahead now, but we'll beat you out in the end!*
2. **beat out of** To achieve or obtain something from something or someone by beating or assaulting: *We beat the dirt out of the rug. The hooligans beat a false confession out of me.*

beat to

1. To get to a place before someone else: *You're fast—I'm sure you can beat all the other runners to the finish line.*
2. To finish or achieve before someone else: *I beat all the other students to the end of the test.*

◆ **become** (bĭ-kŭm′)

became (bĭ-kām′), **become** (bĭ-kŭm′), **becoming** (bĭ-kŭm′ĭng), **becomes** (bĭ-kŭmz′)

become of

To happen to someone or something; be the fate of someone or something: *Nobody really knows what became of the coach after he retired. What has become of the old garden?*

◆ **bed** (bĕd)

bedded (bĕd′ĭd), **bedding** (bĕd′ĭng), **beds** (bĕdz)

bed down

1. To lie down to sleep: *I'm about to bed down for the night.*
2. To furnish someone with a bed or sleeping quarters: *We bedded down our guests in the den. The army bedded down the troops in a temporary shelter.*
3. To put someone or something securely to bed: *The parents bed down their children every night by reading them a story. We bedded the baby down early tonight.*
4. To secure or protect something, especially by covering or enclosing it: *To keep the roots of the plants healthy, bed them down in the winter with an inch of soil. We bedded down our equipment under some leaves while we explored the surrounding woods.*

◆ **beef** (bēf)

beefed (bēft), **beefing** (bē′fĭng), **beefs** (bēfs)

beef up

1. To cause someone or something to become bigger, stronger, or bulkier: *You should beef up your travel report with more descriptions of what you saw. The soup tastes good, but we could beef it up by adding some spices.*
2. To become bigger, stronger, or bulkier: *The actor beefed up over a couple of months so that he could play the part of a boxer.*

◆ **beg** (bĕg)

begged (bĕgd), **begging** (bĕg′ĭng), **begs** (bĕgz)

beg off

To excuse oneself from something, such as an obligation: *We were invited to stay for dinner, but we had to beg off.*

◆ **belly** (bĕl′ē)

bellied (bĕl′ēd), **bellying** (bĕl′ē-ĭng), **bellies** (bĕl′ēz)

belly up

SLANG

To approach closely: *The drunk tourists bellied up to the bar and drank some more. They were shy, but when we asked them over, they eventually bellied up and joined us.*

◆ **belt** (bĕlt)

belted (bĕl′tĭd), **belting** (bĕl′tĭng), **belts** (bĕlts)

belt out

To sing or shout something loudly and forcefully: *The singer belted out the national anthem before the baseball game. He belted his story out so that everyone in the large room could hear him.*

◆ **bet** (bĕt)

bet (bĕt) *or* **betted** (bĕt′ĭd), **betting** (bĕt′ĭng), **bets** (bĕts)

bet on

1. To place a bet of some amount on some event: *I bet $5 on the first race of the evening. I'm not going to bet on the last race.*
2. To place a bet of some amount on some participant in an event: *We bet $200 on the home team, but they lost. Don't bet anything on me in this game; I'm not a very good player. Will you bet on any of the players?*
3. To expect or feel sure that something will happen: *You can bet on Chris being late to the meeting.*

◆ **bid** (bĭd)

bade (băd, bād) *or* **bid** (bĭd), **bidden** (bĭd′n) *or* **bid** (bĭd), **bidding** (bĭd′ĭng), **bids** (bĭdz)

bid on

1. To offer some amount of money for something at an auction: *I won't bid more than $10 on that sofa. Who would like to bid on this beautiful painting?*
2. To respond to some business proposal with a bid: *Four companies are bidding on this contract right now.*

bid up

1. To increase the price of something by offering increasingly high purchase prices for it: *The traders bid up the stocks in oil companies. The buyer bid the artist's paintings up much more than she expected that they would be worth.*
2. To increase some cost by offering increasingly high purchase prices: *There were many potential buyers, and together they bid up the cost of milk to $3 per gallon. The price was low at first, but the buyer bid it up to much more than he could afford.*

◆ **billow** (bĭl′ō)

billowed (bĭl′ōd), **billowing** (bĭl′ō-ĭng), **billows** (bĭl′ōz)

ă	pat	är	car	ī	bite	ô	paw	ŏŏ	took	ûr	urge
ā	pay	ĕ	pet	îr	pier	ôr	core	ŏŏr	lure	zh	vision
âr	care	ē	be	ŏ	pot	oi	boy	ōō	boot	ə	about,
ä	father	ĭ	pit	ō	toe	ou	out	ŭ	cut		item

billow out

1. To surge outward or puff out due to the movement of air: *The sails billowed out as the breeze strengthened.*
2. To cause something to stretch or puff out: *The wind billowed the sails out. The breeze billowed out the sheets that were hung up on the clothesline.*

◆ **bind** (bīnd)

bound (bound), **binding** (bīn′dĭng), **binds** (bīndz)

bind off

To secure some number of stitches in knitting and form an edge by lifting one stitch over the next: *Bind off 12 stitches on the next row to make the neck edge. Make 5 stitches on the next row and bind them off. The scarf is long enough, so you can bind off.*

bind over

To put someone under a financial obligation as a guarantee of that person's appearance at trial or of his or her good behavior for a period of time: *I was arrested for littering, and the court bound me over to keep the peace for six months. After a brief hearing, the judge bound over the accused murderer for trial and set the bail at one million dollars.*

◆ **black** (blăk)

blacked (blăkt), **blacking** (blăk′ĭng), **blacks** (blăks)

black out

1. To stop emitting light; go out: *The traffic lights blacked out when the storm knocked down power lines.*
2. To cause a failure of electrical power in some region: *The strong winds blacked out much of the city.*
3. To lose consciousness or memory temporarily: *The patient felt very dizzy and blacked out for a few minutes.*
4. To suppress some memory from the conscious mind: *The refugees blacked out their wartime experiences.*
5. To prohibit the broadcast or spread of something, especially by censorship: *The government blacked out the news that was broadcast from enemy radio stations.*

◆ **blank** (blăngk)

blanked (blăngkt), **blanking** (blăng′kĭng), **blanks** (blăngks)

blank on

To forget or fail to remember something; draw a blank on something: *I blanked on her name even though we had just been introduced.*

blank out

1. To erase or cover something so that it cannot be seen or read: *Please blank out the incorrect information on this form. I didn't want them to see my letter on the computer screen, so I blanked it out. Some of the words in the document had been blanked out to protect people's privacy.*
2. To suddenly forget what one was about to say: *My neighbor blanks out on my name every time we meet. I was about to say something important, but I blanked out!*

3. To deliberately forget or stop thinking about something, especially something unpleasant: *I've blanked out most of those sad memories. The suffering patient tried to blank out the pain.*

◆ **blare** (blâr)

blared (blârd), **blaring** (blâr′ĭng), **blares** (blârz)

blare out

1. To sound loudly and stridently, especially through a broadcast system: *Music blared out from the speakers while everyone danced.*
2. To proclaim something boldly or flamboyantly: *The newspaper headlines blared out the scandal.*

◆ **blast** (blăst)

blasted (blăs′tĭd), **blasting** (blăs′tĭng), **blasts** (blăsts)

blast off

1. To be launched off the ground. Used of rockets: *The astronauts were strapped in their seats and ready to blast off.*
2. To launch some rocket from the ground: *The space agency needs a new location to blast off its spacecraft. The kids set up their model rockets on the field and blasted them off.*
3. To explode or fire something: *I blasted off some firecrackers during the celebration. I put some bullets in the gun and blasted a few rounds off to test it.*
4. To dislodge or remove something with an explosion: *Be careful not to blast your fingers off with that loaded gun! To make room for the new road, the workers blasted off a large rock from the side of the hill.*
5. SLANG To depart for a destination: *We need to blast off right now if we are going to get to the party on time.*

◆ **bliss** (blĭs)

blissed (blĭst), **blissing** (blĭs′ĭng), **blisses** (blĭs′ĭz)

bliss out

SLANG

1. To cause someone to feel intense happiness and relaxation: *The beautiful sunset blissed me out. The melodies this band writes will bliss out even the most spoiled music fans. I was blissed out by the friendly spirit of the crowd.*
2. To be in a state of intense happiness and relaxation: *I blissed out lying on the beach under the sun.*

◆ **block** (blŏk)

blocked (blŏkt), **blocking** (blŏk′ĭng), **blocks** (blŏks)

block on

To forget or fail to remember something; have a mental block about something: *I had met these people before, but this time I blocked on their names.*

ă	pat	är	car	ī	bite	ô	paw	o͝o	took	ûr	urge
ā	pay	ĕ	pet	îr	pier	ôr	core	o͝or	lure	zh	vision
âr	care	ē	be	ŏ	pot	oi	boy	o͞o	boot	ə	about,
ä	father	ĭ	pit	ō	toe	ou	out	ŭ	cut		item

block out

1. To prevent something from being seen: *The smoke from the volcano blocked out the sun. This Internet filter blocks obscene language out.*
2. To deliberately forget or stop thinking about something, especially something that is unpleasant: *She blocked out the horrible details of the accident. The memories of his childhood were painful, and he blocked them out as much as he could.*
3. To lay out or present the details of something: *The director blocked out the actors' movements on stage. The city council blocked the new budget out.*

block up

1. To obstruct something, as a passageway: *The stalled truck blocked up the road. The old leaves are blocking up the drainage pipes.*
2. To cause something to become obstructed: *The soldiers blocked up the tunnel with barbed wire. A bad head cold has blocked my sinus passages up.*
3. To become obstructed: *My arteries had blocked up, so my doctor put me on a special diet.*

◆ **blow** (blō)

blew (blo͞o), **blown** (blōn), **blowing** (blō′ĭng), **blows** (blōz)

blow away

1. To be carried or pushed away by the force of moving air: *I left the newspaper on the table and it blew away.*
2. To carry or push something away by the force of moving air: *The wind blows the fallen leaves away. The storm blew away all the laundry from the clothesline.*
3. SLANG To affect someone intensely in mind or emotion: *Your wonderful new poems really blow me away. Their amazing performance blew away every member of the audience.*
4. SLANG To kill someone, especially with a firearm: *The gang entered their rival's hideout, ready to blow away everyone. The thieves threatened to blow me away if I didn't tell them where I hid the money.*
5. SLANG To defeat someone or something decisively: *The confident chess player blew away every challenger. The visiting soccer team was much better than our team and easily blew us away.*

blow in

1. To push or carry something inward by the force of moving air: *Close the door; the wind is blowing in a lot of leaves. The breeze picked up a small feather and blew it in through the window.*
2. To be pushed or carried inward by the force of moving air: *I opened the screen and several flies blew in.*
3. To cause something to collapse inwardly due to sudden powerful or violent force: *The force of the explosion blew in the walls of the cave. The huge gust of wind came suddenly, blowing the windows in.*
4. To collapse inwardly from sudden powerful or violent force: *The holes that had been drilled in the oil field blew in during the fire.*
5. To arrive unexpectedly: *My old friend blew in from out of town today and paid me a visit.*

blow off

1. To push or carry something away from something by the force of moving air: *A gust of wind blew my hat off my head. The strong wind blew off the napkins that we had put on the tables.*
2. To be pushed or carried off by the force of moving air: *If I put a weather vane on top of the house, do you think it would blow off?*
3. To remove something with powerful or violent force: *The bomb blasts blew off the side of the building. The exploding car engine blew the hood off.*
4. SLANG To avoid or neglect some responsibility or obligation: *Yesterday I blew off all my work and went to the movies. I know you don't want to go to work today, but if you blow your job off, you'll get fired.*
5. SLANG To fail to keep an appointment with someone: *She's annoyed because her date blew her off. He's pretty reliable, and he won't blow you off.*
6. SLANG To abandon or leave someone behind in a rude way: *The movie star suddenly blew off the waiting crowd and left the building. We set off to go fishing together, but halfway there my friends blew me off and went to the park instead.*
7. SLANG To treat something as unimportant; dismiss or ignore something: *The writer blew off the criticism and continued to write as before. They made an unkind remark, but I just blew it off.*
8. VULGAR SLANG To perform fellatio on someone.

blow out

1. To extinguish something with the breath or a gust of air: *The child blew out the candles on the birthday cake. The lamp was flickering, so I blew it out.*
2. To be extinguished by the breath or a gust of air: *If the wind picks up, our fire will blow out.*
3. To remove or burst something with powerful or violent force: *The blast blew out all the windows on the block. The sudden pressure blew the pipes out.*
4. To cause something to burst: *The glass on the road blew out our tires. A nail got caught under the inner tube and blew it out.*
5. To burst: *The front tire blew out when we were driving down the road.*
6. To cause something to stop functioning suddenly. Used of an electrical apparatus: *Playing your stereo too loudly will blow your speakers out. The surge in current blew out the microchips in my computer.*
7. To stop functioning suddenly. Used of an electrical apparatus: *Because the light bulb was old, it blew out.*
8. To erupt in an uncontrolled manner. Used of a gas or oil well: *If the safety valve breaks, the well might blow out and spill oil everywhere.*

9. To diminish; subside. Used reflexively of windy weather conditions: *Until the storm blows itself out, we'll have to stay inside.*

blow over

1. To upset or tip something or someone by the force of moving air: *The hurricane blew over many large billboards. I set up a flagpole outside, but the wind blew it over.*
2. To be upset or tipped by the force of moving air: *Our tents blew over in the storm.*
3. To subside or wane with little lasting effect; die down: *The storm blew over quickly. The scandal will soon blow over.*

blow up

1. To destroy something or someone by explosion: *The soldiers will blow the bridge up. The dynamite blew up the abandoned building.*
2. To explode: *I pressed the red button, and the bomb blew up.*
3. To start suddenly and with force: *A storm blew up as we were walking home.*
4. To fill something with air or gas; inflate something: *We need to blow up the tires of this old bicycle. The clown blew some balloons up for the kids to play with.*
5. To increase the size or scale of an image of something, as for display or in order to view it more closely: *We blew up the document to make a poster out of it. If we blow the photograph up we can see more detail.*
6. To become very angry: *My date blew up when I suggested we leave the party early.*
7. To exaggerate something: *Don't blow the story up into such a great disaster; it wasn't that bad. It may sound impressive, but I'm sure they're blowing up what really happened.*

◆ **board** (bôrd)
boarded (bôr′dĭd), **boarding** (bôr′dĭng), **boards** (bôrdz)

board up

1. To fill or block an opening with boards: *The carpenter boarded up the hole in the wall to keep the cold air from coming in. Before the storm, we boarded the windows up.*
2. To enclose or seal a building or part of a building with boards: *The landlord boarded up the old building to keep trespassers away. Two weeks after the owners closed the motel, they boarded it up.*

◆ **bob** (bŏb)
bobbed (bŏbd), **bobbing** (bŏb′ĭng), **bobs** (bŏbz)

bob up

To come to the surface quickly, especially after being underneath for a short time: *I didn't think anyone else was swimming in the pond, but then someone's head bobbed up right in front of me.*

◆ **boil** (boil)
boiled (boild), **boiling** (boi′lĭng), **boils** (boilz)

boil down

1. To make an amount of liquid or food less in quantity or more concentrated by boiling it: *You can boil down the leftover juices and make a nice sauce. The soup seemed thin, so I boiled it down.*

2. To condense something to its bare essentials; summarize: *I boiled down my long report into a short two-page report. This plan is too long for me to read; can you boil it down for me?*
3. To have something as a basic or root cause: *All of the complaints at work boil down to a lack of good leadership.*

boil over

1. To rise and flow over the sides of a container while boiling. Used of a liquid: *I turned up the heat too high and the soup boiled over.*
2. To erupt in violent anger: *When I realized I had been robbed, I boiled over and started yelling.*

boil up

1. To prepare some food by boiling it: *I boiled up some lobster for supper. Let's boil the potatoes up and fry them with ham.*
2. To grow rapidly and steadily; escalate: *Hostilities have been boiling up all over that part of the world.*

◆ **bollix** (bŏl′ĭks)

bollixed (bŏl′ĭkst), **bollixing** (bŏl′ĭk-sĭng), **bollixes** (bŏl′ĭk-sĭz)

bollix up

To make a mess of something because of mistakes or poor judgment: *I'm afraid you've bollixed up that job badly! Don't make me paint the chairs; I'll just bollix it up.*

◆ **bomb** (bŏm)

bombed (bŏmd), **bombing** (bŏm′ĭng), **bombs** (bŏmz)

bomb out

1. To cause something to be damaged completely due to bombing. Used chiefly in the passive: *The town was bombed out during the war.*
2. To be compelled or forced to leave some place due to bombardment: *My grandparents' family was bombed out of their house twice during the war. The only way to get the guerillas to leave the area is to bomb them out.*
3. To be compelled or forced to leave some place because of miserable failure: *Because he didn't study enough, he bombed out of college.*

bomb through

1. To drop a bomb or bombs so that they pass through something before detonating: *Due to a storm, the plane was forced to bomb through thick cloud cover.*
2. To penetrate some obstacle with bombs: *The soldiers bombed through the wall of the fortress.*
3. To move rapidly and aggressively through something: *They bombed through the town on motorcycles. The dirt bike bombed through the course.*
4. To accomplish or proceed with something swiftly and aggressively: *The soccer team bombed through the tournament and made it to the finals.*

ă	pat	är	car	ī	bite	ô	paw	ŏŏ	took	ûr	urge
ā	pay	ĕ	pet	îr	pier	ôr	core	ŏŏr	lure	zh	vision
âr	care	ē	be	ŏ	pot	oi	boy	ōō	boot	ə	about, item
ä	father	ĭ	pit	ō	toe	ou	out	ŭ	cut		

◆ **bone** (bōn)
boned (bōnd), **boning** (bō′nĭng), **bones** (bōnz)

bone up
To improve or hone some skill or ability in preparation for some event: *The candidate boned up on foreign policy for the big debate. I wanted a decent grade, so I boned up for the final exam. Before visiting Paris, he boned up on his French.*

◆ **book** (bŏŏk)
booked (bŏŏkt), **booking** (bŏŏk′ĭng), **books** (bŏŏks)

book up
To reserve all the available places or times, such as seats, rooms, or appointment hours, from something or someone: *We couldn't get a place to sit because someone had booked up the entire restaurant. There are only two small hotels on the island, and their regular customers book them up a year in advance. You'll never get an appointment; the doctor is booked up through the next month.*

◆ **boom** (bo͞om)
boomed (bo͞omd), **booming** (bo͞o′mĭng), **booms** (bo͞omz)

boom out
1. To make a loud, deep sound: *Rock music suddenly boomed out from the speakers.*
2. To say something very loudly: *She boomed her speech out to the entire building over the public address system. He boomed out the sermon in his thunderous voice.*

◆ **boot** (bo͞ot)
booted (bo͞o′tĭd), **booting** (bo͞o′tĭng), **boots** (bo͞ots)

boot out
To force someone or something to leave a place or position: *The principal booted the troublemaker out of the school. I booted the peddler out the door. The fan who threw a bottle at the umpire was booted out of the ballpark.*

boot up
1. To cause some computer or similar device to start working and and prepare for operation: *This program will boot up your disk drive automatically. My computer is so badly damaged that I can't even boot it up.*
2. To start working and prepare for operation. Used of computers and related devices: *My new computer boots up in less than 30 seconds.*

◆ **booze** (bo͞oz)
boozed (bo͞ozd), **boozing** (bo͞o′zĭng), **boozes** (bo͞o′zĭz)

booze up
1. To consume alcoholic beverages steadily: *They were boozing up all night and didn't come home until sunrise.*
2. To serve someone enough alcohol to cause drunkenness: *The sales representative was well known for boozing up her clients after a sale. He doesn't seem friendly, but he's more sociable if you booze him up a bit.*
3. To become drunk. Used in the passive: *I was too boozed up to drive home.*

◆ **border** (bôr′dər)

bordered (bôr′dərd), **bordering** (bôr′də-rĭng), **borders** (bôr′dərz)

border on *or* **border upon**

1. To be next to something in location: *New York State borders on Lake Ontario. My property borders upon a small lake.*
2. To come close to being something, especially in association, meaning, or intent; verge on something: *Your harsh criticism borders on being offensive. Some of their jokes were funny, but others bordered upon the ridiculous!*

◆ **bore** (bôr)

bored (bôrd), **boring** (bôr′ĭng), **bores** (bôrz)

bore into

1. To make some hole or perforation in something by piercing, drilling, or digging: *The termite bore little holes into the side of the wooden chest. I used a small drill bit to bore into the wood.*
2. To stare at someone or something intently: *I could sense everyone's eyes boring into my back as I left the room.*

◆ **boss** (bôs)

bossed (bôst), **bossing** (bô′sĭng), **bosses** (bô′sĭz)

boss around

To give someone orders in a forceful and unpleasant way: *My older brothers and sisters are always bossing me around. What gives you the right to boss around everyone on the playground?*

◆ **botch** (bŏch)

botched (bŏcht), **botching** (bŏch′ĭng), **botches** (bŏch′ĭz)

botch up

To make a mess of something because of mistakes or poor judgment: *You've botched up that job and you'll have to start all over again. I won't try painting the chairs—I would just botch them up.*

◆ **bottle** (bŏt′l)

bottled (bŏt′ld), **bottling** (bŏt′l-ĭng), **bottles** (bŏt′lz)

bottle up

1. To store something by putting it in a bottle or bottles: *We will need an hour to bottle up the apple juice. After the wine is fully fermented, we bottle it up and let it age.*
2. To contain or suppress something, especially emotions, and not express or reveal them: *If you keep bottling up what you're thinking, we'll never be able to help you. I was angry, but I bottled my feelings up.*

◆ **bottom** (bŏt′əm)

bottomed (bŏt′əmd), **bottoming** (bŏt′ə-mĭng), **bottoms** (bŏt′əmz)

bottom out

To descend to the lowest point possible, after which only an increase

ă	pat	är	car	ī	bite	ô	paw	ŏŏ	took	ûr	urge
ā	pay	ĕ	pet	îr	pier	ôr	core	ŏŏr	lure	zh	vision
âr	care	ē	be	ŏ	pot	oi	boy	ōō	boot	ə	about,
ä	father	ĭ	pit	ō	toe	ou	out	ŭ	cut		item

is possible: *The company's sales of computers have bottomed out, but they should increase when a new model comes out.*

◆ **bounce** (bouns)

bounced (bounst), **bouncing** (boun′sĭng), **bounces** (boun′sĭz)

bounce around

1. To rebound repeatedly in various directions: *The ball landed in my bedroom and bounced around, knocking over a vase on the shelf.*
2. To cause something to rebound in various directions: *Don't bounce the basketball around in the living room! Let's go outside and bounce around my new rubber ball.*
3. To move about energetically or restlessly in various directions: *The scared mouse bounced around all over the room. The kids are bouncing around in the back seat of the car.*
4. To discuss something with a number of people: *I bounced my new idea around at the meeting, and some people gave me some very interesting comments on it.*
5. To circulate among a number of people. Used of a name, word, or idea: *That rumor has been bouncing around here for years.*

bounce back

1. To rebound after striking an object or a surface: *I threw the tennis ball at the wall, and it bounced back and hit me on the head.*
2. To recover quickly, as from a setback or illness: *Although the surgery was difficult, the patient bounced back to good health very quickly.*

bounce off

1. To cause something to rebound from something: *She bounced the tennis ball off the wall.*
2. To rebound from something or someone: *The basketball hit the rim and bounced off.*
3. To present some idea or thought to someone for comment or approval: *I have been thinking about what we should do next, so let me bounce a few ideas off you.*

◆ **bow** (bou)

bowed (boud), **bowing** (bou′ĭng), **bows** (bouz)

bow down

1. To bend the head or the top part of the body forward as a sign of respect: *The loyal subjects stood before the throne and bowed down to the king and queen.*
2. To submit to someone's orders without offering resistance: *The rebels refused to bow down to a corrupt government.*

bow out

To stop taking part in an activity or give up a position: *Because of my illness, I had to bow out of my role as president. The singer bowed out of the talent show at the last minute.*

◆ **bowl** (bōl)

bowled (bōld), **bowling** (bō′lĭng), **bowls** (bōlz)

bowl out

CHIEFLY BRITISH In the game of cricket, to retire some batsman with a bowled ball that knocks the bails off the wicket. Used chiefly in the passive: *They played well but were bowled out shortly after lunch.*

bowl over

1. To knock someone or something down to the ground: *The kids ran down the hallway, bowling over everyone in their way. A strong wind will bowl that billboard over.*
2. To make a powerful impression on someone; astound someone: *She bowled over everyone at the meeting with her amazing presentation. His new songs bowled me over, so I bought his new CD. You must go hear this poet—you will be bowled over!*

◆ **box** (bŏks)

boxed (bŏkst), **boxing** (bŏk′sĭng), **boxes** (bŏk′sĭz)

box in

1. To trap or confine someone or something in a limited space or region: *We boxed in the left corner of the living room with a new wall and curtains. The enemy forces had boxed us in on all sides.*
2. To prevent someone from acting freely, usually by creating restrictions or obstacles: *Being too strict will box in your students and prevent them from being creative. I want to make some changes at the office, but my boss has boxed me in with too many rules.*

◆ **brace** (brās)

braced (brāst), **bracing** (brā′sĭng), **braces** (brā′sĭz)

brace up

1. To provide something or someone with additional support; prop up someone or something: *We used plywood to brace up the wall paneling. The old tower would have fallen down if we hadn't braced it up.*
2. To prepare or strengthen someone or something to face some challenge: *We braced up the car for the road race. They gave me some encouraging words to brace me up for the interview. I'm glad you were braced up for your exams.*
3. To summon one's strength or endurance; prepare to face a challenge: *I spent all day bracing up for my performance in the concert that evening.*

◆ **branch** (brănch)

branched (brăncht), **branching** (brăn′chĭng), **branches** (brăn′chĭz)

branch off

1. To separate from a main road or path and follow a smaller one: *Take a left where the main trail branches off onto a footpath.*
2. To separate from a primary source or origin and move or develop in a different direction: *After we discovered a new species of insect, some members of our research team branched off and are studying it. A new political group has branched off from the old party.*

ă	pat	är	car	ī	bite	ô	paw	o͝o	took	ûr	urge
ā	pay	ĕ	pet	îr	pier	ôr	core	o͝or	lure	zh	vision
âr	care	ē	be	ŏ	pot	oi	boy	o͞o	boot	ə	about, item
ä	father	ĭ	pit	ō	toe	ou	out	ŭ	cut		

branch out

1. To develop or have many branches or tributaries: *Once this tree reaches a certain size, it will begin to branch out. The river branches out into a great delta before flowing into the sea.*
2. To grow out of a tree trunk or branch: *I like to sit on a large limb that branches out from the apple tree.*
3. To expand the scope of one's interests or activities into a new area or areas: *At first I studied only Latin, but later I branched out and began learning other languages, too.*

◆ **brave** (brāv)

braved (brāvd), **braving** (brā′vĭng), **braves** (brāvz)

brave out

To endure something with great courage: *The explorers braved out the hot weather and dangerous animals during their journey. It will be a tough game against such strong players, but you should brave it out and play as well as you can.*

◆ **brazen** (brā′zən)

brazened (brā′zənd), **brazening** brā′zə-nĭng), **brazens** (brā′zənz)

brazen out

1. To face or endure something boldly: *The determined people brazened out the political crisis. Your first month in the army will be tough, but I know you can brazen it out.*
2. To face or admit to something shameful or untrue without expressing any remorse or shame: *I can't believe that the government would brazen out such a terrible scandal. Instead of admitting that her story was a lie, she brazened it out.*
3. To invent some bold story to cover up something that is embarrassing: *The angry student brazened out a poor excuse for his bad behavior.*

◆ **break** (brāk)

broke (brōk), **broken** (brō′kən), **breaking** (brā′kĭng), **breaks** (brāks)

break away

1. To separate or detach something in order to clear a space: *It was easier to dig through the snow once we had broken the icy crust away.*
2. To separate or detach oneself: *Our politics began to change, so we broke away from the political party we had belonged to. The ice on the shore began to break away once the weather got warmer.*
3. To move rapidly away from or ahead of a group: *The cyclist broke away from the pack and was soon very far ahead.*

break down

1. To cause something to collapse, especially by hitting it: *The firefighters broke down the door of the burning house. The bulldozer pushed at the old wall and broke it down.*
2. To collapse, especially as a result of force or pressure; give way: *The door finally broke down after I kept hitting it with a club.*
3. To cause someone to stop resisting, especially by force or pressure: *The police will break you down and make you talk.*
4. To stop resisting; accede: *My friends kept pleading with me to*

go to the beach, so I finally broke down and went along with them.

5. To destroy or remove something, especially something viewed as a problem: *This political party hopes to break down the barriers between social classes. Let's identify the obstacles and break them down.*
6. To stop functioning: *The elevator broke down, so please use the stairs.*
7. To be a passenger in a vehicle that stops functioning: *We're late because we broke down just outside the city.*
8. To fail despite effort; come to a stop: *The negotiations between the warring nations broke down, and the fighting continued.*
9. To suffer an emotional or mental collapse: *The stress of my new job was so high that I eventually broke down and couldn't go to work for days.*
10. To separate something into parts; take something apart: *When the carnival was over, we broke down all the tents. The workers broke down the equipment and put it into storage.*
11. To examine or explain something by looking at its parts; analyze something: *Break down your story into its main themes and write each part separately. This problem looks very difficult, but if we break it down, it becomes easy to solve.*
12. To be divisible into smaller parts: *The population of the city breaks down into three main groups: the poor, the rich, and the middle class.*

break in

1. To enter a place forcibly or illegally: *While we were out of the house, a thief tried to break in.*
2. To interrupt a conversation or discussion: *We were talking about the weather when my friend broke in and said it was time to leave.*
3. To loosen or soften something with use: *I need to break in my new boots before I take any long hikes.*
4. To train or domesticate an animal: *Be sure to break in your puppies at an early age. The horses were very good to ride once the trainer had broken them in.*
5. To accustom someone to a new task: *The sergeant broke in the new recruits to the army way of life. It was hard to keep up with the work, but my colleagues broke me in gradually.*

break into

1. To enter some place forcibly: *Someone broke into our house while we were gone and stole our TV.*
2. To access a computer or computer network illegally or maliciously: *We believe spies are breaking into the government's computer files.*
3. To interrupt something: *I'm sorry that I have to break into your nap, but it's important that I speak to you now.*

ă	pat	är	car	ī	bite	ô	paw	o͝o	took	ûr	urge
ā	pay	ĕ	pet	îr	pier	ôr	core	o͝or	lure	zh	vision
âr	care	ē	be	ŏ	pot	oi	boy	o͞o	boot	ə	about,
ä	father	ĭ	pit	ō	toe	ou	out	ŭ	cut		item

4. To begin to do something suddenly: *The horse broke into a wild gallop. The upset child broke into a flood of tears.*
5. To enter some established profession or field of activity: *The young writer broke into journalism right after college.*

break off

1. To separate a piece of something from some whole, especially by force: *We broke the icicles off the gutters of the house. I broke off a piece of chocolate and gave it to my friend. The truck hit my rear-view mirror and broke it off.*
2. To become separated from some whole: *A large piece of ice broke off the iceberg and crashed into the water. I dropped my coffee mug and the handle broke off.*
3. To stop or end suddenly. Especially used of communication: *He began the first line of his speech and then mysteriously broke off. Unfortunately, the peace talks between the countries broke off.*
4. To end some relationship: *Although I am angry, I do not want to break off my long relationship with you. The countries broke off all diplomatic ties and went to war.*

break out

1. To escape confinement: *The prisoners dug a tunnel under the prison walls and broke out. He broke out from jail but was immediately caught.*
2. To aid something or someone in escaping confinement: *The gangsters broke their comrade out of jail.*
3. To develop suddenly and forcefully; erupt: *Fighting broke out in the street when the two gangs came together.*
4. To start doing something suddenly or spontaneously: *We were quietly eating dinner when suddenly the kids broke out laughing. The marching soldiers broke out in song.*
5. To bring something forth: *The enemy is attacking; break out the rifles! Let's break out the champagne and celebrate.*
6. To become affected with pimples, hives, acne, or similar skin rash: *Wash your face well in the evening or you'll break out. I accidentally walked through poison ivy and broke out in a bad rash.*

break through

1. To force a path through some obstruction by penetrating and breaking it: *The escaping bank robbers broke through the police barricade by ramming it with their car.*
2. To achieve a major success that permits further progress: *With the discovery of the new drug, the scientists broke through in their fight against cancer.*

break up

1. To divide something into pieces: *He broke up a piece of chocolate and scattered the pieces on top of the cake. She took the damaged table outside and broke it up with an axe for use as firewood.*
2. To separate or shatter into pieces: *The falling rocket broke up before it hit the ground.*
3. To cause a relationship or partnership to end: *Personal tensions*

broke the rock band up. I'm not trying to break up their marriage.

4. To end a relationship or partnership; separate: *I thought they would be married by the end of the year, but they broke up instead.*
5. To cause a crowd or gathering to disperse: *The protest rally was getting very big and noisy when the police came and broke it up. The teacher came outside to break up the group of children that were fighting.*
6. To disperse: *The crowd broke up after the concert was over.*
7. To cause someone to laugh or cry very hard: *That story that you told really broke me up!*
8. To laugh or cry very hard: *She broke up when I told her the joke. He broke up when he heard the sad news.*
9. To be unclear because of technical difficulties. Used of radio and telephone signals: *My radio started breaking up as I drove through the tunnel. There must be something wrong with your phone; your signal is breaking up!*
10. To add variety to something: *The vertical stripes break up the horizontal patterns on the wall. I take a short walk after lunch to break up the routine of the workday.*

break with

1. To discontinue something that has been ongoing or continuous: *This year we broke with tradition and did not get a pumpkin for Halloween. The new farming technology has forced the farmers to break with their old methods.*
2. To stop communicating with someone, especially because of distance or hostility: *The brothers broke with the rest of the family when they moved out of town. I broke with my colleagues for years after our big argument.*

◆ **breathe** (brē*th*)

breathed (brē*th*d), **breathing** (brē′*th*ĭng), **breathes** (brē*th*z)

breathe in

1. To inhale: *Don't forget to breathe in and hold your breath before you jump into the water!*
2. To take something into the lungs by inhaling: *My lungs are unhealthy because I've been breathing in smoke from the factory for so many years. There is poisonous gas here; don't breathe it in.*

breathe out

1. To exhale: *Breathe out slowly, and you will relax more easily.*
2. To expel something from the lungs by exhaling: *I closed my eyes and breathed out a sigh. The yoga instructor told everyone to take a big breath, hold it for ten seconds, and then breathe it out.*

◆ **breeze** (brēz)

breezed (brēzd), **breezing** (brē′zĭng), **breezes** (brē′zĭz)

ă	pat	är	car	ī	bite	ô	paw	ŏŏ	took	ûr	urge
ā	pay	ĕ	pet	îr	pier	ôr	core	ŏŏr	lure	zh	vision
âr	care	ē	be	ŏ	pot	oi	boy	o͞o	boot	ə	about,
ä	father	ĭ	pit	ō	toe	ou	out	ŭ	cut		item

breeze through

1. To pass through some place swiftly and without lingering: *The couple breezed through the room before anyone could say hello to them.*
2. To make progress with something swiftly and effortlessly: *The smart student breezed through the test.*

◆ **brick** (brĭk)

bricked (brĭkt), **bricking** (brĭk′ĭng), **bricks** (brĭks)

brick up

To fill or block an opening with a wall of bricks: *The owners of the old factory bricked up the windows to keep animals and curious children out. The builders bricked the old doorway up and covered it with drywall.*

◆ **brighten** (brīt′n)

brightened (brīt′nd), **brightening** (brīt′n-ĭng), **brightens** (brīt′nz)

brighten up

1. To become brighter or more intense in color: *The sky brightened up quickly as the clouds dispersed.*
2. To make something brighter or more intense in color: *Some red paint will brighten up this dreary room. Put some yellow into the dye to brighten it up.*
3. To become happier; improve one's mood or outlook: *He brightened up after you began talking with him.*
4. To make someone happier or more cheerful: *The sunny weather brightened up the tired travelers. A cool glass of lemonade would brighten me up right now.*

◆ **bring** (brĭng)

brought (brôt), **bringing** (brĭng′ĭng), **brings** (brĭngz)

bring about

To cause something to happen, especially an overall change: *The invention of the internal-combustion engine brought about a huge shift in people's mobility. The new manager decided it was time to bring some changes about.*

bring along

To bring someone or something into one's care or keeping while going somewhere: *I brought a book along for the long flight. The chaperones will bring along 20 children to the museum.*

bring around *or* **bring round**

1. To move or lead something or someone to a particular place: *Please bring the car around to the front of the building. You should bring your kids around to play with our kids sometime.*
2. To distribute something among a group: *The servers will be bringing around refreshments shortly. If you're all hungry, I can bring some sandwiches around.*
3. To direct some conversation toward a particular subject: *At the meeting, I tried to bring the discussion around to our biggest problems, but no one wanted to talk about them.*
4. To persuade someone to adopt a particular point of view or to do something: *The employees tried to bring around their boss to their way of approaching the problem. He was reluctant to come with her, but she brought him around.*

5. To cause someone to recover consciousness: *I had passed out, but the fresh air brought me around.*

bring down

1. To move something or someone from a higher to a lower position: *He brought down the plates from the top shelf. She brought the trunk down from the attic.*
2. To cause something to fall or collapse: *The explosives went off and brought down the old building. That tower is so strong that no wind could bring it down.*
3. To reduce the amount or level of something: *I opened the window to bring down the temperature in my room. Can you bring the volume of the stereo down a bit?*
4. To remove a ruler or government from a position of power: *The rebels intend to bring down the government. A strong opposition to the leaders could bring them down. The president was brought down by the scandal.*
5. Slang To depress or discourage someone: *The argument I had with my friends really brought me down.*

bring forth

1. To present something or someone: *Bring forth the best champagne for our hero!*
2. To give rise to something; produce something: *Our speech brought forth enthusiastic applause.*
3. To give birth to someone: *Eight months after conception, she brought forth a child.*

bring forward

1. To present or produce something or someone: *The lawyer needs to bring forward some real evidence to the court. If you have the information, please bring it forward.*
2. To move an event or engagement to an earlier date or time: *My boss brought forward the conference by three days so I could attend it before I left for vacation. That meeting is scheduled too late; we'll have to bring it forward.*
3. In accounting, to carry a sum from one page or column to another: *I copied the number incorrectly when I brought it forward to the last page. Bring forward your total on this column to line 4 of the next column.*

bring in

1. To move or guide something or someone into some place: *Please bring in the newspaper before you close the door. I brought my child in to wait with me in my office.*
2. To earn or yield a particular amount of money: *Their wise investments have brought in millions of dollars. My second job brings a few extra dollars in.*
3. To attract something or someone, such as business or customers: *The new campaign has brought in thousands of tourists to the city.*

ă	pat	är	car	ī	bite	ô	paw	o͝o	took	ûr	urge
ā	pay	ĕ	pet	îr	pier	ôr	core	o͝or	lure	zh	vision
âr	care	ē	be	ŏ	pot	oi	boy	o͞o	boot	ə	about,
ä	father	ĭ	pit	ō	toe	ou	out	ŭ	cut		item

The movie should bring in big audiences.

4. To include someone in some activity: *Do you think we should we bring him in on this project? The doctor is bringing in a specialist to look at her case.*
5. To arrest someone for a crime: *They brought my neighbor in on counterfeiting charges. The police want to bring in all of the robbery suspects by the end of the day.*
6. To deliver some legal verdict to a court: *The jury brought in their verdict within the hour. Make sure you are all comfortable with the verdict before you bring it in.*

bring off

1. To accomplish something difficult: *The promoters brought off the series of concerts without a single problem. We planned the party well beforehand so that we would be sure we could bring it off.*
2. VULGAR SLANG To cause someone to achieve orgasm.

bring on

To cause something to arise: *Eating ice cream too fast can bring on a headache. My child threw a terrible tantrum, but I don't know what brought it on.*

bring out

1. To move or guide something or someone out of some place, especially to make it available or visible: *He brought out some food when we arrived. Bring the horses out so we can begin our trip.*
2. To reveal or expose something: *These documents brought out the facts. The new evidence will bring the truth out.*
3. To cause something or the quality of something to be more prominent: *I don't like singing this sort of music because it brings out the weaknesses of my voice. Your shirt brings the color of your eyes out.*
4. To produce or publish something: *I hope my favorite author brings out another book this year. The publishing company has just brought a new magazine out.*

bring round

See **bring around.**

bring to

1. To cause a ship to turn toward the wind or come to a stop: *Some lines were dragging overboard, so we brought the ship to and hauled them in again.*
2. To cause someone to recover consciousness: *I fainted, but the smelling salts brought me to right away.*

bring up

1. To move something or someone from a lower to a higher position: *She brought her hand up to shield her eyes from the sun. I requested that a turkey sandwich be brought up to my hotel room.*
2. To raise someone or something up to adulthood: *My parents died when I was a baby, so my aunt and uncle brought me up. You will have to bring up the puppy by yourself.*
3. To mention or introduce something into discussion: *We were having a pleasant chat until someone brought up politics. I had some questions about the lecture, so I*

brought them up during the discussion.

4. To increase the amount or rate of something: *We must bring up productivity in our department. Our last goal brought the score up to 3-1.*
5. To make information appear on a computer screen: *Can you bring up the main menu again? I brought the old webpage up to compare it with the new one.*

◆ **brown** (broun)

browned (bround), **browning** (brou′nĭng), **browns** (brounz)

brown off

CHIEFLY BRITISH SLANG

To anger or irritate someone: *The nasty way that store clerk treated us really browned me off. By the time the traffic jam cleared up, we were pretty browned off.*

◆ **brush** (brŭsh)

brushed (brŭsht), **brushing** (brŭsh′ĭng), **brushes** (brŭsh′ĭz)

brush aside

1. To push or wave something or someone out of the way: *I brushed aside the clutter and put my books on the desk. The police brushed the people aside to make way for the president.*
2. To refuse to listen to someone or something; ignore someone or something: *I continued to complain, but they brushed aside my protests. Whenever people try to bother me at a party, I just brush them aside.*

brush back

1. To displace something with or as if with a brush: *I brushed back my curly locks from in front of my eyes. Your hair looks better when you brush it back.*
2. BASEBALL To force someone at bat to move away from the plate by throwing an inside pitch: *Some pitchers try to brush back the batter on their first pitch. The pitcher decided to intimidate the batter and brushed him back.*

brush off

1. To remove something from a surface by brushing: *Brush off those crumbs from the breakfast table! There's some dust on the desk, but I'll just brush it off.*
2. To clean or clear some surface by brushing it: *Would you please brush off the picnic table?*
3. To dismiss someone or something rudely: *The store owner rudely brushed off the customer who wanted a refund. I'm mad that you brushed me off when I tried to make a helpful suggestion.*

brush up

1. To collect or dispose of something by a using a brush: *I brushed up the crumbs from the table. The kids brushed the leaves up into a pile and played in it.*
2. To refresh something or improve its quality or appearance, especially

ă	pat	är	car	ī	bite	ô	paw	o͝o	took	ûr	urge
ā	pay	ĕ	pet	îr	pier	ôr	core	o͝or	lure	zh	vision
âr	care	ē	be	ŏ	pot	oi	boy	o͞o	boot	ə	about, item
ä	father	ĭ	pit	ō	toe	ou	out	ŭ	cut		

superficially or modestly: *You could brush up your resume with a few style changes. I haven't spoken Italian in many years, but if I brushed it up a little, I think I could speak very well.*

3. **brush up on** To refresh or improve one's facility with something: *I brushed up on my Spanish by reading newspapers from Mexico.*

◆ **bubble** (bŭb′əl)

bubbled (bŭb′əld), **bubbling** (bŭb′ə-lĭng), **bubbles** (bŭb′əlz)

bubble over

1. To rise and spill over the edges of a container while boiling or effervescing: *Soup bubbled over from the hot pan. Better turn the heat down; your stew is bubbling over!*
2. To be full of some emotion, to the point where one cannot resist expressing it: *We were bubbling over with excitement at the good news.*

bubble up

1. To rise due to a bubbling motion: *Water bubbled up through the hole in the boat. Foam always bubbles up onto the counter when I wash the dishes.*
2. To rise or increase steadily in intensity: *Anger bubbled up in his chest when he heard their crude remarks.*
3. To express some positive emotion: *She bubbled up with joy when she got accepted into college.*

◆ **buck** (bŭk)

bucked (bŭkt), **bucking** (bŭk′ĭng), **bucks** (bŭks)

buck up

1. To make one's self feel more heartened or ready to confront a problem: *I eventually bucked up and started doing something about my financial problems.*
2. To make someone feel more heartened or ready to confront a problem: *Getting a good grade on the quiz bucked me up for the big test. The football team bucked up the crowd when they scored a touchdown.*

◆ **buckle** (bŭk′əl)

buckled (bŭk′əld), **buckling** (bŭk′lĭng), **buckles** (bŭk′əlz)

buckle down

1. To secure something or someone with straps that fasten together with buckles: *Don't forget to buckle down the top of the suitcase before we pack it into the car. We took off our backpacks and buckled them down on the roof of the truck.*
2. To apply oneself and start working seriously at something: *I've wasted a lot of time, and now I have to buckle down and finish my homework.*

buckle under

1. To bend, crumple or collapse under some great weight or pressure: *The bridge supports were weakened by rust and buckled under the weight of the heavy truck. The metal chair I was sitting on suddenly buckled under, and I fell to the ground.*
2. To succumb to or be adversely affected by some pressure: *Some schools have buckled under the strain of having too many new*

students. I had fought very hard against their ideas but finally buckled under to them.

buckle up

1. To secure something or someone with straps that fasten together with buckles: *Buckle up your shoes. We buckled the baby up in its car seat.*
2. To fasten one's seat belt: *The first thing I did when I got on the plane was to buckle up.*
3. To bend or fold in half at the middle: *Everyone buckled up with laughter when they heard my jokes.*

◆ **buddy** (bŭd′ē)

buddied (bŭd′ēd), **buddying** (bŭd′ē-ĭng), **buddies** (bŭd′ēz)

buddy up

1. To pair up and work closely with someone: *Each camper had to buddy up with a friend when swimming. The students buddied up when asked to select locker partners.*
2. **buddy up to** To become overly friendly or familiar with someone, especially in order to gain his or her favor: *The new worker buddied up to the office secretary.*

◆ **budget** (bŭj′ĭt)

budgeted (bŭj′ĭ-tĭd), **budgeting** (bŭj′ĭ-tĭng), **budgets** (bŭj′ĭts)

budget for

To set aside some amount of money for something or someone: *For the party, we budgeted $1,000 for musicians and food.*

◆ **bug** (bŭg)

bugged (bŭgd), **bugging** (bŭg′ĭng), **bugs** (bŭgz)

bug off

SLANG

To go away. Used chiefly as a command: *Bug off! I'm trying to get some work done.*

bug out

1. To grow large; bulge outward: *Your eyes will bug out when you see my new car.*
2. SLANG To leave some place, usually in a hurry: *They made it clear they didn't want me there, so I bugged out.*
3. SLANG To be frightened or confused: *I'm afraid of the dark, so I was bugging out during the blackout.*
4. SLANG To cause someone to be frightened or confused: *The thought of surgery bugs me out.*

◆ **bugger** (bŭg′ər)

buggered (bŭg′ərd), **buggering** (bŭg′ə-rĭng), **buggers** (bŭg′ərz)

bugger off

CHIEFLY BRITISH VULGAR SLANG

To go away. Used chiefly as a command.

◆ **build** (bĭld)

built (bĭlt), **building** (bĭl′dĭng), **builds** (bĭldz)

ă	pat	är	car	ī	bite	ô	paw	ŏŏ	took	ûr	urge
ā	pay	ĕ	pet	îr	pier	ôr	core	ŏŏr	lure	zh	vision
âr	care	ē	be	ŏ	pot	oi	boy	ōō	boot	ə	about,
ä	father	ĭ	pit	ō	toe	ou	out	ŭ	cut		item

build around

1. To construct or develop something that surrounds or avoids something else: *They built the highway around the center of town. If we build a fence around the plants, the goats won't be able to eat them.*
2. To develop something based on someone or something: *The story is built around two characters. I built my bookstore around the idea that people like to browse before they buy anything.*

build in

To construct or include something as an integral part of another thing: *When you install the new bathroom, make sure to build in a towel rack. We didn't add shelves to the wall; we built them in when we constructed the house.*

build into

To make something or someone an integral part of something: *We built overhead lights into the ceiling. The president is building you into the framework of the company.*

build on *or* **build upon**

1. To construct something on the base of something else: *She wants to build a new house on that hill. The pioneer built a small cabin upon the plain.*
2. To use something as a basis or foundation on which to develop something else: *The company built its hiring policy on the principle of fairness. The efficiency of our department is built on hard work.*

build up

1. To develop or increase something in stages or by degrees: *I'm building up my endurance for the big race by running every day. We built the family business up over many years.*
2. To accumulate, collect or increase: *Sediment is building up on the riverbank.*
3. To become bigger, stronger, or bulkier, especially through exercise: *I need to build up if I'm going to make the football team this year.*
4. To bolster something: *The company plans to build up their new product with a big advertising campaign. The interview went well and built up my hopes for getting the job.*
5. To fill some region with buildings: *There was a forest here before they started building up the area. The developer bought the farmland and built it up.*

◆ **bulge** (bŭlj)

bulged (bŭljd), **bulging** (bŭl′jĭng), **bulges** (bŭl′jĭz)

bulge out

1. To swell or protrude outward: *I ate so much that my stomach was bulging out.*
2. To bend or warp out of proper shape or alignment: *If it gets too hot, the sides of the stove will bulge out.*

◆ **bulk** (bŭlk)

bulked (bŭlkt), **bulking** (bŭl′kĭng), **bulks** (bŭlks)

bulk up *or* **bulk out**

1. To increase in size or weight: *The weightlifters are exercising in order to bulk out.*

2. To cause someone or something to increase in size, weight, or degree: *I hope all the food I'm eating doesn't bulk me out too much. All of the new employees have bulked out the company's payroll.*

◆ **bump** (bŭmp)

bumped (bŭmpt), **bumping** (bŭm′pĭng), **bumps** (bŭmps)

bump into

1. To collide with someone or something accidentally: *I wasn't looking where I was going and bumped into a garbage can.*
2. To encounter someone or something by chance: *I often bump into my friends at the grocery store.*

bump off

1. To remove someone or something from a list or hierarchy due to lack of time or space: *To make room for people who would pay for seats, the concert manager bumped off everybody on the guest list. The airline had to bump me off because the flight was oversold.*
2. To break someone's connection between a computer and the Internet or other network: *Something strange happened on my computer and it has bumped me off the Internet. I got bumped off before I could finish downloading the file.*
3. SLANG To murder someone: *The gang threatened to bump off anyone who interfered with their plan. The ringleader hired someone to bump his enemies off.*

bump up

1. To damage or batter someone or something: *Whoever tried to park that truck bumped up my car pretty badly. The skiing accident bumped me up a bit, but I'm okay.*
2. To move someone to a higher position in a list: *The doctors bumped up anyone who needed immediate medical attention to the top of the list. My friend at the theater bumped me up in the line for tickets.*
3. To raise something or someone to a higher category or level: *The store had to bump up their prices when the price of heating oil went up. All I had to do was ask, and the airline bumped me up from coach to business class.*

◆ **bunch** (bŭnch)

bunched (bŭncht), **bunching** (bŭn′chĭng), **bunches** (bŭn′chĭz)

bunch up

1. To move close together to form a tight group; cluster: *The kids bunched up in a corner of the room, whispering to each other.*
2. To pack some people or things together tightly: *Bunch up the blankets and stuff them into the bag. I didn't like what I had written on the page, so I bunched it up and threw it out.*

ă	pat	är	car	ī	bite	ô	paw	ŏŏ	took	ûr	urge
ā	pay	ĕ	pet	îr	pier	ôr	core	ŏŏr	lure	zh	vision
âr	care	ē	be	ŏ	pot	oi	boy	ōō	boot	ə	about, item
ä	father	ĭ	pit	ō	toe	ou	out	ŭ	cut		

3. To come together or be more concentrated in one place: *The cloth bunches up at the cuff of my shirt.*

◆ **bundle** (bŭn′dl)

bundled (bŭn′dld), **bundling** (bŭn′dl-ĭng), **bundles** (bŭn′dlz)

bundle off

1. To send something somewhere or to someone in a tightly wrapped package: *Bundle off those boxes of books for storage in the attic. I bundled my laundry off to the cleaners.*
2. To send someone to some place, especially in a hurry or without his or her consent: *She bundled the kids off to their grandparents' house for the holiday.*
3. **bundle off to** To depart for some place: *I bundled off to catch my flight.*

bundle up

1. To gather or tie something together in a tight package: *He bundled up his belongings and left for college. She bundled her manuscript up and sent it to the publisher.*
2. To wrap someone snugly in warm clothes or blankets: *She bundled up the baby and laid him in the crib. He bundled the kids up and sent them out to play in the snow.*
3. To dress snugly in warm clothes or blankets: *I bundled up and went outside.*

◆ **bunk** (bŭngk)

bunked (bŭngkt), **bunking** (bŭng′kĭng), **bunks** (bŭngks)

bunk up

To share a bed or sleeping accommodations, especially temporarily: *Before they moved to a bigger house, she had to bunk up with her sister. The campers would bunk up together if it got too cold.*

◆ **buoy** (bo͞o′ē, boi)

buoyed (bo͞o′ēd, boid), **buoying** (bo͞o′ē-ĭng, boi′ĭng), **buoys** (bo͞o′ēz, boiz)

buoy up

1. To keep something or someone aloft or afloat: *Air currents helped buoy up the glider. The life jacket buoyed me up until I was rescued.*
2. To keep something at a high level; support something: *The advertising campaign buoyed up their sales through the summer. The athlete's endorsement buoyed the politician up.*
3. To hearten or inspire someone or something: *The cheering fans buoyed up the team's spirit. Your kind words have buoyed me up.*

◆ **burn** (bûrn)

burned (bûrnd) *or* **burnt** (bûrnt), **burning** (bûr′nĭng), **burns** (bûrnz)

burn in

1. To engrave or etch something, such as marks or letters, on a surface by the use of intense heat: *I burned in the image of an eagle and then varnished the wood.*
2. To darken or brighten a part of a photographic print or negative by exposing unmasked areas: *Burn in the edges of the picture to create a darkened border. You can burn in the highlights to enhance their effect.*
3. To become a permanently visible image due to constant exposure: *The message was displayed on the*

computer screen so long that it burned in.

4. To implant something firmly in the memory: *I repeated the poem over and over again to burn it in my mind. The image of the forest fire has been burned in my memory.*

burn out

1. To stop burning from lack of fuel: *The candle burned out in a wisp of smoke. The bonfire burned out, and we threw sand on the embers.*
2. To become inoperative as a result of excess heat or friction: *This vacuum cleaner needs to be fixed—I think the motor burned out.*
3. To destroy some structure completely by fire, so that only the frame is left. Used chiefly in the passive: *City hall was burned out in the attack.*
4. To be compelled or forced to leave some place due to fire. Used chiefly in the passive: *The shopkeeper was burned out by arsonists.*
5. To become exhausted, especially as a result of stress or excessive work: *I'm so burned out with work—I could really use a vacation.*
6. To make someone exhausted as a result of stress or excessive work: *Your busy schedule will burn you out if you don't take a break soon. I burned myself out by studying too late into the night.*

burn through

1. To penetrate something with flames: *The flames were burning through the ceiling. The firefighters came too late and the walls were already burned through.*
2. To create some opening by burning: *The sparks hit my sweater and burned a hole through the sleeve.*
3. To expend something completely; use something up: *I burned through all my money in one evening.*

burn up

1. To destroy something or someone by fire or heat: *She burned the contract up. He burned up all the photographs.*
2. To be completely destroyed by fire or heat: *The cabin burned up, leaving only ashes.*
3. To expend something; use something up: *When I was on vacation, I burned up all my money quickly. I'm really burning up calories with this exercise plan.*
4. To make someone angry: *Their rudeness really burns me up.*
5. To travel over or through something at high speed: *The racecars were really burning up the track.*

◆ **burst** (bûrst)

burst (bûrst), **bursting** (bûr′stĭng), **bursts** (bûrsts)

burst in

1. To enter some place suddenly and forcefully: *While the gangsters were playing cards, the police burst in and arrested everyone.*

ă	pat	är	car	ī	bite	ô	paw	o͝o	took	ûr	urge
ā	pay	ĕ	pet	îr	pier	ôr	core	o͝or	lure	zh	vision
âr	care	ē	be	ŏ	pot	oi	boy	o͞o	boot	ə	about, item
ä	father	ĭ	pit	ō	toe	ou	out	ŭ	cut		

2. To interrupt or intrude: *I hate to burst in, but you have an important message from work. He burst in to the meeting to let us know that there was a fire drill.*

burst into

1. To enter some place suddenly and forcefully: *The police burst into the room and conducted a raid.*
2. To start doing something suddenly: *Sometimes we burst into song while we're hiking in the mountains.*

burst out

1. To explode outward: *The container was under so much pressure that it burst out.*
2. To leave some place suddenly and forcefully: *The doors from the bar opened and the crowd burst out. After school, the children burst out onto the playground.*
3. To say something suddenly and loudly: *The defendant burst out at the lawyers from the witness stand.*
4. To start doing something suddenly: *At the end of my story, everyone burst out laughing. The children burst out in song.*

◆ **butt** (bŭt)

butted (bŭt′ĭd) *or* **butt** (bŭt), **butting** (bŭt′ĭng), **butts** (bŭts)

butt in

To intrude upon or interrupt someone or something: *You're always butting in my conversations, and I wish you'd stop. I can't believe that you butted in on that meeting! We were having a good talk until you butt in.*

butt out

SLANG

1. To stop interfering or meddling in someone's affairs. Often used as a command: *Butt out!—This conversation is none of your business! I wish you'd butt out when I'm trying to talk to my boss.*
2. To leave some place hastily; depart: *If anyone sees us, let's butt out of the room. The thieves stole my bag and butted out.*

◆ **butter** (bŭt′ər)

buttered (bŭt′ərd), **buttering** (bŭt′ə-rĭng), **butters** (bŭt′ərz)

butter up

To praise or flatter someone in order to make him or her more receptive or willing: *My coworker, hoping for a raise, is always buttering up the boss. If we butter up the bartender, maybe he'll buy us a drink.*

◆ **button** (bŭt′n)

buttoned (bŭt′nd), **buttoning** (bŭt′n-ĭng), **buttons** (bŭt′nz)

button up

1. To fasten all the buttons on a garment: *He buttoned up the sweater. She buttoned her shirt up.*
2. To stop talking: *The students buttoned up when the principal walked past. Button up!—You're going to get us in trouble.*
3. To close or seal something securely: *We buttoned up the cabin for winter.*
4. To complete the final details of something: *The author is buttoning up the paperback rights before publication.*

◆ **buy** (bī)

bought (bôt), **buying** (bī′ĭng), **buys** (bīz)

buy into

1. To acquire a stake or interest in something, especially a business or organization: *I bought into a risky real estate venture, and fortunately I didn't lose any money.*
2. To believe in something, especially wholeheartedly or uncritically: *I can't buy into your brand of politics.*

buy off

To bribe someone in order to ensure cooperation: *I didn't get a speeding ticket because I bought off the police officer. The mobster avoided jail by buying the judge off.*

buy out

1. To purchase someone's share of stock, business rights, or interests: *I bought my partner out, and now I am the sole owner of the company.*
2. To purchase something entirely or completely: *The investor bought out the company. The larger company intends to buy the smaller one out.*

buy up

1. To purchase something entirely or completely: *The real estate agent bought up all the land in the area. I wanted to get one of those T-shirts, but someone has already bought them up.*
2. To quickly purchase as much of something as possible, especially when supplies are limited: *People are buying up food supplies in case the blizzard hits. I bought all the donuts up at the bakery and took them to work.*

◆ **buzz** (bŭz)

buzzed (bŭzd), **buzzing** (bŭz′ĭng), **buzzes** (bŭz′ĭz)

buzz off

SLANG

To leave quickly; go away. Used chiefly as a command: *Buzz off and leave me alone! I told them to buzz off because I was trying to study.*

ă	pat	är	car	ī	bite	ô	paw	o͝o	took	ûr	urge
ā	pay	ĕ	pet	îr	pier	ôr	core	o͝or	lure	zh	vision
âr	care	ē	be	ŏ	pot	oi	boy	o͞o	boot	ə	about,
ä	father	ĭ	pit	ō	toe	ou	out	ŭ	cut		item

C

◆ **call** (kôl)

called (kôld), **calling** (kô′lĭng), **calls** (kôlz)

call around

1. To telephone several people, usually to get or give some information: *I called around to all the hospitals trying to locate my injured friend.*
2. To invite someone for a visit, especially by calling them on the telephone: *I've been trying to call you around for dinner, but you never seem to be home!*

call back

1. To contact, or attempt to contact, someone who has called previously, especially by telephone: *When I got home from work, I called back my mother, who had left a message on my answering machine. I left a message asking the manager to call me back as soon as possible. I'll call back tonight when your parents are home.*
2. To summon someone back to a previous situation or location: *Just as I started walking away, the teacher called me back. The workers who were laid off are hoping that management will call them back as soon as the economy improves.*
3. To recall something defective for repair: *The company has called back all models of this car built in 2002. After discovering that the toy was unsafe for small children, the company was forced to call it back.*

call down

1. To shout something from a higher level to a lower one: *I called down from the balcony to the people onstage.*
2. To summon someone from a higher level to a lower one: *I was upstairs getting dressed when my dad called me down for dinner. I waited in the bleachers until they called down my group.*
3. To ask for someone's presence at some location; summon someone: *The police called me down to the station to identify the robber. I was called down to the principal's office to explain why I was late.*
4. To criticize or reprimand someone: *The teacher called me down for being late. The grouchy boss took a cruel delight in calling down the members of the staff.*
5. To invoke something, as from heaven: *The prophet called down punishment on the wicked. Their sins called a plague down upon them.*

call for

1. To summon or request someone or something: *As I neared home, I could hear my mother calling for me.*
2. To require or demand something: *The recent surge in crime calls for a strong community response.*

3. To be an appropriate occasion for something: *This happy news calls for champagne.*
4. To come to pick someone up: *The driver will call for you at 7:00.*
5. To say that something is likely to occur: *The weather forecast calls for clouds and rain.*

call forth

1. To summon someone to come forward; beckon someone: *The judge called me forth and asked me to tell what happened at the crime scene. The coach called forth the winners and presented them with a trophy.*
2. To evoke or elicit some result or reaction: *The love song called forth sad memories. I held back my tears through most of the story, but the tragic ending called them forth.*

call in

1. To summon someone into a place: *I went to the window and called the children in for dinner.*
2. To summon someone or something for assistance or consultation: *The hospital called in a specialist from out of town to examine the patient. The soldiers stood ready in case the protests turned violent and the police needed to call them in.*
3. To make a telephone call to a place: *Viewers called in to the television station to complain. Has the boss called in today?*
4. To conduct some transaction by telephone: *I called in my order to the restaurant so that it would be ready when I arrived. The new telephone system will allow customers to call their orders in rather than submitting them by mail.*
5. To withdraw something that one has issued or sent out: *The library called in the book I borrowed because a professor urgently needed it. Coin collectors began saving silver dollars as soon as the government called them in.*

call off

1. To cancel or postpone something: *We called off the trip when two of people who were supposed to go became sick. The union called the strike off after the management gave in to their demands.*
2. To order someone or something to stop attacking or aggressing: *The police called off the dogs after the suspect surrendered. The commander called his troops off when the enemy retreated.*

call on

1. To select or request someone to undertake a particular activity: *The teacher always calls on the students in the back row to answer questions.*
2. To make use of some resource; draw on something: *I called on all my strength to lift the rock that had fallen on my foot.*

ă	pat	är	car	ī	bite	ô	paw	o͝o	took	ûr	urge
ā	pay	ĕ	pet	îr	pier	ôr	core	o͝or	lure	zh	vision
âr	care	ē	be	ŏ	pot	oi	boy	o͞o	boot	ə	about, item
ä	father	ĭ	pit	ō	toe	ou	out	ŭ	cut		

3. To visit someone: *I called on my neighbors last night and returned a book I had borrowed.*
4. To challenge someone on the truth or accuracy of something that has been said: *When the magician boasted that he could juggle blindfolded, we called him on it, and he was forced to admit he was lying.*
5. To tell someone that one has noticed that he or she has done something wrong: *When I called her on her bad behavior, she apologized and said that it would not happen again.*

call out

1. To shout: *When I realized I was trapped, I called out for help. I called out from the porch for lemonade.*
2. To say something in a loud voice; announce something: *The announcer called out the names of the runners as they crossed the finish line. The conductor called the station name out as we pulled up.*
3. To request the services of someone or something: *The mayor called out the guard to suppress the riots. We called the veterinarian out to the farm to examine one of the calves.*
4. To challenge someone or something: *When I insulted his mother, he called me out.*
5. To order food from a restaurant by telephone: *If you don't want to cook, we can just call out for pizza.*

call up

1. To shout something from a lower level to a higher one: *Standing on the sidewalk, I called up to the people on the roof.*
2. To summon someone from a lower level to a higher one: *The speaker called members of the audience up to the stage to receive a prize. After I climbed to the top of the tower and determined that it was safe, I called up the others who had stayed behind.*
3. To telephone someone or something: *As soon as I heard the news, I called up my broker and told her to sell the stock. I called him up to ask if he was free for lunch.*
4. To summon someone to active military service: *The military has called up thousands of reserve troops for active duty. The reservists have begun training in case the military calls them up.*
5. To cause someone to remember something; bring something to mind: *The view of the river called up a painting I had once seen. The therapist was certain that I had repressed memories and that her therapy would call them up.*
6. To bring something forth for action or discussion: *At the meeting, the treasurer called up the budget proposal for review. Supporters of the legislation complained that the senator had never called it up for a vote.*
7. To summon or draw on something: *I called up all my courage and asked the boss for a raise.*

call upon

1. To order or require someone to do something: *I call upon you to tell the truth.*
2. To make a demand or a series of demands on something: *Social in-*

stitutions are often called upon to assist the poor.

3. To visit someone: *I called upon an old friend when I was in New York.*
4. To make use of some resource; draw on something: *I knew the task would call upon my every resource.*

◆ **calm** (kôlm)

calmed (kôlmd), **calming** (kôl′mĭng), **calms** (kôlmz)

calm down

1. To become less agitated, active, or unsettled: *When the wind calmed down, we went outside to assess the storm's damage.*
2. To cause someone or something to become less angry, active, or unsettled: *The leader calmed down the angry mob by addressing their complaints. Listening to music before going to bed calms me down and helps me sleep.*

◆ **camp** (kămp)

camped (kămpt), **camping** (kăm′pĭng), **camps** (kămps)

camp out

1. To sleep outdoors, usually in a tent: *If the weather is nice, we should camp out on the mountain.*
2. To reside at some place temporarily, especially under difficult conditions: *I had to camp out in my cousin's living room until I found an apartment of my own.*

◆ **cancel** (kăn′səl)

canceled *or* **cancelled** (kăn′səld), **canceling** *or* **cancelling** (kăn′sə-lĭng), **cancels** (kăn′səlz)

cancel out

1. To delete or erase something: *I went back to the list and canceled out my name. Realizing the total was incorrect, I canceled it out and recalculated the price.*
2. To equalize or make up for something; offset something: *Today's decline in the stock's price canceled out yesterday's gain. We made record progress last month, but the delays this month have canceled it out. I never go to the beach because the fun of swimming in the ocean and the difficulty of getting to the beach cancel out.*
3. To remove a common factor from both sides of a mathematical equation: *After I canceled out the common factors, I could easily solve for the variable. When two factors are equal, you can cancel them out.*
4. To withdraw from something, as an activity or obligation: *They had dinner reservations with us, but they had to cancel out when they couldn't find a babysitter.*
5. SLANG To murder someone: *The loan shark threatened to cancel me out if I didn't pay him the money. The gangsters vowed to cancel out any rivals.*

ă	pat	är	car	ī	bite	ô	paw	o͝o	took	ûr	urge
ā	pay	ĕ	pet	îr	pier	ôr	core	o͝or	lure	zh	vision
âr	care	ē	be	ŏ	pot	oi	boy	o͞o	boot	ə	about,
ä	father	ĭ	pit	ō	toe	ou	out	ŭ	cut		item

◆ **care** (kâr)
cared (kârd), **caring** (kârʹĭng), **cares** (kârz)

care for

1. To like or love someone or something: *I care for you very deeply.*
2. To provide needed assistance or supervision to someone or something: *The hospital hired more nurses to care for the sick. My sister cares for my dog when I'm out of town.*
3. To like or have an attachment to someone or something. Usually used in the negative: *I don't really care for strawberry ice cream.*

◆ **carry** (kărʹē)
carried (kărʹēd), **carrying** (kărʹē-ĭng), **carries** (kărʹēz)

carry away

1. To pick something up and move away with it: *The garbage collectors carried away the trash. I forgot to tie the canoe to the dock, and the river carried it away.*
2. To steal something: *The looters carried away everything in the store. The thieves carried the diamonds away.*
3. To be moved to excess or be greatly excited. Used in the passive: *The lovers were carried away by desire. Don't get carried away with the frosting; we need to save some for the other cake.*

carry forward

1. In accounting, to transfer some entry to the next column, page, or book, or to another account: *The company decided to carry their losses forward to offset future profits.*
2. To succeed or make progress with something: *I thought of the plan, and my assistant carried it forward.*

carry off

1. To pick up something or someone and move away: *The wind carried off the balloon. The criminal frowned as the police carried him off.*
2. To steal something or someone: *The bandits broke into the farmyard and carried off the chickens. The painting was the city's most treasured possession until thieves carried it off.*
3. To handle or accomplish something successfully: *The performance was unrehearsed, but we carried it off without a problem. The host carried off the event beautifully.*
4. To win something, as an award or prize: *The film carried off four of the top prizes. The prize was $10,000, and I was determined to carry it off.*
5. To cause the death of someone: *Heart disease finally carried him off. Many pioneers were carried off by fever.*

carry on

1. To continue or resume doing something: *After speaking with us briefly, the captain told us to carry on, and we went back to work. Our class is proud to carry on the university's tradition of academic excellence.*
2. To maintain something: *The cabinetmaker has carried on a thriving business for the past 50 years.*

3. To engage in something: *Archaeological evidence suggests that the two communities carried on an active trade for centuries.*
4. To persevere: *Despite protests from our families, we carried on with our plans to marry.*
5. To behave in an excited, improper, or silly manner: *The bar was full of old friends making toasts and carrying on.*
6. **carry on about** To complain vocally about someone or something: *We were all tired of listening to him carrying on about his personal problems.*
7. **carry on with** To flirt with someone: *The maids gossiped that the lady of the house had been carrying on with the gardener.*

carry out

1. To lift and move something or someone out of a place: *The firefighter carried the dog out of the burning building. I'll carry out the trash as soon as I finish the newspaper.*
2. To put something into practice or effect; implement something: *The citizens hoped that the government would carry out the reforms it had promised. She planned the crime but hired thugs to carry it out.*
3. To follow or obey something: *I carried out her request without asking any questions. The judge had pronounced the prisoner's sentence as death, and the executioner carried it out.*
4. To bring something to fruition; accomplish something: *The institute carried out a series of studies to determine the effect of music on shoppers. The design was so challenging that only the very best architects and contractors could have carried it out.*

carry over

1. To transport something or someone from one place to another: *After I finished eating, I carried my plate over to the sink.*
2. To transfer some account from one column or category to another one relating to the same account: *The company carried its losses over to the next year for tax purposes. The accountant carried over the balance to the next statement.*
3. To retain merchandise or other goods for a subsequent (usually the next) season: *The store disappointed many of its fashionable customers when it carried over its fall collection. Because of the weak market, farmers carried a billion bushels of corn over from last year.*
4. To persist to another time or situation: *The confidence gained in remedial classes carried over into the children's regular schoolwork.*
5. To defer something to another time: *We will carry over all unfinished business to the next meeting. Can we carry this conversation over to another time?*

carry through

1. To bring something to completion; accomplish something: *Although at times it seemed as though we'd never finish, we carried the project through by the deadline.*
2. To survive; persist: *Some traditions have carried through over the centuries.*
3. To enable someone to endure; sustain someone: *Their strong faith carried them through the horrible ordeal.*

◆ **cash** (kăsh)

cashed (kăsht), **cashing** (kăsh′ĭng), **cashes** (kăsh′ĭz)

cash in

1. To exchange something for its equivalent value in currency: *After winning a big hand at the blackjack table, I cashed in my chips. As soon as I got to Italy, I cashed my traveler's checks in and went shopping.*
2. To withdraw from some venture by or as if by settling one's account: *The business was starting to lose money, and I cashed in before the other investors noticed.*
3. To exploit some situation in order to profit financially from it: *Gas retailers cashed in during the gasoline shortage by raising prices.*
4. SLANG To die: *My uncle finally cashed in after a long illness.*

cash out

1. To count the money made by a business at the end of the day: *When the last customer leaves the store, the owner locks the doors and cashes out.*
2. To sell some asset in order to have access to cash: *Some farmers are tempted to cash out by selling their valuable land.*

◆ **cast** (kăst)

cast (kăst), **casting** (kăs′tĭng), **casts** (kăsts)

cast about for

1. To devise a means of doing something; contrive something: *The general cast about for methods of defeating the enemy.*
2. To search for someone or something: *We cast about for a good campsite. The agency has been casting about for new ideas ever since their last advertising campaign failed.*

cast aside

1. To throw or push something or someone out of the way: *I cast my coat aside so that he could sit down. She cast aside the boxes in front of the door.*
2. To reject or disregard something or someone: *The commander cast aside all caution and ordered the troops to charge the fort. I knew you would cast me aside once you became famous.*

cast off

1. To discard or reject something: *Each year the principal would cast off her role as disciplinarian and perform in the school play. The load was too heavy, so we cast it off and left it behind.*
2. To let something go; set something loose: *I cast off the bow line and let the boat drift in the current. The crew grabbed the lines and cast them off as the captain started the engines. The crew re-*

mained on the boat, ready to cast off at the first sign of trouble.*

3. To estimate the space some manuscript will occupy when set into type: *The publisher cast off the manuscript to see how long the book would be. We cast each chapter off separately in order to save time.*
4. CHIEFLY BRITISH To secure some number of stitches in knitting and form an edge by lifting one stitch over the next: *When the scarf was the correct length, I cast off. Cast off 12 stitches on the next row to make the neck edge. Make 5 stitches on the next row and cast them off.*

cast on

1. To cause something to fall upon or come into contact with something: *The moon cast its light on the snowy countryside.*
2. To cause or give rise to some critical valuation about something or someone: *These facts cast doubt on the suspect's story.*
3. To make the first row of stitches in knitting by putting some number of stitches on a knitting needle: *Be careful not to cast on too tightly or it will be difficult to knit the first row. Start by casting on 18 stitches. Make 4 loops and cast them on.*

cast out

To drive someone or something out by force; expel someone or something: *The board of directors cast out the company president after a trading scandal. When I questioned their methods, they cast me out of the group.*

◆ catch (kăch)

caught (kôt), **catching** (kăch′ĭng), **catches** (kăch′ĭz)

catch on

1. To snag something on something: *I caught the sleeve of my jacket on a branch, and it ripped.*
2. To understand or figure something out: *We played a practice game so that the new players could catch on before we started betting. We were slow to catch on to the swindler's tricks.*
3. To become popular or fashionable: *Since the time when skateboarding first caught on, there have been many improvements in wheel design.*

catch out

To detect or expose the error, wrongdoing, or shortcoming of someone: *The test is designed to catch you out with trick questions. I got caught out in a lie.*

catch up

1. To move fast enough to attain the same progress as someone or something: *The runner caught up to the leader on the last lap of the race.*
2. To become equal or on a par with someone or something: *I finally*

ă	pat	är	car	ī	bite	ô	paw	ŏŏ	took	ûr	urge
ā	pay	ĕ	pet	îr	pier	ôr	core	ŏŏr	lure	zh	vision
âr	care	ē	be	ŏ	pot	oi	boy	ōō	boot	ə	about, item
ä	father	ĭ	pit	ō	toe	ou	out	ŭ	cut		

caught up with my brother in height.

3. To bring some activity to completion or to a state of currentness: *On the weekends, I catch up on reading the daily newspapers because I don't have time during the week.*
4. To bring someone up to date; brief someone: *Let me catch you up on all the gossip. I read the Sunday newspaper to catch up on the news.*
5. To seize or lift something suddenly: *The wind caught up the umbrella and carried it off. I wasn't holding onto the balloon very tightly, and the wind caught it up and sent it sailing away.*
6. To involve someone in something, often unwillingly. Used chiefly in the passive: *The senator was caught up in the scandal.*
7. To captivate or enthrall someone. Used chiefly in the passive: *Perhaps I shouldn't have proposed to you, but I was caught up in the mood of the evening.*

◆ **cave** (kāv)

caved (kāvd), **caving** (kā′vĭng), **caves** (kāvz)

cave in

To give way; collapse: *The sides of the snow fort caved in. The mine shaft caved in on a group of miners, but fortunately they were rescued.*

◆ **center** (sĕn′tər)

centered (sĕn′tərd), **centering** (sĕn′tə-rĭng), **centers** (sĕn′tərz)

center around

1. To be primarily concerned with something: *The plot of this story centers around the life of a cowboy.*
2. To make or do something that is primarily concerned with something else: *We centered our discussion around the problem of homelessness.*

center on

1. To be concerned primarily with something: *This chapter centers on the childhood of one of the characters.*
2. To make or do something that is concerned primarily with something else: *We centered our analysis on the best pieces of evidence.*
3. To place something at the center of some location: *We centered the painting on the wall.*

◆ **chalk** (chôk)

chalked (chôkt), **chalking** (chô′kĭng), **chalks** (chôks)

chalk up

1. To earn or score something: *The baseball team chalked up four runs in the last inning.*
2. To credit or ascribe something: *Let's just chalk the mistakes up to experience and try to do better on the next project.*

◆ **chance** (chăns)

chanced (chănst), **chancing** (chăn′sĭng), **chances** (chăn′sĭz)

chance on *or* **chance upon**

To find or meet someone or something accidentally; happen upon someone or something: *While in Atlanta we chanced on two old friends. I chanced upon my neighbor while I was shopping at the mall.*

◆ **change** (chānj)

changed (chānjd), **changing** (chānj′ĭng), **changes** (chānj′ĭz)

change down

To switch to a lower gear when driving a motor vehicle: *The driver changed down to third gear coming into the turn.*

change into

1. To transform from one state to some other: *The caterpillar will soon change into a moth.*
2. To transform something from one state to some other: *The alchemist tried to change lead into gold.*
3. To put on some other clothing: *After my workout at the gym, I showered and changed into regular clothes.*

change off

1. To alternate with someone in performing some task: *I changed off washing the dishes with my brother. If you two change off once in a while, the work will be less tiring.*
2. To perform two tasks at once by alternating, or perform a single task by alternate means: *Every so often I changed off between pushing and pulling the cart up the hill.*

change out of

To take off some clothing and put on other clothing: *You should change out of those wet clothes before you catch a cold!*

change up

1. To alter something: *The cafeteria changed up the menu after people complained that they were tired of macaroni and cheese. When the other team discovered our strategy, we had to change it up.*
2. To switch to a higher gear when driving a motor vehicle: *When you accelerate, you have to change up or the car will stall.*

◆ **chat** (chăt)

chatted (chăt′ĭd), **chatting** (chăt′ĭng), **chats** (chăts)

chat up

1. To engage someone in light, casual talk, especially in order to gain his or her favor: *The salesperson chatted us up for an hour before we finally decided to buy something. I chatted up the director, hoping to get a part in the film.*
2. To talk amorously to someone, usually without serious intentions; flirt with someone: *Many people go to the bar just to chat up the attractive bartenders. By their false smiles, we could tell they were coming over to chat us up.*

◆ **cheat** (chēt)

cheated (chē′tĭd), **cheating** (chē′tĭng), **cheats** (chēts)

cheat on

1. To behave fraudulently during some process or activity: *The*

ă	pat	är	car	ī	bite	ô	paw	ŏŏ	took	ûr	urge
ā	pay	ĕ	pet	îr	pier	ôr	core	ŏŏr	lure	zh	vision
âr	care	ē	be	ŏ	pot	oi	boy	ōō	boot	ə	about,
ä	father	ĭ	pit	ō	toe	ou	out	ŭ	cut		item

teacher caught the student cheating on the test.

2. To be unfaithful to someone, especially a spouse or lover: *I hired a private detective to see if my spouse was cheating on me.*

◆ **check** (chĕk)

checked (chĕkt), **checking** (chĕk′ĭng), **checks** (chĕks)

check in

1. To register or record one's arrival somewhere, as at a hotel or airport: *The airline requires you to check in at least an hour before your flight. I entered the hotel, went to the registration desk, and checked in.*
2. To register or record the arrival of someone, as at a hotel or airport: *The hotel receptionist checked us in and gave us the key to our room. The ticket agent checked in the passengers and gave them their boarding passes.*
3. To return or deposit something somewhere, and have its receipt recorded: *I checked the book in to the library a few days late. When we arrived at the airport, we checked in our luggage and proceeded to the plane.*
4. To record that something has been returned or deposited somewhere: *The librarian checked in the stack of books that people had returned. The porter checked our bags in for the flight.*

check into

1. To investigate something; look into something: *I checked into the rumor that the band was going on tour, and the rumor turned out to be false.*
2. To register and gain admittance to one's room upon arrival at a hotel or other place of lodging: *When I arrived in New York, I checked into the hotel and went straight to bed.*

check off

To put a check mark on or next to some item on a list to indicate that it has been reviewed or completed: *Don't forget to check off the task after you have completed it. As I put the groceries in the cart, I checked them off on my list.*

check on *or* **check up on**

To inspect someone or something that one is supervising or watching over: *I checked on the meatloaf in the oven to see if it was ready to eat. Go upstairs to check up on the children and make sure they're all asleep.*

check out

1. To inspect something so as to determine accuracy, quality, or other condition; test something: *The technician checked out the computer system to make sure there were no errors in the software. I heard a strange noise, so I went downstairs to check it out.*
2. To be verified or confirmed; pass inspection: *Although we doubted it at first, the suspect's story checked out.*
3. To look at someone or something that is surprising, interesting, or attractive: *If you liked that movie, you should check out the director's other films. Check out the size of that diamond! I became jealous when I saw my spouse checking the lifeguard out.*

4. To settle one's bill and leave a hotel or other place of lodging: *The hotel requires that guests check out by noon so that the rooms can be cleaned before the next guests arrive.*
5. To record and sum the prices of and receive payment for something being purchased or the items someone is purchasing at a retail store: *The cashier checked out and bagged my order. We brought our items to the counter, and the sales clerk checked us out.*
6. To undergo the process of purchasing some selected item or items from a retailer: *It took us an hour to check out because there was only one register.*
7. To borrow some item, as from a library, with the lender registering or keeping track of the borrowing: *I checked out all four volumes, but could only read the first before they were due. If you don't finish that book before the library closes, you will have to check it out. I went to the video store and checked out two movies.*
8. To lose awareness of one's surroundings; become inattentive: *I got bored at the meeting and checked out until someone punched me on the arm.*
9. SLANG To die: *When I check out, I want to be buried in a fancy coffin.*

check over

To examine something or someone closely: *I checked over the bill to make sure it was accurate. The teacher checked the students' papers over for errors.*

check through

1. To examine something or a group of things: *I checked through the drawer to see if I had left my keys there.*
2. To allow someone to pass through some place after examining tickets, papers, or passes: *The security guards checked us through the gate.*
3. To have someone's travel be arranged so that the traveller may present a ticket or check in only at the beginning of a journey and not at each leg: *You don't need to go to the ticket counter when you change planes; we already checked you through.*
4. To have something, especially luggage, sent along each leg of a journey to some destination, without requiring that a person pick it up and check it again at each leg of the journey, as when changing airplanes, trains, or buses: *You should check your luggage through, or else you'll have to carry your bags with you in the airport.*

check with

1. To consult someone, as before deciding or answering: *I'll check with my boss to see if that time is good for a meeting.*
2. To correspond with something: *The suspect's fingerprints checked with those from the crime scene.*

ă	pat	är	car	ī	bite	ô	paw	o͝o	took	ûr	urge
ā	pay	ĕ	pet	îr	pier	ôr	core	o͝or	lure	zh	vision
âr	care	ē	be	ŏ	pot	oi	boy	o͞o	boot	ə	about,
ä	father	ĭ	pit	ō	toe	ou	out	ŭ	cut		item

◆ **cheer** (chîr)

cheered (chîrd), **cheering** (chîr′ĭng), **cheers** (chîrz)

cheer on

To encourage someone with or as if with cheers: *The spectators cheered the runners on as they passed by. I always cheer on the team that is losing.*

cheer up

1. To become happier or more cheerful: *I cheered up once the weather got warmer.*
2. To make someone happier or more cheerful: *The fine spring day cheered me up. The hospital staged a musical to cheer up the sick patients.*

◆ **chew** (cho͞o)

chewed (cho͞od), **chewing** (cho͞o′ĭng), **chews** (cho͞oz)

chew on

1. To bite and grind something with the teeth: *If we give the puppy a bone, maybe it will stop chewing on our shoes.*
2. To meditate or ponder something; think about something: *I chewed on the question for a full minute before answering.*

chew out

SLANG

To scold or reprimand someone: *The teacher chewed us out for being late.*

chew over

1. To think about or discuss something for a period of time: *Your plan sounds good, but I'll have to chew it over. I chewed over the idea for a few days, but decided against it.*
2. To criticize or berate someone strongly: *They really chewed me over for forgetting to write the report. When we were kids, my parents would chew over all of us whenever we made a big mess.*

◆ **chicken** (chĭk′ən)

chickened (chĭk′ənd), **chickening** (chĭk′ə-nĭng), **chickens** (chĭk′ənz)

chicken out

SLANG

To decide not to do or complete an activity due to fear: *My friends dared me to jump into the pond, but I chickened out and climbed down from the tree.*

◆ **chill** (chĭl)

chilled (chĭld), **chilling** (chĭl′ĭng), **chills** (chĭlz)

chill out

SLANG

To relax: *We hung out by the pool and chilled out all day long.*

◆ **chime** (chīm)

chimed (chīmd), **chiming** (chī′mĭng), **chimes** (chīmz)

chime in

1. To join in harmoniously with someone or something: *The carolers began singing and everyone chimed in.*
2. To interrupt someone or join a conversation suddenly, especially with an uninvited opinion: *The kids were talking among themselves when the teacher chimed in.*

◆ **chip** (chĭp)
chipped (chĭpt), **chipping** (chĭp′ĭng), **chips** (chĭps)

chip away

1. To fall or break off in small pieces: *The old paint chipped away from the frame when we opened the window.*
2. To break off small pieces of something: *Don't chip away the paint with a screwdriver. I chipped the enamel away with a scraper.*
3. **chip away at** To reduce or make progress on something incrementally: *We chipped away at the problem until it was solved. I chipped away at the dried cement on the tiles.*

chip in

1. To contribute something toward some general pool or effort: *They chipped a few bucks in for snacks. We all chipped in $5 for supplies. Everybody ought to chip in so that no one gets stuck with all of the costs.*
2. To put up chips or money as one's bet in poker and other games: *After each player chipped in $1, I dealt the cards. You're not getting any cards until you chip in.*
3. To interrupt a conversation with comments; interject: *I wanted to chip in, but I couldn't get a word in edgewise. You can chip in any time.*

chip off

1. To break away from a surface in small, flat pieces: *The cold weather has caused the paint on the bench to chip off.*
2. To break off a small, flat piece of something from some whole: *She chipped off a small piece of ice from the block. He chipped the hard coating off the pipe with a screwdriver.*

◆ **choke** (chōk)
choked (chōkt), **choking** (chō′kĭng), **chokes** (chōks)

choke back

To suppress or hold something back, especially with great effort: *I choked back tears as I told my family the sad news.*

choke off

To prevent or stop the free flow of something: *High tariffs choked off trade between the two countries. The car accident in the middle of the road choked the traffic off, and no one could get through.*

choke up

1. To be unable to speak because of strong emotion: *The speaker choked up when he tried to talk about his grandparents' journey to America.*
2. To cause someone to be unable to speak because of strong emotion: *Their generosity choked me up. Whenever I hear the national anthem, I get choked up.*
3. **choke up on** To grip some implement that is used to strike something, such as a baseball bat or a

ă	pat	är	car	ī	bite	ô	paw	o͝o	took	ûr	urge
ā	pay	ĕ	pet	îr	pier	ôr	core	o͝or	lure	zh	vision
âr	care	ē	be	ŏ	pot	oi	boy	o͞o	boot	ə	about,
ä	father	ĭ	pit	ō	toe	ou	out	ŭ	cut		item

hammer, at a point closer to where contact is made:*The child had to choke up on the golf club because it was too large.*

◆ **choose** (cho͞oz)

chose (chōz), **choosing** (cho͞o′zĭng), **chooses** (cho͞o′zĭz)

choose up

To select players and form sides, teams, or some other group for a game or competition: *The two captains chose up sides for the baseball game.*

◆ **chop** (chŏp)

chopped (chŏpt), **chopping** (chŏp′ĭng), **chops** (chŏps)

chop off

To cut something short by or as if by chopping; curtail something: *The barber chopped my ponytail off. The butcher chopped off a hunk of meat for me.*

chop out

To remove something by chopping or cutting; excise something: *I chopped out a big piece of wood from the log. The editor always chops all the jokes out of the manuscripts.*

chop up

1. To cut something into small pieces with a sharp tool: *The cook chopped up the parsley. I chopped an onion up and added it to the soup.*
2. To divide something into smaller segments: *The editor chopped the manuscript up into distinct chapters. I chopped up the long drive by making frequent stops.*

◆ **chow** (chou)

chowed (choud), **chowing** (chou′ĭng), **chows** (chouz)

chow down

To eat something greedily or voraciously: *We chowed down on the wild berries until the bush was bare. I dropped my sandwich on the ground and the dog chowed it down.*

◆ **churn** (chŭrn)

churned (chŭrnd), **churning** (chŭr′nĭng), **churns** (chŭrnz)

churn out

To produce something in an abundant and automatic manner: *The author churns out four novels a year. Although the chairs look handmade, the company churns them out in a factory.*

◆ **cinch** (sĭnch)

cinched (sĭncht), **cinching** (sĭn′chĭng), **chinches** (sĭn′chĭz)

cinch up

To tighten some drawstring or strap, especially a saddle girth: *I cinched up the saddle girth before mounting the horse. I cinched up the hood of my jacket to keep the rain out.*

◆ **circle** (sûr′kəl)

circled (sûr′kəld), **circling** (sûr′kə-lĭng), **circles** (sûr′kəlz)

circle around

1. To proceed in a circle around someone or something: *We circled around the block until they were ready to be picked up.*

2. To move something in a circle around someone or something: *We circled the dish around the table so everyone could try some.*
3. To wrap or place something in a circle around someone or something: *We circled the ribbon around the pole.*
4. To form a circle around someone or something: *The children circled around the storyteller.*
5. To proceed in a circle: *The plane circled around until it was cleared for landing.*
6. To be centered around someone or something: *These movie stars think everything circles around them.*
7. To come by way of rotation: *When the holiday season circles around, I want to have all my shopping done.*

circle in

1. To make a circle or other closed loop around something: *Circle in the part of the picture that you want to darken.*
2. To surround and confine someone or something within a limited area: *The bandits circled us in so that we couldn't escape.*
3. To proceed in a circle or spiral path toward a destination: *The plane circled in for a landing.*

◆ **clam** (klăm)

clammed (klămd), **clamming** (klăm′ĭng), **clams** (klămz)

clam up

SLANG

To refuse to talk or to stop talking suddenly: *The politician clammed up when the reporters started to ask about the scandal.*

◆ **clamp** (klămp)

clamped (klămpt), **clamping** (klăm′pĭng), **clamps** (klămps)

clamp down

1. To press down tightly on something: *Clamp down the pipe securely before you try to drill a hole in it. I glued the strip of wood to the surface and clamped it down while it dried.*
2. To prevent or regulate something with increased strictness: *The cartel clamped down on oil production in order to raise prices.*
3. To punish or repress someone or something with increased strictness: *The government plans to clamp down on tax fraud with tough new laws. Crime began to increase, so the police started clamping down.*

◆ **clean** (klēn)

cleaned (klēnd), **cleaning** (klē′nĭng), **cleans** (klēnz)

clean out

1. To rid the inside of something of dirt, rubbish, or impurities: *The zookeepers clean out the cages once a day. I cleaned the pan out with a scrub brush.*

ă	pat	är	car	ī	bite	ô	paw	o͝o	took	ûr	urge
ā	pay	ĕ	pet	îr	pier	ôr	core	o͝or	lure	zh	vision
âr	care	ē	be	ŏ	pot	oi	boy	o͞o	boot	ə	about, item
ä	father	ĭ	pit	ō	toe	ou	out	ŭ	cut		

2. To empty some area of contents or occupants: *The looters cleaned out the house. The comedian's bad jokes cleaned the place out.*
3. SLANG To drive or force out someone or some group: *The police were determined to clean out the gangs. When the cowboys became too rowdy, the bartender picked up his shotgun and cleaned them out.*
4. SLANG To leave someone or something completely without money or material wealth: *The robbery cleaned us out. The stock market crash cleaned out even careful investors.*
5. SLANG To deplete or use up all of some resource or supply: *The thieves stole my bank card and cleaned out my account. Emergency supplies were already low, and the hurricane cleaned them out.*

clean up

1. To make someone or something clean, neat, or presentable: *My brother stayed late and helped me clean up the apartment after the party. After I got home from work, I cleaned myself up for dinner.*
2. To get rid of dirt, rubbish, or impurities: *Volunteers helped clean up the oil spill. I cleaned the broken glass up before anyone could step on it.*
3. To rid something or some place of crime or immoral behavior: *The government promised to clean up the corrupt judicial system. The mayor cleaned the neighborhood up and made it safe for residents.*
4. SLANG To make a large amount of money, often in a short period of time: *Investors cleaned up when the company struck oil.*

◆ **clear** (klîr)
cleared (klîrd), **clearing** (klîr′ĭng), **clears** (klîrz)

clear away

1. To remove something that is covering some area, especially something that is no longer being used: *She cleared away the snow on the sidewalk so that no one would slip. I cleared the dishes away after dinner.*
2. To move away from some place: *He cleared away from the dangerous cliff. The crowd cleared away when the police arrived.*
3. To make someone or some group move away from some place: *The troopers cleared the crowd away from the crime scene. The police cleared away the crowd in preparation for the celebrity's arrival.*

clear off

1. To remove something that is covering some area: *She cleared off the papers that were cluttering her desk. He cleared the dirt off the windowsill.*
2. To clean some area by removing items that are there: *He cleared off the worktable to make room for the new equipment. She cleared the counter off and wiped it with a sponge.*

clear out

1. To empty something of its contents or occupants: *We cleared the living room out and turned it into a dance floor. Emergency crews cleared out the village ahead of the hurricane.*

2. To remove some contents or occupants from a container or region: *I opened up the old cabin and cleared the cobwebs out with a broom. We finally cleared out the junk in the attic.*
3. To become free of occupants: *The theater cleared out when the show ended.*
4. To leave a place, usually quickly: *The embassy advised us to clear out before the war started.*

clear up

1. To remove obstructions, unwanted objects, or imperfections from something: *Could you help me clear up the table after dinner? The allergy medication cleared my sinuses up.*
2. To remove some obstructions, unwanted objects, or imperfections: *Firefighters quickly cleared up the accident, and traffic returned to normal. When I got poison ivy, the doctor gave me a medicinal cream to clear it up.*
3. To become free of obstructions, unwanted objects, or imperfections: *My skin has cleared up since I started using that acne medication.*
4. To go away; disappear: *I hope the traffic clears up before I have to drive home.*
5. To clarify something: *This article should clear up some of the confusion surrounding my new theory. The origin of the artifact remained a mystery, and we hoped that the professor could clear it up.*
6. To become more apparent or easily perceptible: *As we discussed the issue, it began to clear up.*
7. To become brighter and more pleasant. Used especially of the weather: *We can go to the beach if the weather clears up.*

◆ **clock** (klŏk)

clocked (klŏkt), **clocking** (klŏk′ĭng), **clocks** (klŏks)

clock in

1. To begin an activity at some recorded time, as by stamping the time on a timecard: *The workers must clock in before 8:00.*
2. To be measured as having some speed: *The fastest bicycle riders clocked in at over 40 miles per hour.*
3. To complete a task or activity after some duration of time: *The slowest cars in the race clocked in at 12 minutes.*

◆ **clog** (klŏg)

clogged (klŏgd), **clogging** (klŏg′ĭng), **clogs** (klŏgz)

clog up

1. To obstruct some passageway: *The fallen leaves clogged up the drainpipe. The sediment clogged the pipe up.*
2. To cause something to become obstructed: *I clogged up the sink with some leftover food. This nagging cold has clogged my sinuses up.*

ă	pat	är	car	ī	bite	ô	paw	ŏŏ	took	ûr	urge
ā	pay	ĕ	pet	îr	pier	ôr	core	ŏŏr	lure	zh	vision
âr	care	ē	be	ŏ	pot	oi	boy	ōō	boot	ə	about,
ä	father	ĭ	pit	ō	toe	ou	out	ŭ	cut		item

3. To become obstructed: *Call the plumber; the toilet clogged up again.*

◆ **close** (klōz)

closed (klōzd), **closing** (klō′zĭng), **closes** (klō′zĭz)

close down

1. To stop operating permanently or for an extended period of time. Used especially of businesses: *After decades of serving the community, the gymnasium closed down.*
2. To force someone or something, as a business, to stop operating: *The cops closed down our poker game. I'd like to keep the shop running, but the recession will probably close my business down.*

close in

1. To surround and advance on a person or thing: *The police located the escaped prisoner and closed in. Scientists closed in on the cause of the disease.*
2. To appear to be coming in from all sides: *Problems of every sort are closing in on me.*
3. To be about to occur; be imminent: *We had better hurry, the deadline is closing in.*

close off

To prevent passage along or through something: *The police closed off the main avenue for a parade. Park rangers closed the lake off to motorboats.*

close out

1. To block someone or something from entering some place: *I shut the windows to close out the light. The management closed the striking union out from the factory.*
2. To refuse to include someone in a group or activity: *The tour guide had to close out many people who wanted to come on the trip because the bus was full. The school closed me out of the class because I registered too late.*
3. To discontinue the sale of some merchandise: *The store is closing out its old line of hiking boots, so they're on sale. This is a good brand of refrigerator, so buy one before the store closes them out.*
4. To terminate something, as a business or an account, by disposing of all its assets: *She opened a new bank account and closed out the old one. He closed his savings account out and bought a new car.*
5. To bring some activity to an end: *This performance will close out our program for the evening. Just when we thought the tennis match might go to a third set, one of the players closed it out with two aces.*

close up

1. To shut something completely: *The doctor closed up the cut with stitches. I closed the box up with wire and tape.*
2. To become shut completely: *My eye closed up because of the infection.*
3. To shut and lock a building for a period of time: *It's my job to close up the store for the night because I'm always the last one to leave. At the end of August, we'll close the cottage up for the winter.*

◆ **clue** (klo͞o)

clued (klo͞od), **clueing** or **cluing** (klo͞o′ĭng), **clues** (klo͞oz)

clue in

To provide someone with important or exclusive information about something: *I hoped my friend who worked for a senator would clue me in to what the government was planning to do. My friend clued me in on the local club scene.*

◆ **color** (kŭl′ər)

colored (kŭl′ərd), **coloring** (kŭl′ə-rĭng), **colors** (kŭl′ərz)

color in

To cover completely the bounded surface of something with a color: *The child colored in an outline of a tree with green crayon. We traced the stencil and colored it in.*

◆ **come** (kŭm)

came (kām), **come** (kŭm), **coming** (kŭm′ĭng), **comes** (kŭmz)

come about

1. To happen; come to pass: *It came about that John and Mary got married and had three children.*
2. To change tack. Used of sailing vessels: *We were about to come about when the wind suddenly died down.*

come across

1. To arrive by crossing something: *To get to our house, it's fastest to come across the south bridge.*
2. To meet or find by chance: *I came across my old college roommate in town today.*
3. To encounter something: *We came across a few small mistakes in the students' work.*
4. To give an impression: *I hope I didn't come across as rude.*
5. To be clear or manifest: *It did not really come across that they were only trying to help.*
6. To pay something that is demanded: *You had better come across with the check by tomorrow.*

come after

1. To occur following something: *The letter C comes after the letter B.*
2. To be less important than something: *Doing it well comes after getting it done.*
3. To chase or pursue someone or something: *Look out, the mosquitos are coming after us!*

come along

1. To go with someone else who takes the lead: *If you go swimming, I'll come along.*
2. To make advances to a goal; progress: *Our projects are coming along very well. How is your remodeling coming along?*
3. To make an appearance; show up: *Don't take the first offer that comes along.*

come apart

1. To be separated into parts; disintegrate; break apart: *The roof of the*

ă	pat	är	car	ī	bite	ô	paw	o͝o	took	ûr	urge
ā	pay	ĕ	pet	îr	pier	ôr	core	o͝or	lure	zh	vision
âr	care	ē	be	ŏ	pot	oi	boy	o͞o	boot	ə	about, item
ä	father	ĭ	pit	ō	toe	ou	out	ŭ	cut		

old building is starting to come apart and needs to be replaced.

2. To be capable of being separated into parts: *This picnic table comes apart into five pieces that easily fit in the car.*
3. To begin to fail, especially by losing coherence or due to internal conflict: *My schedule is getting so busy that my plan to visit Poland is coming apart. Halfway through the proposal, their arguments in favor of buying the house came apart.*
4. To be suddenly unable to cope with negative emotions; have an emotional breakdown: *When I heard the news about their death, I completely came apart.*

come around *or* **come round**

1. To approach or arrive following some curved path: *He came around the bend in the road carrying a large box.*
2. To approach or arrive by avoiding something: *The swamp was too dangerous, so she came around it.*
3. To visit or pay a call to someone, especially informally: *Why don't you come around sometime and have supper with us?*
4. To come to pass. Used of times, seasons, or scheduled events: *When April comes around, we'll work in the garden again. The World Series is coming around soon.*
5. To recover; revive: *I fainted at the bad news but soon came around and felt better.*
6. To change one's opinion or position: *You'll come around after you hear the whole story.*

come at

1. To approach or address something, especially some situation or problem: *This is a difficult problem, but we all came at it with interesting ideas.*
2. To bombard or assail someone repeatedly or persistently: *Questions came at the mayor one after the other, but she answered them all confidently.*
3. To rush at someone, especially to attack: *They came at me with knives, so I ran away.*

come away

1. To leave, relinquish, or abandon a place in favor of another place: *Come away with me to New York. We should come away to the country more often.*
2. To be removed from a surface: *When I sprayed water on the table, the dust came away very easily.*
3. **come away with** To finish a process or event, having something as a result: *Luckily, the driver came away from the accident with only a broken finger. She came away with first place in the competition.*

come back

1. To return to some place: *I came back to Montana last year. I hope my dog comes back.*
2. To become present again: *That unpleasant feeling came back to me when I found out they were lying again.*
3. To begin to be remembered; recur to the memory: *What happened last night is coming back to me now.*
4. To return to or regain past success after a period of misfortune: *After*

years of living in obscurity, the rock singer came back more popular than ever.

5. **come back with** To retort; reply: *She came back with a clever answer that subtly insulted him.*

come before

1. To occur sooner or earlier in a sequence than something: *Easter comes before April this year. The letter B comes before the letter C.*
2. To be more important than something: *Playing fairly comes before winning the game.*
3. To present oneself to some group: *They came before the court on Wednesday, and the trial was finished by the end of the week.*

come between

1. To be situated before part of some group and after another part: *A quiet section of this piece comes between the loud introduction and the end of the first movement.*
2. To be a source of conflict or disruption for someone or something: *I didn't want the dispute about money to come between us.*

come by

1. To visit someone: *I told them to come by for dinner some evening.*
2. To pass into a region: *A nice breeze came by and the campers felt cooler.*
3. To gain possession of something; acquire something: *We don't know how our neighbor came by all that money.*
4. To find something: *Really good movies are hard to come by.*

come down

1. To descend: *The snow is coming down hard.*
2. To lose wealth or position: *He has really come down in the world.*
3. To pass or be handed down by tradition: *The family loved traditions that came down from their ancestors.*
4. To be handed down from a higher authority: *An indictment came down on the case of corruption.*
5. SLANG To happen; occur: *What's coming down tonight?*
6. To experience diminishing effects of a recreational or hallucinogenic drug: *He felt giddy and sick from the overdose, but he eventually came down and felt better.*
7. **come down on** To descend upon something or someone: *The rain came down on us suddenly.*
8. **come down on** To criticize or punish someone harshly: *He came down hard on anyone who was late to his meetings.*
9. **come down to** To be passed on to someone; inherited by someone: *I believe those antiques came down to them from their grandparents.*
10. **come down to** To depend on the answer to or outcome of something: *The situation comes down to whether we can finish on time.*
11. **come down with** To develop an ailment: *She came down with a nasty cold and stayed in bed all day.*

ă	pat	är	car	ī	bite	ô	paw	o͝o	took	ûr	urge
ā	pay	ĕ	pet	îr	pier	ôr	core	o͝or	lure	zh	vision
âr	care	ē	be	ŏ	pot	oi	boy	o͞o	boot	ə	about,
ä	father	ĭ	pit	ō	toe	ou	out	ŭ	cut		item

come forth

1. To reveal oneself or make an appearance: *Several students came forth from the audience and asked questions.*
2. To issue out of something: *A large amount of water came forth from the ruptured tank.*

come forward

1. To step out and present oneself: *The teacher asked the three boys to come forward and receive their award.*
2. To offer information or assistance: *After the fire, several families came forward with some money for the victims.*

come from

1. To arrive from some location: *We just came from New York.*
2. To originate in some location, especially where one was born, grew up, or currently lives: *I come from Buenos Aires, which is also where I went to college.*
3. To have something as an origin or cause; stem from something: *That bad cough comes from too much smoking.*
4. To have an attitude or opinion because of some situation: *You must understand that I'm coming from seven years of hard work on this project. I don't see why he makes these suggestions; I just don't know where he's coming from.*

come in

1. To enter some enclosed region: *You may open the door and come in.*
2. To arrive or become available: *We don't have any summer hats now, but a new shipment will be coming in soon. Some important information just came in that we think you should know about.*
3. To arrive at an airport, harbor, or other central location. Used especially of modes of transportation: *The flight comes in at 6:00.*
4. To approach or encroach upon a shoreline: *The tide is coming in after noon. Big waves will come in for some time after the storm.*
5. To arrive, among those who finish a contest or race, at some rank with respect to the others: *My friend came in fifth place in the spelling contest, and I came in last. These two runners will come in ahead of the others.*
6. To be received. Used of wireless communications: *The radio signal is not coming in well because of the electrical storm.*
7. To take on a specified role: *You don't have to help move the boxes; come in when we need you for the furniture. Chapter five of the book is where the main character comes in.*
8. **come in at** To be measured or evaluated as having some value: *The heaviest of the parcels came in at more than ten pounds.*
9. **come in for** To be subject to something: *The engineers came in for high praise with their clever design. The officials will come in for sharp criticism by the newspapers.*
10. **come in with** To join some group in some endeavor or toward achieving something: *Do you want to come*

in with us to buy a birthday present for Timmy?

come into

1. To enter some enclosed space or region: *When the president came into the room, everyone stood up.*
2. To acquire something, especially by good fortune: *Since her parents were so rich, she came into a fortune on her twenty-first birthday. The store managed to come into a huge number of winter hats, so they were put on sale.*
3. To attain some state or condition: *After some rearrangement, our plans came into good shape.*

come of

To be the result, outcome, or outgrowth of something or someone: *We were hopeful at first, but ultimately not much came of our grandiose plans. Nothing much will come of you if you drop out of school now.*

come off

1. To become detached from something: *Three of the buttons have come off my coat. The dirt came off the table easily with a brush.*
2. To have an effect that is felt to have some quality: *His remarks came off as unfriendly. The dinner party came off very well.*
3. To happen; occur: *Her trip came off on time.*

come on

1. To begin by degrees: *Darkness came on quickly that evening. I have a terrible sore throat; I feel the flu coming on.*
2. To begin to be broadcast or communicated, as of television or radio programs: *My son's favorite show doesn't come on until 7:30.*
3. To connect to a channel of communication: *We had been talking for an hour when my cousin came on the phone and asked us to stop.*
4. To activate or be activated: *The room was dark when the lights suddenly came on.*
5. To hurry up; move rapidly. Used chiefly as a command: *Would you please come on? We'll be late!*
6. To stop an inappropriate behavior; abandon a position or an attitude; be obliging. Used chiefly as a command: *Come on; you've been using the same feeble excuse for weeks.*
7. To convey a particular personal image: *The fellow comes on as an old-fashioned reactionary, but he's actually quite open-minded.*
8. SLANG **come on to** To show sexual interest in someone: *Two people tried to come on to me at the party.*

come out

1. To leave some enclosed space: *The dog went into the shed, but he won't come out.*
2. To go and spend time outside of where one lives: *Every summer we*

ă	pat	är	car	ī	bite	ô	paw	o͝o	took	ûr	urge
ā	pay	ĕ	pet	îr	pier	ôr	core	o͝or	lure	zh	vision
âr	care	ē	be	ŏ	pot	oi	boy	o͞o	boot	ə	about,
ä	father	ĭ	pit	ō	toe	ou	out	ŭ	cut		item

come out to the country to get fresh air. Why don't you come out with us after work and see the play?

3. To appear or come into view: *Look, the stars are coming out!*
4. To have a visibly successful outcome: *None of my photographs of the UFO came out.*
5. To become known: *The whole story came out at the trial.*
6. To be issued or brought out: *The author's new book just came out.*
7. To declare oneself publicly: *The governor came out in favor of tax breaks.*
8. To reveal that one is a gay man, a lesbian, or a bisexual: *The celebrity came out on national television.*
9. To make a formal social debut: *She came out at age 18 in New York City.*
10. To end up in some state; result in being something: *I hope everything comes out well. My painting came out a big mess.*
11. **come out to** To result in some total amount; sum up to some amount: *The bill for the dinner comes out to $15 per person.*
12. **come out with** To offer something new for sale: *The band is coming out with a new record next week.*

come over

1. To arrive somewhere by crossing something: *The settlers came over the bridge.*
2. To change sides in a conflict or argument: *After hearing our speech, the group came over to our side and voted for us.*
3. To pay a casual visit: *Come over for lunch tomorrow.*
4. To influence or overwhelm someone strongly but temporarily, without that person being conscious of it: *Something came over me, and I lost my patience for a while.*

come round

See **come around**.

come through

1. To arrive or approach by entering and crossing something; pass through the middle of something: *We came through Albany. A cold front came through last night.*
2. To do what is required or anticipated: *Whenever I ask for help, my friends come through for me.*
3. To become clear or manifest: *The parents' tenderness comes through in their facial expressions.*
4. To communicate clearly: *The radio signal is not coming through. Am I coming through to you?*

come to

1. To arrive at a place: *We came to this city looking for a new life.*
2. To come to the mind of someone; occur to someone: *An interesting idea just came to me.*
3. To have some sum as a total: *The bill for dinner came to $40.*
4. To arrive at some final state; amount to something: *What will these strange events come to? So far, my miserable life has come to nothing.*
5. To recover consciousness: *The fainting victim came to.*
6. NAUTICAL To bring the bow into the wind: *We should stop right here, so come to and we'll let the sails luff.*
7. NAUTICAL To anchor: *We came to in the cove and spent the night there.*

come up

1. To rise or ascend: *When the girl prodded the bottom of the pond with the stick, bubbles came up. I called into the basement and the children came up.*
2. To appear above the horizon. Used of the sun, moon, and stars: *The sun came up.*
3. To become higher in value: *Their grades came up once they started studying more.*
4. To rise in status or rank: *This general came up from the lower ranks very quickly.*
5. To travel to a town or city, especially for a visit: *Why don't you come up to New York for the weekend?*
6. To travel to and arrive at a northern place: *We came up to Canada to look for wolves.*
7. To draw near to something or someone; approach something or someone: *They came up and said hello to us.*
8. To occur or arise, especially unexpectedly. Used of situations, issues, and problems: *The principal couldn't go to the meeting because something important had come up at home. We never considered whether the kids should go with us; the question never came up.*

come upon

To discover or meet someone or something by accident: *While walking down the road, I came upon a strange old house.*

come with

1. To accompany someone; go along with someone: *I didn't go to the mall alone—some friends came with me.*
2. Regional (Chicago & Milwaukee) To accompany; go along. Used intransitively: *I'm going to the store; do you want to come with?*

◆ **confess** (kən-fĕs′)

confessed (kən-fĕst′), **confessing** (kən-fĕs′ĭng), **confesses** (kən-fĕs′ĭz)

confess to

1. To admit to doing something: *The kids confessed to eating all the ice cream. I will not confess to a crime I did not commit!*
2. To admit something to someone: *The thief confessed the crime to the police.*

◆ **conk** (kŏngk)

conked (kŏngkt), **conking** (kŏng′kĭng), **conks** (kŏngks)

conk out

Slang

1. To fail to function; cease to be useful, effective, or operable: *My computer conked out on me. The car's engine conked out halfway through the race.*
2. To go to sleep, especially due to exhaustion: *I conked out after studying all night.*
3. To lose consciousness or awareness: *He conked out after being hit by the ball. She took some medicine and conked out.*

ă	pat	är	car	ī	bite	ô	paw	ŏŏ	took	ûr	urge
ā	pay	ĕ	pet	îr	pier	ôr	core	ŏŏr	lure	zh	vision
âr	care	ē	be	ŏ	pot	oi	boy	ōō	boot	ə	about, item
ä	father	ĭ	pit	ō	toe	ou	out	ŭ	cut		

4. To cause someone or something to lose consciousness or awareness: *The ball hit the goalie's head and conked her out. The mugger conked him out and grabbed his briefcase.*

◆ **consist** (kən-sĭst′)

consisted (kən-sĭs′tĭd), **consisting** (kən-sĭs′tĭng), **consists** (kən-sĭsts′)

consist of

To have something as components; be made up of something: *The English test consisted of four essays.*

◆ **contract** (kən-trăkt′, kŏn′trăkt′)

contracted (kən-trăk′tĭd, kŏn′trăk′tĭd), **contracting** (kən-trăk′tĭng, kŏn′trăk′tĭng), **contracts** (kən-trăkts′, kŏn′trăkts′)

contract out

To engage another person or company by contract to undertake some job that is typically considered part of one's business: *Many companies contract out administrative tasks in order to concentrate on sales and marketing.*

◆ **converge** (kən-vûrj′)

converged (kən-vûrjd′), **converging** (kən-vûr′jĭng), **converges** (kən-vûr′jĭz)

converge on

1. To come together from various places and assemble somewhere for a common purpose: *Protesters converged on the park for a peace rally.*
2. To attack someone or something from all sides: *The police converged on the suspect.*

◆ **cook** (ko͝ok)

cooked (ko͝okt), **cooking** (ko͝ok′ĭng), **cooks** (ko͝oks)

cook out

1. To extract or remove something from something, such as food, by heating: *The chef cooked the flavor out of the vegetables. We cooked out the juices from the meat on the grill.*
2. To cook and eat food outdoors: *Let's cook out for the Fourth of July.*

cook up

1. To prepare some food: *We cooked up a pizza for dinner. I cooked hamburgers up on the grill.*
2. SLANG To fabricate or concoct something; make up something: *Don't cook up an excuse just because you're late. The suspect cooked up an alibi at the last minute.*

◆ **cool** (ko͞ol)

cooled (ko͞old), **cooling** (ko͞o′lĭng), **cools** (ko͞olz)

cool down

1. To become cooler: *We sat in the shade to cool down. As soon as the pie cools down, we can eat it.*
2. To make something cooler: *She cooled down her coffee with an ice cube. He turned on the fan to cool the room down.*
3. To gradually relax after a period of physical exertion: *We walked around the track to cool down after our two-mile run.*
4. To become less angry or contentious: *Let's discuss this after you cool down a bit.*
5. To cause someone or something to become less angry or contentious:

The mediator cooled down the disputing parties. The principal cooled the angry students down.

cool off

1. To cool to a comfortable and agreeable degree of heat: *The kids jumped in the lake to cool off.*
2. To cool something or someone to a comfortable and agreeable degree of heat: *The air conditioner cooled off the building. My soup was hot, but blowing on it cooled it off.*
3. To become calm after a period of anger or conflict: *Have things cooled off in that part of the world?*
4. To calm someone or something that is angry or contentious: *The coach took the angry players aside and cooled them off. The counselor cooled off the fighting campers.*
5. To have a period of outstanding performance come to an end: *They scored ten points in the first half of the game but cooled off in the second. The stock market cooled off after the latest unemployment report was released.*
6. To lose passion: *Their romance has cooled off.*

◆ **cop** (kŏp)

copped (kŏpt), **copping** (kŏp′ĭng), **cops** (kŏps)

cop out

To avoid fulfilling some commitment or responsibility: *I was too tired to go out, so I copped out on my friends. The students copped out of cleaning up after the party.*

◆ **copy** (kŏp′ē)

copied (kŏp′ēd), **copying** (kŏp′ē-ĭng), **copies** (kŏp′ēz)

copy down

To write something exactly as it is said or written somewhere else; transcribe something: *I'll be out tomorrow, so please copy down what the teacher says. Copy the instructions down so you don't forget them.*

◆ **cotton** (kŏt′n)

cottoned (kŏt′nd), **cottoning** (kŏt′n-ĭng), **cottons** (kŏt′nz)

cotton onto

To come to understand something: *I finally cottoned onto the new method.*

cotton to

1. To take a liking to someone or something: *That dog doesn't cotton to strangers.*
2. To come to understand something: *I finally cottoned to the new computer system.*

cotton up

To attempt to be friendly to someone or something: *The teachers all cottoned up to the new principal.*

◆ **cough** (kôf)

coughed (kôft), **coughing** (kô′fĭng), **coughs** (kôfs)

ă	pat	är	car	ī	bite	ô	paw	o͝o	took	ûr	urge
ā	pay	ĕ	pet	îr	pier	ôr	core	o͝or	lure	zh	vision
âr	care	ē	be	ŏ	pot	oi	boy	o͞o	boot	ə	about, item
ä	father	ĭ	pit	ō	toe	ou	out	ŭ	cut		

cough up

1. To force something from the throat or lungs and out of the mouth by coughing: *After years of smoking, he started coughing up blood. The medicine loosened the phlegm so she could cough it up.*
2. SLANG To pay or hand over something, as money, often reluctantly: *Cough up the money or you're going to jail. I know you're short on the rent money, but you'll have to cough it up.*
3. SLANG To confess or disclose something: *When the police arrived, we coughed up the details of the incident. When the lawyers threatened me for not disclosing the tax returns, I coughed them up.*

◆ **count** (kount)
counted (koun′tĭd), **counting** (koun′tĭng), **counts** (kounts)

count against

1. To be a liability to someone; weigh against someone: *The team's inexperience will count against them when they play more difficult opponents.*
2. To hold something against someone: *The teacher counted my absences against me.*

count among

1. To consider someone or something a part of some group: *The company counts many important people among its clients.*
2. To be considered a part of some group: *The new novel counts among the author's greatest works.*

count down

1. To count backward to zero, especially when leading to the start of an important event: *With only ten seconds until midnight, the crowd counted down to the beginning of the new year.*
2. To anticipate something eagerly: *The children are counting down to their summer vacation.*

count off

1. To recite numbers in turn, as when dividing people or things into groups: *The 24 children counted off by twos, forming a dozen pairs.*
2. To count to an agreed upon number so that some group begins an activity at the same time: *The conductor counted the band off, and they began to play. The director counted off the choir, and they began to sing. The conductor counted off, and the band began to play.*
3. To decrease the score or evaluation of someone by some amount: *The professor will count you off five points if you skip a class.*
4. To deduct some amount from a score or evaluation: *The teacher counted off one point for each mistake. The Olympic judges counted a tenth of a point off for the gymnast's wobbly landing. The teacher counts off for misspelled words.*

count on

1. To rely or depend on someone or something: *I was counting on getting a raise when I made the decision to purchase a house.*
2. To be confident of something; anticipate something: *We are count-*

ing on a great vacation this summer.

count out

1. To enumerate a quantity of something unit by unit: *The clerk counted out 12 roses and wrapped them in paper. I counted $5.38 out and handed it to the cashier.*
2. To exclude someone from a group or activity: *You can count me out if you plan to go swimming in this weather.*
3. To eliminate something or someone as a possibility; disregard something or someone: *I wouldn't count them out after that comeback last year. Don't count out the older competitors—they're the ones with experience.*
4. To declare some boxer to have been knocked out by counting out loud the number of seconds by which the boxer must resume fighting: *The boxer fell to the mat, and the ref counted him out to end the fight.*

◆ **cover** (kŭv′ər)

covered (kŭv′ərd), **covering** (kŭv′ə-rĭng), **covers** (kŭv′ərz)

cover up

1. To spread or extend something over someone or something in order to protect or conceal: *We covered up the furniture with a drop cloth before painting the walls. The children covered themselves up with leaves while playing hide and seek.*
2. To conceal something, especially wrongdoing or error: *The criminal tried to cover up the crime by destroying the evidence. I accidentally overcharged a customer, and my boss told me to cover it up.*
3. To put on or wear clothing: *My grandmother covers up before going outside to protect herself from the sun.*

◆ **crack** (krăk)

cracked (krăkt), **cracking** (krăk′ĭng), **cracks** (krăks)

crack down

1. To increase the intensity or severity involved in preventing or regulating something: *The police are cracking down on drunk driving and issuing stiffer penalties. The police cracked down after the murder last week.*
2. To increase the intensity or severity involved in punishing or repressing someone: *The government has cracked down on protesters.*

crack up

1. To damage something or someone, as in an accident: *I cracked up the car when I hit a tree. We gave him a remote control plane for his birthday, but he cracked it up on his very first flight.*
2. To become damaged or wrecked: *The plane cracked up when it hit the ground.*
3. To praise someone or something highly, especially incorrectly. Often used in the passive: *I am simply*

ă	pat	är	car	ī	bite	ô	paw	o͝o	took	ûr	urge
ā	pay	ĕ	pet	îr	pier	ôr	core	o͝or	lure	zh	vision
âr	care	ē	be	ŏ	pot	oi	boy	o͞o	boot	ə	about, item
ä	father	ĭ	pit	ō	toe	ou	out	ŭ	cut		

not the genius I'm cracked up to be. His friend cracked him up to be a great mechanic, but I thought his work was shoddy.

4. To have a mental or physical breakdown: *We were afraid that the pilot might crack up under the stress.*
5. To laugh very hard: *She cracked up when I told her the joke.*
6. To cause someone to laugh very hard: *The funny movie cracked us up. The comedian cracked up the audience.*

◆ **cramp** (krămp)

cramp (krămpt), **cramping** (krăm′pĭng), **cramps** (krămps)

cramp up

1. To suffer muscle cramps: *I cramped up while swimming today.*
2. To cause someone or something to suffer muscle cramps: *That lousy meal cramped me up.*
3. To squeeze something tightly into a restrictive space or position: *There are too many subjects cramped up together under the same heading. I was cramped up in the back seat of a compact car for hours.*

◆ **crank** (krăngk)

cranked (krăngkt), **cranking** (krăng′kĭng), **cranks** (krăngks)

crank out

To produce, especially mechanically and rapidly: *The secretary cranked out one memo after another. I know you're tired of stuffing envelopes, but you need to crank them out.*

crank up

1. To cause a machine to start working by or as if by turning a crank: *The mechanic cranked up the antique car to show us how it worked. We waved goodbye as the pilot cranked the engines up.*
2. To put something into action: *The producers cranked up a massive publicity campaign before releasing the film.*
3. To motivate someone: *I could barely crank myself up to get to school this morning. An emcee came out before the performance and cranked up the crowd.*
4. To cause something to intensify, as in volume or force: *I cranked up the stereo when my favorite song came on. We cranked the motor up to 4200 rpm.*

◆ **crap** (krăp)

crapped (krăpt), **crapping** (krăp′ĭng), **craps** (krăps)

crap out

1. To lose on a roll of dice when playing craps and leave the game: *My first time playing craps, I placed my chips in the come box, rolled a 12, and crapped out.*
2. Vulgar Slang To cease functioning; break down: *My car crapped out on the freeway, and I had to get it towed.*
3. Vulgar Slang To back out of doing something: *They were supposed to go to the movies with me, but they crapped out at the last minute.*

crap up

Vulgar Slang

1. To bungle or make a mess of something: *I really crapped up the*

project. It looks like they crapped it up again.

2. To fail to function properly: *My computer crapped up on me, and I had to shut it down.*

◆ **crawl** (krôl)

crawled (krôld), **crawling** (krô′lĭng), **crawls** (krôlz)

crawl with

To be swarming or covered with moving things: *The accident scene was crawling with police officers.*

◆ **crop** (krŏp)

cropped (krŏpt), **cropping** (krŏp′ĭng), **crops** (krŏps)

crop up

To happen or appear, often unexpectedly: *Errors have cropped up in the report despite all our proofreading.*

◆ **cross** (krôs)

crossed (krôst), **crossing** (krô′sĭng), **crosses** (krô′sĭz)

cross out

1. To draw a line or lines on something to delete or obscure it, or to indicate that it should be canceled or ignored: *The student crossed out so many words that the essay was difficult to read. I crossed the sentence out and rewrote it.*
2. To remove someone or something from a list or record: *The teacher crossed out the name of each student who had left the school. We crossed them out of the database when they left the neighborhood.*

cross over

1. To move from one side of something to another: *Let's cross over the bridge.*
2. To change from one condition or loyalty to another: *The political party was furious when the senator crossed over and voted against the bill.*
3. To extend success or popularity in one field into another: *The actor successfully crossed over from the stage to the movies.*
4. To extend the success or popularity of someone in one field into another: *The jazz musician hoped the media exposure would cross her over to a pop audience.*
5. To die: *My uncle finally crossed over after a long illness.*

cross up

1. To confuse someone by acting in a way that is contrary to what is expected: *The pitcher threw a wild pitch that crossed up the catcher and allowed the runner to steal a base. The quarterback crossed us up with a fake handoff.*
2. To cause some bicycle or motor vehicle to turn about the vertical axis so that it is no longer oriented in the direction that it is moving, often resulting in an abrupt stop. Used chiefly in the passive: *On the last jump, my motorcycle became crossed up in the air, and I landed sideways.*

3. To turn about the vertical axis so that one is no longer oriented in the direction that one is moving, often resulting in an abrupt stop: *The car crossed up in the last turn, and the other car rammed into the side of it.*

◆ **cruise** (kro͞oz)

cruised (kro͞ozd), **cruising** (kro͞o′zĭng), **cruises** (kro͞o′zĭz)

cruise by

1. To pass quickly, as of a moving object or an interval of time: *The vacation cruised by, and when I returned to work, it seemed as though I had never left.*
2. To pass someone or something quickly and easily: *The second-place car cruised by the leader on the final lap.*
3. To visit briefly, often unexpectedly: *My friend cruised by for a cup of coffee. I cruised by the office to pick up my briefcase.*

cruise through

1. To move rapidly through something or some place: *The motorcycle cruised through the tunnel.*
2. To accomplish or proceed with something swiftly or energetically: *We cruised through the project and went home early.*
3. To read something quickly and easily: *I cruised through the chapter because I was already familiar with the subject.*

◆ **cry** (krī)

cried (krīd), **crying** (krī′ĭng), **cries** (krīz)

cry down

To belittle or disparage someone or something: *The rowdy children cried down anyone who attempted to quiet them. The opposition cried us down at every opportunity.*

cry off

To decide to break a commitment or promise: *My volleyball partner cried off at the last moment and forced me to cancel the game.*

cry up

1. To make a strong case for something; try to make others enthusiastic about something: *The governor spent a lot of time crying up the new tax bill. The company hires celebrities to cry its products up.*
2. To praise or extol something: *The sports commentators are crying up the new players on the soccer team. The new romantic comedy didn't look very good, but the film critics sure cried it up.*

◆ **cue** (kyo͞o)

cued (kyo͞od), **cueing** (kyo͞o′ĭng), **cues** (kyo͞oz)

cue in

1. To give a signal to someone at a specified time, especially a signal to begin: *The conductor cued in each section of the choir one by one. Cue me in when it's time to say my lines.*
2. To give information or instructions to someone, such as a latecomer: *I cued in my coworker about the items that we discussed at the beginning of the meeting. She cued me in to what happened in the first five minutes of the movie.*

cue up

1. To position an audio or video recording in readiness for playing:

The DJ cued up the next record on the turntable as the song came to an end. I wanted to show scenes from the film during my presentation, so I cued them up ahead of time.

2. To form or get into a waiting line; queue up: *The customers cued up for tickets long before the box office was open.*

◆ **curl** (kûrl)

curled (kûrld), **curling** (kûr′lĭng), **curls** (kûrlz)

curl up

1. To twist, bend, or roll something into a curved or spiral form: *She curled up the poster and slipped it into a tube. He waxed the ends of his moustache and curled them up.*
2. To assume a curved or spiral form: *The pages of the book had curled up at the edges.*
3. To assume a position with the legs drawn up: *I curled up in an armchair to read a book.*

◆ **cut** (kŭt)

cut (kŭt), **cutting** (kŭt′ĭng), **cuts** (kŭts)

cut across

1. To travel across some region, rather than around it: *We can get to the house faster if we just cut across the front lawn.*
2. To affect or concern a number of different groups of persons or things: *The issue of health care cuts across all social classes.*

cut back

1. To shorten something, as a plant, by cutting; prune something: *If I don't cut back the weeds, they will choke the flowers. Let's cut the vines back.*
2. To reduce or decrease the amount of something: *The factory cut back production because of budget problems. The company cut salaries back this year.*

cut down

1. To chop something down: *The loggers cut down trees from the forest. I cut the overgrown shrubs down.*
2. To reduce the amount of something done, used, or taken: *I need to cut down on shopping this month. They need to cut their drinking down. We've been gambling too much—we need to cut down.*
3. To reduce something, as a price: *They're cutting down all the prices at the mall. The company is cutting bonuses down this year.*
4. To kill or incapacitate someone: *The troops were cut down in battle. Before there were vaccines, many people were cut down by polio.*
5. To belittle or discredit someone or something, especially in front of others: *The boss cut me down in front of my subordinates. The prosecutor cut down the defendant's testimony.*

ă	pat	är	car	ī	bite	ô	paw	o͝o	took	ûr	urge
ā	pay	ĕ	pet	îr	pier	ôr	core	o͝or	lure	zh	vision
âr	care	ē	be	ŏ	pot	oi	boy	o͞o	boot	ə	about,
ä	father	ĭ	pit	ō	toe	ou	out	ŭ	cut		item

6. To alter something by removing extra or additional fittings: *The shop cut down my car for racing. Let's buy those old trucks and cut them down for work on the back roads.*

cut in

1. To step into some line in front of others: *He cut in the line when he joined his friends. She was late, so I let her cut in.*
2. To interrupt someone or something with a comment: *During the debate my opponent kept cutting in.*
3. To drive into the space between two moving cars, often suddenly and recklessly: *I almost ran off the road when that car cut in right in front of me.*
4. To interrupt a dancing couple in order to dance with one of them: *May I cut in? That guy cut in on me and my partner at the dance. I wanted to finish the dance, but she cut in.*
5. To include someone in a plan, especially among those profiting: *We'll cut you in if you help us.*
6. To become operative automatically: *The air conditioning will cut in as soon as the room gets too hot.*
7. To mix something in with or as if with cutting motions: *Measure out the flour and use a pair of knives to cut the shortening in.*

cut off

1. To remove something by cutting: *I cut off the tree branch. He cut his beard off.*
2. To interrupt someone who is speaking: *Don't cut me off like that. The speaker was cut off by the crowd. The principal cut off the discussion when the assembly started.*
3. To separate someone from others; isolate someone: *I don't want to cut my brother off from his friends. She was cut off from her family while she was gone. All contact was cut off.*
4. To stop something from functioning by disconnecting it from its source of power: *Cut the power off. The landlord cut off the heat. The lights got cut off.*
5. To interrupt the course or passage of something: *The infielder cut off the throw to the plate. The police cut all the routes of escape off.*
6. To interrupt or break the line of communication of someone: *The telephone operator cut us off. The storm cut off the phone lines.*
7. To stop or come to an end suddenly: *The music suddenly cut off.*
8. To change from one direction to another: *The road goes straight over the hill and then cuts off to the right around the pond.*
9. To disinherit someone: *They cut their heirs off without a cent. My parents changed their will and cut me off after I left home.*
10. To discontinue the funding for something, such as a government program: *School breakfasts were cut off after the funding cuts. The mayor cut off free school lunches from the budget.*
11. To drive into the space in front of a moving car, often suddenly and recklessly: *That taxi cut me off on*

the highway. The truck cut off the small car abruptly.

cut out

1. To remove something by or as if by cutting: *The children cut out the stencils. We cut the pictures out.*
2. To form or shape by or as if by cutting: *The hikers cut out a path in the bush. I cut a circle out from the paper.*
3. To make something unnecessary: *The lower plane fares cut out the need for long train trips.*
4. To be fit for or suited to something by nature: *I'm not cut out to be a hero.*
5. To predetermine something; assign something beforehand or by necessity. Used in the passive: *Our task has been cut out for us.*
6. To exclude something: *The coach cut us out of all the fun. I've had to cut out sweets from my diet.*
7. To stop or cease doing something: *Cut out that horseplay! Cut it out or you'll have to leave. They were acting badly, but they cut it out when the teacher walked into the room.*
8. To depart hastily: *We cut out of the party early.*
9. To disengage some device by breaking its connection to a power source: *The electrician cut out all of the power. Cut the lights out.*
10. To stop working suddenly: *The engine cut out while I was waiting at the stoplight.*

cut through

1. To penetrate or slice through something: *He cut through the tough steak with a knife.*
2. To avoid or bypass something complicated; circumvent something: *Lets cut through the red tape and get this matter resolved.*
3. To travel across some region, rather than around it: *We cut through the field to get to school. The snow isn't deep here; let's cut through.*
4. To create a passageway through something by cutting: *Someone had cut a path through the woods.*
5. To interrupt something: *The judge's gavel cut through my objections.*

cut up

1. To slice or chop something into smaller pieces: *The electrician cut up the wires. We cut the newspapers up.*
2. To wound someone by cutting or gashing, especially in multiple places: *The mobster grabbed a knife and cut up the witness.*
3. To behave in a playful, comic, or boisterous way; clown: *That clown cut us all up. The new teacher cut up the class.*
4. Slang To criticize someone or something severely: *The teacher cut up the lazy student. The judge cut me up for arriving late.*

ă	pat	är	car	ī	bite	ô	paw	o͝o	took	ûr	urge
ā	pay	ĕ	pet	îr	pier	ôr	core	o͝or	lure	zh	vision
âr	care	ē	be	ŏ	pot	oi	boy	o͞o	boot	ə	about, item
ä	father	ĭ	pit	ō	toe	ou	out	ŭ	cut		

D

◆ **dabble** (dăb′əl)

dabbled (dăb′əld), **dabbling** (dăb′ə-lĭng), **dabbles** (dăb′əlz)

dabble in

To do some activity occasionally, superficially, or without ambition: *I've dabbled in painting, but I'm not very good.*

◆ **dash** (dăsh)

dashed (dăsht), **dashing** (dăsh′ĭng), **dashes** (dăsh′ĭz)

dash off

1. To depart in a hurry: *When the bell rang, he excused himself from the lunch table and dashed off to class.*
2. To write or draw something hurriedly: *She dashed off a note that explained where she was going. He dashed a memo off to the staff explaining the new dress code.*

◆ **dawn** (dôn)

dawned (dônd), **dawning** (dô′nĭng), **dawns** (dônz)

dawn on *or* **dawn upon**

To begin to be perceived or understood by someone; become apparent to someone: *It dawned on me that I had forgotten to pick up some milk. A possible motive for the crime dawned upon the detective.*

◆ **deal** (dēl)

dealt (dĕlt), **dealing** (dē′lĭng), **deals** (dēlz)

deal in

1. To include someone in a card game by giving that player cards: *Deal me in—I'm just getting up to get some potato chips. The dealer dealt in all the players who sat at the table.*
2. To be in some particular line of work or pursuit: *She deals in computer hardware. The gangster dealt in stolen goods.*

deal out

1. To exclude someone from a card game by not giving that player cards: *Deal me out—I have to go to the bathroom.*
2. To distribute something to someone: *The dealer dealt the cards out. The politician dealt out pamphlets explaining her position on the issues. Deal out another hand; I'm ready to play.*

deal with

1. To be about something; have to do with something: *This report deals with teaching students how to read.*
2. To confront or grapple with something: *I can't deal with all of these problems at the same time. These researchers are dealing with the most difficult issues in the field. You dealt with their hostility very well.*

◆ **decide** (dĭ-sīd′)

decided (dĭ-sī′dĭd), **deciding** (dĭ-sī′dĭng), **decides** (dĭ-sīdz′)

decide on *or* **decide upon**

To choose something or someone after deliberation: *We decided on green as the color for the nursery. I've decided upon the red shoes; you can put the black ones back.*

◆ **dedicate** (dĕd′ĭ-kāt′)

dedicated (dĕd′ĭ-kā′tĭd), **dedicating** (dĕd′ĭ-kā′tĭng), **dedicates** (dĕd′ĭ-kāts′)

dedicate to

1. To address or inscribe something to someone as a mark of respect or affection: *The author dedicated the book to her nephew. This monument is dedicated to prisoners of war.*
2. To set something apart for some deity or for religious use; consecrate something: *The parish dedicated the new church to St. Peter. The temple was dedicated to Ra, the Egyptian sun god.*
3. To set something apart for some special use: *The convention organizers have dedicated this table to publishers who want to sell their books. This lane of traffic is dedicated to city buses.*
4. To commit someone to some course of thought or action: *The candidate dedicated herself to fixing social security. The mayor is dedicated to lowering taxes.*

◆ **delight** (dĭ-līt′)

delighted (dĭ-lī′tĭd), **delighting** (dĭ-lī′tĭng), **delights** (dĭ-līts′)

delight in

To derive great pleasure or joy from something or someone: *The happy couple delighted in taking romantic walks through the park.*

◆ **deliver** (dĭ-lĭv′ər)

delivered (dĭ-lĭv′ərd), **delivering** (dĭ-lĭv′ə-rĭng), **delivers** (dĭ-lĭv′ərz)

deliver on

To do something one has promised or is expected to do: *The contractor delivered on his promises to get the work done by Friday. Our office manager delivers on everything she says she will do.*

◆ **depend** (dĭ-pĕnd′)

depended (dĭ-pĕn′dĭd), **depending** (dĭ-pĕn′dĭng), **depends** (dĭ-pĕndz′)

depend on *or* **depend upon**

1. To be contingent upon something or someone for an outcome: *Whether or not we go on the picnic depends on the weather.*
2. To rely on something or someone, especially for support or maintenance: *Children depend on adults for food and shelter.*
3. To place trust or confidence in someone or something: *You can depend upon my honesty.*
4. To have a chronic or compulsive need for something; be addicted to something: *As time went by, he*

ă	pat	är	car	ī	bite	ô	paw	o͝o	took	ûr	urge
ā	pay	ĕ	pet	îr	pier	ôr	core	o͝or	lure	zh	vision
âr	care	ē	be	ŏ	pot	oi	boy	o͞o	boot	ə	about,
ä	father	ĭ	pit	ō	toe	ou	out	ŭ	cut		item

began to depend on painkillers to get him through the day.

◆ **deprive** (dĭ-prīv′)

deprived (dĭ-prīvd′), **depriving** (dĭ-prī′vĭng), **deprives** (dĭ-prīvz′)

deprive of

To keep someone from possessing or enjoying something; take something away from someone: *The war had deprived the refugees of a normal childhood.*

◆ **derive** (dĭ-rīv′)

derived (dĭ-rīvd′), **deriving** (dĭ-rī′vĭng), **derives** (dĭ-rīvz′)

derive from

1. To obtain or receive something from some source: *I derive great pleasure from listening to music.*
2. To issue or originate from some source: *The word "peninsula" derives from the Latin words for "almost" and "island."*
3. To trace the origin or development of something, as a word, from some source: *The language scholar derived the word from ancient Greek.*

◆ **despair** (dĭ-spâr′)

despaired (dĭ-spârd′), **despairing** (dĭ-spâr′ĭng), **despairs** (dĭ-spârz′)

despair of

To lose all hope for something or someone: *The shipwrecked sailors despaired of being rescued. I have seen so much unfairness that I despair of a just world.*

◆ **detract** (dĭ-trăkt′)

detracted (dĭ-trăk′tĭd), **detracting** (dĭ-trăk′tĭng), **detracts** (dĭ-trăkts′)

detract from

To reduce a quality, importance, or some other value; diminish something: *The dent on the side of the car detracts from its overall value. The politician's uneven voting record detracted from his chances of winning the election.*

◆ **deviate** (dē′vē-āt′)

deviated (dē′vē-ā′tĭd), **deviating** (dē′vē-ā′tĭng), **deviates** (dē′vē-āts′)

deviate from

1. To wander or turn aside from some path, course, or way: *The hiker deviated from the trail and got lost. The riverbank deviates from the side of the ridge where the sediment has built up.*
2. To depart or stray from some subject or matter of discussion: *The teacher deviated from the topic of the lecture.*

◆ **devote** (dĭ-vōt′)

devoted (dĭ-vō′tĭd), **devoting** (dĭ-vō′tĭng), **devotes** (dĭ-vōts′)

devote to

1. To commit someone or something to some task: *She devoted herself to finishing the project. Don't devote all your time to that one project. I'm devoted to finishing this book by Friday.*
2. To commit someone loyally to someone or something: *She devoted herself to her family. He was entirely devoted to his parents.*
3. To set something apart for a specific purpose or use: *I'm devoting Saturday to cleaning the house. This knife is devoted to cutting cheese.*

4. To set something apart by or as if by a vow or solemn act; consecrate something: *The priest devoted the Mass to the veterans in the parish.*

◆ **dial** (dīl)

dialed *or* **dialled** (dīld), **dialing** *or* **dialling** (dī′lĭng), **dials** (dīlz)

dial up

To telephone someone or something: *I dialed up my dentist and made an appointment. Would you dial your sister up and ask her what time she's coming over?*

◆ **dictate** (dĭk′tāt′)

dictated (dĭk′tā′tĭd), **dictating** (dĭk′tā′tĭng), **dictates** (dĭk′tāts′)

dictate to

1. To say or read something aloud to someone, especially for it to be written down or notated: *The executive dictated the letter to the secretary.*
2. To issue orders or commands to someone: *The manager dictated the new company policy to the staff.*

◆ **die** (dī)

died (dīd), **dying** (dī′ĭng), **dies** (dīz)

die back

To be affected by the gradual dying of plant shoots, starting at the tips and working back, as a result of weather conditions, natural growth cycle, or disease: *Aerate the soil weekly when the flowers bloom and until they die back.*

die down

To lose strength gradually; subside: *The airplanes won't take off until the winds die down.*

die off

To become extinct gradually: *The dodo died off in the 1600s. Wolves were dying off in the formerly rural area as new subdivisions were built.*

die out

1. To become extinct: *The dinosaurs died out millions of years ago. These tribal customs died out centuries ago.*
2. To diminish and finally cease functioning or existing: *With a few final flickers, the candles died out.*

◆ **differ** (dĭf′ər)

differed (dĭf′ərd), **differing** (dĭf′ə-rĭng), **differs** (dĭf′ərz)

differ from

To have qualities that are not the same as those of something else: *My results differed from the results of everyone else who conducted the experiment. Sopranos differ from altos in having higher voices.*

◆ **dig** (dĭg)

dug (dŭg), **digging** (dĭg′ĭng), **digs** (dĭgz)

ă	pat	är	car	ī	bite	ô	paw	ŏŏ	took	ûr	urge
ā	pay	ĕ	pet	îr	pier	ôr	core	ŏŏr	lure	zh	vision
âr	care	ē	be	ŏ	pot	oi	boy	o͞o	boot	ə	about,
ä	father	ĭ	pit	ō	toe	ou	out	ŭ	cut		item

dig in

1. To plunge the hands into something, especially to search for something: *Dig in your pockets for some change.*
2. To push something into some other thing: *The robbers dug a gun in my back and demanded my wallet.*
3. To dig trenches for protection: *The troops dug in and waited for the enemy to attack.*
4. To hold on to something stubbornly, as to a position; entrench oneself: *The two sides have dug in and refuse to compromise.*
5. To begin to work intensively: *I gathered all the materials for the project and dug in.*
6. To begin to eat heartily: *As soon as everyone got their food, we dug in.*

dig into

1. To plunge the hands into something, especially to search for something: *She dug into her bookbag and pulled out a pen.*
2. To push something into some other thing: *I dug two posts into the ground and hung a volleyball net between them.*

dig out

1. To create a space or structure by digging: *The fox dug a shelter out of the dense earth. The workers dug out a moat around the castle.*
2. To create some pathway that leads from some place by digging: *The prisoners dug a tunnel out of the dungeon.*
3. To expose, gain access to, or free something by digging and removing what surrounds it: *They worked around the clock to dig out the city after the blizzard. The nurse dug the splinter out of my finger with a needle.*
4. To emerge or become accessible by or as if by digging: *It took three weeks for the village to dig out after the mudslide.*

dig up

1. To unearth or expose and gain access to something by digging: *The scientists dug up a dinosaur fossil. The landscapers dug the tree up and replanted it.*
2. To scatter earth, snow, or another substance on some surface by digging into it: *The woodchucks dug up my lawn last night.*
3. To discover or find something through concerted effort: *I dug up some old photos that were in the back of my closet. The detective intended to dig the truth up.*

◆ **dip** (dĭp)
dipped (dĭpt), **dipping** (dĭp′ĭng), **dips** (dĭps)

dip into

1. To plunge something briefly into a liquid: *I dipped the donut into the coffee.*
2. To take a small amount of something from where it is stored: *We have been dipping into the olives you bought all day, but there are still some left.*
3. To withdraw a small amount from some place where it is stored or kept: *We dipped into our savings account to buy the car.*
4. To browse something: *I dipped into the book, but I didn't read the whole thing.*
5. To investigate some subject superficially; dabble in something: *I've*

dipped into psychology, but it never really interested me.

◆ **dish** (dĭsh)

dished (dĭsht), **dishing** (dĭsh′ĭng), **dishes** (dĭsh′ĭz)

dish out

1. To distribute some food from a container: *The hosts dished out lots of steaming vegetables to the dinner guests. Could you dish the soup out while I pour the drinks?*
2. To distribute something: *The company dished out some $10 million in bribes. We made copies of our performance and dished them out to our friends.*

◆ **dispense** (dĭ-spĕns′)

dispensed (dĭ-spĕnst′), **dispensing** (dĭ-spĕn′sĭng), **dispenses** (dĭ-spĕn′sĭz)

dispense with

To get rid or do away with something; forgo something: *The restaurant dispensed with its dress code in order to appeal to a younger crowd.*

◆ **dispose** (dĭ-spōz′)

disposed (dĭ-spōzd′), **disposing** (dĭ-spō′zĭng), **disposes** (dĭ-spō′zĭz)

dispose of

1. To throw out or get rid of something: *The government hired contractors to dispose of the nuclear waste.*
2. To settle or attend to some problem, question, or situation: *We quickly disposed of the problem before anyone found out.*
3. To transfer or part with something, as by giving away or selling it: *The bank disposed of its bad loans.*
4. To kill or destroy someone: *The dictator disposed of all his enemies.*

◆ **dive** (dīv)

dived (dīvd) *or* **dove** (dōv), **dived** (dīvd), **diving** (dī′vĭng), **dives** (dīvz)

dive in

1. To plunge one's body into something: *The swimmer stood at the edge of the pool and dived in. The bird flew up suddenly before diving in the water.*
2. To start enthusiastically: *The teacher laid out the chemistry equipment, and the students dived in.*
3. To start eating eagerly: *I'm getting hungry, I can't wait to dive in. Here's the pizza; dive in!*

dive into

1. To plunge one's body into something: *The swimmer dived into the pool.*
2. To start doing something enthusiastically: *The class dived into the science experiment.*
3. To start eating or drinking something eagerly: *The hungry children dove into the pizza.*

ă	pat	är	car	ī	bite	ô	paw	o͝o	took	ûr	urge
ā	pay	ĕ	pet	îr	pier	ôr	core	o͝or	lure	zh	vision
âr	care	ē	be	ŏ	pot	oi	boy	o͞o	boot	ə	about,
ä	father	ĭ	pit	ō	toe	ou	out	ŭ	cut		item

◆ **divvy** (dĭv′ē)

divvied (dĭv′ēd), **divvying** (dĭv′ē-ĭng), **divvies** (dĭv′ēz)

divvy up

To divide something into parts or portions for distribution: *The thieves went back to the cabin to divvy up the loot. My grandparents gave me $100, and I divvied it up among my brothers, sisters, and me.*

◆ **do** (do͞o)

did (dĭd), **done** (dŭn), **doing** (do͞o′ĭng), **does** (dŭz)

do by

To behave in some manner with respect to someone or something: *The children have done well by their attentive parents.*

do in

1. To tire someone completely; exhaust someone: *The marathon did me in. Those difficult exercises did in the students who were out of shape.*
2. To kill someone: *Those cigarettes will do you in if you smoke too many of them. That powerful poison did in every one of the cockroaches.*
3. To ruin someone or something: *Huge losses on the stock market did many investors in. The hurricane did in many of the stores along the coast.*

do up

1. To adorn or dress someone or something lavishly: *I did the kids up in Halloween costumes for the party. Let's do up the living room with some new paint. The children were all done up in matching outfits.*
2. To wrap and tie something, such as a package: *She did up the birthday presents in beautiful bows and ribbons. I took all the packages to the post office, did them up with twine, and sent them right away.*
3. To fasten completely some item or part of clothing: *She did up the buttons on her dress and put on her shoes. He did his trousers up and left the changing room.*

do with

To manage with something that is not optimal: *We don't have time to order new parts; we must do with the parts that we have.*

do without

To manage despite the absence of something: *Since we're short of money for supplies, you'll have to do without. We had to do without a telephone on the island.*

◆ **doctor** (dŏk′tər)

doctored (dŏk′tərd), **doctoring** (dŏk′tə-rĭng), **doctors** (dŏk′tərz)

doctor up

1. To falsify or change something in such a way as to make it favorable: *The corrupt lawyer doctored up the evidence. I doctored the photo up to make myself look younger.*
2. To modify something so as to improve or conceal its taste or appearance: *The chef doctored up the bland fish by seasoning it heavily. I doctored the eggs up with a little oregano.*

◆ **dole** (dōl)

doled (dōld), **doling** (dō′lĭng), **doles** (dōlz)

dole out

To distribute something: *The government doles out cheese to the needy. The teacher doled pencils out to the students.*

◆ **doll** (dŏl)

dolled (dŏld), **dolling** (dŏl′ĭng), **dolls** (dŏlz)

doll up

SLANG

1. To dress someone in fancy or ostentatious clothes, especially for a special occasion: *The parents dolled up their child in sailor outfits. The costume designer dolled me up in 19th-century clothing. I got all dolled up for the big Halloween party.*
2. To add embellishing details to something in order to make it more attractive: *I dolled up the boring lecture by adding a lot of jokes. There wasn't much content in the manuscript, so the author had tried to doll it up with interesting stories.*

◆ **dope** (dōp)

doped (dōpt), **doping** (dō′pĭng), **dopes** (dōps)

dope out

SLANG

1. To work or figure something out: *The math student doped out the difficult homework problem. We need to come up with ways to pay for more police officers, and it's up to the mayor to dope it out.*
2. To intoxicate someone strongly. Used of drugs: *That allergy medicine really dopes me out. I left the party because everyone there was doped out.*

dope up

1. To administer drugs to someone or something: *The coach doped the athletes up before the race, in violation of the rules. The nurse doped me up after my surgery.*
2. To intoxicate someone with some drug: *The kidnappers doped up their victim on sedatives. She doped herself up and went to a party. Does he always have to get doped up in order to enjoy himself?*
3. To become intoxicated by taking some drug: *The nervous passenger doped up on tranquilizers before the flight.*

◆ **dote** (dōt)

doted (dō′tĭd), **doting** (dō′tĭng), **dotes** (dōts)

dote on

To show excessive fondness or love to someone: *My grandmother dotes on all of her grandchildren.*

◆ **double** (dŭb′əl)

doubled (dŭb′əld), **doubling** (dŭb′ə-lĭng), **doubles** (dŭb′əlz)

ă	pat	är	car	ī	bite	ô	paw	ŏŏ	took	ûr	urge
ā	pay	ĕ	pet	îr	pier	ôr	core	ŏŏr	lure	zh	vision
âr	care	ē	be	ŏ	pot	oi	boy	ōō	boot	ə	about, item
ä	father	ĭ	pit	ō	toe	ou	out	ŭ	cut		

double as

To serve in some additional capacity: *The high school principal doubles as the soccer coach.*

double back

1. To turn around and move back in the opposite direction: *Since we got lost, we'll need to double back and start over.*
2. To turn sharply or reverse course completely, as of a path: *The road doubles back, following the course of the river. The trail up the mountain doubles back on itself several times.*

double down

To double one's original bet after being dealt the first two cards in a game of blackjack: *The dealer dealt me a good hand, so I doubled down.*

double over

1. To bend or fold something back upon itself at the middle: *We had to double over the invitations to fit them in the envelopes. I doubled my ticket over and stuck it in my pocket.*
2. To bend or fold in half at the middle: *These lawn chairs double over so you can store them in a small space.*
3. To cause someone to bend over from the waist: *The bad smell doubled the kids over when they entered the school. The comedian's funny jokes doubled us over.*
4. To bend over from the waist: *When he got the bad news, he just doubled over. She was so sick from the flu that she doubled over.*

double up

1. To bend at the waist suddenly, out of pain or intense laughter: *We doubled up in laughter watching the old movies.*
2. To cause someone to bend at the waist suddenly, as out of pain or intense laughter: *That joke absolutely doubled me up!*
3. To arrange something in pairs: *We doubled up the children in the downstairs bedrooms.*
4. To be arranged in pairs: *The children doubled up, and each pair took a turn on the swings. If the crew doubles up, they can finish this job in half the time.*
5. To do or use twice as much of something as usual: *I didn't go to the gym yesterday, so I'm doubling up on my workout today. The clothes are filthy, so double up on detergent.*
6. To share between two people something meant for one: *There aren't enough beds for everyone, so they had to double up.*
7. To perform two functions simultaneously: *The new band has a lead singer who doubles up on keyboards. My key ring doubles up as a bottle opener.*

◆ **doze** (dōz)

dozed (dōzd), **dozing** (dō′zĭng), **dozes** (dō′zĭz)

doze off

To fall into a light sleep: *I dozed off in front of the TV for a few minutes.*

◆ **draft** (drăft)

drafted (drăf′tĭd), **drafting** (drăf′tĭng), **drafts** (drăfts)

draft up

To write or devise some preliminary version or plan: *I drafted up a speech to give at the banquet. The architect came up with a basic plan and drafted it up to show the client.*

◆ **drag** (drăg)

dragged (drăgd), **dragging** (drăg′ĭng), **drags** (drăgz)

drag down

1. To pull something or someone from a higher to a lower position: *She dragged down the boxes from the attic. Help me drag the camping gear down the hill.*
2. To lower the quality, character, or value of something or someone: *His disruptions are dragging down the performance of the other students. Recent events have dragged prices down.*
3. SLANG To exhaust, discourage, or depress someone: *All this work is really dragging me down. The lowered salaries have dragged down morale.*

drag out

1. To prolong something tediously: *The teacher dragged out the lecture with boring stories. The director dragged the rehearsal out until late in the evening.*
2. To be prolonged to the point of tedium: *The movie dragged out and I fell asleep.*
3. To extract some information from someone by means of a long, drawn-out process: *The police dragged the confession out of the suspect. The prosecutor dragged out the truth from the witnesses.*

drag up

To bring some unpleasant thought or topic back to mind or discussion: *Why did you have to drag those old secrets up? The principal dragged up my bad grades from last year.*

◆ **draw** (drô)

drew (dro͞o), **drawn** (drôn), **drawing** (drô′ĭng), **draws** (drôz)

draw away

1. To pull something away: *I drew the dogs away from the creek. The babysitter drew away the children from the stranger.*
2. To pull back from someone or something: *The jury drew away from the bloody photograph. The man reached toward us, but we drew away.*
3. To move ahead of competitors, as in a race: *In the last lap, the leader drew away from the pack.*
4. To lure or attract something away from someone or something: *Her speech drew attention away from the honoree. The national election drew away interest in our local news.*

draw back

1. To retreat: *The soldiers drew back after a night of intense fighting.*

When the general gave the order, the regiment drew back.

2. To recoil from someone or something: *The dog drew back when my friend moved to pet it. He reached out to me, but I drew back.*
3. To decide not to follow a planned course of action: *The politician drew back from seeking candidacy this year.*

draw down

1. To pull something down, especially by extending it: *Draw down the shades so I can get dressed. The stagehand drew the curtain down after the first act.*
2. To deplete something by consuming or spending: *The embargo drew down our food reserves. The increased costs drew our budget down.*

draw on

1. To put lines, pictures, or some other markings on some surface, using a pen, pencil, or other marking implement: *The kids are drawing clowns on the the walls! In my art class we drew on big pieces of paper.*
2. To use something as a resource: *If I run out of cash, I'll have to draw on my savings account. I drew on my old scout training to make that fire.*
3. To approach: *The lost campers became more worried as nighttime drew on.*
4. To pass gradually: *The storm gradually lessened as the night drew on.*

draw out

1. To pull something out of some other thing: *The sheriff drew a gun out of a holster. The burglar drew out a knife.*
2. To lure someone or something out of some state or place: *The teacher's voice drew me out of my daydream. The hunters tried to draw deer out into the open.*
3. To make something longer than usual or necessary; prolong something: *The emcee drew out his introduction until the performers were ready. The speaker drew the lecture out so that it would last the entire class.*
4. To induce someone to speak freely: *The doctor managed to draw the shy child out. The staff's kindness drew out the reserved patient.*
5. To extract information from someone: *The police drew out the truth from the suspect. The kids' parents drew the real story out from them.*

draw up

1. To compose or write something in a set form: *My lawyer will draw up a contract. The committee drew the list of nominees up.*
2. To pull something close by: *Draw up a chair and join us!*
3. To bring oneself to an erect posture, often as an expression of dignity or indignation: *She drew up to her full height. He drew up out of his chair in protest.*
4. To come to a halt, as a vehicle: *The truck drew up at the curb.*
5. To bring something to a halt, as a vehicle: *I drew the car up in front of the house. We drew up the van to the curb.*
6. To bring troops into order: *The prince drew up the soldiers and praised their courage.*

◆ **dream** (drēm)

dreamed (drēmd) *or* **dreamt** (drĕmt), **dreaming** (drē′mĭng), **dreams** (drēmz)

dream on

SLANG

To fantasize about something that is improbable or unrealistic. Used chiefly as a scornful command: *So you want to move to Hollywood and become a movie star? Dream on!*

dream up

To concoct something, especially a plan or idea that is viewed as impractical: *We dreamed up a plan to take over the company. They dreamed a plan up that would allow them to retire next year. What happens in the book is more magical than anything I could dream up.*

◆ **dredge** (drĕj)

dredged (drĕjd), **dredging** (drĕj′ĭng), **dredges** (drĕj′ĭz)

dredge up

1. To deepen some body of water by digging and removing material from its bottom: *They'll have to dredge up the river, or else the larger ships won't be able to pass through. Because the stream was hard to navigate, the farmer paid someone to dredge it up.*
2. To raise something from the bottom of a body of water: *The workers dredged up a car from the bottom of the lake. They dredged a lot of garbage up from the bottom of the canal.*
3. To bring something back into discussion or importance, especially something unpleasant: *I wish you hadn't dredged up that issue with our boss. I had been content to forget about the accident until my neighbor dredged it up by asking me questions about it.*

◆ **dress** (drĕs)

dressed (drĕst), **dressing** (drĕs′ĭng), **dresses** (drĕs′ĭz)

dress down

1. To scold or reprimand someone: *The teacher dressed down the students for arriving to class late. My parents dressed me down for being rude.*
2. To wear informal clothes, befitting an occasion or location: *I dressed down for the casual party.*

dress up

1. To clothe someone or something: *They dressed their dolls up in outfits they made themselves. The store owner dressed up the mannequin and put it in the window of the store.*
2. To wear formal or fancy clothes: *The students dressed up and went to the prom.*
3. To dress someone in clothes suited for some particular occasion or situation: *We dressed up the children for the cold weather. We'll need to dress ourselves up for wet*

ă	pat	är	car	ī	bite	ô	paw	o͝o	took	ûr	urge
ā	pay	ĕ	pet	îr	pier	ôr	core	o͝or	lure	zh	vision
âr	care	ē	be	ŏ	pot	oi	boy	o͞o	boot	ə	about,
ä	father	ĭ	pit	ō	toe	ou	out	ŭ	cut		item

weather. I can see you're dressed up to go hiking.

4. To wear clothes suited for some particular occasion or situation: *People usually dress up in white to play tennis.*
5. To make something appear more interesting or attractive than it actually is: *The real estate agent dressed up the truth about the old house. The story of my trip was pretty boring, so I dressed it up with colorful exaggerations.*

◆ **drift** (drĭft)

drifted (drĭf′tĭd), **drifting** (drĭf′tĭng), **drifts** (drĭfts)

drift off

1. To move away slowly, especially while being carried by currents of air or water: *The stick drifted off with the river current. The child let go of the balloon and it drifted off toward the horizon.*
2. To walk slowly toward some other place or area: *As they left the cafeteria, the students started drifting off toward the gym.*
3. To fall asleep gradually: *I drifted off while watching television. I was so tired that I drifted off.*
4. To stop listening or paying attention to someone or something: *The professor noted that most of the students had drifted off during the lecture.*

◆ **drill** (drĭl)

drilled (drĭld), **drilling** (drĭl′ĭng), **drills** (drĭlz)

drill into

1. To penetrate some surface by boring: *The geologist drilled into the Earth's crust.*
2. To teach or inculcate something to someone by constant, intense repetition: *The teacher drilled the multiplication tables into the bored students. The teacher tried to drill into our heads the capital of every country.*

◆ **drink** (drĭngk)

drank (drăngk), **drunk** (drŭngk), **drinking** (drĭng′kĭng), **drinks** (drĭngks)

drink in

To take something in eagerly through the senses or the mind: *The campers drank in the view of the sunset over the mountain lake. The shoreline was so beautiful that I stopped for a while to drink it in.*

drink up

To drink something completely: *She drank the coffee up and set the cup on the counter. He drank up his milk and asked for more. Drink up—it's time to go.*

◆ **drive** (drīv)

drove (drōv), **driven** (drĭv′ən), **driving** (drī′vĭng), **drives** (drīvz)

drive at

To mean to do or say something; have something as a point: *I don't understand what you're driving at—just tell me what you mean.*

drive away

1. To leave a place in a vehicle: *We got in our car after the party and drove away.*
2. To take someone or something away in a vehicle: *The farmer drove the puppies away to their*

new home. The police drove away the criminals in their van.

3. To repel someone or something: *We drove the bugs away with insect repellent. The smell drove away trespassers.*

drive down

1. To drive a vehicle downward, southward, or along some path: *We drove down to Florida for winter break. They drove down the street in the van.*
2. To drive some vehicle downward, southward, or along some path: *My sister drove my car down to Florida. She drove the motorcycle down the road.*
3. To cause something to decrease rapidly: *The increase in supply drove down the costs. The ongoing war drove travel down.*

drive off

1. To leave a place in a vehicle: *I got in my car and drove off.*
2. To repel someone or something: *We drove the bugs off with fly swatters. The police drove off the angry crowd with tear gas.*
3. To hit a golf ball off something, especially a tee, at the start of a hole: *I drove off the tee and ended up in a sand trap.*

drive out

1. To force someone or something to leave some place: *The rising cost of rent drove the tenants out. The pesticide drove out the insects.*
2. To travel to some destination in a vehicle: *We might drive out to the country this weekend. I was driving out toward Denver when the blizzard hit.*

drive to

1. To travel to some destination in a vehicle: *She drove to the beach in her truck. He drove to the mall.*
2. To travel in some vehicle to some destination: *We drove the car to the store for groceries.*
3. To force or impel someone to some action or condition: *I didn't want to have to say it, but you drove me to it. This paperwork is driving the staff to insanity.*

drive up

1. To arrive at a destination in a vehicle: *I was standing in front of the house when they drove up.*
2. To drive a vehicle upward, northward, or along some path: *We drove up the mountain. The fire engines were driving up the street.*
3. To drive some vehicle upward, northward, or along some path: *Let's drive the van up to Canada. We were driving our new sports car up the street.*
4. To cause something to increase rapidly: *The scarce supply of oil is driving up prices. The interest in the new toy drove up sales.*

◆ **drop** (drŏp)
dropped (drŏpt), **dropping** (drŏp′ĭng), **drops** (drŏps)

ă	pat	är	car	ī	bite	ô	paw	o͝o	took	ûr	urge
ā	pay	ĕ	pet	îr	pier	ôr	core	o͝or	lure	zh	vision
âr	care	ē	be	ŏ	pot	oi	boy	o͞o	boot	ə	about, item
ä	father	ĭ	pit	ō	toe	ou	out	ŭ	cut		

drop back

1. To take a position behind some group by moving more slowly: *I dropped back behind the group of my friends and walked alone on the beach.*
2. FOOTBALL To back away from the line of scrimmage: *The quarterback dropped back to throw a pass.*

drop behind

1. To fail to keep up a pace; fall behind: *The slow runner dropped behind the others. I had the lead, but I got tired and dropped behind.*
2. To fail to maintain a desired level of performance: *She dropped behind the rest of the class during her illness. He had been the best musician in the band, but after he missed so many rehearsals, he dropped behind.*

drop by

To pay a casual visit to some place: *He dropped by the hospital to visit his aunt. She dropped by the office during her vacation to see if she had received any important mail.*

drop in

1. To let something fall into some other thing: *I dropped some spare change in the beggar's cup. I took some rocks to the hole and dropped them in. Don't push the latch down into the lock; just let it drop in.*
2. To come to some place for a casual visit: *We'll drop in and see how you're doing tomorrow. Should we drop in on our neighbors tonight?*

drop off

1. To fall off something: *The box must have dropped off the back of the truck.*
2. To cause something to fall off something: *The hiker dropped the rock off the cliff's edge.*
3. To deliver something to some place: *Drop those DVDs off at the video store on your way home. We'll drop off the gifts at your house later.*
4. To decline: *Sales dropped off in December.*
5. To fall asleep: *The movie was so dull that I dropped off for a while.*

drop out

1. To fall out of something: *My card must have dropped out of the bag at some point.*
2. To make or let something or someone fall out of something: *I dropped the stones out of the window.*
3. To withdraw from participation in something, as a game, club, or school: *The committee is trying to determine why so many students were dropping out. I dropped out of algebra because it was too hard. I dropped history out of my schedule this term.*
4. To withdraw from established society, especially due to disillusionment with conventional values: *My cousin dropped out and moved to the tropics.*
5. To omit something: *This computer drops out the semicolons. The old stereo drops the bass out.*
6. To be omitted: *When words are contracted, some sounds or letters drop out.*

◆ **drown** (droun)

drowned (dround), **drowning** (drou′nĭng), **drowns** (drounz)

drown out

To muffle or mask some sound with a louder sound: *I turned up my TV in order to drown out the noise coming from next door. The protesters drowned the speaker out.*

◆ **drum** (drŭm)

drummed (drŭmd), **drumming** (drŭm′ĭng), **drums** (drŭmz)

drum up

1. To bring something about by continuous, persistent effort: *The advertising firm drummed up new business for us. The manager tried to drum interest up in the computer training classes.*
2. To obtain or resourcefully put together something that one needs; come up with something: *The witness drummed up an alibi during the trial. We drummed some volunteers up for the project.*

◆ **dry** (drī)

dried (drīd), **drying** (drī′ĭng), **dries** (drīz)

dry out

1. To become free of liquid or moisture: *If you sit in the sun, your wet hair will dry out.*
2. To remove the moisture from something: *Dry out your clothes on the line. We'll dry the rags out on the lawn.*
3. Slang To become sober: *I need a few hours to dry out before I go out again.*
4. Slang To make someone become sober: *The crisp morning air has dried me out a bit.*
5. Slang To undergo a cure for alcoholism: *My uncle went to a clinic to dry out.*

dry up

1. To become devoid of liquid or moisture: *During the drought, the pond dried up.*
2. To cause something to become devoid of liquid or moisture: *She dried up the wet table with a towel. He spilled some water on his pants and dried it up with a hair dryer.*
3. To become unavailable gradually: *The money for the grant dried up because of funding problems.*
4. To stop talking suddenly: *The suspect realized he was talking to the police without his lawyer and quickly dried up.*

◆ **duck** (dŭk)

ducked (dŭkt), **ducking** (dŭk′ĭng), **ducks** (dŭks)

duck out

1. To sneak out of some place: *The shy student ducked out of the school dance early. When no one was looking, I ducked out.*
2. To avoid or neglect some responsibility or obligation: *I ducked out*

ă	pat	är	car	ī	bite	ô	paw	o͝o	took	ûr	urge
ā	pay	ĕ	pet	îr	pier	ôr	core	o͝or	lure	zh	vision
âr	care	ē	be	ŏ	pot	oi	boy	o͞o	boot	ə	about,
ä	father	ĭ	pit	ō	toe	ou	out	ŭ	cut		item

of mowing the lawn and headed to the beach. My kids were supposed to clean the garage this morning, but they ducked out by claiming they were too tired.

◆ **dumb** (dŭm)

dumbed (dŭmd), **dumbing** (dŭm′ĭng), **dumbs** (dŭmz)

dumb down

SLANG

To simplify something excessively in order to make it suitable for a less educated or less sophisticated audience: *The researchers dumbed down the report before releasing it to the public.*

◆ **dummy** (dŭm′ē)

dummied (dŭm′ēd), **dummying** (dŭm′ē-ĭng), **dummies** (dŭm′ēz)

dummy up

1. To refuse to talk or to stop talking suddenly: *I was told to dummy up until my lawyer arrived.*
2. To make a model of some publication or page layout: *Dummy up the first page and I'll look at it. If you're finished proofreading the article, dummy it up.*

◆ **dump** (dŭmp)

dumped (dŭmpt), **dumping** (dŭm′pĭng), **dumps** (dŭmps)

dump on

1. To discard or discharge something onto some other thing: *We weren't allowed to dump trash on the premises. Someone dumped this package on my front porch.*
2. To tell all one's problems to someone: *After he was fired, he dumped his problems on me for hours. She dumped on me when her boyfriend left.*
3. To criticize someone severely and unfairly: *You're dumping on me because you're in a bad mood, not because I did anything wrong.*
4. To assign some job to someone, often inconveniently and unfairly: *The boss dumped the filing on the new employee. The most menial work was dumped on the interns.*

◆ **dust** (dŭst)

dusted (dŭs′tĭd), **dusting** (dŭs′tĭng), **dusts** (dŭsts)

dust off

1. To remove dust from something or someone by brushing or wiping: *I dusted off the old trunk in the attic. We picked up the antiques and dusted them off.*
2. To restore something to use: *The mechanic dusted off that old engine and sold it. I dusted off last year's winter coat and put it on.*

◆ **dwell** (dwĕl)

dwelt (dwĕlt) *or* **dwelled** (dwĕld), **dwelling** (dwĕl′ĭng), **dwells** (dwĕlz)

dwell on

To think or talk about something to an excessive degree: *The teacher dwelled on the subject of tardiness for several minutes.*

E

◆ **ease** (ēz)

eased (ēzd), **easing** (ē′zĭng), **eases** (ē′zĭz)

ease back

1. To move something backward slowly and gently: *The pilot eased back the control stick and the plane began to rise. You'll be more comfortable in the airplane if you ease the seat back and take a nap. I realized I was speeding, so I eased back on the accelerator.*
2. To act with less intensity or severity: *The school has eased back on punishments for being late. The teachers were criticizing the students very harshly, so the principal asked them to ease back.*

ease off

1. To diminish gradually in intensity or severity: *My headache eased off after I took an aspirin.*
2. To move away from someone or something slowly and carefully: *The snake eased off from the mongoose. Better ease off—they have a gun.*
3. To treat someone less severely: *The principal eased off on the student and only gave a warning. The coach has made us practice very hard and hasn't eased off for days.*

◆ **eat** (ēt)

ate (āt), **eaten** (ēt′n), **eating** (ē′tĭng), **eats** (ēts)

eat in

To eat at home, rather than in a restaurant: *It's raining outside, so let's eat in tonight.*

eat out

1. To eat at a restaurant or away from one's home: *I'm tired of cooking; let's eat out tonight.*
2. VULGAR SLANG To perform cunnilingus on someone.

eat up

1. To devour something completely: *The children ate up all the food in the house. If you leave cookies out, the dog will eat them up.*
2. To consume a large amount of something: *The repair bills for maintaining this old car really eat up my savings account. Driving so fast ate all our gas up very quickly.*
3. SLANG To obsess or bother someone: *That snide remark you made is still eating me up.*
4. SLANG To receive or enjoy something enthusiastically or avidly: *That television celebrity really eats up the publicity. The kids love those jokes—they eat them right up.*

ă	pat	är	car	ī	bite	ô	paw	o͝o	took	ûr	urge
ā	pay	ĕ	pet	îr	pier	ôr	core	o͝or	lure	zh	vision
âr	care	ē	be	ŏ	pot	oi	boy	o͞o	boot	ə	about, item
ä	father	ĭ	pit	ō	toe	ou	out	ŭ	cut		

5. SLANG To believe something without question: *He'll eat up whatever his broker tells him. I said I was very rich and she ate it right up.*

◆ **edge** (ĕj)
edged (ĕjd), **edging** (ĕj′ĭng), **edges** (ĕj′ĭz)

edge out

1. To move something gradually: *He edged the car out of the garage.*
2. To displace or surpass someone or something gradually: *The large company began to edge out its competitors one by one. One of my coworkers is trying to edge me out of my job.*
3. To surpass or beat someone by a small margin: *The incumbent edged out the challenger by 200 votes. The runner edged her opponent out at the last moment.*

◆ **edit** (ĕd′ĭt)
edited (ĕd′ĭ-tĭd), **editing** (ĕd′ĭ-tĭng), **edits** (ĕd′ĭts)

edit in

To insert something during the course of editing: *The sound mixer edited in the soundtrack after the video was shot. Before the show was aired, an additional scene was edited in.*

edit out

To delete something during the course of editing: *To shorten the film, they decided to edit out one musical number from each scene. The censor insisted that the author edit the controversial paragraph out.*

◆ **egg** (ĕg)
egged (ĕgd), **egging** (ĕg′ĭng), **eggs** (ĕgz)

egg on

To encourage, goad, or incite someone into action: *I didn't want to sing karaoke, but my friends egged me on. She egged on her coworkers to sign the petition.*

◆ **empty** (ĕm′tē)
emptied (ĕm′tēd), **emptying** (ĕm′tē-ĭng), **empties** (ĕm′tēz)

empty out

1. To remove all the contents of something: *I emptied out the trash barrel. The trash can is full—please empty it out.*
2. To remove something from a container, leaving the container empty: *I emptied the trash out of the can into a plastic bag. If you empty out all that junk from the garage, there will be some room for my bicycle.*
3. To become devoid of people: *The room emptied out after the mayor's speech.*

◆ **encroach** (ĕn-krōch′)
encroached (ĕn-krōcht′), **encroaching** (ĕn-krō′chĭng), **encroaches** (ĕn-krō′chĭz)

encroach on *or* **encroach upon**

To advance or extend toward or into something beyond its proper or former limits: *The weeds in my neighbor's yard are encroaching on my lawn. At the edge of the village, the desert encroaches upon grassland.*

◆ **end** (ĕnd)

ended (ĕn′dĭd), **ending** (ĕn′dĭng), **ends** (ĕndz)

end up

1. To bring something to a close: *The manager ended up the meeting by thanking us for all of our hard work.*
2. To arrive somewhere, especially when not anticipated: *We lost our way and ended up downtown. If you end up in our area tonight, feel free to drop in.*
3. To arrive in some situation or condition as a result of a course of action: *If you keep going outside in this weather without shoes, you'll end up catching a cold.*

◆ **engage** (ĕn-gāj′)

engaged (ĕn-gājd′), **engaging** (ĕn-gā′jĭng), **engages** (ĕn-gā′jĭz)

engage in

1. To participate in some activity: *The soldiers engaged in combat. The law students engaged in a mock trial.*
2. To involve or draw someone or something into some activity: *I engaged the new student in conversation. I was engaged in deep thought when the fire alarm went off.*

◆ **enter** (ĕn′tər)

entered (ĕn′tərd), **entering** (ĕn′tə-rĭng), **enters** (ĕn′tərz)

enter into

1. To participate or take an active interest in something: *After college, she entered into politics. The union and management have decided to enter into negotiations in order to settle the strike.*
2. To enroll or register someone or something in some activity: *I'm going to enter my dog into the competition.*
3. To become party to a contract: *The nations entered into a trade agreement.*
4. To become a part of something: *Financial matters entered into the discussion.*

enter on

1. To begin or set out on something: *With the assassination of the prime minister, the country entered on four years of civil unrest.*
2. To begin considering something; take up something: *After approving the budget proposal, the committee entered on the problem of raising taxes.*
3. To take possession of something: *When my uncle passed away, I entered on his estate and began managing the family business.*

enter upon

To begin or set out on something: *We have entered upon a challenging period in our lives.*

◆ **even** (ē′vən)

evened (ē′vənd), **evening** (ēv′n-ĭng), **evens** (ē′vənz)

ă	pat	är	car	ī	bite	ô	paw	o͝o	took	ûr	urge
ā	pay	ĕ	pet	îr	pier	ôr	core	o͝or	lure	zh	vision
âr	care	ē	be	ŏ	pot	oi	boy	o͞o	boot	ə	about,
ä	father	ĭ	pit	ō	toe	ou	out	ŭ	cut		item

even out

1. To make something more balanced or equitable: *The typesetter evened out the columns so that they were both 60 lines long. The barber evened my hair out in back.*
2. To become more balanced or equitable: *I'll pay for the appetizers and dessert if you pay for the meal—that way everything evens out.*

even up

1. To make something balanced or equal: *The bookie evened the odds up. The carpenter evened up the legs of the chair so that it would stop wobbling.*
2. To become balanced or equal: *The home team was ahead for the first half of the game, but the score evened up after the second half started.*

◆ **explain** (ĭk-splān′)

explained (ĭk-splānd′), **explaining** (ĭk-splā′nĭng), **explains** (ĭk-splānz′)

explain away

To dismiss or minimize the significance of something by explanation: *The candidate tried to explain his earlier misstatements away. The researcher explained away the criticisms that were raised against her hypothesis.*

◆ **extend** (ĭk-stĕnd′)

extended (ĭk-stĕn′dĭd), **extending** (ĭk-stĕn′dĭng), **extends** (ĭk-stĕndz′)

extend to

1. To stretch out to some point: *The road extends to the next city.*
2. To lengthen or prolong something to some point: *We extended the table's legs to raise its height. I'd like to extend my holiday to the weekend.*
3. To include someone or something in a sphere of influence: *These rules extend to applications submitted before this morning.*
4. To offer something to someone: *Extend my best wishes to your family.*

F

◆ **face** (fās)

faced (fāst), **facing** (fā′sĭng), **faces** (fā′sĭz)

face down

1. To confront someone in a resolute or determined manner: *The incumbent faced down the opponent in a debate. The soldiers faced the enemy down.*
2. To position something so that its front surface is oriented downward: *I faced the picture down so that I wouldn't be reminded of my dead parents.*

face off

1. To begin a confrontation or competition: *The troublemakers had just faced off when the playground aide noticed them.*
2. To begin to confront or compete with someone: *Those in favor of the proposal faced off with their opponents yesterday. The incumbent faced off against the challenger in a televised debate.*
3. To cause something or someone to begin a confrontation or competition with or against something or someone: *The organizers faced the finalists off against each other. The organizers faced each finalist off with the other. The organizers faced these two teams off early in the competition.*
4. Sports To start play in ice hockey, lacrosse, and similar games by releasing the puck or ball between two opposing players: *In hockey, the teams face off at the start of each period.*

face out

1. To be placed so that a front surface shows: *The paintings on the wall face out.*
2. To place something so that its front surface is exposed: *Keep the two parts of the sign folded together while it's raining, but face them out so we can read them when the rain stops. The window dresser faced the mannequins out so that passersby could see the clothing.*
3. To confront directly and engage with someone or something, often to resolve or get through a conflict or a problem: *Don't be afraid of them; you should face them out and defend yourself. I faced out my fear of flying and walked on the plane.*

face up

1. To position something so that its front surface is oriented upward: *The designer faced the mirror up to reflect the sunlight.*

ă	pat	är	car	ī	bite	ô	paw	o͝o	took	ûr	urge
ā	pay	ĕ	pet	îr	pier	ôr	core	o͝or	lure	zh	vision
âr	care	ē	be	ŏ	pot	oi	boy	o͞o	boot	ə	about,
ä	father	ĭ	pit	ō	toe	ou	out	ŭ	cut		item

2. **face up to** To confront an unpleasant situation; accept responsibility, blame, or a particular reality: *The manager finally faced up to the problem of theft.*

face with

1. To cover the surface of something using a substance: *The builders faced the front wall with marble. The facade was faced with terra cotta.*
2. To force someone to confront or deal with something or someone. Used chiefly in the passive: *When I'm faced with a problem, I ask my parents for advice.*

◆ **factor** (făk′tər)

factored (făk′tərd), **factoring** (făk′tə-rĭng), **factors** (făk′tərz)

factor in

1. To take something into account; take something into consideration; figure something in: *We factored sick days and vacations in when we prepared the work schedule. The boss factored in overtime when giving out bonuses.*
2. To be taken into account or consideration; to be figured in: *These observations are interesting, but they don't really factor in.*

factor out

1. To reanalyze a situation or problem in order to remove something from consideration: *If we factor out personal details, it seems that everyone has the same story. If we factor the bad data out, the results are predictable.*
2. MATHEMATICS To rewrite an expression so that something, especially a constant or variable, appearing more than once in the expression appears only once: *By factoring the shared terms out of the expression, we can easily solve the equation. The teacher factored out 3x from both sides of the equation* $6x^3 + 9x^2 + 12x = 24x$.

◆ **fade** (fād)

faded (fā′dĭd), **fading** (fā′dĭng), **fades** (fādz)

fade away

To dissipate or fade slowly and completely: *As I got older, my memories faded away.*

fade back

1. In American football, to move away from the line of scrimmage, opposite to the direction of the overall offensive play, in order to gain time to make a forward pass: *The quarterback faded back and looked downfield for an open receiver.*
2. To move something backwards into some space: *After she took the medicine, the rash faded back to just her finger.*

fade in

To cause something, especially sound, light, or a cinematic or television image, to appear or be heard gradually: *At the beginning of the play, a voice mutters quietly as the lights fade in.*

fade into

To gradually assume a new degree or quality of visibility, brightness, or color: *Each scene of the movie fades into black before the next one starts.*

fade out

1. To disappear gradually: *The final scene of the movie faded out.*
2. To cause something, especially a sound or a cinematic or television image, to disappear gradually: *The technician will fade out the lights when the speaker gets off the stage. I faded the spotlight out at the end of the act.*

fade up

1. To increase in intensity: *The sound of the drums fades up as the piece begins.*
2. To cause something to increase in intensity: *The director said we should fade the lights up on the back of the stage. The picture faded up as the movie began.*

◆ **fail** (fāl)

failed (fāld), **failing** (fā′lĭng), **fails** (fālz)

fail in

1. To fail to achieve some goal or effort: *I am failing in all of my attempts to win the contest.*
2. To achieve unsatisfactory grades in an academic subject: *Because I am failing in math, I am seeing a tutor.*
3. To give someone an unsatisfactory grade in an academic subject: *My teacher failed me in algebra despite my hard work.*

fail out

To be forced to leave an academic institution because of unsatisfactory grades: *My cousin is failing out of law school.*

◆ **fake** (fāk)

faked (fākt), **faking** (fā′kĭng), **fakes** (fāks)

fake out

To fool someone into expecting that you will act in one manner, only to act in another: *He faked me out by looking to the right but jumping to the left. The lights came on briefly to fake out the audience, but then they went out and the band returned to the stage.*

◆ **fall** (fôl)

fell (fĕl), **fallen** (fô′lən), **falling** (fô′lĭng), **falls** (fôlz)

fall apart

1. To disintegrate, collapse, or break into pieces: *The rickety chair fell apart when I sat on it.*
2. To suffer a nervous breakdown: *The political prisoner fell apart after years in solitary confinement.*
3. To lose structure or continuity: *Our vacation plans fell apart because we couldn't agree on which country to visit.*

fall away

1. To become gradually diminished in size, amount, or intensity: *Company revenues have been falling away in recent years. The sound of the car fell away into the distance.*

ă	pat	är	car	ī	bite	ô	paw	ŏŏ	took	ûr	urge
ā	pay	ĕ	pet	îr	pier	ôr	core	ŏŏr	lure	zh	vision
âr	care	ē	be	ŏ	pot	oi	boy	ōō	boot	ə	about, item
ä	father	ĭ	pit	ō	toe	ou	out	ŭ	cut		

2. To drift off an established course or pattern: *I slowly fell away from my work in chemistry and spent more time writing fiction.*
3. To be shed, lost, or discarded: *Before we knew it, the summer days had fallen away. As I exercised, inches fell away from my waistline.*
4. To drop off or become steeper at a distance: *The road falls away just past the meadow.*

fall back

1. To give ground; retreat: *After an unsuccessful attempt to retake the city, the soldiers fell back.*
2. To recede: *The waves fell back, leaving frothy white bubbles on the sand.*
3. **fall back on** To use something as a substitute or backup: *If we run out of cash, we will have to fall back on the money in our savings account.*
4. **fall back on** To rely on someone or something for support: *At least I can fall back on my friends in times of need.*

fall behind

1. To fail to keep up a pace; lag behind: *Despite a strong performance in the beginning, he fell behind in the second half of the race and finished last.*
2. To fail to maintain a desired level of performance: *She missed two classes and fell behind in her reading assignments.*
3. To be financially in arrears: *After losing my job, I fell behind on the mortgage payments.*

fall down

To drop or tip over: *I slipped on the ice and fell down the steps. A lot of trees fell down during the hurricane.*

fall for

1. To feel love for someone; be in love with someone: *I fell for you the first time I saw you in the park. They immediately fell for each other.*
2. To be deceived or swindled by something: *The gullible dupe fell for the con artist's scheme and lost $200,000.*

fall in

1. To take one's place in military formation, especially a line. Used of soldiers: *The troops fell in immediately upon the command of their sergeant.*
2. To sink inward; cave in: *Under the weight of the snow, the roof of the old barn finally fell in.*
3. **fall in with** To become associated with some group of people: *They fell in with the wrong crowd and were eventually arrested for armed robbery.*

fall into

1. To descend or drop freely or effortlessly into something: *I was so tired that I went to my bedroom and fell into bed.*
2. To come to assume a configuration, pattern, or order: *The lines of text fell into neat rows. After a quick meeting, our plans fell into place.*
3. To come upon, receive, or become involved with something, especially by chance: *They fell into a lot of money unexpectedly, so they bought a new car.*
4. To undergo a change of state or emotion, especially a negative change: *I took one look at my*

class schedule and fell into a bad mood. The tenants complained when the apartment building fell into disrepair.

fall off

1. To drop or descend from the top of something: *I fell off the ladder and bruised my knee.*
2. To become less; decrease: *Stock prices fell off markedly, resulting in a loss for thousands of accounts. The number of staff meetings fell off after a few months as our initial enthusiasm waned. I started a new diet and the pounds fell off.*
3. To lose weight. Used of livestock: *Toward the end of the dry season, the cattle fall off rapidly.*
4. NAUTICAL To change course to leeward: *We have a lot of pressure on the sail; let's fall off a little.*

fall on *or* **fall upon**

1. To drop or descend from one location to a lower one: *My coat got dirty when it fell on the muddy floor. The leaves fell upon the ground underneath the tree.*
2. To occur at some particular point in time: *My birthday falls on a Thursday this year. Their anniversary falls upon a Saturday this year.*
3. To be passed on to someone, especially as a responsibility or burden: *It falls on me now to maintain order here. It fell upon the president to solve the crisis.*
4. To attack or beset someone or something suddenly and intensely: *Insurgent forces fell on the unlucky patrol. A massive hurricane fell upon the coastal town.*
5. To experience or enter into something, especially a negative state of affairs: *The stockbrokers made a lot of money for a while, but fell on hard times during the recession. After he lost his job, he fell upon a difficult period.*

fall out

1. To drop from something: *I accidentally knocked my toolbox over and all of my nails fell out.*
2. To come out of place. Used of teeth: *When I was 12, my last baby tooth fell out. If you don't get your cavity filled, your tooth will fall out!*
3. To occur as a natural consequence; turn out: *These results fall out directly from the experimental evidence.*
4. To come or be revealed to be known, especially by chance: *Over the course of their conversation, it fell out that they had all once lived in Chicago.*
5. To break a relationship or form a negative relationship as a result of a dispute: *The siblings fell out over the inheritance. The law firm was disbanded after the partners fell out.*
6. **fall out with** To break a relationship or form a negative relationship with someone: *After John fell out with Alice, they sold their house.*

ă	pat	är	car	ī	bite	ô	paw	o͝o	took	ûr	urge
ā	pay	ĕ	pet	îr	pier	ôr	core	o͝or	lure	zh	vision
âr	care	ē	be	ŏ	pot	oi	boy	o͞o	boot	ə	about,
ä	father	ĭ	pit	ō	toe	ou	out	ŭ	cut		item

fall outside

To fail to be within or classified within some range, limit, or category: *That behavior falls outside of what is allowed here. The proposed budget falls outside the guidelines.*

fall over

1. To tip over; fall from an upright position to a flat one: *The vase fell over after I bumped into the table.*
2. To stumble over something or someone: *I fell over the skates that you left on the stairs.*
3. To attempt eagerly or frantically to accomplish something. Used reflexively: *I fell over myself trying to please my guests.*

fall through

1. To drop through some object or surface: *The skaters fell through the thin ice.*
2. To fail to occur: *The trip fell through due to lack of interest.*
3. To fail to be carried out: *Our plans fell through at the last minute.*

fall to

1. To be passed on to someone as a duty or responsibility; be incumbent upon someone: *Now that your brothers and sisters are at college, it falls to you to mow the lawn.*
2. To begin an activity energetically: *When I entered high school, I fell to soccer with a passion.*

fall under

1. To be classified or considered as something, or to be represented by something: *These animals fall under the classification "endangered species."*
2. To be controlled or deeply swayed by something; be mesmerized: *We fell under the magic spell of the singer's performance.*

fall within

To be within or to be classified as within a range, limit, or category: *The number of storms this year fell within the normal range.*

◆ **fan** (făn)

fanned (fănd), **fanning** (făn′ĭng), **fans** (fănz)

fan out

1. To move or project outward from a central source or point: *The troops landed on the beachhead and fanned out.*
2. To lay out or place something in a fanlike shape: *I fanned the cards out on the table. They fanned out the photos on the desk so we could see them.*

◆ **fare** (fâr)

fared (fârd), **faring** (fâr′ĭng), **fares** (fârz)

fare against

To perform or function at a level comparable with that of something or someone else: *I wonder how well the new car models fare against the old ones.*

fare up

To perform or function successfully at a level comparable with or equal to that of something or someone else; fare against: *They worked hard to win the competition, but in the end they didn't fare up. My performance didn't fare up to that of the other players.*

◆ **farm** (färm)

farmed (färmd), **farming** (fär′mĭng), **farms** (färmz)

farm out

1. To distribute or delegate something, especially a task or responsibility: *The camp counselor farmed out the cleaning tasks to the campers. We farmed the chores out to the kids.*
2. BASEBALL To demote a major-league player to a minor-league team: *The coach decided to farm the catcher out until he improved. The struggling pitcher was farmed out yesterday.*

◆ **fart** (färt)

farted (fär′tĭd), **farting** (fär′tĭng), **farts** (färts)

fart around

VULGAR SLANG

To fritter time away; fool around.

◆ **feed** (fēd)

fed (fĕd), **feeding** (fē′dĭng), **feeds** (fēdz)

feed off

To be nourished, sustained, or fueled by something: *The microbes feed off the decaying seaweed. The politicians are feeding off of the public's fear.*

feed on

To be nourished or sustained by something. Used especially of animals: *Pigs feed on corn husks.*

◆ **feel** (fēl)

felt (fĕlt), **feeling** (fē′lĭng), **feels** (fēlz)

feel around

To explore something by the sense of touch, especially when seeking an item: *If you feel around in the sock drawer, you'll probably find your missing earrings.*

feel for

To sympathize or empathize with someone: *I feel for the employees that were laid off.*

feel like

1. To desire to do something: *We all got bored and felt like leaving. I feel like ordering a cup of coffee.*
2. To desire to have something: *I feel like a cup of coffee.*

feel out

1. To examine or investigate the opinion or nature of someone or something: *We need to feel out the landlord about lowering the rent. My friends felt me out to see if I wanted to go to the carnival with them.*
2. To find a path, especially through physical exploration of one's surroundings: *We felt our way out of the dark room. They felt out a path to the edge of the underbrush.*

feel up

1. VULGAR SLANG To touch or fondle someone sexually.

ă	pat	är	car	ī	bite	ô	paw	ŏŏ	took	ûr	urge
ā	pay	ĕ	pet	îr	pier	ôr	core	ŏŏr	lure	zh	vision
âr	care	ē	be	ŏ	pot	oi	boy	ōō	boot	ə	about,
ä	father	ĭ	pit	ō	toe	ou	out	ŭ	cut		item

2. **feel up to** To feel ready to experience, do, or accomplish something; to feel capable of doing something: *I'm tired, so I don't feel up to going to the movies. Once we felt up to confronting our boss, we drafted a letter of complaint.*

◆ **fend** (fĕnd)

fended (fĕn′dĭd), **fending** (fĕn′dĭng), **fends** (fĕndz)

fend against

To protect from something: *We wear heavy parkas to fend against the cold wind.*

fend for

To provide for, take care of, or defend someone without assistance: *We watched the bear fending for her cubs as the hunters approached. I had to fend for myself when I arrived in Europe alone.*

fend off

1. To try to prevent something; avert something: *To fend off cavities, brush your teeth regularly.*
2. To turn something aside; repel something: *The troops fended the enemy off. My neighbor fended off the reporters who blocked her driveway.*

◆ **ferret** (fĕr′ĭt)

ferreted (fĕr′ĭ-tĭd), **ferreting** (fĕr′ĭ-tĭng), **ferrets** (fĕr′ĭts)

ferret out

To uncover or extract something by searching or questioning: *The detective ferreted out the sequence of events by questioning all of the witnesses. We ferreted the truth out after we finished our investigation.*

◆ **fess** (fĕs)

fessed (fĕst), **fessing** (fĕs′ĭng), **fesses** (fĕs′ĭz)

fess up

SLANG

To admit to something; confess something: *The treasurer fessed up when confronted with the evidence of fraud. The gangster fessed up to the crime.*

◆ **fetch** (fĕch)

fetched (fĕcht), **fetching** (fĕch′ĭng), **fetches** (fĕch′ĭz)

fetch up

1. To move fast enough to attain the same progress as another; catch up: *They struggled to fetch up with the leader of the hike.*
2. To make something equal or on a par with something else: *You'd better fetch up your grades to the class average. Fetch your scores up to our median and you'll have a good chance for admission.*
3. To bring something forth; to produce something: *We fetched up a basketful of blueberries to make a pie. Please fetch some tomatoes up from the garden.*
4. To reach a stopping place or goal; end up: *I fell over my skis and fetched up in a heap on the snow.*
5. To bring something to a halt; to stop something: *Please fetch up the noise; I can't hear.*

◆ **fiddle** (fĭd′l)

fiddled (fĭd′ld), **fiddling** (fĭd′l-ĭng), **fiddles** (fĭd′lz)

fiddle around

To act foolishly, playfully, or without a clear sense of purpose: *If you don't stop fiddling around and start working, we'll never get home.*

fiddle away

To waste or squander some period of time: *I fiddled away the afternoon surfing the Internet. The lazy student fiddled the night away instead of doing homework.*

fiddle with

1. To make unskilled or experimental efforts at repairing or improving something: *I fiddled with the broken toaster, but I couldn't fix it.*
2. To manipulate something without a clear sense of purpose: *Stop fiddling with the remote or you'll break it.*

◆ **fight** (fīt)

fought (fôt), **fighting** (fī′tĭng), **fights** (fīts)

fight amongst *or* **fight among**

To engage in mutual hostilities; squabble. Used reflexively: *The siblings fought amongst themselves constantly. During our meetings, we always fight among ourselves.*

fight off

To defend against or drive back someone or something, such as a hostile force or an infection: *The enemy is advancing, but the troops will fight them off. The doctor told me to rest so I can fight off this cold.*

fight out

To engage in some dispute or fight for the purpose of resolving an issue or determining a winner: *We fought out our disputes during dinner. The last two contestants will fight their final match out on Saturday night.*

◆ **figure** (fĭg′yər)

figured (fĭg′yərd), **figuring** (fĭg′yə-rĭng), **figures** (fĭg′yərz)

figure in

1. To be included or require inclusion in order to make a calculation or conclusion: *The profit reports will figure in the final budget decision.*
2. To include something in making a calculation or conclusion: *They failed to figure in all of their travel expenses. Don't forget to figure these numbers in when you write your report.*

figure into

1. To include something in making a calculation or drawing a conclusion: *We have to figure the possibility of a flat tire into our travel plans.*
2. To be included or require inclusion in order to make a calculation or conclusion: *The decline in profits figured into the manager's recent decision.*

ă	pat	är	car	ī	bite	ô	paw	o͝o	took	ûr	urge
ā	pay	ĕ	pet	îr	pier	ôr	core	o͝or	lure	zh	vision
âr	care	ē	be	ŏ	pot	oi	boy	o͞o	boot	ə	about, item
ä	father	ĭ	pit	ō	toe	ou	out	ŭ	cut		

figure on

1. To depend on something: *We figured on your support when we made up the plans.*
2. To guess that something will transpire; estimate: *I figured on traffic being heavy, so I left early.*
3. To plan on doing something; anticipate: *We figure on leaving for the store at noon.*

figure out

1. To discover or decide something: *Let's figure out a way to help. We figured out when to hold the next meeting.*
2. To solve or decipher something: *Can you figure this puzzle out? Late into the night, I figured out my homework assignment.*

figure up

To calculate something, especially by addition: *That's all of the supplies we need; can you figure up the total for us? We figured up the bill incorrectly; everyone owes another $10.*

◆ **file** (fīl)

filed (fīld), **filing** (fī′lĭng), **files** (fīlz)

file away

1. To rub against something with or as if with a file until it is smooth or gone: *I filed the rough skin away with a pumice stone. The foot doctor filed away my bone spurs.*
2. To file some document or other material into the appropriate place: *The secretary filed the legal documents away. The receptionist filed away the important memos.*

file down

To cause wear on something by rubbing against or filing it, reducing its size: *I filed down my fingernails before the party. The dentist filed the jagged tooth down.*

file under

To store some document or information in a place with some name, label, or symbol associated with it: *The contract was filed under her married name. The lawyer filed the documents under the appropriate heading.*

◆ **fill** (fĭl)

filled (fĭld), **filling** (fĭl′ĭng), **fills** (fĭlz)

fill in

1. To provide someone with essential or newly acquired information: *I didn't receive the information in the mail—could you fill me in? Please fill in the new secretary about our rules.*
2. To provide something, especially required information, in written form or on a document: *The applicant filled the answers in on the registration form. The students filled in the test forms.*
3. To cover completely the bounded surface of something: *Fill in all the rectangles on the page with blue ink. The artist filled all the stencils in with pastels.*
4. To act as a substitute; stand in: *When I was sick, my colleague filled in. The understudy filled in for the sick actor last night.*

fill out

1. To provide required information in written form on something, such as a document: *She carefully filled out the job application. He filled the voter registration form out.*

2. To become larger, fuller, or fatter: *The child filled out after he reached puberty.*
3. To cause something to become larger, fuller, or fatter: *The reporter filled out the article with extra anecdotes. The speaker filled the lecture out with a slide show.*
4. To be large enough to fit some article of clothing properly: *You don't really fill out that dress—it is a little baggy in places.*

fill up

1. To become full: *The bucket filled up with rain. The train filled up quickly, so we had to stand in the aisle.*
2. To cause something to become full: *I filled up the sink with soapy water. We inflated the pool and filled it up with water.*
3. To fill some vehicle with fuel: *I said to the mechanic, "Fill it up!" You'd better fill up the car soon. If we don't fill up now, we could run out of gas.*

◆ **filter** (fĭl′tər)

filtered (fĭl′tərd), **filtering** (fĭl′tə-rĭng), **filters** (fĭl′tərz)

filter down

To pass or spread downward from an upper level to lower levels, as through a filter: *The information slowly filtered down from management to the hourly employees.*

filter out

To prevent something from passing through, being communicated, or being perceived: *My new glasses filter out ultraviolet rays. These headphones filter unwanted noise out.*

filter through

To be allowed to pass through something or to find a way through something, especially an obstacle: *The sunlight filtered through the thin curtains.*

◆ **find** (fīnd)

found (found), **finding** (fīn′dĭng), **finds** (fīndz)

find against

To decide that someone or something is guilty, as in a court of law: *The jury found against the defendants.*

find for

To decide that someone or something is innocent, as in a court of law: *The judge found for the plaintiff after the hearing.*

find out

1. To ascertain something, as through examination or inquiry: *I found out the phone number by looking it up. We found the answer out in the dictionary. I'm not sure of the location of the bus stop, but I'll try to find out.*
2. To detect or expose the true nature or character of something or someone: *My plan to trick my*

ă	pat	är	car	ī	bite	ô	paw	o͝o	took	ûr	urge
ā	pay	ĕ	pet	îr	pier	ôr	core	o͝or	lure	zh	vision
âr	care	ē	be	ŏ	pot	oi	boy	o͞o	boot	ə	about,
ä	father	ĭ	pit	ō	toe	ou	out	ŭ	cut		item

roommate ended when he found me out. Liars risk being found out.

◆ **finish** (fĭn′ĭsh)

finished (fĭn′ĭsht), **finishing** (fĭn′ĭ-shĭng), **finishes** (fĭn′ĭ-shĭz)

finish off

1. To complete the last part of a task or process: *The staff finished off the final items on the agenda and ended the meeting. The crew finished the cleaning tasks off before leaving for the day.*
2. To consume the last part of something, such as food or a resource: *I finished off that last piece of bread. We finished the cake off.*
3. To finish something in a particular way: *We finished off the hot day with one final swim. The teacher finished the semester off with a big party.*

finish up

1. To conclude something; bring something to an end: *We finished up dinner and took the dirty dishes to the kitchen. The council finished the meeting up by stating when the next meeting would occur.*
2. To conclude; end: *The meeting finished up at 11:00. Finish up reading your book, already—it's late!*

◆ **fire** (fīr)

fired (fīrd), **firing** (fī′rĭng), **fires** (fīrz)

fire away

1. To start to ask questions or talk. Often used as a command: *I know you have questions, so fire away. As soon as the candidate finished his speech, the pundits fired away with their commentaries.*
2. To begin to shoot with a weapon: *The troops landed on the beach and started firing away. I fired away at the burglar as he ran from the house.*
3. To use up something by shooting it from a weapon: *The recruits fired away all of the ammunition during practice. We fired the last bullets away at the range.*

fire off

1. To say or ask something rapidly, especially a question or command: *The prosecutor fired questions off to the witness. My parents fired off reasons why my plan wouldn't work.*
2. To write and send a communication quickly: *I fired off a positive reply to the job offer. My friend fired an angry letter off to the editor.*
3. To shoot something from a weapon, especially in quick succession: *The police officer fired off warning shots when the suspect approached them. At the parade, the color guard fired three shots off.*

fire up

1. To set something going, especially a machine; start the operation of something: *She fired up the furnace as soon as she entered the old house. The driver fired the engine up and we took off.*
2. To make someone or something excited or enthusiastic: *The review fired me up about the author's new book. The cheerleaders fired up the crowd.*

3. To light a cigarette, cigar, or similar product: *The comedian fired up a cigar and began his act. The patient fired the cigarette up despite the doctor's warnings.*

◆ **firm** (fîrm)

firmed (fîrmd), **firming** (fîr′mĭng), **firms** (fîrmz)

firm up

1. To become firm or firmer: *My vacation plans firmed up, so I bought airline tickets.*
2. To cause something, such as a shape or a plan, to become definite or firm: *I want to firm up our vacation plans before I call the travel agent. Let's firm our route up and get on the road.*

◆ **fish** (fĭsh)

fished (fĭsht), **fishing** (fĭsh′ĭng), **fishes** (fĭsh′ĭz)

fish around

To seek within some place by or as if by probing: *She was fishing around in her pocket for a quarter. He fished around for compliments after the meeting.*

fish for

To seek something by or as if by probing: *I fished for my blue socks in the top drawer of the dresser. Instead of just fishing for compliments, you should try to get constructive criticism.*

◆ **fit** (fĭt)

fitted (fĭt′ĭd) *or* **fit** (fĭt), **fitted** (fĭt′ĭd), **fitting** (fĭt′ĭng), **fits** (fĭts)

fit in

1. To be easily accommodated; fit: *The puzzle piece fits in here.*
2. To belong to a group or to have similarities with members of a group: *I never fit in with the popular crowd at school. The kids felt awkward in their new school, but soon they found that they fit in well.*
3. To be logically or seamlessly related to something; mesh: *My role as supervisor fits in with my authoritative personality.*
4. To cause something to be placed or accommodated within specific limits: *I don't know if we can fit the paragraph in the space provided. We can fit you in at noon.*

fit out

To dress or decorate something or someone: *We'll fit you out with an excellent suit for the party. The tailor fit out the entire bridal party yesterday.*

◆ **fix** (fĭks)

fixed (fĭkst), **fixing** (fĭk′sĭng), **fixes** (fĭk′sĭz)

fix on

1. To determine something conclusively; settle on: *We need to fix on a date for the next meeting.*
2. To direct something toward a particular point, purpose, or focus of

ă	pat	är	car	ī	bite	ô	paw	o͝o	took	ûr	urge
ā	pay	ĕ	pet	îr	pier	ôr	core	o͝or	lure	zh	vision
âr	care	ē	be	ŏ	pot	oi	boy	o͞o	boot	ə	about, item
ä	father	ĭ	pit	ō	toe	ou	out	ŭ	cut		

attention: *They fixed their eyes on each other from across the room. The photographer's lens fixed on the nest of eagles.*

fix up

1. To improve the appearance or condition of something; refurbish something: *We fixed up the apartment before we moved in. The company fixed up the old theater.*
2. To prepare or provide someone or something with another thing: *The counselor fixed the campers up with some bag lunches. My parents fixed me up with a few months of rent.*
3. To provide a companion on a date for; set up: *My cousins fixed me up with their roommate for the big dance. I fixed up my neighbor with one of my coworkers.*

fix with

To gaze intently at someone or something in a particular way: *I fixed the guard with a long stare.*

◆ **fizzle** (fĭz′əl)

fizzled (fĭz′əld), **fizzling** (fĭz′ə-lĭng), **fizzles** (fĭz′əlz)

fizzle out

To come gradually to an end by growing fainter, weaker, less active, or less frequent: *I lit the fuse of the firecracker, but it fizzled out. The party finally fizzled out after midnight.*

◆ **flag** (flăg)

flagged (flăgd), **flagging** (flăg′ĭng), **flags** (flăgz)

flag down

To signal something or someone to stop: *I flagged down a taxi when it started raining. When we ran out of gas, we flagged the police officer down to ask for help.*

◆ **flail** (flāl)

flailed (flāld), **flailing** (flā′lĭng), **flails** (flālz)

flail about *or* **flail around**

To engage in rapid, frantic, undirected movements or activity: *The baby cried and flailed about as we looked for the bottle. After I caught the fish, it flailed around in the bottom of the boat.*

◆ **flake** (flāk)

flaked (flākt), **flaking** (flā′kĭng), **flakes** (flāks)

flake off

1. To break away from a surface in small, flat pieces: *Rust is flaking off of the old pipes. Paint chips are flaking off from the ceiling.*
2. SLANG To fail to do something out of lack of interest; blow something off: *Last night I flaked off doing the dishes because I was tired.*

flake out

SLANG

1. To act oddly or eccentrically: *I flaked out after hearing the bad news.*
2. To lose interest or nerve: *We wanted to go skydiving, but at the last minute we flaked out.*
3. To fall asleep or collapse from fatigue or exhaustion: *After driving for ten hours, I stopped and flaked out.*
4. To fail to live up to an expectation or responsibility: *I wouldn't have assigned you such an important task if I knew you were going to*

flake out like that. My contractor flaked out on me, and now I need to find a new one.

◆ **flame** (flām)

flamed (flāmd), **flaming** (flā′mĭng), **flames** (flāmz)

flame out

1. To fail: *Their new Internet company flamed out after only a few months.*
2. To emit a flame that causes a malfunction; to burn out. Used of engines: *I tried to restore that old car, but the engine flamed out.*

◆ **flare** (flâr)

flared (flârd), **flaring** (flâr′ĭng), **flares** (flârz)

flare out

1. To curve away distinctly: *This skirt flares out below the knee.*
2. To emit a flame or something shaped like a flame: *The candles we were carrying flared out in the night. A beacon flared out from the lighthouse.*
3. To make a sudden, angry verbal attack: *The sergeant flared out at the troops.*

flare up

1. To begin to increase in intensity: *My rash flared up when I went outdoors into the sunshine.*
2. To express sudden, strong negative emotions, especially anger or hate: *The store manager flared up when the employee started talking back.*

◆ **flash** (flăsh)

flashed (flăsht), **flashing** (flăsh′ĭng), **flashes** (flăsh′ĭz)

flash back

1. To undergo a change of scene to a previous point in time as a narrative device: *In this chapter, the main character flashes back to her youth.*
2. To remember or reexperience a previous point in time, usually suddenly: *Whenever he hears sirens, he flashes back to his service in Vietnam.*

flash forward

To undergo a change of scene to a future point in time as a narrative device: *The first scene of the movie shows a boy playing with a ball, and then the next scene flashes forward to the character's adulthood.*

◆ **flatten** (flăt′n)

flattened (flăt′nd), **flattening** (flăt′n-ĭng), **flattens** (flăt′nz)

flatten out

1. To become completely flat: *The graph indicated that sales were strong in July but that they flattened out in August.*
2. To make something completely flat: *I flattened out the crumpled paper and wrote on it. The iron flattened the wrinkly fabric out.*
3. To knock someone to the ground: *The boxer flattened out his oppo-*

ă	pat	är	car	ī	bite	ô	paw	o͝o	took	ûr	urge
ā	pay	ĕ	pet	îr	pier	ôr	core	o͝or	lure	zh	vision
âr	care	ē	be	ŏ	pot	oi	boy	o͞o	boot	ə	about, item
ä	father	ĭ	pit	ō	toe	ou	out	ŭ	cut		

nent. The bicyclist flattened the pedestrian out.

◆ **flesh** (flĕsh)
fleshed (flĕsht), **fleshing** (flĕsh′ĭng), **fleshes** (flĕsh′ĭz)

flesh out
To fill in, enrich, or build on the content or structure of something: *At the meeting, we fleshed out the plans for our trip. This paragraph is not specific enough—you should flesh it out.*

◆ **flick** (flĭk)
flicked (flĭkt), **flicking** (flĭk′ĭng), **flicks** (flĭks)

flick off
1. To remove something from a surface with a quick, brief sweeping motion: *I flicked off the cat hair from my sweater before I went outside. The tailor flicked some loose threads off before giving me the suit.*
2. To deactivate by using a switch; switch off: *He flicked the light off and shut the door. She flicked off the bright lights to conserve energy.*

flick on
To activate by switch; switch on: *We flicked on the lights and entered the attic. Flick the heat on when you get home.*

◆ **flicker** (flĭk′ər)
flickered (flĭk′ərd), **flickering** (flĭk′ə-rĭng), **flickers** (flĭk′ərz)

flicker out
To waver in intensity and then completely subside: *The candle burned for an hour and then flickered out.*

◆ **flip** (flĭp)
flipped (flĭpt), **flipping** (flĭp′ĭng), **flips** (flĭps)

flip for
1. To determine who gets to have something or do something by flipping a coin: *Both of us wanted the last slice of pie, so we flipped for it.*
2. To react enthusiastically or passionately to someone or something: *I flipped for the new bartender. Sunbathers will flip for these new stylish swimsuits.*

flip off
1. To deactivate using a switch; switch off: *Could you please flip off the lights before you go to sleep? I flipped the TV off because no one was watching it.*
2. Slang To make an obscene hand gesture to someone or something: *The driver cursed, flipped me off, and drove straight into the oncoming truck. Whenever I try to take his picture, he flips off the camera or makes a face.*

flip on
To activate by switch; switch on: *We flipped the lights on the moment the raccoon emerged from the bushes. I flipped on the radio to hear the news.*

flip out
Slang
1. To go crazy: *The neighbors flipped out when my oak tree crashed onto their property.*

2. To react strongly and especially enthusiastically; flip: *When the broker showed me the spacious new apartment, I flipped out. The customer flipped out over the luxurious black convertible.*

flip over

1. To reverse orientation so that the top surface or part faces down: *The tables flipped over in the strong breeze.*
2. To reverse the orientation of something so that its top surface or part faces down: *I flipped the record over to listen to the other side. I flipped over the card to reveal the ace of spades. The children flipped the toy train over to look at its underside.*
3. To be astounded by and react strongly to something: *The children flipped over the large stuffed bear in the store window and asked their parents to buy it.*

flip through

To go through some printed material quickly, rapidly turning from page to page: *I was flipping through the magazine when I spotted an article on comets.*

◆ **float** (flōt)

floated (flō′tĭd), **floating** (flō′tĭng), **floats** (flōts)

float around

1. To be or move in a nonspecific or unknown location: *That pen must be floating around here somewhere. The travelers floated around the countryside, stopping here and there to eat and rest.*
2. To move around while suspended on the surface of a fluid without sinking; float in no particular direction: *Empty bottles and other debris float around in the cove at low tide.*

◆ **flood** (flŭd)

flooded (flŭd′ĭd), **flooding** (flŭd′ĭng), **floods** (flŭdz)

flood out

To force something out or away from some place due to a current or influx of water: *The torrential rains flooded out most of the coastal residents. High tides regularly flood the smaller animals and insects out of spaces between the rocks. We were flooded out by the broken water line.*

◆ **flow** (flō)

flowed (flōd), **flowing** (flō′ĭng), **flows** (flōz)

flow from

To originate in and develop from something; stem from: *The second paragraph does not flow from the first in logical sequence. Many interesting discussions flowed from our initial conversation.*

◆ **flub** (flŭb)

flubbed (flŭbd), **flubbing** (flŭb′ĭng), **flubs** (flŭbz)

ă	pat	är	car	ī	bite	ô	paw	o͝o	took	ûr	urge
ā	pay	ĕ	pet	îr	pier	ôr	core	o͝or	lure	zh	vision
âr	care	ē	be	ŏ	pot	oi	boy	o͞o	boot	ə	about,
ä	father	ĭ	pit	ō	toe	ou	out	ŭ	cut		item

flub up

1. To make a mistake, especially out of confusion or ignorance: *He tried to tell the joke, but he flubbed up the punch line. She is nervous about giving the toast and will probably flub it up. My taxes were incorrect because my accountant flubbed up.*
2. To cause someone or something to blunder: *I tried to hold my camera steady for the shot, but all the insects buzzing around flubbed me up. The constant distractions flubbed up the actor.*

◆ **fluff** (flŭf)

fluffed (flŭft), **fluffing** (flŭf′ĭng), **fluffs** (flŭfs)

fluff up

To shake or ruffle something, especially something with feathers or fur, to make it softer, puffier, or larger: *When my canary fluffs up its feathers, it looks round and fat. I fluffed up the cat's fur with a hairbrush. The pillows will be more comfortable if you let me fluff them up.*

◆ **flunk** (flŭngk)

flunked (flŭngkt), **flunking** (flŭng′kĭng), **flunks** (flŭngks)

flunk out

To expel or be expelled from a school or course because of work that does not meet requirements or standards: *His grade-point average was less than 2.0, so the college flunked him out. Students lacking adequate math skills will flunk out of the physics program.*

◆ **flush** (flŭsh)

flushed (flŭsht), **flushing** (flŭsh′ĭng), **flushes** (flŭsh′ĭz)

flush out

1. To empty or clean something by a flow of water or liquid: *After coming in contact with the caustic substance, she flushed out her eye, which was red and puffy. The school nurse flushed the child's eyes out after he got ink in them.*
2. To cause something to leave or be removed from something with a flow of water or liquid: *She ran to the sink to flush out the dirt from her cut. My tears flushed the sand out of my eye.*
3. To frighten someone or something from a concealed place: *The golden retriever jumped into the reeds and flushed out the ducks. The passing car flushed the birds out of the thicket.*
4. To drive or force someone into the open: *The sniper is hiding in one of the buildings to the south and won't be easy to flush out. The army pledged to flush all insurgents out of the village.*

◆ **fly** (flī)

flew (flo͞o) [*or, in baseball sense* **flied** (flīd)], **flown** (floun) [*or, in baseball sense* **flied**], **flying** (flī′ĭng), **flies** (flīz)

fly at

To attack something or someone fiercely; assault someone or something: *The dogs flew at each other's throats. My roommate flew at me in a fit of rage and ripped the letter from my hands.*

fly by

1. To pass quickly, as of a moving object or an interval of time: *The*

summer months flew by, leaving us only a few days warm enough for swimming.

2. To visit briefly, often unexpectedly: *Some of my old school friends flew by for a short visit last week.*
3. To move past in flight: *Several geese flew by as we climbed the hill.*

fly off

1. To fly away: *After the gunshot, the birds flew off.*
2. To depart and travel by flying: *My parents flew off to Miami for the weekend.*
3. To suddenly and expressively enter an excited, especially negative, emotional state: *When the child was told to sit down, he flew off into a rage.*

fly out

1. To move through the air, leaving some location: *The birds flew out of their nest. Yesterday we flew out of London and arrived in New York. The pilot flew the soldiers out quickly.*
2. To operate aircraft using some place as a central landing area: *This new airline flies out of Boston and already has 20 destination cities.*
3. BASEBALL To be called out by hitting a fly ball that is caught by the other team: *The batter swung at the first pitch and flied out.*

◆ **foam** (fōm)

foamed (fōmd), **foaming** (fō′mĭng), **foams** (fōmz)

foam up

To become more foamy: *Shaving cream foams up when you spray it from the can.*

◆ **fob** (fŏb)

fobbed (fŏbd), **fobbing** (fŏb′ĭng), **fobs** (fŏbz)

fob off

1. To dispose of something by fraud or deception; palm off: *The jeweler fobbed off the zircon as a diamond. The crook fobbed the broken computer off as functional.*
2. To put someone off or appease someone by deceit or evasion: *He wanted to go on a date, but she fobbed him off with excuses. The landlord fobbed off the tenants' complaints for another month.*

◆ **focus** (fō′kəs)

focused *or* **focussed** (fō′kəst), **focusing** *or* **focussing** (fō′kə-sĭng), **focuses** *or* **focusses** (fō′kə-sĭz)

focus on

1. To orient or adjust something toward some particular point or thing: *I focused the camera on the car across the street.*
2. To direct someone or something at a particular point or purpose: *The company director wanted to focus the staff's attention on finding a solution to the problem.*
3. To be directed at some particular point or purpose: *The manager focused on the sales force's performance.*

ă	pat	är	car	ī	bite	ô	paw	ŏŏ	took	ûr	urge
ā	pay	ĕ	pet	îr	pier	ôr	core	ŏŏr	lure	zh	vision
âr	care	ē	be	ŏ	pot	oi	boy	ōō	boot	ə	about,
ä	father	ĭ	pit	ō	toe	ou	out	ŭ	cut		item

◆ **fog** (fôg)

fogged (fôgd), **fogging** (fôg′ĭng), **fogs** (fôgz)

fog in

1. To surround something with fog: *The descending mists fogged in the little village. The storm clouds fogged us in on the mountaintop. Because the airport was fogged in, all of the flights were canceled.*
2. To cause something to be unable to move safely due to fog. Used chiefly in the passive: *The airplane was fogged in and could not land.*

fog up

1. To become covered with condensation: *The bathroom mirror fogged up after I took a shower.*
2. To cause something to become covered with condensation: *The steam from the kettle fogged up the kitchen windows. Don't breathe on the lens—you'll fog it up.*
3. To become teary-eyed out of a strong sense of emotion: *I fogged up when my parents' photo was unveiled.*

◆ **foist** (foist)

foisted (fois′tĭd), **foisting** (fois′tĭng), **foists** (foists)

foist off on

To force something, especially something unwanted, worthless, or false, on someone: *She foisted off the furniture on the new owners. The peddler foisted his wares off on the unsuspecting crowd.*

◆ **fold** (fōld)

folded (fōl′dĭd), **folding** (fōl′dĭng), **folds** (fōldz)

fold up

1. To bend or fold something so that it is closed or made compact: *My roommate folded the letter up. Fold up that box and put it away.*
2. To be able to be bent or folded to become closed or made compact: *This table folds up so you can put it in the trunk of a small car.*
3. To go out of business: *Three of my favorite stores on this street folded up last summer.*

◆ **follow** (fŏl′ō)

followed (fŏl′ōd), **following** (fŏl′ō-ĭng), **follows** (fŏl′ōz)

follow along

1. To accompany by following: *I went for a walk in the woods, and my cats followed along. Our guide led the hike and we followed him along.*
2. To move or act in conjunction with an activity by following an example: *The teacher sang and the children followed along.*
3. To move or act in conjunction or in parallel with someone or something: *I followed along with the speaker by reading the transcript.*

follow out

1. To fulfill something, especially a command or request; carry something out: *The colonel expected the troops to follow out every order without question.*
2. To exit a location by following someone or something: *The fans followed the movie star out of the studio.*

follow through

1. To complete fully something that has been planned or is in process:

She passed the remaining work on to him, but he didn't follow through right away. I followed through on the report and finished it the next day.

2. SPORTS To complete a stroke or swing fully after hitting or releasing a ball or other object: *My tennis instructor taught me how to follow through after I served the ball. When you're batting, don't forget to follow through on your swing.*

follow up

1. To finish something by means of some final action: *They followed the performance up with a stunning encore. The writer followed up his first book with a great sequel.*
2. **follow up on** To enhance the effectiveness of something by means of further action: *I followed up on the job interview with an email. Did you follow up on their request?*

◆ fool (fo͞ol)

fooled (fo͞old), **fooling** (fo͞o′lĭng), **fools** (fo͞olz)

fool around

1. SLANG To engage in frivolous activity; goof off: *The children are fooling around in the yard.*
2. SLANG **fool around with** To manipulate or work with something without a clear purpose; toy with something: *Who's been fooling around with my briefcase?*
3. VULGAR SLANG To engage in casual, often promiscuous sexual activity.
4. VULGAR SLANG To be sexually unfaithful.

fool with

1. To alter something improperly: *Did someone fool with the computer settings?*
2. To tease someone: *Don't mind your uncle—he's just fooling with you.*

◆ foot (fo͝ot)

footed (fo͝ot′ĭd), **footing** (fo͝ot′ĭng), **foots** (fo͝ots)

foot up

To calculate something, especially by addition: *The waiter footed up the bill at the end of the meal. Our producer footed the expenses up after the closing night of the play.*

◆ force (fôrs)

forced (fôrst), **forcing** (fôr′sĭng), **forces** (fôr′sĭz)

force back

1. To make someone or something retreat or return: *A terrible storm forced the soldiers back to the camp. Hard up for money, the strikers were forced back to work.*
2. To prevent the expression of one's own emotions: *She forced back her laughter as she listened to the debate. He forced his anger back when he read the editorial.*

ă	pat	är	car	ī	bite	ô	paw	o͝o	took	ûr	urge
ā	pay	ĕ	pet	îr	pier	ôr	core	o͝or	lure	zh	vision
âr	care	ē	be	ŏ	pot	oi	boy	o͞o	boot	ə	about, item
ä	father	ĭ	pit	ō	toe	ou	out	ŭ	cut		

force down

1. To cause someone or something to descend or land by use of force: *Engine failure forced down the aircraft. On sighting the hostile helicopter, the soldier engaged it and forced it down.*
2. To swallow something that one does not want to swallow: *To be polite, I forced down the awful-tasting food. I forced the unpleasant cough syrup down.*

force on

1. To require someone or something to accept or confront something: *The people in charge always force the least pleasant jobs on us. The unexpected guests forced themselves on us, and we ended up cooking them dinner. The tax was forced on both rich and poor for the benefit of the king.*
2. To force or require someone or something to continue: *Although we were almost too exhausted to move, hunger forced us on. After ten miles some prisoners collapsed, but the captors forced on the rest.*

force out

1. To make someone or something leave by use of force or out of necessity: *She was forced out of the game by a leg injury. The scandal forced him out of the company. The fire forced the animals out of the forest.*
2. To cause a runner in baseball to be called out when that player cannot act in any way to prevent it: *The catcher forced him out at the plate. She was forced out at second base.*

◆ **forge** (fôrj)

forged (fôrjd), **forging** (fôr′jĭng), **forges** (fôr′jĭz)

forge ahead *or* **forge on**

To continue moving forward or making progress: *The reporters forged ahead with the investigation. The weary troops forged on despite the snow.*

◆ **fork** (fôrk)

forked (fôrkt), **forking** (fôr′kĭng), **forks** (fôrks)

fork out

1. To distribute or supply something, especially money: *The government forks out millions of dollars to maintain the royal palace. The town finally forked the cash out for a new high school.*
2. To split or diverge; fork: *The river forks out in numerous places in the delta.*

fork over *or* **fork up**

To give or transfer something, especially in a reluctant, unenthusiastic, or automatic way: *I thought the rug was overpriced, but I forked the cash over. We forked over our admission tickets to the usher and walked into the theater.*

◆ **form** (fôrm)

formed (fôrmd), **forming** (fôr′mĭng), **forms** (fôrmz)

form up

1. To come together into an organized shape or formation: *At the sergeant's command, the troops formed up into a single line. Our plans formed up quickly after we reviewed the possibilities.*

2. To cause something to be created by arranging or organizing: *We formed up several teams of players. The marines formed the captives up into two columns and marched them forward.*

◆ **foul** (foul)

fouled (fould), **fouling** (fou′lĭng), **fouls** (foulz)

foul out

1. SPORTS To be put out of a game for exceeding the number of permissible fouls: *After committing his fifth foul, the center fouled out and walked off the court.*
2. BASEBALL To strike out by hitting a fly ball that goes foul but is still caught: *He fouled out on a pop fly near the dugout on the third base line.*

foul up

1. To blunder because of mistakes or poor judgment: *I've tried many times to pass this test, but this time I really fouled up.*
2. To cause someone or something to blunder: *The howling dogs distracted me and fouled up my concentration. The pain in my hand fouled me up and I couldn't aim my camera.*
3. To clog or became entangled in something: *The seaweed fouled up the propeller blades. The dangling cables fouled the machinery up, thereby causing the breakdown.*

◆ **found** (found)

founded (foun′dĭd), **founding** (foun′dĭng), **founds** (foundz)

found on *or* **found upon**

To establish the basis of something with some other thing; base something on something else: *The original inhabitants founded their community on the basis of shared labor. The laws are founded upon deep principles of justice.*

◆ **freak** (frēk)

freaked (frēkt), **freaking** (frē′kĭng), **freaks** (frēks)

freak out

SLANG

1. To lose control of one's emotions: *I freaked out when I saw my low test score.*
2. To cause someone to lose control of his or her emotions: *The dentist really freaked me out with that needle. The rock band freaked out the crowd when they started letting audience members onstage.*

◆ **free** (frē)

freed (frēd), **freeing** (frē′ĭng), **frees** (frēz)

free up

To make something available that was previously occupied or in use: *A few passengers decided to take the next bus, which freed up seats for my friend and me. Connecting my computer to a separate net-*

ă	pat	är	car	ī	bite	ô	paw	o͝o	took	ûr	urge
ā	pay	ĕ	pet	îr	pier	ôr	core	o͝or	lure	zh	vision
âr	care	ē	be	ŏ	pot	oi	boy	o͞o	boot	ə	about,
ä	father	ĭ	pit	ō	toe	ou	out	ŭ	cut		item

work connection has freed my phone line up.

◆ **freeze** (frēz)

froze (frōz), **freezing** (frē′zĭng), **freezes** (frē′zĭz)

freeze out

To shut out or exclude someone by cold or unfriendly treatment: *The popular kids tried to freeze me out of the conversation. The group froze out the new employees at the meeting.*

freeze over

1. To freeze completely at the surface: *Once the pond freezes over we can go skating.*
2. To become covered with a layer of ice: *The bridge has frozen over, so drive very carefully.*

freeze up

1. To become completely frozen: *The water in the ice trays hasn't frozen up yet.*
2. To cause something to freeze completely: *We froze up the water for ice cubes. Freeze the juice up and we'll have some frozen treats!*
3. To become fixed in place or unable to move: *The lock froze up due to rust. When I noticed that I was being watched, I froze up.*
4. To cause something to become fixed in place or unable to move: *The subzero temperatures froze up the water pipes. The rust froze the gears up.*

◆ **freshen** (frĕsh′ən)

freshened (frĕsh′ənd), **freshening** (frĕsh′ə-nĭng), **freshens** (frĕsh′ənz)

freshen up

1. To clean oneself, rearrange one's clothing, or reapply makeup: *I went upstairs to freshen up quickly before we left for the party.*
2. To rearrange or renew something in order to make it more attractive or comfortable: *Putting new pillows on the couch really freshened the room up. I freshened up the apartment by making new curtains.*

◆ **frighten** (frīt′n)

frightened (frīt′nd), **frightening** (frīt′n-ĭng), **frightens** (frīt′nz)

frighten away *or* **frighten off**

To cause someone or something to leave or to stay away due to fear: *The sound of my shotgun frightened the crows away. The alarm frightened away the burglar. The big dog frightens off unwanted guests. The scary-looking house frightened neighborhood children off.*

◆ **fritter** (frĭt′ər)

frittered (frĭt′ərd), **frittering** (frĭt′ə-rĭng), **fritters** (frĭt′ərz)

fritter away

To gradually use something up, especially wastefully or without serious purpose: *They frittered away their inheritance. I frittered my lottery winnings away on bad investments. I frittered away my vacation time watching television.*

◆ **frizz** (frĭz)

frizzed (frĭzd), **frizzing** (frĭz′ĭng), **frizzes** (frĭz′ĭz)

frizz up

1. To become completely frizzy: *When the air is humid, my hair frizzes up.*
2. To cause something to become completely frizzy: *The humidity frizzes up my hair. Sitting by the pool will frizz my hair up.*

◆ **front** (frŭnt)

fronted (frŭn′tĭd), **fronting** (frŭn′tĭng), **fronts** (frŭnts)

front for

1. To appear to operate with a legitimate purpose in order to conceal the operation of something or someone: *The grocery store was actually fronting for a group of smugglers.*
2. To serve as a cover for or representative of someone or something: *Leave the negotiations up to me—I'll front for you.*

front onto

To be facing something. Used especially of buildings: *The living room windows front directly onto the street.*

◆ **frost** (frôst)

frosted (frôs′tĭd), **frosting** (frôs′tĭng), **frosts** (frôsts)

frost over

To become covered with frost: *The blades of grass frosted over in the cold night air.*

frost up

1. To become covered with frost: *The windows frosted up quickly when the temperature dropped.*
2. To cause something to become covered with frost: *The freezing air frosted up the windows. Our breath frosted the mirrors up.*

◆ **froth** (frôth)

frothed (frôtht), **frothing** (frô′thĭng), **froths** (frôths)

froth up

1. To become frothy or foamy: *The vinegar quickly frothed up when I added the baking soda.*
2. To cause something to become frothy or foamy: *The spinning blades of the blender frothed up the juice. You need to stir vigorously in order to froth the sauce up.*

◆ **frown** (froun)

frowned (fround), **frowning** (frou′nĭng), **frowns** (frounz)

frown on *or* **frown upon**

To disapprove of something: *The administration frowns on late submissions of the required forms. My parents frown upon loud music.*

◆ **fry** (frī)

fried (frīd), **frying** (frī′ĭng), **fries** (frīz)

fry up

To prepare or make something by frying: *I'll fry up some pancakes*

ă	pat	är	car	ī	bite	ô	paw	o͝o	took	ûr	urge
ā	pay	ĕ	pet	îr	pier	ôr	core	o͝or	lure	zh	vision
âr	care	ē	be	ŏ	pot	oi	boy	o͞o	boot	ə	about,
ä	father	ĭ	pit	ō	toe	ou	out	ŭ	cut		item

for breakfast. They fried some bacon up for the sandwiches.

◆ **fuel** (fyo͞ol)

fueled (fyo͞old), **fueling** (fyo͞o′lĭng), **fuels** (fyo͞olz)

fuel up

To fill the gas tank of a vehicle with gasoline or other fuel: *The family fueled up the car before leaving for the lake. I fueled the truck up so we wouldn't have to stop. It's time to go; let's fuel up.*

◆ **function** (fŭngk′shən)

functioned (fŭngk′shənd), **functioning** (fŭngk′shə-nĭng), **functions** (fŭngk′shənz)

function as

To serve a purpose or play a role similar to that of something else: *The beaks of some wading birds function as spears for catching fish.*

◆ **fuss** (fŭs)

fussed (fŭst), **fussing** (fŭs′ĭng), **fusses** (fŭs′ĭz)

fuss over

To handle or deal with something or someone in an overly attentive or nervous way: *Don't fuss over every detail—just get the main idea across for now. The grandparents fussed over their new grandchild.*

fuss with

To handle or manipulate something excessively and unnecessarily, especially when overly concerned or nervous: *The contestants fussed with their outfits before the pageant began.*

◆ **futz** (fŭts)

futzed (fŭtst), **futzing** (fŭt′sĭng), **futzes** (fŭt′sĭz)

futz around

SLANG

1. To act foolishly, playfully, or without a clear sense of purpose; goof off: *The kids were futzing around so much that they didn't finish their chores.*
2. To manipulate something without a clear sense of purpose: *Stop futzing around with the door handle, or you'll break it.*

futz up

SLANG

To fail at or make a mess of something: *I read the speech as well as I could, but I futzed it up. We futzed up the trip because we got lost. Don't drink before going onstage—you'll futz up.*

futz with

SLANG

To manipulate something without a clear sense of purpose: *The child futzed with the toy, and then it broke.*

G

◆ **gain** (gān)

gained (gānd), **gaining** (gā′nĭng), **gains** (gānz)

gain in

To increase with respect to something: *The athlete gained in strength, but lost in agility.*

gain on

To get closer to something or someone, often in pursuit; close a gap: *Run faster—the stampeding cattle are gaining on us!*

◆ **gamble** (găm′bəl)

gambled (găm′bəld), **gambling** (găm′blĭng), **gambles** (găm′bəlz)

gamble on

1. To wager something on the outcome of some event: *I gambled all my money on the first race. They don't like to gamble on poker games; they just play for fun.*
2. To wager something on some participant in an event: *I gambled $50 on my favorite horse.*
3. To anticipate or foresee something: *I didn't gamble on it raining, so I hadn't brought an umbrella.*

◆ **gang** (găng)

ganged (găngd), **ganging** (găng′ĭng), **gangs** (găngz)

gang up

1. To join together to attack or address some problem or issue: *The various police agencies ganged up to fight the illegal drug trade.*
2. **gang up on** To join together to bother, harm, or attack someone or something: *The older children were always ganging up on the little ones.*
3. **gang up against** To join together in opposition to someone or something: *Whenever one corporation became too powerful, the others ganged up against it.*

◆ **gas** (găs)

gassed (găst), **gassing** (găs′ĭng), **gases** (găs′ĭz) *or* **gasses** (găs′ĭz)

gas up

1. To supply gasoline or fuel to a vehicle: *The tank was almost empty, so we stopped at a service station and gassed up.*
2. To supply some vehicle or machine with gasoline or fuel: *We gassed up the car before the road trip. After fixing the lawn mower, I gassed it up and tried to start it.*

◆ **gather** (găth′ər)

gathered (găth′ərd), **gathering** (găth′ə-rĭng), **gathers** (găth′ərz)

ă	pat	är	car	ī	bite	ô	paw	ŏŏ	took	ûr	urge
ā	pay	ĕ	pet	îr	pier	ôr	core	ŏŏr	lure	zh	vision
âr	care	ē	be	ŏ	pot	oi	boy	ōō	boot	ə	about, item
ä	father	ĭ	pit	ō	toe	ou	out	ŭ	cut		

gather around *or* **gather round**

1. To come to some place and form a group; assemble at: *The cowboys gathered round the campfire.*
2. To cause some people or things to come to a place; bring some people or things together around a place: *We gathered the tour group around the exhibit and began our talk.*

gather up

1. To bring together or collect something that is distributed or scattered: *I gathered up my dress and stepped over the puddle. I gathered the papers up and put them in my briefcase.*
2. To come together or be more concentrated in one place: *The cloth gathers up at the hem of this dress.*

◆ **gear** (gîr)

geared (gîrd), **gearing** (gîr′ĭng), **gears** (gîrz)

gear toward *or* **gear to**

To alter something in order to meet needs, requirements, or expectations of someone or something: *We must gear our presentation toward the younger members of the audience. The redesign of the aircraft was geared to making it use fuel more efficiently.*

gear up

1. To get ready for something, especially an upcoming action or event; prepare for something: *The investors geared up for the merger of the two companies.*
2. To get something ready for an upcoming action or event: *The company is gearing up its marketing team for the release of the new film. We geared the truck up for the journey.*

◆ **get** (gĕt)

got (gŏt), **gotten** (gŏt′n) *or* **got** (gŏt), **getting** (gĕt′ĭng), **gets** (gĕts)

get about

To be out of bed and beginning to walk again, as after an illness: *Many days passed after the heart operation before I was able to get about.*

get above

1. To come to a position over or on top of something: *I finally got above the wave and gasped for air.*
2. To assume a superior attitude toward something so that one is no longer concerned with its problems and no longer worrying about it: *Once you get above all this bickering, the answer should become clear.*

get across

1. To cross something; traverse something: *How are we going to get across the swamp? The bridge was long, but once we got across, we were treated to a view of the cliffs.*
2. To cause someone or something to cross something: *The tow truck driver got the stalled car across the bridge.*
3. To make something understandable or clear; successfully communicate something: *I got my point across by giving lots of examples. You'll get your message across if you speak clearly.*
4. **get across to** To find a way to communicate convincingly: *Once the*

teacher was able to get across to the students, the lessons went very well.

get after

1. To urge or scold someone: *You should get after the kids to mow the lawn.*
2. To pursue something that is a problem or menace: *If you don't get after those termites, your house will be destroyed.*

get ahead

1. To come to a position in front of or in advance of something or someone: *We tried to get ahead of the heavy traffic by taking a short-cut.*
2. To make progress with something or advance in something, especially a career, income, or quality of life: *I took a second job to get ahead and was able to save up enough money to buy a house.*

get along

1. To be or continue to be on harmonious terms with someone: *I never got along with the mail carrier. Do you think the cats and dogs will get along if we put them in a cage together?*
2. To manage or fare, especially with reasonable success: *There's no way I can get along on those wages. How are you getting along these days?*
3. To advance or make progress, especially in age: *He's not as athletic as he was before, but he is getting along in age.*
4. To go away; leave: *She told the children to get along and leave her to her work.*

get around

1. To travel from place to place in some region: *I use a bicycle to get around my neighborhood. It is hard to get around town without a car.*
2. To become known; circulate: *The rumors got around quickly. It eventually got around that the movie star had been arrested.*
3. To be known to many different people in different social settings: *You certainly get around; you seem to know everybody!*
4. SLANG To engage in numerous amorous affairs with a variety of people; be promiscuous: *The team captain really gets around.*
5. To circumvent, avoid, or evade something: *The debater managed to get around the real issues.*
6. To cause someone to circumvent or evade something: *Your advice got me around the problem easily.*
7. To do something when the right opportunity arises or when it is convenient: *I haven't gotten around to finishing my schoolwork yet. Eventually we'll get around to building a new balcony.*
8. To convince someone; change someone's mind: *My friends' constant pleas finally got me around to joining them on their trip.*

ă	pat	är	car	ī	bite	ô	paw	o͝o	took	ûr	urge
ā	pay	ĕ	pet	îr	pier	ôr	core	o͝or	lure	zh	vision
âr	care	ē	be	ŏ	pot	oi	boy	o͞o	boot	ə	about, item
ä	father	ĭ	pit	ō	toe	ou	out	ŭ	cut		

get at

1. To reach something or someone: *The cat hid where we couldn't get at it.*
2. To annoy or bother someone: *The noise from the construction site is really getting at me.*
3. To express or try to express something; hint at something: *The way you've phrased this doesn't get at the main point. I don't know what you're getting at.*
4. To discover or understand something: *We finally got at the cause of the problem.*
5. SLANG To bribe or influence by improper or illegal means: *He got at the judge, and the charges were dismissed.*

get away

1. To leave or go away, especially to make an excursion: *I'd really like to get away to a nice warm beach this year. We need a vacation; let's get away.*
2. To cause something or someone to leave or go away: *Get those ugly lizards away from here!*
3. To leave a particular location where one has a responsibility or duty to be: *Work has been busy, so I'll go to lunch with you if I can get away.*
4. To escape or avoid capture: *The thieves were able to get away in their car before anyone knew they had left.*
5. To succeed in some wrongdoing without being accused or without being punished: *The merchants always got away with overcharging the customers.*
6. To succeed at something that would typically be expected to fail: *We got away with driving the old car all the way across the country without once checking our oil.*

get back

1. To have something returned to one's possession: *I shouldn't have let the dog run away with the ball; now we'll never get it back. Don't give him that box; I'll never get back the books.*
2. To return to some place, condition, or activity, or to someone's possession: *How will we get back to the city if the road is closed? Let's get back to the subject that we were discussing earlier.*
3. To return someone or something: *I'll go with you if you can get me back to the office by 2:00. Please get the kids back by lunchtime.*
4. To resume doing something: *I'll get back to reading this book when my chores are done.*
5. To renew a relationship with someone: *The drummer got back with the jazz band after a short career as a violinist. A few days after their argument, Pat got back together with Chris.*
6. To retaliate or punish someone in return for some wrongdoing: *You may have won this fight, but I'll get you back tomorrow!*
7. To respond or react to someone, especially in retaliation for some wrongdoing: *She wrote a critical article about him, but he got back at her by ignoring it completely.*
8. **get back into** To resume some regular activity, or renew an interest in something, after not having been involved with it for a period of time: *I got back into bicycling after many years of doing nothing in my spare time but swim. They got*

back into rock music after losing interest in jazz.

9. **get back to** or **get back with** To make contact with someone or something at a later time: *They said they would get back to me once they had decided whether or not they would buy my car. I have to leave right now, but I'll get back with you with a response after lunch.*

get behind

1. To lend support to some cause or effort: *It was easy to finish the project once the whole community got behind it.*

2. To come to a position to the rear of or following something or someone: *The child got behind the tree where no one could see him.*

get by

1. To find a way past or around something: *The store was so crowded that it was hard to get by the entranceway.*

2. To go unnoticed or ignored by someone: *The mistake got by the editor, but the proofreader caught it.*

3. To cause something to pass unnoticed or ignored by someone: *The smuggler failed to get the drugs by the inspector.*

4. To succeed at a level of minimal acceptability or with the minimal amount of effort: *When I was in college I just barely got by. There's no way to get by with just half a bottle of cream for the dessert tonight.*

5. To succeed in managing; survive: *We can get by if we save our money carefully.*

get down

1. To descend or climb off of something: *He got down off the table and stood in the middle of the kitchen. Get down off the roof before you fall!*

2. To cause someone or something to descend or climb off of something: *I tried to get the cat down from the tree.*

3. To lower oneself by crouching or lying, especially on the ground or the floor: *When the thieves started shooting, we all got down and covered our heads.*

4. SLANG To exhaust, discourage, or depress someone: *The awful heat was getting me down.*

5. To swallow something: *I got the pill down by taking it with a large glass of water.*

6. To master something: *I finally got my Latin vocabulary down, and I'm ready for the test.*

7. To put something in written form; to write down: *I couldn't get down her name before my pen broke. The teacher spoke so fast that the students couldn't get it all down.*

8. **get down to** To begin putting effort into something: *We need to get down to work.*

9. **get down to** To begin focusing attention on something: *Let's get down to the basic facts and find out what really happened.*

10. SLANG To lose one's inhibitions; en-

ă	pat	är	car	ī	bite	ô	paw	o͝o	took	ûr	urge
ā	pay	ĕ	pet	îr	pier	ôr	core	o͝or	lure	zh	vision
âr	care	ē	be	ŏ	pot	oi	boy	o͞o	boot	ə	about,
ä	father	ĭ	pit	ō	toe	ou	out	ŭ	cut		item

joy oneself wholeheartedly: *Let's just get down and enjoy the party.*

11. SLANG To start dancing with great gusto and style: *After they ate, the guests got down and boogied.*

get in

1. To enter something: *Please get in the back seat. We opened the door of the car and got in.*
2. To arrive: *He got in late last night.*
3. To become accepted to some institution, such as a school or club: *I applied to cooking school and, fortunately, I got in.*
4. To cause someone or something to come to or be admitted to a place: *Please get the children in before noon. The standards of the school are high, but your good grades will get you in.*
5. To succeed in making or doing something within a restricted period of time: *The milk truck got six deliveries in before noon. The postal carrier got in the entire route before 2:00.*
6. To attain some condition, especially unwittingly: *The hooligans got in trouble for disrupting the picnic.*
7. To put something into some condition: *We got the car in good condition for the long trip. The runner got in great shape for the marathon.*
8. **get in on** To gain access to or knowledge of something: *At the dance club, we got in on the latest dance moves. Everybody wanted to get in on the secret.*
9. **get in with** To become involved with something, especially with some group: *She got in with a bad group of people.*

get into

1. To attain some condition: *The kids got into trouble for being late. I got into good physical shape by running every day.*
2. To cause someone or something to enter or be admitted to some place: *This round key will get you into the house. My good grades got me into a good school.*
3. To put something into some condition: *We need to get your papers into proper order.*
4. SLANG To become interested in or enthusiastic about something: *They got into gourmet cooking.*

get off

1. To remove oneself from something that supports, carries, or holds: *I got off my chair and ran down the hall. After we got off the plane, we picked up our baggage. Get off the couch!*
2. To remove something from a supporting, carrying, or holding thing: *Get the cat off the table!*
3. To start, as on a trip; leave. *It took so long to pack that we didn't get off until noon.*
4. To send something; transmit something: *I'll get a letter off to you next week.*
5. To cause something to be emitted, as when firing a weapon: *The hunter got off two shots before the deer disappeared. The archer got three arrows off before hitting the bull's-eye.*
6. To escape, as from punishment or danger: *They thought the judge would sentence them harshly, but somehow they got off.*
7. To obtain a release or lesser penalty for someone: *The attorney got her client off with just a small fine.*

8. To get permission to leave one's workplace: *The sales crew got off early and went out for a walk.*
9. SLANG To stop pressuring, pestering, or domineering someone: *The boss thought the employees were lazy and didn't get off them the whole day. Get off me!—I can't work with you watching over me.*
10. SLANG To feel great pleasure or gratification from something: *They really got off on that roller coaster ride at the amusement park. I don't really get off on photography.*
11. SLANG To cause someone to feel great pleasure or gratification; satisfy someone: *That movie really didn't get me off.*
12. VULGAR SLANG To achieve orgasm.
13. VULGAR SLANG To cause someone to achieve orgasm.

get on

1. To place oneself on something that supports, holds, or carries: *I got on the train to California. The bus was packed, but I was still able to get on.*
2. To place something on some object that supports, holds, or carries: *Once I got the kids on the bus, I was alone for the day.*
3. To place something, especially clothing, on oneself: *I got my coat and hat on and left the dull party. The kids got on their boots and played in the snow.*
4. To be or continue to be on harmonious terms with someone; get along: *I always got on well with my roommate. Our children get on very well together.*
5. To manage or fare reasonably well: *How are you getting on?*
6. To make progress with something; continue something: *Stop complaining about the work and get on with it. I'll get right on your request!*
7. To approach old age: *My grandparents are getting on in years, so they bought a condominium in Arizona.*
8. **get on to** To acquire understanding or knowledge of something; catch on to something: *We eventually got on to the way our landlord was manipulating us.*

get out

1. To leave or escape: *I got out of the car and followed them. I'm stuck in this terrible job and I can't get out. Someone left the door open and the cat got out.*
2. To cause to leave or escape: *I got them out of the car just in time.*
3. To bring something into the open; expose something in order to use it: *The students got their notebooks out and began writing. The reporters got out their equipment and started recording.*
4. To express some feeling, emotion, or condition: *If something is bothering you, you should get it out so we can discuss it.*
5. To become known: *Somehow our secret got out.*
6. To cause something to become known; disseminate something: *We*

ă	pat	är	car	ī	bite	ô	paw	o͝o	took	ûr	urge
ā	pay	ĕ	pet	îr	pier	ôr	core	o͝or	lure	zh	vision
âr	care	ē	be	ŏ	pot	oi	boy	o͞o	boot	ə	about, item
ä	father	ĭ	pit	ō	toe	ou	out	ŭ	cut		

need to get this important information out. Let's get out the news as quickly as possible.

7. To produce or manufacture something: *The factory got out 5,000 parts just in time. The publisher got 25 new titles out last year.*

get over

1. To traverse something or reach the other side of something: *How do we get over the river? This bridge is too icy; how do we get over?*
2. To cause something or someone to traverse or reach someone or something: *Please get that money over to me as soon as you can.*
3. To recover from something, especially emotionally: *They both finally got over their divorce. Your dog ran away a month ago; it's time for you to get over it.*
4. To cause someone to recover from something: *The beautiful summer weather got me over the sad events of the spring.*
5. To overcome or prevail against something: *We got over the storm, but the flooding that followed was even worse. The kids never got over their fear of large dogs.*
6. To cause someone to prevail against or be sustained through something; tide someone over: *I didn't have a job, but the money I had saved got me over.*
7. To come to understand or no longer be surprised by something. Used in the negative: *I can't get over the fact that he's still living in that awful apartment.*
8. **get over with** To complete some task or ordeal that one does not want to face: *Once we get over with the interview, the rest will be easy. If you have to have your tooth pulled, you should go to the dentist and get it over with.*

get past

1. To reach the other side of something: *It was raining hard, but once we got past the floodplains, we felt safer.*
2. To cause something to reach the other side of something: *If you can get the supplies past the guards, the prisoners can take them and no one will notice.*
3. To overcome something; no longer need to deal with something: *Your advice helped me get past my problems.*
4. To cause someone to overcome some obstacle: *The cash advance got me past the winter.*

get through

1. To arrive at the end of something, especially something difficult; finish something: *I got through the speech without making a single mistake. It took me a week to get through the book.*
2. **get through with** To bring something to an end; complete something: *You can go outside as soon as you get through with your homework.*
3. **get through with** To complete an assault or attack on someone: *As soon as I get through with this guy, I'm coming after you. You'll be penniless after my lawyers get through with you.*
4. To manage or survive through some ordeal: *The company got through the war by manufacturing uniforms. The tornado destroyed our house, but somehow we got through unharmed.*

5. To cause or help someone to manage or survive some period of time: *The snowstorm trapped us in the cabin, but our ample supplies of food and firewood got us through. The well-stocked library got me through many boring nights.*
6. To succeed in making contact with someone or something; reach someone or something: *I tried to get through to an operator, but I couldn't get past the recording. If the line is busy, keep calling until you get through.*
7. To make oneself understood by someone: *I warned the children about the dangers of playing in the street, but I am afraid that I didn't get through. The teacher hoped to get through to the students by relating the subject to popular music.*

get to

1. To arrive at some place: *Our plane got to Miami at noon.*
2. To begin doing something: *After visiting the orphanage, I got to thinking about my own childhood.*
3. To start to deal with something: *I couldn't get to the assignment until Sunday because I was busy with other work.*
4. To influence or affect someone, especially adversely: *The sound of crying babies really gets to me. Don't let their teasing get to you.*

get together

1. To come together as a group; meet: *Let's get together for lunch next week. The president got together with his advisers to discuss the bill.*
2. To bring some set of people or things together; gather some things or people together: *She got the children together for a game of soccer. My best friend from high school got me together with the woman I later married.*
3. To organize something or sort something out, especially a state of affairs: *If you don't get your romantic life together, you'll never be happy.*
4. To agree to cooperate: *The two parties finally got together after weeks of debating. The staff got together to buy me a retirement gift. We got together with a technology company to offer our customers Internet services.*

get up

1. To arise from bed or rise to one's feet: *We must be quiet until the babies get up from their nap. I got up from the chair and turned the light on. During intermission I got up and went to the lobby.*
2. To go to or over the top of something: *You can reach the higher shelf if you get up on that stool.*
3. To reach some particular level or place: *The temperature got up to 100 degrees. This floor is restricted—How did you get up here? It took an hour to get up the mountain.*

ă	pat	är	car	ī	bite	ô	paw	o͝o	took	ûr	urge
ā	pay	ĕ	pet	îr	pier	ôr	core	o͝or	lure	zh	vision
âr	care	ē	be	ŏ	pot	oi	boy	o͞o	boot	ə	about,
ä	father	ĭ	pit	ō	toe	ou	out	ŭ	cut		item

4. To act as the creator or organizer of something: *We got up a petition against the plan for a new garbage dump.*
5. To build up or achieve some mental state that is needed to do something: *I stood on the edge of the diving board until I got the courage up to jump. I finally got up the strength to tell my boss I needed a raise.*
6. To dress or adorn oneself. Used chiefly reflexively: *She got herself up in a bizarre outfit.*

get with
SLANG

To become involved with or attuned to some activity; be properly engaged with something: *You need to get with the project and start helping us.*

◆ **give** (gĭv)

gave (gāv), **given** (gĭv′n), **giving** (gĭv′ĭng), **gives** (gĭvz)

give away

1. To relinquish something; give something to another: *The store is giving away free samples of cheese. I gave my old clothes away to charity.*
2. To present a bride to her bridegroom at a wedding ceremony: *Very often, the father gives away the bride. I gave my daughter away at her wedding.*
3. To reveal something or make something known, often accidentally; divulge something: *The preview gave away the film's surprise ending. The tone of the teacher's voice gave the answer away.*
4. To betray someone: *I tried to pass for a local resident, but my accent gave me away.*

give back

To return something: *Don't forget to give the books back when you're done with them. I gave back the hammer when the job was done.*

give in

1. To submit something; hand in something: *She gave in her report. You can't change the grades after you've given them in, so make sure they are correct.*
2. To cease opposition; yield: *They will try to make you change your mind, but don't give in. The opposition finally gave in to our demands.*
3. To give way; collapse: *The floor gave in under the weight of the heavy sculpture.*

give of

1. To devote or contribute something: *She really gave of her time to help.*
2. To devote oneself to something. Used reflexively: *They give of themselves to improve the quality of education.*

give off

To emit, release, or radiate something: *This chemical reaction gives off a lot of energy. The refrigerator gave off a strange odor.*

give on

To pretend something in order to deceive another: *The con artist gave on that he was a car salesman, although in fact he knew very little about cars.*

give out

1. To allow or cause something to be known; declare something publicly:

The professor gave out the bad news.

2. To emit or radiate something; give something off: *My car engine gave out a steady buzzing.*
3. To distribute something: *The homeless shelter gave out food and blankets. The teacher gave the homework assignment out.*
4. To stop functioning; fail: *The dishwasher finally gave out last week.*
5. To become used up or exhausted; run out: *Their determination finally gave out.*

give over

1. To hand something over; entrust something: *The landlord gave over the keys after we paid the deposit. She gave the package over to the courier for delivery.*
2. To devote something to a particular purpose or use: *Because we won, we gave the day over to merrymaking.*
3. To surrender or abandon oneself completely. Used reflexively: *When the funeral was finished, I finally gave myself over to grief.*

give up

1. To surrender: *The suspects gave up. The fugitives gave themselves up.*
2. To admit defeat: *Okay, let me go; I give up.*
3. To cease to do or perform something, especially before completion or success: *We gave up our search for the missing earrings. I tried to learn chess, but I was so bad that I gave it up.*
4. To desist from doing something; stop doing something: *My friend gave up smoking. I've been trying to give this habit up for years.*
5. To abandon what one is planning to do: *The author gave up writing the novel. Don't give up on this project!*
6. To part with something; relinquish something: *We gave the apartment up when the landlord raised the rent. They gave up all hope of ever finding their dog again.*
7. To completely devote oneself to something. Used reflexively: *The librarian gave himself up to his work.*
8. **give up on** To lose faith or confidence in someone or something: *After the sixth inning, our team gave up on winning the game. I gave up on my brother when he failed to return my letters.*
9. **give up on** To lose hope that someone or something will appear: *We'd given up on you an hour ago.*
10. **give up for** To believe someone will not appear because he or she is in some debilitated state: *You were so late to the party, we had given you up for lost. The lonely soldiers gave up their colonel for dead.*

give way

1. To cease resisting or holding: *The roof gave way under the weight of the snow, and the whole building collapsed.*

ă	pat	är	car	ī	bite	ô	paw	o͝o	took	ûr	urge
ā	pay	ĕ	pet	îr	pier	ôr	core	o͝or	lure	zh	vision
âr	care	ē	be	ŏ	pot	oi	boy	o͞o	boot	ə	about,
ä	father	ĭ	pit	ō	toe	ou	out	ŭ	cut		item

2. To yield, make space for, or accommodate something: *The old computer system must give way in order to meet the new hardware requirements.*

◆ **glance** (glăns)

glanced (glănst), **glancing** (glăn′sĭng), **glances** (glăn′sĭz)

glance over

To take a brief look at something: *I picked up the book and glanced it over, but it didn't look very interesting. We glanced over the paperwork before buying the car.*

◆ **glare** (glâr)

glared (glârd), **glaring** (glâr′ĭng), **glares** (glârz)

glare down

1. To shine on or illuminate someone or something strongly from above: *The sun glared down on the nomads crossing the desert.*
2. To intimidate someone or cause someone to submit by staring: *The lawyer glared me down until I was unable to speak.*
3. To look directly at someone or something disapprovingly or disappointedly: *I glared down on my dog, whom I'd caught chewing on the curtains. The dog glared down at the bone, which had sunk to the bottom of the swimming pool.*

◆ **glass** (glăs)

glassed (glăst), **glassing** (glăs′ĭng), **glasses** (glăs′ĭz)

glass in

To surround or enclose something with glass: *We glassed in the side porch to keep it warmer in winter.*

glass over

1. To cover something with glass or fiberglass: *We glassed the surface over to keep water from seeping in.*
2. To come to appear expressionless or lifeless. Used of the eyes: *You should get some sleep—your eyes have glassed over.*

◆ **glaze** (glāz)

glazed (glāzd), **glazing** (glā′zĭng), **glazes** (glā′zĭz)

glaze over

1. To cover the surface of something with a glaze or similar substance: *We glazed the cake over with chocolate frosting. The pastry chef glazed over doughnuts with hazelnut creme. The road was dangerously glazed over with frost.*
2. To come to appear expressionless or lifeless: *Her eyes glazed over when we talked about her last book. His expression always glazes over when he gets bored.*

◆ **glean** (glēn)

gleaned (glēnd), **gleaning** (glē′nĭng), **gleans** (glēnz)

glean from

1. To learn something or figure something out using some information gathered bit by bit: *We were able to glean information about their past from the conversation we overheard. I gleaned from these various articles that there was serious trouble brewing in the government.*
2. To gather grain left behind by reapers: *The farmers have gleaned their final harvests from their fields of wheat.*

◆ **gloat** (glōt)

gloated (glō′tĭd), **gloating** (glō′tĭng), **gloats** (glōts)

gloat over

To feel or express great pleasure or self-satisfaction about something, especially smugly or maliciously: *I wish you wouldn't gloat over winning that chess game.*

◆ **glory** (glôr′ē)

gloried (glôr′ēd), **glorying** (glôr′ē-ĭng), **glories** (glôr′ēz)

glory in

To take great pleasure or pride in something; revel in something: *The composer gloried in the beauty of his own compositions.*

◆ **gnaw** (nô)

gnawed (nôd), **gnawing** (nô′ĭng), **gnaws** (nôz)

gnaw at

1. To bite or chew on something, removing small pieces of it a bit at a time: *The mice gnawed at the corner of the box until they had made a small hole in it.*
2. To cause someone or something to have or feel persistent discomfort, anxiety, or guilt: *His harsh criticism gnawed at me the rest of the day. Hunger was gnawing at my stomach.*

gnaw away

1. To bite or chew something a bit at a time: *The fox gnawed the tough meat away first, and then bit into the bone.*
2. To bite or chew on something repeatedly in order to grind it down or to remove small pieces from it a bit at a time: *The kids gnawed away at the cobs of fresh corn. That dog will gnaw away at that bone until it gets to the marrow inside.*
3. To cause someone or something to have or feel persistent discomfort, anxiety, or guilt: *Dark thoughts gnawed away at my mind.*

gnaw on

1. To bite or chew on something, either without eating it or removing small pieces of it a bit at a time: *The dog has been gnawing on that bone for days.*
2. To cause someone or something to have or feel persistent discomfort, anxiety, or guilt: *Unpleasant dreams gnawed on me all night and I couldn't sleep.*

◆ **go** (gō)

went (wĕnt), **gone** (gôn), **going** (gō′ĭng), **goes** (gōz)

go about

1. To go from place to place in some area, doing something openly and habitually: *All summer, the bees go about the garden collecting pollen.*
2. To execute some routine: *From my office on the top floor, I could observe all the city's workers going about their business.*

ă	pat	är	car	ī	bite	ô	paw	o͝o	took	ûr	urge
ā	pay	ĕ	pet	îr	pier	ôr	core	o͝or	lure	zh	vision
âr	care	ē	be	ŏ	pot	oi	boy	o͞o	boot	ə	about,
ä	father	ĭ	pit	ō	toe	ou	out	ŭ	cut		item

3. To walk around or appear in public, especially in a particular state of dress: *I don't know why you always go about in that silly hat.*
4. To undertake something in a particular way: *How does one go about finding an apartment? Your application could take weeks if you don't go about it in the right way.*

go after

1. To depart later than some specific time: *Don't go after 7:00, because the store will be closed.*
2. To perform an activity after someone else: *Since we have only one shower, I go after my brother, and my sister goes after me.*
3. To chase or pursue someone or something: *The dogs went after the cats down the alley.*

go against

1. To oppose or be in conflict with something, especially a directive or a set of beliefs: *Telling such lies goes against my religious beliefs. They went against their lawyers' recommendations, and now they're in jail.*
2. To decide someone or something is wrong or guilty, especially in a court of law: *This case finally went against the defendants, and they had to pay a fine.*

go ahead

1. To move forward in front of someone or something: *We moved to the right lane to let the faster cars go ahead of us. I went ahead to find seats while my friends bought popcorn.*
2. To continue despite a concern or hesitation: *The game will go ahead as scheduled even if it rains. If you want to take an apple, go ahead.*
3. To begin, especially after waiting or planning. Often used in conjunction with another verb: *I have to work late tonight—go ahead and eat without me.*
4. **go ahead of** To perform an action before someone else: *Whenever we play chess, my sister always goes ahead of me.*
5. **go ahead with** To continue doing something, especially after a delay or despite a concern: *The students went ahead with the prank despite the principal's warnings.*

go along

1. To form or follow a path at the edge of something or parallel to something: *The trail goes along the rim of the canyon. I built a railing that goes along the side of the porch.*
2. To proceed on some path or in some way: *Go along the boulevard until you come to an intersection, and take a right onto Elm Street. No need to explain the rules to me—I'll just learn them as we go along. The trip was going along nicely until you lost the map.*
3. To participate in someone's plan or activity: *We knew their scheme was dishonest, but we went along with it anyway. Your friends are going to the movies—aren't you going along?*
4. To accept something that has been stated or suggested: *We didn't know any good restaurants in the area, so we just went along with the newspaper's suggestion. I didn't understand what they were going to make us do, but I just went along.*

5. To be in accord with something: *The results of the study go along with our previous observations. I wouldn't wear that hat with that tie—they don't go along.*
6. To combine with some set so that a balanced or harmonious result is achieved: *The film won many minor awards to go along with its two Oscars. I bought a new suit and some fancy shoes to go along.*
7. To be a secondary effect of something: *The government was concerned about the rise in smoking and all the costs that go along with it. I enjoy the satisfaction that goes along with making my own furniture.*

go around *or* **go round**

1. To form or follow an indirect path that avoids something: *Go around the fence if the gate is locked. Don't try to cross the marsh—go around.*
2. To form or follow some circular path; loop around something: *The cars have already gone around the track 200 times. Our bus almost tipped over when it went around the turn. This bracelet goes around your ankle.*
3. To move in a circle around something: *The earth goes around the sun once every 365 days. Could you go around to the back of the barn and get the ladder?*
4. To rotate: *We went to the back of the boat and watched the paddle wheel go around.*
5. To go here and there; move from place to place: *We went around the city with the tour group. I went around to all the shops looking for a particular type of perfume.*
6. To walk around, or appear in public, especially in a particular state of dress: *I used to go around in a bright yellow coat.*
7. To pass or be passed from place to place or from person to person: *A flu is going around, so make sure you wash your hands frequently. There are some strange stories going around about that empty house. A box of pencils is going around—please take one and pass it on.*
8. To do something regularly or as a matter of course, especially in a carefree or selfish manner: *He goes around boasting about his new watch. You can't go around expecting people to pay for you.*
9. To satisfy the needs of a group. Used with the infinitive: *There were not enough chairs to go around, so some of us sat on the floor. There is plenty of popcorn to go around.*

go at

1. To undertake something or work on something, especially with enthusiasm or drive: *She went at the job with a lot of energy. He went at that stain on the table with extra soap.*

ă	pat	är	car	ī	bite	ô	paw	o͝o	took	ûr	urge
ā	pay	ĕ	pet	îr	pier	ôr	core	o͝or	lure	zh	vision
âr	care	ē	be	ŏ	pot	oi	boy	o͞o	boot	ə	about, item
ä	father	ĭ	pit	ō	toe	ou	out	ŭ	cut		

2. To attack something, especially with energy: *My cat suddenly leaped up and went at the squirrel.*

go away

1. To leave a place: *The pigeons wouldn't go away once the children fed them. Go away and stop bothering me!*
2. To make an excursion; get away: *We went away to the beach for a couple of days. I have to go away on business next week, but I'm available the following Tuesday. It's boring at home—let's go away for the holidays.*
3. To lose all intensity or diminish in intensity: *I took one aspirin and my headache went away. We emptied the garbage can, but the smell still hasn't gone away.*

go back

1. To return or revert to something: *I'd never go back to that restaurant after the awful meal we had. After lunch, I went back home and slept. The children go back to school in the fall. That book needs to go back to the library.*
2. To reverse direction: *We were going to drive across the bridge, but it was so windy, we decided to go back.*
3. **go back to** To resume some activity: *After looking around, the deer went back to eating. I turned off my alarm and went back to sleep.*
4. **go back to** To return one's attention to something; refer to something: *Let's go back to an interesting comment you made earlier. If we go back to her earlier books, you can see how her style has changed.*
5. To consider or refer to some past time, especially in a narrative: *In chapter four, the book goes back to the main character's childhood.*
6. To have existed since some time; date back: *This house goes back to the 1800s. That idea goes back to Thomas Aquinas.*
7. To have been acquainted for some period of time: *We're old friends—we go back at least 20 years. He and I go way back—we used to play together as children.*
8. **go back on** To fail to carry out some promise or commitment: *I hope you don't go back on your promise to help me out.*
9. **go back on** To claim that something said earlier is untrue; retract or take back something: *The witness went back on his story when the lawyer questioned him. The researcher said she would not go back on her original claim.*

go by

1. To approach someone or something and then move past; pass something: *I could smell the fresh bread as we went by the bakery. The goalie stumbled, and the ball went right by her. We sat near the window so that we could watch the people going by on the sidewalk.*
2. To elapse; pass. Used of periods of time: *Time goes by quickly if you're busy. Three years have gone by since we last spoke to each other.*
3. To pay a short visit to some place: *On my way to work, I went by the post office to mail a package. My parents were not at home when we went by last week.*
4. To make a judgment or proceed on the basis of some property or observation: *When I'm choosing a*

pair of boots, I go by quality and price, not the way they look. If you want to play this game with us, you must go by the rules. Should we go by the recipe in the cookbook or the recipe on the package? They have a good chance of winning the tournament, if their performance in the last few games is something to go by.

5. To be known as having some name: *My real name is Theodore, but I also go by "Teddy."*

go down

1. To proceed along some path: *We went down the street.*
2. To descend something: *Let's go down the stairs rather than taking the elevator. Go down and see if they need any help in the kitchen. I went down to the cellar to fetch a bottle of wine.*
3. **go down to** To reach or extend to some lower point: *This path goes down to the bottom of the canyon. The thermometer goes down to -15 degrees.*
4. To fall to the ground; plummet: *The helicopter went down when the rotor malfunctioned. The boxer went down in the fourth round.*
5. To sink: *The ship went down in the storm, but the crew survived.*
6. To travel south: *I go down to the tropics every winter. I went down and visited my family in Mexico.*
7. To go to a city or town center, or some central location: *We went down to the park to meet our friends. My friend got arrested, so I went down and bailed him out.*
8. To drop toward or below the horizon; set. Used especially of the sun and moon: *The crickets began to chirp after the sun went down.*
9. To experience defeat or ruin: *The company went down after the stock market crashed.*
10. To fail to operate; break down: *The computers went down due to a software problem.*
11. To permit swallowing: *This cough syrup goes down readily.*
12. To diminish in intensity or volume: *The lights went down and the movie began. Put some ice on your injured elbow to help the swelling go down. When they returned to their car, they saw that the tires had gone down.*
13. To decrease in value: *Bond prices often go up as stocks go down. Last night, the temperature went down to 10 degrees.*
14. To occur; happen. Used especially of interesting or important events: *When the police officers saw the limousines arrive at the mobster's hideout, they knew something big was going down.*
15. To be accepted or tolerated: *My announcement that the show would be canceled did not go down well with the audience.*
16. To come to be remembered in posterity: *This remarkable debate will go down as a turning point in the campaign. The day we signed the treaty will go down in history.*

ă	pat	är	car	ī	bite	ô	paw	o͝o	took	ûr	urge
ā	pay	ĕ	pet	îr	pier	ôr	core	o͝or	lure	zh	vision
âr	care	ē	be	ŏ	pot	oi	boy	o͞o	boot	ə	about,
ä	father	ĭ	pit	ō	toe	ou	out	ŭ	cut		item

17. VULGAR SLANG **go down on** To perform oral sex on someone.

go for

1. To reach or move toward something or someone: *When the police officer looked away, the thief went for the door.*
2. To reach or move toward something or someone in order to attack or injure: *The angry dog went straight for my leg. The debater went for her opponents weaknesses.*
3. To try to grab something quickly, especially a weapon: *The soldier went for the knife on the table, but slipped and fell down.*
4. To make a concerted effort to achieve some goal: *I am going for my second tournament win. If you think you have a chance of winning, go for it. The running back saw an opening and went for it. Whenever I see an opportunity to make more money, I go for it.*
5. To try to attain or produce some condition: *The restaurant is going for a rustic atmosphere. Today's fashions are going for a colorful look.*
6. To choose something: *After trying all the different flavors, I went for the vanilla ice cream.*
7. To have a special liking for something; enjoy something: *My parents go for the older styles of jazz. I could really go for a beer right now.*
8. To leave temporarily in order to fetch or get something: *We're going for pizza; do you want to come along?*
9. To apply or be relevant to someone or something: *These rules go for the adults as well as the children. It's hard to eat pizza without making a mess, and the same goes for ice cream cones.*
10. To be sold or available for purchase at some price: *This phone normally goes for $100, but we'll give it to you for $60. How much did that old house finally go for? That painting will probably go for $1000 at auction, but I wouldn't pay one cent.*
11. To be of support or value to someone: *She had everything going for her after the success of her last album, but she threw it all away on drugs and alcohol. The team has a lot going for them. The one thing going for him is his talent for making people laugh; otherwise he's a failure.*

go forward

1. To move in the direction in which one is facing: *I stepped on the accelerator and the car went forward.*
2. To begin as planned: *The demolition of the old building went forward despite protests from the local historical society.*
3. To continue; make progress: *We need to watch the budget for this project as we go forward.*
4. To advance to the next in a sequence of levels: *Whoever wins this competition will go forward to the final round. Only two of the contestants went forward.*
5. To be passed on as a recommendation. Used especially of people's names: *The names of three people went forward as possible candidates for president.*

go in

1. To enter something: *I went in the garage to find a rake. I went in, and there was Grandma, sitting on the sofa. It's too cold on the porch—let's go in. I walked to the pond and went in for a swim.*
2. To enter through something: *If the front door is locked, go in the back door.*
3. To go to a central or particular location: *I called the office and told them I wouldn't be going in today. The car has to go in for service. I went in for surgery.*
4. To belong to or be easily accommodated by some place: *These forks go in the bottom drawer. I tried this key on the lock, but it wouldn't go in.*
5. To be an added ingredient of something: *What kinds of spices go in this sauce?*
6. To be learned or understood: *I explained the procedure to the new mechanic many times, but it didn't go in.*
7. To take part in a cooperative venture: *I went in with my friends to buy a present for our new neighbors. He'll go in with them on the plan. Who wants to go in on a pizza with me?*

go into

1. To enter something: *They went into the tunnel and emerged from the other side an hour later. I went into my suitcase to get my toothbrush. I am going into my final year at school, so I need to start looking for a job.*
2. To go to some central or particular location: *I'll go into the office on Saturday and finish the report. I went into town to buy some clothing. The car went into the shop for repairs.*
3. To impact something, especially unintentionally: *I swerved and went into the stop sign.*
4. To be invested in some activity: *A lot of work has gone into this project. How much money went into fixing the roads last year?*
5. To be added to something: *In this cake recipe, the sugar goes into the batter before the flour.*
6. To be able to enter something; to fit in something: *My suitcases won't go into the overhead compartment.*
7. To be a factor of some number: *Five goes into fifteen three times.*
8. To discuss or investigate something: *The book doesn't go into any of the culture's religious practices. They said they could solve the problem, but they refused to go into the details.*
9. To undertake as a profession or course of study: *After I graduate, I'm going into the family business. I plan to go into law.*
10. To come to be in some condition: *Both patients went into a coma. The audience went into fits of laughter. We went into debt to send the children to college. The company is going into decline.*

11. To begin to undergo some process or use: *Two hundred more airplanes will soon go into production. A new coin went into circulation yesterday.*

go off

1. To go away: *The children all went off to play at the park. Don't go off mad—let me explain!*
2. To stop functioning. Used especially of electrical devices: *The lights went off suddenly, and the performance began right away.*
3. To occur, or be perceived as having occurred, in some particular manner: *I think our party went off very well!*
4. To adhere to the expected course of events or the expected plan: *The project went off smoothly.*
5. To stop taking some drug or medication: *She went off painkillers a few weeks after the operation.*
6. To make a noise; sound: *The siren goes off every day at noon.*
7. To undergo detonation; explode: *If you push this red button, the bomb will go off.*
8. **go off on** To begin to talk extensively about something: *He went off on a series of excuses for his bad behavior.*
9. **go off on** To berate someone directly and loudly: *My boss really went off on me when she learned that I had forgotten to make the phone call.*

go on

1. To move forward; proceed: *The train went on down the tracks. We were tired of walking, but we went on anyway.*
2. To put oneself on some surface: *I went on the roof to fix the leak.*
3. To connect with some computer or computer network: *You can go on the Internet to find rare books.*
4. To stretch or extend from a place. Used of paths of motion: *This road goes on from here through many more towns before reaching the ocean. The river goes on to the lake. The desert goes on for miles in every direction.*
5. To use something as a mode of conveyance: *The buses weren't running, so I went on the train.*
6. To embark on some trip, excursion, or similar activity: *My kids went on a hike. I have always wanted to go on a safari. Let's go on a roller coaster ride.*
7. To be carried away by some emotionally charged activity: *The killer went on a rampage. The reporter remarked about the deranged person who went on a shooting spree.*
8. To take place; happen: *What is going on in that noisy room? There is a lot going on in the market. I couldn't go to the meeting, so please tell me what went on.*
9. To continue: *The speech went on for almost an hour. The temperature will fall as the day goes on. If they go on fighting like this, there will be nothing left when the war is over.*
10. To continue doing something: *I can't go on arguing with you every day. I'm sorry I interrupted you—please go on. We walked until we couldn't go on any longer.*
11. To make an appearance on some public medium, such as a stage or television broadcast: *The actor went on TV to help raise money*

for the charity. You should dress quickly for your performance—you go on in half an hour.

12. To begin. Used especially of performances or broadcasts: *The show goes on at 6:00. The show first went on the air in 1972.*

13. To begin to operate. Used especially of lights and other electrical devices: *After the movie was over, the lights went on.*

14. To begin taking some drug or medication regularly: *I went on a mild painkiller after the operation.*

15. To do something. Used as a command or encouragement: *Go on, have another drink.*

16. To proceed to some place: *We went on to the next exhibition. After a brief stay in Moscow, we went on to St. Petersburg. After high school I went on to a two-year college. The winner of this match will go on to the third round.*

17. To proceed to do something next, often later in life: *Without pausing, she went on to talk about the mountains. He went on to become a senator years later. The winner of this match will go on to face the champion.*

18. To base one's judgment on something; go by something: *Going on the few symptoms that we could observe, we were able to diagnose the patient. Without a witness, the police had nothing to go on.*

19. To talk continuously; rattle on: *Every time we see them, they go on about their child's good grades. Do you have to go on like that?*

20. To stop telling stories that are not believed or are considered preposterous. Used only as a command: *Now go on—you know there are no such things as dragons.*

21. To be close to some age. Used only in the progressive: *My sister is going on 23. I was going on 10 when I changed schools.*

go out

1. To leave a building, region, or other place: *Let's go out and look at the stars. I went out for a cigarette. The children went out to play in the snow. We went out on the porch. Instead of cooking, let's go out for dinner tonight. We ran out of rice, so I went out for some more. The seas are too rough for the ships to go out today.*

2. To exit through something: *Go out the back door so that no one sees you.*

3. To recede from the land. Used of tides: *When the tide goes out, we collect shells along the shore.*

4. To leave the boundary of a game: *If you kick the ball and it goes out, the other team gets control.*

5. To take an active role in accomplishing something. Used with *and: You should go out and get a lawyer if you want to win this case.*

6. To make a trip, especially to some distant or remote location: *We went out to the country to visit the dairy farm. This ferry goes out to the islands.*

ă	pat	är	car	ī	bite	ô	paw	o͝o	took	ûr	urge
ā	pay	ĕ	pet	îr	pier	ôr	core	o͝or	lure	zh	vision
âr	care	ē	be	ŏ	pot	oi	boy	o͞o	boot	ə	about,
ä	father	ĭ	pit	ō	toe	ou	out	ŭ	cut		item

7. To be sent, broadcast, or disseminated: *The package went out last week. The invitations went out two weeks before the party. The word went out that the couple was getting a divorce.*
8. To have something, such as one's thoughts, heart, or sympathy, preoccupied with or affected by someone's suffering: *Our hearts go out to the victims of the fire.*
9. To take part in social life outside the home: *I go out every Friday night. Let's go out tonight and see a movie. On our last date, we went out for ice cream. I'm going out to meet some friends at the mall. I went out to dinner with my parents.*
10. To collapse structurally: *The bridge went out after the heavy rains.*
11. To become extinguished: *The children were frightened when the lights went out. The power went out during the storm. We stayed up and talked until the fire went out.*
12. To become unfashionable: *Big collars are going out of fashion. High boots went out last year.*
13. To be in a steady romantic relationship with someone: *They started going out a couple of months ago, and now they are inseparable. She had been going out with him for three years before they got married.*
14. **go out for** To undergo a competitive qualifying test for some athletic team: *If you plan to go out for the basketball team this year, you had better start practicing. I've gone out for the swim team every year, but I've never made it.*

go over

1. To go to a place: *Let's go over to the store and buy a snack. My friend was feeling lonely, so I went over and cheered him up.*
2. To examine or review something: *We'll go over last week's lesson before we start a new one.*
3. To search something thoroughly: *I went over my entire room, but I couldn't find my wallet.*
4. To perform an action on the entire surface of something: *The table still looked dusty, so I went over it with a damp cloth.*
5. To gain acceptance or garner a reaction or opinions: *The new movie went over superbly. I think your criticism went over well.*
6. **go over with** To gain acceptance or garner a reaction or opinions from someone: *We weren't sure if our play would go over with the critics. Our comments went over badly with the press.*

go through

1. To move or proceed into or within something, especially completely or from one side to the other: *We turned on our headlights when we went through the tunnel. The ink went through the paper and stained the table. The larger fish got caught in the net, but the smaller fish went right through. We went through the field gathering flowers.*
2. To form a path within something, especially completely or from one side to the other: *The tunnel goes through the mountain. Only one path goes through this forest.*
3. To send a message or signal successfully: *My telephone calls*

aren't going through. I sent two e-mails, but neither went through.

4. To use someone or something as an intermediary for interacting or communicating: *All of our customers' orders go through our sales department. Don't buy a car from them—go through a reputable dealer. If you need to contact me, go through my office.*
5. To proceed to the next stage of a process or event: *The winner of this match will go through to the finals.*
6. To be accepted or enacted after going through an approval procedure. Used of proposals: *If the new law goes through, we won't be able to park on that side of the street anymore.*
7. To examine each of some set of things: *I went through the students' papers, looking for the best one. Someone has been going through my mail without permission.*
8. To review or search something completely: *The lawyer went through the documents but couldn't find any useful information. I went through the drawer trying to find the earring I lost.*
9. To experience something, especially something negative: *We went through some tough times when my father lost his job. All our products go through months of testing. They went through a lot to get you that gift, so you'd better thank them.*
10. To perform something from start to finish: *The violinist went through the sonata in 30 minutes. Let's go through the dance from the beginning.*
11. To use something until there is no more of it remaining; use something up: *I went through an entire pack of cigarettes in two hours. My dogs go through two bags of food a week.*
12. **go through with** To finish something, especially something difficult or which one does not want to do: *We intended to eat the rabbit once it got big enough, but after the children gave it a name, we just couldn't go through with it. I decided not to go through with the surgery after I discovered how dangerous it was.*

go together

1. To be matched or suited, especially in appearance; belong together: *Those socks don't go together; they're different colors. This belt goes together with my brown shoes.*
2. To be associated: *Drug abuse and crime often go together.*
3. To have a romantic relationship: *They've only been going together for three weeks, but it looks like they're in love.*

go under

1. To move to a place beneath something: *The dog went under the table.*

ă	pat	är	car	ī	bite	ô	paw	o͝o	took	ûr	urge
ā	pay	ĕ	pet	îr	pier	ôr	core	o͝or	lure	zh	vision
âr	care	ē	be	ŏ	pot	oi	boy	o͞o	boot	ə	about,
ä	father	ĭ	pit	ō	toe	ou	out	ŭ	cut		item

2. To sink or descend below the surface: *The divers went under three times that afternoon. The ship leaked so badly that it finally went under.*
3. To fail. Used especially of businesses and enterprises: *That big department store went under last year because of the fire.*
4. To suffer defeat or destruction: *The enemy went under after a long battle.*
5. To lose consciousness: *The surgeons gave me a strong anesthetic, and I quickly went under.*

go up

1. To ascend something: *It became colder as we went up the mountain. Let's go up to the roof deck and watch the fireworks.*
2. To travel north: *Next summer, let's go up to Alaska where it won't be so hot. We went up and stayed with a friend in Canada.*
3. To go to a less central location in a town or city: *We went up to the new movie theater to see an art film.*
4. To go to some larger town or city: *On the weekends we often go up to New York. We went up and saw a show in the city.*
5. **go up to** To extend or to reach some point or time: *My new calendar only goes up to December.*
6. To approach someone or something: *I went up to the counter and asked for a soda. Your friends have arrived—why don't you go up and say hello?*
7. To increase in value or intensity: *If the temperature goes up, the snow will melt.*
8. To begin to burn: *A spark from the train lit the nearby brush, and the entire field went up.*
9. To be constructed or in the process of construction: *New buildings are going up all over the city.*
10. To occur or arise. Used of noises made by crowds: *We heard a cheer go up whenever the team scored a goal.*
11. **go up against** To be confronted with an opponent or challenge: *In the third round, I went up against the best player in the league.*

go with

1. To proceed in the company of someone or something: *I'll go with you to the supermarket if we also stop by the ice cream shop.*
2. To select or choose something: *We decided to go with the pink wallpaper, even though it doesn't match our carpet.*
3. To be matched or suited to something; belong with something: *The big lid goes with the stock pot. These shoes will go nicely with my red dress. This wine goes well with spicy food.*
4. To be a secondary effect of being something or some way: *The risk of injury goes with being a firefighter. I enjoyed being a politician and especially all the privileges that went with it. There are many health problems that go with obesity.*
5. To combine with something so that a balanced or harmonious result is achieved. Used chiefly in the infinitive: *The museum hosted a series of lectures to go with the art exhibit. I made a sauce to go with the meat.*

6. To be in a romantic relationship with someone: *Mary started going with Bill after she broke up with her boyfriend.*

go without

To proceed without the benefit of something that one needs: *The children went without any shoes for several months. We were always well taken care of and never went without.*

◆ **goad** (gōd)

goaded (gō′dĭd), **goading** (gō′dĭng), **goads** (gōdz)

goad into

To induce someone to do something through prodding or threat of embarrassment: *I didn't want to steal the candy bar, but the other kids goaded me into it.*

goad on

1. To make someone or something move by prodding or poking: *The farmer goaded the cattle on.*
2. To urge someone to continue something through prodding or threat of embarrassment: *I didn't want to sing any more, but the crowd goaded me on.*

◆ **gobble** (gŏb′əl)

gobbled (gŏb′əld), **gobbling** (gŏb′ə-lĭng), **gobbles** (gŏb′əlz)

gobble down

To eat something completely and in haste, especially by swallowing large amounts at a time: *The family gobbled down the peach pie. I was so hungry that when they gave me food, I gobbled it down.*

gobble up

To eat something completely and in haste: *We gobbled up our meal and left for the theater. The babysitter grabbed the brownies and gobbled them up.*

◆ **goof** (go͞of)

goofed (go͞oft), **goofing** (go͞o′fĭng), **goofs** (go͞ofs)

goof around

To act foolishly, playfully, or without a clear sense of purpose: *The students who goofed around all semester failed the course.*

goof off

To waste time, especially by acting foolishly or frivolously: *The students spent their free time goofing off instead of working on the project.*

goof up

1. To make a mistake, especially out of confusion or ignorance: *You really goofed up by not telling your parents you were leaving. I didn't follow the instructions for the job carefully, so I goofed up.*
2. To cause someone or something to blunder: *The directions to the park were confusing and they goofed me up. You're not alone in getting*

ă	pat	är	car	ī	bite	ô	paw	o͝o	took	ûr	urge
ā	pay	ĕ	pet	îr	pier	ôr	core	o͝or	lure	zh	vision
âr	care	ē	be	ŏ	pot	oi	boy	o͞o	boot	ə	about,
ä	father	ĭ	pit	ō	toe	ou	out	ŭ	cut		item

lost; that fork in the road goofs up everybody.

3. To perform something badly; blunder in executing something: *You really goofed up the spelling section of the test. The band didn't rehearse enough before the concert and really goofed the march up.*

◆ **goose** (go͞os)

goosed (go͞ost), **goosing** (go͞o′sĭng), **gooses** (go͞o′sĭz)

goose up

To improve the performance of something; make something more intense, powerful, or remarkable: *Goose up the engine and we'll be on our way. You could goose the pie up with some nutmeg.*

◆ **gorge** (gôrj)

gorged (gôrjd), **gorging** (gôr′jĭng), **gorges** (gôr′jĭz)

gorge on

To eat enthusiastically and in great amounts: *He gorged on pizza. She gorged herself on junk food.*

gorge with

1. To embed something or someone with some object or decoration: *The king's crown was gorged with diamonds.*
2. To indulge something or someone, especially with food or drink: *The hosts gorged the weary travelers with delicacies of every kind. The hotel guests were gorged with hospitality.*
3. To eat enthusiastically and in great amounts. Used reflexively: *They gorged themselves with ice cream.*

◆ **grace** (grās)

graced (grāst), **gracing** (grā′sĭng), **graces** (grā′sĭz)

grace with

1. To lend honor or prestige to someone or some event. Used chiefly in the passive: *We were graced with high praise from our superiors. The ambassadors kindly joined the reception and graced it with their presence.*
2. To decorate, adorn, or benefit something by means of some added feature. Used chiefly in the passive: *The living room of this house is graced with a large fireplace.*
3. To decorate, adorn, or benefit something: *The caterer finished setting the table and graced it with candles.*

◆ **grade** (grād)

graded (grā′dĭd), **grading** (grā′dĭng), **grades** (grādz)

grade down

To give someone a lower rank or score, usually with respect to something evaluated: *The teacher graded me down on my English test because of my terrible penmanship. The driving instructor graded down our group because we weren't listening.*

◆ **graduate** (grăj′o͞o-āt′)

graduated (grăj′o͞o-ā′tĭd), **graduating** (grăj′o͞o-ā′tĭng), **graduates** (grăj′o͞o-āts′)

graduate from

1. To move up from one position, rank, or level, to a higher one: *That year, the athletes graduated*

from amateur to professional status in the competition.

2. To complete the academic requirements of some institution, usually receiving an academic degree: *I graduated from college with a degree in history.*

graduate in

To complete the requirements of an institution and receive an academic degree in some subject: *I graduated in mathematics from the local community college.*

graduate with

To complete the academic requirements of an institution for something, especially a degree or an honor: *I graduated with a degree in mathematics. Few students graduated with honors this year.*

◆ **grapple** (grăp′əl)

grappled (grăp′əld), **grappling** (grăp′ə-lĭng), **grapples** (grăp′əlz)

grapple with

To be engaged with the complications or problems presented by something; struggle with: *Some parts of the world are grappling with overpopulation.*

◆ **grasp** (grăsp)

grasped (grăspt), **grasping** (grăs′pĭng), **grasps** (grăsps)

grasp at

To have a hold on something or take hold of something with the hands: *Afraid of the steep drop-off, I grasped at the railing.*

◆ **grate** (grāt)

grated (grā′tĭd), **grating** (grā′tĭng), **grates** (grāts)

grate on

1. To scrape against something and roughen or remove pieces of a surface: *The fender was grating on the tire of the car.*

2. To irritate someone or something as if by scraping or grating: *These loud noises are starting to grate on me.*

◆ **grease** (grēs, grēz)

greased (grēst, grēzd), **greasing** (grē′sĭng, grē′zĭng), **greases** (grē′sĭz, grē′zĭz)

grease up

To coat something completely with grease; lubricate something with grease: *The mechanic greased up the motor. At the fair, they greased the pigs up and then we chased them.*

◆ **grind** (grīnd)

ground (ground), **grinding** (grīn′dĭng), **grinds** (grīndz)

grind away

1. To remove something by grinding: *You need to grind the spurs away with a file. The optician ground away the glass from the lens.*

2. To devote oneself to study or work: *She ground away at the problem.*

ă	pat	är	car	ī	bite	ô	paw	o͝o	took	ûr	urge
ā	pay	ĕ	pet	îr	pier	ôr	core	o͝or	lure	zh	vision
âr	care	ē	be	ŏ	pot	oi	boy	o͞o	boot	ə	about,
ä	father	ĭ	pit	ō	toe	ou	out	ŭ	cut		item

We told him to get some sleep before the exam, but he kept grinding away.

grind down

1. To cause wear on something by rubbing against it, reducing its size: *The jeweler ground the opals down into beautiful egg-shaped pieces. The miller ground down the wheat for the farmers.*
2. To slow down, as if through a grinding action: *The machine eventually ground down to a halt.*

grind into

1. To change the state of something to some other state by grinding: *In this recipe you have to grind the rice into a fine powder.*
2. To instill or teach something by persistent repetition: *The instructor ground the lessons into their heads.*

grind out

1. To produce mechanically or without inspiration: *The factory grinds out a uniform product. I dread writing my tedious weekly reports, but I grind them out.*
2. To achieve or accomplish something through determination and force: *The team ground out a win. Their running game ground out 50 yards, putting them in position for a field goal. Victory seemed far off, but we managed to grind it out in the last minutes of play.*

◆ **gross** (grōs)

grossed (grōst), **grossing** (grō′sĭng), **grosses** (grō′sĭz)

gross out

SLANG

To fill someone with disgust; nauseate someone: *The pizza they serve at school grosses me out. The gory pictures grossed out our friends.*

◆ **ground** (ground)

grounded (groun′dĭd), **grounding** (groun′dĭng), **grounds** (groundz)

ground out

BASEBALL

To be put out by hitting a ground ball that is caught by the first base player or is thrown to first base by another player: *The game ended when our best batter grounded out on a curve ball.*

◆ **grow** (grō)

grew (gro͞o), **grown** (grōn), **growing** (grō′ĭng), **grows** (grōz)

grow in

To fill an area by growing extensively within it: *We cut down too many of the bushes, but they will grow in again soon.*

grow into

1. To develop so as to become something: *A child grows into an adult. An acorn grows into an oak.*
2. To develop or change so as to fit something: *She grew into her job. He grew into the relationship slowly.*

grow on *or* **grow upon**

1. To be nourished by something and develop in size or quality: *Wheat does not grow on sandy soil. Baby mice grow on only a few drops of milk every hour.*

2. To become gradually more evident to someone: *A feeling of distrust grew on me.*
3. To become gradually more pleasurable or acceptable to someone: *Just wait; the bitter taste will grow on you.*

grow out

1. To extend from a place by growing: *I cut my hair short, but it will grow out again.*
2. To cause something to become longer or thicker by growing it or letting it grow: *I cut my hair short, but I'll grow it out again. He grew out his beard until his chin was completely covered.*
3. **grow out of** To have developed to the point that one is too big or no longer suited to something: *My son grew out of his shoes in three weeks.*
4. **grow out of** To have developed in such a way that something is no longer interesting or appropriate: *When I was young I liked eating bananas with pickles, but I grew out of it.*

grow up

To become an adult: *I want to be a teacher when I grow up.*

◆ **grub** (grŭb)

grubbed (grŭbd), **grubbing** (grŭb′ĭng), **grubs** (grŭbz)

grub for

1. To dig in the ground to get something out of it, especially food: *The bears grubbed for beetles in the soft ground.*
2. To try to achieve or get something by begging, nagging, or acting in a shameless way: *The members of the city council were always grubbing for more power.*

grub up

To procure something by or as if by digging in the ground for it: *The bird grubbed up some worms from under the rock.*

◆ **gum** (gŭm)

gummed (gŭmd), **gumming** (gŭm′ĭng), **gums** (gŭmz)

gum up

1. To cover with a sticky substance: *Gum up the back of the paper so it will stick to the frame. Gum the poster up so it won't fall down.*
2. To become inactive or inoperable because of interference with moving parts: *The cash register gummed up while it was in the attic, and now we can't open it.*
3. To cause complications or inefficiency in something: *These new regulations have gummed our procedures up, and we can't get anything done on time. The extra layer of bureaucracy gummed up the department's ability to process claims quickly.*

◆ **gun** (gŭn)

gunned (gŭnd), **gunning** (gŭn′ĭng), **guns** (gŭnz)

ă	pat	är	car	ī	bite	ô	paw	o͝o	took	ûr	urge
ā	pay	ĕ	pet	îr	pier	ôr	core	o͝or	lure	zh	vision
âr	care	ē	be	ŏ	pot	oi	boy	o͞o	boot	ə	about,
ä	father	ĭ	pit	ō	toe	ou	out	ŭ	cut		item

gun down

1. To cause something to collapse or fall by striking it with bullets, missiles, or some other projectile; shoot down something: *The marines gunned down the attacking airplanes. The soldiers gunned the enemy down.*
2. To kill or incapacitate someone by shooting: *They stormed into the hideout and gunned down all the soldiers there. The assassin tracked down the politicians and gunned them down.*

gun for

1. To pursue someone or something relentlessly in order to overcome or destroy: *Look out; they're jealous of you and they're gunning for you.*
2. To go after something in earnest; set out to obtain something: *Everyone in the office is gunning for a promotion.*
3. To lend encouragement and support to someone or something: *My friends were all gunning for me when I ran in the marathon.*

◆ **gush** (gŭsh)

gushed (gŭsht), **gushing** (gŭsh′ĭng), **gushes** (gŭsh′ĭz)

gush over

To speak or write about something or someone with wild enthusiasm: *They returned from the new store and gushed over the great shoes they had bought.*

◆ **gussy** (gŭs′ē)

gussied (gŭs′ēd), **gussying** (gŭs′ē-ĭng), **gussies** (gŭs′ēz)

gussy up

SLANG

1. To dress someone in special or fancy clothes. Used chiefly in the passive or with a reflexive: *We were gussied up in ball gowns. I gussied myself up for the party.*
2. To add embellishing details to something in order to make it more attractive: *The chef gussied up the meat loaf with a truffle sauce. The decorators gussied the room up for the ceremony.*

H

◆ **hack** (hăk)

hacked (hăkt), **hacking** (hăk′ĭng), **hacks** (hăks)

hack away

1. To remove something with blows from a sharp instrument: *The lumberjack hacked away the larger limbs from the tree before felling it. The gardener used a large pair of shears to hack the dead twigs away.*
2. **hack away at** To reduce or attempt to reduce something in size by chopping off pieces of it: *The butcher hacked away at the side of beef to remove the fat.*
3. **hack away at** To reduce something gradually by working at it continuously: *I'm hacking away at the pile of reports on my desk.*

hack off

1. To cut something off, usually with rough or heavy blows: *The gardener hacked off the branch with a machete. We hacked the old shingles off the side of the house.*
2. CHIEFLY BRITISH To annoy someone: *That attitude really hacks me off. The drunken celebrity really hacked off the entertainment reporter.*

hack out

1. To remove something by chopping or cutting; excise something: *The butcher hacked the bone out from the meat. We hacked out the broken shingles from the roof.*
2. To fashion something by chopping, cutting, or chiseling: *The artist hacked out a statue from a chunk of clay. Let's hack a sculpture out of the ice.*
3. SLANG To produce something hastily or routinely, such as written material: *The reporter hacked out a weekly column. The author hacked three romance novels out every year.*

hack up

1. To cut or chop something into pieces, usually with little care: *The cook hacked up the potatoes and dumped them in the pot. We hacked the wood up and threw it in the fireplace.*
2. To mangle or disfigure something, especially by cutting: *That barber hacked up your hair badly! I accidentally hacked the shrubs up with the electric clippers.*
3. To force something from the throat or lungs and out of the mouth by coughing: *The patient hacked some phlegm up. My cat hacked*

up some blood, so I made an appointment with the vet.

◆ **haggle** (hăg′əl)

haggled (hăg′əld), **haggling** (hăg′ə-lĭng), **haggles** (hăg′əlz)

haggle over

To bargain or negotiate over something, as an item or a price: *The merchant and the buyer haggled over the price of the damaged towels.*

◆ **hail** (hāl)

hailed (hāld), **hailing** (hā′lĭng), **hails** (hālz)

hail as

To praise someone for being something: *The veterans were hailed as heroes when they marched in the parade.*

hail from

To come or originate from some place: *My boss hails from Texas. The governor hails from a small rural town.*

◆ **hammer** (hăm′ər)

hammered (hăm′ərd), **hammering** (hăm′ə-rĭng), **hammers** (hăm′ərz)

hammer away

1. To pound on something with loud, repeated blows: *The kids hammered away at the door until I let them in.*
2. To work at something with determination for an extended period: *We hammered away on our proposal all night.*
3. To talk about something to an excessive and tedious degree: *The committee hammered away at the same subject for hours.*

hammer into

1. To drive something through some surface by striking it with a hammer: *The carpenter hammered a nail into the board.*
2. To teach or inculcate something to someone by constant, intense repetition: *The teacher hammered the multiplication tables into the pupils.*

hammer out

1. To expand the surface area of something, as a metal, by striking it with a hammer: *The artisan hammered out the copper plate before engraving it. The blacksmith started by hammering the iron out.*
2. To arrive at some agreement after much discussion, argument or negotiation: *The warring nations finally hammered out a treaty. The manager hammered a vacation schedule out that everyone liked.*

◆ **hand** (hănd)

handed (hăn′dĭd), **handing** (hăn′dĭng), **hands** (hăndz)

hand down

1. To pass something down from a higher level to a lower one: *Please hand that vase down to me while you're up there. The worker on the scaffold handed down the paint can to the assistant.*
2. To pass something on to someone, especially a younger relative: *My older brother hands all his old clothes down to me. My aunt handed down her necklaces to me.*

The house has been handed down from generation to generation.

3. To make and pronounce an official decision, especially a court verdict: *The jury handed down the verdict. The court handed a decision down yesterday.*

hand in

To deliver or submit something to someone: *I handed in my homework. The committee finally handed the proposal in to the mayor.*

hand on

1. To pass something to someone: *I handed the letter on to my cousin after I read it. The lawyer handed on the contract to each party so that it could be signed.*
2. To bequeath something to someone: *The elders handed on their traditions to the younger generation. My grandparents handed the property on to me in their will.*

hand out

1. To distribute something freely; disseminate something: *He handed out flyers in the street all morning. I gave the flyers to the volunteer and told her to hand them out quickly.*
2. To administer or mete something: *It seemed like the jury handed out an arbitrary verdict. The judge is known for handing tough sentences out to juvenile offenders.*

hand over

1. To give something to someone: *Hand over all your money! I handed my keys over to the valet.*
2. To release or relinquish authority or responsibility to someone or something: *The president handed over power to the militants. The king handed the throne over to his successor.*
3. To pass someone into the authority of another: *The sheriff handed over the suspects to the FBI. The state police handed the escaped prisoner over to the federal authorities.*

◆ **hang** (hăng)

hung (hŭng) *or (execution sense only)* **hanged** (hăngd), **hanging** (hăng′ĭng), **hangs** (hăngz)

hang back

1. To keep a distance behind others; lag: *Everyone surged forward, but I hung back, afraid I'd be crushed. I hung back behind the popular kids as I walked through the hall.*
2. To delay or hesitate on some task; hold off: *You should hang back on filling out college applications until you get better test scores.*

hang in

To persevere: *The politician decided to hang in the campaign despite the negative comments in the press.*

ă	pat	är	car	ī	bite	ô	paw	o͝o	took	ûr	urge
ā	pay	ĕ	pet	îr	pier	ôr	core	o͝or	lure	zh	vision
âr	care	ē	be	ŏ	pot	oi	boy	o͞o	boot	ə	about, item
ä	father	ĭ	pit	ō	toe	ou	out	ŭ	cut		

hang off

1. To be suspended from something: *The ornaments hang off the chandelier.*
2. To hesitate or remain behind: *Hang off on that decision until the boss gets back.*

hang on

1. To affix or mount something to some place or fixture that holds it and prevents it from falling: *Please hang your hats on the hooks of the coat rack. I hung the picture on the wall.*
2. To cling tightly to something: *The cat hung on to the draperies until I was able to get it down.*
3. To wait for a short period of time: *Hang on, would you? I'll be there in a moment.*
4. To continue persistently; persevere: *The family is hanging on despite financial problems.*
5. To depend on something or someone for an outcome: *My whole future could hang on the results of this test.*
6. To blame something on someone, especially unfairly: *We lost the game, but you can't hang that on me.*

hang out

1. To suspend something outdoors or in an exposed way: *The maid hung the clothes out to dry. We hung the socks out on the clothesline. My shirttails were hanging out when I got there.*
2. To spend time with someone or at some place: *My friends and I hung out at the mall.*

hang together

1. To stand united; stick together: *Our band has managed to hang together for five years.*
2. To constitute a coherent totality: *The play had several plot lines that did not hang together.*
3. To spend time together: *My friends and I like to hang together at the mall.*

hang up

1. To suspend something on a hook or hanger: *Please hang your jacket up in the closet. I hung up my bathrobe on the hook.*
2. To replace a telephone receiver on its base or cradle: *I hung up the phone and returned to my chores. Will you hang that phone up and get back to your homework?*
3. To end a telephone conversation: *I said goodbye to my mother and hung up.*
4. To delay or impede something; hinder something: *Budget problems hung up the project for months. Squabbling hung the contract talks up for weeks.*
5. To become snagged or hindered: *The fishing line hung up on a rock.*
6. To stop doing or participating in some activity: *They are planning to hang up their law practice after 40 years. Trying to find your keys in the snow is a lost cause—you might as well hang it up.*
7. SLANG To have emotional difficulties or inhibitions. Used passively: *If you weren't so hung up about your job, you'd be more fun to be around.*
8. SLANG To be obsessed or consumed with something. Used passively:

I'm still hung up on that sale I missed last week.

◆ **happen** (hăp′ən)

happened (hăp′ənd), **happening** (hăp′ə-nĭng), **happens** (hăp′ənz)

happen on *or* **happen upon**

To find or meet someone or something accidentally: *She happened on a $10 bill that lay on the sidewalk. The detective happened upon a clue while searching the cabin.*

◆ **harp** (härp)

harped (härpt), **harping** (här′pĭng), **harps** (härps)

harp on

To talk about something to an excessive and tedious degree; dwell on something: *Every day my teacher harps on the importance of getting to class on time.*

◆ **haul** (hôl)

hauled (hôld), **hauling** (hô′lĭng), **hauls** (hôlz)

haul off

SLANG

1. To carry someone or something away to some place, especially by force: *The police hauled the troublemaker off to jail. The troops hauled off the spy for questioning.*
2. To draw back slightly, as in preparation for initiating an action: *The tormented child hauled off and slugged the bully.*
3. To do something impulsively: *I hauled off and bought a new car last weekend.*
4. To shift operations to a new place; move away: *The company said goodbye to Buffalo and hauled off to Phoenix.*

haul up

1. To pull or hoist something up from below: *The workers hauled the crates up with a pulley. The mail carrier hauled up the mailbag to the second floor.*
2. SLANG To come to a halt: *We hauled up at their front door.*
3. SLANG To force someone to appear in a court of law or before some other authority: *The prosecutor hauled up the CEO on charges of fraud. They hauled her up on charges that would be difficult to prove. He was hauled up on a larceny charge.*

◆ **have** (hăv)

had (hăd), **having** (hăv′ĭng), **has** (hăz)

have at

To engage something in a vigorous, enthusiastic, or aggressive way: *Here's the work you need to do, so have at it! The dog really had at the bones that were left in the garbage. The teacher took me aside and had at me for my bad behavior.*

ă	pat	är	car	ī	bite	ô	paw	o͝o	took	ûr	urge
ā	pay	ĕ	pet	îr	pier	ôr	core	o͝or	lure	zh	vision
âr	care	ē	be	ŏ	pot	oi	boy	o͞o	boot	ə	about,
ä	father	ĭ	pit	ō	toe	ou	out	ŭ	cut		item

have on

1. To be wearing something: *The dancers had on red shoes. The snowman had a scarf on.*
2. To carry something on one's person: *Do you have a toothpick on you?*
3. To have something scheduled: *We have a dinner party on for Friday. Do you have anything on for next weekend?*
4. To possess information, usually damaging, about someone or something: *Don't worry—the investigators have nothing on you. Anything they have on us won't hold up in court.*
5. To tease or mislead by suggesting something is true: *Did you really have dinner with the president, or are you just having me on?*

◆ **head** (hĕd)

headed (hĕd′ĭd), **heading** (hĕd′ĭng), **heads** (hĕdz)

head for

1. To travel toward some destination: *We headed for Houston.*
2. To set something or someone on a course toward some destination, situation, or condition. Used passively: *This bus is headed for New York. You're headed for trouble if you keep telling such lies.*

head off

1. To depart for some destination: *She's heading off to New York City next week. He headed off for the mountains for his annual vacation.*
2. To intercept or divert someone or something: *Try to head them off before they get home. The sheriff headed off the gangsters at the pass.*
3. To block the progress or completion of something: *The town headed off the attempt to build another mall. The city council wanted to pass a restrictive zoning ordinance, but the mayor headed them off.*

head out

1. To depart for some destination: *I'm heading out to the store, do you want anything?*
2. To aim or point something outward: *The teenager headed the car out of the driveway and sped off.*

◆ **heap** (hēp)

heaped (hēpt), **heaping** (hē′pĭng), **heaps** (hēps)

heap up

1. To pile something up: *I heaped up the dirty clothes in the corner of my room. The floodwaters heaped debris up onto the beach.*
2. To accumulate: *Garbage heaped up in the streets.*

◆ **hear** (hîr)

heard (hûrd), **hearing** (hîr′ĭng), **hears** (hîrz)

hear from

1. To get some information or communication from someone: *The jury heard the testimony from the witness.*
2. To be contacted by someone: *I heard from your cousin in Tampa yesterday.*
3. To be reprimanded by someone: *If you don't do your homework, you're going to hear from me.*

hear of

1. To know of the existence of someone or something: *Have you ever heard of this basketball player?*
2. To receive news about something or someone: *This is the first I've heard of your decision. She was last heard of somewhere abroad.*
3. To consider, permit, or consent to something. Used only in the negative: *I won't hear of your going!*

hear out

To listen to someone without interrupting: *Hear me out, I have something important to say. I heard the mediator out, but I didn't agree.*

◆ **heat** (hēt)

heated (hē′tĭd), **heating** (hē′tĭng), **heats** (hēts)

heat up

1. To become hotter: *As stars heat up, they expend more energy.*
2. To cause something to become hotter: *He heated the water up on the stove. She heated up the pizza in the microwave.*
3. To become acute or intense: *The baseball game heated up in the last inning.*
4. SLANG To make someone angry: *That incompetent umpire really heated me up. The newscaster's outlandish comments heated up the audience.*

◆ **heave** (hēv)

heaved (hēvd) [*or, in nautical sense* **hove** (hōv)], **heaving** (hē′vĭng), **heaves** (hēvz)

heave to

To steer a sailing ship directly into the wind so that it stops sailing, especially in order to face a storm or to make repairs: *We hove to so that we could change the torn sail.*

heave up

1. To raise or lift something up, especially with great effort or force: *The campers heaved up the flag. The tow truck heaved our car up.*
2. To vomit: *I heaved up my dinner. The turbulent waves caused the people on the ship to heave their lunch up.*

◆ **help** (hĕlp)

helped (hĕlpt), **helping** (hĕl′pĭng), **helps** (hĕlps)

help out

1. To assist someone in doing some work or activity: *Our children always help us out with the chores. You can help out the neighbors by raking their leaves. This place is a mess—come help out.*
2. To aid someone by providing something: *We helped out my relatives by lending them money after the fire. When my neighbors needed a ladder to fix the roof, I helped them out. After the disaster, we helped out by donating money.*

ă	pat	är	car	ī	bite	ô	paw	o͝o	took	ûr	urge
ā	pay	ĕ	pet	îr	pier	ôr	core	o͝or	lure	zh	vision
âr	care	ē	be	ŏ	pot	oi	boy	o͞o	boot	ə	about, item
ä	father	ĭ	pit	ō	toe	ou	out	ŭ	cut		

3. To assist someone emerging from something or some place: *An assistant helped the injured man out of the car.*

◆ **hem** (hĕm)

hemmed (hĕmd), **hemming** (hĕm′ĭng), **hems** (hĕmz)

hem in

1. To surround and enclose someone or something: *Tall mountains hemmed in the valley. The troops hemmed their enemy in on all sides.*
2. To restrict or confine someone or something: *Don't hem me in with all these regulations. The police hemmed in the rowdy crowd.*

◆ **hew** (hyo͞o)

hewed (hyo͞od), **hewn** ((hyo͞on)) *or* **hewed** (hyo͞od), **hewing** (hyo͞o′ĭng), **hews** (hyo͞oz)

hew to

To conform to some law, set of beliefs, or course of action: *I hope our children will hew to the traditions of our ancestors.*

◆ **hide** (hīd)

hid (hĭd), **hidden** (hĭd′n), **hiding** (hī′dĭng), **hides** (hīdz)

hide away

1. To put something in a place that is concealed or out of sight: *The squirrel hides away nuts underground. I hid the money away in my sock drawer.*
2. To seek refuge in a secret place: *The refugees hid away in a cave.*

hide out

To seek refuge in a secret place, especially to evade a pursuer: *The gangsters hid out in a remote cabin until it was safe to return to the city.*

◆ **hike** (hīk)

hiked (hīkt), **hiking** (hī′kĭng), **hikes** (hīks)

hike up

1. To pull up or raise something with a sudden motion, especially a piece of clothing: *He hiked up his pants when we crossed the stream. She hiked her skirt up so it wouldn't get wet.*
2. To raise or increase something in amount, especially abruptly: *Vendors hiked up prices at the end of summer. The contractor hiked up the estimate of the amount of days needed to build the garage.*

◆ **hinge** (hĭnj)

hinged (hĭnjd), **hinging** (hĭn′jĭng), **hinges** (hĭn′jĭz)

hinge on *or* **hinge upon**

To depend on something or someone. Used of facts, events, and situations: *The success of this play hinges on three weeks of rehearsal. Whether or not we reach our fundraising goal hinges upon our volunteers.*

◆ **hire** (hīr)

hired (hīrd), **hiring** (hīr′ĭng), **hires** (hīrz)

hire out

To grant the services of someone or the temporary use of something for a fee: *The agency hires out temporary workers to local businesses. We hired out the cottage for the summer. My friends hired themselves out as cooks.*

◆ **hit** (hĭt)

hit (hĭt), **hitting** (hĭt′ĭng), **hits** (hĭts)

hit on

1. To strike someone or something in some particular area: *A branch fell off the tree and hit me on the back.*
2. To discover something: *We finally hit on a solution to our financial problems.*
3. Slang To pay unsolicited and usually unwanted sexual attention to someone: *I can't believe that the bartender hit on me!*

hit up

Slang

1. To ask someone for something, especially for money: *My friend tried to hit me up for a loan. I hit up my roommate for some extra cash.*
2. To pay a casual visit to some place: *I plan to hit up a few clubs while I'm in the city.*

◆ **hitch** (hĭch)

hitched (hĭcht), **hitching** (hĭch′ĭng), **hitches** (hĭch′ĭz)

hitch up

1. To pull up something, especially an item of clothing: *I keep hitching up my pants because I forgot to wear a belt today. The pioneers hitched their pantlegs up and crossed the creek.*
2. To attach something or someone to something or someone else with a hitch: *I hitched up the trailer to the car. They hitched the horses up to the wagon.*
3. Slang To marry: *They hitched up last month in Las Vegas.*

◆ **hive** (hīv)

hived (hīvd), **hiving** (hī′vĭng), **hives** (hīvz)

hive off

To set something apart from a group: *The CEO hived off the department into another division. The police academy hived the new recruits off during orientation.*

◆ **hog** (hôg)

hogged (hôgd), **hogging** (hô′gĭng), **hogs** (hôgz)

hog out

Slang

To eat something greedily, ravenously, or voraciously; gorge: *At the picnic we hogged out on hot dogs and fries.*

◆ **hold** (hōld)

held (hĕld), **holding** (hōl′dĭng), **holds** (hōldz)

hold against

1. To place someone on or next to some other thing: *I held the picture against the wall.*
2. To have ill feelings toward someone because of something: *I still hold their unkind insults against them.*

ă	pat	är	car	ī	bite	ô	paw	ŏŏ	took	ûr	urge
ā	pay	ĕ	pet	îr	pier	ôr	core	ŏŏr	lure	zh	vision
âr	care	ē	be	ŏ	pot	oi	boy	ōō	boot	ə	about,
ä	father	ĭ	pit	ō	toe	ou	out	ŭ	cut		item

They arrived late and the supervisor held it against them for months.

hold back

1. To restrain someone or something: *The principal held back the bully. We held the dog back when the guests arrived.*
2. To retain something in one's possession or control: *The witness held back valuable information. I held my tears back when I heard the bad news.*
3. To impede the progress of someone or something: *Your interference is holding me back from completing the job. The manager's incompetence held back the staff from meeting their sales quota.*

hold down

1. To push down on something to prevent it from moving or shifting: *Hold down the rug while we move the furniture. I held the clothes down so the suitcase would close.*
2. To prevent someone or something from advancing: *Once that team gets going, you can't hold them down. Don't hold down everyone else just because you're tired.*
3. To limit the amount or level of something: *Please hold the noise down. Hold down the music.*
4. To keep a job for an extended period of time: *My cousin can't seem to hold down a job for more than a few months. If I could hold a job down, I wouldn't be broke.*
5. To digest food successfully: *I'm so sick, I haven't been able to hold down anything. If you eat slowly, maybe you can hold your food down.*

hold forth

To talk at great length: *The professor held forth on the subject of classical literature for an hour.*

hold off

1. To keep someone or something at a distance; resist someone or something: *The firm's attorney held the creditors off. We held off the reporters as long as we could.*
2. To stop or delay doing something: *Let's hold off until we have more data. I held off buying a house until I had a down payment.*

hold on

1. To maintain a grip on something; cling to something: *I held on to the ledge until someone could pull me to safety. You should hold on to the railing when you walk down the stairs.*
2. To persist or persevere: *Our organization has managed to hold on through some hard times.*
3. To wait for a short time: *Hold on; I'll be with you in a moment. The operator asked me to hold on while processing my request.*

hold out

1. To present or proffer something as being attainable: *I held a carrot out for the rabbit. The valet held out the keys for us.*
2. To continue to be in supply or service; last: *Our food held out during the blizzard.*
3. To continue to resist: *The defending garrison held out for a month.*
4. To refuse to reach or satisfy an agreement: *The union held out for three months without signing the contract.*

hold over

1. To wield something above someone or something: *Hold the flashlight over my head.*
2. To postpone or delay something: *We held the election over until after vacation. The trip was held over because of the rain.*
3. To continue a term of office past the usual length of time. Used chiefly in the passive: *The acting governor's term was held over until a successor was elected.*
4. To prolong the engagement of something: *This show is so popular that they held it over an extra day. The film was held over for weeks.*
5. To control someone by threatening to make use of or reveal damaging information: *He had no choice but to cooperate with the builders, since they held the legal contract over him. Now that they know my secret, they have something to hold over me.*

hold to

1. To place something close to something else: *He held a finger to his lips.*
2. To expect someone to adhere to some agreement or promise: *I'll hold you to your word.*
3. To remain loyal or faithful to something: *She held to her resolutions.*

hold together

1. To keep something from falling apart: *The paper clip held together the memos. The rubber band held the manuscript together.*
2. To remain functional and whole: *I'm surprised that old car is still holding together so well. I hope this computer holds together until I can afford a new one. My family has managed to hold together through some tough times.*
3. To maintain one's composure. Used reflexively: *Hold yourself together. He held himself together after the accident.*
4. To be logically sound: *Your explanation doesn't really hold together.*

hold up

1. To raise something or someone in the air: *I held the baby up over my head. The police officer held up the stop sign so drivers could see it.*
2. To support something or someone in an upright position: *The nurse held the patient up as they walked to the bathroom. The coach held up the injured athlete.*
3. To maintain or adhere to some part of an arrangement or agreement: *You need to hold up your part of the deal, or your partners will lose trust in you. We intend to hold our end of the bargain up.*
4. To obstruct or delay something or someone: *The bad weather is holding flights up. The traffic jam held up thousands of commuters.*
5. To rob someone or some place while armed, often at gunpoint: *The armed robbers held the con-*

ă	pat	är	car	ī	bite	ô	paw	o͝o	took	ûr	urge
ā	pay	ĕ	pet	îr	pier	ôr	core	o͝or	lure	zh	vision
âr	care	ē	be	ŏ	pot	oi	boy	o͞o	boot	ə	about,
ä	father	ĭ	pit	ō	toe	ou	out	ŭ	cut		item

venience store up. The gangsters held up the bank.

6. To offer or present something as an example: *The professor held the essay up as a model for the students. The company president held up his record as one that couldn't be surpassed.*
7. To continue to function without losing force or effectiveness; cope: *The company held up under financial stress. How are you holding up?*
8. **hold up to** To withstand the force of something: *The dye in my sweater can't hold up to the strong chemicals in the detergent.*
9. **hold up to** To withstand comparison with something: *Although I practice every day, my singing can't hold up to your beautiful voice.*

hold with

To support or agree with something. Used chiefly in the negative: *I don't hold with your theories, because you don't have enough evidence to support them.*

◆ **hole** (hōl)

holed (hōld), **holing** (hōl′ĭng), **holes** (hōlz)

hole up

1. To hibernate in or as if in a hole: *The weather outside was cold, so the rabbits holed up in their warren.*
2. To take refuge in or as if in a hideout: *The thieves holed up in a remote cabin until the police stopped looking for them.*

◆ **home** (hōm)

homed (hōmd), **homing** (hōm′ĭng), **homes** (hōmz)

home in

1. To move or advance toward a target or goal: *The missile first homed in, then hit its target. The investigators were homing in on the truth.*
2. To direct one's attention; focus: *Our closing argument should home in on the evidence found.*

◆ **hone** (hōn)

honed (hōnd), **honing** (hōn′ĭng), **hones** (hōnz)

hone in

1. To advance toward some target, goal, or desired state: *The police are honing in on the location of the gang. We don't have the answer yet, but by working together we're definitely honing in.*
2. To direct one's attention; focus: *The lawyer honed in on the discrepancies in my testimony.*

◆ **hook** (ho͝ok)

hooked (ho͝okt), **hooking** (ho͝ok′ĭng), **hooks** (ho͝oks)

hook up

1. To connect or attach something to something else: *We'll hook up these shelves to that wall. The plumber hooked the pipes up to the shower.*
2. To assemble or wire up some mechanism: *Could you help me hook up my stereo? Someone from the cable company stopped by to hook the television up.*
3. To meet or associate with someone: *We agreed to hook up after class. He hooked up with the wrong crowd.*

4. SLANG To get married: *We finally hooked up after five years of living together.*
5. SLANG To become romantically involved with someone: *I joined the dating service to try to hook up with someone.*
6. VULGAR SLANG To become sexually involved with someone.

◆ **hop** (hŏp)

hopped (hŏpt), **hopping** (hŏp′ĭng), **hops** (hŏps)

hop up

SLANG

To stimulate someone with or as if with a drug. Used chiefly in the passive: *The drug addicts were hopped up on cocaine.*

◆ **horn** (hôrn)

horned (hôrnd), **horning** (hôr′nĭng), **horns** (hôrnz)

horn in

To join without being invited; intrude: *The new supervisor horned in on the discussion. We were talking privately when a coworker came over and horned in.*

◆ **horse** (hôrs)

horsed (hôrst), **horsing** (hôr′sĭng), **horses** (hôr′sĭz)

horse around

SLANG

To engage in frivolous or idle activity; goof off: *Stop horsing around and get to work! The kids horsed around in the park all day.*

◆ **huddle** (hŭd′l)

huddled (hŭd′ld), **huddling** (hŭd′l-ĭng), **huddles** (hŭd′lz)

huddle up

1. To move close together to form a tightly packed group: *The football team huddled up to discuss the next play.*
2. To cause a group to come together in a tightly packed crowd: *I huddled the children up in a group in the museum lobby. The police huddled up the protesters and led them into the van.*
3. To assume a position with the limbs drawn up close to the body: *The lost hiker huddled up under a shelter made of branches and leaves.*

◆ **hunker** (hŭng′kər)

hunkered (hŭng′kərd), **hunkering** (hŭng′kə-rĭng), **hunkers** (hŭng′kərz)

hunker down

1. To sit on the heels with the knees bent forward; squat: *My personal trainer hunkered down to help me with the barbells.*
2. To take shelter or refuge: *The campers hunkered down in the cabin during the blizzard.*
3. To hold stubbornly to some position: *The candidates hunkered down and refused to admit their mistakes.*

ă	pat	är	car	ī	bite	ô	paw	o͝o	took	ûr	urge
ā	pay	ĕ	pet	îr	pier	ôr	core	o͝or	lure	zh	vision
âr	care	ē	be	ŏ	pot	oi	boy	o͞o	boot	ə	about,
ä	father	ĭ	pit	ō	toe	ou	out	ŭ	cut		item

4. To apply oneself and start working seriously at something: *You need to hunker down and study if you're going to pass that test.*

◆ **hunt** (hŭnt)

hunted (hŭn′tĭd), **hunting** (hŭn′tĭng), **hunts** (hŭnts)

hunt down

1. To pursue, track, or search for something or someone: *The panther hunted down the deer. The police hunted the kidnappers down.*
2. To find something or someone after a long or difficult search: *I hunted down my watch—it was at the bottom of my sock drawer. After two weeks, the detectives finally hunted the suspect down.*

◆ **hurry** (hûr′ē)

hurried (hûr′ēd), **hurrying** (hûr′ē-ĭng), **hurries** (hûr′ēz)

hurry up

1. To move more quickly: *Hurry up or you'll miss the bus! I hurried up and finished the test.*
2. To make someone move or something happen more quickly: *The coach hurried up the team. The babysitter hurried the children up and took them to school.*

◆ **hush** (hŭsh)

hushed (hŭsht), **hushing** (hŭsh′ĭng), **hushes** (hŭsh′ĭz)

hush up

1. To stop talking; become quiet: *The crowd hushed up as the speaker approached the podium. Hush up—you'll wake the baby!*
2. To make someone stop talking or become quiet: *The guards hushed up the prisoners. Please hush the kids up—I've got a headache.*
3. To prevent something from being talked about; keep something from public knowledge: *The government acted quickly to hush up the scandal. The editor hushed the news story up.*

◆ **hype** (hīp)

hyped (hīpt), **hyping** (hī′pĭng), **hypes** (hīps)

hype up

1. To publicize or promote something or someone, especially by extravagant, inflated, or misleading claims: *The publicist hyped up the new movie. The marketers hyped the new clothing line up.*
2. To stimulate or excite someone: *The news that I got the job hyped me up. The warm-up act hyped up the crowd before the big comedian came onstage.*

I

◆ **ice** (īs)

iced (īst), **icing** (ī′sĭng), **ices** (ī′sĭz)

ice down

1. To cool something or keep something cold with ice: *I iced down a bottle of champagne. Ice the fish down until it's time to cook it.*
2. To soothe something, especially a sore or injured muscle, by applying ice: *The coach iced down the player's injury. Ice your sore muscles down; you'll feel better.*

ice out

SLANG

To cover or decorate something with diamonds: *The medallion was completely iced out. The performers went to the jewelry store and iced out their wrists.*

ice up

1. To become covered with ice: *The road has iced up, so be careful.*
2. To cause something to become covered with ice: *The storm has iced up the bridges. The cold weather iced the pond up, so we decided to go skating.*

◆ **identify** (ī-dĕn′tə-fī′)

identified (ī-dĕn′tə-fīd′), **identifying** (ī-dĕn′tə-fī′ĭng), **identifies** (ī-dĕn′tə-fīz′)

identify with

1. To associate or affiliate someone or something with someone or something else: *The villagers did not trust us because they identified us with the foreigners who had looted their village years ago.*
2. To understand or share the feelings of someone: *I identify with children who have lost their parents because I am an orphan myself.*

◆ **idle** (īd′l)

idled (īd′ld), **idling** (īd′l-ĭng), **idles** (īd′lz)

idle away

To spend some period of time not working or avoiding work: *I idled the day away. The children idled away the summer.*

◆ **immerse** (ĭ-mûrs′)

immersed (ĭ-mûrst′), **immersing** (ĭ-mûr′sĭng), **immerses** (ĭ-mûr′sĭz)

immerse in

1. To submerge someone or something in some liquid: *The cook immersed the dishes in hot water.*
2. To involve someone completely in something: *The teacher immersed the students in every aspect of mathematics. I immersed myself in the family business.*

ă	pat	är	car	ī	bite	ô	paw	o͝o	took	ûr	urge
ā	pay	ĕ	pet	îr	pier	ôr	core	o͝or	lure	zh	vision
âr	care	ē	be	ŏ	pot	oi	boy	o͞o	boot	ə	about,
ä	father	ĭ	pit	ō	toe	ou	out	ŭ	cut		item

◆ **impact** (ĭm-păkt′)

impacted (ĭm-păk′tĭd), **impacting** (ĭm-păk′tĭng), **impacts** (ĭm-păkts)

impact on

To have an effect on someone or something: *The results of the election will impact on upcoming legislation.*

◆ **impinge** (ĭm-pĭnj′)

impinged (ĭm-pĭnjd′), **impinging** (ĭm-pĭn′jĭng), **impinges** (ĭm-pĭn′jĭz)

impinge on *or* **impinge upon**

1. To intrude or encroach upon something: *I disagree with this new law because it impinges on my First Amendment rights.*
2. To strike or collide with something: *Sound waves impinge on the eardrum, causing it to vibrate.*

◆ **impose** (ĭm-pōz′)

imposed (ĭm-pōzd′), **imposing** (ĭm-pō′zĭng), **imposes** (ĭm-pō′zĭz)

impose on *or* **impose upon**

1. To make something prevail over someone or something by authority: *The government imposes a tax on cigarettes. The tribunal imposed a sentence upon the defendant.*
2. To force something, such as a set of rules or opinions, on someone: *Don't impose your views on me.*
3. To be an inconvenience to someone by requesting unreasonable favors: *Our guests imposed on us by staying for three weeks.*

◆ **impress** (ĭm-prĕs′)

impressed (ĭm-prĕst′), **impressing** (ĭm-prĕs′ĭng), **impresses** (ĭm-prĕs′ĭz)

impress on *or* **impress upon**

1. To produce something, as a mark or pattern, on a surface by pressure; imprint something on a surface: *We impressed the stencil outline on the fabric.*
2. To impart a strong or vivid impression of something in the mind of someone: *The singing coach impressed her theories of music on me.*

◆ **improve** (ĭm-pro͞ov′)

improved (ĭm-pro͞ovd′), **improving** (ĭm-pro͞o′vĭng), **improves** (ĭm-pro͞ovz′)

improve on *or* **improve upon**

To make beneficial additions or changes to something; make something better: *We can improve on this room by painting it. I improved upon the recipe by adding more spices.*

◆ **inch** (ĭnch)

inched (ĭncht), **inching** (ĭn′chĭng), **inches** (ĭn′chĭz)

inch up

1. To ascend or advance along something by small degrees or steps: *The worm slowly inched up the side of the tree. That book is inching up the bestseller list.*
2. To cause someone or something to ascend, progress, or approach by small degrees or steps: *I inched up the chair to the table. The soldiers inched the flag up the pole.*

◆ **indulge** (ĭn-dŭlj′)

indulged (ĭn-dŭljd′), **indulging** (ĭn-dŭl′jĭng), **indulges** (ĭn-dŭl′jĭz)

indulge in

To engage or take part in something, especially freely, avidly, and for one's own sake or pleasure: *The college students indulged in childish pranks. Those teenagers indulge in all the latest fads.*

◆ **inflict** (ĭn-flĭkt′)

inflicted (ĭn-flĭk′tĭd), **inflicting** (ĭn-flĭk′tĭng), **inflicts** (ĭn-flĭkts′)

inflict on *or* **inflict upon**

To deal or mete out something that punishes or is burdensome; impose something: *The insurgents inflicted heavy losses on the troops. The hurricane inflicted great damage upon the coastal communities.*

◆ **inform** (ĭn-fôrm′)

informed (ĭn-fôrmd′), **informing** (ĭn-fôr′mĭng), **informs** (ĭn-fôrmz′)

inform on *or* **inform against**

To disclose confidential or incriminating evidence about someone to an authority: *The FBI agent informed on the drug dealers. You can't force me to inform against my own family.*

◆ **inquire** (ĭn-kwīr′)

inquired (ĭn-kwīrd′), **inquiring** (ĭn-kwīr′ĭng), **inquires** (ĭn-kwīrz′)

inquire about

To seek information about something or someone: *I went to the store and inquired about available jobs.*

inquire after

To ask about the health or condition of someone: *My neighbor cordially inquired after my mother, who was in the hospital.*

◆ **insist** (ĭn-sĭst′)

insisted (ĭn-sĭs′tĭd), **insisting** (ĭn-sĭs′tĭng), **insists** (ĭn-sĭsts′)

insist on *or* **insist upon**

1. To demand something firmly and persistently: *I insist on peace and quiet when I'm trying to work!*
2. To continue with some behavior or course of action in spite of the disapproval of others: *He insists on tapping his fingers on the desk, even though I've told him to stop.*

◆ **interest** (ĭn′tər-ĭst, ĭn′trĭst′)

interested (ĭn′tər-ĭs-tĭd, ĭn′trĭs′tĭd), **interesting** (ĭn′tər-ĭs-tĭng, ĭn′trĭs′tĭng), **interests** (ĭn′tər-ĭsts, ĭn′trĭsts′)

interest in

To arouse in someone a curiosity about, or a desire for, doing or acquiring something: *The clerk interested the customer in a new refrigerator. I am interested in French literature.*

◆ **interfere** (ĭn′tər-fîr′)

interfered (ĭn′tər-fîrd′), **interfering** (ĭn′tər-fîr′ĭng), **interferes** (ĭn′tər-fîrz′)

interfere with

1. To serve as a hindrance or obstacle to something: *Don't let football*

ă	pat	är	car	ī	bite	ô	paw	o͝o	took	ûr	urge
ā	pay	ĕ	pet	îr	pier	ôr	core	o͝or	lure	zh	vision
âr	care	ē	be	ŏ	pot	oi	boy	o͞o	boot	ə	about,
ä	father	ĭ	pit	ō	toe	ou	out	ŭ	cut		item

practice interfere with your schoolwork.

2. To tamper with something: *Someone interfered with the alarm system, and now it's broken.*

◆ **invest** (ĭn-vĕst′)

invested (ĭn-vĕs′tĭd), **investing** (ĭn-vĕs′tĭng), **invests** (ĭn-vĕsts′)

invest in

1. To commit money or capital to something in order to gain a financial return: *We lost a lot of the money we had invested in the stock market last year. We invested $1,000 in stocks.*
2. To spend money or time on something that will be beneficial in the future: *Since winter is coming up, you might want to invest in a good coat.*
3. To commit oneself to some purpose. Used reflexively: *The teachers invested themselves in improving the school's curriculum.*

invest with

1. To grant someone some power or authority: *The state invests a justice of the peace with the authority to perform marriages. I am invested with the task of fixing the computers.*
2. To attribute to someone or something some enveloping or pervasive quality: *I invested my friend with virtues that turned out to be products of my own imagination.*

◆ **iron** (ī′ərn)

ironed (ī′ərnd), **ironing** (ī′ər-nĭng), **irons** (ī′ərnz)

iron out

1. To remove some unevenness, such as a wrinkle or crease, from cloth by ironing: *He ironed out the wrinkles from the shirt. She ironed the creases out.*
2. To remove some obstacle or difficulty in the process of solving or compromising: *The mediator ironed out the troubles between management and the union. The teacher ironed the kinks out of the overlapping test schedules.*

J

◆ **jabber** (jăb′ər)

jabbered (jăb′ərd), **jabbering** (jăb′ə-rĭng), **jabbers** (jăb′ərz)

jabber away

To talk rapidly, unintelligibly, or idly: *The friends jabbered away for hours.*

◆ **jack** (jăk)

jacked (jăkt), **jacking** (jăk′ĭng), **jacks** (jăks)

jack off

VULGAR SLANG

To masturbate. Used chiefly of males.

jack up

1. To lift something, especially a vehicle, using a jack: *We jacked up the car to change the tire. I hurt my arm when I jacked the van up.*
2. To raise some price or value by increments: *Because of the drought, the stores jacked up the price of lettuce. That candidate is going to jack taxes up after the election.*
3. To stimulate someone with or as if with a drug: *My friend jacked me up on caffeine the night before exams. The coach jacked up the team with a pep talk before the game.*

◆ **jam** (jăm)

jammed (jămd), **jamming** (jăm′ĭng), **jams** (jămz)

jam up

1. To become blocked, congested, or clogged: *The traffic jammed up on the highway.*
2. To cause something to become blocked, congested, or clogged: *Some hair jammed the pipes up. You jammed up the drain with leftover food.*

◆ **jazz** (jăz)

jazzed (jăzd), **jazzing** (jăz′ĭng), **jazzes** (jăz′ĭz)

jazz up

SLANG

To make something or someone appear more interesting; enliven something or someone: *We jazzed up the apartment with beaded curtains. The caterer jazzed the tables up with candles.*

◆ **jerk** (jûrk)

jerked (jûrkt), **jerking** (jûr′kĭng), **jerks** (jûrks)

jerk around

1. SLANG To waste time: *They jerked around for hours instead of doing their homework.*

ă	pat	är	car	ī	bite	ô	paw	o͝o	took	ûr	urge
ā	pay	ĕ	pet	îr	pier	ôr	core	o͝or	lure	zh	vision
âr	care	ē	be	ŏ	pot	oi	boy	o͞o	boot	ə	about,
ä	father	ĭ	pit	ō	toe	ou	out	ŭ	cut		item

2. Slang To take unfair advantage of someone, especially by deception or manipulation: *Don't jerk me around; tell me what's going on. The con artist jerked around the unsuspecting tourists at the carnival.*

jerk off
Vulgar Slang

To masturbate. Used chiefly of males.

◆ **jet** (jĕt)
jetted (jĕt′ĭd), **jetting** (jĕt′ĭng), **jets** (jĕts)

jet off

To depart and travel by airplane: *They jetted off to Los Angeles for the weekend.*

◆ **jibe** (jīb)
jibed (jībd), **jibing** (jī′bĭng), **jibes** (jībz)

jibe with

To be in accord with something; agree with something: *My calculations jibe with the ones that the accountant made.*

◆ **join** (join)
joined (joind), **joining** (join′ĭng), **joins** (joinz)

join in

To take part in something; participate in something: *The tenors started singing, and then the sopranos joined in. The adults joined in the celebration.*

join up

1. To become a member of some group or organization: *After the recruiter's speech, I decided to join up.*
2. To collaborate or team up with someone: *The advertising firm joined up with the baseball team to promote the new manager.*
3. To connect together: *The points join up to form a straight line.*
4. To connect something with some other thing: *Join up the dots, and you'll see a picture. When we join these pieces up, the puzzle will be completed.*

◆ **joke** (jōk)
joked (jōkt), **joking** (jō′kĭng), **jokes** (jōks)

joke around

1. To act amusingly and without seriousness: *We didn't mean to appear rude—we were just joking around.*
2. To fool someone lightheartedly: *I was just joking around with you when I said that I cut my hair.*

◆ **jot** (jŏt)
jotted (jŏt′ĭd), **jotting** (jŏt′ĭng), **jots** (jŏts)

jot down

To write down something briefly or hastily: *The secretary jotted the message down. I jotted down the homework assignment.*

◆ **juice** (jo͞os)
juiced (jo͞ost), **juicing** (jo͞o′sĭng), **juices** (jo͞o′sĭz)

juice up
Slang

1. To make something more interesting or lively: *The writers juiced up*

the plot line. The comedian juiced his act up.

2. To make something more powerful: *I juiced up the punch with more rum. We need to juice the engine up with a tune-up.*
3. To drink to the point of intoxication: *The clients juiced up at the bar after the conference.*
4. To become drunk. Used in the passive: *He got juiced up on cheap wine last night.*

◆ **jumble** (jŭm′bəl)

jumbled (jŭm′bəld), **jumbling** (jŭm′bə-lĭng), **jumbles** (jŭm′bəlz)

jumble up

To mix some things up in a random, confused, or disorderly manner: *The toddler jumbled up the puzzle pieces. The cat jumbled the yarn up.*

◆ **jump** (jŭmp)

jumped (jŭmpt), **jumping** (jŭm′pĭng), **jumps** (jŭmps)

jump at

1. To leap or bound toward someone or something: *The security guard jumped at the attacker.*
2. To take advantage of something enthusiastically, as an opportunity; respond quickly to something: *We jumped at the chance to invest in the project.*
3. To make a sudden verbal attack on someone; lash out at someone: *The students jumped at the speaker during the lecture.*

jump in

1. To leap or bound in or into something: *The lake is nice and warm; jump in! Don't jump in the water here; there are rocks below.*
2. To enter something quickly, especially a vehicle: *She jumped in, I hit the gas, and we took off. Jump in the car and let's go.*
3. To join some activity that is already in progress: *I like your project; do you think I could jump in? I jumped in on their card game in the third round.*
4. To interrupt someone or join a conversation suddenly, especially with an uninvited opinion: *I wanted to finish the meeting quickly, but people kept jumping in. My neighbor jumped in with a strong objection at our town meeting.*

jump off

1. To leap or bound off something: *The parachuter jumped off the cliff.*
2. To get started: *The event jumped off at 3:00 this afternoon.*

jump on

1. To leap, bound, or pounce on or onto something: *The kids were jumping on the bed and laughing. Jump on the wagon, and let's go for a ride!*
2. To become involved in something promptly: *The boss handed me the assignment and I jumped on it right away. She jumped on to help us out with the project.*

ă	pat	är	car	ī	bite	ô	paw	o͝o	took	ûr	urge
ā	pay	ĕ	pet	îr	pier	ôr	core	o͝or	lure	zh	vision
âr	care	ē	be	ŏ	pot	oi	boy	o͞o	boot	ə	about,
ä	father	ĭ	pit	ō	toe	ou	out	ŭ	cut		item

3. To attack someone verbally: *The students jumped on the college president after he spoke.*

jump up

1. To leap or bound upward from the ground: *I jumped up to swat the flies above the window.*
2. To stand up suddenly from a sitting, lying, or crouching position: *Everyone jumped up when they heard the gunshot.*
3. To ascend rapidly in some series or hierarchy: *She jumped up the ranks in the organization due to her outstanding performance.*

◆ **jut** (jŭt)

jutted (jŭt′ĭd), **jutting** (jŭt′ĭng), **juts** (jŭts)

jut out

To stick outward; protrude: *The puppet's nose jutted out from its face.*

K

◆ **keel** (kēl)

keeled (kēld), **keeling** (kē′lĭng), **keels** (kēlz)

keel over

1. To fall over; capsize: *The ship keeled over when it hit the iceberg.*
2. To collapse or fall into or as if into a faint: *I keeled over when I heard the bad news.*

◆ **keep** (kēp)

kept (kĕpt), **keeping** (kē′pĭng), **keeps** (kēps)

keep ahead

1. To remain in front of something, especially when moving: *We tried to keep ahead of the truck, but it eventually passed us.*
2. To have completed all or more than is required of some task in order to be prepared to face more work: *I can't keep ahead of all my homework; every day I get more.*

keep at

1. To continue putting effort into something; persevere in something: *The crossword puzzle was difficult, but she kept at it and finally solved it.*
2. To prod or remind someone persistently to do something: *You'll have to keep at me about that yard work.*

keep away

1. To remain at a distance from something, especially something that should be avoided: *You should keep away from fallen electrical wires after storms so that you don't get electrocuted. The dog is in a bad mood, so you should keep away.*
2. To cause someone or something to remain at a distance from something: *Keep your cat away from my dog! Keep the candy away—I'm on a diet.*
3. To refrain from using or doing something, especially something harmful: *The doctor said I should keep away from alcohol.*
4. To cause someone or something to refrain from doing something: *Nothing could keep me away from a quick trip to visit you. I love to ski in the winter, and nothing could keep me away.*

keep back

1. To remain out of the way: *The spectators at the film shoot kept back. Passengers are requested to keep back behind the yellow line.*
2. To cause someone or something to remain out of the way: *The police*

ă	pat	är	car	ī	bite	ô	paw	ŏŏ	took	ûr	urge
ā	pay	ĕ	pet	îr	pier	ôr	core	ŏŏr	lure	zh	vision
âr	care	ē	be	ŏ	pot	oi	boy	ōō	boot	ə	about,
ä	father	ĭ	pit	ō	toe	ou	out	ŭ	cut		item

kept the onlookers back so that the paramedics could do their job. The fine mesh kept back the debris.

3. To fail to advance someone to the next grade or class of school; flunk: *The teacher kept three struggling students back. A tutor helped each student who was kept back.*

keep behind

1. To hold or maintain someone or something to the rear of something else: *I keep my car behind the garage.*
2. To remain to the rear of something: *We didn't want them to see us, so we kept behind the barn when they arrived.*
3. To fail to advance someone to the next grade or class of school; flunk. Usually used in the passive: *After a year of doing poorly in class, the troubled student was kept behind.*

keep down

1. To remain in a lower position: *We heard gunfire overhead, so we kept down for a while.*
2. To cause something to remain in a lower position: *I keep the blinds down in my apartment during the summer. We kept down the shades so no one would see.*
3. To prevent something from growing, accomplishing, or succeeding: *These unfair wages are keeping people like us down. The new policies are keeping down the poor.*
4. To hold something under control or at a reduced level: *Keep your voice down, or you'll wake the baby. Keep down the noise, or you'll have to leave.*
5. To refrain from vomiting something: *Although I was seasick, I managed to keep my food down. The patient kept down the medicine.*

keep from

1. To prevent someone or something from doing something: *The tape is there to keep the pages from falling apart. This constant noise is keeping me from my work.*
2. To refrain from doing something: *I couldn't keep from having a little snack before dinner.*
3. To prevent some information from becoming known by someone or something: *They kept the news of the accident from the newspapers.*

keep in

1. To hold or maintain someone or something inside of something else: *I wish you wouldn't keep the onions in the same drawer as the bread.*
2. To restrain someone or something within some place: *It's raining very hard, so keep the cat in tonight. I couldn't keep in my laughter when I heard the joke.*
3. To provide someone with some information needed to take part in a group activity: *We met with them every week to keep them in on the job that we were doing.*

keep off

1. To remain away from some surface or place: *You should keep off the stairs; they might break.*
2. To hold or maintain something away from some surface or place: *Keep your dogs off my lawn.*
3. To prevent something, especially something that is not wanted, from

staying or accumulating on something: *Try to keep those thoughts off of your mind. I've been exercising every day, but I can't keep the weight off.*

4. To cause something to be non-operational by having it remain switched off: *I always keep the lights off when I look out the window at the stars. Keep off the lights to save electricity.*
5. To refrain from indulging in something unhealthy, such as food or drugs: *I've kept off cigarettes for three years now. Keep off of junk food and you'll lose some weight.*

keep on

1. To hold or maintain something using something else as a support: *I keep the peanut butter on the top shelf.*
2. To hold or maintain the aim or sight of something toward some object or goal: *Keep your eyes on the road when you're driving. I kept my attention on my book, despite the children's screaming.*
3. To continue doing something: *I was getting increasingly tired, but I kept on walking. Keep on working.*
4. To have something remain operational, switched to an on position: *I always keep one light on when I go to bed. The custodian keeps on the heat at night.*
5. To remind someone repeatedly about something: *Why do I always have to keep on you about handing your homework in on time?*

keep out

1. To prevent something or someone from entering a space: *The lid keeps the flies out of the jar. I have a screen door to keep out stray animals.*
2. To remain in an external place: *I respect your privacy; I'll keep out of your room. There are a dangerous animals in that cage, so keep out!*
3. **keep out of** To refrain from interfering with something, especially someone's affairs: *I think they should keep out of our argument. Keep the children out of it.*
4. **keep out of** To prevent someone from interfering with something: *I tried to keep the children out of our family's problems.*

keep to

1. To refrain from venturing away from some place or activity: *Because of the rain, the kids mostly kept to their rooms.*
2. To adhere to some plan; stick with something: *We should ignore these new projects and keep to the original purpose of our organization.*
3. To remain private, unsociable, or uncommunicative. Used reflexively: *The people at the party were not very friendly, so I kept to myself.*

keep up

1. To preserve or sustain something: *We kept up the appearance of friendship even though we were mad at each other. The couple*

ă	pat	är	car	ī	bite	ô	paw	o͝o	took	ûr	urge
ā	pay	ĕ	pet	îr	pier	ôr	core	o͝or	lure	zh	vision
âr	care	ē	be	ŏ	pot	oi	boy	o͞o	boot	ə	about,
ä	father	ĭ	pit	ō	toe	ou	out	ŭ	cut		item

kept appearances up even though they had separated.

2. To maintain something in good condition: *He did a good job of keeping up the property. The community kept up the old church.*
3. To persevere in doing something; carry on doing something: *I asked her to stop yelling, but she kept it up. Keep up the good work!*
4. To continue at a steady level or pace, especially a significant level or pace: *The snow kept up all day.*
5. To maintain a value or level equal to that of something, even as that value or level increases: *The number of new TVs that arrived didn't keep up with the demand. The scarcity of available land keeps up the demand for it.*
6. To match some competitor or perceived competitor: *I kept up with the leader of the race until the very end, and so I came in second place.*
7. To cause someone to remain awake: *The noise from the construction site outside my window kept me up all night.*
8. **keep up on** To remain adequately informed: *He loved to keep up on the gossip by reading the tabloids.*

◆ **key** (kē)

keyed (kēd), **keying** (kē′ĭng), **keys** (kēz)

key in

1. To enter something as data into a computer system or program using a keyboard; input something: *The scientist keyed the statistics in and analyzed the patterns. The researcher keyed in the results of the experiment and printed out a copy.*
2. To become aware of or responsive to someone or something: *If they are going to be good leaders, they need to key in to the needs of the voters. We stated our complaints very clearly, but the manager hasn't keyed in.*
3. To cause someone to become aware of or responsive to someone or something: *We don't know the strategy yet, but you can key us in. The manager keyed in the employees to the new dress code.*

key to

To make something correspond to something else: *I wrote up a teaching guide and keyed it to the materials for each lesson. The worksheets were keyed to the requirements for each course.*

key up

To cause someone to be intense, excited, or nervous: *The coffee has really keyed me up. Thinking about the party tonight has keyed up the kids. The audience was all keyed up, waiting to find out who won the award.*

◆ **kick** (kĭk)

kicked (kĭkt), **kicking** (kĭk′ĭng), **kicks** (kĭks)

kick around

1. To kick something back and forth casually: *The players warmed up by kicking the ball around. The children kicked around a soccer ball on the playground.*
2. To move from place to place casually or occasionally, usually within some region or place: *Those old books have been kicking around the house for years.*

3. To give thought or consideration to something; ponder or discuss something: *We've been kicking around the names that you gave us, but none seems appropriate for the position. Chris and I have kicked the idea around, and we both agree that we should buy a new car.*
4. To hassle or bully someone: *Don't let your colleagues kick you around—stand up for yourself! The seniors and juniors are always kicking around the sophomores and freshmen.*
5. SLANG To continue to be alive or active: *My grandfather is still kicking around at the age of 80.*

kick back

1. To return something by kicking it: *I'll roll the ball to you, and then you can kick it back to me. The goalie kicked back the soccer ball.*
2. To recoil unexpectedly and violently: *Be careful with that power saw—if it kicks back, you could injure yourself badly. Hold the rifle tightly—otherwise it will kick back and bruise your shoulder.*
3. To relax, especially by resting: *I was too tired to work last night, so I just kicked back at home and watched TV.*
4. SLANG To pay someone in return for an illegal favor: *The corrupt official kicked $1,000 back to the politicians who helped him get the grant money. If you can kick back some of your profits, I'll make sure you win that contract.*

kick in

1. To break or smash a hole in something with a kick: *The police kicked in the door. The burglar kicked the windows in to enter the house.*
2. To contribute something, especially money: *The boss kicked in $20 for the office party. I kicked a few bucks in to buy them a gift.*
3. To become operative or take effect: *I got dizzy when the medication kicked in.*

kick off

1. To begin; start: *The party will kick off around 4:00, so we need to leave here at 3:30.*
2. To begin something; cause something to start: *The author kicked off the book tour with a press conference. Our annual film festival starts tomorrow, and we will be kicking it off with a screening of contemporary African films.*
3. To expel someone from some official group: *I was such a bad player that they finally kicked me off the team. I served on the committee for a few months, but they soon kicked me off for not going to the meetings. I got kicked off the swim team for drinking alcohol during the season.*
4. To suddenly disconnect someone from some computer network. Used chiefly in the passive: *I was*

ă	pat	är	car	ī	bite	ô	paw	o͝o	took	ûr	urge
ā	pay	ĕ	pet	îr	pier	ôr	core	o͝or	lure	zh	vision
âr	care	ē	be	ŏ	pot	oi	boy	o͞o	boot	ə	about,
ä	father	ĭ	pit	ō	toe	ou	out	ŭ	cut		item

kicked off the Internet while I was downloading some software.

5. Sports To begin or resume play by kicking a ball: *The home team kicked off at the top of the second half.*

kick out

Slang

To dismiss or expel someone; throw someone out: *If you make too much noise in the movie theater, they'll kick you out. I got kicked out of French class for making fun of the teacher.*

kick over

1. To kick something so that it falls on its side: *Don't put your glass on the carpet—someone might accidentally kick it over. The playful children kicked over the statue, and it shattered into pieces.*
2. To begin to fire or turn. Used of engines: *We gave it one last crank, and the old engine kicked over.*

kick up

1. To increase the amount or force of something by some degree; intensify something by some amount: *We were a little chilly, so I kicked the temperature up three degrees. Kick up the tempo during the chorus of the song.*
2. To increase in amount or force; intensify: *The waves at the beach really kicked up in the afternoon breeze.*
3. To begin to take place spontaneously: *A sandstorm kicked up when we were driving through the desert.*
4. To arouse some activity: *Those troublemakers kick up trouble wherever they go.*
5. To show signs of activity, especially of disorder: *His ulcer has kicked up again.*

◆ **kid** (kĭd)

kidded (kĭd′ĭd), **kidding** (kĭd′ĭng), **kids** (kĭdz)

kid around

1. To act amusingly and without seriousness: *We didn't mean to appear rude; we were just kidding around.*
2. To fool someone lightheartedly: *At first she thought we were serious, but she finally realized we were just kidding around. I was kidding around with my brother, telling him that our parents had won the lottery.*

◆ **kill** (kĭl)

killed (kĭld), **killing** (kĭl′ĭng), **kills** (kĭlz)

kill off

1. To destroy some form of life in such large numbers that none is left: *The poisonous chemicals have killed off the fish that once lived in this pond. The pesticides killed the crops off.*
2. To destroy or eliminate something, especially plans, ideas, or activities: *Your insolent behavior has killed off any desire I might have had to help you. The disinfectant killed the odor off.*

◆ **kiss** (kĭs)

kissed (kĭst), **kissing** (kĭs′ĭng), **kisses** (kĭs′ĭz)

kiss off

Slang

1. To be forced to give something up or regard it as lost: *After being late*

so much, he can kiss off that promotion. The producers can kiss that award off.

2. To leave or disappear from notice: *The athlete got bad press by telling the reporters to kiss off.*

kiss up
SLANG

To praise or flatter someone excessively in order to gain his or her favor: *You'll get the job if you kiss up enough. Stop kissing up to them and tell them what you really think.*

◆ **knit** (nĭt)

knitted (nĭt′ĭd), **knitting** (nĭt′ĭng), **knits** (nĭts)

knit together

1. To join some pieces of material by knitting: *It's easier to knit each part of the sweater separately and then knit them together. After adding the fringe, knit together the two sections of the blanket.*
2. To become fused together. Used of broken bones that are healing: *If the doctor sets the two pieces of bone just right, they should knit together in three weeks.*

knit up

To create something by knitting, especially quickly or easily: *I knitted up some mittens for my grandchildren. I knitted some hats up for the church sale.*

◆ **knock** (nŏk)

knocked (nŏkt), **knocking** (nŏk′ĭng), **knocks** (nŏks)

knock around

1. To be rough or brutal with someone; mistreat someone: *When he got drunk, he would knock me around. They were in a small boat, and the waves really knocked them around.*
2. To wander from place to place in some area: *I spent my summer knocking around Europe.*
3. To discuss or consider something: *We met to knock around some ideas. I'm not sure of this proposal—let's knock it around for a few days.*

knock back

1. To hit someone or something abruptly, repelling it: *With a swing of the racket, she knocked the ball back to her opponent. The blast from the explosion knocked me back into the fence. The post was crooked, so I got a hammer and knocked it back into place.*
2. To drink something, especially an alcoholic drink, quickly or in large amounts: *After he knocked back six beers, we took his car keys away. She knocked the rest of the bottle back and went to bed.*

knock down

1. To bring something or someone to the ground with a blow; topple something or someone: *The strong wind knocked down the power*

lines. The car went through the stop sign and almost knocked me down. We knocked down part of the wall and put in a door.

2. To cause something or someone to fall off or along something: *The raccoons climbed on our roof and knocked some loose bricks down the chimney. I knocked the croquet balls down the lawn.*
3. To disassemble something into parts, as for storage or shipping: *I knocked down the tables and put them back in the closet. The vendors knock their stalls down at the end of the day.*
4. To declare that a lot has been sold at an auction, as by striking a blow with a gavel: *When the highest bid is called three times without an answer, the auctioneer knocks the lot down and the bidding is over. The auctioneer knocked down the lot to the highest bidder.*
5. To reduce the price of something by some amount: *The store has knocked all software down from $25 to just $15. We'll knock down your next purchase an additional 10 percent.*
6. To reduce the level or value of something: *I went to the thermostat and knocked the temperature down a few degrees. The company has knocked down the price of all their old products. For you, we'll knock the price down to $30.*
7. To persuade someone to reduce an asking price: *The owners wanted $100 for the furniture, but I knocked them down to $80. A good bargainer can knock down even the most resistant sellers.*
8. Slang To receive some amount or rate as wages; earn something: *Some bartenders knock down $200 an hour in tips alone.*
9. Slang To intoxicate someone: *Whatever was in that drink really knocked me down last night. A glass of this liquor will knock down even the biggest drinkers.*

knock off

1. To hit something abruptly and dislodge it or remove it from something else: *I accidentally knocked the vase off the shelf as I walked by. Knock off the mud on your shoes before you come in. The low branch knocked my hat off.*
2. Slang To take a break or rest: *Let's knock off for a few minutes and get something to eat.*
3. Slang To stop doing some kind of labor for the day: *We knocked off work at noon and went fishing. Let's knock off early today and go out for a drink.*
4. Slang To complete, accomplish, or dispose of something hastily or easily; finish something quickly or easily: *That author knocks off three books a year. Once we knock the project off, we can eat lunch.*
5. Slang To eliminate something; get rid of something: *The sales person knocked $50 off the price of the stereo. Knock off 12 pounds in just one month with our exclusive diet plan!*
6. Slang To overcome or defeat someone or something: *They knocked off the two best teams in the league. They were the better team, but somehow we knocked them off by almost 20 points.*
7. Slang To kill someone: *The sniper knocked off three of our best sol-*

diers. I was afraid that they would knock me off if I told the police.

8. SLANG To rob some place: *He went to jail for knocking off a bank.*
9. SLANG To copy or imitate something, especially without permission: *He made a career out of knocking off other people's ideas. The new car design really just knocks off last year's model.*

knock out

1. To hit something abruptly and cause it to move beyond a border: *The batter knocked the baseball out of the stadium. I removed the filter and knocked out the dust.*
2. To cause someone to be eliminated from some competition: *An engine malfunction knocked the car out of the race. We knocked out last year's champions in the quarterfinals.*
3. To render someone unconscious: *The thief knocked the guards out before they could call for help. Those sleeping pills could knock out a horse! I banged my head on the car door and knocked myself out.*
4. To defeat someone in boxing with a punch from which he or she cannot recover: *The new champion has knocked out the last three opponents. The boxer knocked the opponent out in the first round.*
5. To render something useless, inoperative, or ineffective: *The storm knocked the phone lines out across the state. High winds knocked out the power to all the homes in the valley.*
6. To exert or exhaust someone thoroughly in order to accomplish something. Used reflexively: *She always knocks herself out to be ready on time. Try to clean the house for the party, but don't knock yourself out.*
7. To produce something in abundance: *The workers knocked out 500 parts in an hour. We used to make the parts by hand, but the machine can knock them out much faster.*
8. SLANG To impress someone greatly: *Your new poems knock me out!*

knock over

1. To hit something abruptly and cause it to topple or fall to its side: *I moved the lamp because every time I walked by it, I knocked it over. Don't knock over the block tower your sister built.*
2. To make a strong and surprising impression on someone, especially a positive impression: *The band's amazing performance knocked me over completely. The candidate's qualifications knocked over the interviewer, who was expecting much less.*

knock together

1. To strike some pair or set of things against each other abruptly: *We didn't have a drum to keep the beat, so I knocked a couple of sticks together. The guide showed*

ă	pat	är	car	ī	bite	ô	paw	ŏŏ	took	ûr	urge
ā	pay	ĕ	pet	îr	pier	ôr	core	ŏŏr	lure	zh	vision
âr	care	ē	be	ŏ	pot	oi	boy	ōō	boot	ə	about,
ä	father	ĭ	pit	ō	toe	ou	out	ŭ	cut		item

us how to start a fire by knocking together certain kinds of rock.

2. To collide, especially repeatedly or glancingly: *The two boats knocked together in the narrow channel.*
3. To make, assemble, or build something quickly or carelessly: *The editor knocked an article together for the front page. I knocked together a makeshift table out of some old lumber.*

knock up

1. VULGAR SLANG To make someone pregnant.
2. CHIEFLY BRITISH To wake up or summon someone, as by knocking at the door: *The hotel clerk knocked me up at 7:00 in the morning.*

◆ **knot** (nŏt)

knotted (nŏt′ĭd), **knotting** (nŏt′ĭng), **knots** (nŏts)

knot up

1. To tangle or tie something in a knot or knots: *The wind knotted my hair up. Don't let the kittens knot up the yarn.*
2. To become tangled or tied in a knot or knots: *My shoelaces knotted up. If you don't comb your hair, it will knot up.*
3. To make something or someone painfully tense, as from illness or grief: *Something I ate has knotted up my stomach. The sad scene at the end of the movie knotted me up. I get all knotted up when I think of the terrible accident.*
4. To equal an opponent's score in some contest: *The home team knotted up the game. The hockey player knotted it up with a last-minute goal. The game was knotted up at 2–2.*

◆ **knuckle** (nŭk′əl)

knuckled (nŭk′əld), **knuckling** (nŭk′lĭng), **knuckles** (nŭk′əlz)

knuckle down

To apply oneself earnestly to a task: *We've been relaxing too long—it's time for us to knuckle down and finish this work.*

knuckle under

To yield to some opposing force: *The union knuckled under to pressure from the company. I've made up my mind on this matter, and I will not knuckle under.*

◆ **kowtow** (kou′tou′)

kowtowed (kou′toud′), **kowtowing** (kou′tou′ĭng), **kowtows** (kou′touz′)

kowtow to

To show someone or something excessive respect and obedience in order to gain or maintain favor: *The peasants had to kowtow to the dictator. The staff kowtowed to every plan their boss proposed.*

L

◆ **lace** (lās)

laced (lāst), **lacing** (lā′sĭng), **laces** (lā′sĭz)

lace into

To attack or assail someone: *The captain laced into me for getting to practice so late.*

lace up

1. To fasten shoes or clothing by tightening and tying laces: *I laced up my skates before my lesson. We laced our hiking boots up before we headed out.*
2. To tighten and tie the laces on someone's shoes or clothing: *Come over here so I can lace you up. The assistant laced up the skater before the beginning of the competition.*

◆ **lack** (lăk)

lacked (lăkt), **lacking** (lăk′ĭng), **lacks** (lăks)

lack for

To be in need of something or someone. Used chiefly in the negative: *She is very popular and does not lack for friends. Because he's rich, he doesn't lack for luxuries.*

◆ **lade** (lād)

laded (lā′dĭd), **laden** (lād′n) *or* **laded** (lā′dĭd), **lading** (lā′dĭng), **lades** (lādz)

lade with

1. To load some vessel or carrier with some cargo. Used chiefly in the passive: *The ship is laden with timber.*
2. To burden someone or something. Used chiefly in the passive: *The thief was laden with guilt.*

◆ **lag** (lăg)

lagged (lăgd), **lagging** (lăg′ĭng), **lags** (lăgz)

lag behind

1. To fail to maintain the pace or progress of someone or something; straggle: *I lagged behind the rest of the hikers and got lost in the forest. Don't forget to do your readings for class, or you'll lag behind.*
2. To proceed or develop with comparative slowness: *Sales are lagging behind this year compared to last year.*

◆ **lance** (lăns)

lanced (lănst), **lancing** (lăn′sĭng), **lances** (lăn′sĭz)

ă	pat	är	car	ī	bite	ô	paw	ŏŏ	took	ûr	urge
ā	pay	ĕ	pet	îr	pier	ôr	core	ŏŏr	lure	zh	vision
âr	care	ē	be	ŏ	pot	oi	boy	ōō	boot	ə	about,
ä	father	ĭ	pit	ō	toe	ou	out	ŭ	cut		item

lance through

1. To pierce through something or someone: *My spear lanced through the fish.*
2. To permeate something or someone thoroughly and sharply: *Pain lanced through the runner's body during the marathon.*

◆ **land** (lănd)

landed (lăn′dĭd), **landing** (lăn′dĭng), **lands** (lăndz)

land in

1. To come down and settle in something after traveling through the air: *The fly landed in my soup.*
2. To arrive in some situation or condition as a result of a course of action: *I landed in court after they fired me.*
3. To cause someone or something to arrive in some situation or condition: *The company's poor fiscal policies landed it in bankruptcy.*

land up

To arrive somewhere, especially when not anticipated: *We got lost and landed up miles from home. An accident shut down the freeway, and I landed up downtown.*

◆ **lap** (lăp)

lapped (lăpt), **lapping** (lăp′ĭng), **laps** (lăps)

lap up

1. To eat or drink something completely by licking: *The kitten lapped up the milk in the saucer. The cat lapped the water up.*
2. To receive something eagerly or greedily: *The author lapped up the audience's praise. The runner lapped the medals up at the banquet.*

◆ **lard** (lärd)

larded (lär′dĭd), **larding** (lär′dĭng), **lards** (lärdz)

lard with

1. To cover or coat something with lard or a similar fatty substance: *The cook larded the rice with pork fat.*
2. To enrich or embellish something thoroughly with extra material: *The performer larded the monologue with boring stories. The report was larded with unnecessary quotations.*

◆ **lash** (lăsh)

lashed (lăsht), **lashing** (lăsh′ĭng), **lashes** (lăsh′ĭz)

lash out

1. To aim a sudden blow; strike: *The horse lashed out with its hind legs.*
2. To make a scathing verbal or written attack on someone or something: *The mayor lashed out at her critics during the interview. The defendant lashed out when asked about his arrest record.*

◆ **last** (lăst)

lasted (lăs′tĭd), **lasting** (lăs′tĭng), **lasts** (lăsts)

last out

1. To endure or survive for some period of time: *The patient is comatose and won't last the night out. The recruit is determined to last out the training.*
2. To continue to be in supply or service for some period of time: *Our water supply is barely going to*

last the week out. I hope these old shoes can last out the month.

◆ **lather** (lă*th*′ər)

lathered (lă*th*′ərd), **lathering** (lă*th*′ə-rĭng), **lathers** (lă*th*′ərz)

lather up

1. To cover some surface with lather or foam: *He lathered up his chin and shaved the stubble. She lathered her hair up with the new shampoo.*
2. To produce or become filled or covered with lather or foam: *This shaving cream lathers up as soon as you put it on your skin.*

◆ **laugh** (lăf, läf)

laughed (lăft, läft), **laughing** (lăf′ĭng, lä′fĭng), **laughs** (lăfs, läfs)

laugh at

1. To laugh in response to something intended to be humorous: *I always laugh at that TV show.*
2. To mock or make fun of someone or something: *They laughed at me when I said I wanted to become an astronaut.*
3. To treat someone or something lightly; scoff at someone or something: *That daredevil laughs at danger.*

laugh off *or* **laugh away**

1. To dismiss something or someone as ridiculous or laughable: *She laughed off the critic's conclusion that the show was a flop. The landlord wanted more money, but I laughed him away.*
2. To force someone to leave some area because of laughter or ridicule: *The audience laughed the singer off the stage. The other team laughed us away from the field.*

◆ **launch** (lônch)

launched (lôncht), **launching** (lôn′chĭng), **launches** (lôn′chĭz)

launch into

To start saying or doing something enthusiastically; plunge into something: *The professor launched into the topic after a brief introduction.*

◆ **lavish** (lăv′ĭsh)

lavished (lăv′ĭsht), **lavishing** (lăv′ĭ-shĭng), **lavishes** (lăv′ĭ-shĭz)

lavish on

To give or bestow something in abundance to someone or something: *The critics lavished praise on the new movie. The pundits lavished scorn on the new mayor.*

lavish with

To enhance or praise something or someone with something: *The teacher lavished the best students with praise. The tables were lavished with decorations.*

◆ **lay** (lā)

laid (lād), **laying** (lā′ĭng), **lays** (lāz)

ă	pat	är	car	ī	bite	ô	paw	o͝o	took	ûr	urge
ā	pay	ĕ	pet	îr	pier	ôr	core	o͝or	lure	zh	vision
âr	care	ē	be	ŏ	pot	oi	boy	o͞o	boot	ə	about,
ä	father	ĭ	pit	ō	toe	ou	out	ŭ	cut		item

lay aside

1. To stop being actively engaged with something: *I will lay aside my reading and go for a walk when I finish this chapter. The lifeguard laid the binoculars aside and jumped in the water.*
2. To abandon something, especially a plan, hope, or desire; give up something: *The marooned sailors had lain aside any hope of being saved. When the loan fell through, they laid their plans of buying a house aside.*
3. To save something for the future: *I lay aside part of my paycheck every week to save for a new car. Let's lay part of your allowance aside to pay for the movies.*

lay away

1. To reserve something for the future; save something: *I'm laying away $500 just in case my car ever breaks down. The bride laid the dishes away for her trousseau.*
2. To have something held for future delivery, especially by paying partly for it beforehand: *I gave the salesman a check for $100, and he laid the carpet away for me. The manager laid away the oven until we could get to the store.*

lay by

To save something for future use: *After she had laid by a good sum of money, the lawyer bought a new condo for use as her office. The mechanic packed up his tools and laid them by for the next project.*

lay down

1. To put something in a horizontal or lying position: *You can lay down the newspaper on the table. Lay the baby down in the crib.*
2. To put down some weapon in order to surrender: *The militants laid down their weapons. The protesters laid their signs down when the mayor came out to speak to them.*
3. To specify something firmly: *The first thing the counselor did was to lay down the rules for the campers. The club owner laid the business policies down for the employees.*

lay for

To be waiting to attack someone: *Muggers were laying for the unsuspecting pedestrian in the dark alley.*

lay in

1. To place something and embed it in a surface: *The roofer laid the new shingles in yesterday. We should lay in the tiles before cleaning them.*
2. To store something for future use: *The northern explorers had to lay in supplies for the Arctic winter. We harvested a lot of potatoes and laid them in for the long winter ahead.*

lay into

1. To embed something by penetrating some surface: *The builders laid the first stones into the ground for a foundation yesterday. The ceremony started when a stake was laid into the soil.*
2. To begin to penetrate or undertake something, especially resolutely: *The ceremony started when the dignitary laid into the soil with a shovel. I sat down and laid into my work right away.*

3. To scold someone sharply: *The sergeant laid into the private for being late.*

4. To attack someone physically; beat someone up: *They punched me on the chin and then really laid into me.*

lay off

1. To terminate someone's employment, especially temporarily; suspend someone from work: *The company had to lay off two dozen workers or it would have gone bankrupt. They had to lay the clerk off for stealing mail.*

2. To mark the boundaries of some region and reserve that region; mark something off: *We laid off the front part of the yard for a garden and left the back for a lawn. We used lime to lay the field off for the game.*

3. To stop using or doing something: *I'm going to have to lay off the cigarettes; they're making me sick.*

4. SLANG To stop bothering someone. Used chiefly as an angry command: *Look, I'm trying to work, so just lay off me, okay?*

lay on

1. To place or spread something on a flat surface: *I laid my notebooks on my desk and sat down to work.*

2. To apply some modification to appearance or behavior: *The concierge laid on a strong French accent to fool us. She laid the charm on pretty thick, but I saw through it.*

3. To prepare something, usually in an elaborate fashion; arrange something: *The caterers laid on cocktails for 50 guests at the last minute.*

4. SLANG To present or reveal something to someone thoroughly or heavily; confront someone with something: *He laid his standard questions on them. The reviewer certainly laid on the criticism, didn't she? I want to know everything that happened, so lay it on me.*

lay out

1. To make something explicit, especially an idea or plan: *Let me lay out my ideas for our next move. The architect laid the plans out for the new building.*

2. To clothe and prepare someone who is dead for burial: *The funeral home laid the body out for visitation. The mortician laid out the body for the family to view.*

3. To rebuke someone harshly: *She laid me out for breaking the vase. The coach laid out the team for its mistakes.*

4. To knock someone to the ground, especially to knock someone unconscious: *She laid him out with an unexpected punch in the gut. The police officer laid out the attacker with a swift kick.*

5. To expend something; spend something: *The rich couple laid out a fortune on jewelry for the*

ă	pat	är	car	ī	bite	ô	paw	o͝o	took	ûr	urge
ā	pay	ĕ	pet	îr	pier	ôr	core	o͝or	lure	zh	vision
âr	care	ē	be	ŏ	pot	oi	boy	o͞o	boot	ə	about,
ä	father	ĭ	pit	ō	toe	ou	out	ŭ	cut		item

wedding. We can't lay that much money out without more information.

6. To put something on display: *It's time to lay out the merchandise for the new season. Every day the jeweler lays the watches out in the display case.*

lay over

To temporarily interrupt or delay someone's journey in order to rest, refuel, do repairs, or change vehicles. Used chiefly in the passive: *Because it was snowing, we were laid over in Albany for four hours.*

lay up

1. To store or stock something for future use: *We must lay up many supplies for our long journey. We bought a bushel of seed and laid half of it up for planting next year.*
2. To confine someone with an illness or injury: *A bad flu can lay you up for two weeks. Yellow fever laid up many of the people who worked on the Panama Canal. I was laid up for a month.*
3. To put some sailing vessel in dock, as for repairs: *We laid up the ship in Anchorage for six months. Let's lay the boat up at the next port.*
4. To dock for repairs: *The sailboat laid up in Charleston to have the rigging fixed.*
5. To hit a golf shot less far than one is able so as to avoid a hazard: *I was afraid of hitting the sand trap, so I laid up a bit.*

◆ **lead** (lēd)

led (lĕd), **leading** (lē′dĭng), **leads** (lēdz)

lead into

1. To guide someone into something or some place: *The guide led the tourists into the cave.*
2. To make a transition into something; segue into something: *The ballad leads into a dance number.*

lead off

1. To cause something to begin or start; inaugurate something: *Do you want me to lead off the discussion with some comments? The secretary led the meeting off with some announcements.*
2. To guide someone or something away: *The counselor led the campers off to their bunks.*
3. BASEBALL To be the first batter in an inning: *The batter who led off in the first inning scored a home run.*

lead on

1. To guide someone forward: *The general led the troops on to battle.*
2. To mislead or deceive someone: *It's not right to lead your date on when you're not really interested. I thought they would buy the house, but they were leading on the realtor.*
3. To keep someone in a state of expectation or hope; entice someone: *That recruiter led me on with promises of employment. The college counselor led on the students with anecdotes of successful applicants.*

lead to

1. To guide someone to something or someone: *Our teacher led the children to the museum. This path leads to the other side of the forest.*

2. To have something as a goal or result: *Exercise leads to better health.*

◆ **leaf** (lēf)

leafed (lēft), **leafing** (lē′fĭng), **leafs** (lēfs)

leaf through

To go through some reading material quickly or superficially, turning from page to page, as in searching or browsing: *On Sunday mornings, I leaf through the newspaper while eating breakfast.*

◆ **leak** (lēk)

leaked (lēkt), **leaking** (lē′kĭng), **leaks** (lēks)

leak out

1. To flow out through some breach or flaw in a container; seep out: *Water leaked out the crack in the pipe. As the air leaked out of the balloon, it got smaller and smaller.*
2. To become known to the public through a breach of secrecy: *We were supposed to keep the date a secret, but it leaked out.*
3. To release secret information to the public through unofficial channels: *A disgruntled worker leaked the scandalous information out to the reporter. Someone leaked out news of the fraudulent business deal to the newspapers.*

◆ **lean** (lēn)

leaned (lēnd), **leaning** (lē′nĭng), **leans** (lēnz)

lean on

1. To rest on or be supported by something: *I leaned on the crutch to rest my injured foot.*
2. To place something so that it rests on or is supported by some other thing: *Don't lean the ladder on the awning—you might damage it.*
3. To rely on someone for assistance or support: *When I became sick, I leaned on my family for support.*
4. SLANG To pressure someone to do something: *The mobsters leaned on the store owner to sell his business.*

◆ **leap** (lēp)

leaped (lēpt) *or* **leapt** (lĕpt), **leaping** (lē′pĭng), **leaps** (lēps)

leap at

1. To spring or bound toward someone or something: *The cat leaped at the mouse.*
2. To accept something eagerly, as an opportunity: *I leaped at the chance to be an intern at the publishing company.*

leap in

1. To spring or bound in or into something: *I couldn't resist leaping in the big pile of raked leaves on the ground. The couch looked so comfortable that we just leapt in.*
2. To join some activity that is already in progress: *I leapt in the game they had been playing. Whenever you feel like joining us, just leap in!*

ă	pat	är	car	ī	bite	ô	paw	ŏŏ	took	ûr	urge
ā	pay	ĕ	pet	îr	pier	ôr	core	ŏŏr	lure	zh	vision
âr	care	ē	be	ŏ	pot	oi	boy	ōō	boot	ə	about,
ä	father	ĭ	pit	ō	toe	ou	out	ŭ	cut		item

leap out

1. To spring or bound outward: *The cat leaped out from behind the bush and pounced on the mouse.*
2. To draw immediate attention; be immediately apparent: *That red lettering really leaps out from the page. If the answers don't leap out at you, you probably didn't study enough.*

◆ **lease** (lēs)
leased (lēst), **leasing** (lē′sĭng), **leases** (lē′sĭz)

lease up

1. To fully lease some building: *The housing agency leased up the new apartment building in record time. After the new building had been on the market for only one week, the real estate agent had leased it up. The retail spaces were leased up before construction even started.*
2. To become fully leased: *The new office building leased up in less than a week.*

◆ **leave** (lēv)
left (lĕft), **leaving** (lē′vĭng), **leaves** (lēvz)

leave behind

1. To depart from some place, especially in order to begin a new stage of a journey: *We left Paris behind and went on to Warsaw.*
2. To abandon, neglect, or forego someone or something: *I can't believe you would leave behind your whole family. We boarded the plane to Tahiti and left all our troubles behind. The teacher was afraid that the younger students were getting left behind.*
3. To have someone or something remaining after one's death: *When she died, she left behind two young children. Many of the soldiers who died in the war left families behind. The actor left behind a legacy when he died.*
4. To depart or disappear, leaving something as a result: *When the glacier receded, it left behind many small lakes.*
5. To surpass someone or something: *This new product will leave the competition behind.*

leave off

1. To fail to include something or someone in something, as a list; omit something or someone: *We left them off the guest list because of their behavior at our last party. You've left off a zero from the end of this number.*
2. To stop doing or using something: *I picked up my book and began reading from where I left off. I left off writing my term paper and watched TV for a while.*
3. To deliver something or someone to a place while underway somewhere else: *I'll leave you off at my parents' house on the way to my house. My car wouldn't start after I left off the kids at school.*

leave on

1. To continue wearing something: *I accidentally left my watch on when I went swimming. There's broken glass on the floor, so leave on your shoes.*
2. To have something remain operational, switched to an on position: *She leaves the radio on all night when she goes to sleep. He left on*

some lights because he knew he'd return after dark.

leave out

1. To allow something or someone to remain outdoors: *I left the dog out last night.*
2. To allow something to remain in plain sight: *Who left the dirty dishes out on the kitchen counter?*
3. To fail to include or mention something; omit something: *We weren't sure if the facts were correct, so we left that section out of the report. You've left out the decimal point on this price tag.*

◆ **lessen** (lĕs′ən)

lessened (lĕs′ənd), **lessening** (lĕs′ə-nĭng), **lessens** (lĕs′ənz)

lessen up

To diminish; abate: *The wind lessened up, and the surf died down.*

◆ **let** (lĕt)

let (lĕt), **letting** (lĕt′ĭng), **lets** (lĕts)

let down

1. To cause to fall to a lower level; lower something: *The tailor let down the hem of my new pants. If you let your hair down, I can braid it. It's time to let down the sails.*
2. To fail to meet the expectations of someone; disappoint someone: *The contractor really let us down when the kitchen wasn't ready in time for Thanksgiving. When the school board had to cancel the sports program, they really let down the community.*
3. To hinder the success or progress of someone or something: *It would have been a good book, but the slow pacing lets it down a bit.*
4. To be released from the breast as breast milk: *She tried to breastfeed her newborn infant, but her milk wouldn't let down.*

let in

1. To allow someone or something to enter some place; admit someone or something: *We don't usually let the cat in the house. I opened a window to let in some fresh air. There was no answer at the door, so I got the key from under the mat and let myself in.*
2. **let in for** To make oneself subject or vulnerable to something: *I didn't know the trouble I was letting myself in for when I accepted that invitation.*
3. **let in on** To tell someone something that has been kept private: *I'll let you in on a secret if you promise not to tell anyone. They won't let me in on their plans.*

let off

1. To allow someone to disembark from a vehicle: *My house is just down the street, but you can let me off at the corner. The bus driver let off the passengers at the terminal.*
2. To excuse or pardon someone from something unpleasant, as punishment or work: *I'm going to let you*

ă	pat	är	car	ī	bite	ô	paw	ŏŏ	took	ûr	urge
ā	pay	ĕ	pet	îr	pier	ôr	core	ŏŏr	lure	zh	vision
âr	care	ē	be	ŏ	pot	oi	boy	ōō	boot	ə	about,
ä	father	ĭ	pit	ō	toe	ou	out	ŭ	cut		item

off this once, but if I catch you cheating again, you're going to be expelled. The police arrested the leader and let off the rest of the gang with only a warning.

3. To emit something, as heat, gas, or sound: *The stove lets off a lot of heat.*
4. To detonate or discharge something: *The police officer let off a warning shot. We let a fire-cracker off in the park.*

let on

To allow something to be known; admit or give away something: *Don't let on that you know the undercover police officer.*

let out

1. To allow someone or something to exit from some place; release someone or something: *My neighbor let out the dog for the night. After the party, we let the helium out of the balloons.*
2. To make some sound: *I let a sigh of relief out when I saw my test score. I let out a shriek when I saw the mouse.*
3. To come to a close; end: *School let out early.*
4. To make something known; reveal something: *Who let that story out? If you let out the secret, our team will lose.*
5. To increase the size of a garment by undoing its seams: *The tailor let out my new coat. The kids grew so much this year that I had to let all the hems out on their jeans.*
6. To rent or lease something to someone: *We decided to let the apartment out for extra income. The neighbors let out the space over the garage to students.*

let up

1. To allow something or someone to go or get up: *Stop wrestling me and let me up!*
2. **let up on** To release or diminish the pressure on someone or something; ease up on something: *Let up on the clutch slowly or you'll stall out the engine. Let up on the new workers; they're doing the best they can.*
3. To slow down; diminish: *The weather got cold, but the protesters didn't let up in their efforts.*
4. To come to a stop; cease: *The rain let up, so we went outside and played.*

◆ **level** (lĕv′əl)

leveled *or* **levelled** (lĕv′əld), **leveling** *or* **levelling** (lĕv′ə-lĭng), **levels** (lĕv′əlz)

level at

To direct something toward someone or something: *The reporter leveled charges of corruption at the committee. The robber leveled the gun at the victim's head.*

level off

1. To come to follow an even, flat path after rising or falling to some level: *The airplane leveled off at 5,000 feet.*
2. To stop changing after rising or falling to some level: *Milk prices leveled off at $2 per gallon.*
3. To make something smooth or flat: *The carpenter used a plane to level off the top of the cabinet. I placed the uneven piece of molding in the vise and leveled it off with a file.*

level up

1. To make something even or equal: *One more goal from the visiting*

team leveled up the score. I used a scraper to level the wet cement up.

2. To advance to the next level. Used especially of role-playing and video games: *The scenarios became more complex and difficult as I leveled up. After solving the first puzzle, my character leveled up to level 2.*

◆ **lick** (lĭk)

licked (lĭkt), **licking** (lĭk′ĭng), **licks** (lĭks)

lick up

To eat or drink something completely by licking: *The kitten licked up the milk. The dog licked the spilled food up.*

◆ **lie** (lī)

lay (lā), **lain** (lān), **lying** (lī′ĭng), **lies** (līz)

lie down

To place the body in a flat, horizontal position; recline: *The dog usually lies down in front of the fireplace. After lunch, I lay down under a tree and fell asleep. I had just lain down when the phone rang.*

lie in

1. To recline or rest in something: *He lies in bed. The book lay in a puddle of mud.*
2. To consist of or have something as a basis: *Our continued success lies in our commitment to service.*

lie with

1. To be decided by, dependent on, or up to someone or something: *Most of the country's wealth still lies with the elite. The fault lies with the negligent parents, not with the children. The prisoner's fate now lies with the governor.*
2. ARCHAIC To have sexual intercourse with someone.

◆ **lift** (lĭft)

lifted (lĭf′tĭd), **lifting** (lĭf′tĭng), **lifts** (lĭfts)

lift off

1. To pick something up from some surface: *I lifted the lid off the pan to let the heat escape. I unfastened the tarp and lifted it off from the tent.*
2. To leave the ground and begin flight: *The spacecraft will lift off at noon.*

◆ **light** (līt)

lighted (lī′tĭd) *or* **lit** (lĭt), **lighting** (lī′tĭng), **lights** (līts)

light into

To attack someone or something verbally or physically; assail someone or something: *The two movie stars lit into the reporters for following them around.*

light out

To leave someplace hastily: *With only 30 minutes to get to the airport, we grabbed our bags and lit out. The robbers lit out of the bank once the alarm went off.*

light up

1. To illuminate or be illuminated: *All the neon signs along the street light up at night.*
2. To cause something to illuminate or be illuminated: *The morning sun lit up the room. The miners lit their headlamps up and descended into the shaft.*
3. To begin to burn: *The gas burners lit up on the first try.*
4. To cause something to burn; ignite something: *I lit up a match and started the fire. I'll get some wood and light a fire up.*
5. To ignite and begin smoking something, especially a cigarette, cigar, or pipe: *I went out to the porch and lit up a cigar. He lit his pipe up with a match. She took a cigarette from the case and lit up.*
6. To become animated or cheerful: *The children's eyes lit up when they saw the size of the cake.*
7. To cause someone or something to become animated or cheerful: *The presence of the movie star lit up the room. He was feeling sad, but the surprise party lit his face up.*

◆ **lighten** (līt′n)
lightened (līt′nd), **lightening** (līt′n-ĭng), **lightens** (līt′nz)

lighten up

1. To make something appear lighter in shade: *The artist lightened up the paint by mixing in some white. Those mirrors really lighten the room up.*
2. To become lighter in shade: *These pants are too dark now, but they will lighten up after they've been washed a lot.*
3. To make something more pleasant and less serious or depressing: *The jokes lightened up the tone of the meeting. I didn't mean to be disrespectful—I was just trying to lighten things up.*
4. To take matters less seriously: *Everything will work out fine, so stop worrying and lighten up.*

◆ **line** (līn)
lined (līnd), **lining** (lī′nĭng), **lines** (līnz)

line up

1. To form a line: *The students lined up at the front of the classroom. People are lining up to get tickets to the game.*
2. To arrange some people or things in a line: *The police lined the suspects up against the wall. We lined up some chairs in front of the stage. Customers were lined up waiting for the stores to open.*
3. To organize something or someone for an event or activity; schedule something or someone: *I've lined two interviews up for next week. The organizers lined up some great speakers for the rally. The senator is lining up support for the bill.*
4. To straighten something, or put it in the correct position in relation to some other thing: *I lined the text up with the edge of the page. The sniper lined up the rifle and fired two shots at the middle of the target. We lined up the holes and put the bolt through.*
5. To be straight or in the correct position in relation to some other thing: *The holes don't line up—I*

can't get the bolt in. Does this painting line up with the ceiling?

6. In American football, to take one's position in a formation before a snap or kickoff: *The players lined up at the scrimmage line.*

◆ **link** (lĭngk)

linked (lĭngkt), **linking** (lĭng′kĭng), **links** (lĭngks)

link up

1. To collaborate or team up: *The two minority parties linked up to oppose the ruling party. Two popular bands have linked up for a nationwide tour.*
2. To introduce someone into a relationship or collaboration with others: *Can you link me up with a good financial adviser? I linked them up last year and now they are partners. The convention links up buyers and sellers.*
3. To join together: *The two trains linked up to form one long train. This road links up with the highway in six miles.*
4. To connect something with some other thing: *We linked the trailer up to the truck. I linked up four extension cords and plugged the vacuum cleaner in. They linked the computers up so that they could share files.*
5. To meet with someone, especially in order to do something: *Let's link up next week and discuss the report. I linked up with my friends after the concert.*

◆ **liquor** (lĭk′ər)

liquored (lĭk′ərd), **liquoring** (lĭk′ə-rĭng), **liquors** (lĭk′ərz)

liquor up

1. To cause or encourage someone to consume alcohol: *They liquored me up and asked me where I hid the money. My boss is at a bar liquoring up some potential investors.*
2. To become drunk. Used in the passive: *I got liquored up on whiskey and started a fight.*
3. To consume alcoholic beverages steadily: *They've been liquoring up in the bar all day.*

◆ **listen** (lĭs′ən)

listened (lĭs′ənd), **listening** (lĭs′ə-nĭng), **listens** (lĭs′ənz)

listen for

To listen attentively to hear some sound; wait expectantly to hear something or someone: *Listen for the doorbell—the pizza should be here soon.*

listen in

1. To listen to something or to someone conversing without participating in the conversation: *It is rude to listen in on other people's conversations. We put our ears to the door and listened in.*
2. To tune in and listen to a broadcast: *Listen in next week to the conclusion of our jazz concert series!*

ă	pat	är	car	ī	bite	ô	paw	o͝o	took	ûr	urge
ā	pay	ĕ	pet	îr	pier	ôr	core	o͝or	lure	zh	vision
âr	care	ē	be	ŏ	pot	oi	boy	o͞o	boot	ə	about, item
ä	father	ĭ	pit	ō	toe	ou	out	ŭ	cut		

listen up

To pay attention closely; be attentive. Used chiefly as a command: *Listen up—I'm only going to tell you this once! I want you to listen up and do what I tell you to do.*

◆ **live** (lĭv)

lived (lĭvd), **living** (lĭv′ĭng), **lives** (lĭvz)

live down

To overcome or reduce some negative feeling about a negative event for which one is known. Used chiefly in the negative: *You'll never live down the embarrassment of losing your bathing suit in the pool. I know you're not proud of your past, but you can't live it down by lying about it.*

live for

To be enthusiastic about something: *He lives for mountain climbing.*

live in

To reside in the place where one is employed: *They were wealthy enough to afford household servants who lived in.*

live off

1. To survive or provide for one's needs by benefiting from someone or something: *I'm living off my savings until I find a job. It's shameful to live off your parents at your age!*
2. To eat some type of food frequently or exclusively: *In the winter, some animals live off collections of food that they gathered during the warmer months.*

live on

1. To survive or provide for one's needs by using some resource: *The retiree had to live on a fixed income. The family lived on $30,000 a year.*
2. To persist; endure: *Although The Beatles broke up decades ago, their music lives on.*

live out

1. To live outside one's place of domestic employment: *You have to get home on time when you have a nanny who lives out.*
2. To experience the passing and completion of some period of time or the attainment of something planned, desired, or imagined: *She hopes to live out her dreams of becoming a famous author. He lived his last days out on a remote tropical island.*

live together

1. To dwell in the same house or premises: *My children, parents, grandparents, and I all live together in one big house. We live together with my cats and dogs.*
2. To cohabit with someone, especially in a sexual relationship when not legally married: *We might get married someday, but right now we are living together. I've been living together with my partner for a year.*

live with

1. To dwell in the same house or premises as someone else: *I live with my parents and my grandmother.*
2. To cohabit with someone, especially in a sexual relationship when not legally married: *They're not*

just dating—she actually lives with him.

3. To put up with something; resign oneself to something: *My friends don't like the dormitory, but they have to live with it for the rest of the year.*

◆ **liven** (lī′vən)

livened (lī′vənd), **livening** (lī′və-nĭng), **livens** (lī′vənz)

liven up

1. To become more lively, interesting, or exciting: *The party livened up when the music got better.*
2. To make something or someone more lively, interesting, or exciting: *I livened up the crowd by suggesting that we play charades. The yellow paint livened the room up.*

◆ **load** (lōd)

loaded (lō′dĭd), **loading** (lō′dĭng), **loads** (lōdz)

load down

1. To give someone or something too much weight to carry: *The driver loaded the truck down with cement. I loaded down the car with crates of groceries. The students' backpacks are loaded down with books.*
2. To give someone too much work to do: *My boss loaded me down with a lot of paperwork. The new professor loaded down the class with homework.*

load up

1. To fill something up with something that it carries: *We'll leave as soon as we finish loading up the car with the bags. Let's load the van up and get going.*
2. **load up on** To gather and store a supply of something; stock up on something: *I loaded up on shampoo because the store was having a sale.*
3. **load up on** To become drunk or intoxicated. Used in the passive: *That guy is loaded up on vodka.*

◆ **loan** (lōn)

loaned (lōnd), **loaning** (lō′nĭng), **loans** (lōnz)

loan out

To lend something; loan something: *I loaned out my cookbook to my neighbor. The school loaned a computer out to us.*

◆ **lock** (lŏk)

locked (lŏkt), **locking** (lŏk′ĭng), **locks** (lŏks)

lock away

1. To put something in a locked space or container, especially for safekeeping: *Fortunately, we had locked away most of our valuables before the burglary. I always lock my jewelry away in a safe.*
2. To put someone in confinement, especially prison; incarcerate someone: *After I threatened to jump off a building, they locked me away in the asylum. The secret*

ă	pat	är	car	ī	bite	ô	paw	o͝o	took	ûr	urge
ā	pay	ĕ	pet	îr	pier	ôr	core	o͝or	lure	zh	vision
âr	care	ē	be	ŏ	pot	oi	boy	o͞o	boot	ə	about,
ä	father	ĭ	pit	ō	toe	ou	out	ŭ	cut		item

police would lock away anyone who criticized the president.

3. To seclude oneself: *I'm going to lock myself away and finish this book.*

lock in

1. To lock a door to a place leaving someone or something inside: *My parents often locked me in my bedroom as punishment. We accidentally locked in the cat when we left.*
2. To guarantee something for the duration of a contract: *You can lock in this interest rate for the life of the loan. When interest rates fell, I locked them in at a lower rate.*
3. To bind someone by contract: *The contract locks us in for two years, during which time we cannot work for anyone else. Once you sign the agreement, you will be locked in for the next ten years.*
4. To invest some money in such a way that it cannot easily be converted into cash. Used chiefly in the passive: *The money is locked in until I turn 65.*
5. To bind in close struggle or battle. Used chiefly in the passive: *The wrestlers were locked in combat. The two sides were locked in a heated debate.*
6. **lock in on** To focus on someone or something; target someone or something: *The fighter pilot locked in on an enemy target and fired. The review locked in on the crude set design and failed to mention the great acting.*

lock on

1. To aim something at a moving target so as to follow it automatically: *The pilot locked the heat-seeking missile on its target.*
2. To stare at someone or something intently; fix one's gaze on someone or something: *The detective's eyes locked on the suspicious package under the desk.*

lock out

1. To prevent someone or something from entering a place by locking a door or entrance: *The committee locked out the protesters from the meeting hall. I left the keys in the car and accidentally locked myself out.*
2. To withhold work from some employees during a labor dispute: *The company bosses locked the auto workers out. The management will lock out the pilots' union until an agreement is reached.*
3. To exclude someone from something, as a competition. Used chiefly in the passive: *Professional athletes were locked out of the competition.*

lock up

1. To shut or make something secure with or as if with locks: *We locked the house up and went on vacation. I locked up my bike and went into the store. The owner locks up every day at 5:00.*
2. To confine or exclude something or someone by or as if by means of a lock: *We locked up the dog for the night. The guards locked the criminal up in the cell. All our savings are locked up in a retirement account.*
3. To become fixed in place so that movement or escape is impossible; be immobilized: *I was so nervous that my knees locked up and I*

couldn't walk. The car's brakes locked up, and it skidded to a halt.

◆ **log** (lŏg)

logged (lŏgd), **logging** (lŏg′ĭng), **logs** (lŏgz)

log in

1. To provide the necessary information to a computer for someone to be allowed to access computer resources; log on: *I'll log you in so that you can access the library's resources. I sat at the terminal and logged in using my student account.*
2. To spend some amount of time working: *We've logged in 100 hours working on this project.*

log into

To provide the necessary information to a computer for someone to be allowed access to some set of computer resources: *I logged into my student account to see if I owed any money to the university. This new software will automatically log you into the company's private website.*

log on

To provide the necessary information to a computer for someone to be allowed to access computer resources: *Let me log you on so that you can access the files yourself. You can't use this program until you log on.*

log out *or* **log off**

To disconnect someone from some computer resource to which one has been connected or logged on: *If you use the computer longer than one hour, it will automatically log you out. Don't log out of your account yet—I want to check something.*

◆ **long** (lông)

longed (lôngd), **longing** (lông′ĭng), **longs** (lôngz)

long for

To desire greatly or yearn for something, especially something that is difficult or impossible to obtain: *I long for the carefree days of my youth.*

◆ **look** (lo͝ok)

looked (lo͝okt), **looking** (lo͝o′kĭng), **looks** (lo͝oks)

look after

To take care of someone or something: *I looked after my younger brother and sister while my parents were working.*

look ahead

1. To cast one's gaze forward: *The passengers looked ahead toward the horizon to keep from getting seasick.*
2. To think about the future: *After months of work, we looked ahead to summer vacation.*

ă	pat	är	car	ī	bite	ô	paw	o͝o	took	ûr	urge
ā	pay	ĕ	pet	îr	pier	ôr	core	o͝or	lure	zh	vision
âr	care	ē	be	ŏ	pot	oi	boy	o͞o	boot	ə	about, item
ä	father	ĭ	pit	ō	toe	ou	out	ŭ	cut		

look back

1. To direct one's gaze backward: *The travelers looked back to the city as they boarded the ship.*
2. To think about the past; retrospect: *At the high school reunion, everyone looked back at the good times they had shared.*

look down

1. To view something from above: *We looked down at the rocky coast and watched the waves crash onto the shore.*
2. **look down on** To be situated so as to provide a view of something from above: *The living room of my apartment looks down on a parking lot.*
3. **look down on** To disapprove of something or someone: *My boss looks down on tardiness. The landlord looked down on tenants who could not pay rent on time.*

look for

1. To search for something or someone; seek something or someone: *I was late because I was looking for my keys.*
2. To hope for or expect something: *Look for a change of weather in March.*

look into

1. To investigate something; check into something: *The police looked into the disturbance.*
2. To direct one's gaze toward an inner area or room: *He looked into the cupboard and decided to make some soup.*

look on

1. To watch an incident or event without participating in it: *The firefighters battled the blaze while dozens of neighbors looked on. I looked on while my teacher prepared the lesson.*
2. To regard someone or something in a certain way: *The boss looked on the new employee as incompetent.*

look out

To be watchful or careful; take care: *If you don't look out, you could fall on the ice. The campers looked out for each other on the hike.*

look over

1. To direct one's gaze in some specified direction or at some specified thing: *I heard a strange noise to my left, and when I looked over, I saw that the television was on.*
2. To examine or inspect something, often briefly or casually: *We looked over the proposal before the meeting. I picked up the receipt and looked it over before signing it.*

look through

1. To peer through or as if through something: *The astronomer allowed us to look through the telescope.*
2. To go through something quickly or superficially, especially when searching: *I looked through the book, but I haven't had a chance to read it.*

look to

1. To rely on someone or something: *He looks to his parents for support when things get tough.*
2. To expect or hope for something: *She looked to hear from the doctor within a week.*

look up

1. To direct one's gaze upward: *Look up at that cloud; it looks like a dog!*
2. To search for information about someone or something from a reference source, such as a book or a file system: *He looked up the word "gullible" in the dictionary. I forgot her phone number, so I looked it up on the Internet.*
3. To seek out and visit or contact someone: *We looked up an old friend when we visited Boston. I looked my college roommate up, and we got together to talk about the old days.*
4. To become better; improve: *Things are looking up now that the weather's better.*
5. **look up to** To hold someone in high regard: *I look up to my parents.*

look upon

To regard someone or something in a certain way: *The parents looked upon their children as their pride and joy.*

◆ **loosen** (lo͞o′sən)

loosened (lo͞o′sənd), **loosening** (lo͞o′sə-nĭng), **loosens** (lo͞o′sənz)

loosen up

1. To cause someone or something to become more loose or relaxed: *After the big meal, I loosened up my belt. The trainer loosened me up with a massage before the fight.*
2. To become more loose or relaxed: *The knots loosened up, and the captives worked themselves free. They seemed shy at first, but by the end of the dinner, the guests had really loosened up.*

◆ **lop** (lŏp)

lopped (lŏpt), **lopping** (lŏp′ĭng), **lops** (lŏps)

lop off

To cut something off; chop off: *The barber lopped my ponytail off. The gardener lopped off the dead branches.*

◆ **lose** (lo͞oz)

lost (lŏst), **losing** (lo͞o′zĭng), **loses** (lo͞o′zĭz)

lose in

To cause someone, especially oneself, to become so mentally involved in something as to lose all awareness of everything else: *After a hard day at work, I went home and lost myself in a book. I tried to ask her a question, but she was lost in thought.*

lose out

1. To fail to achieve or receive an expected gain: *Your sister got here first, so I'm giving her the money—I guess you lose out. The town will lose out on a lot of tax revenue if the factory is shut down.*
2. **lose out to** To be defeated or surpassed by someone or something; lose to someone or something: *Local companies are losing out to*

ă	pat	är	car	ī	bite	ô	paw	o͝o	took	ûr	urge
ā	pay	ĕ	pet	îr	pier	ôr	core	o͝or	lure	zh	vision
âr	care	ē	be	ŏ	pot	oi	boy	o͞o	boot	ə	about,
ä	father	ĭ	pit	ō	toe	ou	out	ŭ	cut		item

foreign companies in the competition for government contracts.

◆ **louse** (lous)
loused (loust), **lousing** (lou′sĭng), **louses** (lou′sĭz)

louse up
To cause something to fail because of poor handling; botch something: *The president loused up the merger, costing the company millions of dollars. Let me tell the story—you always louse it up.*

◆ **lube** (lo͞ob)
lubed (lo͞obd), **lubing** (lo͞o′bĭng), **lubes** (lo͞obz)

lube up
1. To coat something thoroughly with a lubricating substance; make something slippery to prevent damage or irritation from friction: *The mechanic lubed up the engine. I took the gears out of the motor, lubed them up, and put them back in.*
2. To be drunk. Used in the passive: *I was pretty lubed up, so I took a taxi home.*

◆ **luck** (lŭk)
lucked (lŭkt), **lucking** (lŭk′ĭng), **lucks** (lŭks)

luck out
SLANG
To gain success or a thing that was desired by chance; experience good luck: *I lucked out and got tickets for tonight's baseball game.*

◆ **lump** (lŭmp)
lumped (lŭmpt), **lumping** (lŭm′pĭng), **lumps** (lŭmps)

lump together
To put people or things in the same group or category indiscriminately: *The teacher lumped the puzzles and the books together in the toy box. Those students are friends, but I wouldn't lump them together in the same clique.*

lump with
To put someone or something in the same group or category as some other person or thing: *My roommates lumped their CD collection with mine. The uniforms from the visiting team got lumped with ours after the game.*

◆ **lust** (lŭst)
lusted (lŭs′tĭd), **lusting** (lŭs′tĭng), **lusts** (lŭsts)

lust after
1. To desire someone sexually: *My college roommate lusts after the resident assistant.*
2. To have an overwhelming desire or craving for something: *I lust after chocolate, and I'm always snacking on fudge.*

M

◆ **major** (mā′jər)

majored (mā′jərd), **majoring** (mā′jə-rĭng), **majors** (mā′jərz)

major in

To complete a long-term course of study in some subject that is one's main focus: *In high school I was interested in math, but in college I majored in history.*

◆ **make** (māk)

made (mād), **making** (mā′kĭng), **makes** (māks)

make away with

To steal something: *The robbers made away with $2,000 from the store.*

make for

1. To move in the direction of something; head for something: *When the fire broke out, everybody made for the door.*
2. To have or produce something as an effect or result: *Paying attention to small details makes for a more enjoyable trip. Speaking clearly makes for better communication.*

make of

1. To create or fashion something from something else: *All that practice will make a good player of you. This statue is made of clay.*
2. To consider something to be true of something or someone. Used chiefly as a question or in the passive: *What do you make of these little pieces of wood? Not much was made of the evidence they found.*

make off

1. To depart in haste; run away: *He certainly made off in a hurry!*
2. **make off with** To steal something: *Someone entered the room and made off with my hat.*

make out

1. To discern or see something, especially with difficulty: *It was hard to make out the traffic signs because of the rain. The patient tried to read the doctor's handwriting, but couldn't make it out.*
2. To hear something well enough to understand it: *He simply could not make out what she said. The voice over the public address system was so garbled that I couldn't make it out.*
3. To write something out; draw something up: *The shopkeeper stayed late to make out the invoices. We drew up a guest list so we could make the invitations out.*

ă	pat	är	car	ī	bite	ô	paw	o͝o	took	ûr	urge
ā	pay	ĕ	pet	îr	pier	ôr	core	o͝or	lure	zh	vision
âr	care	ē	be	ŏ	pot	oi	boy	o͞o	boot	ə	about, item
ä	father	ĭ	pit	ō	toe	ou	out	ŭ	cut		

4. To represent or describe someone or something as being or doing something. Used with an infinitive clause: *Their inaccurate description made me out to be a liar. The commercial made out the candidate to be a real hero.*
5. To try to establish or prove that something is true: *We made out that we were innocent.*
6. To get along in some way; fare in some way: *The family made out well in their business.*
7. **make out of** To create or fashion something from something else: *We made a birdcage out of the leftover wood. The jewelry was made out of copper.*
8. Slang To kiss deeply and passionately; neck: *The couple made out in the back seat of the car.*
9. Vulgar Slang To have sexual intercourse.

make over

1. To renovate something; give something a new appearance: *We need to make over the whole living room. The house is really shabby, but we plan to make it over.*
2. To change or transfer the ownership of something by means of a legal document: *I made over the property to my children in the will. My parents intend to make the house over to me.*

make toward

To move in the direction of something, especially when fleeing or trying to leave a place; try to reach something; make for something: *When the alarm went off, everyone made toward the rear door.*

make up

1. To constitute or form something: *Ten years make up a decade. The committee is made up of scientists and politicians.*
2. To put something together; construct, arrange, or compose something: *The doctor made up a prescription for my cough. We can make a bed up in the living room if you'd like to stay.*
3. To prepare or alter one's appearance by applying cosmetics: *The makeup artist made up the actor and sent him on to wardrobe. After she made herself up, she put on her dress and went downstairs.*
4. To devise some fiction or falsehood; invent something: *If you don't know any scary stories, just make one up. I didn't want to go to the party, so I made up an excuse.*
5. To compensate for something, such as a previous debt or bad behavior: *They didn't charge me the right amount last month, but made up the difference in this month's bill. I'm sorry I forgot your birthday—I'll make it up to you by taking you out to dinner.*
6. To take some examination or course again or at a later time because of previous absence or failure: *When will you make up the exam that you missed? If you fail the course, you must make it up over the summer.*
7. To resolve a quarrel or conflict: *My husband and I often fight about money, but we always make up right away. I made up with my sister after several years of not speaking to her.*
8. **make up to** To make ingratiating or fawning overtures to someone: *I*

have seen you make up to the boss, hoping to get a promotion.

9. To set something in order: *I'll make up the bedroom before the guests arrive. We made the room up with clean linens and fresh flowers.*

make with

SLANG

To put forth something; produce something: *Our teacher is always making with the jokes.*

◆ **map** (măp)

mapped (măpt), **mapping** (măp′ĭng), **maps** (măps)

map out

1. To plan something explicitly: *Let's map out a way to accomplish this project. We mapped the trip out so we wouldn't get lost.*
2. To incorporate or lay out some set of things into an explicit map, plan, or order: *I've mapped out the beginning and end of each project on this timeline. The houses on these city blocks have been mapped out for demolition.*

◆ **march** (märch)

marched (märcht), **marching** (mär′chĭng), **marches** (mär′chĭz)

march on

1. To continue to march: *The militia marched on despite the jeers from the people on the sidewalk.*
2. To assemble and walk to some place in order to express an opinion, especially opposition, to people of power there: *The employees' union marched on the state capitol.*

◆ **mark** (märk)

marked (märkt), **marking** (mär′kĭng), **marks** (märks)

mark down

1. To write a description or symbol for something observed; make a note of something: *I marked down the characteristics of every bird I saw in the woods. Did you mark the directions down?*
2. To lower the price of something offered for sale: *The department store marked down all of its shoes last week by 20 percent. The baker marks the bread down an hour before closing.*

mark off

1. To indicate the boundary of some region: *The rows of trees on either side of the property mark off our part of it. The lime marks the playing field off.*
2. To make a mark or sign by the name of someone or something on some list, especially to indicate completion of a task or an intention to do a task: *As I delivered each package, I marked off the name of the addressee to make sure I hadn't forgotten anyone. Well, that task is finished, so let's mark it off the list.*
3. To lower someone's score or grade by some amount due to some error:

ă	pat	är	car	ī	bite	ô	paw	ŏŏ	took	ûr	urge
ā	pay	ĕ	pet	îr	pier	ôr	core	ŏŏr	lure	zh	vision
âr	care	ē	be	ŏ	pot	oi	boy	ōō	boot	ə	about,
ä	father	ĭ	pit	ō	toe	ou	out	ŭ	cut		item

My professor marked me off a grade for being late. The teacher marks off five points for each spelling error. The judges marked the dancers off for dancing over the time limit.

mark out

To establish explicitly the outline, boundary, or shape of some region or thing, by or as if by drawing lines or points around it: *We marked out the territory we wanted to explore on the map. Let's mark out the boundaries of the new garden.*

mark up

1. To cover something with marks, especially defacing it: *The rubber balls the kids threw in the hallway marked up the walls. The broken vacuum cleaner marked the floors up.*
2. To write comments or corrections directly on some document: *The teacher had marked up everyone's papers before passing them back to us. The committee marked the report up with comments and questions.*
3. To raise the price of something put on sale: *You'd better buy the shoes now before they mark them up. The new owners marked up the entire inventory.*

◆ **marvel** (mär′vəl)

marveled *or* **marvelled** (mär′vəld), **marveling** *or* **marvelling** (mär′və-lĭng), **marvels** (mär′vəlz)

marvel at

To be astonished or impressed by something: *We walked through the carnival and marveled at all the rides and amusements.*

◆ **mash** (măsh)

mashed (măsht), **mashing** (măsh′ĭng), **mashes** (măsh′ĭz)

mash up

1. To combine some recordings to produce a composite recording: *The DJ mashed popular songs up. The DJ mashed up two songs by The Beatles. The DJ mashed the popular song up with an old blues song.*
2. To mash something completely: *The cook mashed up the potatoes. I threw the turnips into a bowl and mashed them up.*

◆ **match** (măch)

matched (mächt), **matching** (măch′ĭng), **matches** (măch′ĭz)

match against

1. To compare something with something else to see whether their parts correspond: *We matched our list of attendees against the invited guests. Match the list of workers against the checks to see what's missing.*
2. To set someone or something in competition with someone or something else: *The sports league tries to match each team against other teams of the same ability. We were matched against a much smarter team for the debate.*

match up

1. To be the same, comparable, or in agreement: *There's some kind of mistake—the numbers on these two forms don't match up.*

2. To cause something to be the same, comparable, or in agreement: *He matched up the edges of the books on the bookcase. Would you please match the pictures up?—They're crooked.*
3. To form a pair or group from some set of people or things: *I have to thank the dating service for matching us up. I matched up the socks.*
4. **match up with** To be the same as, comparable with, or in agreement with something else: *Each number on this list must match up with the numbers on the other list exactly.*
5. **match up with** To take something as a corresponding element or partner: *The teacher asked each student to match up with one other student and form a double line.*

match with

1. To be the same as, comparable with, or in agreement with something: *The results of our study matched with the previous results perfectly.*
2. To compare something with something else to see whether their parts correspond: *Match your scorecard with mine to see whether there is any disagreement.*
3. To set someone or something in competition with someone or something else: *I don't know why they matched us with a team that is so much stronger than we are; we'll only lose.*

◆ **max** (măks)

maxed (măkst), **maxing** (măk′sĭng), **maxes** (măk′sĭz)

max out

1. To achieve a maximum value, especially as a final value: *The rocket kept accelerating for a while, but finally maxed out at 6,000 miles per hour.*
2. To cause something to achieve a maximum value, especially as a final value: *I think I've maxed out the number of favors I can ask of my cousin. If you keep your foot on the accelerator pedal, you'll max the engine out.*
3. To extend some source of credit to a maximum value or degree: *I can't pay for this—I have no cash, and I maxed out my credit card. We maxed our credit line out, so we can't afford to do any more home improvements. Don't use the credit card again—we'll max out.*

◆ **measure** (mĕzh′ər)

measured (mĕzh′ərd), **measuring** (mĕzh′ə-rĭng), **measures** (mĕzh′ərz)

measure off

To isolate, define, or identify some region within another by measurement: *The surveyors measured off the part of the property where the house was going to be built. The builders measured each section off precisely before pouring the concrete.*

ă	pat	är	car	ī	bite	ô	paw	o͝o	took	ûr	urge
ā	pay	ĕ	pet	îr	pier	ôr	core	o͝or	lure	zh	vision
âr	care	ē	be	ŏ	pot	oi	boy	o͞o	boot	ə	about,
ä	father	ĭ	pit	ō	toe	ou	out	ŭ	cut		item

measure out

To dispense some specific, measured amount of something: *The cook measured out four cups of flour into the bowl. The tailor measured two yards of material out and cut it from the bolt.*

measure up

To be the equal of something or someone; be of equal or sufficient quality for something or someone: *This team easily measures up to any of the others in the league. I wanted the job, but I just didn't measure up.*

◆ **meet** (mēt)

met (mĕt), **meeting** (mē′tĭng), **meets** (mēts)

meet up

1. To come together at a place, especially in order to accomplish something; meet: *Let's meet up after the meeting and discuss this further.*
2. **meet up to** To have some required level of quality: *I think our performance will meet up to your expectations. I hope my new car will meet up to the demands of all the driving that I have to do for my job.*
3. **meet up with** To come together with someone or something, especially in order to accomplish something; meet with someone or something: *We'll meet up with the others later and decide where to eat dinner.*

meet with

1. To come together with someone or something, especially in order to discuss or accomplish something: *The president met with the staff to analyze the new budget.*
2. To experience or undergo something: *Strong statements often meet with harsh criticism. You can meet your obstacles with bitterness or with determination.*
3. To be experienced by something or someone. Used passively: *Visitors to the impoverished city are often met with many problems, such as high prices and crime.*

◆ **mellow** (mĕl′ō)

mellowed (mĕl′ōd), **mellowing** (mĕl′ō-ĭng), **mellows** (mĕl′ōz)

mellow out

SLANG

1. To make someone relax; cause someone to become more genial and pleasant: *A nice cool drink would mellow me out right now. A nap might mellow out the kids.*
2. To relax; become genial and pleasant: *Hey, don't get so upset; just mellow out! We stayed at home and mellowed out all day.*
3. To make something less intense or less striking: *I added some white to the paint to mellow the color out a little bit. We added candles to mellow out the atmosphere.*

◆ **melt** (mĕlt)

melted (mĕl′tĭd), **melting** (mĕl′tĭng), **melts** (mĕlts)

melt away

1. To dissipate or fade away by or as if by melting: *As the sun rose, the fog melted away.*
2. To cause something to dissipate or fade away by or as if by melting: *The medication melted my anxiety away. The soothing words melted away the child's fears.*

melt down

1. To melt from a solid into a liquid: *As ice cubes melt down, the water level in the glass remains constant.*
2. To cause something to melt from a solid into a liquid: *The sun melted the snowman down into a puddle. I melted down the ice on the window with a hair dryer.*
3. To overheat severely and melt, resulting in the escape of radiation from a nuclear reactor core: *The nuclear reactor melted down, and thousands of people had to evacuate the area.*
4. Slang To have an emotional breakdown: *I was dealing with a lot of stress, and I melted down on the subway when it stopped between stations.*

◆ **mess** (mĕs)

messed (mĕst), **messing** (mĕs′ĭng), **messes** (mĕs′ĭz)

mess around

1. Slang To waste time: *Stop messing around and finish your chores!*
2. **mess around with** Slang To manipulate or work with something without a clear sense of method: *I messed around with the TV controls, but the picture still looks too green.*
3. Vulgar Slang To engage in casual, often promiscuous sexual activity.

mess up

1. To make a mistake, especially from nervousness or confusion: *The runner scored because I messed up and dropped the ball.*
2. To spoil something by making mistakes: *I really messed up that chemistry test. That problem was difficult—I think I messed it up.*
3. To cause someone or something to blunder or fail: *I tried to pass the ball to the other player, but the loud shouting from the fans messed me up.*
4. Slang To beat someone up; handle roughly: *The bullies really messed up a couple of kids in a fight after school. If I told anyone what they did, they'd mess me up.*
5. To cause something to be messy, tangled, or in disarray; muss something up: *The kids messed up my hair, so I had to comb it all over again.*
6. To injure, damage, or negatively interfere with something: *Sitting in that uncomfortable chair really messed up my back. I messed my knee up when I fell down on the ice. Don't take those drugs; they will really mess you up.*

mess with

1. To alter something improperly: *Don't mess with the arrangement of the chairs—they're all set up for the meeting.*
2. To deceive or confuse someone or something: *The horrible accident really messed with my head.*

◆ **mete** (mēt)

meted (mē′tĭd), **meting** (mē′tĭng), **metes** (mēts)

ă	pat	är	car	ī	bite	ô	paw	o͝o	took	ûr	urge
ā	pay	ĕ	pet	îr	pier	ôr	core	o͝or	lure	zh	vision
âr	care	ē	be	ŏ	pot	oi	boy	o͞o	boot	ə	about,
ä	father	ĭ	pit	ō	toe	ou	out	ŭ	cut		item

mete out

To distribute and apply a measure or judgment of something: *The cook meted out small portions of soup to the soldiers. Our school principal metes out strict punishment to those who break the rules. The central office gathers information and metes it out to the departments that need it.*

◆ **minor** (mī′nər)

minored (mī′nərd), **minoring** (mī′nə-rĭng), **minors** (mī′nərz)

minor in

To complete a long-term course of study in some subject that is one's secondary focus: *My main course of study is biology, and I'm minoring in philosophy.*

◆ **miss** (mĭs)

missed (mĭst), **missing** (mĭs′ĭng), **misses** (mĭs′ĭz)

miss out

To be unable or fail to participate in something: *I missed out on last month's concert because I was out of town. There's a lot going on at the fair, so set aside the whole day or you'll miss out!*

◆ **mist** (mĭst)

misted (mĭs′tĭd), **misting** (mĭs′tĭng), **mists** (mĭsts)

mist over *or* **mist up**

1. To cover something with fine droplets of water or some other misty substance: *The sprinkler automatically mists over the plants in the greenhouse every day. The humid air misted the mirrors up.*
2. To become covered with fine droplets of water or some other misty substance; fog up: *The cold windshield misted over with our moist breath. I turned on the blower because the car windows had misted up.*
3. To become full of tears: *As they sang the old songs, my eyes misted over. I mist up whenever I think of home.*

◆ **mistake** (mĭ-stāk′)

mistook (mĭ-sto͝ok′), **mistaken** (mĭ-stā′kən), **mistaking** (mĭ-stā′kĭng), **mistakes** (mĭ-stāks′)

mistake for

To wrongly perceive that someone or something is someone or something else: *I'm sorry to have bothered you—I mistook you for a friend of mine. Don't mistake the poison ivy for a box elder vine!*

◆ **mix** (mĭks)

mixed (mĭkst), **mixing** (mĭk′sĭng), **mixes** (mĭk′sĭz)

mix down

1. To combine all of the audio components of some recording into a single final soundtrack or mix: *We recorded the last guitar part toward the end of the song, and now we can mix the song down. It can be difficult to mix down 24 tracks.*
2. To reduce the volume of some component of an electrical or audio signal relative to other components: *The drums sounded too loud in the recording studio, so we mixed them down. The sound engineer mixed down the vocals.*

mix up

1. To cause the elements of something to be intermingled: *Mix up the eggs and sugar before you pour them into the flour. Mix the batter up thoroughly before pouring it into the pan.*
2. To prepare something by mixing: *I mixed some eggs up for breakfast. I mixed up a cake for her birthday.*
3. To confuse someone; confound someone: *His explanation just mixed me up more. The confusing directions mixed up all the party guests.*
4. To mistake something or someone for something or someone else: *I always mix up the twins. I mixed the twins up because they were wearing the same thing.*
5. To involve or implicate someone in the activities of someone or something, especially something negative: *Don't mix yourself up with that crowd. She mixed him up in the whole mess. He got mixed up with the wrong people.*
6. To increase the volume of some component of an electrical or audio signal relative to other components: *Your singing sounds too quiet—we should mix it up. Mix up the microphones when the announcer begins speaking.*

◆ **mock** (mŏk)

mocked (mŏkt), **mocking** (mŏk′ĭng), **mocks** (mŏks)

mock up

To make a model of something, especially as part of a presentation: *We mocked up our ideas for the stage scenery to see if it would be hard to build. Take these building plans and mock them up for the presentation.*

◆ **model** (mŏd′l)

modeled *or* **modelled** (mŏd′ld), **modeling** *or* **modelling** (mŏd′l-ĭng), **models** (mŏd′lz)

model on

To form, develop, or found something on the basis of something else: *The architect modeled the plans for the new school on a beautiful old building.*

◆ **mouth** (mou*th*)

mouthed (mou*th*d), **mouthing** (mou′*th*ĭng), **mouths** (mou*th*z)

mouth off

SLANG

To express one's opinions or complaints in a loud, indiscreet manner: *Quit mouthing off about what you think is wrong, and go do something about it! Don't mouth off to your parents like that!*

◆ **move** (mo͞ov)

moved (mo͞ovd), **moving** (mo͞o′vĭng), **moves** (mo͞ovz)

move in

1. To come nearer or encroach: *The soldiers slowly moved in on the*

ă	pat	är	car	ī	bite	ô	paw	o͝o	took	ûr	urge
ā	pay	ĕ	pet	îr	pier	ôr	core	o͝or	lure	zh	vision
âr	care	ē	be	ŏ	pot	oi	boy	o͞o	boot	ə	about, item
ä	father	ĭ	pit	ō	toe	ou	out	ŭ	cut		

enemy's fort. I think it will rain—I see dark clouds moving in.

2. To begin to occupy a residence or place of business: *We bought the house last week, but we won't move in until next month.*

move out

1. To begin to leave: *This cold weather is finally moving out. The troops will move out at dawn.*
2. To stop occupying a residence or place of business and go elsewhere: *She bought a new house up the street, and she's moving out of her apartment this weekend.*
3. SLANG To move extremely quickly: *I couldn't catch that thief running down the street—he was really moving out!*

move up

1. To cause something to change or move to a higher or more advanced position: *Please move these boxes up to the top shelf. The attic lacked furniture, so we moved up some old chairs.*
2. To change or move to a higher or more advanced position or value: *She couldn't see the football game well from the field, so she moved up to the stands. He waited in line for a long time before he moved up at all. Stock prices have moved up recently.*
3. To attain higher status, income, or social standing: *I started my job here as a clerk, but I moved up quickly and now I own the company.*
4. To change the date or time of some scheduled event to an earlier date or time: *Several of our friends were leaving town in July, so we moved up our party to early June. To avoid staying too late tonight, we should move the meeting up a few hours.*

◆ **mow** (mō)

mowed (mōd), **mowed** *or* **mown** (mōn), **mowing** (mō′ĭng), **mows** (mōz)

mow down

1. To trim back or cut down something that grows from the ground: *Unfortunately, you didn't just cut the grass—you mowed down all the potato plants. We mowed the brush down with scythes.*
2. To destroy or incapacitate someone or something as if by cutting or driving into the ground: *The machine gunners mowed down hundreds of enemy troops within the first ten minutes of fighting. I tried to tackle the runner, but he just mowed me down. The gang drove by with machine guns and mowed the informant down in front of his house.*
3. To overwhelm someone or something: *The experienced debater mowed down the opposition with persuasive arguments.*

◆ **muck** (mŭk)

mucked (mŭkt), **mucking** (mŭk′ĭng), **mucks** (mŭks)

muck around *or* **muck about**

To spend time idly; putter: *We spent our summer afternoons mucking around in the fields and ponds. I stayed home and mucked around all day.*

muck up

SLANG

1. To make something dirty or contaminated, especially with mud,

grime, or a similar substance: *Don't step in that puddle; you'll muck up your shoes. The gears in the car's transmission were all mucked up.*

2. To make some liquid unclear or unusable by stirring up elements settled on the bottom: *Unfortunately, all the dredging in the river has mucked up the water so much that we can't go swimming. The rains mucked the water up, making it difficult for scuba divers to see.*
3. To make something unusable by disrupting what should remain undisturbed: *I tried to incorporate these ideas into my paper at the last minute, but all they did was to muck it up. The editor stopped the author from mucking up the book with needless revisions.*

◆ **muddle** (mŭd′l)

muddled (mŭd′ld), **muddling** (mŭd′l-ĭng), **muddles** (mŭd′lz)

muddle through

To do some task poorly or without strong motivation: *I forgot the cookbook, so we just muddled through the recipe without it.*

◆ **muster** (mŭs′tər)

mustered (mŭs′tərd), **mustering** (mŭs′tə-rĭng), **musters** (mŭs′tərz)

muster in

1. To enlist someone in military service. Used chiefly in the passive: *Once the men were mustered in, they got their heads shaved.*
2. To enlist in military service: *In the US, you can't officially muster in until you're 18 years old.*

muster out

1. To discharge someone from military service. Used chiefly in the passive: *The last of the soldiers who fought in that battle were mustered out last week.*
2. To be discharged from military service: *I mustered out last month, and I'm proud that I had the chance to serve my country.*

muster up

To gather up some force of will to do something: *I couldn't muster up the courage to tell them about my terrible mistake. Although the team lost, they mustered some good cheer up and went to the party.*

ă	pat	är	car	ī	bite	ô	paw	o͝o	took	ûr	urge
ā	pay	ĕ	pet	îr	pier	ôr	core	o͝or	lure	zh	vision
âr	care	ē	be	ŏ	pot	oi	boy	o͞o	boot	ə	about, item
ä	father	ĭ	pit	ō	toe	ou	out	ŭ	cut		

N

◆ **nail** (nāl)

nailed (nāld), **nailing** (nā′lĭng), **nails** (nālz)

nail down

1. To secure something or make it unable to move by driving nails through it and into another object: *On the passenger ship, the workers nailed the tables down so that they wouldn't slide around during the storm. We examined the deck and nailed down all loose boards.*
2. To specify or fix something: *After months of evading the question, the candidate finally nailed down her position on the war. We can't release the schedule until we've nailed it down.*
3. To discover or establish something conclusively: *The reporter nailed down the story by checking all the facts. We looked for the source of the problem but couldn't nail it down.*
4. To win something decisively: *She nailed down her sixth win of the season with a birdie on the 18th hole. We nailed the top spot down by defeating the two best teams in the league.*

◆ **natter** (năt′ər)

nattered (năt′ərd), **nattering** (năt′ə-rĭng), **natters** (năt′ərz)

natter on

To talk continuously: *My neighbor nattered on about life in the 1950s.*

◆ **nibble** (nĭb′əl)

nibbled (nĭb′əld), **nibbling** (nĭb′ə-lĭng), **nibbles** (nĭb′əlz)

nibble at

1. To eat something by taking small bites: *The mice have been nibbling at the curtains.*
2. To eat a small amount of something, especially unenthusiastically: *She only nibbled at her peas.*
3. To bite something but not break the surface; nip at something: *My date nibbled at my ear during the movie.*

nibble on

1. To eat something by taking small, quick bites, often as a snack or a light meal: *Dinner wasn't for another two hours, so I nibbled on some potato chips. The rabbit nibbled on a carrot.*
2. To bite something but not break the surface: *Nervously, I nibbled on my pencil's eraser during the test.*

◆ **nip** (nĭp)

nipped (nĭpt), **nipping** (nĭp′ĭng), **nips** (nĭps)

nip at

1. To grab and pinch or bite: *The fish nipped at our feet when we walked in the pond.*
2. To bite or sting with the cold: *The wind was nipping at our nose.*
3. To sip some drink, often alcoholic, in small amounts: *They were*

caught nipping at the whiskey again.

nip on

1. To grab and pinch or bite: *The fish nipped on the wader's feet.*
2. To sip some drink, often alcoholic, in small amounts: *The guests nipped on their eggnog all night long. I nipped on my soda while waiting for my date to show up.*

◆ **nod** (nŏd)

nodded (nŏd′ĭd), **nodding** (nŏd′ĭng), **nods** (nŏdz)

nod off

To fall asleep, especially without intending to do so: *Some of the students nodded off during the lecture.*

nod out

SLANG

To fall asleep without intending to do so, especially as a result of taking a drug or medicine: *The medicine made me so tired that I nodded out on the subway.*

◆ **nose** (nōz)

nosed (nōzd), **nosing** (nō′zĭng), **noses** (nō′zĭz)

nose in on

To listen in on or get involved in something where one's presence is not wanted: *You're always nosing in on my conversations, and I wish you'd stop.*

nose out

1. To defeat someone or something by a narrow margin: *We nosed out the opposing team for the win. In the last inning, we took the lead and nosed them out.*
2. To perceive or detect someone or something by or as if by sniffing: *The police dogs nosed out the drugs hidden in the car. The criminals left very few clues, but the police were still able to nose them out.*

◆ **nosh** (nŏsh)

noshed (nŏsht), **noshing** (nŏsh′ĭng), **noshes** (nŏsh′ĭz)

nosh on

To eat something as a snack or a light meal: *At the reception, the guests noshed on bagels, cream cheese, and lox.*

ă	pat	är	car	ī	bite	ô	paw	ŏŏ	took	ûr	urge
ā	pay	ĕ	pet	îr	pier	ôr	core	ŏŏr	lure	zh	vision
âr	care	ē	be	ŏ	pot	oi	boy	ōō	boot	ə	about,
ä	father	ĭ	pit	ō	toe	ou	out	ŭ	cut		item

O

◆ **object** (əb-jĕkt′)

objected (əb-jĕk′tĭd), **objecting** (əb-jĕk′tĭng), **objects** (əb-jĕkts′)

object to

To express disagreement with or disapproval of something: *The city council objects to vulgar art displays in public buildings.*

◆ **occupy** (ŏk′yə-pī′)

occupied (ŏk′yə-pīd′), **occupying** (ŏk′yə-pī′ĭng), **occupies** (ŏk′yə-pīz′)

occupy with

1. To fill, hold, or control some place through some set of things or people: *The army occupied the town with their third division. The town built new office buildings and occupied them with workers from the health department.*
2. To fill some period of time by engaging in or with something: *I occupied my spare time with books. You'll never be able to occupy your entire morning with writing.*
3. To engage someone in some activity or some object of attention: *The teacher occupied the students with their science projects for the morning. During the cold winter afternoons, we occupied ourselves with card games.*

◆ **occur** (ə-kûr′)

occurred (ə-kûrd′), **occurring** (ə-kûr′ĭng), **occurs** (ə-kûrz′)

occur to

To come to someone's mind: *When it occurred to me that I could leave the party whenever I wanted, I felt more at ease.*

◆ **offer** (ô′fər)

offered (ô′fərd), **offering** (ô′fə-rĭng), **offers** (ô′fərz)

offer up

To submit something as an offering, especially in worship or devotion: *At the memorial, they offered prayers up for the victims. Let's offer up free meals during the holidays.*

◆ **oil** (oil)

oiled (oild), **oiling** (oi′lĭng), **oils** (oilz)

oil up

To coat something thoroughly with oil: *The mechanic oiled up the engine. The therapist oiled my back up and worked out the knots in my muscles.*

◆ **open** (ō′pən)

opened (ō′pənd), **opening** (ō′pə-nĭng), **opens** (ō′pənz)

open out

1. To become wider: *The river opens out as it heads toward the bay.*
2. To unfold or expand so that inner parts are displayed; spread out: *The couch opened out into a bed.*

3. To unfold or expand something; spread something out: *I opened the couch out into a bed. Let's open out the model to see how it works.*
4. **open out on** To be a passage or opening to some larger external space: *After we remodel, the living room will open out on to the kitchen.*

open up

1. To release something from a closed or fastened position: *Please open up the cabinet and take out the plates. We opened the trunk up and found some old clothing.*
2. To remove obstructions from something; clear something: *The change in weather opened up my sinuses. The cancellation of that meeting opened my schedule up.*
3. To become free from obstruction: *After the debris was removed from the road, the traffic opened up.*
4. To spread out; unfold: *A green valley opened up before us.*
5. To begin operation, as a business or office: *The new store opens up next month.*
6. To begin firing: *The artillery opened up at dawn.*
7. To speak freely and candidly: *At last the frightened witness opened up and told the truth.*
8. To make an opening in something or someone by cutting: *The surgeon opened up the patient's chest. I opened the package up with a box cutter.*
9. To make something available or accessible: *The new CEO plans to open up markets overseas. The snow opens the possibility up of a good ski season.*
10. To accelerate. Used of a motor vehicle: *The sports car opened up and roared down the road.*

◆ **opt** (ŏpt)

opted (ŏp′tĭd), **opting** (ŏp′tĭng), **opts** (ŏpts)

opt for

To choose something, especially over some other option: *I opted for a king-sized bed when I made my hotel reservation.*

opt out

To choose not to participate in something: *When she rented the car, she opted out of the extra insurance. Everyone on my baseball team is going to run in the marathon, but I opted out.*

◆ **order** (ôr′dər)

ordered (ôr′dərd), **ordering** (ôr′də-rĭng), **orders** (ôr′dərz)

order around

To issue commands to someone in a forceful and unpleasant way; boss someone around: *The lieutenant ordered the new recruits around. The nanny ordered around the children.*

order out

To request that some food be delivered from a restaurant to another place, such as one's home or office: *We wanted to stay home, so we ordered out for pizza. Let's order out some Thai food tonight. We didn't cook this food; we ordered it out. I have to stay late at work tonight, so I'm going to order out.*

◆ **orient** (ôr′ē-ĕnt′)

oriented (ôr′ē-ĕn′tĭd), **orienting** (ôr′ē-ĕn′tĭng), **orients** (ôr′ē-ĕnts′)

orient to

1. To position something or someone with respect to a point or system of reference: *We oriented the telescope to the southern parts of the sky. The tent's opening is oriented to the sunlight.*
2. To make someone familiar with something, as facts, principles, or a situation: *I oriented the staff to the new computer system.*
3. To become familiar with something, as facts, principles, or a situation: *The rookie needs time to orient to the schedule.*
4. To focus something on some topic or on the interests of some group: *We should orient our meeting to any new problems that have arisen since last week. The afterschool program is oriented to elementary school students.*

◆ **overflow** (ō′vər-flō′)

overflowed (ō′vər-flōd′), **overflowing** (ō′vər-flō′ĭng), **overflows** (ō′vər-flōz′)

overflow with

1. To be filled beyond capacity with something: *Their mugs overflowed with beer.*
2. To have a boundless supply of something: *The hospital room overflowed with flowers. Our wonderful hosts were overflowing with generosity to us.*

◆ **owe** (ō)

owed (ōd), **owing** (ō′ĭng), **owes** (ōz)

owe to

1. To be in debt by some amount to someone: *I owe $100 to my brother.*
2. To have something because of something or someone else: *The family owed its wealth to oil. I owe my rosy complexion to my mother.*

◆ **own** (ōn)

owned (ōnd), **owning** (ōn′ĭng), **owns** (ōnz)

own up

To confess to something; admit something: *If the person who stole the erasers doesn't own up, recess will be canceled. The thief owned up to the crime.*

P

◆ **pace** (pās)

paced (pāst), **pacing** (pā′sĭng), **paces** (pā′sĭz)

pace out *or* **pace off**

To measure some distance by counting the number of strides taken while walking across it: *We paced out 100 feet when making the course for the race. The counselors paced the boundaries of the field out before marking them.*

◆ **pack** (păk)

packed (păkt), **packing** (păk′ĭng), **packs** (păks)

pack away

1. To put something in a container for storage: *We packed away the winter clothes for summer. After the trip, I packed my souvenirs away.*
2. To fit into a container for storage: *The shaving kit packs away easily into your suitcase.*
3. To eat a large amount of something: *We packed it away at the banquet. The kids really packed away those hot dogs!*

pack in

1. To fit something into some enclosed space for storage or travel: *I packed our sandwiches in the picnic basket.*
2. To fit something into some limited space: *Do you think you could pack in a few more pairs of socks in your bag? There was not much room in the trunk for the bags, but I was able to pack them in.*
3. To stop doing something, as a job or habit; retire from doing something: *He packed in his career as a railroad engineer when the trains were sold. She wasn't making any money through her work, so she decided to pack it in.*
4. To attract a large number of people: *The speaker's seminars have been packing in audiences all month. Good marketing will pack audiences in at the premiere.*

pack into

1. To fit, fill, or squeeze something into something else: *The students packed their books into the trunk. She sure packed a lot of information into a two-minute speech.*
2. To enter and occupy some space fully: *The students packed into the assembly hall.*

pack off

To send someone away to some place, especially in a hurry or without his or her consent: *The neighbors packed their children off to boarding school. When I went on*

ă	pat	är	car	ī	bite	ô	paw	o͝o	took	ûr	urge
ā	pay	ĕ	pet	îr	pier	ôr	core	o͝or	lure	zh	vision
âr	care	ē	be	ŏ	pot	oi	boy	o͞o	boot	ə	about, item
ä	father	ĭ	pit	ō	toe	ou	out	ŭ	cut		

vacation, I packed off the dogs to the kennel before leaving.

pack up

1. To put the belongings one is traveling with into some container that will be used to transport them: *We packed the car up and left for Canada. I packed up my suitcase and put it in the car.*
2. To gather or tie some group of things together in a package: *I packed up your books in that box for you. I packed my old clothes up and sent them to the shelter.*

◆ **pad** (păd)
padded (păd′ĭd), **padding** (păd′ĭng), **pads** (pădz)

pad out

1. To line or stuff something with soft material to make it fuller, puffier, or fluffier: *I padded the pillow out with extra down. If you don't like the shape of this coat, we can pad out the shoulders for a fuller look.*
2. To lengthen or increase something, especially with something extraneous: *The director padded out the movie with several extra scenes so that it would be 90 minutes long. The lazy student wrote a short report and padded it out with useless facts.*

◆ **page** (pāj)
paged (pājd), **paging** (pā′jĭng), **pages** (pā′jĭz)

page through

To go through some reading material quickly or superficially, turning from page to page, as in searching or browsing: *I paged through the magazine to see if there were any interesting articles in it. You'll find some interesting things on that website if you page through it for a while.*

◆ **pair** (pâr)
paired (pârd), **pairing** (pâr′ĭng), **pairs** (pârz)

pair off

1. To arrange some things or people in groups of two: *The drama coach paired off the students to rehearse scenes. The organizer paired the partygoers off and sent them on a treasure hunt.*
2. To form pairs: *The dance students paired off and practiced waltzing.*

pair up

1. To arrange some things or people in groups of two: *The gym teacher paired up the students and started a badminton tournament. The organizer paired the volunteers up.*
2. To form pairs or a pair: *The dance students paired up and practiced waltzing. My best friend and I paired up when our class chose locker partners.*

◆ **pal** (păl)
palled (păld), **palling** (păl′ĭng), **pals** (pălz)

pal around

To spend time or do things with someone in a friendly or informal manner: *My roommates and I pal around together all the time.*

◆ **palm** (päm)
palmed (pämd), **palming** (pä′mĭng), **palms** (pämz)

palm off

To get rid of or dispose of something by fraud or deception; fob off: *The crooked merchant palmed off a lot of fake diamonds before being caught. Someone tried to palm some old coins off on me yesterday, saying they were rare and valuable.*

◆ **pan** (pă̆n)

panned (pă̆nd), **panning** (pă̆n′ĭng), **pans** (pă̆nz)

pan out

1. To prove successful, effective, or satisfactory; turn out well: *I'm glad to see that your business plan has panned out.*
2. To have some specified result: *My plans panned out poorly.*

◆ **pander** (pă̆n′dər)

pandered (pă̆n′dərd), **pandering** (pă̆n′də-rĭng), **panders** (pă̆n′dərz)

pander to

To cater to or indulge someone's lower tastes or desires, especially in order to win his or her favor or gain an advantage: *This bawdy television show panders to people with sophomoric senses of humor.*

◆ **paper** (pā′pər)

papered (pā′pərd), **papering** (pā′pə-rĭng), **papers** (pā′pərz)

paper over

1. To cover something unpleasant, such as a blemish on a wall, with paper: *He papered over the cracks in the ceiling. She papered the walls over to hide the stains.*
2. To put or keep something out of sight; downplay something: *The accountant papered the deficit over with questionable calculations. The principal papered over the school's problem with drugs when questioned by the press.*

◆ **parcel** (pär′səl)

parceled *or* **parcelled** (pär′səld), **parceling** *or* **parcelling** (pär′sə-lĭng), **parcels** (pär′səlz)

parcel out

To divide something into parts or portions for distribution: *The teacher parceled out the cookies to the pupils. I parceled the free tickets out to my friends.*

parcel up

To gather or tie something together in a tight package; wrap up: *He parceled up the clothes and took them to the yard sale. She is going to parcel those dry goods up and deliver them to the shelter.*

◆ **pare** (pâr)

pared (pârd), **paring** (pâr′ĭng), **pares** (pârz)

pare down

1. To reduce the size of something by cutting or shaving off its outer layers; trim something: *I pared down the tiles so that they would fit snugly together. The pegs were too*

ă	pat	är	car	ī	bite	ô	paw	o͝o	took	ûr	urge
ā	pay	ĕ	pet	îr	pier	ôr	core	o͝or	lure	zh	vision
âr	care	ē	be	ŏ	pot	oi	boy	o͞o	boot	ə	about,
ä	father	ĭ	pit	ō	toe	ou	out	ŭ	cut		item

big for the holes, so I pared them down with a pocketknife.

2. To reduce the size or amount of something by gradually taking away parts of it: *We should pare down the supplies we keep in our storage room until we have only what we absolutely need. The article was too long, and it took me a long time to pare it down.*

◆ **park** (pärk)

parked (pärkt), **parking** (pär′kĭng), **parks** (pärks)

park in

To prevent some parked vehicle from being able to leave by blocking it with another vehicle: *The van stopped in the right lane of traffic and parked a small car in. I honked my horn until the people who parked me in moved their car. My car was parked in, so I took a cab to my appointment.*

◆ **parlay** (pär′lā′, pär′lē′)

parlayed (pär′lād′, pär′lēd′), **parlaying** (pär′lā′ĭng, pär′lē′ĭng), **parlays** (pär′lāz′, pär′lēz′)

parlay into

To work with or manipulate some quality in order to make it something of value: *She parlayed her ability to make people feel comfortable into a successful career as a therapist. The politician was able to parlay the people's complaints into a successful campaign strategy.*

◆ **part** (pärt)

parted (pär′tĭd), **parting** (pär′tĭng), **parts** (pärts)

part with

1. To leave the company of someone; go away from someone: *After months of negotiations, we've decided to part with the company.*
2. To give up or let go of something; relinquish something: *It's hard for me to part with old mementos.*

◆ **partake** (pär-tāk′)

partook (pär-to͝ok′), **partaken** (pär-tā′kən), **partaking** (pär-tā′kĭng), **partakes** (pär-tāks′)

partake in

To participate in some activity; share in something: *The reporter criticized the company that partook in the secret meeting with government officials.*

partake of

To use, consume, or participate in something shared with others: *I hope that the guests will partake of the delicious dinner I prepared.*

◆ **partition** (pär-tĭsh′ən)

partitioned (pär-tĭsh′ənd), **partitioning** (pär-tĭsh′ə-nĭng), **partitions** (pär-tĭsh′ənz)

partition off

To divide or separate something by or as if by means of a partition: *The construction workers partitioned off each office with drywall. My vacation was almost ruined when my wallet was stolen, but I've partitioned that event off from my memories of the trip.*

◆ **partner** (pärt′nər)

partnered (pärt′nərd), **partnering** (pärt′nə-rĭng), **partners** (pärt′nərz)

partner up

1. To arrange some things or people in groups of two: *The gym teacher partnered up the students and started a tennis tournament. The organizer partnered us up with some new volunteers.*
2. To form pairs or a pair; become partners: *The dance students partnered up and started to waltz.*

◆ **party** (pär′tē)

partied (pär′tēd), **partying** (pär′tē-ĭng), **parties** (pär′tēz)

party down

SLANG

To celebrate or carouse at a party: *The team partied down after winning the championship.*

◆ **pass** (păs)

passed (păst), **passing** (păs′ĭng), **passes** (păs′ĭz)

pass around

1. To transfer something from one person to another: *We passed around each plate of food that was brought to us. The teacher gave the book to the students and told them to pass it around.*
2. To be transferred from one person to another; circulate: *The bottle of wine passed around the table.*
3. To offer something to each person in a group: *I brought a handful of fliers to the meeting and passed them around to everyone. The clowns passed around pieces of candy to the children.*

pass as

To give some unreal impression that is accepted as real; pass for something: *Although he was 30, he could easily pass as a teenager when he shaved his beard.*

pass away

1. To die: *My grandfather passed away last year.*
2. To pass out of existence; end: *The years of famine passed away and were followed by years of prosperity.*

pass by

1. To move or travel past someone or something: *You'll pass by many herds of cattle on your trip through the plains. We passed by Toledo on our way to Chicago.*
2. To go past someone or something without stopping or acknowledging: *We waved at the approaching truck, but it passed us by.*
3. To move past in time; elapse: *Many weeks passed by with no rain.*

pass down

1. To transfer something from a higher level to a lower one: *I passed the can of paint down to my friend who was painting the window. The main office passes down simple requests to our help department.*
2. To transfer something to the next member of a sequence: *Each player takes one card and passes it down to the next player.*

ă	pat	är	car	ī	bite	ô	paw	o͝o	took	ûr	urge
ā	pay	ĕ	pet	îr	pier	ôr	core	o͝or	lure	zh	vision
âr	care	ē	be	ŏ	pot	oi	boy	o͞o	boot	ə	about, item
ä	father	ĭ	pit	ō	toe	ou	out	ŭ	cut		

3. To bestow something to someone, especially a younger relative: *I passed down my old clothes to my younger sister. My parents passed a strong work ethic down to all of my brothers and sisters.*

pass for

To be accepted as something; be believed to be something: *The fake painting passed for an original. If you wore that heavy coat and fur hat, you could pass for a Russian.*

pass in

1. To deliver or submit some assignment or work: *The students passed their assignments in. The researchers passed in their reports.*
2. To achieve satisfactory grades in an academic subject: *I passed in algebra, English, and history.*
3. To give someone a satisfactory grade in an academic subject: *The teacher passed 15 students in calculus.*

pass off

1. To offer, sell, or circulate something that is an imitation as though it were genuine: *Some dishonest merchants are able to pass off glass as a gemstone.*
2. To present someone as something else. Often used reflexively: *He tried to pass himself off as a banker, even though he has no experience in finance. The clever spy passed herself off as a store clerk. My friend passed the refugee off as a visiting cousin when the landlord asked who he was.*
3. To disregard or ignore something by considering it to have some negative quality: *I passed his snide comment off as a joke. They pass off everything I say as ignorant.*

pass on

1. To transmit or convey something that one has received or acquired to someone else: *My boss passed the assignment on to me.*
2. To bestow something to someone, especially a younger relative: *I intend to pass my wedding ring on to my granddaughter.*
3. To convey some item of information that one has received or acquired to someone else: *Please pass on any important information to me. I passed the news on to the neighbors.*
4. To transmit some disease or sickness to someone: *The child passed on the cold to the whole family. Don't go to work with a bad cold, or you'll pass it on to everyone else.*
5. To give something to someone else, especially after having used or partaken of it: *Could you pass the book on to me after you've read it? Take one cupcake from the tray and pass it on.*
6. To die: *At the age of 92, he passed on.*
7. To refuse something politely; decline something: *I passed on going to the movie with my friends because I was feeling sick.*

pass out

1. To lose consciousness: *Some of the football players passed out from the heat. The bar owner had to throw out patrons who would pass out after drinking.*
2. To go to sleep: *I went home and passed out after a long day at work.*

3. To distribute something: *The teacher passed out the test results. Our troop leader passed the cookies out.*

pass over

1. To move or travel above something or someone: *The plane passed over our heads while we were talking.*
2. To avoid or bypass something, especially something difficult or unpleasant: *We tried to pass over the subject of the divorce. The report passed over the events leading up to the war.*
3. To disregard or ignore someone or something: *I can't believe they passed me over for that promotion again! I wanted the panel to appoint me to the committee, but they passed over me completely.*

pass up

1. To transfer something from a lower level to a higher one: *I passed the can of paint up to my friend who was painting the ceiling. The help department passes up serious complaints to the main office.*
2. To transfer something to the next member of a sequence: *We cleared the earth by forming a line and passing up buckets of dirt. Each person signed the document and passed it up to the next person on the list.*
3. To reject or refuse someone or something: *I passed up a chance for promotion because I didn't want to move across the country. That job offer sounds very good—don't pass it up!*

◆ **pat** (păt)

patted (păt′ĭd), **patting** (păt′ĭng), **pats** (păts)

pat down

1. To flatten or mold something by tapping it gently with the hands or a flat implement: *The baker patted down the dough with a rolling pin. We patted the clay down before shaping it.*
2. To search someone or something with the hands, especially for weapons or illegal substances: *The police patted down the suspect for guns. The customs officials patted us down.*

◆ **patch** (păch)

patched (păcht), **patching** (păch′ĭng), **patches** (păch′ĭz)

patch up

1. To mend or fix something that has separated or has holes by using some material to reconnect its parts: *I patched up my jeans with that fabric. I bought a sewing kit and patched my jacket up.*
2. To cover some hole or gap with some material: *She patched up the hole in my jeans. He patched up the rip in the drapes.*
3. To resolve some problem or conflict: *The delegates must patch up their differences.*

ă	pat	är	car	ī	bite	ô	paw	ŏŏ	took	ûr	urge
ā	pay	ĕ	pet	îr	pier	ôr	core	ŏŏr	lure	zh	vision
âr	care	ē	be	ŏ	pot	oi	boy	ōō	boot	ə	about,
ä	father	ĭ	pit	ō	toe	ou	out	ŭ	cut		item

◆ **pattern** (păt′ərn)

patterned (păt′ərnd), **patterning** (păt′ər-nĭng), **patterns** (păt′ərnz)

pattern on *or* **pattern after**

To form, develop, or found something on the basis of something else; fashion something after something else: *The country patterned its legal system on French civil law. These lesson plans are patterned after the ones I learned at graduate school.*

◆ **pave** (pāv)

paved (pāvd), **paving** (pā′vĭng), **paves** (pāvz)

pave over

1. To cover thoroughly some surface of land with asphalt, concrete, or other hard surface: *The contractor paved over the meadow in order to expand the mall's parking lot. The city paved the dirt road over to accommodate more traffic.*
2. To willfully ignore or hide some obvious issue or problem: *The politician paved over the whole issue of his voting record in his speech. Instead of simply telling us the real story, she tends to pave it over, even if she did nothing wrong.*

◆ **paw** (pô)

pawed (pôd), **pawing** (pô′ĭng), **paws** (pôz)

paw at

1. To strike or scrape something repeatedly with a paw or paws: *The cat pawed at the ball of string and chased it around the room.*
2. To handle someone or something clumsily, rudely, or with too much familiarity: *Stop pawing at all the fruit in the store! I was annoyed because my date kept pawing at me.*

◆ **pawn** (pôn)

pawned (pônd), **pawning** (pô′nĭng), **pawns** (pônz)

pawn off

To get rid of or dispose of something deceptively by misrepresenting its true value: *The clerk tried to pawn off the fake gemstone as a diamond. They almost pawned the counterfeit bills off on unsuspecting tourists.*

◆ **pay** (pā)

paid (pād), **paying** (pā′ĭng), **pays** (pāz)

pay back

1. To return some amount of money that has been borrowed: *Will you pay back the $60 I gave you last month? They finally paid the money back.*
2. To repay someone an amount of money: *I might not have enough money to pay them back. We need to pay back the bank.*
3. To reward or punish someone for something: *After all their hard work, the team was paid back with a victory. After they beat us, we paid them back by winning the series.*

pay for

1. To give some amount of money in return for something: *I paid $12 for those gloves. Did you pay for our meal yet?*
2. To bear a cost or penalty as a result of some action: *You will pay for*

your laziness when you take your exams and do badly.

pay off

1. To pay the full amount of some debt: *She paid off the mortgage ahead of schedule. He paid his college debt off six years after he graduated.*
2. To result in profit; be lucrative: *Your efforts will eventually pay off.*
3. To result in some degree of profit or loss: *My unwise bet paid off very badly.*
4. To pay the wages that are due to an employee upon discharge: *We were fired, so they paid us off and we left the building. The company didn't fire the workers because it couldn't afford to pay them off.*
5. To bribe someone in order to ensure cooperation: *The owner of the factory paid off the inspectors so that they wouldn't report the safety violations. I won't allow anyone to cheat here, and no one can pay me off.*

pay out

1. To disburse money to someone who is owed the money: *We paid $2,000 out to the contractor. The clients paid out for our services in advance.*
2. To spend money, especially a large amount: *I paid out $20,000 for my new car. My parents paid a bundle out for my tuition.*
3. To unwind or slowly add slack to some rope or line: *He paid out the line after each cast. She paid the leash out bit by bit to allow the dog to explore in the park.*

pay up

To pay some amount that is demanded in full: *If you don't pay up by the end of the week, you'll be evicted.*

◆ **peck** (pĕk)

pecked (pĕkt), **pecking** (pĕ′kĭng), **pecks** (pĕks)

peck at

To eat something unenthusiastically by taking small bites: *The sullen child only pecked at his carrots.*

peck out

To remove something by pecking: *The birds pecked the worms out of the apples. The vultures pecked out the dead rabbit's innards.*

◆ **peel** (pēl)

peeled (pēld), **peeling** (pē′lĭng), **peels** (pēlz)

peel off

1. To strip some outer layer, surface, or covering away from something in thin strips or pieces: *I peeled off the wrapping from my new CD case and took out the CD. You have to peel the skin off before you eat a banana.*
2. To come off from a surface in thin strips or pieces: *My skin peeled off after I got a sunburn. The labels peeled off from the file folders.*

ă	pat	är	car	ī	bite	ô	paw	o͝o	took	ûr	urge
ā	pay	ĕ	pet	îr	pier	ôr	core	o͝or	lure	zh	vision
âr	care	ē	be	ŏ	pot	oi	boy	o͞o	boot	ə	about,
ä	father	ĭ	pit	ō	toe	ou	out	ŭ	cut		item

3. To take off clothes, especially when they fit tightly: *It was so hot, we peeled off our jackets. Eventually, the campers peeled their shoes and socks off as they sat on the beach.*
4. To leave a flight formation in order to land or make a dive. Used of an aircraft: *The plane peeled off from the rest of the formation and did a trick.*
5. To leave a group and move in a different direction: *The members who voted against me peeled off and formed their own school.*

peel out

To drive a vehicle away suddenly and quickly, especially by spinning and skidding the tires loudly: *The angry teenager left the house quickly and peeled out of the driveway.*

◆ **peep** (pēp)

peeped (pēpt), **peeping** (pē′pĭng), **peeps** (pēps)

peep out

1. To become partially visible behind a cover or obstacle: *The moon peeped out from behind the clouds.*
2. To give a quick look from behind a cover or obstacle: *The child peeped out at us from behind the door.*

◆ **peg** (pĕg)

pegged (pĕgd), **pegging** (pĕg′ĭng), **pegs** (pĕgz)

peg up

1. To hang or post something up with or as if with a peg: *I pegged the laundry up on the clothesline. The artist pegs up his canvasses to dry.*
2. To raise some amount, rate, or value suddenly: *The store had to peg up the price of milk.*
3. To achieve something: *The team pegged up their first win halfway through the season. This successful record has pegged up more than a million dollars in sales.*
4. To play golf: *She has the opportunity to peg up in a professional tournament.*

◆ **pen** (pĕn)

penned (pĕnd), **penning** (pĕn′ĭng), **pens** (pĕnz)

pen in

To confine someone or something in or as if in a pen: *The farmer penned the pigs in for the night. If you don't pen in the chickens, the wolves will get them.*

◆ **pencil** (pĕn′səl)

penciled *or* **pencilled** (pĕn′səld), **penciling** *or* **pencilling** (pĕn′sə-lĭng), **pencils** (pĕn′səlz)

pencil in

1. To write something in with a pencil: *The assistant penciled in the editorial changes on the manuscript. After the teacher reviewed my test, I penciled the corrections in.*
2. To schedule something tentatively: *The secretary penciled in a staff meeting for 3:00. The band penciled a rehearsal in on Friday.*
3. To schedule a tentative appointment with someone: *We penciled him in for lunch next Monday. The interviewers penciled in the applicant for the end of the week.*

◆ **pep** (pĕp)

pepped (pĕpt), **pepping** (pĕp′ĭng), **peps** (pĕps)

pep up

1. To cause something to become more exciting or interesting: *A little spice will pep up the flavor of the stew. We could use a good comedian to pep this party up!*
2. To cause someone to become more alert and energetic: *I drank coffee to pep myself up as the night wore on. A little music might pep up our bored guests.*

◆ **pepper** (pĕp′ər)

peppered (pĕp′ərd), **peppering** (pĕp′ər-ĭng), **peppers** (pĕp′ərz)

pepper with

1. To intersperse something with something else, especially to make it more exciting, interesting, or colorful: *She peppers her stories with interesting details. Our vacation consisted of long days at the beach peppered with exciting trips to the city.*
2. To sprinkle liberally with something; dot with something: *The kids have peppered the backyard with lost marbles.*
3. To be sparsely distributed across something; dot something. Used in the passive: *The green plain was peppered with small yellow shrubs.*
4. To attack someone or something with or as if with small missiles: *The attackers peppered the castle wall with a hail of bullets.*

◆ **perk** (pûrk)

perked (pûrkt), **perking** (pûr′kĭng), **perks** (pûrks)

perk up

1. To become more lively, cheerful, or attentive: *We perked up when we heard the good news. The students perked up when the professor began the lecture.*
2. To cause someone or something to become more lively, cheerful, or attentive: *The morning coffee really perked me up! I perked up the kitten by feeding it catnip.*
3. To refresh the appearance of something: *New furniture and paint have perked up the room. Washing the windows has really perked the kitchen up.*

◆ **pertain** (pər-tān′)

pertained (pər-tānd′), **pertaining** (pər-tā′nĭng), **pertains** (pər-tānz′)

pertain to

To be relevant to or concerned with something: *In chemistry the word "basic" pertains to substances with a pH factor greater than 7.*

◆ **peter** (pē′tər)

petered (pē′tərd), **petering** (pē′tər-ĭng), **peters** (pē′tərz)

peter out

1. To cause someone to lose all energy; tire someone out: *That long*

ă	pat	är	car	ī	bite	ô	paw	ŏŏ	took	ûr	urge
ā	pay	ĕ	pet	îr	pier	ôr	core	ŏŏr	lure	zh	vision
âr	care	ē	be	ŏ	pot	oi	boy	ōō	boot	ə	about,
ä	father	ĭ	pit	ō	toe	ou	out	ŭ	cut		item

run petered me out. You'll get petered out if you work too fast.

2. To lose all energy; tire out: *I petered out toward the end and lost the race.*
3. To diminish slowly and come to an end; dwindle: *The flow of water petered out as the valves were closed.*

◆ **phase** (fāz)
phased (fāzd), **phasing** (fā′zĭng), **phases** (fā′zĭz)

phase in
To introduce something or someone gradually or in stages: *The government is now phasing in a new immigration policy. We should phase the new regulations in slowly so that businesses can get used to them.*

phase out
To take something or someone out of service gradually or in stages: *The company phased out the old model of vacuum cleaner, and it's hard to find any in the stores now. We will gradually phase the old schedule out to create a more efficient one.*

◆ **phone** (fōn)
phoned (fōnd), **phoning** (fō′nĭng), **phones** (fōnz)

phone in
1. To relay some information by telephone: *I phoned in my credit card number so the company could bill me directly. She couldn't go to the meeting, so she just phoned her report in using a speaker phone.*
2. To perform something halfheartedly or carelessly without full concentration or passion: *After playing the same role for a year, the actor started to phone in his performances.*

phone up
To telephone someone or something: *I didn't understand the contract, so I phoned up my lawyer for help. She told her client that she would phone him up after lunch to review what they had discussed.*

◆ **pick** (pĭk)
picked (pĭkt), **picking** (pĭk′ĭng), **picks** (pĭks)

pick apart
1. To pull something or someone to pieces: *The vultures picked apart the deer carcass. The children picked the bread apart, trying to remove all the raisins.*
2. To find flaws in something or someone by close examination: *The lawyer picked apart the witness's testimony. The candidate picked her opponent's speech apart.*

pick at
1. To pluck or pull at something, especially with the fingers or with a pick: *The musician picked at the guitar strings. The farmer picked at the bugs in the sheep's wool.*
2. To eat something sparingly or without appetite: *The child picked at the vegetables but ate all of the hamburger.*
3. To nag someone: *Don't pick at me—I'm doing the best I can!*

pick off

1. To remove or pluck something from a surface: *I picked off the price tag before wrapping the gift. We picked the dead leaves off the plant.*
2. To shoot and kill something or someone with a gun, especially from a distance: *The hunter picked the ducks off one by one. The sniper picked off an enemy soldier.*
3. BASEBALL To throw the ball to an occupied base and put out a runner who is taking a lead: *The catcher picked off the runner as he was trying to steal a base. The runner took a big lead, and the pitcher picked her off at first base.*
4. SPORTS To intercept something, as a pass in American football: *The cornerback picked off an errant pass and ran it back for a touchdown. The quarterback threw a low pass and a linebacker picked it off.*

pick on

To treat someone badly or unfairly, especially by teasing or bullying: *My big sister always picks on me. The kids at school pick on him for wearing glasses.*

pick out

1. To choose something or someone from a set of options; select something or someone: *We went to the video store and picked out a movie to watch. I picked this fabric out because it was the most colorful.*
2. To discern something or someone from the surroundings; distinguish something or someone: *From the plane, she was able to pick out her house on the ground. The victim picked his attacker out of the lineup.*
3. To play a piece of music tentatively, especially on a guitar or piano: *He picked out the song on the guitar, trying to remember the notes. I hummed the tune for her, and she picked it out on the piano.*

pick over

1. To sort through something carefully: *We picked over the grapes before buying them. Many of these archaeological sites have been picked over by tourists, and few artifacts remain.*
2. To examine or analyze something carefully: *The committee picked over the budget, looking for ways to save money.*

pick through

To search carefully through something, especially a disorganized mass: *I picked through the pile of clothes, looking for a pair of matching socks.*

pick up

1. To lift something or someone up, especially with the hands: *He bent over and picked the child up. She hasn't picked up the violin in years. I picked up the phone and answered it. After the tackle, I*

ă	pat	är	car	ī	bite	ô	paw	o͝o	took	ûr	urge		
ā	pay	ĕ	pet	îr	pier	ôr	core	o͝or	lure	zh	vision		
âr	care	ē	be	ŏ	pot	oi	boy	o͞o	boot	ə	about,		
ä	father	ĭ	pit	ō	toe	ou	out	ŭ	cut		item		

picked myself up off the ground and walked to the scrimmage line.

2. To collect someone; call for someone: *He left to pick up the children from school. I'll stop by your house at 8:00 and pick you up for the movie.*
3. To collect or gather something: *We picked up all the trash after the barbecue. Please pick your toys up so I can vacuum.*
4. To tidy up some thing or place: *You can't go outside until you pick up your room. I'm tired of picking up after you.*
5. To take on passengers or freight, as of a vehicle: *The bus picks up commuters at five stops. The truck will pick its cargo up in Miami.*
6. To purchase something casually or by chance: *Let's pick up a couple of magazines for the train ride. I picked this coat up at the sale.*
7. To acquire knowledge or habits through practice or experience: *My parents were afraid that I would pick up bad habits at summer camp. She never studied French in school—she just picked it up when she was working in Paris.*
8. To claim something: *She picked up her car at the repair shop. He dropped off his clothes at the dry cleaners and picked them up the following day.*
9. To improve in condition or activity: *Sales picked up last fall.*
10. To acquire speed: *The wind is starting to pick up. The bike picks up speed on the hill.*
11. To cause some speed or rate to increase: *The runners picked up the pace. Improvements to efficiency have picked the rate of production up.*
12. To contract something, as a disease: *I picked up a rare disease while I was traveling in Asia. The children must have picked the virus up at school.*
13. To earn, gain, or garner something: *Qualified specialists can pick up over $100 an hour.*
14. To take someone into custody; arrest someone: *The agents picked up two of the smugglers at the border. The police picked me up for questioning.*
15. Vulgar Slang To make casual acquaintance with someone, usually in anticipation of sexual relations.
16. To detect something: *The crew picked up two submarines on sonar. The signal is so weak that only a special antenna can pick it up. The dogs picked up the scent of the ducks.*
17. **pick up on** To notice something: *I picked up on my roommate's bad mood and left him alone.*
18. To continue with something after a break: *Let's pick up the discussion after lunch. She opened the book and picked the story up where she left off. The sequel picks up ten years after the death of the character in the last book.*
19. To prepare a sudden departure: *She just picked up and left without telling anyone.*

◆ **piece** (pēs)

pieced (pēst), **piecing** (pē′sĭng), **pieces** (pē′sĭz)

piece together

To join or unite the pieces of something: *We pieced the broken vase together. The detective pieced together the sequence of events leading up to the accident by interviewing witnesses.*

◆ **pig** (pĭg)

pigged (pĭgd), **pigging** (pĭg′ĭng), **pigs** (pĭgz)

pig out

SLANG

To eat greedily, ravenously, or voraciously; gorge: *The food was free, so I pigged out. We pigged out on ice cream until we all felt sick.*

◆ **pile** (pīl)

piled (pīld), **piling** (pī′lĭng), **piles** (pīlz)

pile in

1. To enter something or some place in a disorderly mass or group: *All six of us piled in the car. The subway doors opened and the passengers piled in.*
2. To move some people into something or some place in a disorderly fashion: *Pile the kids in the van and let's go. I opened the cellar door and piled the logs in. The truck is full and I don't think we can pile in any more rugs.*

pile out

To exit something or some place in a disorderly mass or group: *When we reached the store, the kids piled out of the van. I opened the door and the crowd piled out.*

pile up

1. To arrange something into a pile: *We piled up the firewood in the garage. I piled the dirty dishes up in the sink.*
2. To accumulate: *My bills piled up while I was in the hospital.*
3. To cause something to accumulate: *The company is piling up debt with its risky investments. The team piled 40 points up in the first half of the game.*
4. To crash into each other; collide. Used especially of vehicles: *Because of the thick fog, dozens of cars piled up on the freeway.*

◆ **pin** (pĭn)

pinned (pĭnd), **pinning** (pĭn′ĭng), **pins** (pĭnz)

pin down

1. To secure or fasten something using a pin or pins: *The tailor pinned down the patch before sewing it on. I pinned my tie down to stop it from flapping in the wind.*
2. To render someone or something immobile by or as if by holding down: *We pinned down the tarp with four heavy rocks. They pinned me down on the table while the doctor removed the bullet from my leg. The platoon was pinned down by heavy machine-gun fire.*
3. To establish something clearly: *Doctors finally pinned down the cause of the disease. I had a strange feeling about the old house, but I couldn't pin it down.*
4. To compel someone to give firm opinions or precise information: *The reporter pinned the governor*

ă	pat	är	car	ī	bite	ô	paw	o͝o	took	ûr	urge
ā	pay	ĕ	pet	îr	pier	ôr	core	o͝or	lure	zh	vision
âr	care	ē	be	ŏ	pot	oi	boy	o͞o	boot	ə	about,
ä	father	ĭ	pit	ō	toe	ou	out	ŭ	cut		item

down on the issue of raising taxes. The newspaper tried to pin down the candidates on their positions regarding capital punishment.

pin on

1. To hang or secure something onto someone or something using a pin or pins: *I pinned a flower on my hat. I pinned on a corsage to my sleeve.*
2. To ascribe responsibility for something, especially something that is worthy of blame, to someone: *The detective pinned the murder on the wrong suspect.*

◆ **pine** (pīn)

pined (pīnd), **pining** (pī′nĭng), **pines** (pīnz)

pine away

To wither or waste away from longing or grief: *After its owner was killed, the old dog pined away and died.*

pine for

To long or grieve intensely for someone or something: *All summer he sat in the garden pining for his girlfriend back home. Many teachers pine for the days when students were better behaved.*

◆ **pipe** (pīp)

piped (pīpt), **piping** (pī′pĭng), **pipes** (pīps)

pipe down

SLANG

To stop talking; become quiet: *Pipe down—I'm trying to sleep!*

pipe up

To join a conversation with an opinion, especially unexpectedly: *You should have piped up if you didn't agree with us.*

◆ **piss** (pĭs)

pissed (pĭst), **pissing** (pĭs′ĭng), **pisses** (pĭs′ĭz)

piss away

VULGAR SLANG

To waste or squander something.

piss off

VULGAR SLANG

1. To make someone angry.
2. To go away. Often used as an angry command.

◆ **pit** (pĭt)

pitted (pĭt′ĭd), **pitting** (pĭt′ĭng), **pits** (pĭts)

pit against

To set someone or something in competition with or opposition to someone or something else: *The civil war pitted brother against brother. The match will pit the two greatest boxers against each other. The grading system pits one student against another and discourages cooperation.*

◆ **pitch** (pĭch)

pitched (pĭcht), **pitching** (pĭch′ĭng), **pitches** (pĭch′ĭz)

pitch in

1. To contribute something toward some general pool or effort: *We all pitched in $10 to buy the couple a wedding gift. After the earthquake, local businesses pitched in with donations of food and water. When it was time to clean up the park, the neighbors pitched in.*

2. To set to work vigorously: *The grass had to be cut, so I started the lawn mower and pitched in.*

pitch into

1. To throw or toss something or someone into something: *She pitched the plastic cup into the garbage can.*
2. To attack someone verbally or physically; assault someone: *They pitched into the photographer for taking their picture without permission.*

pitch on

1. To throw or toss something onto something: *I pitched my jacket on the chair and sat down.*
2. To choose or achieve something, usually quickly: *We pitched on the terrace as the proper location for the ceremony.*

pitch upon

To choose or achieve something, usually quickly: *After a brief discussion of the problem, we pitched upon a good solution.*

◆ **pivot** (pĭv′ət)

pivoted (pĭv′ə-tĭd), **pivoting** (pĭv′ə-tĭng), **pivots** (pĭv′əts)

pivot on *or* **pivot around**

1. To rotate or spin around while remaining centered on some point: *The chair pivots on a steel post.*
2. To depend on something or someone for success or failure: *This business deal pivots on whether or not we are willing to change the name of our product.*
3. To develop from a central idea: *The plot of the show pivots on the effects of drug addiction.*

◆ **place** (plās)

placed (plāst), **placing** (plā′sĭng), **places** (plā′sĭz)

place out of

To qualify for a waiver of some requirement or prerequisite: *If you've placed out of introductory biology, you can take an advanced course. The school has a language requirement, but since I know Spanish, I placed out.*

◆ **plague** (plāg)

plagued (plāgd), **plaguing** (plā′gĭng), **plagues** (plāgz)

plague with

To pester, trouble, or harass someone or something with something: *Reporters plague me with questions everywhere I go. The production was plagued with problems from the start.*

◆ **plan** (plăn)

planned (plănd), **planning** (plăn′ĭng), **plans** (plănz)

plan ahead

To make arrangements in advance: *I planned ahead and bought my tickets a month in advance, which saved me a lot of money.*

plan for

To prepare for something: *Many people don't plan for retirement and then find that they haven't saved enough money.*

plan on

1. To intend to do something: *I plan on buying a house as soon as I get a promotion.*
2. To anticipate or expect something: *We planned on 50 people coming to our party, so we bought a lot of food. I didn't plan on being stuck in traffic for two hours.*

plan out

To formulate a detailed scheme or plan for something: *Every Monday we have a meeting to plan out the week. The suspects said the murder was an accident, but the police claimed they had planned it all out.*

◆ **play** (plā)

played (plād), **playing** (plā′ĭng), **plays** (plāz′)

play along

1. To cooperate or pretend to cooperate with someone: *We decided to play along with their silly plans for a while. If you don't play along, we'll never get the job done.*
2. To accompany someone or something by playing a musical instrument: *I listen to the radio and play along with the songs on my guitar.*

play around

1. To engage in frivolous or idle activity; goof off: *Stop playing around and get to work.*
2. **play around with** To manipulate or work with something without a clear sense of method: *We played around with the old television set, trying to see if we could make it work.*
3. SLANG To engage in romantic or sexual relations with someone; fool around: *I think those two are playing around. Who is he playing around with now?*

play at

1. To pretend to be or to do something for amusement or out of curiosity: *He was just playing at being a cowboy.*
2. To do or take part in something halfheartedly: *You're playing at your work and not taking it seriously enough.*

play back

1. To replay something that has been recorded: *After recording the interview, the reporter played back the tape to find a quotation for the article. The instructors videotaped the performance and played it back for the class in slow motion.*
2. To withdraw or lower the emphasis of something: *You should play back the budget questions in your presentation and concentrate on hiring decisions. The coach played the defense back for a while and concentrated on scoring goals.*

play down

To minimize something or the importance of something: *She played down the importance of her own research and credited her colleagues instead. When the reporters asked the mayor about the city's growing debt, she played it down, assuring them that she would not raise taxes.*

play off

1. SPORTS To play a game that breaks a tie in ranking: *The top two teams play off tonight to determine the champion.*
2. To perform an action in response to some other action, exploiting it advantageously: *A good tennis player plays off every move the opponent makes. We make a good team, since we play off each other perfectly.*
3. **play off against** To set something in opposition to, or working in a different direction than, something else in order to gain an advantage: *The queen played the nobles off against each other, telling each of them that the others were plotting against him.*

play on *or* **play upon**

1. To take advantage of some attitude or feeling for one's own interests: *Many politicians play on popular fears by exaggerating the threat of crime and terrorism.*
2. To perform some trick or joke at someone's expense: *They're always playing little tricks on me, like stealing one of my shoes.*
3. To improvise playfully or mockingly with something: *The comedian played on what I had said and made me sound very foolish.*

play out

1. To use something until there is none left; use up something: *The boxer's strength was played out early in the match.*
2. To proceed through a course of progression or development. Used of situations: *We'll have to see how the situation in my office plays out before we know whether we can take a vacation.*

play over

1. To consider something; give thought to something: *It's a very tough question, and I've been playing it over for a long time. I continue playing over the accident, wondering if I could have prevented it.*
2. To be repeatedly recalled or relived in the mind; occupy the mind repeatedly: *Our kiss last night keeps playing over in my head.*

play up

To emphasize something or the importance of something in order to make a better impression: *The newspaper played up the scandal in order to excite its readers. Your experience with computers is your strongest qualification, so be sure to play that up in the interview.*

play with

1. To engage in a sport, game, or other recreation with someone: *I played chess with my brother until midnight.*
2. To amuse or distract oneself by manipulating something: *He sat playing with a rubber band throughout the lecture.*

ă	pat	är	car	ī	bite	ô	paw	o͝o	took	ûr	urge
ā	pay	ĕ	pet	îr	pier	ôr	core	o͝or	lure	zh	vision
âr	care	ē	be	ŏ	pot	oi	boy	o͞o	boot	ə	about,
ä	father	ĭ	pit	ō	toe	ou	out	ŭ	cut		item

3. To jest with someone: *I was just playing with you when I said I was angry.*
4. To tamper with something: *Someone played with my computer while I was gone.*
5. To treat something casually or without seriousness; flirt with something: *She played with the idea of going back to college.*
6. To experiment with something: *He played with many different hairstyles before choosing one he liked.*
7. To manipulate or arrange something in a skillful manner: *I like the way your poem plays with language.*

◆ **plot** (plŏt)
plotted (plŏtʹĭd), **plotting** (plŏtʹĭng), **plots** (plŏts)

plot against
To establish a plan to overthrow or ruin someone or something: *The spies plotted against the government.*

plot out
1. To place something on a graph: *The students plotted out the equation and determined that it was a parabola. We determined the coordinates and plotted them out on the graph.*
2. To establish some plan, path, or course: *We plotted out the best route through the mountains. The captain plotted the ship's course out on the chart.*
3. To make a thorough analysis of some plan: *The governor met with his top advisers to plot out a new strategy. Before we started the company, we spent six months just plotting it out.*

◆ **plow** (plou)
plowed (ploud), **plowing** (plouʹĭng), **plows** (plouz)

plow back
To reinvest some earnings or profits in one's business: *After plowing back its profits for years, the company finally decided to pay dividends to its investors. The owners plowed the profits back into the business, using the money to buy new equipment.*

plow into
1. To strike someone or something with force: *The truck slid on the ice and plowed into a brick wall.*
2. To cause something to strike someone or something with force: *The driver plowed the SUV into the wall.*
3. To undertake something, as a task, with eagerness and vigor: *I went to the library and plowed into my research paper.*
4. To invest some amount of money into something: *The company plowed its excess cash into stocks. I just plowed $200,000 into a new house.*

plow under
1. To work something into the earth by turning up soil over it: *Low grain prices have forced many farmers to plow their crops under. Many wetlands were plowed under to make more farmland.*
2. To overwhelm someone or something: *My teachers have plowed me under with work this*

week. We were plowed under with dirty laundry.

◆ **plug** (plŭg)

plugged (plŭgd), **plugging** (plŭg′ĭng), **plugs** (plŭgz)

plug in

1. To insert a part of some object into another, especially to make a mechanical or electrical connection: *He plugged in the iron and waited for it to get hot. If you don't plug the phone in, you won't get any telephone calls.*
2. To function by being mechanically or electrically connected to another object: *That radio plugs in, but it can also run on batteries.*

plug into

To insert a part of some object into an outlet, socket, or some other receptacle, especially to make a mechanical or electrical connection: *Plug the iron into the electrical outlet. I plugged the speakers into the back of the receiver.*

plug up

1. To obstruct the path or passageway through, into, or out of something: *An orange rind plugged up the sink. Leaves have plugged the storm drain up.*
2. To be obstructed so that substances cannot pass through: *The hose plugged up and eventually burst.*
3. To cause the path through, into, or out of something to become obstructed: *They plugged up the leaks in the boat with tar. We plugged the hole up with a cork.*

◆ **plump** (plŭmp)

plumped (plŭmpt), **plumping** (plŭm′pĭng), **plumps** (plŭmps)

plump up

1. To become more plump or chubby: *I went off my diet and immediately plumped up.*
2. To make something rounded or full in form: *We plumped up the dried cherries by soaking them in water. The nurse brought me a pillow and plumped it up before putting it behind my head.*

◆ **plunge** (plŭnj)

plunged (plŭnjd), **plunging** (plŭn′jĭng), **plunges** (plŭn′jĭz)

plunge in

1. To submerge something quickly into something else: *The cook plunged the hot eggs in the cold water to stop them from cooking.*
2. To jump or throw oneself into something: *I walked up to the swimming pool and plunged in.*
3. To fall into something: *The child slipped and plunged in the well.*

plunge into

1. To fall or dive into some place or thing: *I jumped off the diving board and plunged into the warm water.*
2. To thrust or throw something forcefully into some place or thing: *I plunged the shovel into the soil.*

ă	pat	är	car	ī	bite	ô	paw	o͝o	took	ûr	urge
ā	pay	ĕ	pet	îr	pier	ôr	core	o͝or	lure	zh	vision
âr	care	ē	be	ŏ	pot	oi	boy	o͞o	boot	ə	about, item
ä	father	ĭ	pit	ō	toe	ou	out	ŭ	cut		

3. To enter earnestly or wholeheartedly into some activity or situation: *After the vacation, I plunged into my studies with renewed energy.*
4. To send someone or something into some condition or situation: *My gambling losses plunged me into debt.*
5. To fall into some state or condition: *After my divorce, I plunged into a deep depression.*

◆ **ply** (plī)

plied (plīd), **plying** (plī′ĭng), **plies** (plīz)

ply with

To give someone substantial amounts of something, such as drinks or other favors, especially to encourage cooperation or to manipulate: *She plied the spy with wine, hoping that he would reveal his true identity.*

◆ **point** (point)

pointed (poin′tĭd), **pointing** (poin′tĭng), **points** (points)

point out

To bring something to the attention of others; indicate something: *No one likes him because he always points out everyone's mistakes. As we drove by her old house, she pointed it out to me.*

point to

1. To indicate the location of something: *The arrows on the map point to the places where we camped overnight.*
2. To make a gesture indicating the location of something: *He told the dog to go outside and pointed to the door.*
3. To suggest something as a likely possibility or conclusion: *The chewed-up bones in the kitchen point to the dog, not the child. All indications point to an early spring.*

point toward

1. To indicate the direction in which something lies: *The sign points toward the center of the city.*
2. To make a gesture indicating the direction in which something lies: *The farmer pointed toward the fields across the road.*
3. To be suggestive of the idea that something is a possibility or correct conclusion: *The fact that the door wasn't broken points toward the theory that the thief had a key.*
4. To cause someone to consider something to be a possibility or correct conclusion: *These facts point us toward a new explanation.*

◆ **poke** (pōk)

poked (pōkt), **poking** (pō′kĭng), **pokes** (pōks)

poke out

1. To stick outward; protrude: *A tag is poking out of your shirt. They were so thin that their bones were poking out.*
2. To cause something to be dislodged by prodding it: *Be careful with that ice pick—you might poke out your eye. I poked the ants out of the hole with a stick.*
3. To extend something through some gap or hole, especially cautiously: *The gopher poked its head out the entrance of its tunnel.*

◆ **polish** (pŏl′ĭsh)

polished (pŏl′ĭsht), **polishing** (pŏl′ĭ-shĭng), **polishes** (pŏl′ĭ-shĭz)

polish off

1. To make something clean or shiny: *The student polished off the apple and handed it to the teacher. I polished the vase off with a cloth and set it on the table.*
2. To eliminate something, such as rust or a stain by rubbing: *Please polish that spot off the doorknob. After much scrubbing, I finally polished off the stain.*
3. SLANG To finish or consume something enthusiastically: *I polished off that last piece of cake. After we polish this pizza off, let's get dessert.*

polish up

1. To make something smooth and shiny by rubbing or chemical action: *The jeweler polished up the stones and made them into a necklace. She cleaned the mud off her shoes and polished them up.*
2. To improve one's knowledge of something, especially through study and practice: *I've been polishing up on my Spanish because I'm going to Mexico. My dancing skills weren't that good, so I took a class to polish them up.*
3. To improve or refine something: *The mayor tried to polish up his image after the scandal. The manuscript is good, but you need to polish it up if you want it to be published.*

◆ **pony** (pō′nē)

ponied (pō′nēd), **ponying** (pō′nē-ĭng), **ponies** (pō′nēz)

pony up

SLANG

To pay some amount of money that is owed or due: *I had to pony up $6 for a hot dog at the airport. The star was charging $100 for an autograph, but fans gladly ponied it up. You said you'd repay me last week, so pony up!*

◆ **pooch** (po͝och)

pooched (po͝ocht), **pooching** (po͞o′chĭng), **pooches** (po͞o′chĭz)

pooch out

SLANG

To swell or protrude outward: *I need to go on a diet—my stomach is starting to pooch out.*

◆ **pool** (po͞ol)

pooled (po͞old), **pooling** (po͞o′lĭng), **pools** (po͞olz)

pool up

1. To accumulate in pools of liquid: *Because the seal around the bathtub leaks, water pools up on the floor every time I shower.*
2. To group some resources for the common advantage of the participants or contributors: *We pooled our money up so that we could buy a new TV. If the kids pool up their allowances, they could buy a baseball bat.*

ă	pat	är	car	ī	bite	ô	paw	o͝o	took	ûr	urge
ā	pay	ĕ	pet	îr	pier	ôr	core	o͝or	lure	zh	vision
âr	care	ē	be	ŏ	pot	oi	boy	o͞o	boot	ə	about,
ä	father	ĭ	pit	ō	toe	ou	out	ŭ	cut		item

◆ **poop** (po͞op)
pooped (po͞opt), **pooping** (po͞o′pĭng), **poops** (po͞ops)

poop out
SLANG
1. To make someone exhausted; tire someone out: *That long walk uphill really pooped me out.*
2. To quit something because of exhaustion: *Too tired to continue, he pooped out of the race.*
3. To decide not to participate, especially at the last moment: *She was going to help me, but she pooped out and didn't come.*

◆ **pop** (pŏp)
popped (pŏpt), **popping** (pŏp′ĭng), **pops** (pŏps)

pop for
SLANG
To pay for something: *I'll pop for the video if you buy some snacks.*

pop in *or* **pop by**
To come to some place for a quick or casual visit: *Can you pop by my house for lunch? I just popped in to say hello.*

pop into
1. To visit some place briefly: *I'm going to pop into the store for a moment.*
2. To put or throw something into something suddenly: *He watched the movie while popping marshmallows into his mouth. She popped the DVD into the DVD player.*

pop off
1. To burst off with a short, sharp, explosive sound: *If the pressure in the bottle gets too high, the top will pop off.*
2. SLANG To leave abruptly or hurriedly: *She popped off a few minutes ago, but I don't know where she went. He popped off to the store.*
3. SLANG To speak thoughtlessly in a burst of released anger: *The movie star popped off at the reporters who were hounding him.*
4. SLANG To die suddenly: *The book is about a rich man who pops off and leaves his family millions of dollars.*
5. SLANG To kill someone: *The gangster popped off the witness outside of the courtroom. She learned that he was a double agent, and so she popped him off the next time she saw him.*

pop out
1. To jump or burst out of something: *I wound the jack-in-the-box until the puppet popped out.*
2. To appear suddenly from within or behind something: *Suddenly, a bear popped out from the bushes.*
3. To cause something to be removed or released, especially with a small, quick push: *The kids accidentally popped out the bottom pane of the window. The memory chip in my computer was broken, so I popped it out and installed a new one.*
4. To leave briefly: *He'll be back in a minute—he just popped out to get some coffee.*

pop up
1. To cause something to jump upwards, often with a short, sharp, explosive sound: *The batter popped up a fly ball to center field, where it was caught. I*

wedged a crowbar under the lid of the crate and popped it up.

2. To appear suddenly or unexpectedly: *He dived under the water and popped up at the other end of the pool. The doctor told me to call her if any new symptoms pop up.*

◆ **pore** (pôr)

pored (pôrd), **poring** (pôr′ĭng), **pores** (pôrz)

pore over

To read or study something carefully and thoroughly: *The engineers pored over their calculations looking for errors.*

◆ **pork** (pôrk)

porked (pôrkt), **porking** (pôr′kĭng), **porks** (pôrks)

pork out

SLANG

1. To eat greedily, ravenously, or voraciously; gorge: *After we porked out at the buffet, we didn't have room for dessert. I went to my favorite restaurant and porked out on pizza.*
2. To become fat: *I porked out over the holidays, and now I can barely fit into my pants.*

◆ **portion** (pôr′shən)

portioned (pôr′shənd), **portioning** (pôr′shə-nĭng), **portions** (pôr′shənz)

portion out

To divide something into parts or shares for distribution: *The charity raises money and then portions it out among the most needy places. We portioned out the equipment according to how much weight each person could carry.*

◆ **pounce** (pouns)

pounced (pounst), **pouncing** (poun′sĭng), **pounces** (poun′sĭz)

pounce on

1. To jump, leap, or bound onto something or someone: *The cat pounced on the mouse and killed it. We saw a falcon pounce on a rabbit.*
2. To criticize or attack someone verbally: *He suddenly pounced on me for not returning his book.*
3. To take advantage of something enthusiastically, as an opportunity; jump at something: *She pounced on the chance to move to New York and go to law school.*

◆ **pound** (pound)

pounded (poun′dĭd), **pounding** (poun′dĭng), **pounds** (poundz)

pound out

1. To expand the surface area of something, as a metal, by striking it: *The artist pounded out the metal plate until it was flat. The blacksmith pounded the iron out.*
2. To arrive at some agreement after much discussion, argument, or negotiation: *The warring nations finally pounded out a treaty. The manager pounded a vacation schedule out that everyone liked.*

ă	pat	är	car	ī	bite	ô	paw	ŏŏ	took	ûr	urge
ā	pay	ĕ	pet	îr	pier	ôr	core	ŏŏr	lure	zh	vision
âr	care	ē	be	ŏ	pot	oi	boy	ōō	boot	ə	about,
ä	father	ĭ	pit	ō	toe	ou	out	ŭ	cut		item

3. To write something very quickly, especially using a keyboard: *The author pounded out the last chapter of her novel in one day. The article was due in two hours, so I went to my computer and pounded it out.*

◆ **power** (pou′ər)

powered (pou′ərd), **powering** (pou′ər-ĭng), **powers** (pou′ərz)

power down

1. To stop the operation of something, especially when a special process is required: *The engineers powered down the generator to repair the wires. After we were finished with the computer, we powered it down.*
2. To stop operating, especially when a special process is required: *The computer powers down automatically if not used for four hours.*

power up

1. To activate some device and prepare it for operation: *The pilot powered up the engines and prepared to take off. I replaced the memory chip and powered the computer up to see if it worked.*
2. To start operating and become ready for use: *You have to wait a few seconds for the computer to power up.*

◆ **preside** (prĭ-zīd′)

presided (prĭ-zī′dĭd), **presiding** (prĭ-zī′dĭng), **presides** (prĭ-zīdz′)

preside over

To have or exercise authority over something or someone; be in charge of something or someone: *The vice president presided over the committee meeting because the president was absent.*

◆ **press** (prĕs)

pressed (prĕst), **pressing** (prĕs′ĭng), **presses** (prĕs′ĭz)

press for

To entreat or require someone to provide something: *The reporters pressed the politician for a reply.*

press on

1. To apply direct pressure to something: *I pressed on the edge of the table, and it tipped over.*
2. To continue doing something with determination and despite setbacks: *Despite their exhaustion, the climbers pressed on toward the summit.*

◆ **pretty** (prĭt′ē)

prettied (prĭt′ēd), **prettying** (prĭt′ē-ĭng), **pretties** (prĭt′ēz)

pretty up

To improve the appearance or style of someone or something; doll someone or something up: *We prettied up the guest room with some new curtains. My parents prettied me up in a satin dress for the piano recital.*

◆ **prevail** (prĭ-vāl′)

prevailed (prĭ-vāld′), **prevailing** (prĭ-vā′lĭng), **prevails** (prĭ-vālz′)

prevail on *or* **prevail upon**

To successfully persuade or induce someone to do something: *We prevailed on the committee to stop the developers from building a shopping mall. Lobbyists pre-*

vailed upon the president to veto the legislation.

◆ **prey** (prā)

preyed (prād), **preying** (prā′ĭng), **preys** (prāz)

prey on

1. To hunt and kill something for food: *Owls prey on mice.*
2. To exploit or make a profit at the expense of someone; take advantage of someone: *Pickpockets often prey on unsuspecting tourists.*
3. To exert a harmful or injurious effect on something or someone: *Guilt preyed on him and eventually led him to confess.*

◆ **print** (prĭnt)

printed (prĭn′tĭd), **printing** (prĭn′tĭng), **prints** (prĭnts)

print out

1. To produce something by printing or with a printer: *The student printed out two copies of the document by hand. This printer prints out ten pages a minute.*
2. To reproduce some image or document stored on a computer by printing it on paper or displaying it on a screen: *She printed my files out for me. He printed out some pictures. You can set up this program so that it prints everything out in a single window.*
3. To be reproduced with a printer or by display on a computer screen: *After these documents print out, put them in an envelope and leave it on my desk. My documents have been printing out crooked—is something wrong with the printer?*

print up

To produce something by printing or with a printer: *He printed up two copies of the document. She printed some flyers up and distributed them at the meeting.*

◆ **proceed** (prō-sēd′)

proceeded (prō-sē′dĭd), **proceeding** (prō-sē′dĭng), **proceeds** (prō-sēdz′)

proceed from

1. To set out or embark from some place: *We proceeded from the bus station toward our hotel.*
2. To have something as an origin or cause; have developed from something: *Most of our mistakes proceed from carelessness.*

proceed with

To begin or continue some action or process: *The company proceeded with its plan to fire the workers, despite opposition from the union.*

◆ **prop** (prŏp)

propped (prŏpt), **propping** (prŏp′ĭng), **props** (prŏps)

prop up

1. To support something with or as if with a prop: *I propped up the leg of my desk with some cardboard to keep it from wobbling. She sat*

ă	pat	är	car	ī	bite	ô	paw	ŏŏ	took	ûr	urge
ā	pay	ĕ	pet	îr	pier	ôr	core	ŏŏr	lure	zh	vision
âr	care	ē	be	ŏ	pot	oi	boy	ōō	boot	ə	about,
ä	father	ĭ	pit	ō	toe	ou	out	ŭ	cut		item

down in the chair and propped her feet up on the table. He propped the ladder up against the wall and climbed up to the roof.

2. To provide temporary or partial support to something that is failing or needs assistance: *Foreign investors propped up the currency by purchasing more government bonds. The company would go bankrupt if the government didn't prop it up with special tax breaks.*

◆ **provide** (prə-vīd′)

provided (prə-vī′dĭd), **providing** (prə-vī′dĭng), **provides** (prə-vīdz′)

provide against

To take measures to deal with or prevent some unforeseen occurrence: *Our homeowner's insurance provides against damage from flooding.*

provide for

1. To supply someone or something with basic necessities, as food, shelter, and clothing: *How long do you have to work every week to provide for such a large family?*
2. To take measures in preparation for something: *Our forecast provides for a 6 percent decrease in sales next year.*
3. To set something down as a stipulation: *Their employment contract provides for two weeks of vacation every year.*

◆ **pry** (prī)

pried (prīd), **prying** (prī′ĭng), **pries** (prīz)

pry out

1. To extract something with or as if with a lever: *I pried out the staples from the thick report. They pried the microphone out of my hands to stop me from singing.*
2. To obtain something from someone with effort or difficulty: *The detectives finally pried a confession out of the suspect. They kept questioning me until they had pried out all the information.*

◆ **psych** (sīk)

psyched (sīkt), **psyching** (sī′kĭng), **psyches** (sīks)

psych out

To undermine the confidence of someone by psychological means; intimidate someone: *The admissions officer really psyched me out during the interview. They psyched out the other team by chanting.*

psych up

To prepare someone mentally for some task or activity: *The preview psyched us up to see the film. The coach's speech psyched up the team for the game.*

◆ **puff** (pŭf)

puffed (pŭft), **puffing** (pŭf′ĭng), **puffs** (pŭfs)

puff out

1. To extend, stretch, or swell, by or as if by being filled: *The sails puffed out as the breeze strengthened.*
2. To cause something to extend, stretch, or swell outward: *The wind puffed out the sheets that were hanging on the clothesline. Male birds will puff their chests out to appear larger.*

◆ **puke** (pyo͞ok)

puked (pyo͞okt), **puking** (pyo͞o′kĭng), **pukes** (pyo͞oks)

puke up

VULGAR SLANG

To eject some contents of the stomach by vomiting: *I became sick on the carnival ride and puked up my dinner. The cat puked a hairball up.*

◆ **pull** (po͝ol)

pulled (po͝old), **pulling** (po͝ol′ĭng), **pulls** (po͝olz)

pull apart

1. To pull pieces or components from something; take something apart: *I pulled the computer apart and replaced some damaged chips. Our dogs pulled apart the couch while we were away.*
2. To separate some people or things: *The teacher pulled apart the fighting students. I pulled the two stuck pages apart.*
3. To cause someone deep emotional turmoil: *Her guilt was pulling her apart.*

pull around

1. To bring some vehicle to a location, especially to load or unload it: *The valet pulled our car around, and we all got in.*
2. To gradually return to a sound state of health; recover: *Now that her fever is gone, the patient is really starting to pull around.*
3. To reverse a decline in the value, performance, or health of something; turn something around: *The company is almost bankrupt—I don't see how the new president can pull it around.*

pull away

1. To draw or haul something or someone away from something or someone: *She opened the box and gently pulled away the layers of tissue paper. He pulled the child's hand away from the hot stove.*
2. To move away or backward; withdraw: *When I leaned over to wipe the child's face, he pulled away. She tried to stop him from going, but he pulled away from her.*
3. To start moving away, as a vehicle: *She noted the car's license plate as it was pulling away. We waved goodbye as the boat pulled away from the dock.*
4. To move ahead: *The horse pulled away in the final stretch and won the race.*

pull back

1. To haul or tug something or someone backward: *I pulled my hair back and put it in a ponytail. She pulled back the curtain and looked outside. He pulled me back from the edge of the cliff.*
2. To withdraw or retreat: *The firefighters pulled back when the fire reached the gas tanks.*
3. To order someone to withdraw or retreat: *The commander pulled the*

ă	pat	är	car	ī	bite	ô	paw	o͝o	took	ûr	urge
ā	pay	ĕ	pet	îr	pier	ôr	core	o͝or	lure	zh	vision
âr	care	ē	be	ŏ	pot	oi	boy	o͞o	boot	ə	about,
ä	father	ĭ	pit	ō	toe	ou	out	ŭ	cut		item

troops back to a safer position. Aid organizations are pulling back volunteers until the fighting in that area stops.

pull down

1. To bring something down from a higher level to a lower one: *Could you pull that book down from the shelf for me? After the concert, we went around town and pulled down all the advertisements.*
2. To demolish or destroy some structure; raze something: *They're pulling down the movie theater and putting in a shopping mall. When someone got injured on the old water tower, the city council decided to pull it down.*
3. To reduce something to a lower amount: *Lower wages have not pulled down the price of consumer goods, and many people can no longer afford the bare necessities. Airline ticket prices have risen over the past year, but lower fuel costs should soon pull them down.*
4. To depress someone, as in spirits or health: *This fight with his parents is really pulling him down.*
5. To draw some amount of money as wages; earn something: *She pulls down a hefty salary as a lawyer.*

pull for

To give encouragement and support to someone or something; root for someone or something: *Good luck in the game tomorrow—we're all pulling for you!*

pull in

1. To draw or haul something or someone inward or inside: *When I offered to help him get out of the pool, he pulled me in. She grabbed my hand and pulled me in the room. The fishermen pulled in the nets and collected the fish.*
2. To arrive at a place. Used of vehicles, passengers, or drivers: *I got to the station just as the train was pulling in. We pulled in after midnight and quietly shut the car doors so we wouldn't wake anyone.*
3. To involve someone in an activity or situation. Used chiefly in the passive: *I got pulled into the scam because I thought I was going to make money.*
4. To restrain someone; rein someone in: *The commander pulled in the maverick officer.*
5. To arrest someone: *The police pulled me in for questioning. The police pulled in two of the suspects on drug charges.*
6. To earn or yield some amount of money: *The film has pulled in $30 million since its release.*

pull off

1. To remove something by pulling: *I sat down and pulled off my boots. Someone pulled the antenna off your car.*
2. To extract, remove, or take someone or something from something, such as an assignment or public posting: *The network pulled the show off the air when viewers began to complain. The editor pulled the reporter off the story.*
3. To exit some roadway or lane of traffic: *The car pulled off the highway, and the police followed it onto a country road. Let's pull off at the next rest area and get something to eat.*
4. To perform something in spite of difficulties or obstacles; bring

something off: *The team pulled off a last-minute victory after being down 15 points at halftime. We didn't think we could complete the project before the deadline, but somehow we pulled it off.*

pull on

1. To pull something directly; tug something: *Please don't pull on my hair; it hurts.*
2. To put something on by pulling: *I pulled on my boots and stepped outside. We pulled our jackets on when the sun went down.*
3. To take a long puff or sip of something: *My friends and I pulled on the cold beer with gusto.*
4. To draw out a weapon and threaten someone: *The intruder pulled a knife on me.*

pull out

1. To remove something: *I pulled out the splinter with a pair of tweezers. The chef pulled a lobster out of the tank.*
2. To bring something forth; produce something: *She reached into her purse and pulled out her wallet. The mugger pulled a knife out and threatened us.*
3. To leave or depart. Used of a vehicle, passenger, or driver: *The train pulls out at noon. We pulled out of town in the evening.*
4. To enter a lane of traffic: *The car pulled out onto the highway. The truck pulled out in front of us.*
5. To withdraw from some situation or commitment; get out of some situation: *The troops will pull out from the occupied area as soon as peace is restored. After the crash, many Wall Street investors pulled out. The pilot pulled out of a nose dive.*
6. To withdraw something or someone, as from a situation or commitment: *The government pulled out its ambassador before the war began. We pulled the children out of school and educated them at home.*

pull over

1. To draw or drag something over someone or something: *The children pulled the covers over their heads.*
2. To bring some vehicle to a stop at a curb or at the side of a road: *When we drove up the coast, we pulled over at a lookout and watched the sunset. I pulled the car over to the side of the road to let the fire truck pass.*
3. To instruct or force a driver to bring a vehicle to a stop at a curb or at the side of a road: *The state trooper pulled the motorist over for driving too fast. We saw a police car pulling over a truck.*

pull through

1. To successfully endure or survive something difficult, as trouble or illness: *The patient's fever is still high, but the doctor says that she'll pull through. The company barely pulled through the recession.*

ă	pat	är	car	ī	bite	ô	paw	o͝o	took	ûr	urge
ā	pay	ĕ	pet	îr	pier	ôr	core	o͝or	lure	zh	vision
âr	care	ē	be	ŏ	pot	oi	boy	o͞o	boot	ə	about, item
ä	father	ĭ	pit	ō	toe	ou	out	ŭ	cut		

2. To help someone endure something difficult, as trouble or illness: *The disease almost killed the patient, but the doctors pulled him through. My sense of humor has pulled me through some difficult times.*

pull together

1. To draw some things closer to each other: *We pulled our chairs together so that we could talk.*
2. To bring together things gathered from several sources; compile something: *The report pulls together findings from previous studies. The way you've written the ending is good—it pulls the whole story together. The tragedy has pulled the community closer together.*
3. To make a joint effort toward a common goal; cooperate: *The whole community pulled together to rebuild the school that had burned down.*
4. To make oneself calm and tranquil. Used reflexively: *Stop crying and pull yourself together!*

pull up

1. To obtain something by drawing or pulling upwards: *I pulled up a large fish yesterday with my new fishing pole. I'll tie the bucket to the rope, and you pull it up to the roof.*
2. To uproot something, especially a plant: *We pulled up several large weeds from the garden. If you want to get rid of the ivy, you can't just cut it down, you have to pull it up.*
3. To draw something close by and make it available for use: *I pulled up a chair and sat down. Let's pull a few more seats up to the table for the new guests.*
4. To bring some vehicle to a halt alongside something: *The drivers must pull up their trucks to the curb before loading them. She pulled the bus up to the school entrance to let the children out.*
5. To come to a halt alongside something. Used of vehicles and riders: *The truck pulled up to the gas pump. I pulled up to the tollbooth and paid the toll.*
6. To move to a position or place ahead, as in a race; catch up: *The track star pulled up and passed the leader in the final lap, winning the race.*

◆ **pump** (pŭmp)
pumped (pŭmpt), **pumping** (pŭm′pĭng), **pumps** (pŭmps)

pump out

1. To force or suck something, as a liquid or gas, out of something by means of a pump: *The contractors pumped the water out of the ditch. They pumped out the sewage that had flooded the basement.*
2. To force the liquid or gas out of something by means of a pump: *When the rain finally stopped, we rented a sump pump and pumped out our basement. The holes had filled with water, so the contractors pumped them out before pouring the concrete footings.*
3. To flow out of something rapidly and forcefully: *When the firefighters arrived, smoke was pumping out of the windows. Blood was pumping out, so the doctor tied a tourniquet around the patient's arm.*

4. To produce something continuously and in large amounts: *That factory pumps out a lot of toxic waste. Movie sequels continue to make money, and studios continue to pump them out.*

pump up

1. To inflate something with gas by using a pump: *We pumped up a new basketball before the game. One of my tires was getting low, so I stopped at a gas station and pumped it up.*
2. To force or suck something, as a liquid or gas, from beneath a surface by using a pump: *This well pumps up oil from underground. We pump the water up from the lake to tanks on the hillside.*
3. SLANG To fill someone with enthusiasm, strength, and energy; psych someone up: *The crowd's chants pumped up the players. The coach pumped us up for the big game with a rousing speech.*
4. SLANG To be actively involved in bodybuilding exercises: *The football players are always pumping up at the gym.*
5. SLANG To strengthen something: *Pump up the volume on that stereo—I can't hear it. The economy was declining, but investors hoped that a favorable exchange rate would pump it up.*

◆ **punch** (pŭnch)

punched (pŭncht), **punching** (pŭn′chĭng), **punches** (pŭn′chĭz)

punch in

1. To check in formally at a job upon arrival, especially by stamping the arrival time on a timecard: *I punched in ten minutes late this morning and the company fired me.*
2. To enter some data on a keypad or similar device: *I punched in my access code and I was allowed through the door.*

punch out

1. To check out formally from a job upon departure, especially by stamping the departure time on a timecard: *If we punch out after 5:00, the company has to pay us for overtime.*
2. To knock someone unconscious with a punch: *The thief punched out the security guards and broke into the safe. He punched me out, and when I woke up, I was lying on the ground.*
3. SLANG To eject from a military aircraft: *The pilots punched out just before the missile struck their plane.*

◆ **push** (po͝osh)

pushed (po͝osht), **pushing** (po͝osh′ĭng), **pushes** (po͝osh′ĭz)

push around

To give someone orders in a forceful or unpleasant way; bully someone: *The seniors and juniors pushed around the younger students. You shouldn't let your boss push you around like that!*

ă	pat	är	car	ī	bite	ô	paw	o͝o	took	ûr	urge
ā	pay	ĕ	pet	îr	pier	ôr	core	o͝or	lure	zh	vision
âr	care	ē	be	ŏ	pot	oi	boy	o͞o	boot	ə	about, item
ä	father	ĭ	pit	ō	toe	ou	out	ŭ	cut		

push back

1. To move or force something backward by applying pressure: *Push that glass back from the edge of the table. The police managed to push back the protestors by using tear gas.*
2. To delay something until a future time; postpone something: *We should push back the deadline so that we have more time to work on the project. They pushed the meeting back to Thursday because two of the officers were sick.*

push for

To request or demand something insistently: *Taxpayers are pushing for tax reforms.*

push forward

1. To advance something or someone ahead by exerting pressure: *They are trying to push forward reforms despite resistance from the older members. The teacher asked for volunteers, and as a joke someone pushed me forward.*
2. To advance despite difficulty or opposition: *The explorers pushed forward through the thick underbrush. The committee pushed forward with their plan to demolish the building.*
3. To change the scheduled time of some event to an earlier time: *They pushed the meeting forward from 3:00 to 1:30.*

push off

1. To shove or thrust something or someone from a place: *She climbed up to the roof and pushed off the snow. He pushed a glass off the table, and it shattered.*
2. To set out; depart: *The infantry patrol pushed off before dawn.*
3. To launch or move away by pushing against a surface: *I can jump higher when I push off the ground with my left foot. We got in the boat and pushed off from the dock.*

push on

1. To apply pressure to something: *Push on the green button to open the door.*
2. To continue in a determined manner, despite setbacks or difficulties: *The terrain was rugged, but the travelers pushed on. I have to push on with my final term paper.*

push over

1. To cause someone or something to topple by thrusting or shoving: *The winning team pushed over the two goalposts. The cat pushed the vase over.*
2. To move someone or something over something by exerting upward pressure: *They lifted me up on their shoulders and pushed me over the wall.*

push through

1. To force something or someone to penetrate or pass through something: *The clerk pushed the bulky envelope through the mail slot.*
2. To force or work one's way through something: *We pushed through the heavy snow.*

◆ **put** (po͝ot)

put (po͝ot), **putting** (po͝ot′ĭng), **puts** (po͝ots)

put about

1. To reverse direction: *When the troops saw the enemy approaching, they put about and fled.*
2. To cause something to reverse direction. Used chiefly of sailing vessels: *The captain put the ship about and we sailed back home.*
3. To spread some information or rumor: *The boss put about the rumor that there was a major policy change for next year. Your story is inaccurate, and I wish you hadn't put it about without talking to me.*

put across

1. To place something so that it traverses something else: *I put one leg across the other because it was more comfortable to sit that way.*
2. To state or describe something clearly to others: *The council put its views across during the hearing. The students will put across their opinions at the meeting.*

put aside

1. To move something to the side in order to clear a space: *We put the books on the shelf aside and made room for the picture. I put aside my homework and cleaned the table.*
2. To stop discussing or paying attention to something: *Let's put these problems aside. Put aside your differences and work together.*
3. To save something for use at a later time: *I put aside a little cash for an emergency. You should take some of your earnings and put it aside for college.*

put at

To determine or estimate some quantity to have some value: *The forecasters put the price of corn next year at $8 per bushel.*

put away

1. To put something in a place where it is kept when not in use: *Remember to put away the milk when you are finished with it. Please put your toys away.*
2. To stop thinking about something: *Put that old daydream away and use your imagination. We put away our fear of losing and just concentrated on doing our best.*
3. To eat or drink something completely, readily, and quickly: *They put away two bottles of wine over lunch. I ordered a large pizza and put it away in five minutes.*
4. To confine to a prison, mental health facility, or other institution: *If you get caught stealing again, they will put you away. The judicial system puts away both drug dealers and drug users.*
5. To bury someone: *They put the preacher away in that cemetery next to the church.*

put back

1. To return something to the position from which it was taken: *No, you may not eat another cookie, so*

ă	pat	är	car	ī	bite	ô	paw	o͝o	took	ûr	urge
ā	pay	ĕ	pet	îr	pier	ôr	core	o͝or	lure	zh	vision
âr	care	ē	be	ŏ	pot	oi	boy	o͞o	boot	ə	about, item
ä	father	ĭ	pit	ō	toe	ou	out	ŭ	cut		

put it back! I put back the books I'd taken from the shelf.

2. To drink completely: *I put back four bottles of beer with dinner.*
3. To reschedule something to an earlier time: *They put the meeting back from 3:00 to noon. Let's put back the date a few weeks.*
4. To cause someone or something to be delayed: *We hoped to start painting the house this week, but the bad weather put us back several days. The lack of funds put back the project a few months.*
5. To cause someone or something to be offended. Used chiefly in the passive: *I was put back by their uncaring remarks.*

put before

1. To place something in front of someone or something, especially as an offering: *The waiters put plates of cheese before us.*
2. To present some information or argument to someone or something for consideration: *The lawyer put the evidence before the judge. The final arguments were put before the jury.*
3. To consider someone or something as being more important than someone or something else: *He always put his family before his career as an artist.*

put behind

1. To place something to the rear of something or someone: *I put the wires behind the bookcase, where no one can see them.*
2. To provide something to someone or something as a means of support or assistance: *The corporation put one million dollars behind the reconstruction project.*
3. To consciously stop worrying or thinking about some unpleasant experience: *I'm glad you put those bad days behind you and finished your studies.*
4. To place someone in some lower or less advanced grade or class, especially due to inadequate performance: *I couldn't pass all the required tests, so they had to put me behind with the beginners.*

put by

1. To place something at the side of something else: *We put the plates by the cake.*
2. To save something for later use: *The family put by the extra wrapping paper for next year.*

put down

1. To set something on the surface of something: *They put the boxes down on the floor. I put down my pen and looked up. We put a new carpet down.*
2. To write down: *I grabbed a piece of paper and quickly put down what she had just said. He put his address down on a slip of paper and handed it to me.*
3. To assign someone to some task or obligation: *We put John down to do the laundry and Mary to do the dishes. You can put me down for a $20 donation, and I'll send you a check next week.*
4. To render something ineffective; repress something: *We should put down any rumors that we might be leaving town. When the peasants organized a revolution, the dictator called in the army to put it down.*
5. To criticize, berate, or insult someone or something: *My boss is al-*

ways putting me down for small mistakes. The teachers put down our knowledge of literature.

6. To kill some animal, especially a domesticated animal that is sick or suffering: *We had to put down several cows that had gotten very ill. The vet put our dog down when it became too sick.*
7. To put some child to bed: *We put the baby down for a nap.*
8. To land: *The plane put down at O'Hare Airport.*
9. To land some aircraft: *The pilot put the plane down in a field.*
10. To make some down payment: *We just put down a deposit on a new house. If I put $100 down today, can I pay the rest next month?*
11. **put down to** To attribute some event to some cause: *They put the boating accident down to the captain's inexperience.*

put forth

1. To propose something; offer something for consideration: *Who first put forth the idea that the Earth is round rather than flat? At the hearing, the lawyer put it forth that the witnesses were all lying.*
2. To exert something: *You should put forth more effort at school.*
3. To grow some new part, such as leaves, roots, or shoots. Used of plants: *The bulb will put forth a shoot if you water it every day.*

put forward

1. To move something into a position in the front part of a thing or a region: *There was no more room in the back of the boat, so we put the rest of the cargo forward.*
2. To propose something; offer something for consideration: *They put forward a proposal to increase teachers' salaries. We put two ideas forward, but both were rejected by the council.*
3. To propose that someone be considered: *The committee put forward two candidates as possible replacements for the retiring manager. After the battle, the captain put one of his officers forward for a medal.*
4. To change the scheduled time of some event to an earlier time: *They put the meeting forward from 4:00 to 2:30.*
5. To postpone some event: *We put the surprise party forward by an hour so everyone could attend.*

put in

1. To place someone or something on the inside of or within something: *Put the key in the ignition and start the car. Let me put these flowers in water. The recipe says to put in two cups of sugar. They put them in jail for robbery.*
2. To set something into some state or position: *She put the car in first gear and drove away. During the summer, I usually put my hair in a ponytail.*
3. To make a formal offer of something: *The defendant put in a plea of not guilty. I put an offer in on the house.*

ă	pat	är	car	ī	bite	ô	paw	o͝o	took	ûr	urge
ā	pay	ĕ	pet	îr	pier	ôr	core	o͝or	lure	zh	vision
âr	care	ē	be	ŏ	pot	oi	boy	o͞o	boot	ə	about, item
ä	father	ĭ	pit	ō	toe	ou	out	ŭ	cut		

4. To introduce some information, as in a conversation: *Will you put in a good word for me at the next meeting?*
5. To spend or expend something at some task: *I put in eight hours at the office. You should put more effort in this project. The actor put in a strong performance.*
6. To plant or build something, especially on the ground: *We put in 20 rows of pine trees. They tore the shed down and put a pool in.*
7. To install something: *We put in a new washing machine. The electrician put a new outlet in.*
8. To enter a port or harbor. Used of sailing vessels: *The freighter put in at San Diego to refuel.*
9. **put in for** To apply for something: *I put in for a pay raise, but I doubt I'll get it.*

put into

1. To place someone or something on the inside of or within something: *He put the plates into the dishwasher. Don't put too many eggs into the batter. Her family put her into a sanatorium when she contracted tuberculosis.*
2. To set something into some state or position: *Put the car into reverse and back out of the driveway. I can't put my ideas into words.*
3. To spend or expend something at some task: *I put all of my spare time into fixing the roof.*
4. To enter some port or harbor. Used of sailing vessels: *The ship will put into Boston Harbor tomorrow.*

put off

1. To delay or postpone something: *I always put off paying the bills and end up paying a late fee. If you keep putting your homework off, you won't get it done.*
2. To persuade someone or something to postpone an activity: *I managed to put off the creditors for another week. We succeeded in putting the meeting off until next week.*
3. To cause someone to be offended, disgusted, and repelled: *His indifferent attitude has put us off. Her arrogance put off the interviewers.*
4. To discourage someone from doing something: *The bad weather put us off from trying to climb the mountain.*
5. To cause someone to be distracted from something and perform poorly: *That athlete is sensitive, and too much crowd noise puts off his game. She throws the ball pretty well, but the pain in her arm put her aim off.*

put on

1. To place something so that it is supported by something else: *The children put the flowers on a string and made a necklace. Please put the plates on the table.*
2. To clothe oneself with something; don something: *Don't forget to put on a warm coat. I put my sunglasses on because the sun was too bright.*
3. To apply or activate something: *I put on the brakes and the car slowed down. Put the emergency brake on when you park on a hill.*
4. To assume some style or behavior affectedly: *Don't put on that English accent! I put a smile on my face and greeted the customer.*
5. To tease or mislead someone: *You're putting me on!*
6. To tease or mislead by suggesting

something is true: *They put on that they were hunting for treasure, when they were really just looking for something to do.*

7. To add some quantity of weight: *I must have put on five pounds over the holidays. You've put some weight on since I last saw you.*

8. To produce or perform some event: *The children put on a puppet show. There is a concert this weekend, but I'm not sure which organization is putting it on.*

9. To make someone or something available for listening to, talking to, or watching via some broadcast or communication medium: *Let's put on some music while we work. Will you put your mother on the phone?*

10. To prescribe or administer a medicine or some other corrective that is taken or undertaken routinely: *The doctor put the patient on antibiotics. I put my dog on a diet because he was getting fat.*

11. To wager some stake on something; bet on something: *I went to the track and put $50 on a horse.*

put out

1. To remove something from within some space or region; place something outside: *The dog likes to put its head out the window. I put the cat out before we left. Don't forget to put out the garbage.*

2. To extend something: *I put out my hand, but the man refused to shake it. The doctor asked me to put my tongue out.*

3. To place something on display; make something accessible or visible: *Put some cups and spoons out so people can serve themselves. We put out fliers on the table.*

4. To extinguish something: *Put out that fire now, before it goes out of control. The principal told them to put the cigarettes out.*

5. To expel someone or something from a premises: *They had to put out the drunk. The guard put out the rowdy students.*

6. To publish something or make it publicly available: *Our club puts out a weekly newsletter. The president put a statement out explaining the company's annual report.*

7. To inconvenience someone: *Did our early arrival put you out? I hope you didn't put yourself out to get us those tickets.*

8. To make someone unhappy through inconsiderate behavior: *That comment about my mother really put me out.*

9. To make an effort: *They really put out for their team.*

10. NAUTICAL To leave, as a port or harbor; depart: *The ship put out to sea.*

11. BASEBALL To retire some runner: *The pitcher put the runner out with a hard throw to first base. The shortstop put out the runner at second base.*

12. VULGAR SLANG To provide sex.

13. **put out of** To remove someone or something from participation in or engagement with something: *The*

ă	pat	är	car	ī	bite	ô	paw	o͝o	took	ûr	urge
ā	pay	ĕ	pet	îr	pier	ôr	core	o͝or	lure	zh	vision
âr	care	ē	be	ŏ	pot	oi	boy	o͞o	boot	ə	about,
ä	father	ĭ	pit	ō	toe	ou	out	ŭ	cut		item

mistake put the team out of medal contention. Large retailers have put all the independent shops out of business.

put over on

To communicate something to someone, especially in order to deceive: *He tried to put a lie over on me, but I wasn't fooled.*

put past

To believe some action, especially an extreme action, to be of a kind that someone would not do. Often used negatively: *I wouldn't put it past those kids to try to climb to the top of the flagpole. Would you put murder past these thugs?*

put through

1. To cause something to pass from one side of a boundary, threshold, or opening to the other: *I put the thread through the eye of the needle.*
2. To bring something to completion: *They put the project through on time.*
3. To cause someone or something to complete a process, especially a process of approval: *Congress has recently put through a number of new laws. I had to work two jobs to put my child through college.*
4. To cause someone or something to undergo or experience something unpleasant or difficult: *They put me through a lot of trouble. We put all our products through a series of tests.*
5. To connect some telephone call or caller: *Can you put the call through to my office? The operator put me through on the office line.*

put to

1. To place something in some direction: *Put those books to the left of the shelf.*
2. To cause something to be considered or evaluated by someone or by some means: *The committee put the matter to a vote. Several questions were put to me, and I couldn't answer any of them.*
3. To make a formal or strong claim to someone that something is true, especially in a court of law: *I put it to you that you were not, in fact, at home when the fire broke out.*
4. To add something to, or associate something with, something else: *I can't put my name to this poor proposal. She remembered his face, but couldn't put a name to it.*
5. To have someone perform some task: *The company put the new employee to work immediately.*
6. To head for shore. Used of boats and ships: *The ship put to and was home in four hours.*

put together

1. To construct or create something out of pieces or parts: *The carpenter put together a new bookcase. The broker put a revised insurance package together.*
2. To group together some set of people or things: *Let's put the children together in the guest room.*
3. To understand something by considering many pieces of information or ideas: *The police reviewed the clues presented by the evidence, but couldn't put them together. The jury tried to put together all of the facts.*

put toward

To provide or secure something to obtain something else or to serve some purpose: *We've put $500 toward a new car. I put my efforts toward improving my grades.*

put up

1. To place something in a high or upright position: *I put the books up on the shelf. I put up the hood on my rain jacket. I put my hair up in a bun.*
2. To place something in a prominent position: *They put signs up all over town, hoping someone would recognize their lost cat. The superintendent put up a notice on the door advising residents to conserve water.*
3. To erect some structure: *They're going to put up three new apartment buildings on this street. The children put a tent up in the backyard and slept outside.*
4. To nominate someone: *The committee put up three new candidates for mayor. The Green Party put candidates up in many races.*
5. To preserve some food by jarring, canning, or salting: *He put up six jars of jam. She put half the cucumbers up for pickles.*
6. To provide some amount of money for some purpose: *The company put up half of the money for the new park. The agency put $1,000 up toward the scholarship fund.*
7. To provide lodgings for someone: *Could you put me up for the night? I put up my guests in the spare bedroom.*
8. To startle deliberately some animal that one is hunting: *We put up the pheasants but didn't manage to shoot any.*
9. To offer something, especially for sale: *I put up some of my antique furniture to raise money for my trip. They put their house up for sale and moved to Houston.*
10. To make a display or appearance of something: *They put up a good bluff, but I knew they were lying.*
11. To engage in something; carry on something: *The boxer certainly put up a good fight.*
12. **put up to** To persuade someone to commit some funny, mischievous, or malicious act: *My older brother put me up to making a prank telephone call.*
13. **put up with** To tolerate someone or something: *I can't put up with that awful noise from next door.*

put upon

To impose on someone; overburden someone. Used chiefly in the passive: *My teacher is often put upon by the students.*

◆ **puzzle** (pŭz′əl)

puzzled (pŭz′əld), **puzzling** (pŭz′ə-lĭng), **puzzles** (pŭz′əlz)

puzzle out

To come to a conclusion by thinking carefully: *I puzzled out the murderer's identity before finishing the novel. The answer escaped me at first, but I finally puzzled the problem out.*

ă	pat	är	car	ī	bite	ô	paw	ŏŏ	took	ûr	urge
ā	pay	ĕ	pet	îr	pier	ôr	core	ŏŏr	lure	zh	vision
âr	care	ē	be	ŏ	pot	oi	boy	ōō	boot	ə	about,
ä	father	ĭ	pit	ō	toe	ou	out	ŭ	cut		item

Q

◆ **qualify** (kwŏl′ə-fī′)

qualified (kwŏl′ə-fīd′), **qualifying** (kwŏl′ə-fī′ĭng), **qualifies** (kwŏl′ə-fīz′)

qualify for

1. To be competent or eligible for something, such as an office, job, or benefit: *After one year on the job, you will qualify for a raise.*
2. To cause someone to be eligible for something: *That certificate qualifies you for a promotion.*

◆ **quarrel** (kwôr′əl)

quarreled *or* **quarrelled** (kwôr′əld), **quarreling** *or* **quarrelling** (kwôr′ə-lĭng), **quarrels** (kwôr′əlz)

quarrel over

To have an argument or dispute about something: *The siblings quarreled over their inheritance.*

quarrel with

1. To have an argument or dispute with someone: *The coach quarreled with the umpire.*
2. To have a complaint about something; disagree with something: *I can't quarrel with the test results.*

◆ **queue** (kyo͞o)

queued (kyo͞od), **queueing** (kyo͞o′ĭng), **queues** (kyo͞oz)

queue up

1. To form an ordered sequence or line; line up: *The patrons queued up outside the theater. The customers queued up at the ticket booth.*
2. To order some set of things to deal with them in sequence; line up something: *Queue up the children, and I'll serve them lunch. We'll queue the applicants up and interview them one at a time.*

◆ **quiet** (kwī′ĭt)

quieted (kwī′ĭ-tĭd), **quieting** (kwī′ĭ-tĭng), **quiets** (kwī′ĭts)

quiet down

1. To become less noisy or more relaxed; calm down: *When the class quiets down, we can proceed. Quiet down now.*
2. To cause someone or something to become less noisy or more relaxed: *Please quiet down those children or you will have to leave. We need to quiet the dogs down.*

◆ **quit** (kwĭt)

quit *or* **quitted** (kwĭt′ĭd), **quitting** (kwĭt′ĭng), **quits** (kwĭts)

quit on

1. To stop helping or working with someone, especially when the support or assistance is needed: *My friends quit on me when I really needed them.*
2. To stop functioning properly for someone; give out on someone: *The car's battery quit on us when we were a mile from the city. My knee quit on me in the last mile of the marathon.*

R

◆ **rack** (răk)

racked (răkt), **racking** (răk′ĭng), **racks** (răks)

rack up

1. To accumulate or score a number of something: *The home team racked up 64 points. Our team did badly in the first half, but in the second half we really racked the points up.*
2. To set up billiard balls for a game of billiards or pool by placing them in the rack: *He racked up the balls at the start of the game. She picked up the balls, racked them up, and cued off.*

◆ **raffle** (răf′əl)

raffled (răf′əld), **raffling** (răf′l-ĭng), **raffles** (răf′əlz)

raffle off

To offer something as a prize in a lottery in which a number of persons buy chances to win: *The theater is raffling off tickets to its upcoming plays. The school raffled a new car off to raise money for a new swimming pool.*

◆ **rag** (răg)

ragged (răgd), **ragging** (răg′ĭng), **rags** (răgz)

rag on

SLANG

1. To tease or taunt someone: *My older cousins used to rag on me when I was young.*
2. To criticize someone severely; berate or scold someone: *The supervisor ragged on the workers for being lazy.*

◆ **rage** (rāj)

raged (rājd), **raging** (rā′jĭng), **rages** (rā′jĭz)

rage against

To protest something angrily or violently: *The marching protestors were raging against the new taxes.*

rage at

To express or direct strong anger toward someone or something: *The sergeant raged at the troops for falling behind the rest of the platoon.*

◆ **rail** (rāl)

railed (rāld), **railing** (rā′lĭng), **rails** (rālz)

rail against

To protest something vehemently, especially using strong language: *The students railed against the change to a longer school year.*

ă	pat	är	car	ī	bite	ô	paw	o͝o	took	ûr	urge		
ā	pay	ĕ	pet	îr	pier	ôr	core	o͝or	lure	zh	vision		
âr	care	ē	be	ŏ	pot	oi	boy	o͞o	boot	ə	about,		
ä	father	ĭ	pit	ō	toe	ou	out	ŭ	cut		item		

rail at

To criticize someone or something in harsh, bitter, or abusive language: *The workers railed at the new contract that cut medical benefits.*

◆ **rain** (rān)

rained (rānd), **raining** (rā′nĭng), **rains** (rānz)

rain down

1. To fall as rain: *It rained down hard all day, so we had to cancel the picnic.*
2. To fall in large quantities: *The rice container tipped over on the top shelf and rice rained down on me.*
3. To throw or hurl something down upon someone: *The boxer rained blows down on his opponent's head for several seconds. The soldiers rained down arrows from the top of the castle.*

rain in

1. To cause something to remain inside due to rain: *We wanted to go hiking, but we were rained in.*
2. To cause something to take place inside due to rain. Used chiefly in the passive: *Our outdoor party was rained in, but we still managed to have fun.*

rain out

To force the cancellation or postponement of some event because of rain. Used chiefly in the passive: *If the parade is rained out, it will be held the following week.*

◆ **raise** (rāz)

raised (rāzd), **raising** (rā′zĭng), **raises** (rā′zĭz)

raise on

1. To help someone or something grow by feeding it something: *You can't raise chickens on just corn—they need other food too. I was raised on a healthy diet.*
2. To accustom someone to something from an early age. Used chiefly in the passive: *He knows so much about pop culture because he was raised on TV.*

◆ **rake** (rāk)

raked (rākt), **raking** (rā′kĭng), **rakes** (rāks)

rake in

To win, earn, or gain something in abundance: *You certainly raked in a lot of prizes at the carnival last night! We raked a lot of money in when our new product sold well.*

rake over

To revisit or reexamine something in detail, especially something that is unpleasant: *I don't want to rake over past arguments. They insisted on raking the story over many times.*

rake up

1. To collect or gather something with or as if with a rake: *After I had cut the grass, I raked up the trimmings and piled them in a heap. We raked the leaves up.*
2. To revive or bring something to light; uncover something: *When he runs out of things to say, he rakes old stories up from his days in the army. She is sure to rake up an embarrassing story or two about me!*

◆ **ram** (răm)

rammed (rămd), **ramming** (răm′ĭng), **rams** (rămz)

ram down

1. To break something down by pounding with or as if with a ram: *The attacking army rammed down the fortress wall using a huge log. The truck rammed the tree down.*
2. To force the passage or acceptance of something into something: *The plumber rammed the plunger down the pipe.*

◆ **ramp** (rămp)

ramped (rămpt), **ramping** (rămp′ĭng), **ramps** (rămps)

ramp up

To increase the volume, amount, or rate of something: *The factory must ramp up production due to increased demand for its products. I added a new card to my computer memory to ramp it up.*

◆ **rat** (răt)

ratted (răt′tĭd), **ratting** (răt′ĭng), **rats** (răts)

rat on

To disclose incriminating information about someone; betray someone by giving incriminating information: *The hoodlum ratted on the rest of the gangsters. It was mean of you to rat on your friends.*

rat out

To expose or reveal incriminating or embarrassing information about someone: *The newspapers ratted out the people who were involved with the scam.*

◆ **ratchet** (răch′ĭt)

ratcheted (răch′ĭ-tĭd), **ratcheting** (răch′ĭ-tĭng), **ratchets** (răch′ĭts)

ratchet up

1. To cause something to increase in increments: *The motor was running too slow to run the pump, so we ratcheted up the speed until it worked. We won't resolve our disagreements if you ratchet up our discussions into big arguments.*
2. To increase by increments: *The tension ratcheted up as the hostage crisis wore on.*

◆ **ration** (ră′shən)

rationed (ră′shənd), **rationing** (ră′shə-nĭng), **rations** (ră′shənz)

ration out

To distribute a fixed portion of something, especially food that is allotted to persons in military service or to civilians in times of scarcity: *The government rationed out flour and sugar during the war. The hikers had very little water and had to ration it out carefully.*

◆ **rattle** (răt′l)

rattled (răt′ld), **rattling** (răt′l-ĭng), **rattles** (răt′lz)

ă	pat	är	car	ī	bite	ô	paw	ŏŏ	took	ûr	urge
ā	pay	ĕ	pet	îr	pier	ôr	core	ŏŏr	lure	zh	vision
âr	care	ē	be	ŏ	pot	oi	boy	ōō	boot	ə	about,
ä	father	ĭ	pit	ō	toe	ou	out	ŭ	cut		item

rattle off

To recite something rapidly and easily; reel something off: *She rattled off the names of people who had recently applied for the job opening. He knows every state capital and can easily rattle them off if you ask him to.*

rattle on

To talk continuously about something, especially to others not as interested in the subject as the speaker is: *They kept rattling on about how much fun they had at the party, but I didn't really care.*

◆ **rave** (rāv)

raved (rāvd), **raving** (rā′vĭng), **raves** (rāvz)

rave about *or* **rave over**

To speak or write about something or someone with wild enthusiasm: *The dinner guests raved about the roasted duck. The critic raved over the new movie.*

◆ **reach** (rēch)

reached (rēcht), **reaching** (rē′chĭng), **reaches** (rē′chĭz)

reach out

1. To extend one's grasp outward: *The vines along the path were full of grapes, so I reached out and grabbed some. I reached out for the boy's hand and pulled him out of the water.*
2. To extend one's grasp thorough something: *They kids reached out the car window and the clerk handed them each an ice cream cone.*
3. To extend one's circle of friends, contacts, or experiences: *He has been rather isolated, but now he's reaching out and meeting new people.*
4. To strive toward something; aspire to something: *She is reaching out for a job that is more challenging.*
5. **reach out for** To seek help, comfort, or support from someone: *Given the way you wrote this letter, it seems that you're reaching out for someone to talk to.*

◆ **read** (rēd)

read (rĕd), **reading** (rē′dĭng), **reads** (rēdz)

read for

1. To study for something, as an examination, degree, or certification: *They are in the library reading for their exams next week.*
2. To read or examine something in order to look for something specific: *I read the text once for comprehension and a second time for pleasure. The writer hired an assistant to read for errors. The tracker read the trail for signs of foxes.*
3. To audition for some acting role: *Five people read for the part of Hamlet in the school play.*

read into

To attribute some interpretation or meaning to something, especially an unintended meaning: *He's reading things into the text that the author never intended. Don't read too much into her remark—it is hardly representative of her opinion.*

read off

1. To read aloud some items in a list, one by one: *Could you read off the*

last four digits of the number again? As I read your name off, please come up to the stage and collect your certificate.

2. To read some information that is printed or displayed on something: *The nurse read off my temperature from the thermometer. I read the number off the box.*

read over

To read something thoroughly and carefully: *The lawyer read over the contract before signing it. The teacher read each essay over and marked all mistakes with a red pen.*

read up on

To study or learn something by reading: *I read up on the places I plan to visit before I travel.*

◆ **rear** (rîr)

reared (rîrd), **rearing** (rîr′ĭng), **rears** (rîrz)

rear up

1. To rise on the hind legs, as of a horse: *A rattlesnake slithered out from behind the bush, and the horse reared up.*
2. To arise or appear suddenly or unexpectedly: *We can handle any problems that rear up.*

◆ **reason** (rē′zən)

reasoned (rē′zənd), **reasoning** (rē′zə-nĭng), **reasons** (rē′zənz)

reason out

To determine or conclude something by logical thinking: *The detective reasoned out the killer's motive. The mechanics were able to reason out the problem from the little I told them. Rather than worrying about the decision, let's sit down and reason it out.*

reason with

To attempt to come to an agreement or understanding with someone through logical discussion: *The kids did not want to learn to swim, but I reasoned with them until they agreed to take lessons.*

◆ **reckon** (rĕk′ən)

reckoned (rĕk′ənd), **reckoning** (rĕk′ə-nĭng), **reckons** (rĕk′ənz)

reckon on

To expect and take something into account; bargain on something: *The farmers hadn't reckoned on an early frost. Reckon on spending $250 for a hotel room in New York.*

reckon with

To take someone or something into account; deal with someone or something: *The new governor will have to reckon with a large budget deficit. Now that this candidate has the support of the unions, she is definitely someone to be reckoned with.*

ă	pat	är	car	ī	bite	ô	paw	ŏŏ	took	ûr	urge
ā	pay	ĕ	pet	îr	pier	ôr	core	ŏŏr	lure	zh	vision
âr	care	ē	be	ŏ	pot	oi	boy	ōō	boot	ə	about,
ä	father	ĭ	pit	ō	toe	ou	out	ŭ	cut		item

reckon without

To fail to consider or deal with someone or something; ignore someone or something: *They thought it would be an easy victory, but they had reckoned without the determination of their enemy.*

◆ **reduce** (rĭ-do͞os′)

reduced (rĭ-do͞ost′), **reducing** (rĭ-do͞o′sĭng), **reduces** (rĭ-do͞o′sĭz)

reduce to

1. To decrease something to some level: *The drought reduced the stream to a trickle.*
2. To bring someone to some humbler, weaker, difficult, or forced state or condition: *The illness had reduced them almost to emaciation. The sight of her mother reduced her to tears. The army reduced him from a command post to a desk job.*
3. To bring someone to such a humble, weak, or desperate state or condition that he or she does something drastic: *The Depression reduced many to begging on the street.*
4. To damage or destroy something, leaving it in some lesser state: *The blaze reduced the warehouse to ashes.*
5. To make something shorter and simpler; summarize something: *Their entire business philosophy can be reduced to "The customer is always right."*

◆ **reek** (rēk)

reeked (rēkt), **reeking** (rē′kĭng), **reeks** (rēks)

reek of

1. To give off or have some strong, unpleasant odor: *The kitchen reeks of rotten eggs.*
2. To be full of something distasteful or offensive: *The report reeks of bigotry. The whole incident reeks of corruption.*

◆ **reel** (rēl)

reeled (rēld), **reeling** (rē′lĭng), **reels** (rēlz)

reel in

1. To draw or haul something inward by winding on a reel: *It took me two hours to reel in the giant fish. I reeled the line in slowly, pulling the lure along the bottom.*
2. To attract someone or something, such as business or customers: *Their excellent pizza is reeling customers in. The fundraising campaign reeled in $10 million.*

reel off

To recite something quickly and easily: *She reeled off the names of all the presidents from memory. The actor reeled his lines off without hesitating.*

◆ **refer** (rĭ-fûr′)

referred (rĭ-fûrd′), **referring** (rĭ-fûr′ĭng), **refers** (rĭ-fûrz′)

refer to

1. To mention or reference someone or something: *When you say he's clumsy, are you referring to what he did the other day? When we are in the meeting, refer to me as your colleague and not as your sister.*
2. To signify something or someone directly; denote something or

someone: *The red line on the graph refers to the birth rate and the blue line to the death rate.*

3. To pertain to something or someone; concern something or someone: *I have a question referring to yesterday's lecture.*
4. To direct someone to someone or something for help, support, or information: *My doctor couldn't find the problem, so she referred me to a specialist.*
5. To have recourse to someone or something for help, support, or information; turn to someone or something: *Whenever I encounter a word that I don't know, I refer to a dictionary.*
6. To direct the attention of someone to something: *The instructor referred us to the third page of the manual.*

◆ **reflect** (rĭ-flĕkt′)

reflected (rĭ-flĕk′tĭd), **reflecting** (rĭ-flĕk′tĭng), **reflects** (rĭ-flĕkts′)

reflect on *or* **reflect upon**

1. To think carefully about something: *He sat in the garden and reflected on what he had just read.*
2. To express carefully considered thoughts about something: *In the essay, she reflects on her long career and offers advice for young writers.*
3. To give evidence of the characteristics or qualities of someone or something: *The student's performance reflects well on the whole school. Hasty preparation of the report will reflect badly on you.*
4. To appear as a reflected image on some surface: *The trees are reflecting on the water.*
5. To cause something to appear as a reflected image on some surface: *The window reflected wavy lines on the floor.*

◆ **refrain** (rĭ-frān′)

refrained (rĭ-frānd′), **refraining** (rĭ-frā′nĭng), **refrains** (rĭ-frānz′)

refrain from

To make a conscious decision not to do something: *All passengers must refrain from smoking during the flight.*

◆ **reign** (rān)

reigned (rānd), **reigning** (rā′nĭng), **reigns** (rānz)

reign over

1. To have authority or control over someone or something; rule over someone or something: *The same family has reigned over this island for ten generations.*
2. To be prevalent or predominant in some place or situation: *Chaos reigned over the city during the power outage.*

◆ **rein** (rān)

reined (rānd), **reining** (rā′nĭng), **reins** (rānz)

rein in

1. To restrain or control something or someone: *The coalition tried to*

ă	pat	är	car	ī	bite	ô	paw	ŏŏ	took	ûr	urge
ā	pay	ĕ	pet	îr	pier	ôr	core	ŏŏr	lure	zh	vision
âr	care	ē	be	ŏ	pot	oi	boy	ōō	boot	ə	about,
ä	father	ĭ	pit	ō	toe	ou	out	ŭ	cut		item

rein in its more militant members. I reined my anger in and refused to fight.

2. To make a horse move more slowly or stop by pulling back on reins: *Rein in your horse while this truck goes by. The horses wanted to break free, but the rancher reined them in.*

◆ **rejoice** (rĭ-jois′)

rejoiced (rĭ-joist′), **rejoicing** (rĭ-joi′sĭng), **rejoices** (rĭ-joi′sĭz)

rejoice in

To feel joyful or delighted about something or someone: *All the fans rejoiced in the team's success.*

◆ **relate** (rĭ-lāt′)

related (rĭ-lā′tĭd), **relating** (rĭ-lā′tĭng), **relates** (rĭ-lāts′)

relate to

1. To have a connection, relation, or reference to something: *My question relates to your earlier work.*
2. To establish a connection, relation, or reference between one thing and another: *She related the painful experience to having a tooth pulled at the dentist.*
3. To narrate or relay some information to someone; tell something to someone: *When he related the story to us, he left out the part about himself.*
4. To have or establish a reciprocal relationship with someone; interact with someone: *Your child seems to relate well to her peers.*
5. To empathize or identify with someone or something: *I simply can't relate to such an extreme viewpoint.*

◆ **relieve** (rĭ-lēv′)

relieved (rĭ-lēvd′), **relieving** (rĭ-lē′vĭng), **relieves** (rĭ-lēvz′)

relieve of

1. To take or lift a burden from someone: *The bellhop relieved us of our heavy luggage. Their rudeness relieved me of the burden of having to invite them.*
2. To dismiss someone from a job, office, or position: *After the scandal, the army relieved him of his post.*
3. To rob or deprive someone of something: *Pickpockets relieved the tourist of her money.*

◆ **rely** (rĭ-lī′)

relied (rĭ-līd′), **relying** (rĭ-lī′ĭng), **relies** (rĭ-līz′)

rely on

1. To be dependent upon something or someone for support, help, or supply: *Some people still rely on coal to heat their houses. He relies on his parents for tuition.*
2. To place trust or confidence in someone or something: *He was relying on the meeting being canceled and didn't prepare his speech. I can always rely on her to get here on time.*

◆ **remember** (rĭ-mĕm′bər)

remembered (rĭ-mĕm′bərd), **remembering** (rĭ-mĕm′bə-rĭng), **remembers** (rĭ-mĕm′bərz)

remember to

To deliver greetings from someone to someone else: *Please remember me to your family.*

◆ **remind** (rĭ-mīnd′)

reminded (rĭ-mīn′dĭd), **reminding** (rĭ-mīn′dĭng), **reminds** (rĭ-mīndz′)

remind of

1. To cause someone to remember something; bring to someone's mind some thought or memory: *Your story reminds me of the time I went to Texas.*
2. To appear to someone to resemble something or someone else: *That woman reminds me of my mother.*

◆ **remit** (rĭ-mĭt′)

remitted (rĭ-mĭt′ĭd), **remitting** (rĭ-mĭt′ĭng), **remits** (rĭ-mĭts′)

remit to

1. To transmit money to someone: *You must remit the tuition to the registrar today.*
2. To refer a legal case to another court for further consideration or action: *The judge remitted the case to the state court.*

◆ **renege** (rĭ-nĕg′, rĭ-nĭg′)

reneged (rĭ-nĕgd′, rĭ-nĭgd′), **reneging** (rĭ-nĕg′ĭng, rĭ-nĭg′ĭng), **reneges** (rĭ-nĕgz′, rĭ-nĭgz′)

renege on

To fail to carry out some promise or commitment; go back on a promise or commitment: *If I had known that you would renege on your contract, I never would have hired you.*

◆ **rent** (rĕnt)

rented (rĕn′tĭd), **renting** (rĕn′tĭng), **rents** (rĕnts)

rent out

To grant temporary occupancy or use of some property or some service to someone in exchange for regular payments: *I rented out the extra room over the garage to a college student. My parents rented our cabin out to one of my cousins.*

◆ **repair** (rĭ-pâr′)

repaired (rĭ-pârd′), **repairing** (rĭ-pâr′ĭng), **repairs** (rĭ-pârz′)

repair to

To move oneself to some place; go somewhere: *The lawyers repaired to the judge's chamber for further discussion.*

◆ **reside** (rĭ-zīd′)

resided (rĭ-zī′dĭd), **residing** (rĭ-zī′dĭng), **resides** (rĭ-zīdz′)

reside in

1. To dwell in some place permanently or for an extended period; live in some place: *I resided in Chicago during the 1990s.*
2. To be inherent in something or someone; exist in something or someone: *These teaching methods will unleash the enormous potential that resides in these children.*
3. To be vested in something or someone, as a power or right: *By the*

ă	pat	är	car	ī	bite	ô	paw	o͝o	took	ûr	urge
ā	pay	ĕ	pet	îr	pier	ôr	core	o͝or	lure	zh	vision
âr	care	ē	be	ŏ	pot	oi	boy	o͞o	boot	ə	about,
ä	father	ĭ	pit	ō	toe	ou	out	ŭ	cut		item

authority that resides in me, I now pronounce you husband and wife.

reside with

1. To dwell in the same house or premises with someone permanently or for an extended period: *My mother resides with us during the winter.*
2. To be vested in something or someone, as a power or right: *In the end, the final decision resides with my supervisor.*

◆ **resign** (rĭ-zīn′)

resigned (rĭ-zīnd′), **resigning** (rĭ-zī′nĭng), **resigns** (rĭ-zīnz′)

resign to

To submit oneself passively to something; give in to doing something: *Everyone had left for the movie, so I resigned myself to washing the dishes.*

◆ **resonate** (rĕz′ə-nāt′)

resonated (rĕz′ə-nā′tĭd), **resonating** (rĕz′ə-nā′tĭng), **resonates** (rĕz′ə-nāts′)

resonate with

1. To sound with some particular tone: *The house resonated with the final chime of the grandfather clock.*
2. To correspond closely or harmoniously with something: *My ideas for the film resonated with what the producers had in mind.*
3. To evoke a feeling of shared emotion or belief with someone: *His book mostly resonated with young adults.*
4. To feel shared emotions or beliefs with something or someone: *Everywhere she speaks, millions resonate with her message.*

◆ **resort** (rĭ-zôrt′)

resorted (rĭ-zôr′tĭd), **resorting** (rĭ-zôr′tĭng), **resorts** (rĭ-zôrts′)

resort to

To adopt some less desirable course of action due to difficult circumstances; have recourse to something: *When the electricity went out, we resorted to heating water in the fireplace.*

◆ **rest** (rĕst)

rested (rĕs′tĭd), **resting** (rĕs′tĭng), **rests** (rĕsts)

rest on

1. To place, lay, or lean something on some other thing for support, ease, or repose: *She rested the vase on the table.*
2. To be supported by or based on something: *The flowerpot rests on the shelf.*
3. To be contingent upon something or someone; depend on something or someone: *Whether or not we have a picnic rests on the weather.*

rest up

To relax and replenish energy in preparation for later strenuous activity: *The baseball players rested up for the big game.*

◆ **retch** (rĕch)

retched (rĕcht), **retching** (rĕch′ĭng), **retches** (rĕch′ĭz)

retch up

To eject some contents of the stomach by vomiting: *I retched up my dinner. The baby retched the mashed carrots up.*

◆ **rev** (rĕv)

revved (rĕvd), **revving** (rĕv′ĭng), **revs** (rĕvz)

rev up

SLANG

1. To make some engine work faster by injecting it with fuel: *The mechanic revved up the engine before the race. We revved the engine up and sped off.*
2. To work faster due to an injection of fuel: *The old car's engine revved up when I pushed the accelerator.*
3. To make someone or something more lively or productive: *We had a pep rally to rev ourselves up for the game. The administration is making efforts to rev up the economy.*
4. To increase in rate, amount, or activity: *Production revved up after the war started.*
5. To improve the quality of something: *We need to add something to this batter to rev up the flavor. Those candles really revved up the festive atmosphere.*

◆ **revel** (rĕv′əl)

reveled *or* **revelled** (rĕv′əld), **reveling** *or* **revelling** (rĕv′ə-lĭng), **revels** (rĕv′əlz)

revel in

To take great pleasure or pride in something: *The actor reveled in the critic's praise.*

◆ **revert** (rĭ-vûrt′)

reverted (rĭ-vûr′tĭd), **reverting** (rĭ-vûr′tĭng), **reverts** (rĭ-vûrts′)

revert to

1. To return to some former condition, practice, subject, or belief: *When the computerized accounting system failed, we reverted to using paper spreadsheets.*
2. To return to some former owner or the heirs of the former owner. Used of money or property: *At the end of 100 years, all privately held land in the park will revert to the government.*

◆ **revolve** (rĭ-vŏlv′)

revolved (rĭ-vŏlvd′), **revolving** (rĭ-vŏl′vĭng), **revolves** (rĭ-vŏlvz′)

revolve around

1. To orbit around something: *The planets revolve around the sun.*
2. To be primarily concerned with something: *This discussion will revolve around the causes of the problem. Not everything revolves around you, so stop thinking of yourself all the time!*

◆ **rid** (rĭd)

rid *or* **ridded** (rĭd′ĭd), **ridding** (rĭd′ĭng), **rids** (rĭdz)

rid of

1. To make someone or something become free of something else: *The peace movement hoped to rid the world of violence. I was finally able to rid myself of all financial*

ă	pat	är	car	ī	bite	ô	paw	o͝o	took	ûr	urge
ā	pay	ĕ	pet	îr	pier	ôr	core	o͝or	lure	zh	vision
âr	care	ē	be	ŏ	pot	oi	boy	o͞o	boot	ə	about, item
ä	father	ĭ	pit	ō	toe	ou	out	ŭ	cut		

worries. I can't seem to get rid of this cold.

2. To throw out something; dispose of something. Used in the passive with **get**: *I got rid of the old magazines that were cluttering up my office.*

◆ **riddle** (rĭd′l)

riddled (rĭd′ld), **riddling** (rĭd′l-ĭng), **riddles** (rĭd′lz)

riddle with

1. To pierce something in many places, especially with bullets or some other projectile: *The troops riddled the side of the tank with gunfire.*
2. To be permeated with some kind of puncture or hole. Used in the passive: *The side of the house was riddled with bullet holes.*
3. To be permeated in many places by something, especially by flaws. Used in the passive: *That report was riddled with errors.*

◆ **ride** (rīd)

rode (rōd), **ridden** (rĭd′n), **riding** (rī′dĭng), **rides** (rīdz)

ride on

1. To travel on something: *She rode on a bicycle. He rode on a horse all around the ranch.*
2. To continue traveling onward: *Some of the cyclists stopped by the river to rest, but others rode on. The trucker rode on to Chicago.*
3. To be contingent upon something or someone for an outcome; depend on something or someone: *Whether or not I go to college rides on my getting a scholarship.*
4. To make progress by virtue of something: *I was able to ride on my past achievements to secure the promotion.*

ride out

1. To travel out of or to a place in a vehicle or on horseback: *The doctor rode out to the ranch to check on his patient. I just rode out here from Cincinnati on the bus. The cowboy rode out of town on a large black horse.*
2. To survive or outlast something; endure something: *I rode out the war as a nurse. Many people left before the storm, but we stayed and rode it out. Only two companies managed to ride out the depression—all the rest went bankrupt.*

ride up

To slide upward across the surface of something and become bunched together. Used especially of fabric or clothing: *My sleeves always ride up my arms when I wear this coat. I don't like this brand of underwear—they ride up and are really uncomfortable.*

◆ **rifle** (rī′fəl)

rifled (rī′fəld), **rifling** (rī′flĭng), **rifles** (rī′fəlz)

rifle through

To search through something quickly and vigorously: *I rifled through the drawer looking for my car keys.*

◆ **rig** (rĭg)

rigged (rĭgd), **rigging** (rĭg′ĭng), **rigs** (rĭgz)

rig up

1. To equip something: *She took the fishing rod out of the case and*

rigged it up. He rigged up the guitar with some new strings.

2. To make or construct something in haste or in a makeshift manner: *We rigged up a pulley to lift the shingles to the roof. They rigged a tent up using a sheet and three thick sticks.*
3. To connect something to something in haste or in a makeshift manner: *Let's rig the computer up to the stereo so we can play music off the hard drive. I rigged up the old record player and put on an album.*
4. **rig up in** To dress, clothe, or adorn someone in something: *They rigged the dancers up in elaborate gowns.*

◆ **ring** (rĭng)

rang (răng), **rung** (rŭng), **ringing** (rĭng′ĭng), **rings** (rĭngz)

ring back

1. To telephone someone who has called previously: *The store clerk rang back the customer who had left a message. I listened to the voice mail that my father had left, and then I rang him back.*
2. To telephone someone or someplace again: *She could tell he was busy, so she told him she would ring him back later. When I called I got the answering machine, so I left a message saying I'd ring back the next day.*

ring out

1. To sound with a clear, resonant tone: *The monk pulled on the rope, and the bells rang out.*
2. To mark or celebrate the end of something: *We rang out the old year with a champagne toast.*

ring up

1. To record the sale of something, especially by using a cash register: *She had already rung up the sale when I discovered that I didn't have enough money. I placed the items on the counter, and the cashier rang them up.*
2. To record a sale to someone, especially by means of a cash register: *I rang up the last two customers and closed the store. He can ring you up on the second register.*
3. To call someone on the telephone: *I'll ring you up this weekend. She rang up an old friend and asked him to dinner.*
4. To amass some number or quantity of points or wins: *They rang up seven consecutive victories before losing a game.*
5. To amass some amount or quantity of credits or debits: *The company rang up $2 billion in profits last year. With all the food that we ate, we rang a hefty bill up.*

◆ **rinse** (rĭns)

rinsed (rĭnst), **rinsing** (rĭn′sĭng), **rinses** (rĭn′sĭz)

rinse off

1. To remove dirt, soap, or some other residue from the surface of something by washing with water or other liquid: *Please rinse off the detergent before you dry the*

ă	pat	är	car	ī	bite	ô	paw	o͝o	took	ûr	urge
ā	pay	ĕ	pet	îr	pier	ôr	core	o͝or	lure	zh	vision
âr	care	ē	be	ŏ	pot	oi	boy	o͞o	boot	ə	about,
ä	father	ĭ	pit	ō	toe	ou	out	ŭ	cut		item

dishes. I rinsed the soap off the frying pan.

2. To wash something lightly with water or other liquid to remove residue: *I rinsed the dishes off and put them in the rack to dry. I rinsed off the deck chairs with a hose.*

rinse out

1. To remove dirt, soap, or some other residue within something by washing with water or other liquid: *I rinsed the soap out of the rags. Take these old cans and rinse out the dirt. I used turpentine on the brushes to rinse the paint out.*
2. To wash something lightly with water or other liquid to remove residue from within it: *I rinsed out the glasses and put them on the rack to dry. The inside of the bowl was full of dust, so I rinsed it out before I used it.*

◆ **rip** (rĭp)

ripped (rĭpt), **ripping** (rĭp′ĭng), **rips** (rĭps)

rip into

1. To attack someone or something with great vigor or violence; tear into: *The lion ripped into the deer carcass.*
2. To criticize someone or something vehemently: *The candidate ripped into her opponent's political record.*

rip off

1. To remove something from something by ripping or tearing: *I ripped the tag off the pillow. Rip off a few more bits of cloth to make rags.*
2. To remove something quickly: *She ripped her shoes off and threw them under the bed. He ripped off his shirt and threw it into the hamper.*
3. To steal from someone or something: *The thieves ripped off the unsuspecting tourist. The crook ripped the cashier off.*
4. To steal something: *The shoplifter ripped off five shirts. The thief ripped a car off from the lot.*
5. To exploit, swindle, cheat, or defraud someone or something: *The false advertising campaign ripped off a lot of people who bought the product. I think the person at the ticket booth ripped me off.*

rip on

SLANG

To ridicule someone harshly; tease someone: *The older kids ripped on me because my clothes weren't fashionable.*

rip up

1. To tear something roughly or energetically into small pieces: *He ripped up the letter and threw it away. She ripped the contract up and left the office.*
2. To pull or remove something violently from the ground or floor: *When I ripped up the carpet, I could see that the wooden floor was in good condition. The gophers ripped my lawn up.*

◆ **rise** (rīz)

rose (rōz), **risen** (rĭz′ən), **rising** (rī′zĭng), **rises** (rī′zĭz)

rise above

1. To move upward above something: *The balloon rose above the trees.*

2. To extend upward; be prominent over something: *The tower rises above the hill.*
3. To be superior to something or someone: *Her performance rises above that of her peers.*
4. To adopt a better attitude in order to avoid being burdened or concerned with something: *He rose above the silly arguing among his classmates and thought of his own ideas.*

rise up

1. To assume a standing position after lying, sitting, or kneeling: *The kindergartners rose up after naptime and resumed their activities.*
2. To travel upward: *The hot air balloon is rising up above the clouds.*
3. To rise into view, especially from below the horizon: *The campers were eating breakfast when they saw the sun rise up over the mountains.*
4. To increase in pitch or volume; swell: *In the final chorus, the altos rose up above the other voices.*
5. To surge from an inner source; well up: *Even though the situation seemed desperate, I felt hope rise up within me.*
6. To stage a resistance or revolt; rebel: *The migrant workers rose up against the unfair wages.*

◆ **roar** (rôr)

roared (rôrd), **roaring** (rôr′ĭng), **roars** (rôrz)

roar back

To have great success after a period of weak performance; make a dramatic recovery: *The tennis player lost the first set but roared back to win the match.*

◆ **rob** (rŏb)

robbed (rŏbd), **robbing** (rŏb′ĭng), **robs** (rŏbz)

rob of

1. To deprive someone of something by stealing it: *The thief robbed us of our money. I was robbed of my car.*
2. To deprive something or someone of something, to injurious effect: *This parasite robs trees of sap. The malicious rumor robbed me of my professional standing.*

◆ **rock** (rŏk)

rocked (rŏkt), **rocking** (rŏk′ĭng), **rocks** (rŏks)

rock out

SLANG

To play or listen to rock music enthusiastically: *It was an awesome concert—the band really rocked out.*

◆ **roll** (rōl)

rolled (rōld), **rolling** (rōl′ĭng), **rolls** (rōlz)

roll around

To come to pass. Used of times, seasons, or scheduled events: *When the holidays roll around, I'll go*

ă	pat	är	car	ī	bite	ô	paw	o͝o	took	ûr	urge
ā	pay	ĕ	pet	îr	pier	ôr	core	o͝or	lure	zh	vision
âr	care	ē	be	ŏ	pot	oi	boy	o͞o	boot	ə	about,
ä	father	ĭ	pit	ō	toe	ou	out	ŭ	cut		item

visit my family. When June rolls around, I'll go swimming in the lake.

roll back

1. To reduce the power or influence of something: *The government tried to roll back the growing student movement. When the union achieved a more powerful position, management tried to roll it back.*
2. To reduce something, as a price or value, to a previous lower level: *We had to roll back prices to compete with the discount stores. After the store owner raised prices on toasters, no one bought them, so she had to roll them back.*

roll out

1. To move out of something or some place by rolling: *The ball rolled out the door and down the steps.*
2. To unfold and spread out something that has been rolled up: *We rolled out our sleeping bags on the ground. The coach rolled the mats out for the gymnastics competition.*
3. To make something flat by rolling a cylindrical object over it: *The pastry chef rolled the dough out. The sculptor rolled out the clay.*
4. To present something; to make something available: *A lot of stores roll out their best bargains at the end of the year.*
5. To get out of bed: *We didn't get to bed until almost sunrise, and we finally rolled out at noon.*

roll over

1. To shift one's position by turning from one side to the other: *The dog rolled over on the carpet.*
2. To shift the position of someone or something by turning from one side to the other: *We rolled over the rug in order to move the furniture. The toddler rolled the ball over to me.*
3. To defer or postpone payment of an obligation: *The bank says it will roll over our debt until next year. They couldn't pay the bill, so the agency agreed to roll it over until the following month.*
4. To reinvest funds from a maturing security or from a tax-deferred account into a similar security or account: *When I left my job, I rolled over my 401K account into an IRA. If you roll the money over into an IRA, you can defer your taxes until after you retire.*
5. To consent or comply passively or without protest; acquiesce: *You shouldn't just roll over and give in when your kids want something!*

roll up

1. To fold or turn something inward several times in order to make it more compact: *Please roll up the poster before it gets torn. We rolled the carpet up so we could dance on the wooden floor.*
2. To assume a coiled or spiral form: *The snail rolled up in its shell.*
3. To arrive in a vehicle: *The celebrity rolled up to the theater in a white limousine.*
4. To envelop or enfold something in a covering: *Roll the dirty laundry up in a sheet. I rolled up the rags in a tarp and threw them out.*
5. To accumulate or amass something: *The investors rolled up a large fortune.*

◆ **root** (ro͞ot, ro͝ot)

rooted (ro͞o′tĭd, ro͝o′tĭd), **rooting** (ro͞o′tĭng, ro͝o′tĭng), **roots** (ro͞ots, ro͝ots)

root for

1. To dig in the earth with or as if with the snout or a paw in order to find something: *The pigs rooted for truffles.*
2. To lend encouragement and support to someone or something: *We all rooted for our school's football team.*

root in

1. To cause something, as a plant, to grow roots in something: *The gardener rooted the plant in good soil.*
2. To have something as a primary source or origin. Used in the passive: *Homelessness is very often rooted in poverty. The word "tantalize" is rooted in Greek mythology.*

root out

1. To uncover or expose the source of something: *The government agents rooted out the source of the drug money. The mayor hated corruption and vowed to root it out.*
2. To incapacitate or destroy something at its source: *The exterminator was unable to root out the last few mice from the kitchen. The gophers are making a mess of the lawn—we need to root them out!*

root up

1. To remove something by the roots: *We had to root up the tree stumps in our new yard. Let's root these weeds up before it rains.*
2. To unearth or expose some cause, solution, or basis: *The public health officials rooted up the cause of the pandemic. I don't know what the answer is, but I'm sure we can root it up on the Internet.*

◆ **rope** (rōp)

roped (rōpt), **roping** (rō′pĭng), **ropes** (rōps)

rope in

1. To catch and draw something in with a rope or lasso: *The cowboy roped in the stray calf. We set up a barrel and practiced roping it in with a lasso.*
2. To recruit or enlist someone to participate: *I roped in a few bystanders to help me fix the flat tire. She didn't want to go to the store with him, but he roped her in.*

rope into

To persuade someone to do something by means of trickery or deception: *A dishonorable salesman roped us into buying worthless property.*

rope off

To restrict or reserve some location or area by encircling it with rope: *The ushers roped off the first three*

ă	pat	är	car	ī	bite	ô	paw	o͝o	took	ûr	urge
ā	pay	ĕ	pet	îr	pier	ôr	core	o͝or	lure	zh	vision
âr	care	ē	be	ŏ	pot	oi	boy	o͞o	boot	ə	about,
ä	father	ĭ	pit	ō	toe	ou	out	ŭ	cut		item

rows of seats for special guests. The guards roped the stairway off.

◆ **rot** (rŏt)

rotted (rŏt′ĭd), **rotting** (rŏt′ĭng), **rots** (rŏts)

rot out

1. To become completely hollow or ruined by decay or decomposition: *If you don't see a dentist, your teeth will rot out. The abandoned building might collapse because its walls have rotted out.*
2. To cause something to become completely hollow or ruined by decay or decomposition: *The water from the leaky sink rotted out the floor boards. All that candy will rot your teeth out.*

◆ **rough** (rŭf)

roughed (rŭft), **roughing** (rŭf′ĭng), **roughs** (rŭfs)

rough out

To prepare or indicate something in an unfinished form; make a preliminary sketch or plan of something: *We met to rough out the agenda for the upcoming week. They roughed a plan out and estimated how long the project would take.*

rough up

1. To cause something to become less smooth: *Rough the wood up so that the glue will hold better. The ice skates roughed up the surface of the ice.*
2. To treat someone roughly or with physical violence; manhandle someone: *The bully roughed up one of the kids on the playground. They threatened to rough me up if I didn't give them the money.*

◆ **round** (round)

rounded (roun′dĭd), **rounding** (roun′dĭng), **rounds** (roundz)

round on

To assail someone suddenly; turn on someone: *The entire group rounded on me when I questioned their motives.*

round out

To bring some event or achievement to a pleasing conclusion or completeness, especially by enhancing it: *This last song will round out our performance for this evening. Let's round the meal out with a glass of wine.*

round up

1. To herd some cattle together from various places: *In the evening it's time to round up the herd. The ranchers rounded the younger cattle up to brand them.*
2. To seek out and bring some people or things together; gather some people or things: *We rounded up all of our neighbors to help clean the park. Go out and round the kids up for dinner.*
3. To change some exact number to the nearest whole number above it: *The statistician rounded 4.612 up to 5. When you take the test, round up your answers.*

◆ **rub** (rŭb)

rubbed (rŭbd), **rubbing** (rŭb′ĭng), **rubs** (rŭbz)

rub down

1. To rub someone or something thoroughly in order to dry, polish, or

coat the surface: *I stepped out of the shower and rubbed myself down with a towel. Grab that towel and help me rub down the car. I rubbed down the top of the table with sandpaper. I rubbed myself down with suntan lotion.*

2. To massage someone or something thoroughly: *The trainer rubbed the boxer down after the match. The hotel masseuse can rub down 20 tourists a day.*
3. To work something, such as seasoning, into food by rubbing: *It's best to rub the meat down with pepper before cooking. Rub down the surface of the bread with garlic.*

rub in

1. To work something into a surface by rubbing: *I put lotion on my hands and rubbed it in. Don't try to clean the shirt now—you will only rub in the stain.*
2. To talk deliberately and excessively about something unpleasant in order to make another person feel bad: *She always rubs in the fact that she has more money than me. I know I made a mistake—there's no need to rub it in.*

rub off

1. To remove or erase something from a surface by or as if by rubbing: *The mechanic grabbed a rag and rubbed off the grease. Don't scrub too hard, or you'll rub the paint off the car.*
2. To be removed or be capable of being removed from a surface by rubbing: *The ink on the table won't rub off. The newsprint rubbed off on my fingers.*
3. To pass from one person to another through direct association, as of a quality: *We hope some of her enthusiasm rubs off. I'm glad to see their good manners have rubbed off on you.*

rub out

1. To erase or obliterate something by or as if by rubbing: *He tried to rub the paint out from the fabric. She rubbed out the grease with a sponge.*
2. SLANG To kill someone; murder someone: *The gangsters rubbed out one of the witnesses.*

◆ **ruffle** (rŭf′əl)

ruffled (rŭf′əld), **ruffling** (rŭf′lĭng), **ruffles** (rŭf′əlz)

ruffle up

To make some surface less smooth by partially lifting the individual parts that make up that surface: *The wind ruffled up the bird's feathers. Don't ruffle my hair up.*

◆ **rule** (ro͞ol)

ruled (ro͞old), **ruling** (ro͞o′lĭng), **rules** (ro͞olz)

rule against

To deliver a judgment that is not favorable to someone or something: *The court ruled against*

ă	pat	är	car	ī	bite	ô	paw	o͝o	took	ûr	urge
ā	pay	ĕ	pet	îr	pier	ôr	core	o͝or	lure	zh	vision
âr	care	ē	be	ŏ	pot	oi	boy	o͞o	boot	ə	about, item
ä	father	ĭ	pit	ō	toe	ou	out	ŭ	cut		

the plaintiff, and no damages were awarded.

rule for

To deliver a judgment that is in favor of someone or something: *The court ruled for the plaintiff and awarded damages in the amount of $10,000.*

rule out

1. To prevent or preclude something: *The snowstorm ruled out their weekly meeting. Our lack of funds ruled the vacation plans out.*
2. To eliminate something from consideration; exclude something: *The referee has ruled out the option of starting over. I wanted to drop the course, but school policy ruled that option out.*
3. To draw a line or lines through something to delete or obscure it; cross something out: *The copyeditors ruled out all of our mistakes on the manuscript.*

rule over

To have authority or control over someone or something: *A single dynasty once ruled over most of central Asia.*

◆ **run** (rŭn)

ran (răn), **run** (rŭn), **running** (rŭn′ĭng), **runs** (rŭnz)

run across

To find someone or something by chance; come upon someone or something: *I ran across some old friends at the store.*

run after

1. To chase or pursue someone or something: *The fox ran after the rabbit.*
2. To follow something, always lagging behind: *Stock prices have been running after bond prices for a while.*
3. To seek the company or attention of someone for purposes of romance: *She finally became tired of running after him. I can't believe the way he runs after her.*

run against

1. To work against something or someone; oppose something or someone: *The company's policies are running against public opinion.*
2. To compete with someone for an elected position: *I plan to run against my old rival in the election.*
3. To encounter some unexpected obstacle: *The contractor ran against some difficulties in trying to complete the project.*

run along

To go away; leave. Used chiefly as a command: *Why don't you run along and play outside now?*

run around *or* **run round**

1. To run in a space in many different directions: *The kids ran around in the park while we relaxed.*
2. To be very busy doing something, especially when moving from place to place in order to do it: *I've been running around getting ready for the party.*
3. **run around after** To try hurriedly to obtain or catch something or someone: *How long have you been running around after that pair of shoes?*
4. **run around with** To associate or engage in activities with someone or

something: *I don't like the people you've been running around with—they're a bad influence!*

run away

1. To flee; escape: *As the soldiers approached the town, many people ran away. The mouse ran away from the cat.*
2. To secretly leave one's home to escape it: *Every year, many teenagers run away and never return home.*
3. To secretly leave one's home to elope or have a romantic relationship: *They didn't want to deal with a big wedding, so they ran away to Las Vegas.*
4. **run away with** To surpass an opponent and attain some prize: *They ran away with the championship, defeating every opponent handily.*

run by

1. To run near or alongside someone or something: *We were walking in the woods when suddenly a big moose ran by.*
2. To encounter something while walking or running: *We ran by two waterfalls during our hike in the mountains.*
3. To tell, explain, or demonstrate something to someone: *Please run those instructions by me again—I didn't hear them all.*
4. To come to some place for a brief period of time: *I ran by the store after work to pick up some milk.*

run down

1. To stop because of lack of force or power: *The battery ran down, causing the clock to stop.*
2. To make someone or something tired or worn; cause someone or something to lose vigor: *All of that work ran me down. The headlights ran down the battery.*
3. To collide with and knock down or damage someone or something: *That speeding car almost ran me down. The bus ran down a pedestrian.*
4. To chase and capture someone or something: *The detectives ran down the suspects and had them arrested. The wolves separated one of the elk from the herd and ran it down.*
5. To trace the source of something: *The police ran down all possible leads in the case. We had the license plate number, so we ran it down and got the name of the driver.*
6. To disparage someone or something: *Don't run her down—she is very talented.*
7. To review something from top to bottom, such as a list; go over something: *Let's run down the list of new members and see who has paid the membership fee.*
8. Baseball To put a runner out after trapping him or her between two bases: *The visiting team managed to run down three players in one inning. The runner tried to get to*

ă	pat	är	car	ī	bite	ô	paw	o͝o	took	ûr	urge
ā	pay	ĕ	pet	îr	pier	ôr	core	o͝or	lure	zh	vision
âr	care	ē	be	ŏ	pot	oi	boy	o͞o	boot	ə	about,
ä	father	ĭ	pit	ō	toe	ou	out	ŭ	cut		item

third base, but the shortstop caught the ball and ran him down.

run for

1. To flee toward something or some place, especially for shelter or safety: *When it started to rain, we ran for shelter.*
2. To compete to be elected to some office or position: *Four nominees ran for club treasurer.*

run in

1. To quickly or briefly enter some place on foot: *I'm going to run in the house and get my jacket. We stopped at the store, and I ran in and bought some milk.*
2. To drive someone to the center of a place: *Don't walk all the way to town—I can run you in on my way to work.*
3. SLANG To arrest someone; take someone into legal custody: *I had no identification with me, so the police ran me in. The police ran in the suspects for further questioning.*
4. To make a solid body of text without a paragraph or other break: *All of the paragraphs on this page run in, so it's very hard to read.*
5. To cause some printed material to make a solid body of text without a paragraph or other break: *The editor ran in the final paragraph so that it would fit on the page. There was no reason to split this text into two paragraphs, so I ran the second one in.*

run into

1. To go quickly into some place on foot: *The wild horses ran into the woods.*
2. To enter quickly or briefly some place on foot: *I ran into the department store for some new socks.*
3. To collide with something: *I drove off the road and ran into a tree.*
4. To drive or propel something and cause it to collide with something else: *I ran my car into a tree. The truck ran the pedestrian into the guardrail.*
5. To drive someone to some central place: *I'll run you into the center of town and you can walk home from there.*
6. To meet or find someone or something by chance: *We ran into some old friends at the bar. I ran into a quaint restaurant outside of town.*
7. To encounter some unpleasant or unfavorable situation: *The travelers ran into some bad weather on their way over the mountains.*
8. To amount to some quantity: *His net worth runs into the millions.*

run off

1. To move away suddenly on foot; run away: *The scarecrow frightened the approaching children and they ran off. He suddenly remembered something and ran off.*
2. To cause someone or something to leave or run away from some place: *The angry farmer ran us off his land. The security guard ran off the trespassers.*
3. To create some copy or printout of a document: *I ran off 200 copies of the report. Please run another copy off.*
4. To flow off something; drain away from something: *The rainwater runs off the roof into the gutter.*
5. To decide a contest or competition from among the leading

participants: *The two candidates who received the highest votes in the special election will be running off for county commissioner.*

6. To operate using something as a source of power: *This CD player is portable and runs off batteries.*
7. To leave a relationship or place to elope or have a romantic relationship: *They ran off together and got married. I think she's going to run off with the guy she's been seeing secretly.*
8. **run off with** To steal something; make off with something: *The thief ran off with my book bag.*

run on

1. To continue for a long time: *That movie ran on too long.*
2. To talk or complain excessively about something: *He is always running on about his tax problems.*
3. To continue a text without a formal break: *The editor marked all of the instances where the text ran on incorrectly.*
4. To operate using something as a source of power: *This new car runs on electricity.*

run out

1. To hasten on foot to an exterior or distant place: *Let's run out to the lake and swim.*
2. To make a brief trip to fetch or buy something, especially by car: *I'll run out for some more beer.*
3. To be used until nothing remains: *Our supplies finally ran out and we had nothing to eat.*
4. To use something until there is none left: *I think we've run out of toothpaste. Bring enough money so that you don't run out before your return.*
5. To compel someone to leave by force or threat: *The sheriff ran the gangsters out of town. We sneaked into the yard to get the ball, and a pair of vicious dogs ran us out.*
6. To become void, especially through the passage of time: *Our insurance policy will run out next week.*

run over

1. To collide with, knock down, and often pass over someone or something: *That car almost ran me over! I accidently ran over the flower pot with the lawn mower. The football player ran over an opponent and continued down the field for a touchdown.*
2. To move or flow over the surface of something: *The creek runs over the rocks of the old riverbed.*
3. To cause something to move or flow over or across the surface of something: *I ran cold water over my burned hand.*
4. To read or review something quickly: *Let's run over the song one more time before we record it.*
5. To overflow: *Stop pouring the water in—the bucket is running over.*

6. To make a brief trip, especially by car: *I'll run over to the grocery store after work.*
7. To go beyond a limit: *The meeting ran over by 30 minutes.*

run past

1. To run near or alongside someone or something from one side to the other: *A flock of wild turkeys ran past the barn.*
2. To overtake someone or something by running: *I was leading in the race, but then someone ran past me.*
3. To continue later than some time: *I will be late for dinner because our meeting will run past 7:00.*
4. To tell, explain, or demonstrate something to someone: *He ran many ideas past us, but we disliked them all.*

run through

1. To run in some passageway or from one side of something to another: *The ink runs through the nib of the pen. The children ran through the field.*
2. To review the main points of something from beginning to end: *The crew ran through the preflight procedures. We ran through the witness's testimony before presenting it in court.*
3. To permeate or extend throughout something: *A dark mood runs through all of Poe's works.*
4. To use something until there is no more left: *She ran through all of her money in five days.*
5. To rehearse something without stopping: *Let's run through the first act again.*
6. To impale someone: *He ran the soldier through with a bayonet.*

run to

1. To make a brief trip somewhere, especially by motor vehicle: *I'll run to the store and pick up some vegetables for dinner.*
2. To amount to some maximal quantity: *The bill for the flowers for the wedding ran to $900.*

run up

1. To cause some debt to accumulate: *Don't run up such a big bill next time you go out to eat! He has been running a large debt up for months.*
2. To increase some value: *The craze for this company's stock will run up its price. The bidders ran the price up to $100.*

run with

1. To accompany and participate in the activities of someone or something: *Those teenagers run with a wild crowd.*
2. To float or sail in the same direction as something:*The sailboat ran with the wind all the way to the beach. On the trip back, we can run with the current, and we won't have to paddle the canoe.*
3. To adopt something or take something as one's own and then proceed with it: *I took their idea for a novel and ran with it.*

◆ **rush** (rŭsh)

rushed (rŭsht), **rushing** (rŭsh′ĭng), **rushes** (rŭsh′ĭz)

rush in

1. To enter some place hurriedly or quickly: *I rushed in the house to pick up my wallet.*
2. To cause someone to enter some place in a hurry: *We were late for*

the concert, so the ushers rushed us in.

3. To do something impulsively or without careful consideration; act rashly: *It's best to shop around a bit rather than rushing in and buying the first car you see.*

rush into

1. To enter some place hurriedly or quickly: *The firefighters rushed into the burning building.*
2. To cause someone to enter some place in a hurry: *The teacher rushed the students into the gymnasium so they could play games before lunch.*

rush off

1. To depart in a hurry: *It's too bad you have to rush off right after the movie.*
2. To send or transmit something hurriedly: *As soon as your payment clears, we'll rush off your package to you. I'm sorry you left your book here; we'll rush it off to you in the mail.*

rush through

1. To do or complete something in a hurry: *The staff rushed through the meeting because they had started late. I rushed through the test and got a lot of answers wrong.*
2. To cause someone to do or complete something in a hurry: *The tour guide rushed us through the exhibit too quickly.*

◆ **rust** (rŭst)

rusted (rŭs′tĭd), **rusting** (rŭs′tĭng), **rusts** (rŭsts)

rust up

1. To become thoroughly corroded: *The walls of the old ship had rusted up.*
2. To become immobile or stuck due to corrosion: *The bolts have rusted up; I can't remove them.*
3. To cause something to be thoroughly corroded: *Don't use these chemicals; they will rust up the tank. Exposure to salt rusted the fender up.*

◆ **rustle** (rŭs′əl)

rustled (rŭs′əld), **rustling** (rŭs′ə-lĭng), **rustles** (rŭs′əlz)

rustle up

To gather something or some people together, especially energetically or quickly: *Go rustle up the kids and let's go for a drive. I went to the kitchen to rustle some dinner up.*

ă	pat	är	car	ī	bite	ô	paw	o͝o	took	ûr	urge
ā	pay	ĕ	pet	îr	pier	ôr	core	o͝or	lure	zh	vision
âr	care	ē	be	ŏ	pot	oi	boy	o͞o	boot	ə	about,
ä	father	ĭ	pit	ō	toe	ou	out	ŭ	cut		item

S

◆ **sack** (săk)

sacked (săkt), **sacking** (săk′ĭng), **sacks** (săks)

sack out

SLANG

To sleep or go to sleep: *After a long day at work, I sacked out on the couch.*

◆ **saddle** (săd′l)

saddled (săd′ld), **saddling** (săd′l-ĭng), **saddles** (săd′lz)

saddle up

1. To put a saddle on a horse: *The cowboys saddled up and rode off.*
2. To put a saddle on some animal: *The cowboy saddled up three horses for the other riders. Some camels don't like it if you saddle them up at night.*

saddle with

To load or burden someone or something; weigh down someone or something: *My boss saddled me with a large amount of work. The recent college graduate was saddled with debt.*

◆ **sail** (sāl)

sailed (sāld), **sailing** (sā′lĭng), **sails** (sālz)

sail into

1. To move across the surface of water into some place. Used especially of a sailing vessel or its crew: *The ship sailed into the harbor.*
2. To move into some place smoothly or effortlessly: *The student sailed into the room five minutes late.*
3. To attack or criticize someone vigorously: *The supervisor sailed into the workers for the shoddy job they were doing.*

sail through

1. To pass through something quickly and without pausing or lingering: *The car sailed through the red light.*
2. To make progress with something quickly and easily: *Because I had studied for so long, I was able to sail through the exam.*

◆ **salivate** (săl′ə-vāt′)

salivated (săl′ə-vā′tĭd), **salivating** (săl′ə-vā′tĭng), **salivates** (săl′ə-vāts′)

salivate over

To be very eager about, excited about, or desirous for something: *The fans of the rock group salivated over the newest CD.*

◆ **salt** (sôlt)

salted (sôl′tĭd), **salting** (sôl′tĭng), **salts** (sôlts)

salt away

To save or store something for future use: *I salted away money from my summer job to pay for college. I bought 20 packs of paper towels that were on sale, and I salted them away.*

salt down

To cover something completely in salt in order to preserve it, flavor it, or dry it: *The cook salted the eggplant down for four days. Pioneers would salt down meat for the winter.*

◆ **sass** (săs)

sassed (săst), **sassing** (săs′ĭng), **sasses** (săs′ĭz)

sass back

To respond to someone rudely or inappropriately: *If you sass back to your teacher, you'll get sent to the principal's office.*

◆ **save** (sāv)

saved (sāvd), **saving** (sā′vĭng), **saves** (sāvz)

save on

1. To conserve money by purchasing something at a discount: *Save on all kitchen appliances during our special clearance sale!*
2. To conserve some amount of money by purchasing something at a discount: *I saved a dollar on my purchase by using a coupon.*

save up

To collect something for future use; accumulate something: *I haven't saved up enough money yet to buy a new TV. You should save your money up for college. We've been saving up to buy a new car.*

◆ **savor** (sā′vər)

savored (sā′vərd), **savoring** (sā′və-rĭng), **savors** (sā′vərz)

savor of

1. To have some taste or smell: *This dish savors of curry.*
2. To display some quality or characteristic: *Your attitude savors of vanity.*

◆ **say** (sā)

said (sĕd), **saying** (sā′ĭng), **says** (sĕz)

say for

To say or indicate something in support of someone or something: *What do you have to say for yourself? Their legal problems don't say much for their company.*

◆ **scab** (skăb)

scabbed (skăbd), **scabbing** (skăb′ĭng), **scabs** (skăbz)

scab over

To become covered by a scab: *The wound scabbed over and eventually healed.*

◆ **scale** (skāl)

scaled (skāld), **scaling** (skā′lĭng), **scales** (skālz)

scale back

To reduce the scope or extent of something according to a standard or by degrees; reduce something in calculated amounts: *The company scaled back the scheduled pay in-*

ă	pat	är	car	ī	bite	ô	paw	o͝o	took	ûr	urge
ā	pay	ĕ	pet	îr	pier	ôr	core	o͝or	lure	zh	vision
âr	care	ē	be	ŏ	pot	oi	boy	o͞o	boot	ə	about,
ä	father	ĭ	pit	ō	toe	ou	out	ŭ	cut		item

crease. After reviewing its budget, the school scaled its sports activities back.

scale down

1. To climb down something; descend something: *The climber carefully scaled down the cliff.*
2. To reduce the scope or extent of something according to a standard or by degrees; reduce something in calculated amounts: *The lawyer advised them to scale down their demands. We decided our travel plans were unrealistic, so we scaled them down.*

scale up

1. To climb up something; ascend something: *The hikers scaled up the side of the mountain.*
2. To increase the scope or extent of something according to a standard or by degrees; increase something in calculated amounts: *The company scaled up its operations to meet the growing demand. The city scaled its efforts up to reduce crime.*

◆ **scan** (skăn)

scanned (skănd), **scanning** (skăn′ĭng), **scans** (skănz)

scan in

To encode something digitally with an optical scanner: *I scanned in all my old photos and saved them on my hard drive. They scanned the text in and then edited it on the computer.*

◆ **scare** (skâr)

scared (skârd), **scaring** (skâr′ĭng), **scares** (skârz)

scare away *or* **scare off**

To cause someone or something to leave or to stay away due to fear: *The kidnappings have scared tourists away. The farmer put up a scarecrow to scare away the birds.*

scare up

To gather or prepare something with a lot of effort or ingenuity: *They managed to scare up some folding chairs for the unexpected crowd. I'll go in the kitchen and try to scare something up from among the leftovers.*

◆ **scarf** (skärf)

scarfed (skärft), **scarfing** (skär′fĭng), **scarfs** (skärfs)

scarf down

To eat or drink something hungrily; devour something: *We scarfed down the piece of chocolate cake and asked for more. I was very hungry, so I made some soup and scarfed it down.*

◆ **scoop** (sko͞op)

scooped (sko͞opt), **scooping** (sko͞o′pĭng), **scoops** (sko͞ops)

scoop up

1. To lift or collect something with a scoop or scooping motion: *I scooped up a handful of jelly beans. The tractor scooped the dirt up and poured it in the hole.*
2. To win or achieve something, especially a prize, easily: *The movie scooped up numerous awards. We scooped another win up on Saturday.*

◆ **scoot** (sko͞ot)

scooted (sko͞o′tĭd), **scooting** (sko͞o′tĭng), **scoots** (sko͞ots)

scoot over

1. To move or slide to the side: *Can you scoot over so that I can sit down?*
2. To move or slide something to the side: *Scoot your chair over so we can talk.*

◆ **scope** (skōp)

scoped (skōpt), **scoping** (skō′pĭng), **scopes** (skōps)

scope out

To make a preliminary inspection of something: *The crew scoped out possible locations for the movie. Before the thieves robbed the bank, they spent weeks scoping it out.*

◆ **scout** (skout)

scouted (skou′tĭd), **scouting** (skou′tĭng), **scouts** (skouts)

scout around

To go from place to place searching: *I'll scout around and see if I can find a place to build our campfire. The reporter went to the party to scout around for some gossip.*

scout out

To go to a place to make a preliminary inspection of someone or something in order to evaluate it for possible use, purchase, or hire, or in order to obtain information ahead of a future encounter: *The college coach went to a high school game to scout out a potential recruit. I went ahead of the other hikers and scouted the trail out.*

◆ **scrape** (skrāp)

scraped (skrāpt), **scraping** (skrā′pĭng), **scrapes** (skrāps)

scrape along

1. To succeed just barely in managing or surviving, especially despite severely limited resources: *We scraped along on very little income until I could find work.*
2. To succeed or manage at a level of minimal acceptability: *The parents were concerned that their child was just scraping along.*

scrape by

1. To succeed just barely in managing or surviving, especially despite severely limited resources: *When I was out of work, my family and I barely scraped by. We scraped by on just $3 a day.*
2. To succeed at a level of minimal acceptability: *The student just scraped by with a D average.*
3. To succeed just barely in passing some obstacle, such as a competition or evaluation: *The tennis player scraped by the third round with a narrow victory.*

scrape through

To succeed just barely in getting through something: *I didn't get a chance to study, and I barely scraped through the final exam.*

ă	pat	är	car	ī	bite	ô	paw	o͝o	took	ûr	urge
ā	pay	ĕ	pet	îr	pier	ôr	core	o͝or	lure	zh	vision
âr	care	ē	be	ŏ	pot	oi	boy	o͞o	boot	ə	about, item
ä	father	ĭ	pit	ō	toe	ou	out	ŭ	cut		

scrape together

To accumulate or produce something with difficulty: *We scraped together just enough cash to pay for the pizza. The kitchen was so empty that we could barely scrape a meal together.*

◆ **scratch** (skrăch)

scratched (skrăcht), **scratching** (skrăch′ĭng), **scratches** (skrăch′ĭz)

scratch off

1. To remove something or an outer layer of something by lightly scraping: *I scratched off the paint that had dripped on the table. The mud on my shoes dried up, so I scratched it off. I scratched off the lottery ticket with a coin.*
2. To remove someone or something from a list or record: *I decided not to sign up for the team, so the coach scratched off my name from the list. We don't need any pickles, so you can scratch that off the shopping list.*
3. To write or draw something hurriedly: *After the party I scratched off a thank-you note. It's a very old essay—I scratched it off when I was in middle school.*

scratch out

1. To draw a line or lines on something to delete or obscure it, or to indicate that it should be canceled or ignored: *Scratch out anything on the shopping list that you think is too expensive. I didn't like the words you had written, so I scratched them out.*
2. To remove someone or something from a list or record: *Scratch out the neighbors from the list—they're not coming to the wedding. I'm not playing tonight, so you can scratch my name out.*
3. To get by with some way of life, especially with very few resources: *We barely scratched out a living during the war.*

◆ **screen** (skrēn)

screened (skrēnd), **screening** (skrē′nĭng), **screens** (skrēnz)

screen off

To separate, hide, or obscure something with a screen or similar barrier: *I screened off the bed from the rest of the room with curtains. A high wall screens the porch off from the view of the ocean.*

screen out

1. To prevent something from passing by using a filter; filter something out: *This glass screens out the harmful ultraviolet rays. The e-mail filter identifies advertisements and screens them out.*
2. To deny someone or something admittance or approval based on certain criteria: *Background checks allow us to screen out all applicants with criminal records. They screened me out because I didn't meet the eligibility requirements.*

◆ **screw** (skro͞o)

screwed (skro͞od), **screwing** (skro͞o′ĭng), **screws** (skro͞oz)

screw around

1. SLANG To engage in frivolous activity: *I spent the day screwing around watching TV. We spent the evening screwing around at the pool hall. Stop screwing around and get to work!*

2. SLANG **screw around with** To manipulate or work with something without a clear sense of method: *Who's been screwing around with my computer?—It's not working properly.*
3. VULGAR SLANG To be sexually unfaithful.

screw over

VULGAR SLANG To treat someone unfairly; take advantage of someone: *The billing department really screwed me over. The new management screwed over the staff with their rigid policies.*

screw up

SLANG

1. To make a mistake; blunder: *I screwed up and delivered the package to the wrong address.*
2. To injure, damage, or interfere negatively with something: *Lifting those boxes really screwed up my back. I gave them detailed instructions, but they still screwed the project up.*
3. To make someone neurotic or mentally disturbed: *War can really screw up the survivors. Prison really screwed him up. She was screwed up by her parents' divorce.*
4. To twist or deform something: *The jester screwed up his face and gave a mocking reply. She screwed her eyes up and tried to read the sign.*
5. To muster or summon up something: *I screwed up my courage and went out on the stage.*

screw with

VULGAR SLANG

1. To alter something improperly, especially on purpose: *Someone must have screwed with the motor, because it's not working now.*
2. To deceive or confuse someone or something, especially for one's amusement: *I thought they might offer me a job, but now I think they were just screwing with me.*

◆ **scribble** (skrĭb′əl)

scribbled (skrĭb′əld), **scribbling** (skrĭb′ə-lĭng), **scribbles** (skrĭb′əlz)

scribble down

To write something quickly without paying attention to readability or style: *She grabbed a piece of paper and scribbled down the address that I told her. He scribbled a number down on his notepad.*

◆ **scrimp** (skrĭmp)

scrimped (skrĭmpt), **scrimping** (skrĭm′pĭng), **scrimps** (skrĭmps)

scrimp on

To consume something sparingly in order to conserve it, or be frugal when buying something in order to save money: *When my salary was cut, I had to scrimp on food in order to pay my rent.*

◆ **scrounge** (skrounj)

scrounged (skrounjd), **scrounging** (skroun′jĭng), **scrounges** (skroun′jĭz)

ă	pat	är	car	ī	bite	ô	paw	o͝o	took	ûr	urge
ā	pay	ĕ	pet	îr	pier	ôr	core	o͝or	lure	zh	vision
âr	care	ē	be	ŏ	pot	oi	boy	o͞o	boot	ə	about,
ä	father	ĭ	pit	ō	toe	ou	out	ŭ	cut		item

scrounge up

To obtain something by or as if by begging, scavenging, or borrowing: *The dog scrounged up a bone in the pile of trash. I didn't have any quarters for the washing machine, but I scrounged some up by looking under the cushions on the sofa.*

◆ **scrub** (skrŭb)

scrubbed (skrŭbd), **scrubbing** (skrŭb′ĭng), **scrubs** (skrŭbz)

scrub up

To wash the hands and arms thoroughly, as before performing or participating in surgery: *The doctors and nurses scrubbed up before entering the operating room.*

◆ **scrunch** (skrŭnch)

scrunched (skrŭncht), **scrunching** (skrŭn′chĭng), **scrunches** (skrŭn′chĭz)

scrunch up

1. To crumple or squeeze something: *She scrunched up her nose like she was going to sneeze. I scrunched my gloves up and put them in my pocket.*
2. To assume a crouched or cramped posture: *The dog scrunched up in the corner to keep warm.*

◆ **seal** (sēl)

sealed (sēld), **sealing** (sē′lĭng), **seals** (sēlz)

seal off

1. To close tightly or surround something or someplace with a barricade or cordon: *The government has sealed off its borders. The police surrounded the building and sealed it off.*
2. To isolate someone or something: *The remote location sealed the village off from the rest of the world.*

◆ **search** (sûrch)

searched (sûrcht), **searching** (sûr′chĭng), **searches** (sûr′chĭz)

search for

To conduct a thorough investigation for someone or something; seek someone or something: *The police are searching for the missing student.*

search out

To seek and find someone or something: *I managed to search out an old jazz album. She lost his address, but she was able to search him out using the Internet.*

◆ **section** (sĕk′shən)

sectioned (sĕk′shənd), **sectioning** (sĕk′shə-nĭng), **sections** (sĕk′shənz)

section off

To separate or divide some area: *A bookcase sectioned off the sitting area from the dining area. The apartment had no rooms, so we sectioned it off with screens.*

◆ **see** (sē)

saw (sô), **seen** (sēn), **seeing** (sē′ĭng), **sees** (sēz)

see about

To investigate something; look into something: *I went to the bank to see about opening an account. The plumber came over today to see about the leak.*

see after

To take care of someone or something: *The babysitter will see after the children while we're out.*

see in

To escort someone or something into a place: *The receptionist sees in our visitors. The butler will see you in.*

see into

1. To escort some visitor into a room or building: *The butler saw the guests into the room.*
2. To perceive the interior of something with or as if with the eye: *From his window, he could see into the neighbor's apartment.*

see off

To be with someone when he or she is leaving in order to say goodbye: *We saw off our guests at the door. They came to the airport to see us off.*

see out

1. To escort some visitor to an exit: *The butler saw out the visitors. Will you please see Dr. Smith out?*
2. To work on some project until completion: *I plan to retire as soon as I see out this project. Despite poor funding, we saw the project out.*
3. To manage or survive for the duration of some period of time: *The doctor doesn't think the patient will see out the week. In this economy, many companies won't see they year out.*

see through

1. To apprehend one's true nature or character despite some affectation or deception: *We saw through his superficial charm.*
2. To cause or help someone to manage or survive: *I have enough savings to see me through a month without work. We'll see you through until you finish college.*
3. To work on some project until completion: *We are determined to see the project through.*

see to

To deal with some duty, assignment, or matter: *See to washing the dishes, will you? You should see to that cut on your finger—it may need stitches. I'll see to it that you never work in this town again!*

◆ **seek** (sēk)

sought (sôt), **seeking** (sē′kĭng), **seeks** (sēks)

seek out

To try to locate or discover someone or something: *The fish sought out sheltered pools to lay their eggs. The teacher will only give help to those who seek it out.*

◆ **seep** (sēp)

seeped (sēpt), **seeping** (sē′pĭng), **seeps** (sēps)

ă	pat	är	car	ī	bite	ô	paw	o͝o	took	ûr	urge
ā	pay	ĕ	pet	îr	pier	ôr	core	o͝or	lure	zh	vision
âr	care	ē	be	ŏ	pot	oi	boy	o͞o	boot	ə	about, item
ä	father	ĭ	pit	ō	toe	ou	out	ŭ	cut		

seep out

1. To escape or pass slowly through small openings or pores: *I think that gas is seeping out through a crack in the tank.*
2. To become known to the public through a breach of secrecy: *The details they refused to talk about will eventually seep out to the press.*

◆ **seize** (sēz)

seized (sēzd), **seizing** (sē′zĭng), **seizes** (sē′zĭz)

seize on *or* **seize upon**

To take notice of something, especially because it can be used to one's advantage: *The newspapers seized on the mayor's foolish remark and said that he wasn't fit for the job.*

seize up

To fuse or stick together with another part and become unable to move normally, especially as a result of high pressure or temperature: *The car's engine seized up due to a loss of oil.*

◆ **sell** (sĕl)

sold (sōld), **selling** (sĕl′ĭng), **sells** (sĕlz)

sell off

To get rid of something, especially investment assets, by selling: *The company had to sell off some assets so that it could pay its debts. The bank foreclosed on my house and sold it off to the highest bidder.*

sell on

To persuade someone to recognize the worth or desirability of something: *They sold me on the usefulness of their new products, so I invested in their company.*

sell out

1. To be sold completely: *The tickets will sell out by tomorrow.*
2. To sell one's entire supply of a particular item: *I'm afraid we sold out all our ice cream, kids! The hardware store sold out of plywood as the hurricane moved closer to shore.*
3. To cause some supply of merchandise to be sold completely. Used in the passive: *We can't get into the theater because the tickets are sold out.*
4. To cause some vendor to sell its entire supply of something. Used in the passive: *I wanted to buy more spoons, but the store was sold out.*
5. To sell one's entire stake in a business or venture: *The owners of the liquor store plan to sell out as soon as they can find a buyer.*
6. To betray one's cause or colleagues, especially for money: *The disloyal baseball player sold out to another team.*
7. To betray someone or something, especially for money: *The manager sold out his staff in order to keep his own job. Our agent sold us out when she moved to a better company and dropped us as a client.*

◆ **send** (sĕnd)

sent (sĕnt), **sending** (sĕn′dĭng), **sends** (sĕndz)

send away

1. To request that someone or something leave or be taken away: *I became sick suddenly and had to*

send my guests away. Send away the servants so we can talk in private.

2. **send away for** To send a request for something, especially by mail: *I sent away for some information on the university's graduate program.*

send back

1. To order someone to return; have someone return: *He came to visit me at a bad time, so I sent him back. She sent the children back to the same school they attended the year before.*
2. To return something, especially as a way of rejecting it: *I went to the post office to send back the broken toaster. The steak was undercooked, and I had to send it back to the kitchen.*
3. To return or reply to someone or something by mail or some other means of communication: *I sent back a reply via fax. Please send a quick message back by e-mail if you can't come to the party.*

send down

CHIEFLY BRITISH

To suspend or dismiss someone from a university: *The university sent the students down for stealing supplies. They sent down two of the students for cheating.*

send for

To request that someone or something come or be brought, especially by means of a message or messenger; summon someone or something: *Send for the doctor if the patient's fever gets any higher.*

send forth

To cause something to go outward from a source: *The rulers sent the army forth to threaten the approaching invaders. The wounded soldier sent forth a cry of pain.*

send in

1. To submit something, especially by mail or by electronic means: *Let's send in a donation this year. I sent my application for college in by e-mail.*
2. To order someone or some group into a place: *Will you please send in the next candidate on your way out of the office? They sent me in the garage to fetch a hammer.*
3. To have someone enter or reenter a contest, conflict, or situation: *The coach is sending in the kicker. The president sent troops in to suppress the riots.*

send off

1. To release or submit something, especially by mail or by electronic means: *I sent off my application last week. I put a stamp on the letter and sent it off.*
2. To order someone to leave in order to do something or to attend some event or place: *The managers ordered a pizza and sent off an assistant to pick it up. My parents sent me off to boarding school when I was only ten years old.*

ă	pat	är	car	ī	bite	ô	paw	o͝o	took	ûr	urge
ā	pay	ĕ	pet	îr	pier	ôr	core	o͝or	lure	zh	vision
âr	care	ē	be	ŏ	pot	oi	boy	o͞o	boot	ə	about,
ä	father	ĭ	pit	ō	toe	ou	out	ŭ	cut		item

3. To assist or be present at someone's departure: *When I retired, my co-workers sent me off with a big party. A crowd gathered at the train station to send off the politician.*
4. **send off for** To send a request for something, especially by mail: *The mechanic sent off for a replacement part.*
5. SPORTS To eject someone from a game, especially for a flagrant violation of the rules: *The referee stopped the game and sent off two of the players for fighting. The umpire sent me off after I threw my tennis racket into the crowd.*

send out

1. To distribute something widely, especially by mail: *We send out birthday cards to all our customers. I taped up the boxes and sent them out.*
2. To emit or broadcast something: *Such an offensive advertisement will send out the wrong message. We convert the sound into an electronic signal, and that radio tower sends it out.*
3. To dispatch someone to do an errand or convey a message: *The company sent out sales representatives to promote the new product. I sent the bellhop out for some cigarettes.*
4. **send out for** To send or phone in an order for something to a nearby place, such as a restaurant, and request that it be delivered to one's location: *Let's send out for pizza.*

send up

1. To send someone to jail: *They sent the crook up for ten years. The cops busted the gang and sent up the leader.*
2. To make a parody of someone or something: *The comedian sends up contemporary culture. I'm not afraid to send myself up to make people laugh.*

◆ **serve** (sûrv)

served (sûrvd), **serving** (sûr′vĭng), **serves** (sûrvz)

serve on

To serve a term of duty as a member of some official body: *Have you ever served on a jury before?*

serve out

To complete some period of service: *The criminal served out his sentence in a minimum security prison. After she serves out her term as governor, she will probably run for the Senate.*

serve up

1. To provide or offer some meal: *Whenever they have guests, they always serve up a feast. That restaurant makes the best barbecue, and they serve it up every day.*
2. To provide or offer some sensual or emotional experience: *The restaurant serves up a night to remember. A comedian serves laughs up every Wednesday night at the bar.*
3. To put some prepared food into a dish to be eaten: *I gathered the plates and served up the potatoes. If the soup is ready, go ahead and serve it up.*
4. SPORTS To throw or kick some ball into the air in such a way that it is easily hit or intercepted: *The soccer player served up a ball to her teammate, who headed it in for a*

goal. The pitcher served a ball up, and it was hit for a home run.

◆ **set** (sĕt)

set (sĕt), **setting** (sĕt′ĭng), **sets** (sĕts)

set about

To start doing something or some task: *After collecting sticks, the campers set about building a fire.*

set against

1. To place something so that it is touching something on the side: *I set my golf clubs against the car and opened the trunk.*
2. To place something against some background: *The author has set the love story against the backdrop of war. In the picture, the old church is set against the large, glass skyscrapers.*
3. To place something in contrast to something else: *The price seems like a bargain when you set it against real estate prices in larger cities.*
4. To incite someone to oppose or resist someone or something: *The civil war set families against one another. The bosses are set against the proposal, so I doubt it will go through.*

set apart

1. To reserve something for a specific use: *The villagers set apart two goats for the sacrifice.*
2. To make someone or something noticeable: *Your spontaneity sets you apart from the other actors.*

set aside

1. To separate and reserve something for a special purpose: *We set aside some time to discuss the new project. The developer set two acres aside for a park.*
2. To discard or reject something: *He set aside his concerns and allowed his child to go on the field trip. She set her fears aside and continued down the dark trail.*
3. To declare something invalid; annul or overrule something: *The judge set aside a lower court ruling. The appellate court set the conviction aside, and the prisoner was released.*

set at

To attack or assail someone or something: *The dogs set at the fox.*

set back

1. To construct something so that it is a certain distance away from the edge of some boundary. Used in the passive: *All houses must be set back 100 feet from the lake. The second tier of the building is set back 10 feet.*
2. To slow down the progress of something; hinder something: *Bad weather set the project back two weeks. The recent attacks have set back the peace process.*
3. To cost someone some amount of money: *That coat set me back $1,000.*
4. To adjust some instrument or device to an earlier reading: *Last fall, I forgot to set back my clock. The*

ă	pat	är	car	ī	bite	ô	paw	ŏŏ	took	ûr	urge
ā	pay	ĕ	pet	îr	pier	ôr	core	ŏŏr	lure	zh	vision
âr	care	ē	be	ŏ	pot	oi	boy	ōō	boot	ə	about, item
ä	father	ĭ	pit	ō	toe	ou	out	ŭ	cut		

dealership set the odometer back and tried to sell the car as new.

set by

To reserve something for future use: *It is wise to set food and money by in case of a future emergency.*

set down

1. To put something on the surface of something: *They set the boxes down on the floor. I set down my book and closed my eyes.*
2. To put something in writing; record something: *I set down some ideas for a novel. The committee set their findings down in a report.*
3. To land some aircraft: *The pilot set the plane down hard. She found a clearing and set down the helicopter.*
4. To land: *The plane set down at a small airport outside the city.*
5. BASEBALL To put out some batter; retire someone. Used of a pitcher: *The pitcher set down the first two hitters. The hitter stepped up to the plate, and the pitcher set him down with a fastball.*
6. **set down as** To regard someone as something: *They set her down as a liar and never trusted her again.*
7. **set down to** To attribute some event to some cause: *Let's set the error down to inexperience.*

set forth *or* **set forward**

1. To present something for consideration; propose something: *In this essay, the author sets forth her philosophy of film. The committee revised the proposal and set it forth for consideration.*
2. To begin a journey: *The scientist set forth into the volcano crater to gather a lava sample.*

set in

1. To insert or fix something securely: *The tailor patched my jacket and set in a new liner. I put the stakes in the ground and set them in with a mallet.*
2. To become established as an internal or external condition, especially one that brings suffering or hardship to a person or group of people: *Panic set in when the people realized the building was on fire. We must put a bandage on your wound before an infection sets in. We need wood for the fire now that winter is setting in.*
3. To move toward the shore. Used of wind or water: *After nightfall, the wind set in.*

set off

1. To give rise to something; cause something to occur: *The heat set off a chemical reaction. A branch fell on my car and set the alarm off.*
2. To cause something to explode: *At midnight, we set off a string of firecrackers. The terrorists were building a bomb and planned to set it off in the train station.*
3. To make someone suddenly or demonstrably angry: *The clerk's indifference finally set me off. The constant delays set off even the most patient passengers.*
4. **set off from** To indicate someone or something as being different; distinguish someone or something: *His strong features set him off from the crowd. Indented margins set off the quotation from the rest of the text.*
5. To direct attention to something by contrast; accentuate something: *The editor suggested that I set off*

the passage with italics. The artist set the photograph off with a black background.

6. To counterbalance, counteract, or compensate for something. Used chiefly in the passive: *Our dismay at her leaving was set off by our knowing that she was happy.*
7. To start on a journey: *When do you set off for China? The soldier set off on a mission.*

set on

1. To attack someone or something: *The lions set on the gazelles.*
2. To urge or incite someone or something to attack someone or something: *The guards set attack dogs on the intruder.*

set out

1. To start a journey: *She set out at dawn for town.*
2. To begin an earnest attempt to do something; undertake something: *Four years ago, we set out to reform the government, and since then, we have accomplished much.*
3. To make something explicit, especially an idea or plan: *In her speech, she set out a plan for her second term in office. He set his ideas out in a detailed report.*
4. To display something for exhibition or sale: *The vendor set out a large display of fruit and vegetables. The children set a pumpkin out for Halloween.*
5. To plant something: *They set out seeds last year, and now the field is full of flowers. We should set some tulip bulbs out this fall.*

set to

1. To begin working energetically: *After we selected the tree, I picked up the ax and set to. We set to cleaning up the mess after the party.*
2. To begin fighting: *With no hope of escape, I put up my fists and set to.*

set up

1. To place something in a high or upright position: *Please set the books up on the top shelf.*
2. To assemble, erect, or organize something: *The kids set up a tent in the backyard. I bought a new table, but I'm not sure how to set it up. We need to set up a good schedule for taking the kids to school. The scientist set up the data in rows and columns. I have all the supplies for the picnic, so let's set them up.*
3. To lay out a plan to do something: *The police caught the gang trying to set up a kidnapping. They didn't commit the crime, but they did set it up.*
4. To establish something; found something: *We used the money to set up a charity. We don't have a separate office for handling taxes, but maybe we should set one up.*
5. To give someone everything that is needed: *Don't worry that you forgot to pack your good clothes; I'll set you up.*

ă	pat	är	car	ī	bite	ô	paw	o͝o	took	ûr	urge		
ā	pay	ĕ	pet	îr	pier	ôr	core	o͝or	lure	zh	vision		
âr	care	ē	be	ŏ	pot	oi	boy	o͞o	boot	ə	about,		
ä	father	ĭ	pit	ō	toe	ou	out	ŭ	cut		item		

6. To establish someone in business by providing capital, equipment, or other backing: *I wanted to start an Italian restaurant, and my grandparents, who were in the business for years, helped set me up. The agency set up the struggling entrepreneurs by providing small loans.*
7. To treat someone, especially to drinks: *The bartender sets up all of his close friends for one beer. If you don't have enough money for another beer, I'll set you up.*
8. To create the needed conditions for something: *The team's defense set up a good play.*
9. SPORTS To make a pass to some other player in order to create an opportunity to score: *I set up the other forward for an easy goal. The best offensive players don't always score the most, but they set their teammates up.*
10. To put someone or something into a position of authority or power; invest someone with power: *The board members set up the former secretary as the company's new president. The leaders of the coup set the general up as a dictator.*
11. To give the impression, especially a false impression, that someone is something: *She set herself up as an authority on Latin, but she really doesn't know that much. The newspapers set him up as a star athlete, but he had only played three professional games.*
12. To put someone into a compromising situation by deceit or trickery: *He set up the tourists by convincing them he needed bus fare to get home, and then he stole their money. Those swindlers have set me up.*
13. To arrange for someone to meet someone as a possible mate: *A friend set me up with his brother. The dating service set us up.*

set upon

To attack someone or something violently: *The gang set upon their victim with clubs.*

◆ **settle** (sĕt′l)

settled (sĕt′ld), **settling** (sĕt′l-ĭng), **settles** (sĕt′lz)

settle down

1. To begin living a stable and orderly life: *She got a nine-to-five job and settled down in the suburbs. I've finally settled down with my sweetheart.*
2. To become calm or composed: *Hours passed before the children finally settled down. I'll have more free time once things settle down at the office. We made some popcorn and settled down to watch the movie.*

settle for

To accept something in spite of not being completely satisfied: *I had to settle for a lower wage than the one I requested.*

settle in

To become established or comfortable in a new environment or circumstance: *It took a month for us to settle in after the move. We'll come visit you after you get settled in.*

settle into

To become established or comfortable in some new environment or circumstance: *She settled into her new job relatively quickly. After a few days at the camp, I settled into a routine.*

settle on *or* **settle upon**

To reach some decision; determine something: *They discussed several choices for vacation and finally settled on a trip to Florida.*

settle up

To balance an account by paying what is owed: *After the poker game, we counted our chips and settled up. I went down to the racetrack and settled up with the bookie.*

◆ **sew** (sō)

sewed (sōd), **sewn** (sōn) *or* **sewed** (sōd), **sewing** (sō′ĭng), **sews** (sōz)

sew up

1. To mend or repair something by sewing: *I sewed up the tear in my pants. The tailor sewed the hole up.*
2. To make certain that some victory or prize is attained or achieved: *The candidate sewed up the election by winning Florida. We sewed the game up with a goal in the fourth quarter.*

◆ **sex** (sĕks)

sexed (sĕkst), **sexing** (sĕk′sĭng), **sexes** (sĕk′sĭz)

sex up

1. To increase the sexual appeal or content of someone or something: *The producer sexed up the music video with scantily clad dancers. Because the club was bland, the owners decided to sex it up.*
2. CHIEFLY BRITISH SLANG To increase the appeal or attractiveness of something; embellish something: *The committee sexed up the report with suggestions of conspiracy. Our website is boring—what if we sex it up with funky icons?*
3. VULGAR SLANG To arouse someone sexually.

◆ **shack** (shăk)

shacked (shăkt), **shacking** (shăk′ĭng), **shacks** (shăks)

shack up

SLANG

1. To live, room, or stay at some place: *She's shacking up at her cousin's house until she finds a place of her own.*
2. To sleep together or live in sexual intimacy with someone without being married: *There's a rumor that the professor is shacking up with one of his colleagues. Do you know if they are shacking up together?*

◆ **shade** (shād)

shaded (shā′dĭd), **shading** (shā′dĭng), **shades** (shādz)

shade in

1. To represent degrees of shade or shadow in some drawing or picture, so as to give the illusion of depth: *The artist shaded in the*

ă	pat	är	car	ī	bite	ô	paw	o͝o	took	ûr	urge
ā	pay	ĕ	pet	îr	pier	ôr	core	o͝or	lure	zh	vision
âr	care	ē	be	ŏ	pot	oi	boy	o͞o	boot	ə	about,
ä	father	ĭ	pit	ō	toe	ou	out	ŭ	cut		item

contours of the model's face in the portrait.

2. To darken some bounded area that is drawn or printed on a surface: *The teacher shaded in the area where the circles overlapped with yellow chalk. I'm going to shade in the left side of this drawing with crosshatches to make it darker.*

shade into

To pass from one quality, color, or thing to some other by very slight changes or degrees: *The hues of the pink sunset shaded into purple.*

◆ **shake** (shāk)

shook (sho͝ok), **shaken** (shā′kən), **shaking** (shā′kĭng), **shakes** (shāks)

shake down

1. To extort money from someone: *The mob regularly sends thugs to shake down local businesses. The blackmailer shook us down for $1000.*
2. To make a thorough search of someone or something: *The guards shook down the prisoners' cells for hidden weapons. The airport security guards shook me down.*
3. To become acclimated or accustomed, as to a new environment or a new job: *We gave the new hire a few weeks to shake down before assigning her to a project.*

shake off

1. To shake something so as to dislodge what is on it: *We shook off the picnic blanket to get rid of the grasshoppers. I picked up the beach towel and shook it off.*
2. To get rid of something by shaking: *The dog climbed out of the creek and shook off the water. I shook the snow off my jacket and hung it up.*
3. To free oneself of something; get rid of something: *We shook off our fear and proceeded into the dark cave. The injured player shook the pain off and continued to play.*

shake on

To make some agreement binding by shaking hands: *Our negotiations went well, and we soon shook on the deal. If you're satisfied with the arrangement, let's shake on it.*

shake up

1. To move something vigorously up and down or from side to side, as in mixing: *I shook up the orange juice before I opened the carton. We shook the ingredients up and poured them into a bowl.*
2. To upset someone by or as if by a physical jolt or shock: *The accident really shook us up. The bad news shook up the whole family.*
3. To subject something to a drastic rearrangement or reorganization: *The new management intends to shake up the company. The CEO's new policies have really shaken things up around here—I now report to a new boss.*

◆ **shape** (shāp)

shaped (shāpt), **shaping** (shā′pĭng), **shapes** (shāps)

shape up

1. To develop: *This football game could shape up to be the most exciting game in years.*

2. To improve one's behavior or actions so as to meet a standard: *If you don't shape up, you're going to be in a lot of trouble.*

◆ **share** (shâr)

shared (shârd), **sharing** (shâr′ĭng), **shares** (shârz)

share in

To have a share or part in something: *When the company began to make money, everyone working there shared in the profits.*

◆ **shave** (shāv)

shaved (shāvd), **shaved** *or* **shaven** (shā′vən), **shaving** (shā′vĭng), **shaves** (shāvz)

shave off

1. To cut something, especially hair, from the surface of the skin with a razor or shaver: *I shaved my beard off. I shaved off the stubble.*
2. To remove or eliminate something in thin strips or small amounts using a blade: *The woodworker used a planer to shave off the bark. I opened the coconut and shaved some of the meat off with a knife.*
3. To eliminate some small amount of a total: *This aerodynamic racing suit will shave off a full second from your time. She shaved ten seconds off the school's 100-meter dash record.*
4. To limit deliberately the number of points scored by one's own team in an athletic contest, as in return for a payment from gamblers to ensure winnings: *The rest of the team was sure that he was missing shots on purpose in order to shave points off for his gambling buddies. The police are investigating her for shaving off points in the championship game.*

◆ **shell** (shĕl)

shelled (shĕld), **shelling** (shĕl′ĭng), **shells** (shĕlz)

shell out

To pay some amount of money, often reluctantly: *I had to shell out $500 on car repairs. We had to shell the full amount of tuition out even though many of the classes had been canceled.*

◆ **shift** (shĭft)

shifted (shĭf′tĭd), **shifting** (shĭf′tĭng), **shifts** (shĭfts)

shift for

To provide for, take care of, or defend oneself without assistance. Used reflexively: *The teenagers went camping, confident that they could shift for themselves.*

◆ **ship** (shĭp)

shipped (shĭpt), **shipping** (shĭp′ĭng), **ships** (shĭps)

ship off

1. To leave, as for a distant place: *The soldier shipped off to the war zone. I said goodbye to my friends*

ă	pat	är	car	ī	bite	ô	paw	ŏŏ	took	ûr	urge
ā	pay	ĕ	pet	îr	pier	ôr	core	ŏŏr	lure	zh	vision
âr	care	ē	be	ŏ	pot	oi	boy	ōō	boot	ə	about,
ä	father	ĭ	pit	ō	toe	ou	out	ŭ	cut		item

because I was shipping off the next day.

2. To send something or someone, as to a distant place: *They shipped the prisoners off to an offshore island. We shipped off the packages.*

ship out

1. To accept a position on board a ship and serve as a crew member: *The sailor shipped out on a tanker.*
2. To leave, as for a distant place: *The troops shipped out for the war zone.*
3. To send something or someone, as to a distant place: *The army shipped out more troops to the war zone. The factory shipped the part out to the dealership.*

◆ **shoot** (sho͞ot)
shot (shŏt), **shooting** (sho͞o′tĭng), **shoots** (sho͞ots)

shoot down

1. To cause something to collapse or fall by striking it with bullets, missiles, or some other projectile; gun down: *They shot down the attacking airplanes. The kids released a balloon and shot it down with an air rifle.*
2. To kill someone by shooting them; gun down: *They stormed into the office and shot down everyone there. The assassin walked up to her target and shot him down.*
3. To discredit someone or someone's proposal: *Whenever I offer an opinion, they just shoot me down. The council shot down the mayor's proposal. I'm afraid this new evidence shoots down our old theory of what happened.*
4. To ruin the aspirations of someone: *Their sneers and insults shot me down. A bad critic can shoot down even a very determined artist.*
5. To put an end to something; defeat something: *The opposition was able to shoot down the proposal. The electorate shot the incumbent down.*

shoot for

To strive or aim for something; have something as a goal: *We were disappointed, since we won only two games, and we were shooting for at least three. I might not have the report finished until Tuesday, but I'm shooting for Monday.*

shoot off

1. To launch some rocket or missile: *We shot off fireworks to celebrate the New Year. I built a rocket and shot it off in my backyard.*
2. To detach or sever something by shooting: *The gunner shot off the plane's wing. I aimed the gun at the padlock and shot it off.*

shoot up

1. To increase dramatically in amount: *The stock shot up after the merger was announced.*
2. To grow or get taller rapidly: *Your daughter has really shot up since I last saw her.*
3. To riddle someone or something with bullets: *The sharpshooter shot up the target. Some gangsters drove by with machine guns and shot him up.*
4. To damage or terrorize something, such as a town, by intense or random gunfire: *The bandits got drunk and shot up the town. The*

gangsters shot the bar up when the owner refused to pay them.

5. SLANG To inject oneself with a drug using a hypodermic needle: *There were drug addicts shooting up in the hallway.*
6. SLANG To inject a drug into someone using a hypodermic needle: *The nurse shot up the patient with a sedative. They shot her up with morphine.*

◆ **shop** (shŏp)

shopped (shŏpt), **shopping** (shŏp′ĭng), **shops** (shŏps)

shop around

1. To go from store to store in search of merchandise or bargains: *We shopped around for the best price before buying. Don't buy the first pair of shoes you see; shop around first.*
2. To look for something better: *I think the receptionist is shopping around for a new job.*
3. To offer something, such as a large block of common stock, for sale to various parties: *They shopped the deal around for a couple of months but couldn't find a buyer.*

◆ **shore** (shôr)

shored (shôrd), **shoring** (shôr′ĭng), **shores** (shôrz)

shore up

To support something with or as if with a prop: *The carpenters shored up the sagging floors. The peace initiative was failing, so the leaders met to shore it up.*

◆ **shout** (shout)

shouted (shou′tĭd), **shouting** (shou′tĭng), **shouts** (shouts)

shout down

To overwhelm or silence someone by shouting loudly: *The crowd shouted down the speaker. The protestors shouted the candidate down.*

shout out

1. To say something loudly and generally; announce something: *The student shouted out the answer to the question. The counselors shouted instructions out as the campers hiked through the woods.*
2. To utter a loud strong cry: *The survivors of the earthquake shouted out in hopes of being rescued.*

◆ **shove** (shŭv)

shoved (shŭvd), **shoving** (shŭv′ĭng), **shoves** (shŭvz)

shove around

To give someone orders in a forceful or unpleasant way; bully someone: *We refuse to allow corporate lawyers to shove us around. The restaurant management shoved around the employees.*

shove off

1. To push some boat away from shore in leaving: *The captain*

ă	pat	är	car	ī	bite	ô	paw	ŏŏ	took	ûr	urge
ā	pay	ĕ	pet	îr	pier	ôr	core	ŏŏr	lure	zh	vision
âr	care	ē	be	ŏ	pot	oi	boy	ōō	boot	ə	about,
ä	father	ĭ	pit	ō	toe	ou	out	ŭ	cut		item

leaned over the gunwale and shoved off from the dock.

2. To leave: *I had better shove off, or I will be late. Shove off!—I'm sick of your complaining!*

◆ **show** (shō)

showed (shōd), **shown** (shōn) *or* **showed** (shōd), **showing** (shō′ĭng), **shows** (shōz)

show around

To introduce someone to some place by visiting various locations: *The real estate agent showed us around the house. The guide showed us around the old part of the city.*

show in

To conduct some visitor into a room or building: *The nurse came out to the waiting area and showed in the next patient. The butler showed the visitors in.*

show into

To conduct some visitor into some room or building: *My assistant will show you into my office.*

show off

1. To display one's ability, beauty, or status in a showy way, so as to attract attention and impress others: *The students were doing handstands to show off for the coaches.*
2. To display some possession or attribute in a showy way, so as to attract attention and impress others: *I wore tight clothing to show off my figure. They are very wealthy, and they show it off with expensive cars.*

show out

To conduct some visitor to an exit: *The assistant showed me out of the building. We showed out the guests and said goodbye.*

show through

To be visible or evident through something: *Her slip shows through her dress. Your arrogance shows through despite your attempts to be friendly.*

show up

1. To be clearly visible: *Will the blue pencil marks show up in the photocopy?*
2. To make an appearance; arrive: *Everyone was waiting for the bride to show up.*
3. To expose or reveal the true character or nature of someone or something: *The other group's success showed up their efforts as a waste of time. I showed the challenger up as a braggart.*
4. To surpass someone or something, as in ability or intelligence: *The students were always trying to show up the teacher with a fact she didn't know. After his performance, a virtuoso came out on stage and showed him up.*

◆ **shower** (shou′ər)

showered (shou′ərd), **showering** (shou′ə-rĭng), **showers** (shou′ərz)

shower on *or* **shower upon**

To bestow an abundance of something on someone: *The director showered praise on the actor. The happy parents showered love upon their child.*

shower with

To give someone an abundance of something: *The parents showered the child with gifts.*

◆ **shrink** (shrĭngk)

shrank (shrăngk) *or* **shrunk** (shrŭngk), **shrunk** *or* **shrunken** (shrŭng′kən), **shrinking** (shrĭng′kĭng), **shrinks** (shrĭngks)

shrink back

To draw back instinctively, as in alarm; recoil: *The dog shrank back in fear when I raised my hand.*

shrink from

1. To draw back instinctively from someone or something; recoil from someone or something: *The cat shrank from my touch.*
2. To show reluctance to engage in or do something; hesitate to perform something, especially out of fear: *I will not shrink from my duty as captain to defend the ship. They will not shrink from prosecuting each of us if they catch us stealing.*

◆ **shrivel** (shrĭv′əl)

shriveled *or* **shrivelled** (shrĭv′əld), **shriveling** *or* **shrivelling** (shrĭv′ə-lĭng), **shrivels** (shrĭv′əlz)

shrivel up

1. To become completely shrunken and wrinkled: *The leaves shriveled up and fell off the tree.*
2. To cause something to become completely shrunken and wrinkled: *The lack of rain shriveled up my roses. Soaking in the tub for too long will shrivel your skin up.*
3. To lose vitality or intensity; dwindle: *The buying power of the dollar shriveled up as inflation worsened.*

◆ **shrug** (shrŭg)

shrugged (shrŭgd), **shrugging** (shrŭg′ĭng), **shrugs** (shrŭgz)

shrug off

1. To dismiss something with a gesture of doubt, disdain, or indifference: *She shrugged off her mother's advice. Rather than respond to their insults, he just shrugged them off and kept walking.*
2. To minimize the importance of something: *The coach shrugged off the defeat and talked about the team's improvement. The politician shrugged the allegations off, calling them absurd.*
3. To get rid of something: *I hope that I can shrug off this cold before the game next weekend. I began to feel sleepy, but I shrugged it off and kept driving.*
4. To wriggle out of some clothing: *He shrugged off his shirt and put it in the laundry basket. She shrugged her coat off and hung it in the closet.*

◆ **shuffle** (shŭf′əl)

shuffled (shŭf′əld), **shuffling** (shŭf′lĭng), **shuffles** (shŭf′əlz)

ă	pat	är	car	ī	bite	ô	paw	o͝o	took	ûr	urge
ā	pay	ĕ	pet	îr	pier	ôr	core	o͝or	lure	zh	vision
âr	care	ē	be	ŏ	pot	oi	boy	o͞o	boot	ə	about,
ä	father	ĭ	pit	ō	toe	ou	out	ŭ	cut		item

shuffle off

1. To go with short sliding steps, without or barely lifting the feet: *The sleepy children shuffled off to bed.*
2. To leave; depart: *Toward the end of the evening, the guests shuffled off one by one.*
3. To rid oneself of something; dispose of or relocate something: *I have not been able to shuffle off my embarrassment. The computer program automatically shuffles the outdated files off to another disk.*
4. To evade or shirk something, such as a responsibility: *He shuffled off his responsibilities and went to the beach. She shuffled her work off onto others because she wasn't feeling well.*

◆ **shut** (shŭt)

shut (shŭt), **shutting** (shŭt′ĭng), **shuts** (shŭts)

shut down

1. To stop the operation of something, especially when a special process is required: *The inspectors shut down the restaurant when they found a rat in the kitchen. I shut the computers down every night.*
2. To stop operating, especially when a special process is required: *The factory shut down for the holiday.*

shut in

To confine someone or something in or as if in a closed space: *My older brother shut me in the attic to frighten me. Shut in the dog when you leave.*

shut off

1. To stop the flow, passage, or operation of something: *The plumber shut off the water by closing a valve. Shut the lights off before you leave.*
2. To stop flowing or operating, especially automatically: *The electricity shuts off at midnight.*
3. To isolate someone or something: *The miser shut himself off from the community.*

shut out

1. To exclude something or someone: *I used earplugs to shut out the noise. The company shut the unions out of the negotiations. Performers must learn to shut out the crowd. Her husband has shut her out ever since the accident.*
2. Sports To prevent some opponent from scoring any runs or points: *Our strong defense shut out the other team. They shut us out 14-0 in a playoff game.*

shut up

1. To stop speaking: *Shut up!—I can't concentrate. We know to shut up when a teacher walks into the room.*
2. To cause someone to stop speaking; silence someone: *Her outstanding performance shut up her critics. The children's yelling was disturbing the neighbors, so I went in and shut them up.*
3. To shut and lock some building for a temporary period of time: *We shut up the camp for the winter. The caretaker shut the cottage up.*

◆ **shy** (shī)

shied (shīd), **shying** (shī′ĭng), **shies** (shīz)

shy away

1. To retreat out of a sense of shyness: *The deer poked its head out from*

the bushes and then shied away when it saw me.

2. To avoid doing something, especially out of caution or anxiety: *The company shied away from giving raises this year.*

◆ **sic** (sĭk)

sicced (sĭkt), **siccing** (sĭk′ĭng), **sics** (sĭks)

sic on

To urge or incite someone or something to attack or go after someone: *The guards sicced dogs on the intruders. They threatened to sic their lawyers on us.*

◆ **side** (sīd)

sided (sī′dĭd), **siding** (sī′dĭng), **sides** (sīdz)

side against

To align oneself against someone or something in a disagreement: *Our opponents will side against the proposal if we don't revise it.*

side with

To align oneself with someone or something in a disagreement: *The stalemate ended when a small group of senators sided with the opposing party.*

◆ **sidle** (sīd′l)

sidled (sīd′ld), **sidling** (sī′dl-ĭng), **sidles** (sīd′lz)

sidle up

To advance in an unobtrusive, furtive, or coy way: *At the train station, swindlers sidled up to the tourists.*

◆ **sift** (sĭft)

sifted (sĭf′tĭd), **sifting** (sĭf′tĭng), **sifts** (sĭfts)

sift out

To separate some class, kind, or size from others with or as if with a sieve: *The jeweler sifted out the larger gems. An insurance investigator sifts the honest claims out from the false ones.*

sift through

To search through some container or collection: *I sifted through the laundry pile to find a pair of socks.*

◆ **sign** (sīn)

signed (sīnd), **signing** (sī′nĭng), **signs** (sīnz)

sign away

To give something up by signing one's name; relinquish something by signature: *When they agreed to settle the lawsuit, they signed away their claim to the estate. If you wanted the right to sell your work independently, you shouldn't have signed it away by joining the organization.*

sign for

To accept some delivery by signing a document: *I went to the door to sign for the package.*

ă	pat	är	car	ī	bite	ô	paw	o͝o	took	ûr	urge
ā	pay	ĕ	pet	îr	pier	ôr	core	o͝or	lure	zh	vision
âr	care	ē	be	ŏ	pot	oi	boy	o͞o	boot	ə	about, item
ä	father	ĭ	pit	ō	toe	ou	out	ŭ	cut		

sign in

1. To record the arrival of someone by signing a register: *We went to the front desk to sign in. I got to the hotel first and signed us in.*
2. To provide the necessary information to a computer for someone to be allowed to access computer resources: *I signed in on the bank's website and checked my account statement. I'll sign you in using my password so you can access the website's subscriber features.*

sign into

1. To ratify some legislation by affixing a signature, seal, or other mark, so as to bring it into some state of existence: *The president signed the bill into law.*
2. To provide the necessary information to a computer for someone to be allowed access to some set of computer resources: *I'll sign you into the website so you can read the whole article. I signed into my account on the website and checked my order status.*

sign off

1. To announce the end of a communication; conclude: *I've come to the end of my message, so now I'm signing off.*
2. To stop transmission after identifying the broadcasting station: *This is your morning radio host, signing off.*
3. **sign off on** To express approval formally or conclusively: *The president got Congress to sign off on the new tax proposal.*

sign on

1. To enlist oneself, especially as an employee: *He signed on for two years with the Peace Corps. She signed on as a sales representative and was soon promoted to district manager.*
2. To start transmission with an identification of the broadcasting station: *Our local public television station signs on every morning at 6:00.*

sign out

1. To record the departure of another or oneself by signing a register: *Go to the front desk and sign out while I take the bags to the car. Don't forget to sign out your guest when you leave the club. I signed myself out as I was leaving.*
2. To borrow some item and register the borrowing by signing one's name: *They signed out all the canoes at the club. If you would like to examine the file more closely, you can sign it out and take it home.*
3. To disconnect someone from some computer resource to which one has been connected or logged on: *Remember to sign out of your account before you leave the computer. The website automatically signs you out after 15 minutes.*
4. To end communication and disconnect officially. Used to notify others: *The trucker radioed the dispatcher and signed out. Now that I've finished my story, I'm signing out!*

sign over

To transfer ownership or possession of something by signing one's name: *He'll have to sign his next two paychecks over to his creditors. She signed over her fortune to charity.*

sign up

1. To register by or as if by signing one's name; enlist: *The army recruiter persuaded me to sign up. I signed up to volunteer at the hospital. Would you like to sign up for our free newsletter?*
2. To register someone or something by or as if by signing one's name; enlist someone or something: *I signed my daughter up for swimming lessons. The telemarketer signed up another four customers.*
3. To hire or engage someone by obtaining a signature on a contract: *The producer is signing up actors for a touring play. The team signed a rookie pitcher up for next season.*

sign with

To sign an employment contract with some organization: *The soccer player signed with a team in Spain.*

◆ **silt** (sĭlt)

silted (sĭl′tĭd), **silting** (sĭl′tĭng), **silts** (sĭlts)

silt up

1. To become filled with silt: *The old canal had silted up.*
2. To fill, cover, or obstruct something with silt: *River sediments gradually silted up the harbor. Parts of the creek were now too shallow for boats because the storm had silted it up.*

◆ **simmer** (sĭm′ər)

simmered (sĭm′ərd), **simmering** (sĭm′ə-rĭng), **simmers** (sĭm′ərz)

simmer down

1. To become calm after excitement or anger: *We left him to simmer down after the argument.*
2. To reduce a liquid by heating it to a simmer and allowing the water to evaporate: *We simmered down the chili until it was thick enough to hold a spoon upright. Return the sauce to the pan and simmer it down to a medium thickness.*

◆ **sing** (sĭng)

sang (săng) *or* **sung** (sŭng), **sung** (sŭng), **singing** (sĭng′ĭng), **sings** (sĭngz)

sing along

To sing in unison with a song or singer that one is listening to: *The performer urged the audience to sing along. I turned up the radio and sang along to the song.*

sing out

1. To sing loudly and clearly: *The choir sang out from the choir loft.*
2. To say something loudly or in a lively manner: *The announcer sang out the name of the winner. The shopkeeper sang a greeting out as we went by.*

◆ **single** (sĭng′gəl)

singled (sĭng′gəld), **singling** (sĭng′gə-lĭng), **singles** (sĭng′gəlz)

ă	pat	är	car	ī	bite	ô	paw	o͝o	took	ûr	urge
ā	pay	ĕ	pet	îr	pier	ôr	core	o͝or	lure	zh	vision
âr	care	ē	be	ŏ	pot	oi	boy	o͞o	boot	ə	about, item
ä	father	ĭ	pit	ō	toe	ou	out	ŭ	cut		

single out

To choose or distinguish someone or something from others: *We singled her out from the list of applicants because she had a college degree. Unable to determine who had committed the offense, the teacher singled out the most mischievous student for punishment.*

◆ **sink** (sĭngk)

sank (săngk) *or* **sunk** (sŭngk), **sunk** (sŭngk), **sinking** (sĭng′kĭng), **sinks** (sĭngks)

sink in

1. To seep or soak; penetrate: *When the floodwaters sink in, the ground will become soft.*
2. To make an impression; become felt or understood: *The meaning of the poem finally sank in after I had thought about it for a while.*

sink into

1. To pass into some condition: *She sank into a deep sleep.*
2. To seep or soak into something; penetrate something: *The water is sinking into the ground.*
3. To invest some resources in something, especially without any prospect of return: *If the city continues to sink money into that new convention center, it will go broke.*

◆ **sip** (sĭp)

sipped (sĭpt), **sipping** (sĭp′ĭng), **sips** (sĭps)

sip at *or* **sip on**

To drink from some beverage in small amounts at a time: *The skier sipped at the hot coffee at the lodge. She was sipping on a cocktail at the bar.*

◆ **siphon** (sī′fən)

siphoned (sī′fənd), **siphoning** (sī′fə-nĭng), **siphons** (sī′fənz)

siphon off

1. To draw off or convey something through or as if through a siphon: *I used a tube to siphon off the excess water in the fish tank. The lawn mower ran out of gas, so we siphoned some off from the car's gas tank.*
2. To appropriate some money illegally or dishonestly: *The managers were siphoning off money from the foundation and putting it into secret accounts. The dictator siphoned millions of dollars off and hid the money in private bank accounts.*

◆ **sit** (sĭt)

sat (săt), **sitting** (sĭt′ĭng), **sits** (sĭts)

sit around

To sit idly near a location: *We sat around the airport waiting for our flight. I've been sitting around waiting for you for almost two hours.*

sit back

To relax or rest in a sitting position, especially by leaning against a backrest or headrest: *After the plane took off, I sat back and fell asleep.*

sit by

To remain uninvolved; refrain from acting: *I did the work while the others sat by and watched.*

sit down

1. To assume a sitting position; take a seat: *She sat down to eat. Let's sit down in front of the television.*
2. To cause someone to assume a sitting position, especially in a mandatory way: *The principal sat me down and began lecturing. You need to sit down all your grandchildren some day and tell them your wonderful story.*
3. **sit down with** To meet with someone in order to deliberate together or compare views: *The foreign ambassador sat down with the president.*

sit for

To pose for someone or something: *The model sat for a painting. I earned extra money by sitting for sculptors.*

sit in

1. To be present or participate as a visitor at a discussion or music session: *The professor allowed me to sit in on one of her lectures. A guitarist will be sitting in with the band today.*
2. To take part in a sit-in or similar organized protest: *The protesters sat in at the construction site.*
3. **sit in for** To act as a substitute: *She will be sitting in for the usual news anchor, who is away on vacation.*

sit on

1. To occupy a seat as a member of some body of officials: *The president of the company sits on the board of directors.*
2. To confer about something: *The committee will sit on the matter tomorrow and make a decision.*
3. To affect someone with or as if with a burden: *Our financial troubles sat heavily on my parents.*
4. To suppress or repress something: *The attorney suspected the prosecution of sitting on evidence that could help her client.*
5. To postpone action or resolution regarding something: *I'm going to sit on the proposal until I have more information. The company is sitting on $500 million in cash, and everyone is wondering what they'll do with it.*

sit out

1. To stay until the end of something: *Let's sit out this act, and then we can leave at intermission. This lecture is really boring—I don't think I can sit it out.*
2. To refrain from taking part in something: *The star pitcher sat out the game with an ankle injury. I'm going to sit this dance out.*

sit through

To stay until the end of something: *The children will never be able to sit through a four-hour movie.*

sit up

1. To rise from lying down to a sitting position: *The patient sat up for her meal.*

ă	pat	är	car	ī	bite	ô	paw	o͝o	took	ûr	urge
ā	pay	ĕ	pet	îr	pier	ôr	core	o͝or	lure	zh	vision
âr	care	ē	be	ŏ	pot	oi	boy	o͞o	boot	ə	about,
ä	father	ĭ	pit	ō	toe	ou	out	ŭ	cut		item

2. To sit with the spine erect: *The nanny told the children to sit up.*
3. To stay up later than the customary bedtime: *My parents sat up waiting for me to come home.*
4. To become suddenly alert: *The students sat up when the teacher mentioned the test.*

sit upon

1. To affect someone with or as if with a burden: *Official duties sat heavily upon the governor.*
2. To occupy a seat as a member of some body of officials: *The former mayor now sits upon the town council.*
3. To confer about something: *The committee will sit upon the matter at the meeting next month.*

◆ **size** (sīz)

sized (sīzd), **sizing** (sī′zĭng), **sizes** (sī′zĭz)

size up

To make an estimate, opinion, or judgment of someone or something: *She sized up her opponent. He sized the location up.*

◆ **sketch** (skĕch)

sketched (skĕcht), **sketching** (skĕch′ĭng), **sketches** (skĕch′ĭz)

sketch in

1. To add a hasty or undetailed drawing or painting of something to a larger work: *The artist sketched in the leaves before painting. We finished sketching the margins in.*
2. To give a general account or presentation of some aspect of a larger idea: *The staff sketched in the details of the proposal. We sat down and sketched the fine points in.*

sketch out

1. To make a hasty or undetailed drawing or painting of something, often as a preliminary study: *The architect sketched out a couple of ideas on a napkin. I sketched the figure out with pencil before I started painting.*
2. To give a brief general account or presentation of something; outline something: *The president sketched out her plan for the following year. Before I started writing my paper, I sat down and sketched my ideas out.*
3. SLANG To cause someone to experience an odd, unusual, and sometimes uneasy sensation: *Their strange customs sketched out the visitors. His creepy smile sketched us out.*

◆ **skim** (skĭm)

skimmed (skĭmd), **skimming** (skĭm′ĭng), **skims** (skĭmz)

skim off

1. To remove some floating matter from a liquid: *They use a net to skim the cranberries off the surface. They skim off the dross before pouring the metal into molds.*
2. To appropriate some money illegally or dishonestly: *The dictator skimmed off over $1 million from international donations and deposited it in personal bank accounts. The company was skimming money off its employees' paychecks and using it to cover losses.*

skim over

To read or consider something superficially and quickly: *I skimmed over the reading assignment be-*

cause I didn't have time to read it carefully.

skim through

To go through some reading material quickly or superficially: *I skimmed through the movie listings to see what was playing.*

◆ **skimp** (skĭmp)

skimped (skĭmpt), **skimping** (skĭm′pĭng), **skimps** (skĭmps)

skimp on

To fail to provide for or supply something appropriately; be stingy with something: *That pizzeria always skimps on the pepperoni.*

◆ **skin** (skĭn)

skinned (skĭnd), **skinning** (skĭn′ĭng), **skins** (skĭnz)

skin up

1. To bruise, cut, or injure the skin or surface of something: *He fell off his skateboard and skinned up his knee. She slipped on the sidewalk and skinned her arm up.*
2. To roll a cigarette: *I pulled out a pouch of tobacco and skinned up.*

◆ **skip** (skĭp)

skipped (skĭpt), **skipping** (skĭp′ĭng), **skips** (skĭps)

skip off

To leave hastily, especially to avoid a problem or a responsibility: *The students skipped off to the beach for the afternoon.*

skip out of

To leave some place hastily and usually secretly, especially in order to avoid problems: *The suspects skipped out of town before the police could catch them.*

skip out on

To fail to attend something: *We skipped out on the lecture and went to a movie instead.*

◆ **slack** (slăk)

slacked (slăkt), **slacking** (slăk′ĭng), **slacks** (slăks)

slack off

1. To decrease in activity or intensity: *Tourism on Cape Cod usually slacks off around September.*
2. To evade work; shirk: *High school seniors tend to slack off once they get accepted to college.*

◆ **slam** (slăm)

slammed (slămd), **slamming** (slăm′ĭng), **slams** (slămz)

slam down

To put something down forcefully so as to produce a loud noise: *I got angry and slammed down the phone. The teacher slammed a book down to get the students' attention.*

slam into

To hit something with force; crash into someone or something: *The truck lost its brakes and slammed into the guardrail.*

ă	pat	är	car	ī	bite	ô	paw	o͝o	took	ûr	urge
ā	pay	ĕ	pet	îr	pier	ôr	core	o͝or	lure	zh	vision
âr	care	ē	be	ŏ	pot	oi	boy	o͞o	boot	ə	about,
ä	father	ĭ	pit	ō	toe	ou	out	ŭ	cut		item

◆ **slap** (slăp)

slapped (slăpt), **slapping** (slăp′ĭng), **slaps** (slăps)

slap around

To be rough or brutal with someone; abuse someone: *The gangsters threatened to slap me around if I didn't get the money by Friday.*

slap down

1. To restrain or correct someone with a sharp blow or forceful censure: *The soldier slapped me down for talking back. The judge slapped down the defendant for speaking out of turn.*
2. To put a sudden end to something; suppress something: *We must slap this behavior down before it gets out of control. The school slapped down roughhousing on the playground after a child had been hurt.*

slap on

1. To apply something quickly or carelessly: *The cook slapped some butter on the toast and put it on the plate. Running late, I slapped on some clothes and hurried off to class.*
2. To impose some legal obligation, such as a tax or fine, on someone or something: *The government slapped a tax on all imports. If your payment is late, the credit card company will slap on a late fee in addition to interest.*

slap with

To subject someone or something to some legal obligation, such as a fine or court order: *The police officer slapped him with a speeding ticket. Her neighbor slapped her with a lawsuit.*

◆ **slate** (slāt)

slated (slā′tĭd), **slating** (slā′tĭng), **slates** (slāts)

slate for

1. To schedule or designate someone or something to take place at some time: *Our professor has slated the history lecture for Thursday afternoon.*
2. To arrange for something to be or to undergo something: *The contractor has slated the building for destruction. This boss has slated me for a promotion.*

◆ **slave** (slāv)

slaved (slāvd), **slaving** (slā′vĭng), **slaves** (slāvz)

slave away

To work very hard or persistently: *I've been slaving away in the garden. The accountant slaved away on the tax returns.*

◆ **sleep** (slēp)

slept (slĕpt), **sleeping** (slē′pĭng), **sleeps** (slēps)

sleep around

1. To be sexually active with more than one partner: *I'm surprised they're getting married, considering how much they both sleep around.*
2. **sleep around on** To be sexually unfaithful to someone: *I am certain my spouse is sleeping around on me.*

sleep in

1. To oversleep: *I missed the morning train because I slept in.*

2. To sleep late on purpose: *After this week's work, I will sleep in on Saturday.*
3. To sleep at one's place of employment: *Their nanny sleeps in so she can take care of the children at night.*

sleep off

To get rid of something while sleeping: *She went home to sleep off her headache. He has a hangover—let him sleep it off.*

sleep on

To think about something overnight before deciding: *If you can't make a decision right now, sleep on it, and give me your answer in the morning.*

sleep out

1. To sleep away from one's home: *I will be sleeping out tonight, so don't wait up.*
2. To sleep at one's own home, not at one's place of employment: *The maid sleeps out Mondays, so we'll have the house to ourselves.*

sleep over

To spend the night as a guest in another's home: *A friend from out of town slept over last night. You can sleep over on the couch if you're too tired to drive home.*

sleep together

1. To share a bed or room for sleeping. *The baby twins sleep together in their crib. Both guests slept together in our spare room.*
2. To have sexual relations: *They didn't sleep together until they were married.*

sleep with

1. To be with something or someone while sleeping: *Small children often like to sleep with a stuffed animal.*
2. To have sexual relations with someone: *My doctor asked me whether I'd ever slept with anyone.*

◆ **slice** (slīs)

sliced (slīst), **slicing** (slī′sĭng), **slices** (slī′sĭz)

slice off

To cut something from a larger piece: *I picked up the knife and sliced off a piece of cheese. The chef held the pineapple down and sliced the top off.*

slice through

1. To cut through something: *The chef sliced through the tomato with a sharp knife.*
2. To move like a knife through something: *The canoe sliced through the water.*

slice up

To cut or divide something into slices: *We sliced up the loaf of bread and made sandwiches. The developer sliced the estate up into three-acre lots.*

ă	pat	är	car	ī	bite	ô	paw	o͝o	took	ûr	urge
ā	pay	ĕ	pet	îr	pier	ôr	core	o͝or	lure	zh	vision
âr	care	ē	be	ŏ	pot	oi	boy	o͞o	boot	ə	about,
ä	father	ĭ	pit	ō	toe	ou	out	ŭ	cut		item

◆ **slick** (slĭk)
slicked (slĭkt), **slicking** (slĭk′ĭng), **slicks** (slĭks)

slick back
To cause something, especially hair, to lie flat by making it moist or oily and brushing it back: *He wet his hands and slicked back his hair. She slicks her curls back with gel.*

◆ **slim** (slĭm)
slimmed (slĭmd), **slimming** (slĭm′ĭng), **slims** (slĭmz)

slim down
To lose weight, as by dieting or exercise: *I was overweight, so I decided to slim down.*

◆ **slip** (slĭp)
slipped (slĭpt), **slipping** (slĭp′ĭng), **slips** (slĭps)

slip away
To escape, as from a grasp, fastening, or restraint: *When no one was looking, the thief quietly slipped away. The suspect slipped away from the police.*

slip by
1. To pass someone or something gradually, easily, or without being noticed: *The thief slipped by the guards. Time slips by when you're enjoying yourself.*
2. To pass something by someone or something gradually, easily, or without being noticed: *We slipped the key by the guards.*

slip in
1. To insert something gradually, easily, or without being noticed: *She took a dollar bill and slipped it in the birthday card. He slipped in a comment during their conversation.*
2. To enter gradually, easily, or without being noticed: *The party had already started, so I slipped in and got a drink. The thief slipped in the back door.*

slip into
To put on some clothing quickly or easily: *After my shower, I slipped into my pajamas.*

slip off
To remove some article of clothing quickly or easily: *They slipped off their shoes. I reached for my ring and slipped it off.*

slip on
1. To slide involuntarily and lose one's balance or footing as a result of stepping on something slippery: *The clown slipped on a banana peel.*
2. To put on some article of clothing quickly or easily: *It was cold, so I slipped on a sweater. I took the ring and slipped it on.*

slip out
1. To remove something from some place gradually, easily, or without being noticed: *I opened the bag and slipped out two pieces of chocolate. The thief slipped the wallet out of my pocket. I grabbed the keys and slipped them out the window.*
2. To leave or become removed from some place gradually, easily, or without being noticed: *The cotter pin slipped out and the trailer rolled away. The fish slipped out*

of my hands. The thief slipped out the door and into the alley.

3. **slip out of** To remove some clothing quickly or easily: *I slipped out of my boots and put on my nice shoes.*

slip through

1. To pass through something gradually, easily, or without being noticed: *We slipped through the crowd into the club.*
2. To pass something through something gradually, easily, or without being noticed: *The tenant slipped the key through the mail slot. He crept up to the barred window of the jail cell and slipped through the keys.*

slip up

1. To make a mistake or blunder; err: *I slipped up when I said my plane would arrive at 6:00* AM—*I meant 6:00* PM.
2. To cause someone to make a mistake or blunder: *The change in plans slipped me up and I went to the wrong subway station. The false clue slipped up the detective.*

◆ **slog** (slŏg)

slogged (slŏgd), **slogging** (slŏg′ĭng), **slogs** (slŏgz)

slog away

To work diligently for a lengthy period of time: *The student slogged away on the algebra assignment.*

slog through

To walk or progress through something with a slow heavy pace: *The explorers slogged through the swamp. I slogged through both volumes of the author's philosophical writings.*

◆ **slough** (slŭf)

sloughed (slŭft), **sloughing** (slŭf′ĭng), **sloughs** (slŭfs)

slough off

1. To shed or peel off some outer layer, especially by rubbing or scraping: *We need to slough the paint off the pipes before we install them. The snake sloughed off its skin against a rock.*
2. To shed or peel off, as an outer layer: *My skin is sloughing off because of the dryness.*
3. To avoid some work or to work lazily: *Your grades are bad because you've been sloughing off your homework a lot recently. After lunch, he sloughed off and played video games.*
4. To leave unnoticed; slip away: *The kids sloughed off into the woods.*

◆ **slow** (slō)

slowed (slōd), **slowing** (slō′ĭng), **slows** (slōz)

slow down

1. To decrease the speed or rate of something: *The chef slowed down the mixer and added some flour to the batter. We slowed the boat down as we entered the harbor.*

ă	pat	är	car	ī	bite	ô	paw	o͝o	took	ûr	urge
ā	pay	ĕ	pet	îr	pier	ôr	core	o͝or	lure	zh	vision
âr	care	ē	be	ŏ	pot	oi	boy	o͞o	boot	ə	about,
ä	father	ĭ	pit	ō	toe	ou	out	ŭ	cut		item

2. To move, work, or happen at a slower rate: *We slowed down so that we could read the road sign.*
3. To delay someone or something; retard someone or something: *An injury slowed down the runner. A virus has slowed my computer down.*

slow up

1. To delay someone or something; retard someone or something: *Bad weather slowed up the project. The accident on the freeway slowed us up.*
2. To move, work, or happen at a slower rate: *Traffic slows up where the two freeways converge.*

◆ **smack** (smăk)

smacked (smăkt), **smacking** (smăk′ĭng), **smacks** (smăks)

smack of

1. To have the distinctive flavor or taste of something: *The soup smacks of garlic.*
2. To give an indication of something; be suggestive of something: *The city's reluctance to investigate the murder smacked of corruption.*

◆ **smart** (smärt)

smarted (smär′tĭd), **smarting** (smär′tĭng), **smarts** (smärts)

smart off

To speak or act impertinently: *One of my coworkers smarted off to the management and was fired. If you smart off in class, the teacher will punish you.*

◆ **smarten** (smär′tn)

smartened (smär′tnd), **smartening** (smär′tn-ĭng), **smartens** (smär′tnz)

smarten up

1. To improve someone or something in appearance or stylishness: *You can smarten up a dull sweater with a fashionable pin. The designer took my original idea for the greeting card and smartened it up.*
2. To improve someone's appearance or stylishness: *I think this colorful new hat will smarten you up! Please try to smarten yourself up before we get to the party.*
3. To improve in appearance or stylishness: *I had to smarten up when I moved to the city, so I bought a new suit.*
4. To make someone more aware, informed, or sophisticated: *I had to smarten up my young cousins about money management. The experiences they had when buying their first home smartened them up.*
5. To become more aware, informed, or sophisticated: *We smartened up after we had been scammed by the salesperson, and never went back to that store again.*

◆ **smell** (smĕl)

smelled (smĕld), **smelling** (smĕl′ĭng), **smells** (smĕlz)

smell of

1. To have an odor suggesting that something or someone is or has been present: *The locker room smells of soap and sweat.*
2. To be suggestive of something; have a tinge or hint of something: *The dark cave smells of terror.*

smell up

To cause something to have a strong foul odor: *The pungent soup I cooked smelled up the kitchen for days. You should wash the T-shirt, since you were the one who wore it to the gym and smelled it up.*

◆ **smile** (smīl)

smiled (smīld), **smiling** (smī′lĭng), **smiles** (smīlz)

smile on

To regard someone or something with favor or approval: *Good fortune smiled on our efforts, and our plan succeeded.*

◆ **smoke** (smōk)

smoked (smōkd), **smoking** (smō′kĭng), **smokes** (smōks)

smoke out

1. To force someone or something out of a place by or as if by the use of smoke: *The groundskeeper smoked out the gopher. The police smoked the fugitives out of their hideout.*
2. To detect and bring someone or something to public view; expose or reveal someone or something: *The media was quick to smoke out the scandal. The ruse was successful in smoking the culprit out.*

smoke up

1. To fill some area with smoke: *We forgot to open the flue, and the fire smoked up the room. The pot roast was left cooking too long, and it smoked the whole house up.*
2. SLANG To smoke marijuana: *The members of the band would smoke up after each show.*
3. SLANG To provide someone or some group of people with marijuana to smoke: *They smoked us up for the party, but it made us fall asleep.*

◆ **smooth** (smo͞o*th*)

smoothed (smo͞o*th*d), **smoothing** (smo͞o′*th*ĭng), **smoothes** (smo͞o*th*z)

smooth away

1. To eliminate some irregularity, roughness, or projection, so as to achieve a smooth surface or consistency: *After you make the bed, run your hand over the blanket to smooth away the wrinkles. Strands of hair were falling across my forehead while I worked, so I smoothed them away with my thumb.*
2. To eliminate some obstruction, hindrance, or difficulty: *It's good to have a mentor to help smooth away the difficulties of a new career. I had some concerns, but my friend spoke with me and smoothed them away.*

smooth out

1. To eliminate some irregularities, roughness, or projections by stretching or spreading, so as to achieve a smooth surface or consistency: *I had no time to iron my shirt, so I just ran my hands over it to smooth out the creases. If you're unhappy with the*

ă	pat	är	car	ī	bite	ô	paw	o͝o	took	ûr	urge
ā	pay	ĕ	pet	îr	pier	ôr	core	o͝or	lure	zh	vision
âr	care	ē	be	ŏ	pot	oi	boy	o͞o	boot	ə	about, item
ä	father	ĭ	pit	ō	toe	ou	out	ŭ	cut		

wrinkles around your eyes, surgery can smooth them out.

2. To rid something of obstructions, hindrances, or difficulties: *Filing taxes was very confusing, but using online forms smoothes out the process. The assembly procedure is too complicated—we need to smooth it out.*
3. To eliminate some obstructions, hindrances, or difficulties: *I've been getting along better with my parents since we smoothed out our differences. Let me know what the problem is and I'll try to smooth it out.*

smooth over

1. To fill or coat something so as to create a smooth surface: *The builder smoothed over the seams in the sheetrock with plaster. For a healthy complexion, smooth some cold cream over your face before bed.*
2. To make some strained relationship more friendly or amiable: *The ambassador smoothed over relations with France. The two players almost got into a fight before the coach smoothed things over between them.*

◆ **smother** (smŭ*th*′ər)

smothered (smŭ*th*′ərd), **smothering** (smŭ*th*′ə-rĭng), **smothers** (smŭ*th*′ərz)

smother with *or* **smother in**

1. To cover something thickly: *The chef smothered the chicken with sauce.*
2. To give someone an abundance or surfeit of some sort of affection: *The grandparents smothered the children in hugs. I was smothered with affection when I visited my old friends.*

◆ **snack** (snăk)

snacked (snăkt), **snacking** (snăk′ĭng), **snacks** (snăks)

snack on

To eat something as a snack: *One way to lose weight is to snack on carrots instead of junk food.*

◆ **snap** (snăp)

snapped (snăpt), **snapping** (snăp′ĭng), **snaps** (snăps)

snap at

1. To bring the jaws briskly together in an attempt to threaten or bite someone or something: *The dog strained at its leash and snapped at us.*
2. To make a sharp, often hostile or scolding remark to someone: *The lifeguard snapped at the child for running near the pool.*

snap back

1. To recover quickly: *The patient snapped back quickly after surgery.*
2. To utter a sharp retort: *I asked a simple question, but the clerk snapped back with a mean remark.*

snap out

1. To utter something abruptly or sharply: *The sergeant snapped out a command. The coach snapped her orders out.*
2. **snap out of** To recover suddenly from some mental state: *Snap out of it! We have a job to do.*
3. **snap out of** To rouse someone suddenly from some mental state:

When he yelled, he snapped me out of my daydream. The magician snapped the audience volunteer out of the hypnotic state.

snap to

To pay attention or begin complying suddenly: *The troops snapped to attention when the general appeared.*

snap up

To acquire someone or something quickly and eagerly: *The fans of the band snapped up all the tickets the day they went on sale. The large corporation snapped many of its competitors up.*

◆ **snarl** (snärl)

snarled (snärld), **snarling** (snär′lĭng), **snarls** (snärlz)

snarl up

1. To become tangled in or as if in a knot: *This new fishing line keeps snarling up.*
2. To tangle or knot something: *The wind snarled up my hair. I snarled the kite up in a tree.*
3. To involve someone or something in or as if in a tangle: *Their lawyers snarled us up in litigation for years. Don't get me snarled up in your affairs. An accident snarled up traffic for hours.*

◆ **snatch** (snăch)

snatched (snăcht), **snatching** (snăch′ĭng), **snatches** (snăch′ĭz)

snatch at

To attempt to grasp or seize something by grabbing at it suddenly: *The police officer snatched at the gun in the robber's hand.*

◆ **sneak** (snēk)

sneaked (snēkt) *or* **snuck** (snŭk), **sneaking** (snē′kĭng), **sneaks** (snēks)

sneak around

1. To move or operate in some place furtively or surreptitiously: *The security guard caught the thief sneaking around the office after closing.*
2. To do something without someone's knowledge, especially to engage in romantic relationships: *I suspect her husband has been sneaking around. I think his wife was sneaking around on him.*

sneak up

1. To move or operate furtively or surreptitiously toward someone: *The thief sneaked up behind the tourists and stole their luggage.*
2. **sneak up on** To approach suddenly and surprisingly: *The first day of spring sneaked up on me and I still hadn't gone skiing yet. Don't sneak up on me like that!*

◆ **sneeze** (snēz)

sneezed (snēzd), **sneezing** (snē′zĭng), **sneezes** (snē′zĭz)

sneeze at

To treat something as unimportant. Used chiefly in the passive with a

ă	pat	är	car	ī	bite	ô	paw	o͝o	took	ûr	urge
ā	pay	ĕ	pet	îr	pier	ôr	core	o͝or	lure	zh	vision
âr	care	ē	be	ŏ	pot	oi	boy	o͞o	boot	ə	about,
ä	father	ĭ	pit	ō	toe	ou	out	ŭ	cut		item

negative word: *The critical nature of the job at hand is not to be sneezed at.*

◆ **sniff** (snĭf)

sniffed (snĭft), **sniffing** (snĭf′ĭng), **sniffs** (snĭfs)

sniff around

To pry; snoop: *The reporters came sniffing around for more details. The detectives sniffed around the basement for clues. The guard caught them sniffing around in the room where the files are kept.*

sniff at

1. To use the sense of smell to investigate something: *I sniffed at the jar to see what it held.*
2. To regard someone or something in a contemptuous or dismissive manner: *The critics sniffed at the film, even though it was very popular. The amount of funds we've managed to raise in a week is nothing to sniff at.*

sniff out

To perceive or detect someone or something by or as if by sniffing: *The dogs sniffed out the trail through the snow. The detectives sniffed the plot out and arrested the criminals.*

◆ **snitch** (snĭch)

snitched (snĭcht), **snitching** (snĭch′ĭng), **snitches** (snĭch′ĭz)

snitch on

To disclose incriminating information about someone: *She snitched on the coworker who had been stealing petty cash. He snitched on his little brother for breaking the vase.*

◆ **snow** (snō)

snowed (snōd), **snowing** (snō′ĭng), **snows** (snōz)

snow in

1. To cause something to be inoperable or unable to move safely due to snow. Used chiefly in the passive: *The airport was snowed in, and no flights left that day. The school buses were snowed in, so classes were canceled.*
2. To cause someone or something to remain inside due to snow: *The blizzard had snowed in all the townspeople, and all the restaurants were closed. A sudden storm had snowed us in, and we were worried that we would run out of food.*
3. To cause something to be surrounded by snow: *The storm snowed in the mountain and confined the climbers to their tents. One winter, a blizzard snowed their cabin in, and they had to tunnel out the window.*

snow out

To force the cancellation or postponement of some event because of snow. Used chiefly in the passive: *With this blizzard coming, the concert will be snowed out.*

snow under

1. To cover or bury someone or something in snow: *A big storm snowed the explorers under in their tents, and they couldn't leave for days. The blizzard snowed under the entire forest. The skiers were snowed under by the avalanche.*

2. To overwhelm someone or something. Used chiefly in the passive: *I was snowed under with homework.*
3. To defeat someone or something by a very large margin. Used chiefly in the passive: *The candidate was snowed under by a margin of 3 to 1.*

◆ **snub** (snŭb)

snubbed (snŭbd), **snubbing** (snŭb′ĭng), **snubs** (snŭbz)

snub out

1. To extinguish a cigarette, cigar, or some other smoking material by stamping the burning end against a surface; stub something out: *When the "No Smoking" sign lit up, we snubbed out our cigarettes. I took the cigarette and snubbed it out on the wall before the teacher saw me.*
2. SLANG To kill someone; murder someone: *The gangsters snubbed the witness out. The mobsters snubbed out the competition.*

snub up

To anchor something, such as a vessel, by wrapping a line around a post or cleat: *The dock workers took a line and snubbed up the boat. I snubbed the boat up and went ashore. As we came in, one of the crew jumped onto the pier, grabbed a line, and snubbed up.*

◆ **snuff** (snŭf)

snuffed (snŭft), **snuffing** (snŭf′ĭng), **snuffs** (snŭfs)

snuff out

1. To extinguish something: *The altar server snuffed out the candles. I saw her snuff a match out with her fingers.*
2. To put a sudden end to something: *The war has snuffed out many young lives. I had a promising career as a dancer, but a tragic injury snuffed it out.*
3. SLANG To kill someone; murder someone: *The police accused the widow of snuffing out her husband. The gangsters snuffed him out before he could testify in court.*

◆ **snug** (snŭg)

snugged (snŭgd), **snugging** (snŭg′ĭng), **snugs** (snŭgz)

snug down

To prepare some vessel to weather a storm, as by taking in sail or securing movable gear: *The sailors snugged down the ship. Let's snug the boat down before the storm comes.*

◆ **snuggle** (snŭg′əl)

snuggled (snŭg′əld), **snuggling** (snŭg′ə-lĭng), **snuggles** (snŭg′əlz)

snuggle up

1. To lie or press close together: *The lovers snuggled up in front of the fire.*
2. To lie or press close to someone or something: *The puppy snuggled up to its mother.*

ă	pat	är	car	ī	bite	ô	paw	o͝o	took	ûr	urge
ā	pay	ĕ	pet	îr	pier	ôr	core	o͝or	lure	zh	vision
âr	care	ē	be	ŏ	pot	oi	boy	o͞o	boot	ə	about,
ä	father	ĭ	pit	ō	toe	ou	out	ŭ	cut		item

3. To curl up closely or comfortably; nestle: *I snuggled up under the covers.*

◆ **soak** (sōk)
soaked (sōkt), **soaking** (sō′kĭng), **soaks** (sōks)

soak in
To penetrate or permeate; seep: *Wait until the dye soaks in before you handle the fabric. The speaker paused to let her words soak in.*

soak out
To remove something, such as a stain, by continued immersion: *She threw her shirt in a tub of water to soak out the pasta sauce before it set. The ink stain looked permanent, but he tried to soak it out anyway.*

soak through
To drench someone or something: *I forgot to cover my backpack, and now my sleeping bag is soaked through. The rainstorm soaked me through to the skin.*

soak up
1. To absorb something, such as a liquid, through or as if through pores: *The towel under the sink soaks the leaking water up. The quilt was in the barn, and it soaked up some of the smell.*
2. To take in or accept something mentally, especially eagerly and easily: *I soaked up the atmosphere as I wandered its streets. The student soaked up everything the teacher said.*

◆ **soap** (sōp)
soaped (sōpt), **soaping** (sō′pĭng), **soaps** (sōps)

soap up
1. To cover someone or something with soap: *We soaped up the car, scrubbed well, and rinsed it clean. I soaped my legs up and shaved them.*
2. To cover oneself with soap: *I soaped up and rinsed off in the shower.*

◆ **sober** (sō′bər)
sobered (sō′bərd), **sobering** (sō′bə-rĭng), **sobers** (sō′bərz)

sober up
1. To have one's feeling of intoxication subside: *I waited until I had sobered up and then drove home.*
2. To cause someone's feeling of intoxication to subside: *The jailer grabbed a pail of water and a cup of coffee to sober up the drunk. That nap really sobered me up, but I still have a hangover.*
3. To overcome an alcohol or drug addiction: *It wasn't until I had sobered up that I was able hold a steady job.*
4. To become serious, grave, or solemn: *Everyone sobered up and felt ashamed when they heard the bad news.*
5. To make someone or something serious, grave, or solemn: *The news of the disaster sobered them up. The accident sobered up the workers, reminding them how dangerous their job was.*

◆ **sock** (sŏk)
socked (sŏkt), **socking** (sŏk′ĭng), **socks** (sŏks)

sock away
To put something valuable in a safe place for future use: *He socked*

away some gold in a mattress in case the bank was robbed. While the rest of us have been blowing our salaries on electronic gadgets, she has been quietly socking hers away.

sock in

To surround or enshroud someone or something with dense clouds or fog, often preventing movement or operation: *Fog socked in the airport. The mountain was socked in with clouds.*

◆ **sod** (sŏd)

sodded (sŏd′ĭd), **sodding** (sŏd′ĭng), **sods** (sŏdz)

sod off

CHIEFLY BRITISH VULGAR SLANG

To go away. Used chiefly as a command.

◆ **soften** (sô′fən, sŏf′ən)

softened (sô′fənd, sŏf′ənd), **softening** (sô′fə-nĭng, sŏf′ə-nĭng), **softens** (sô′fənz, sŏf′ənz)

soften up

1. To make something soft or softer: *He softened up his new baseball glove with some oil. He left the butter out to soften it up.*
2. To undermine or reduce the strength, morale, or resistance of someone or something: *The air force softened up the enemy positions with a heavy bombing campaign. The children gave me a present to soften me up before asking for new bicycles.*

◆ **sop** (sŏp)

sopped (sŏpt), **sopping** (sŏp′ĭng), **sops** (sŏps)

sop up

To take something up by absorption; absorb something: *We sopped up the water with paper towels. I sopped the sauce up with a piece of bread.*

◆ **sort** (sôrt)

sorted (sôr′tĭd), **sorting** (sôr′tĭng), **sorts** (sôrts)

sort out

1. To separate some class, kind, or size from others: *I sorted out the blue socks and washed them separately. We sorted the rotten fruit out from the rest and threw it away.*
2. To arrange some collection according to class, kind, or size: *I sorted out the pile of photos and put them in the appropriate albums. The jeweler sorted the diamonds out by weight and clarity.*
3. To resolve some confusion or conflict: *It took me an hour to sort out the problem with my reservation. The couple almost broke up, but they managed to sort things out.*
4. SLANG To punish someone or correct someone's behavior: *If they keep messing around, I'll have to go sort them out.*

sort through

To go through some container or collection and classify or arrange the contents, especially when searching: *I sorted through the stack of mail looking for the phone bill. We sorted through the box of photos for a picture of the dog.*

◆ **sound** (sound)

sounded (soun′dĭd), **sounding** (soun′dĭng), **sounds** (soundz)

sound off

1. To express one's views vigorously: *We went to the town meeting to sound off about potholes in the roads.*
2. To chant or count in time with one's step when marching in military formation: *We heard the soldiers sounding off as they marched by.*

sound out

1. To pronounce something slowly and carefully: *The student practiced sounding out the English vowels. I sounded the phrase out until I could say it correctly.*
2. To pronounce the letters of some word slowly and in sequence in order to arrive at the pronunciation or meaning of the whole: *If you don't know the word, try to sound it out. I tried to sound out the word, but its spelling didn't match its pronunciation.*
3. To examine or investigate the opinion or nature of someone or something: *The company conducted a survey to sound out public opinion. I tried to sound them out before asking for the favor so that I wouldn't put them in an awkward position.*
4. To project a sound: *The bell sounded out at midnight.*

◆ **soup** (so͞op)

souped (so͞opt), **souping** (so͞o′pĭng), **soups** (so͞ops)

soup up

SLANG

To modify something so as to increase its capacity to perform or satisfy, especially to add horsepower or greater speed potential to an engine or a vehicle: *The mechanic souped the car up with racing tires and a bigger engine. I souped up my computer with a faster processor and a liquid cooling system.*

◆ **space** (spās)

spaced (spāst), **spacing** (spā′sĭng), **spaces** (spā′sĭz)

space out

1. To organize or arrange some things or some people with spaces between: *The tournament organizers spaced the matches out so that players would have time to rest. The police officers spaced themselves out along the parade route.*
2. To stupefy or disorient someone from or as if from a drug: *The medicine spaces me out so I can't think clearly. The summer heat tends to space out the students and makes it difficult to teach.*
3. To lose awareness of one's surroundings: *I stared out the window and spaced out for an hour.*
4. To lose concentration or become inattentive: *I was supposed to*

meet her at 9:00, but I spaced out and didn't get there till 10:30.

◆ **spark** (spärk)

sparked (spärkt), **sparking** (spär′kĭng), **sparks** (spärks)

spark off

1. To ignite some fire: *Forest rangers think that a cigarette sparked off the blaze. After the fire was extinguished, investigators tried to determine what sparked it off.*
2. To set something in motion; trigger something: *The assassination sparked off a revolution. Historians disagree about what sparked the riot off.*

spark up

1. To initiate some conversation, friendship, or debate: *On the train, I sparked up a conversation with the person next to me. The trial sparked a debate up over free speech.*
2. To light some cigarette, cigar, or similar product: *He lit a match and sparked up his pipe. She took a cigar from the case and sparked it up. The smokers went outside to spark up.*

◆ **speak** (spēk)

spoke (spōk), **spoken** (spō′kən), **speaking** (spē′kĭng), **speaks** (spēks)

speak for

1. To act as spokesperson for someone or something: *I speak for the entire staff when I say thank you. I think these photographs will speak for themselves. Hey, speak for yourself—I'm not too old to dance! I can't speak for my competitors, but we take every precaution to ensure the customer's safety.*
2. To make a reservation or request for someone or something. Chiefly used in the passive: *Is this dance spoken for? That painting is already spoken for.*

speak of

1. To speak about someone or something: *She spoke fondly of her childhood home.*
2. To give an indication or suggestion of something: *His biography speaks of great loneliness.*

speak out

To talk freely and fearlessly, as about a public issue: *Only one newspaper spoke out against the dictator. The politician was not afraid to speak out on controversial issues. Everyone was concerned about the problem, but no one spoke out.*

speak to

To address some topic: *The mayor spoke to the issue of tax increases.*

speak up

1. To speak loud enough to be audible: *Speak up—I can't hear you.*
2. To speak without fear or hesitation: *You have to speak up if you want something.*

ă	pat	är	car	ī	bite	ô	paw	o͝o	took	ûr	urge
ā	pay	ĕ	pet	îr	pier	ôr	core	o͝or	lure	zh	vision
âr	care	ē	be	ŏ	pot	oi	boy	o͞o	boot	ə	about,
ä	father	ĭ	pit	ō	toe	ou	out	ŭ	cut		item

◆ **speed** (spēd)

sped (spĕd) *or* **speeded** (spē′dĭd), **speeding** (spē′dĭng), **speeds** (spēdz)

speed by

1. To pass quickly, as of a moving object or an interval of time: *During vacation, the days sped by.*
2. To pass someone or something quickly: *The car sped by me.*

speed off

To leave or drive off rapidly: *She hopped in her car and sped off. The ambulance sped off to the hospital.*

speed through

1. To accomplish or proceed with something swiftly and energetically: *The students sped through the easy assignment.*
2. To move rapidly through something: *The train sped through the countryside.*

speed up

1. To increase the speed or rate of something; accelerate something: *The company sped up production in order to meet the demand for their product. The conveyor belt is moving too slowly—can you speed it up?*
2. To move, work, or happen at a faster rate; accelerate: *As he hiked uphill, his pulse sped up.*

◆ **spell** (spĕl)

spelled (spĕld) *or* **spelt** (spĕlt), **spelling** (spĕl′ĭng), **spells** (spĕlz)

spell down

To defeat someone in a spelling bee: *My cousin spelled down 15 competitors to reach the finals. I finally spelled last year's champion down.*

spell out

1. To name or write in order the letters constituting some word or part of a word: *I spelled out my name for the telephone operator. The student spelled each out each word on the spelling test.*
2. To give a detailed and literal statement of something in order to make it perfectly clear and understandable: *The committee demanded that he spell out his objectives. She didn't understand the penalties at first, but we spelled them out for her.*

◆ **spew** (spyo͞o)

spewed (spyo͞od), **spewing** (spyo͞o′ĭng), **spews** (spyo͞oz)

spew up

1. To eject some contents of the stomach by vomiting: *She spewed up the spoiled chicken. The sick child spewed his lunch up.*
2. To vomit: *I spewed up in the car after the turbulent plane ride.*

◆ **spice** (spīs)

spiced (spīst), **spicing** (spī′sĭng), **spices** (spī′sĭz)

spice up

1. To make something spicy or spicier: *The cook spiced up the chili with some peppers. I added some pepper to the sauce in order to spice it up.*
2. To make something exciting or more exciting: *We spiced up the party by playing some games. That necklace really spices your outfit up.*

◆ **spiff** (spĭf)

spiffed (spĭft), **spiffing** (spĭf′ĭng), **spiffs** (spĭfs)

spiff up

SLANG

To make attractive, stylish, or up-to-date: *The owners spiffed up the old storefront. I found my old bike and spiffed it up.*

◆ **spin** (spĭn)

spun (spŭn), **spinning** (spĭn′ĭng), **spins** (spĭnz)

spin off

To derive something, such as a company or product, from some source: *The television network decided to spin a new show off from its popular comedy series. The media conglomerate spun off its entertainment division.*

spin out

To rotate out of control, as a skidding car leaving a roadway: *The car spun out on the ice and crashed into the ditch.*

◆ **spirit** (spĭr′ĭt)

spirited (spĭr′ĭ-tĭd), **spiriting** (spĭr′ĭ-tĭng), **spirits** (spĭr′ĭts)

spirit away

To carry someone or something off mysteriously or secretly: *The lawyers spirited away the documents. In the folktale, an old giant spirited the children away.*

◆ **spit** (spĭt)

spat (spăt) *or* **spit** (spĭt), **spitting** (spĭt′ĭng), **spits** (spĭts)

spit out

To expel something from the mouth; expectorate something: *The teacher told the child to spit out the gum. The fish wasn't cooked enough, and I spit it out.*

spit up

1. To spit something out of the mouth: *The boxer is spitting up blood.*
2. To vomit something. Used chiefly of an infant: *The child is still hungry because he spit his meal up. The baby spit up on her bib.*

◆ **splash** (splăsh)

splashed (splăsht), **splashing** (splăsh′ĭng), **splashes** (splăsh′ĭz)

splash down

To land in water. Used of a spacecraft or missile: *The spacecraft splashed down in the Atlantic Ocean.*

◆ **split** (splĭt)

split (splĭt), **splitting** (splĭt′ĭng), **splits** (splĭts)

split off

1. To separate something; detach something: *The babysitter split off a piece of fruit and shared it with the child. Before putting the flowers in water, I split the stem ends off.*

ă	pat	är	car	ī	bite	ô	paw	o͝o	took	ûr	urge
ā	pay	ĕ	pet	îr	pier	ôr	core	o͝or	lure	zh	vision
âr	care	ē	be	ŏ	pot	oi	boy	o͞o	boot	ə	about,
ä	father	ĭ	pit	ō	toe	ou	out	ŭ	cut		item

2. To become separated from something: *The political party split off from a broader coalition. As the temperature rose, a large section of the iceberg split off.*

split up

1. To separate someone or something, such as people or groups; disunite someone or something: *Artistic differences split up the band. They've been together too long to let a little argument split them up.*
2. To become divided or part company as a result of discord or disagreement: *My parents split up after 20 years of marriage.*
3. To divide something, as for convenience or proper ordering: *They split up the remainder of the money among themselves and parted ways. We split the project up into stages.*
4. To become divided or be divisible: *Let's split up into teams. This poem doesn't split up into stanzas very well.*

◆ **spoil** (spoil)
spoiled (spoild) *or* **spoilt** (spoilt), **spoiling** (spoi′lĭng), **spoils** (spoilz)

spoil for

To be eager for something, especially a fight: *The drunk soccer players at the bar were spoiling for a fight.*

◆ **sponge** (spŭnj)
sponged (spŭnjd), **sponging** (spŭn′jĭng), **sponges** (spŭn′jĭz)

sponge down

To moisten or wipe the surface of someone or something with or as if with a sponge: *The artist sponged down the canvas with primer before starting the painting. I had a high fever, so the nurse sponged my forehead down.*

sponge off

1. To wipe or clean the surface of someone or something with or as if with a sponge: *After dinner, I cleared all the dishes and sponged off the table. The blackboard was very dirty, so the teacher told me to sponge it off.*
2. To live by relying on the generosity of someone else: *He sponged off his parents for years because they never insisted that he get a job.*

◆ **spoon** (spo͞on)
spooned (spo͞ond), **spooning** (spo͞o′nĭng), **spoons** (spo͞onz)

spoon out

To distribute something from a container with a spoon: *The cook spooned out the soup into a bowl. I spooned the ice cream out to the kids, making sure they all got the same amount.*

◆ **spout** (spout)
spouted (spou′tĭd), **spouting** (spou′tĭng), **spouts** (spouts)

spout off

1. To speak continuously and tediously: *I dread spending an evening with my cousins and listening to them spout off about their last vacation.*
2. To utter something that is long-winded and tedious: *I'd hoped for a simple answer, but the mechanic spouted off a technical explanation that confused me even more. The tour guides have to memorize*

the speech until they can spout it off without effort.

◆ **sprawl** (sprôl)

sprawled (sprôld), **sprawling** (sprô′lĭng), **sprawls** (sprôlz)

sprawl out

1. To cause something to spread out in a straggling or disordered fashion: *The detective sprawled the evidence out on the desk. The mechanic sprawled out the parts so that they would be easy to find. My papers are sprawled out on the desk.*
2. To be spread out in a straggling or disordered fashion: *Shoddy apartment buildings sprawled out across the valley.*
3. To sit or lie with the body and limbs spread out awkwardly: *I sprawled out on the chair, but I sat up straight when my mother walked into the room.*
4. To extend oneself when lying down or sitting so that the body and limbs spread out awkwardly: *I yawned and sprawled myself out in the hammock. The security guard is sprawled out in the chair, fast asleep.*

◆ **spread** (sprĕd)

spread (sprĕd), **spreading** (sprĕd′ĭng), **spreads** (sprĕdz)

spread out

1. To open something to a fuller extent or width; stretch something out: *The bat spread out its wings and flew through the cave. We spread the blanket out and sat down for a picnic.*
2. To be extended or enlarged: *The butter spread out across the frying pan as it melted. The bird's wings spread out to a span of ten feet.*
3. To make wider the gap between some things or people; move some things or people farther apart: *Your hand can cover the hole if you spread out your fingers. The instructor spread the dancers out across the floor.*
4. To become distributed or widely dispersed: *The cracks spread out across the windshield. We spread out to search the field.*
5. To distribute something over a surface in a layer: *The chef spread out the frosting with a spatula. Start by applying a splotch of paint to the wall, and spread it out with a fine brush.*
6. To make a wide or extensive arrangement of something: *The magician spread out the cards and asked an audience member to choose one. We spread the bicycle parts out on the floor.*
7. To be exhibited, displayed, or visible in broad or full extent: *The prairie spread out in front of the pioneers.*
8. To display the full extent of something. Used in the passive: *The vast landscape was spread out before us.*

ă	pat	är	car	ī	bite	ô	paw	o͝o	took	ûr	urge
ā	pay	ĕ	pet	îr	pier	ôr	core	o͝or	lure	zh	vision
âr	care	ē	be	ŏ	pot	oi	boy	o͞o	boot	ə	about, item
ä	father	ĭ	pit	ō	toe	ou	out	ŭ	cut		

◆ **spring** (sprĭng)

sprang (sprăng) *or* **sprung** (sprŭng), **sprung** (sprŭng), **springing** (sprĭng′ĭng), **springs** (sprĭngz)

spring back

To recover quickly and completely: *The softball player sprang back quickly after her injury.*

spring for

To pay for something: *My boss offered to spring for lunch.*

spring from

To have something as an origin or cause; have developed from something: *The taxpayers' anger springs from policies that were made by the previous governor.*

spring on

To present or disclose something to someone unexpectedly or suddenly: *They sprang the news on all their friends that they were having a baby. The company president sprang on us the plan to lay people off.*

spring up

1. To move suddenly upward on or as if on a spring: *The box opened and the puppet sprang up. The contestants sprang up from the crowd when their names were called.*
2. To appear or come into being quickly: *New shopping malls were springing up rapidly on what was once farmland.*

◆ **sprout** (sprout)

sprouted (sprou′tĭd), **sprouting** (sprou′tĭng), **sprouts** (sprouts)

sprout up

1. To emerge from the soil and grow rapidly: *Weeds had sprouted up through the cracks in the pavement.*
2. To emerge and develop rapidly: *Within a few years, strip malls had sprouted up across the county.*

◆ **spruce** (spro͞os)

spruced (spro͞ost), **sprucing** (spro͞o′sĭng), **spruces** (spro͞o′sĭz)

spruce up

To make someone or something neat, elegant, and stylish in appearance: *The new curtains will certainly spruce up this drab room. She spruced herself up and went out to dinner.*

◆ **spur** (spûr)

spurred (spûrd), **spurring** (spûr′ĭng), **spurs** (spûrz)

spur on

1. To urge some horse onward by the use of spurs: *The knight spurred the horse on across the shallow river. I spurred on the horse as fast as it could go.*
2. To stimulate or encourage someone or something: *Low gas prices spurred on the booming economy. We never could have finished the project if our boss hadn't spurred us on.*

◆ **sputter** (spŭt′ər)

sputtered (spŭt′ərd), **sputtering** (spŭt′ə-rĭng), **sputters** (spŭt′ərz)

sputter out

To make irregular spitting or popping sounds and gradually stop functioning: *The motor emitted a puff of smoke and sputtered out.*

◆ **spy** (spī)

spied (spīd), **spying** (spī′ĭng), **spies** (spīz)

spy on *or* **spy upon**

To observe someone or something secretly and closely: *A detective had been spying on the mayor's every move for months. The children spied upon their neighbors from the bushes along the property line.*

spy out

1. To observe some place secretly and closely: *The troops spied out the cave and decided it was safe to hide there. The explorers sent a scout into the valley to spy it out before descending.*
2. To discover something by observing secretly and closely: *Try to spy out what's going on on those rooftops. We followed the other teams' strategies carefully to spy them out.*

◆ **square** (skwâr)

squared (skwârd), **squaring** (skwâr′ĭng), **squares** (skwârz)

square away

To make someone or something ready; put something in order: *I squared away my remaining office work before I went on vacation. Let's square these matters away before we finish the meeting. Our plans should be squared away before they get here.*

square off

1. To make something square or rectangular: *The carpenter squared the plank off with a table saw. The designer has squared off the toe of the shoe.*
2. To assume a fighting stance; prepare to fight: *The two fighters squared off and exchanged blows.*
3. To face someone or something in a competition or debate: *The two candidates will square off in a debate. The team squared off against its longtime rival. The governor prepared to square off with legislators over the new tax bill.*

square up

1. To make something conform to a desired plane, straight line, or right angle: *He squared up the picture and nailed it in place. The golfer squared her feet up to the hole.*
2. To make one's body, especially one's feet or shoulders, conform to a desired plane, straight line, or right angle: *The football players squared up to the line of scrimmage. The basketball player squared up and shot a free throw.*
3. **square up to** To come face to face with someone or something, especially with defiance or hostility; confront someone or something: *The prisoners squared up to the guards and demanded better food.*

ă	pat	är	car	ī	bite	ô	paw	o͝o	took	ûr	urge
ā	pay	ĕ	pet	îr	pier	ôr	core	o͝or	lure	zh	vision
âr	care	ē	be	ŏ	pot	oi	boy	o͞o	boot	ə	about,
ä	father	ĭ	pit	ō	toe	ou	out	ŭ	cut		item

4. To face one another in a competition: *The two teams will square up tonight.*
5. To settle some bill or debt: *We went to the bar to square up our bill from the night before. The landlord demanded that I square up before the end of the month.*

square with

To agree or conform with something: *Your story doesn't square with the facts.*

◆ **squeak** (skwēk)

squeaked (skwēkt), **squeaking** (skwē′kĭng), **squeaks** (skwēks)

squeak by

To manage barely to pass, win, or survive someone or something: *I squeaked by the first round but won the rest of my matches easily. My parents squeaked by on a limited income.*

squeak through

To manage barely to pass, win, or survive something: *The student squeaked through the course with a D minus.*

◆ **squeal** (skwēl)

squealed (skwēld), **squealing** (skwē′lĭng), **squeals** (skwēlz)

squeal on

To disclose incriminating information about someone: *The accountant squealed on her corrupt managers. He squealed on his brother for jumping on the bed.*

◆ **squeeze** (skwēz)

squeezed (skwēzd), **squeezing** (skwē′zĭng), **squeezes** (skwē′zĭz)

squeeze by

1. To force one's way past someone or something: *I had to squeeze by the flight attendant to get to the bathroom. The vote on this bill will be close, but I think we can squeeze it by.*
2. To succeed just barely in passing an obstacle, such as a competition or evaluation: *The student squeezed by with a D minus.*

squeeze in

1. To manage to make room or time for someone or something in a tight space or schedule by or as if by exerting pressure: *I squeezed in a round of golf before work. We squeezed a quick meal in before the bus trip.*
2. To force one's way into a tight space: *Just as the elevator door was closing, one more person squeezed in.*

squeeze into

1. To manage to make room or time for someone or something in some tight space or schedule by or as if by exerting pressure: *She squeezed her books into the briefcase. The dentist can squeeze you into her schedule next week.*
2. To force one's way into some tight space: *He squeezed into the packed subway car.*

squeeze off

To fire some amount of ammunition by squeezing a trigger: *The police officer squeezed off four shots. I squeezed the shots off in rapid succession.*

squeeze out

1. To extract something by or as if by applying pressure: *I cut open a*

lemon and squeezed out the juice. The detective squeezed a confession out of the suspect.

2. To force out or displace someone or something by gaining better access to a limited resource: *The larger puppies squeezed out the smallest as they competed for the mother's milk. The town center was once populated with local artists, but large retail stores have since squeezed them out.*

squeeze through

1. To force one's way through something that is narrow or tightly packed: *We squeezed through the crowd to get to the bar.*
2. To manage narrowly to pass, win, or survive something: *The team squeezed through the first round of the tournament. School was so tough that I barely squeezed through.*

◆ **squirm** (skwûrm)

squirmed (skwûrmd), **squirming** (skwûr′mĭng), **squirms** (skwûrmz)

squirm out

1. To extricate oneself by sly or subtle means from some situation; worm one's way out of some situation: *She squirmed out of the promise she'd made without upsetting anyone. He was supposed to wash the dishes tonight, but somehow he squirmed out.*
2. To free oneself from something by turning, twisting, or writhing the body: *The fish squirmed out of my grasp. I put the snake in a bag, but it squirmed out.*

◆ **squirrel** (skwûr′əl)

squirreled *or* **squirrelled** (skwûr′əld), **squirreling** *or* **squirrelling** (skwûr′ə-lĭng), **squirrels** (skwûr′əlz)

squirrel away

To hide or store something: *They have been squirreling away money in an offshore bank account. The children were squirreling candy away in their rooms.*

◆ **stack** (stăk)

stacked (stăkt), **stacking** (stăk′ĭng), **stacks** (stăks)

stack up

1. To arrange something in a stack; pile something: *I stacked up the magazines in orderly piles. Don't leave newspapers all over the floor; stack them up neatly.*
2. To form into or as if into a stack; accumulate: *I've been away for two weeks, and my mail is stacking up.*
3. To equal or be of similar quality: *The salary and benefits at this company don't stack up against those offered by larger companies.*
4. To rank against one another; bear comparison: *We sent our critic out to see how the local restaurants stack up.*
5. To make sense; add up: *The story he gave the police was full of contradictions—it just didn't stack up.*

ă	pat	är	car	ī	bite	ô	paw	ŏŏ	took	ûr	urge
ā	pay	ĕ	pet	îr	pier	ôr	core	ŏŏr	lure	zh	vision
âr	care	ē	be	ŏ	pot	oi	boy	ōō	boot	ə	about,
ä	father	ĭ	pit	ō	toe	ou	out	ŭ	cut		item

6. To direct or cause some aircraft to circle at different altitudes while waiting to land: *The control tower stacked up the planes until the runway could be cleared. The controllers stacked the planes up because only one runway was open.*

◆ **stake** (stāk)

staked (stākt), **staking** (stāk′ĭng), **stakes** (stāks)

stake on

To gamble or risk something on the success or outcome of something else: *I was convinced that the horse would win, and I staked a lot of money on the race. Unfortunately, the candidate has staked the election on a story that will be difficult to prove. How much did you stake on the football game?*

stake out

1. To mark the location or limits of something with or as if with stakes: *We walked the boundary of the property and staked it out with orange flags. Pioneers raced to stake out a claim in the new territory.*
2. To claim something as one's own: *We ran ahead of the others to stake out a campsite. The new executive staked a place out in the organization as a technology expert.*
3. To keep someone or something under surveillance: *The police staked out the suspect's house. They staked the car out until the owner showed up.*

◆ **stamp** (stămp)

stamped (stămpt), **stamping** (stăm′pĭng), **stamps** (stămps)

stamp out

1. To extinguish or destroy something by or as if by trampling or stepping on it: *I was able to stamp the small fire out. The government aims to stamp out poverty.*
2. To produce something by application of a mold, form, or die: *The baker rolled the dough and stamped out ten heart-shaped cookies. That machine stamps the coins out of the sheet metal.*

◆ **stand** (stănd)

stood (sto͝od), **standing** (stăn′dĭng), **stands** (stăndz)

stand against

1. To stand next to or rest against something: *He stood against the frame of the door.*
2. To oppose something: *Many of the students stood against the war.*
3. To compete with someone in a race for elected office: *She announced her intention to stand against the incumbent in the next election.*

stand around

To stand idly near a location: *That assistant just stands around while other people work. I've been standing around waiting for you. There was nothing to do, so we just stood around.*

stand back

To assume or maintain a position away from something, especially to be out of harm's way: *Stand back; that container is about to explode. The crowd stood back from the accident site.*

stand by

1. To be ready or available to act: *Operators are standing by, ready to take your call.*
2. To wait for a thing, such as a broadcast, to resume: *Our network is experiencing some technical difficulties; please stand by. This train will be standing by until further notice.*
3. To remain uninvolved; refrain from acting: *The security guard just stood by and let the thief get away.*
4. To remain loyal to someone; aid or support someone: *She stood by her friend and defended her throughout the scandal.*
5. To keep or maintain some principle or position on an issue: *I stand by my decision, and I'm willing to defend it.*

stand down

1. To withdraw or resign, as from a political contest: *Because the candidate was behind in the polls, he decided to stand down.*
2. To end a state of readiness or alert: *The troops were ordered to stand down.*
3. To leave a witness stand: *The judge allowed the witness to stand down.*

stand for

1. To represent something; symbolize something: *In military code, "Charlie" stands for the letter C. What does your middle initial stand for?*
2. To advocate or support something: *I stand for freedom of the press.*
3. To tolerate something; put up with something: *We will not stand for rude behavior.*
4. To run in some election or for some elected office: *The incumbent stood for reelection.*

stand in for

To act as a substitute for someone or something, especially for an actor while the lights and camera are adjusted: *The understudy stood in for the lead performer.*

stand off

1. To stay at a distance; remain apart: *She stood off from the group. He stood off by himself.*
2. To maintain a course away from shore. Used of a ship or other vessel: *The ship stood off to sea.*
3. SPORTS To move backward so that one is farther away from some opponent: *The boxer stood off his opponent. The defender stood off the attacker, allowing her a shot on goal.*

stand on

1. To maintain an upright or vertical position on a base or support: *The vase of flowers stands on a pedestal.*
2. To be based on something; depend on something: *The success of the project stands on management's support of it.*

ă	pat	är	car	ī	bite	ô	paw	ŏŏ	took	ûr	urge
ā	pay	ĕ	pet	îr	pier	ôr	core	ŏŏr	lure	zh	vision
âr	care	ē	be	ŏ	pot	oi	boy	ōō	boot	ə	about,
ä	father	ĭ	pit	ō	toe	ou	out	ŭ	cut		item

3. To insist on the observance of something: *They stand on ceremony, so be on your best behavior.*

stand out

1. To be obvious, conspicuous, or prominent: *The moon stands out among the stars. The champion athletes stand out among their peers.*
2. To protrude; project: *The gargoyle stands out from the side of the building.*
3. To maintain a course away from shore. Used of a ship or other vessel: *The ship stood out to sea.*
4. **stand out against** To refuse compliance with or maintain opposition to someone or something: *They are standing out against the verdict.*

stand over

1. To stand adjacent to and look down on someone or something: *She stood over the chess board, contemplating her next move. He stood over the injured patients until help arrived.*
2. To rise above someone or something: *Big Ben stands over the Thames in London.*
3. To watch or supervise someone or something closely: *My boss is always standing over me.*
4. To postpone something: *We were tired of talking about the matter, so we stood it over until the following meeting.*

stand to

To take up positions for military action: *Upon hearing gunfire, the soldiers stood to.*

stand up

1. To rise to an upright position on the feet: *When the judge entered the room, everyone stood up.*
2. To cause something or someone to assume an upright position: *I stood up the book on its end. The police tried to stand the drunken drivers up on their feet.*
3. To remain valid, sound, or durable: *The claim will not stand up in court. Our old car has stood up well over time.*
4. To fail to keep a date or appointment with someone: *My roommate stood up the prospective students who had wanted to tour the campus. My blind date stood me up, so I had to eat alone.*
5. **stand up for** To defend or support someone or something: *If you do not stand up for yourself, people will not respect you. The candidate stood up for the rights of migrant workers.*
6. **stand up to** To confront someone or something fearlessly: *The citizens were too afraid to stand up to the cruel dictator.*
7. **stand up with** To act as best man, maid of honor, or matron of honor for some groom or bride at a wedding: *I stood up with my old college roommate when he got married. She stood up with her sister at the wedding.*

◆ **stare** (stâr)
stared (stârd), **staring** (stâr′ĭng), **stares** (stârz)

stare down

To intimidate someone or cause someone to submit by staring: *I was able to stare down the lion, and it turned and ran away. If your enemies try to stare you down, just smile back at them.*

◆ **start** (stärt)
started (stär′tĭd), **starting** (stär′tĭng), **starts** (stärts)

start at

1. To have some value as a minimum: *This line of new cars starts at $22,000.*
2. To begin some job at some initial salary: *I started at $8.00 per hour, but I get more now.*
3. To move suddenly or involuntarily: *The horses started at the loud noise.*

start back

To begin a return journey: *We had better start back soon or we won't get home before dark.*

start in

1. To begin something with determination: *She dumped the puzzle pieces on the table and started in. After she had prepared the appetizers, the chef started in on the main course.*
2. **start in on** To criticize someone harshly: *As soon as I walked in the door, my parents started in on me for being late.*

start off

1. To begin in a specified way: *The company started off with only two employees. Let's start off with an appetizer. The director of the play had started off as a stagehand 30 years ago.*
2. To begin a journey: *The climbers started off after breakfast.*

start on

1. To begin doing some project: *After dinner, I started on my homework.*
2. To cause someone to begin some diet, medication, or other corrective action taken or undertaken routinely: *The doctor started me on antibiotics.*

start out

1. To have something as an origin; to have begun in some original form or manner: *The owner started out working in the kitchen. Butterflies start out as caterpillars.*
2. To begin some activity or movement: *At sunrise, the hikers started out for the mountain.*

start over

1. To begin again: *After the waves wrecked my sandcastle, I started over on higher ground.*
2. To cause something to begin again: *We started the movie over when the last guest arrived.*

start up

To set something into motion, operation, or activity: *I started up the car and let the motor run for a few minutes. When did you start this company up?*

ă	pat	är	car	ī	bite	ô	paw	ŏŏ	took	ûr	urge
ā	pay	ĕ	pet	îr	pier	ôr	core	ŏŏr	lure	zh	vision
âr	care	ē	be	ŏ	pot	oi	boy	ōō	boot	ə	about, item
ä	father	ĭ	pit	ō	toe	ou	out	ŭ	cut		

◆ **starve** (stärv)

starved (stärvd), **starving** (stär′vĭng), **starves** (stärvz)

starve for

To cause someone or something to suffer from lack of something. Used in the passive: *The dog was starved for attention.*

starve of

To deprive someone or something of some resource, resulting in its depletion: *Doctors tried to destroy the cancerous cells by starving them of oxygen. The agency has been starved of money by people in Congress who oppose it.*

starve out

To force someone or something to surrender by depriving them of food, as in a siege: *The police starved out the criminals, who had refused to leave their apartment. If they refuse to surrender the garrison, we'll just starve them out.*

◆ **stave** (stāv)

staved (stāvd) *or* **stove** (stōv), **staving** (stā′vĭng), **staves** (stāvz)

stave in

To break or smash a hole in something: *The firefighters staved the door in. I staved in the barrel with an axe.*

stave off

To keep or hold someone or something off; repel someone or something: *I staved the attackers off with my umbrella. Health officials are trying to stave off an outbreak of disease.*

◆ **stay** (stā)

stayed (stād), **staying** (stā′ĭng), **stays** (stāz)

stay ahead

1. To remain in front of something, especially when moving: *The horse managed to stay ahead of the others. Our friends in the other car were following us, so we stayed ahead for the whole trip.*
2. To complete all or more than is required of some task in order to be prepared to face more work: *I try to stay ahead of my work. There is so much to do that it's very hard to stay ahead.*

stay away

1. To remain at a distance from something or someone, especially from a place where one should not be: *Stay away—my cold is contagious! I warned the children to stay away from the abandoned mine.*
2. **stay away from** To refrain from doing, using, or engaging in something: *My parents warned me to stay away from drugs.*

stay back

1. To refrain from approaching. Used chiefly as a command: *Stay back!—I've got a knife.*
2. To repeat a grade level in school: *The teacher suggested that our child stay back a year.*

stay behind

To remain in a place that others have left: *I stayed behind because I had too much work to do.*

stay in

To remain at home and refrain from taking part in social activities:

I stayed in last night and rented a movie.

stay off

1. To remain away from some surface or region: *Stay off the grass! The spectators must stay off of the playing field.*
2. To refrain from indulging in something unhealthy, such as food or drugs: *I'm trying to stay off fatty foods.*

stay on

1. To remain in a place as a visitor or resident: *After the convention in London finished, I stayed on for a few days to see the sights. He stayed on in Germany after the war.*
2. To continue working for an organization: *She resigned her position but stayed on as an adviser.*
3. To continue a course of study at a university: *I stayed on to get my PhD.*

stay out

1. To remain in an external place: *You'll catch my cold, so please stay out! Stay out of the cookie jar!*
2. To remain outside the home, taking part in social activities: *I stayed out much too late last night.*
3. **stay out of** To refrain from becoming involved in something: *Stay out of my life—it's none of your business who my friends are! My mother warned me to stay out of trouble.*

stay over

To spend the night: *The roads were icy, so we urged our guests to stay over. We stayed over in Denver and left the following morning.*

stay up

1. To remain awake: *I stayed up all night reading.*
2. To remain on display: *Their Christmas tree stayed up until February.*
3. To remain well informed: *They stay up on current trends by reading fashion magazines. I don't know how doctors stay up with all the new research.*

stay with

1. To remain next to or in attendance of someone or something: *Stay with the suitcases while I check the train schedule.*
2. To remain or sojourn as someone's guest or lodger: *I'm staying with my brother until I find an apartment.*
3. To adhere to some plan; keep at something: *I played piano for a couple of years, but I couldn't stay with it.*
4. To match some competitor or perceived competitor: *I tried to stay with the lead runner, but she was just too fast.*
5. To remain in one's thoughts or memory: *That poem has stayed with me since I first heard it.*

◆ **steal** (stēl)

stole (stōl), **stolen** (stō′lən), **stealing** (stē′lĭng), **steals** (stēlz)

ă	pat	är	car	ī	bite	ô	paw	o͝o	took	ûr	urge
ā	pay	ĕ	pet	îr	pier	ôr	core	o͝or	lure	zh	vision
âr	care	ē	be	ŏ	pot	oi	boy	o͞o	boot	ə	about,
ä	father	ĭ	pit	ō	toe	ou	out	ŭ	cut		item

steal away

To leave quietly without being noticed: *During the party, the lovers stole away to the garden.*

◆ **steam** (stēm)

steamed (stēmd), **steaming** (stē′mĭng), **steams** (stēmz)

steam up

1. To fill some area with steam: *The shower always steams up the mirror. The pot of boiling water is steaming the room up.*
2. To make someone very angry. Used chiefly in the passive: *I was really steamed up over the insult.*

◆ **steep** (stēp)

steeped (stēpt), **steeping** (stē′pĭng), **steeps** (stēps)

steep in

To expose someone or something to something else in order to imbue some quality: *The teacher steeped the students in classic literature. The university is steeped in tradition.*

◆ **stem** (stĕm)

stemmed (stĕmd), **stemming** (stĕm′ĭng), **stems** (stĕmz)

stem from

To have something as an origin or cause; have developed from something: *Most prejudice stems from fear.*

◆ **step** (stĕp)

stepped (stĕpt), **stepping** (stĕp′ĭng), **steps** (stĕps)

step aside

1. To take a step or to walk to the side so as to give way to another: *I stepped aside to let the jogger pass.*
2. To resign from a post, especially when being replaced: *The chairman of the board asked the executive to step aside for his appointed successor. At the end of her term, she stepped aside and allowed the new appointee to take over.*

step back

1. To move backward by taking one or more steps: *I stepped back from the edge of the cliff. The police officer told the crowd to step back.*
2. To withdraw from something, especially to consider it from a wider perspective: *Let's step back from the project for a moment and admire all that we have accomplished. Rather than arguing about every detail, they should step back and determine what is really important.*

step down

1. To descend with a step: *The speaker stepped down from the platform. The carpenter stepped down off the ladder.*
2. To resign from a high post: *The mayor stepped down after two years in office.*
3. To reduce, especially in stages: *The scientists stepped down the temperature in the chamber and repeated the test. The transformer steps the power down from 110 volts to 24 volts.*

step in

1. To enter into an activity or a situation: *A substitute stepped in for the injured player.*
2. To intervene: *The government stepped in to end the strike.*

step into

To intervene in some matter: *The arbitrator stepped into the dispute to resolve the differences between the union and management.*

step off

1. To take a step so that one is no longer on something: *The politician stepped off the plane and waved to the crowd.*
2. SLANG To leave someone or something alone. Used chiefly as a command: *Step off—I saw that clock first, and I'm going to buy it!*

step out

1. To go outside for a short time: *I stepped out for a cigarette. They stepped out of the meeting to discuss the proposal.*
2. To go out for a special evening of entertainment: *We're stepping out for a wild night on the town.*
3. To withdraw from something; quit something: *The candidate stepped out of the race. The player stepped out.*
4. **step out with** To date someone: *She is stepping out with a younger man.*

step up

1. To increase something, especially in stages: *The factory stepped up production to meet the growing demand. The runners stepped their pace up for the last two laps.*
2. To come forward: *When I call your name, please step up and be counted. The speaker stepped up to the podium and addressed the crowd.*
3. To improve one's performance or take on more responsibility, especially at a crucial time: *You need to step up and take responsibility for your actions. The player stepped up at a crucial moment and scored the winning point.*

◆ **stick** (stĭk)

stuck (stŭk), **sticking** (stĭk′ĭng), **sticks** (stĭks)

stick around

To remain or linger in some place: *I stuck around the lobby while my friend used a pay phone. We stuck around after the show to meet the band. They stuck around in the apartment until the delivery person arrived.*

stick by

1. To remain loyal or faithful to someone: *Her family stuck by her through hard times.*
2. To keep or maintain something: *He is sticking by his opinion despite the new evidence.*

ă	pat	är	car	ī	bite	ô	paw	o͝o	took	ûr	urge
ā	pay	ĕ	pet	îr	pier	ôr	core	o͝or	lure	zh	vision
âr	care	ē	be	ŏ	pot	oi	boy	o͞o	boot	ə	about,
ä	father	ĭ	pit	ō	toe	ou	out	ŭ	cut		item

stick on

1. To be very fond of someone. Used in the passive: *The doctor is stuck on the new medical intern.*
2. To be dedicated or committed to some plan or idea. Used in the passive: *My boss is stuck on the idea, despite its obvious drawbacks.*

stick out

1. To project or protrude: *The tag is sticking out of your shirt. A flagpole stuck out from the front of the house.*
2. To cause something to project or protrude: *The child stuck out her hand for candy. He stuck his tongue out at me.*
3. To be prominent; be conspicuous: *Do you think a pink suit will stick out too much? This essay stuck out from the other submissions.*
4. To endure something: *We stuck out two years without electricity or running water. There was only one month left of school, so I stuck it out and transferred the following year.*
5. **stick out for** To resist capitulating in negotiations so as to achieve some more favorable terms: *The striking workers stuck out for better wages.*

stick to

1. To tend to remain in contact with and attached to something: *Peanut butter sticks to the top of your mouth.*
2. To adhere to some plan and not deviate from it: *The writer stuck to her original idea when her friends made other suggestions. We stuck to the main roads and avoided any dark alleys. You should stick to doing what you know best.*

stick together

1. To join or put someone or something together with or as if with an adhesive material: *I stuck the pieces together with glue. The hotel stuck us all together in one room.*
2. To become or remain attached or in close association by or as if by adhesion: *Two dollar bills stuck together, and I accidently counted them as one. Let's stick together so we don't get lost in the crowd.*

stick up

1. To project or protrude upwards: *When I woke up this morning my hair was sticking up.*
2. To cause something to project or protrude upwards: *The mayor stuck up her hands and waved to the crowd. Stick 'em up—this is a robbery!*
3. To rob someone or something, especially at gunpoint: *A robber stuck up the bank and stole thousands of dollars. Two people with shotguns walked into the store and stuck it up.*
4. To post something with or as if with an adhesive: *They stuck up posters all around the neighborhood. I stuck the photos up on my website.*
5. **stick up for** To defend or support someone or something: *I stuck up for my little brother whenever the other kids teased him. You should stick up for yourself and not let people spread rumors about you.*

stick with

1. To stay with or remain loyal to someone or something: *Stick with*

the person who has the map so you don't get lost. My friends stuck with me through the entire ordeal.

2. To remain consistent or loyal in one's behavior concerning something: *He offered to loan me a chain saw, but I stuck with my ax.*
3. To adhere to some plan; keep at something: *The pianist stuck with the song until she had mastered it.*
4. To remain in someone's thoughts or memory: *That poem stuck with her, and she used it in a speech years later.*
5. To give someone something or someone that is unwanted: *My friends left the bar and stuck me with the bill. The dealer stuck us with shoddy merchandise that we can't sell. Our team got stuck with the worst player in the entire school.*

◆ **sting** (stĭng)

stung (stŭng), **stinging** (stĭng′ĭng), **stings** (stĭngz)

sting for

To charge someone some surprisingly large amount of money: *The airline stung us for $100 to change our ticket.*

◆ **stink** (stĭngk)

stank (stăngk) *or* **stunk** (stŭngk), **stunk** (stŭngk), **stinking** (stĭng′kĭng), **stinks** (stĭngks)

stink up

1. To cause something to have a strong foul odor: *The garbage is stinking up the kitchen. Keep your shoes on so you don't stink the car up with your smelly feet!*
2. To perform very poorly in some place: *The movie is stinking up theaters across the US. That band really stunk the joint up last night.*

◆ **stir** (stûr)

stirred (stûrd), **stirring** (stûr′ĭng), **stirs** (stûrz)

stir in

To introduce something, such as an ingredient, into a liquid or mixture while stirring: *The fruit punch tasted a bit bland, so I stirred in a cup of grape juice. Once the sauce is simmering, stir some parsley in.*

stir up

1. To mix something before cooking or use: *You must stir up the concrete thoroughly before you start paving the path. I poured the batter into a bowl and stirred it up vigorously.*
2. To churn or agitate something into a state of turbulence: *The storm stirred up the normally placid lake. The wind stirs the leaves up.*
3. To cause something to form by churning or agitating: *The truck zoomed off, stirring a cloud of dust up behind it. I stirred up a batch of concrete in the mixer and got to work paving the driveway.*

ă	pat	är	car	ī	bite	ô	paw	o͝o	took	ûr	urge
ā	pay	ĕ	pet	îr	pier	ôr	core	o͝or	lure	zh	vision
âr	care	ē	be	ŏ	pot	oi	boy	o͞o	boot	ə	about, item
ä	father	ĭ	pit	ō	toe	ou	out	ŭ	cut		

4. To rouse the emotions of someone or something; excite someone or something: *The protesters hope to stir up the public through this demonstration. The teacher stirred the students up when she threatened to give them more work.*
5. To summon some collective emotion or sentiment by exciting a group of people: *The court's verdict was certain to stir up controversy. The tourism board is trying to stir up interest in the city.*
6. To evoke some mental image or remembrance: *That old picture stirs up many memories for me.*

◆ **stitch** (stĭch)

stitched (stĭcht), **stitching** (stĭch′ĭng), **stiches** (stĭch′ĭz)

stitch up

1. To mend or repair something with or as if with stitches: *The tailor stitched up the rip in the jacket. The cut over my eye was deep, but the doctor stitched it up in a matter of minutes.*
2. To reach some official agreement: *I've stitched up a deal with my mechanic so that I pay only for parts and not labor. The agreement was easy to make; we stitched it up in a day.*

◆ **stock** (stŏk)

stocked (stŏkt), **stocking** (stŏk′ĭng), **stocks** (stŏks)

stock up

1. To provide or furnish something with supplies: *The bartender stocked up the bar with vodka. We stocked the house up with emergency supplies.*
2. **stock up on** To gather and store a supply of something: *We stocked up on canned goods before the storm came.*

◆ **stoke** (stōk)

stoked (stōkt), **stoking** (stō′kĭng), **stokes** (stōks)

stoke up

1. To feed or stir some fire or furnace: *Lee had to go down to the basement several times to stoke up the furnace. The fire started going out, so I stoked it up with some logs.*
2. To make some emotion or conflict more violent; intensify something: *The accusations stoked up the tension that already existed between the groups. The argument was winding down when your insensitive comments stoked it up again.*
3. To eat heartily: *The boxer stoked up before the fight in order to maintain his strength. The runner stoked up on carbohydrates the day before the race.*

◆ **stoop** (sto͞op)

stooped (sto͞opt), **stooping** (sto͞o′pĭng), **stoops** (sto͞ops)

stoop to

To do something degrading or reprehensible to achieve one's ends: *It's a shame that the museum has to stoop to cheap gimmicks in order to attract visitors.*

◆ **stop** (stŏp)

stopped (stŏpt), **stopping** (stŏp′ĭng), **stops** (stŏps)

stop by

To interrupt one's course or journey briefly in order to visit or do business somewhere: *I stopped by my friend's house on the way home from work. On our way to the party, we need to stop by the store and get a gift. Why don't you stop by sometime for lunch?*

stop down

To reduce the aperture of some lens: *The photographer stopped the lens down in order to increase the picture's depth of field. If your photograph is too bright, you should stop down the aperture.*

stop in

To interrupt one's course or journey briefly in order to visit or do business somewhere: *The next time you're nearby, stop in for dinner. I stopped in at the office on my way to the airport.*

stop off

To interrupt one's course or journey briefly in order to visit or do business somewhere: *I stopped off at the gas station on my way home. We stopped off in San Francisco for a night before continuing on to Honolulu.*

stop out

1. To come to a stop on a racetrack, typically due to a mechanical malfunction. Used of a racecar or racecar driver: *The car stopped out on the track. I was leading the race until I suddenly stopped out halfway through the second lap.*
2. To sell a stock automatically when it reaches a specified price; execute someone's stop order. Used chiefly in the passive: *We were stopped out of the stock at $92.06 for a considerable gain.*
3. **stop out of** To withdraw temporarily from some institution of learning: *My adviser recommended that I stop out of college for a semester to travel a bit.*

stop over

To interrupt one's course or journey briefly somewhere: *We stopped over in Athens for a few days on our way to India.*

stop up

1. To obstruct some passageway: *The fallen leaves stopped up the drainpipe. This nagging cold has stopped my sinuses up.*
2. To cause something to become obstructed: *The reason the engine malfunctioned was that some mud had stopped up its vents. My sloppy roommate stopped the sink up with leftover food.*
3. To become obstructed: *Call the plumber; the sink stopped up again.*
4. To become constipated: *I had stopped up, so I took some laxatives.*

◆ **store** (stôr)

stored (stôrd), **storing** (stôr′ĭng), **stores** (stôrz)

ă	pat	är	car	ī	bite	ô	paw	o͝o	took	ûr	urge
ā	pay	ĕ	pet	îr	pier	ôr	core	o͝or	lure	zh	vision
âr	care	ē	be	ŏ	pot	oi	boy	o͞o	boot	ə	about, item
ä	father	ĭ	pit	ō	toe	ou	out	ŭ	cut		

store away

To put away or reserve something for future use: *We ate one cookie each and stored away the rest for the next day. Don't carry those important documents with you; you should store them away in a safe place.*

store up

To accumulate and maintain a supply of something for future use: *I recharged my phone battery to allow it to store up power for the long trip. Ants gather food all summer and store it up for the winter.*

◆ **stow** (stō)

stowed (stōd), **stowing** (stō′ĭng), **stows** (stōz)

stow away

1. To put something away or store something, especially to keep a place uncluttered or in order: *The platoon leader ordered the soldiers to stow away their sleeping bags and secure the campsite. My lawyer has stowed those papers away in a drawer somewhere.*
2. To hide aboard a conveyance in order to obtain free transportation: *Unable to afford tickets, the youths stowed away on a tanker.*
3. To consume some food or drink greedily: *For someone so tiny, you certainly stow away a lot of food! You must have liked that pork; you certainly stowed it away.*

◆ **straighten** (strāt′n)

straightened (strāt′nd), **straightening** (strāt′n-ĭng), **straightens** (strāt′nz)

straighten out

1. To extend or smooth something until straight: *The reception on my radio was poor, so I straightened out the antenna. I think my arm is broken; I can't straighten it out.*
2. To resolve some confusion or conflict: *We had to share a room until the hotel could straighten out the mix-up with our bookings. There was confusion among the athletes about the order of the races, so the coach came and straightened it out.*
3. To make someone conform to a certain viewpoint or set of principles: *We need better rehabilitation programs to straighten out these criminals. If your behavior doesn't improve, we'll have to send you to military school to straighten you out.*

straighten up

1. To stand erect: *The drill sergeant ordered the recruits to straighten up when they started slouching in formation.*
2. To put someone or something in order: *I straightened up my bookshelves. The room was starting to look like a disaster zone, so we had to straighten it up. I hired a housekeeper to straighten up around the house once a week. We need to straighten up before your parents arrive.*
3. To begin behaving properly: *The principal cautioned the students to straighten up or face suspension.*

◆ **strain** (strān)

strained (strānd), **straining** (strā′nĭng), **strains** (strānz)

strain at

To pull or push on something, trying to make it yield or give way: *The dog barked viciously and strained at its leash. The angry crowd strained at the barriers.*

strain off

To separate some liquid from a solid by filtration: *After boiling the rice, I strained off the excess water in the pot. The chemist strained the water off from the top of the solution in the beaker.*

strain out

To separate some solid from a liquid by filtration: *The cook strained out the noodles from the broth. There was some sediment in the concoction, but the chemist strained it out.*

◆ **strap** (străp)

strapped (străpt), **strapping** (străp′ĭng), **straps** (străps)

strap in

1. To secure someone or something with a strap, especially a seat belt: *Be sure to strap in the children before the car starts moving. We loaded the baggage onto the truck and strapped it in with a cord.*
2. To secure oneself with a strap, especially a seat belt: *The pilot climbed into the cockpit and strapped in.*

◆ **stress** (strĕs)

stressed (strĕst), **stressing** (strĕs′ĭng), **stresses** (strĕs′ĭz)

stress out

SLANG

1. To subject something to extreme stress, as from working too much: *The tight deadlines are stressing out everybody in the office. I might not be cut out for this job; the demanding schedule stresses me out. Don't stress yourself out trying to finish the project; I'll take care of it.*
2. To undergo extreme stress, as from working too much: *You're always stressing out about things that can't be changed.*

◆ **stretch** (strĕch)

stretched (strĕcht), **stretching** (strĕch′ĭng), **stretches** (strĕch′ĭz)

stretch out

1. To lengthen, widen, or distend something: *The shoulders of the old coat were stretched out of shape. Don't put your big feet in my shoes or you'll stretch them out!*
2. To become lengthened, widened, or distended: *The sweater stretched out because it was hung on a hanger.*
3. To reach or put something forth; extend something: *The firefighters stretched out their hands to pull the child out of the well. Your elbow is probably not broken if you can stretch your arm out like that.*
4. To extend oneself when lying down: *Feel free to stretch yourself out on the couch. I had just*

ă	pat	är	car	ī	bite	ô	paw	o͝o	took	ûr	urge
ā	pay	ĕ	pet	îr	pier	ôr	core	o͝or	lure	zh	vision
âr	care	ē	be	ŏ	pot	oi	boy	o͞o	boot	ə	about,
ä	father	ĭ	pit	ō	toe	ou	out	ŭ	cut		item

stretched out on the sofa when the doorbell rang.

5. To lie down at full length: *The cat stretched out on the bed.*
6. To prolong: *I was supposed to be back at work yesterday, but I decided to stretch out my vacation. The film was too short, so the director added new scenes to stretch it out to 90 minutes.*

◆ **strew** (stro͞o)

strewed (stro͞od), **strewn** (stro͞on) *or* **strewed** (stro͞od), **strewing** (stro͞o′ĭng), **strews** (stro͞oz)

strew with

To cover some area or a surface with something scattered or sprinkled: *The baker strewed the top of the cake with chopped nuts. The aisle of the church was strewn with rose petals.*

◆ **strike** (strīk)

struck (strŭk), **struck** *or* **stricken** (strĭk′ən), **striking** (strī′kĭng), **strikes** (strīks)

strike back

To deliver a return attack; counterattack: *The rebels struck back at the government forces.*

strike down

1. To cause someone or something to fall by a blow: *Boxing experts are predicting that the champion will strike down the contender in the third round. I grabbed a wrench and struck the intruder down with a blow to the head.*
2. To incapacitate or kill someone. Used chiefly in the passive: *Hundreds of civilians were struck down during the first week of the war. Smokers need to realize that heart disease can strike them down in the prime of their lives.*
3. To render something ineffective; cancel something: *The committee struck down the proposal we've worked so hard on, so we'll have to start all over again. The Supreme Court determined that the law was unconstitutional and struck it down accordingly.*

strike into

1. To thrust something, such as a weapon, into someone or something: *The knight struck the sword into the dragon.*
2. To cause some strong emotion to penetrate someone or something deeply: *The noise struck terror into their hearts.*

strike off

To start a journey or proceed in a new direction: *The hikers struck off into the forest.*

strike on *or* **strike upon**

To discover something suddenly or unexpectedly: *In the course of their research, the scientists struck on an entirely new approach. The detective struck upon a clue.*

strike out

1. To begin a course of action: *After hatching, the baby turtles struck out toward the ocean. After the band broke up, the lead singer struck out on her own. We struck out on a mission to find the lost treasure.*
2. To make an attempt to hit someone: *The suspect struck out at the police officer.*

3. BASEBALL To pitch three strikes to some batter, putting the batter out: *The pitcher struck out the batter to end the inning. The pitcher struck the batter out with two curve balls and a fastball.*
4. BASEBALL To be put out at bat with three strikes: *The batter struck out and returned to the dugout.*
5. To fail in an endeavor: *They struck out in their attempt to raise taxes. The network struck out with its new television show and canceled it after the third week. The car salesman struck out with his first five customers.*
6. To eliminate or delete something from a document or record: *The editor struck out the final paragraph and rewrote it. The lawyer struck a clause out of the contract.*
7. To put some claim or action out of a court of law without further hearing: *The court struck out the claim when the plaintiff failed to produce enough evidence. The judge found the accusation unclear, so she struck it out.*

strike up

1. To initiate or begin some conversation or relationship: *They often see each other on the bus, but neither of them ever strikes up a conversation. My best friend and I struck it up while working together in the Peace Corps.*
2. To reach some agreement: *You might be able to get a discount if you strike up a deal with the storekeeper.*
3. To start to play or sing something: *A few of the musicians struck up a waltz. Everybody got up to dance once the band struck up.*
4. To cause something to start to play or sing: *Strike up the orchestra and let the celebration begin!*

strike with

1. To afflict someone or something suddenly with some disease or impairment. Used chiefly in the passive: *That doctor treats patients who are stricken with cancer.*
2. To cause someone to be overcome with some emotion. Used chiefly in the passive: *She was struck with alarm at the news. The sight of the ghost struck him with terror.*

◆ **string** (strĭng)
strung (strŭng), **stringing** (strĭng′ĭng), **strings** (strĭngz)

string along

1. To keep someone waiting or in a state of uncertainty: *The company strung along the job candidate for two weeks before hiring someone else. After I proposed, my girlfriend strung me along for a month before rejecting me.*
2. To fool, cheat, or deceive someone: *I am worried that they have no intentions of buying the house at all, but are just stringing us along. The con artist strung along the tourists for an hour before they caught on.*
3. To agree; go along: *They strung along with the plan despite its obvious flaws.*

ă	pat	är	car	ī	bite	ô	paw	o͝o	took	ûr	urge
ā	pay	ĕ	pet	îr	pier	ôr	core	o͝or	lure	zh	vision
âr	care	ē	be	ŏ	pot	oi	boy	o͞o	boot	ə	about, item
ä	father	ĭ	pit	ō	toe	ou	out	ŭ	cut		

string out

1. To make something longer than usual or necessary; prolong something: *The prosecution strung out the trial hoping to get the time to gather more evidence. We've already said everything that needs to be said in this conversation, so why do you keep trying to string it out?*
2. To spread out in a line. Used in the passive: *From the plane, we could see small villages that were strung out along the coast.*
3. Slang To become intoxicated, especially with an addictive opiate or stimulant. Used in the passive: *He was so strung out that he couldn't talk. People started to suspect that the athlete was strung out on coke or booze, or both.*

string together

1. To arrange something in a string or series: *This sentence makes no sense—you've just strung a bunch of words together at random! They worked all night stringing the flowers together to make those garlands.*
2. To produce something by arranging in a string or series: *I was able to string together a flimsy excuse for my chronic lateness. How do you expect to be a successful lawyer when you can barely string an argument together?*

string up

1. To hang something by a string: *All of the neighbors on my street string up the flag in their front yards. The Christmas lights look great—how long did it take to string them up?*
2. To equip something with a string: *They strung up their fishing rods and headed to the lake to catch some trout. I just bought my first guitar, but I don't know how to string it up or tune it. The band couldn't start the set on time because the fiddle player needed a few minutes to string up.*
3. To kill someone by hanging: *Do you know what we do to traitors here?—We string them up! The accused murderer was strung up without a fair trial.*

◆ **strip** (strĭp)
stripped (strĭpt), **stripping** (strĭp′ĭng), **strips** (strĭps)

strip away

1. To remove some covering or layer: *Most bullies are really cowards once you strip away their tough façade. We hated the wood paneling on the walls so much that we stripped it away and painted the whole room.*
2. To take some rights or privileges away: *The state strips away felons' right to vote. I had power of attorney over the property until the court stripped it away.*

strip down

1. To reduce something to essential or minimal features: *The director decided to strip down the production in order to reduce costs. If you strip them down to their bare essentials, most religions really believe the same things.*
2. To remove one's clothing: *I stripped down and stepped into the shower.*
3. **strip down to** To remove layers of one's clothing until only some

clothing remains: *The models stripped down to their underwear for the photo shoot.*

4. To remove someone's clothing: *The babysitter stripped down the kids and drew the bath water. Airport security guards are authorized to detain suspicious individuals and strip them down for searching.*
5. **strip down to** To remove layers of someone's clothing until only some clothing remains: *I stripped the children down to their swimsuits so they could play in the water.*

strip of

1. To deprive someone or something of some covering or ornament: *The tornado stripped the tree of its leaves. The manuscript was stripped of its academic jargon.*
2. To deprive someone of some honor, rank, office, privilege, or possession: *Losing my job and my house stripped me of my dignity. The officers were court-martialed and stripped of their ranks.*

strip off

1. To remove some clothing or outer layer: *When the students got to the beach, they stripped off their uniforms and headed for the water. I stripped the blankets off the bed.*
2. To remove some exterior coating, as of paint or varnish: *I bought a strong cleanser to strip off the grime from the stove. You'll have to strip the old paint off before you repaint that wall.*

strip out

1. To remove the interior of something, such as a building; gut something: *The new owners plan to strip out the building to expose the original red brick walls and concrete ceilings. This old car can run like new if you strip it out and refit it with a new engine and suspension.*
2. To remove some component from a system, such as from a building, text, or calculation: *The electricians stripped out the old wiring. The contract lawyers stripped out all references to royalties. The electricians stripped the old wiring out and installed a new network.*

◆ **strut** (strŭt)

strutted (strŭt′ĭd), **strutting** (strŭt′ĭng), **struts** (strŭts)

strut out

To display something in order to impress others: *Don't strut out your resume until you have more accomplishments to list. I couldn't wait to put on my new suit and strut it out at work.*

◆ **stub** (stŭb)

stubbed (stŭbd), **stubbing** (stŭb′ĭng), **stubs** (stŭbz)

stub out

To extinguish some cigarette, cigar, or similar smoking material by stamping the burning end against a surface: *There were no ashtrays around, so I stubbed out the ciga-*

ă	pat	är	car	ī	bite	ô	paw	o͝o	took	ûr	urge
ā	pay	ĕ	pet	îr	pier	ôr	core	o͝or	lure	zh	vision
âr	care	ē	be	ŏ	pot	oi	boy	o͞o	boot	ə	about, item
ä	father	ĭ	pit	ō	toe	ou	out	ŭ	cut		

rette on the heel of my shoe. If you had told me the smoke from my cigar was bothering you, I would have stubbed it out.

◆ **stuff** (stŭf)
stuffed (stŭft), **stuffing** (stŭf′ĭng), **stuffs** (stŭfs)

stuff up

1. To pack or fill something completely with a large quantity of something: *I can't eat any more—that big meal stuffed me up. We stuffed up the closet with all our old magazines.*
2. To cause someone's sinus or nasal passages to be clogged: *The flu really stuffed me up. I was stuffed up with a bad cold.*
3. To be clogged. Used especially of sinus and nasal passages: *My nose stuffs up whenever I catch a cold.*

◆ **stumble** (stŭm′bəl)
stumbled (stŭm′bəld), **stumbling** (stŭm′blĭng), **stumbles** (stŭm′bəlz)

stumble across

To come upon someone or something accidentally or unexpectedly: *I had given up finding my keys when I stumbled across them lying under the dresser. On my way to work this morning, I stumbled across an old friend I hadn't seen in years.*

stumble on *or* **stumble upon**

1. To trip and almost fall on account of hitting the foot or stepping on something: *He stumbled on the curb and fell. She stumbled upon a tree root.*
2. To come upon something accidentally or unexpectedly: *I happened to stumble on my jacket when I wasn't even looking for it. The detective stumbled upon the truth while thinking about something else.*

◆ **stump** (stŭmp)
stumped (stŭmpt), **stumping** (stŭm′pĭng), **stumps** (stŭmps)

stump up

1. To provide some funds or capital: *An investor stumped up the money to expand the business.*
2. To pay some amount of money, often reluctantly: *We had to stump up $30 just to get inside.*

◆ **subject** (səb-jĕkt′)
subjected (səb-jĕk′tĭd), **subjecting** (səb-jĕk′tĭng), **subjects** (səb-jĕkts′)

subject to

To cause someone to undergo or experience something: *The commander subjected the troops to daily inspections. The oil platform was subjected to extreme weather.*

◆ **submit** (səb-mĭt′)
submitted (səb-mĭt′ĭd), **submitting** (səb-mĭt′ĭng), **submits** (səb-mĭts′)

submit to

1. To give in to some authority, power, or desire of another: *The children are at a rebellious age and refuse to submit to the wishes of their parents.*
2. To allow oneself to be subjected to something: *The pledges submitted to the humiliation of the fraternity's hazing rituals.*

◆ **subscribe** (səb-skrīb′)
subscribed (səb-skrībd′), **subscribing** (səb-skrī′bĭng), **subscribes** (səb-skrībz′)

subscribe to

1. To have some periodical delivered or made available on a regular basis: *Since you're building a lot of furniture, you should subscribe to the new woodworking magazine that comes out every month. I subscribe to an Internet news site.*
2. To feel or express hearty approval for something: *Corporal punishment is not an idea I personally subscribe to, but I can see how others might approve of it.*

◆ **subsist** (səb-sĭst′)

subsisted (səb-sĭs′tĭd), **subsisting** (səb-sĭs′tĭng), **subsists** (səb-sĭsts′)

subsist on

To survive by using something as a source of food: *The people of the war-torn region subsisted on bread, water, and cheese for several months.*

◆ **succeed** (sək-sēd′)

succeeded (sək-sē′dĭd), **succeeding** (sək-sē′dĭng), **succeeds** (sək-sēdz′)

succeed in

To accomplish something desired or intended: *I'm sure you will succeed in your new project. They succeeded in convincing the jury of their innocence.*

succeed to

To replace another in some office or position: *The princess succeeded to the throne after her father's death and became queen.*

◆ **suck** (sŭk)

sucked (sŭkt), **sucking** (sŭk′ĭng), **sucks** (sŭks)

suck in

1. To draw or pull something in by or as if by suction: *The pump occasionally sucks in dirt. The filter sucks air in through a vent. I sucked in my stomach so I would look thinner.*
2. To take advantage of someone; cheat or swindle someone: *The greedy lawyer sucked us in with false promises. This scam sucks in many unsuspecting tourists.*

suck off

Vulgar Slang

To perform fellatio on someone.

suck up

1. To draw or pull something in by or as if by suction: *I sucked up the soda through a straw. There was a lot of dirt on the floor, but the vacuum cleaner sucked it up quickly.*
2. Slang To suppress some pain or emotion: *I thought that job was beneath me, but I really needed the money, so I sucked up my pride and accepted it. I know the pain you're feeling is intense, but you have to suck it up until we get to the hospital!*
3. Slang **suck up to** To behave obsequiously; fawn: *I was unable to ask any good questions in class without my peers saying that I was sucking up to the teacher.*

ă	pat	är	car	ī	bite	ô	paw	o͝o	took	ûr	urge
ā	pay	ĕ	pet	îr	pier	ôr	core	o͝or	lure	zh	vision
âr	care	ē	be	ŏ	pot	oi	boy	o͞o	boot	ə	about,
ä	father	ĭ	pit	ō	toe	ou	out	ŭ	cut		item

◆ **sucker** (sŭk′ər)

suckered (sŭk′ərd), **suckering** (sŭk′ə-rĭng), **suckers** (sŭk′ərz)

sucker into

To cause someone to do or believe something by deceptive or fraudulent means: *The con artist tried to sucker me into revealing my credit card number.*

◆ **sue** (so͞o)

sued (so͞od), **suing** (so͞o′ĭng), **sues** (so͞oz)

sue for

1. To institute legal proceedings against some person for some redress of grievances: *The actor is suing a former TV star for $30 million. Their aunt and uncle sued for custody of the children.*
2. To make an appeal or entreaty for something: *The people of this country are suing for peace.*

◆ **suffer** (sŭf′ər)

suffered (sŭf′ərd), **suffering** (sŭf′ə-rĭng), **suffers** (sŭf′ərz)

suffer from

To be sick with or afflicted by some condition: *I suffer from many different allergies. The country is suffering from a drought.*

◆ **sugar** (sho͝og′ər)

sugared (sho͝og′ərd), **sugaring** (sho͝og′ə-rĭng), **sugars** (sho͝og′ərz)

sugar off

To make maple syrup or maple sugar by boiling maple sap: *The farmer had gathered all the sap, and it was now time to sugar off.*

◆ **suit** (so͞ot)

suited (so͞o′tĭd), **suiting** (so͞o′tĭng), **suits** (so͞ots)

suit to

To make someone or something appropriate or suitable for something; adapt someone or something to something: *We started with the basic recipe, and suited it to our own tastes. The camel is suited to its environment.*

suit up

1. To put on clothing designed for a special activity: *We suited up in our riding clothes.*
2. To dress someone in clothing designed for a special activity: *We suited up the children in their Halloween costumes. The soldiers were suited up for night patrol.*

◆ **sum** (sŭm)

summed (sŭmd), **summing** (sŭm′ĭng), **sums** (sŭmz)

sum up

1. To present the substance of something in a condensed form; summarize something: *At the end of the radio program, they sum up the day's news. Here's what I learned—I'll sum it up for you. At the end of the lecture, the professor summed up.*
2. To describe or assess something concisely: *This poem sums up my feelings perfectly.*
3. To add some set of numbers together: *The teacher challenged the students to sum up the numbers from 1 to 100 as fast as possible. I wrote down all of our expenses for the week and summed them up.*

4. To calculate something, especially by addition: *We need to sum up our total costs for this trip. I'm sure this answer is correct—I summed it up myself.*

◆ **summon** (sŭm′ən)

summoned (sŭm′ənd), **summoning** (sŭm′ə-nĭng), **summons** (sŭm′ənz)

summon up

To call something forth; evoke something: *I summoned up my courage and dove into the deep water. At first I couldn't remember the telephone number, but I summoned it up by concentrating very hard.*

◆ **surrender** (sə-rĕn′dər)

surrendered (sə-rĕn′dərd), **surrendering** (sə-rĕn′də-rĭng), **surrenders** (sə-rĕn′dərz)

surrender to

1. To relinquish possession or control of something to someone or something because of demand or compulsion: *The commander surrendered the valley to the opposing forces.*
2. To submit to the control or authority of someone or something: *The army surrendered to the enemy after they lost the key battle. I hope the suspect surrenders to the police soon.*
3. To give over or resign oneself, as to an emotion. Used reflexively: *When I lost my parents, I surrendered myself to grief.*

◆ **suss** (sŭs)

sussed (sŭst), **sussing** (sŭs′ĭng), **susses** (sŭs′ĭz)

suss out

SLANG

1. To infer or discover something; figure something out: *The spy sussed out our plans before we began. I don't know his intentions, but I plan to suss them out.*
2. To study and evaluate someone; size someone up: *They sussed me out and decided I was trustworthy. She's good at sussing out people who apply for the job.*

◆ **swab** (swŏb)

swabbed (swŏbd), **swabbing** (swŏb′ĭng), **swabs** (swŏbz)

swab down

To clean a surface with a swab: *The sailor swabbed down the deck. If the table is dirty, swab it down with lots of soap.*

swab out

To clean the inside of something with a swab: *I used this cloth to swab out the rifles. The doctor swabbed my ear out.*

◆ **swap** (swŏp)

swapped (swŏpt), **swapping** (swŏp′ĭng), **swaps** (swŏps)

swap around

1. To exchange some set of things, moving each into the position of another: *I swapped the screws*

ă	pat	är	car	ī	bite	ô	paw	o͝o	took	ûr	urge
ā	pay	ĕ	pet	îr	pier	ôr	core	o͝or	lure	zh	vision
âr	care	ē	be	ŏ	pot	oi	boy	o͞o	boot	ə	about,
ä	father	ĭ	pit	ō	toe	ou	out	ŭ	cut		item

around in the holes until I had them all in the right places. We bought several books from the bookstore and swapped them around between us.

2. To trade places: *We each wanted to sit on the other side of the table, so we swapped around. I asked the man sitting in the window seat if he would swap around with me so I could see the ocean.*

swap out

To remove something and replace or exchange it: *The program swapped out the contents of memory to make space for more data. I swapped the memory card out for a newer one.*

swap over

1. To exchange a part with some similar part: *She swapped the flashlight's batteries over to see if the bulb had burned out. He swapped over the memory card for a new one.*
2. CHIEFLY BRITISH To exchange positions or functions: *When we reach London, let's swap over; you drive and I'll read the map.*

◆ **swarm** (swârm)

swarmed (swârmd), **swarming** (swâr′mĭng), **swarms** (swârmz)

swarm with

To be full of some things or some people; abound or teem with some things or some people: *The rotten log swarmed with insects. The courtroom is swarming with reporters.*

◆ **swathe** (swŏ*th*, swā*th*)

swathed (swŏ*th*d, swā*th*d), **swathing** (swŏ*th*′ĭng, swā′*th*ĭng), **swathes** (swŏ*th*z, swā*th*z)

swathe in

To wrap or bind with or as if with some bandages: *The doctor swathed the patient's arm in gauze.*

◆ **swear** (swâr)

swore (swôr), **sworn** (swôrn), **swearing** (swâr′ĭng), **swears** (swârz)

swear at

To use abusive, violent, or blasphemous language against someone or something; curse someone or something: *The child swore at the teacher and was sent to the principal's office.*

swear by

1. To have great reliance on or confidence in someone or something: *He swears by his personal physician. She swears by the new computer program.*
2. To have reliable knowledge of something; be sure of something: *I think that's the person who stole my purse, but I couldn't swear by it.*
3. To take an oath by something: *I swore by all the angels and saints of heaven that I wouldn't reveal the secret to anyone.*

swear in

To administer a legal or official oath to someone: *The police department swore in 15 new officers. The Chief Justice will swear the new President in.*

swear off

To pledge to renounce or give up something: *I have sworn off cigarettes and alcohol.*

swear out

To obtain some warrant for arrest by making a charge under oath: *The victims swore out a warrant against their attacker.*

swear to

To utter or bind someone to some oath: *She swore her friends to secrecy before telling them what happened. The man wanted to confess, but he was sworn to silence.*

◆ **sweat** (swĕt)

sweated (swĕt′ĭd) *or* **sweat** (swĕt), **sweating** (swĕt′ĭng), **sweats** (swĕts)

sweat off

1. To cause something to be washed off the skin by sweating: *The actor sweated off his makeup while acting under the hot lights. The children had sweated the sunscreen lotion off, so I made them reapply it.*
2. To shed some weight by sweating: *I fell asleep in the sauna, and I feel like I sweated off five pounds. Eat dessert tonight, and then sweat it off at the gym tomorrow.*

sweat out

SLANG

1. To endure something anxiously: *I sweated out a three-hour history exam. We sweated the week out, wondering if the police would find us.*
2. To await something anxiously: *I've been sweating out my final grades all week. The patient was sweating the test results out in the waiting room.*
3. To purge the body of some liquid by sweating: *I just sweated all the water out that I drank today. They are in the sauna trying to sweat out the booze.*

◆ **sweep** (swēp)

swept (swĕpt), **sweeping** (swē′pĭng), **sweeps** (swēps)

sweep along

To cause someone or something to be carried along by or as if by a current: *The current swept the raft along. Most of the debris was swept along by the river.*

sweep aside

1. To displace someone or something from consideration, contention, or relevance: *Our team continues to sweep aside all competition as we head toward the finals. You can get things done in this city if you have enough money to sweep the law aside.*
2. To refuse to accept or recognize something; reject something: *The chief financial officer swept aside allegations of fraud. I considered the thought of quitting my job for a moment, but I quickly swept it aside.*

ă	pat	är	car	ī	bite	ô	paw	ŏŏ	took	ûr	urge
ā	pay	ĕ	pet	îr	pier	ôr	core	ŏŏr	lure	zh	vision
âr	care	ē	be	ŏ	pot	oi	boy	ōō	boot	ə	about,
ä	father	ĭ	pit	ō	toe	ou	out	ŭ	cut		item

sweep away

1. To cause someone or something to be carried away by or as if by a current: *The storm swept away the dock. The tornado swept the barn away. I was so swept away by the music that I forgot where I was for a moment.*
2. To eliminate something all at once: *The accident swept away all my dreams. When the school rejected my admissions application, I felt like they had swept all my hard work away in a matter of seconds.*

sweep into

1. To cause something or someone to reach some position decisively or swiftly: *The torrential rains swept the houses into the valley below. Their strong campaign swept the candidate into office.*
2. To reach some position decisively or swiftly: *The Republican Party swept into power. The horse came from behind and swept into first place.*

sweep out

1. To clean the inside of something by sweeping: *I swept out the garage. No one goes in that room except for the janitor, who sweeps it out every week.*
2. To cause something to be carried outward by some current: *The abandoned surfboard was swept out to sea. A gust of wind swept the leaves out of the gutter and into the air.*
3. To cause someone to be removed from office or power, especially in a decisive election. Used chiefly in the passive: *The politician was swept out of office because the citizens had lost faith in the government.*

sweep up

1. To clean or clear some surface with or as if with a broom or brush: *I swept up the kitchen because there were crumbs on the floor. Whenever the barbershop floor became messy, I would sweep it up.*
2. To remove something by sweeping it into a dustpan and discarding it: *You should sweep up those shards of glass before someone steps on them. The custodian noticed candy wrappers on the floor and swept them up.*
3. To lift something or someone up with a swift, brushing motion: *The gambler swept up her winnings from the table and left the casino. He swept the child up into his arms.*
4. To cause something or someone to become lifted and carried by a current: *The wind swept the dust up into the air. The floodwaters swept up the car and carried it away.*
5. To cause someone to be enthralled by and compelled to join in a collective emotion, action, or activity: *The defendant claimed to have been swept up in the heat of passion.*
6. To win some set of competitive events completely and decisively: *He swept up the running events and won four medals. She entered every competition and swept them all up.*
7. To win a large amount of money: *He swept up at the casino last week.*

◆ **sweeten** (swēt′n)

sweetened (swēt′nd), **sweetening** (swēt′n-ĭng), **sweetens** (swēt′nz)

sweeten up

1. To make something sweet or sweeter: *The recipe instructs to sweeten up the sauce with a tablespoon of sugar. I usually add some honey to my tea to sweeten it up.*
2. To make some offer more appealing: *The phone company sweetened up their deal by throwing in a free phone. If you're still unimpressed with our proposal, we can sweeten it up with a great benefits package.*

◆ **swell** (swĕl)

swelled (swĕld), **swelled** *or* **swollen** (swō′lən), **swelling** (swĕl′ĭng), **swells** (swĕlz)

swell up

1. To become swollen: *I put ice on my injured ankle so that it wouldn't swell up.*
2. To become filled, as with pride, arrogance, or anger: *The new parents swelled up with pride.*
3. To rise or surge from an inner source: *After I was fired unjustly, rage swelled up within me.*

◆ **swill** (swĭl)

swilled (swĭld), **swilling** (swĭl′ĭng), **swills** (swĭlz)

swill down

1. To drink something quickly: *After the toast, we swilled down our beers. I poured a tall glass of orange juice and swilled it down.*
2. **swill down with** To follow the ingestion of something, such as food, with the ingestion of some liquid: *We swilled down the hot dogs with beer. I swilled the bitter medicine down with a glass of water.*

swill out

To empty or clean something by a flow of water or liquid: *After you finish washing the dishes, swill out the sink with water. I swilled the cup out and poured myself a glass of milk.*

◆ **swim** (swĭm)

swam (swăm), **swum** (swŭm), **swimming** (swĭm′ĭng), **swims** (swĭmz)

swim in

1. To be covered or flooded with or as if with some liquid: *This roast beef is swimming in gravy.*
2. To possess a large amount of something; abound in something: *After winning the lottery, she was swimming in money.*

◆ **swing** (swĭng)

swung (swŭng), **swinging** (swĭng′ĭng), **swings** (swĭngz)

swing around

1. To turn rapidly around something: *The car swung around the corner and almost hit a pedestrian.*
2. To turn rapidly to face the opposite direction: *When I heard footsteps behind me, I swung around.*

ă	pat	är	car	ī	bite	ô	paw	o͝o	took	ûr	urge
ā	pay	ĕ	pet	îr	pier	ôr	core	o͝or	lure	zh	vision
âr	care	ē	be	ŏ	pot	oi	boy	o͞o	boot	ə	about,
ä	father	ĭ	pit	ō	toe	ou	out	ŭ	cut		item

swing at

To attempt to hit someone or something with a sweeping stroke: *If a batter swings at the ball and misses, it counts as a strike. One of the kids got angry and swung at me with his fist.*

swing by

To visit some place for a brief amount of time, especially as a deviation from a direct course: *On my way home, I swung by the post office to buy some stamps. We swung by a friend's house on our way to the beach. Why don't you swing by for some coffee?*

◆ **swipe** (swīp)

swiped (swīpt), **swiping** (swī′pĭng), **swipes** (swīps)

swipe at

1. To attempt to hit someone or something with a sweeping stroke: *The cat swiped at the string. The hockey player swiped at the puck.*
2. To attack someone verbally; criticize someone sharply: *The candidate took every opportunity to swipe at her opponent.*

◆ **swirl** (swûrl)

swirled (swûrld), **swirling** (swûr′lĭng), **swirls** (swûrlz)

swirl around

1. To move with a twisting or whirling motion; eddy: *It's hard to fly a kite when the wind swirls around like this.*
2. To move around something with a twisting or whirling motion, as in an eddy: *As I stood in the river, the water swirled around my legs. The snow swirled around us.*
3. To apply something in swirls over some area: *The baker swirled the icing around the cake. I swirled syrup around the pancakes.*
4. To circulate among some group of people in response to a particular subject: *Rumors swirled around Hollywood.*
5. To circulate or occur in response to something or someone that is controversial, provocative, or secretive: *Rumors swirled around the governor. Controversy swirled around the new budget.*

◆ **switch** (swĭch)

switched (swĭcht), **switching** (swĭch′ĭng), **switches** (swĭch′ĭz)

switch around

1. To alter something by shifting its components: *The baseball manager switched the lineup around so that the best batter would go first. The decorator switched around the room to make it feel less cramped.*
2. To swap someone or something with another: *The decorator switched the chair around with the bookcase. The manager switched the two players around.*

switch off

1. To deactivate something using a switch: *We switched off the lights before we left the house. Switch that vacuum cleaner off so you can hear what I'm saying.*
2. To stop paying attention; lose interest: *The whole class switched off when the professor started talking about accounting.*
3. To alternate performing some task with another person: *We switch off the baby-sitting every Friday so that one of us can go to the mov-*

ies. It's a long drive, but if we switch off we won't get tired.

switch on

To activate something using a switch: *We switched on the lights and entered the room. I switched the fan on to cool down the kitchen.*

switch over

1. To make or undergo a shift from one thing to another: *I switched over to the trumpet from the saxophone. Some groups have started using the new operating system, but our division won't switch over until next year.*
2. To shift someone or something from one thing to another: *The IT department switched our division over to the new operating system. A better medicine came out, so the doctor switched over all her patients.*
3. To change channels: *I switched over to the classical music station when I got bored with the news.*

◆ **swoop** (swo͞op)

swooped (swo͞opt), **swooping** (swo͞o′pĭng), **swoops** (swo͞ops)

swoop down

To make a rush or an attack with or as if with a sudden sweeping movement: *An owl swooped down on the rabbit.*

◆ **sync** *or* **synch** (sĭngk)

synced *or* **synched** (sĭngkt), **syncing** *or* **synching** (sĭng′kĭng), **syncs** *or* **synchs** (sĭngks)

sync up *or* **synch up**

To coordinate something with something else so that they operate at the same rate and in correspondence with each other: *The film editor synced up the sound and video. I synced the file on my home computer up with the more recent file on my laptop. The sound on my TV doesn't sync up with the video.*

ă	pat	är	car	ī	bite	ô	paw	o͝o	took	ûr	urge
ā	pay	ĕ	pet	îr	pier	ôr	core	o͝or	lure	zh	vision
âr	care	ē	be	ŏ	pot	oi	boy	o͞o	boot	ə	about,
ä	father	ĭ	pit	ō	toe	ou	out	ŭ	cut		item

T

◆ **tack** (tăk)

tacked (tăkt), **tacking** (tăk′ĭng), **tacks** (tăks)

tack on

1. To attach something to a surface using a tack, pin, or nail: *I tack my children's drawings on the kitchen door. The teacher set up a big corkboard, and each child tacked on a poem.*
2. To add or append something additional: *The hotel tacked on a five percent service fee. I read my essay again and tacked an introduction on.*

tack up

1. To post something with or as if with a tack: *I tacked up a poster of my favorite band. The teacher tacked the best students' essays up on the wall.*
2. To outfit a horse with a harness and saddle: *The cowboy tacked up the horse. We can take the horses out for a ride after you've tacked them up.*

◆ **tag** (tăg)

tagged (tăgd), **tagging** (tăg′ĭng), **tags** (tăgz)

tag along

To follow after; accompany: *If you're going to the mall, do you mind if I tag along? My sister tagged along with me to the beach.*

tag on

To add or append something: *She tagged an extra paragraph on the letter. Before sending the package, he tagged on a little note.*

tag out

Baseball

To touch some base runner with the ball in order to put that player out: *The shortstop tagged out the runner at second. I tagged the player out and ended the inning.*

tag up

Baseball

To return to and touch a base with one foot before running to the next base after a fielder has caught a fly ball: *The runner ran back, tagged up at first base, and then continued on to second.*

◆ **tail** (tāl)

tailed (tāld), **tailing** (tā′lĭng), **tails** (tālz)

tail after

To follow someone or something: *The ducklings tailed after their mother. The detective tailed after the suspected criminal.*

tail away *or* **tail off**

1. To diminish gradually; dwindle or subside: *The singer's voice tails away at the end of the song. The fireworks tailed off into darkness.*
2. Sports To veer from a straight course. Used of a ball that has been

hit or thrown: *The pitcher snapped his wrist when throwing the ball, and it tailed away as it approached home plate. The wind caused the football to tail off and the receiver couldn't catch it. The uneven table caused the pool ball to tail off.*

tail into

To flow into something. Used of a tributary: *Two rivers tail into the bay.*

tail out

1. To become more dispersed or less frequent and eventually disappear: *We drove away from the city until the houses tailed out and we had reached the country.*
2. To become lengthened or spaced when moving in a line: *The patrol tailed out in pairs as they marched along the road.*

◆ **take** (tāk)

took (to͝ok), **taken** (tā′kən), **taking** (tā′kĭng), **takes** (tāks)

take after

1. To resemble someone, especially a parent, grandparent, or other predecessor, in appearance, temperament, or character: *She takes after her grandfather in her talent for design. You take after your mother—you have her nose and eyes.*
2. To follow someone or something as an example: *Don't take after your older brother—he's a bad influence.*

take along

To bring someone or something into one's care or keeping while going somewhere: *If we go to the movies, you may take along your friends. I took some books along on my bus trip.*

take apart

1. To disconnect the parts of something; disassemble something: *I took apart the radio to find out what was wrong. The plumber took the drain apart to fix it.*
2. To dissect or analyze something in an effort to understand it: *He took apart my theory and found a few flaws. The professor took my conclusions apart and said they were invalid.*
3. To criticize something or someone severely: *The boss didn't like my report much and really took it apart. The committee took apart my budget as being too wasteful.*
4. SLANG To beat someone severely; thrash someone: *I'm going to take you apart in this fight. Go take apart that bully!*

take around *or* **take round**

1. To bring someone somewhere: *I'll take you around to my favorite restaurant sometime.*
2. To introduce someone to some place by visiting various locations: *Let's take the new neighbors around the town this weekend.*

ă	pat	är	car	ī	bite	ô	paw	o͝o	took	ûr	urge
ā	pay	ĕ	pet	îr	pier	ôr	core	o͝or	lure	zh	vision
âr	care	ē	be	ŏ	pot	oi	boy	o͞o	boot	ə	about, item
ä	father	ĭ	pit	ō	toe	ou	out	ŭ	cut		

Let's take around the exchange students and show them the city.

take aside

To take someone away from a group in order to speak privately: *The teacher took me aside and told me not to tease the other students. The principal took aside the troublemakers who were causing problems.*

take away

1. To remove something: *Someone took my books away. Can you take away the trash?*
2. To have something as the effect of an experience: *I did not take away a good impression of the way things are run there. He took away a black eye from that fight.*
3. To take someone along to a new place: *I wish you would take me away with you.*
4. To arrest someone or send them to prison or another place of incarceration: *The police were threatening to take me away, so I left the country. The police took away the suspects to the courthouse.*
5. To awe someone; cause someone to be emotionally captivated: *The final scene of the movie took me away.*
6. To win something easily, by a wide margin, or dramatically: *It was a tense series of games, but our team took it away in the end. That film took away five Oscars.*
7. CHIEFLY BRITISH To buy food at a restaurant and take it somewhere else to eat: *Let's take away some Chinese food for lunch.*
8. **take away from** To detract from something: *Drab curtains took away from the otherwise lovely room.*

take back

1. To retrieve and regain possession of something: *I had to take back my jacket from your closet because I need to wear it. I took my book back because I forgot that I had written some notes in the margins. The store won't take back clothing if it has been worn.*
2. To return something to some location: *I took the book back to the library. The toaster I bought didn't work, so I had to take it back.*
3. To cause someone to return in thought to a past time: *That old song sure takes me back. The smell of the ocean takes me back to our first trip to the beach.*
4. To retract something stated, written, or done: *What a terrible thing to say—I demand that you take it back. After your bad behavior, I take back all the nice things I said about you. I wish I could take back my embarrassing performance.*

take down

1. To bring something to a lower position from a higher one: *Take the book down from the shelf. The store took down all the signs after the sale ended.*
2. To dismantle something that is standing: *In the morning, we took down the tents and put them in our backpacks. The workers took the Halloween display down and put up one for Thanksgiving.*
3. To lower someone's arrogance or self-esteem: *The opposing team really took him down during the*

final game. They were so good that they took down each member of our debate team.

4. To write something one has heard or observed: *I took down every word they said so I could review the conversation later. The stenographer took the speech down and transcribed it.*

take for

To think someone or something is someone or something else: *I'm sorry I called you the wrong name—I took you for one of your coworkers. Do you take me for a fool?*

take in

1. To allow something to enter or flow in: *The boat took in 40 gallons of water before we could fix the leak. Roots take nutrients in from the soil.*
2. To admit someone. Used of institutions: *The academy takes in only four new students per year. The university took the transfer student in.*
3. To have someone or something live or lodge in one's house: *We took in several refugees during the war. The foster family took the runaway in.*
4. To deliver something or someone to a place of treatment or repair: *The car's brakes aren't working well, so we have to take it in.*
5. To convey someone who has been arrested to a police station: *If the police find out that your driver's license has expired, they will take you in. They took in that suspect who jumped bail.*
6. To include or constitute something: *The United States takes in the land north of Mexico and south of Canada.*
7. To understand or appreciate something that one is hearing or experiencing: *I couldn't take in everything they said. I went to the countryside and took in the beauty of the landscape. The lecture was so profound that I couldn't take it all in.*
8. To deceive or swindle someone. Used chiefly in the passive: *I was taken in by a confidence artist.*
9. To accept some work to be done in one's house for pay: *Why don't you take in a typing job to get extra money for school?*
10. To make some article of clothing smaller, narrower, or shorter: *I took in the waist on that pair of pants. The tailor took the shorts in.*

take into

1. To move something to the interior of something: *We took the boxes into the garage.*
2. To have someone or something live or lodge in one's house: *We took three kittens into our home.*
3. To change the state or condition of something or someone: *The sudden gust of wind took the airplane into a tailspin. The sheriff took the suspect into custody.*

ă	pat	är	car	ī	bite	ô	paw	o͝o	took	ûr	urge
ā	pay	ĕ	pet	îr	pier	ôr	core	o͝or	lure	zh	vision
âr	care	ē	be	ŏ	pot	oi	boy	o͞o	boot	ə	about,
ä	father	ĭ	pit	ō	toe	ou	out	ŭ	cut		item

take off

1. To remove something from something that is supporting it: *I took the books off the shelf. I took off all the vases from the ledge and dusted them. Please take the clothes off the clothesline.*
2. To remove some article of clothing: *She took her coat off. I'll take off my boots.*
3. To release something that holds or restrains: *I took the brake off and the car began to roll. Take the top straps off your boots and you'll be more comfortable. The driving instructor never takes off the seatbelt in the car.*
4. To deduct some amount from some quantity: *The discount dealer took ten percent off the normal price. The teacher takes off five points for each mistake on the quiz.*
5. To leave, especially quickly: *As soon as I told them you were coming, they took off. We took off to the beach for the weekend.*
6. To rise into the air or begin flight: *The plane took off on time.*
7. To increase greatly in activity, success, or number: *The actor's career took off. That new movie really took off. Sales took off around the holidays.*
8. To proceed further on the basis of something; elaborate on something: *The writer took off on my story and wrote a whole novel. I started the project, but my sister really took off with it.*
9. To begin expressing oneself strongly: *I told him about the new tax laws, and he took off about how much more money he would have to pay.*
10. To withhold service due, as from one's work: *I'm taking off three days during May. I'm taking a couple of days off from work to spend with my children.*
11. To stop prescribing or administering to someone some medicine or other corrective that is taken or undertaken routinely: *The doctor took me off the medicine when I got healthy.*
12. **take off on** To mock something by imitating it: *The comedy show took off on the evening news.*

take on

1. To acquire some cargo or burden: *The freighter took on 1,000 tons of wheat. The bus can't take any more passengers on. We hit an iceberg, and the ship is taking on water.*
2. To undertake or begin to handle something: *After her husband's death, she had to take on extra responsibilities. Only a few construction companies are big enough to take the project on.*
3. To hire someone; engage someone: *The farms take on more workers during the harvest. We took him on as a laborer but soon promoted him to supervisor.*
4. To oppose someone in competition: *The unions were prepared to take on the company bosses. I can't play chess, but I'll take you on in checkers.*
5. To acquire some characteristic: *Over the years, he has taken on the look of a banker. The competition takes on more importance now that the title is at stake.*
6. SLANG To display violent or passionate emotion: *Don't take on like that.*

take out

1. To remove or extract something: *My mother took the splinter out of my finger. I opened the camera and took out the film.*
2. To remove something to the outside: *I forgot to take the trash out last night. Take out the garbage before the trash can gets too full.*
3. To withdraw some amount of money from an account: *I went to the ATM and took out $20. She took $500 out of her bank account.*
4. To borrow something from a library: *I took out a book from the library. You can only take three books out at a time.*
5. To give vent to some negative emotion; allow some emotion to be relieved by expressing it: *Don't take out your frustration so aggressively. He took his anger out on his poor dog.*
6. To invite someone as a date or companion and escort them: *I'd like to take you out tonight if you're free. We took the children out to a movie.*
7. To order some food from a restaurant and eat it elsewhere: *We took out some Japanese food and ate at home.*
8. To obtain something as an equivalent in a different form: *They took out the money we owed in babysitting services.*
9. To except something from consideration; not consider something: *It was a good summer if you take out those three days when I was sick. Take the acting out, and tell me what you thought of the plot.*
10. To begin a course; set out: *The police took out after the thieves.*
11. To secure some document or license by application to an authority: *I took out a restraining order against my neighbor. She took a real estate license out and started selling houses.*
12. To secure something, as a loan, from a financial institution: *Let's take out a loan and buy that car. I took a mortgage out on my house.*
13. To destroy or incapacitate something: *The explosion took out the ship's radar. The plane flew over the enemy bunker and took it out with a missile.*
14. SLANG To kill or incapacitate someone: *Two snipers took out the entire enemy platoon. He took me out with a single punch.*

take over

1. To bear something over or across something: *The boat took the passengers safely over the shoals.*
2. To bear something to some other place: *Would you take these blankets over to our neighbor? The painters might get paint on the floor; please take over these newspapers and put them underneath the ladder.*
3. To assume control of, management of, or responsibility for something: *She took over the job after he left. I took the position over from my*

ă	pat	är	car	ī	bite	ô	paw	o͝o	took	ûr	urge
ā	pay	ĕ	pet	îr	pier	ôr	core	o͝or	lure	zh	vision
âr	care	ē	be	ŏ	pot	oi	boy	o͞o	boot	ə	about,
ä	father	ĭ	pit	ō	toe	ou	out	ŭ	cut		item

aunt after she retired. The vice president will take over as president.

4. To become dominant: *Our defense took over in the second half of the basketball game.*
5. To take the place of something: *Computers have largely taken over typewriters. Do you think India will take China over as the country with the largest population?*

take round

See **take around.**

take to

1. To change the location or status of something or someone: *I took flowers to my friend's house. Her comments took the discussion to a more sophisticated level.*
2. To escape or have recourse to something or some place: *They knew we were on their trail, so they took to the woods.*
3. To start doing something as a habit or a steady practice: *After I graduated from college, I slowly took to waking up early.*
4. To become fond of or attached to someone or something: *That child has really taken to her. He took to the piano as if he were born to play it.*

take up

1. To bear or convey something to a higher place: *Please take these books up to the attic. When you go to the attic, don't forget to take up those old lamps.*
2. To remove something from a surface: *He took up the rug so that the dog's muddy paws wouldn't stain it.*
3. To absorb or adsorb something: *Leaves take up carbon dioxide from the air. There's a wine stain on the rug, but this absorbing cleaner will take it up.*
4. To assume or adopt some character or manner: *He later took up a friendly attitude, but he was still unhappy.*
5. To assume some position, structure, or method: *The soldiers took up positions along the river. The executive took up a new post as CFO. The statistical technique developed by physicists was taken up by economists.*
6. To reduce some article of clothing by some amount in size; shorten or tighten something: *I'll need to take these sleeves up about a half inch. The tailor took up the hem two inches.*
7. To accept some offer or challenge: *I took up the offer to go out to dinner. He took her challenge up, and they agreed to meet that night to play darts.*
8. **take up on** To accept from someone some offer or challenge: *I am going to take you up on that invitation to your cottage on the lake.*
9. To resume something; pick up something: *The narrator took up the story at the point where she had stopped for a break.*
10. To use up, consume, or occupy some period of time or space: *Homework took up most of the kids' afternoons. The chores took all my time up. My suitcase takes up too much space.*
11. To develop an interest in some activity and devote time to it: *Later in life they both took up mountain climbing. I took yoga up because it relaxes me.*

12. To enter into some profession or business: *She took up engineering after college. He took chemistry up after realizing he didn't like physics.*
13. To deal with something: *Let's take up each problem one at a time. We'll take each issue up separately.*
14. **take up for** To support some person or group in an argument: *The politician took up for the protesters and pleaded their case before the committee.*
15. **take up with** To bring something to someone for advice: *I'm going to take the matter up with my lawyer.*
16. **take up with** To begin to associate with some person or group; consort with some person or group: *She's taken up with a fast crowd and no longer calls me.*

◆ **talk** (tôk)

talked (tôkt), **talking** (tô′kĭng), **talks** (tôks)

talk around

1. To speak indirectly about something: *The politician just talked around the issue and never answered the question.*
2. To persuade someone of something: *I talked them around to my point of view. They disagreed with me at first, but I talked them around.*

talk at

To speak to someone without regard for or interest in a reaction or response: *Don't talk at me—talk to me!*

talk back

1. To respond to someone rudely or inappropriately: *The servants were not supposed to talk back to their masters.*
2. To make a hostile response: *The enemy's guns are talking back.*
3. To respond to a signal or transmission, especially through a path of electronic communication: *My computer is sending information through the modem, but the network computer is not talking back.*

talk down

1. To try to convince others that something is minor or insignificant: *The company president talked down the importance of the move. The sales manager talked the changes down so the staff wouldn't worry.*
2. To cause the price or value of a particular investment to decrease by talking about it or factors affecting it: *The investors talked down the airline's stock price, spreading rumors about the management so that they could purchase the stock at a discount.*
3. To persuade someone to reduce an asking price: *The customer talked the salesman down to $50 from a list price of $75. I managed to talk down the price of the used car.*
4. To speak in an overtly simple manner that betrays a feeling of

ă	pat	är	car	ī	bite	ô	paw	ŏŏ	took	ûr	urge
ā	pay	ĕ	pet	îr	pier	ôr	core	ŏŏr	lure	zh	vision
âr	care	ē	be	ŏ	pot	oi	boy	ōō	boot	ə	about, item
ä	father	ĭ	pit	ō	toe	ou	out	ŭ	cut		

superiority: *The unpopular principal talked down to the students.*

5. To silence someone, especially by speaking in a loud and domineering manner: *Every time we tried to say anything, they just talked us down. The crowd talked down the speaker.*
6. To direct and control the flight of some aircraft or of some pilot during an approach for landing by radioed instructions from either the ground or a nearby aircraft: *The control tower talked down the damaged plane. The air controllers talked the shaken pilot down.*

talk into

1. To direct one's voice toward some device, such as a microphone: *The radio announcer talked clearly into the microphone. Talk directly into my tape recorder or it won't pick up your voice.*
2. To persuade someone to do something: *The salesperson talked us into buying the car. I tried to talk them into my plan, but they wouldn't cooperate.*

talk out

1. To discuss some matter completely: *I talked out the problem with a therapist. The company executives talked the proposal out behind closed doors.*
2. To resolve or settle something by discussion: *Rather than fight, they agreed to talk it out. The counselor urged the couple to talk their problems out.*
3. **talk out of** To persuade someone not to do something: *I was going to move, but my parents talked me out of it.*
4. CHIEFLY BRITISH To block some proposed legislation by filibustering: *Certain members of Parliament talked the bill out. The bill was talked out by an MP from Manchester.*

talk over

1. To consider something thoroughly in conversation; discuss something: *We talked the matter over. The panel talked over the proposal.*
2. To succeed in gaining the favor or support of someone by persuasion: *We talked them over to our side.*
3. To speak and be heard amid some loud noise: *It is impossible to talk over the noise of the machines.*

talk through

1. To discuss something thoroughly in order to come to some resolution: *At the meeting, the employees talked through the issues and came up with a solution. We rarely fight, because we talk our problems through.*
2. To guide someone through some process: *The fire chief talked us through the exit procedure step by step.*

talk up

1. To speak in favor of someone or something; promote someone or something: *The mayor talked the candidate up. The publicist talked up the new product.*
2. To cause the price or value of a particular investment to increase by publicly talking about it or factors affecting it: *Officials talked up the price of gas by warning of a shortage. The oil speculators are talking prices up.*

◆ **tally** (tăl′ē)

tallied (tăl′ēd), **tallying** (tăl′ē-ĭng), **tallies** (tăl′ēz)

tally up

To calculate something, especially by addition: *The waiter tallied up our bill at the end of the meal. The election officials tallied the votes up and announced the winner.*

◆ **tamper** (tăm′pər)

tampered (tăm′pərd), **tampering** (tăm′pə-rĭng), **tampers** (tăm′pərz)

tamper with

To interfere with something in a harmful manner: *Someone has been tampering with my mail—these letters have been opened! When jurors reported that they had been offered bribes, the judge told the defense not to tamper with the jury.*

◆ **tangle** (tăng′gəl)

tangled (tăng′gəld), **tangling** (tăng′gə-lĭng), **tangles** (tăng′gəlz)

tangle up

1. To mix something together or intertwine it in a confused mass; snarl something: *I accidentally tangled that rope up with the others. You've tangled up all the paper clips and now I can't separate them. The telephone cord is tangled up in a knot.*
2. To catch and hold something in or as if in a net; entrap something: *The children tangled the kite up in the branches. I tangled up the fishing lure as I was pulling it through the weeds. A dolphin became tangled up in the fishing net.*
3. To involve someone in awkward or unsavory circumstances. Used chiefly in the passive: *How did a good kid like you get tangled up with criminals? No politician would want to be tangled up in this sordid affair.*

tangle with

To enter into argument, dispute, or conflict with someone or something: *The tenants were afraid to tangle with their landlord's expensive lawyers.*

◆ **tank** (tăngk)

tanked (tăngkt), **tanking** (tăng′kĭng), **tanks** (tăngks)

tank up

1. To fill the tank of a motor vehicle with gasoline: *Gas prices are so high, I can barely afford to tank up. Don't tank up with low-quality gasoline.*
2. To eat, drink, or accumulate a supply of food or drink: *Midway through the hike, we stopped by a stream to tank up on water. The travelers pulled into a roadside diner and tanked up.*
3. SLANG To intoxicate someone: *Someone poured a bottle of vodka in the punch and tanked up the unsuspecting partygoers. The kids got tanked up on soda pop and*

ă	pat	är	car	ī	bite	ô	paw	ŏŏ	took	ûr	urge
ā	pay	ĕ	pet	îr	pier	ôr	core	ŏŏr	lure	zh	vision
âr	care	ē	be	ŏ	pot	oi	boy	ōō	boot	ə	about, item
ä	father	ĭ	pit	ō	toe	ou	out	ŭ	cut		

ran around in the yard. Many of the revelers were too tanked up to drive home.

4. SLANG To drink to the point of intoxication: *The losing team is tanking up at the bar.*
5. SLANG To be consumed to the point of intoxicating someone: *That last glass of whiskey really tanked me up.*

◆ **tap** (tăp)

tapped (tăpt), **tapping** (tăp′ĭng), **taps** (tăps)

tap for

To select someone for something, such as an appointment to an office: *The mayor tapped his top aide for the position of communications director.*

tap into

1. To gain access to some resource: *The building tapped into the city's water supply.*
2. To take advantage of some sentiment: *The politician tapped into voter anger and won the election.*

tap out

1. To produce something with a succession of light taps: *She tapped out a rhythm with her pencil. The captain tapped out a distress signal in Morse code. I tapped the letter out on my computer.*
2. To submit in a fight, wrestling match, or other contest by tapping the ground with the hand: *Unable to free himself from the choke hold, the wrestler tapped out.*
3. BASEBALL To hit the ball weakly so that one is put out at first base: *The batter tapped out, and the inning was over. The hitter tapped out with a ground ball to third base.*
4. To deplete some resource or the resources of someone or something: *The hurricane tapped out the city's emergency funds. The medical expenses tapped us out. The housing market is tapped out now that so many new houses have been built.*

◆ **tape** (tāp)

taped (tāpt), **taping** (tā′pĭng), **tapes** (tāps)

tape off

To restrict or reserve some location or area by encircling it with tape: *The police taped off the crime scene. We taped the bench off so that no one would sit on the wet paint.*

◆ **taper** (tā′pər)

tapered (tā′pərd), **tapering** (tā′pə-rĭng), **tapers** (tā′pərz)

taper off

1. To narrow, diminish, or lessen gradually: *The rod tapers off to a point at one end. The rain finally tapered off, and we went back outside.*
2. To cause something to narrow, diminish, or lessen gradually: *I tapered off the end of a stick and drove it into the ground. The doctor tapered the medication off as the patient recovered.*
3. To gradually reduce someone's medication: *After my symptoms disappeared, the doctor tapered me off the medication.*

◆ **tart** (tärt)
tarted (tär′tĭd), **tarting** (tär′tĭng), **tarts** (tärts)

tart up
To dress someone up or make something fancy in a tawdry, garish way: *We tarted up the apartment with a pink shag carpet. The dancers tarted themselves up in feathers and sequins.*

◆ **task** (tăsk)
tasked (tăskt), **tasking** (tăs′kĭng), **tasks** (tăsks)

task with
To give someone or something some task: *The president tasked the committee with investigating the accident. The accounting group was tasked with the responsibility of producing a budget report.*

◆ **tattle** (tăt′l)
tattled (tăt′ld), **tattling** (tăt′l-ĭng), **tattles** (tăt′lz)

tattle on
To inform that someone has misbehaved: *My brother tattled on me for spilling the glue.*

◆ **team** (tēm)
teamed (tēmd), **teaming** (tē′mĭng), **teams** (tēmz)

team up
1. To form or join a team or an association: *We decided to team up and combine our resources. The police are teaming up with schools to prevent violence.*
2. To combine someone into a team or an association: *The coach teamed me up with two of the worst athletes in the school. My boss teamed up the best workers for the project.*

◆ **tear** (târ)
tore (tôr), **torn** (tôrn), **tearing** (târ′ĭng), **tears** (târz)

tear apart
1. To destroy something by or as if by tearing: *The explosion tore the building apart. The tornado tore apart the barn.*
2. To separate someone from someone else: *Don't let your anger tear you apart from me. We can't tear the happy couple apart.*
3. To criticize something harshly: *The committee tore apart my report. The professor tore the student's paper apart.*

tear around
1. To move about in excited, often angry haste: *The coach tore around after his team lost. The boss is tearing around the office in a fury.*
2. To lead a wild life: *It's really frightening the way those teenagers tear around.*

tear at
1. To pull at or attack something violently: *The dog tore at the meat.*

ă	pat	är	car	ī	bite	ô	paw	o͝o	took	ûr	urge
ā	pay	ĕ	pet	îr	pier	ôr	core	o͝or	lure	zh	vision
âr	care	ē	be	ŏ	pot	oi	boy	o͞o	boot	ə	about,
ä	father	ĭ	pit	ō	toe	ou	out	ŭ	cut		item

2. To distress someone or something greatly: *Their sad story tore at my heart. When I told a lie, it tore at my conscience.*

tear away

1. To remove someone or something by force: *The mugger tore my bag away from me. The security guard tore away the passenger's knife.*
2. To remove someone unwillingly or reluctantly: *The book was so suspenseful that I couldn't tear myself away from it. We can't tear the children away from the video games, so we bought a system for the car.*
3. To leave or drive off rapidly: *When the stoplight turned green, the taxi tore away.*

tear between

To put someone in the position of having to choose between some equally desirable or undesirable options or loyalties. Used chiefly in the passive: *The soldier was torn between staying on duty or going home.*

tear down

1. To demolish something; raze something: *The city tore down the old warehouses. I put up posters, but my opponents tore them down.*
2. To take something apart; disassemble something: *The mechanic tore down the engine. We took out the motor and tore it down to find out what was wrong with it.*
3. To make vicious and damaging statements about someone or something; denigrate someone or something: *The speakers tried to change the audience's opinion, but the audience tore the speakers down.*

tear into

To attack someone or something with great vigor or violence: *The bear tore into the meat. The boxer tore into his opponent at the match.*

tear off

1. To remove something by ripping or tearing: *She reached for the gift and tore off the wrapping paper. He grasped the sales tag and tore it off.*
2. To remove something quickly: *I unbuttoned my jacket and tore it off. The feverish patient tore off the covers.*
3. To leave or drive off rapidly: *The painting crew tore off in their van.*
4. To produce something hurriedly and casually: *The new reporter tears off article after article.*

tear through

1. To rip or lacerate something: *The nail tore through my stocking. The hook caught on my shirt and tore it through.*
2. To move through something with heedless speed; rush headlong through something: *The student tore through the park on a bicycle.*
3. To move through something with destructive force: *The fire tore through the house.*
4. To proceed with or accomplish something rapidly or hurriedly: *The study group tore through the book the night before the final.*

tear up

1. To tear something to pieces: *The principal tore up the note so no*

one could read it. I tore the newspaper up to make a nest for my pet hamster.

2. To nullify some legal agreement: *The parties reached a compromise and tore up the old contract. We couldn't settle the case, so we tore the agreement up.*
3. To make an opening in something: *The workers tore up the sidewalk to add a drain. The committee condemned the unsafe playground and had some workers come to tear it up.*
4. To damage someone or something by or as if by tearing: *The puppy tore up the furniture. The kids tore the couch up when they were jumping on it.*
5. To ravage or devastate something: *The typhoon tore up the islands. This beach has eroded because a storm tore it up.*
6. To distress someone greatly: *It tears me up to think he won't be coming home. It tears up the students when they think about the football game that they lost in the final minute.*
7. To excel at some place or competition: *The team tore up the chess tournament and won a medal. Our school had the winning team—we tore the competition up.*

◆ **tear** (tîr)

teared (tîrd), **tearing** (tîr′ĭng), **tears** (tîrz)

tear up

1. To have tears well in the eyes: *During the funeral, the mourners started to tear up.*
2. To cause someone to have tears well in the eyes: *I always bring tissues to sad movies because they really tear me up.*

◆ **tease** (tēz)

teased (tēzd), **teasing** (tē′zĭng), **teases** (tē′zĭz)

tease out

To remove or obtain something by or as if by untangling or releasing with a pointed tool or device: *I teased the knot out with a pair of tweezers. The interviewer finally teased the truth out of the politician.*

◆ **tee** (tē)

teed (tēd), **teeing** (tē′ĭng), **tees** (tēz)

tee off

1. To drive a golf ball from the tee: *The golfer teed off with a 300-yard drive.*
2. To hit something or someone solidly with a sweeping blow or stroke: *The batter teed off on the very first pitch and the ball flew over the outfield wall. The boxer was staggering, and his opponent teed off with a hard right-hand punch.*
3. To start or begin something: *They teed off the fundraising campaign*

ă	pat	är	car	ī	bite	ô	paw	o͝o	took	ûr	urge
ā	pay	ĕ	pet	îr	pier	ôr	core	o͝or	lure	zh	vision
âr	care	ē	be	ŏ	pot	oi	boy	o͞o	boot	ə	about,
ä	father	ĭ	pit	ō	toe	ou	out	ŭ	cut		item

with a dinner. We teed the evening off with cocktails at the hotel.

4. To start; begin: *The conference will tee off Saturday morning.*
5. SLANG To make someone angry or disgusted: *These phone solicitations really tee me off. The rude remarks teed off the speaker.*
6. **tee off on** SLANG To attack someone verbally: *Critics teed off on the mayor for failing to balance the budget.*

tee up

To place some ball on a tee: *The golfer bent over and teed the ball up. The kicker teed up the football and stepped backward. The golfer pulled out a golf club and teed up.*

◆ **teem** (tēm)

teemed (tēmd), **teeming** (tē′mĭng), **teems** (tēmz)

teem with

To be full of something; abound or swarm with something: *The rotten log is teaming with insects. The airport is teaming with police.*

◆ **tell** (tĕl)

told (tōld), **telling** (tĕl′ĭng), **tells** (tĕlz)

tell against

To have an adverse impact on someone or something: *Their lack of experience may tell against them during the job interview.*

tell apart

To perceive something as being different or distinct from something else: *I couldn't tell apart the real $20 bill from the counterfeit one. The twins were identical, and we couldn't tell them apart.*

tell from

To perceive something as being different or distinct from something else: *I couldn't tell the homemade cookies from the ones that were bought at the store.*

tell off

To reprimand someone or something; rebuke someone or something: *The customer told off the rude clerk. I was so mad at my roommate for forgetting to pay the rent each month that I finally told him off.*

tell on

1. To inform some authority that someone has behaved badly or illegally: *The janitor told the teacher on me for writing on the desk. We didn't want to tell on our friends for shoplifting. I promised not to tell on my brother for eating cookies before dinner.*
2. To have an effect or impact on someone or something: *The stress of working long hours began to tell on the store's owner.*

◆ **tend** (tĕnd)

tended (tĕn′dĭd), **tending** (tĕn′dĭng), **tends** (tĕndz)

tend to

To apply one's attention to something; attend to something: *I must tend to my chores before I can go outside.*

tend toward

1. To have a tendency toward something: *Most kinds of paint tend toward peeling over time.*

2. To be disposed or inclined toward something: *Many children tend toward exaggeration.*
3. To move or extend in some direction: *Our ship tended toward the northern coast.*

◆ **tense** (tĕns)

tensed (tĕnst), **tensing** (tĕn′sĭng), **tenses** (tĕn′sĭz)

tense up

1. To become tense: *The deer tensed up when it heard my footsteps.*
2. To make something tense: *I tensed up my wrist just before making contact with the ball. The muscle in my calf hurts whenever I tense it up.*

◆ **tent** (tĕnt)

tented (tĕn′tĭd), **tenting** (tĕn′tĭng), **tents** (tĕnts)

tent out

1. To sleep outdoors in a tent: *We tented out in Acadia National Park.*
2. To be extended outwards by a prop so as to create a cavity underneath. Used of a layer or sheet of material: *The wallpaper is tenting out because of a loose nail.*
3. To push out some layer or sheet of material so as to create a cavity underneath: *A loose spring in the cushion is tenting the fabric out. We used ski poles to tent out the sides of the tarp.*

◆ **test** (tĕst)

tested (tĕs′tĭd), **testing** (tĕs′tĭng), **tests** (tĕsts)

test for

To administer a test to someone or something in order to determine the presence of something: *The technician tested the blood sample for leukemia. The doctor tested the children for head lice. This procedure tests for the presence of harmful substances.*

test out

1. To test or use something experimentally: *Test out your new sleeping bag at home before taking it on a camping trip. I tested my speech out on my friends before delivering it at the meeting.*
2. To qualify for a waiver of a requirement or prerequisite by taking and passing a test: *I tested out of the beginning level of Spanish. You don't have to take geography because you tested out.*

◆ **testify** (tĕs′tĭ-fī′)

testified (tĕs′tĭ-fīd′), **testifying** (tĕs′tĭ-fī′ĭng), **testifies** (tĕs′tĭ-fīz′)

testify to

1. To make a statement based on personal knowledge in support of some asserted fact; bear witness to something: *Many astronauts have testified to the thrill of weightlessness. The witness testified to the accuracy of the defendant's story.*

ă	pat	är	car	ī	bite	ô	paw	ŏŏ	took	ûr	urge
ā	pay	ĕ	pet	îr	pier	ôr	core	ŏŏr	lure	zh	vision
âr	care	ē	be	ŏ	pot	oi	boy	ōō	boot	ə	about,
ä	father	ĭ	pit	ō	toe	ou	out	ŭ	cut		item

2. To serve as evidence: *The wreckage testifies to the strength of the storm.*

◆ **thaw** (thô)

thawed (thôd), **thawing** (thô′ĭng), **thaws** (thôz)

thaw out

1. To change from a frozen solid to a liquid by gradual warming: *The lake won't thaw out until the middle of April.*
2. To lose stiffness, numbness, or impermeability by being warmed: *The skiers gathered around the fireplace to thaw out.*
3. To cause something to lose stiffness, numbness, or impermeability by being warmed: *The hot sun thawed out the frozen ground. Get another stick of butter from the freezer, and thaw it out in the microwave.*
4. To become less formal, aloof, or reserved: *The new babysitter looked stern but quickly thawed out after meeting the children.*

◆ **thicken** (thĭk′ən)

thickened (thĭk′ənd), **thickening** (thĭk′ə-nĭng), **thickens** (thĭk′ənz)

thicken up

1. To become thicker or denser: *The gravy thickened up.*
2. To cause something to become thicker or denser: *I thickened the batter up by adding more flour. The cook thickened up the fudge.*

◆ **thin** (thĭn)

thinned (thĭnd), **thinning** (thĭn′ĭng), **thins** (thĭnz)

thin down

1. To make someone or something thin or thinner: *The painter thinned down the paint with turpentine. The designers thinned the shape of the boat down so that it could go faster.*
2. To become thin or thinner: *I thinned down over the summer, and now my pants are too big.*

thin out

1. To make something less dense or concentrated: *A harsh winter thinned out the herd of deer. The chef thinned the sauce out with water.*
2. To become less dense or concentrated: *The air thinned out as we climbed up the mountain.*

◆ **think** (thĭngk)

thought (thôt), **thinking** (thĭng′kĭng), **thinks** (thĭngks)

think ahead

To consider or think about the future; think proactively: *I thought ahead and brought a snack in case I got hungry.*

think back

To consider or think about the past; recollect: *Think back to that time we went to the zoo. I thought back on all the the things we've done for the company.*

think of

1. To weigh or consider some idea: *I'm thinking of moving to New York.*
2. To bring some thought to mind by imagination or invention: *No one thought of that idea before I did.*

3. To recall some thought or image to mind: *I thought of my childhood when I saw the movie.*
4. To consider something to be of some quality. Used with an adverb: *My friend thinks highly of your writing and wants to meet you. I hope they don't think badly of me for being so late.*
5. To have care or consideration for someone or something: *You should think of your family when you choose a place to go on vacation.*

think out

To develop some idea or plan fully: *We thought out a new strategy after we lost the game. The author thought the plot out before starting to write the book.*

think over

To consider or reflect on something, especially in order to make a decision: *The students thought over the story they had just read. Here's my proposal—think it over, and let me know how you feel.*

think through

To reason about or reflect on something, considering every detail and consequence: *Make sure you think through the consequences before you act. Don't make the decision to quit your job right away—think the matter through.*

think up

To devise or develop something: *She thought up a plan to make more money. He thought the design up all by himself.*

◆ **thirst** (thûrst)

thirsted (thûrs′tĭd), **thirsting** (thûrs′tĭng), **thirsts** (thûrsts)

thirst for *or* **thirst after**

To have a strong craving for something; yearn for something: *The oppressed people thirst for freedom.*

◆ **thrash** (thrăsh)

thrashed (thrăsht), **thrashing** (thrăsh′ĭng), **thrashes** (thrăsh′ĭz)

thrash out

1. To discuss or examine something fully: *The committee thrashed out the new budget. The politician thrashed the issue out with her advisers.*
2. To come to some agreement or solution through intense debate: *The two sides finally thrashed out a compromise. The defense thrashed a deal out with the prosecution.*

◆ **threaten** (thrĕt′n)

threatened (thrĕt′nd), **threatening** (thrĕt′n-ĭng), **threatens** (thrĕt′nz)

threaten with

To express a threat against someone by some means or action: *The principal threatened the rowdy students with expulsion.*

◆ **thresh** (thrĕsh)

threshed (thrĕsht), **threshing** (thrĕsh′ĭng), **threshes** (thrĕsh′ĭz)

ă	pat	är	car	ī	bite	ô	paw	o͝o	took	ûr	urge
ā	pay	ĕ	pet	îr	pier	ôr	core	o͝or	lure	zh	vision
âr	care	ē	be	ŏ	pot	oi	boy	o͞o	boot	ə	about, item
ä	father	ĭ	pit	ō	toe	ou	out	ŭ	cut		

thresh out

1. To beat the stems and husks of some grain or cereal plant with a machine or flail to separate the grains or seeds from the straw: *I threshed out the ears of corn. We threshed the stalks out and collected the seeds.*
2. To separate some grains or seeds by beating the stems and husks with a machine or flail: *The farmers threshed out the grain. We might have broken some of the kernels when we threshed them out.*
3. To discuss or examine something fully: *We can thresh out our differences in a civil manner. The two of you will have to thresh this problem out between yourselves. This issue will be threshed out in court.*
4. To formulate or develop something through intense debate: *We held a meeting to thresh out a plan. The committee is still threshing the details out.*

◆ **thrill** (thrĭl)

thrilled (thrĭld), **thrilling** (thrĭl′ĭng), **thrills** (thrĭlz)

thrill to

To be greatly excited by someone or something: *Audiences thrilled to the spectacular performance.*

◆ **thrive** (thrīv)

thrived (thrīvd) *or* **throve** (thrōv), **thrived** *or* **thriven** (thrĭv′ən), **thriving** (thrī′vĭng), **thrives** (thrīvz)

thrive on

To flourish by or as if by feeding on something: *The bears thrived on a rich harvest of berries.*

◆ **throttle** (thrŏt′l)

throttled (thrŏt′ld), **throttling** (thrŏt′l-ĭng), **throttles** (thrŏt′lz)

throttle back *or* **throttle down**

1. To decrease the speed of an engine with a throttle: *The captain throttled back when we entered the harbor.*
2. To decrease the speed of some engine with a throttle: *The captain throttled back the engine as we approached the dock. The pilot throttled the engine back to idle.*

◆ **throw** (thrō)

threw (thro͞o), **thrown** (thrōn), **throwing** (thrō′ĭng), **throws** (thrōz)

throw around

1. To scatter something by or as if by throwing: *The guests threw around confetti to make the room more festive. The kids threw sand around the beach.*
2. To throw or exchange something back and forth casually: *Let's go outside and throw around the ball for a while. We threw some ideas around until we came up with a solution.*

throw aside

To discard or reject something or someone: *The clerk threw aside the receipt. The officer gave me a ticket, but I threw it aside.*

throw at

1. To engage oneself with someone or something with energy or determination. Used reflexively: *The prisoners threw themselves at the judge and begged for mercy. They threw themselves at the problem until it was solved.*

2. To make an overt attempt to attract or interest someone. Used reflexively: *I think everyone noticed how you threw yourself at the professor.*

throw away

1. To get rid of something as useless; discard something: *I threw away yesterday's newspaper. They gave us extra tickets, but we threw them away.*
2. To fail to take advantage of something: *They threw away a chance to make a fortune. The students had an opportunity for a great education, but they threw it away.*
3. To waste or use something in a foolish way: *He threw away his inheritance on poor investments. She won some money in the lottery, but she threw it away.*
4. To utter or perform something in an offhand, seemingly careless way: *The play's villain throws away the news that the house has burned down.*
5. SPORTS To throw some football so that the pass is ruled incomplete: *Unable to find an open receiver, the quarterback threw the ball away. The quarterback threw away the football to stop the clock.*

throw back

1. To return something with a throw: *The catcher threw the ball back. The players threw back the ball to the coach.*
2. To fling something, such as a body part, backward: *I threw back my head in laughter at that scene. The player threw his arm back to catch that ball.*
3. To return some fish to the water after catching it: *When you throw a fish back, hold it in the current until it recovers. Throw back the trout—it's too small to keep.*
4. To hinder the progress of someone or something; check someone or something: *The lack of money threw back the project. The storm threw the schedule back.*
5. SLANG To drink something, especially alcohol, in one draft by suddenly tilting: *We threw back a couple of beers. The club members are at the bar throwing shots back.*
6. **throw back on** To cause someone to depend on someone or something; make someone reliant on someone or something: *The economic downturn threw us back on our own resources.*

throw down

1. To hurl or fling someone or something down with great force or speed: *The card player threw down her fists in anger. The wrestler threw his opponent down on the mat.*

ă	pat	är	car	ī	bite	ô	paw	o͝o	took	ûr	urge
ā	pay	ĕ	pet	îr	pier	ôr	core	o͝or	lure	zh	vision
âr	care	ē	be	ŏ	pot	oi	boy	o͞o	boot	ə	about, item
ä	father	ĭ	pit	ō	toe	ou	out	ŭ	cut		

2. To have a fist fight: *You should watch your words unless you're prepared to throw down.*

throw in

1. To insert or introduce something into the course of an activity, performance, or conversation: *The lawyer threw in a few snide comments while we conversed. The team threw in a new goalie halfway through the game. Let me throw my two cents in.*
2. To add some extra thing or amount with no additional charge: *If you order within the next 15 minutes, we'll throw in a book bag. The car salesperson threw the snow tires in for free.*
3. To engage something, such as a clutch: *He threw in the clutch and drove off. Be careful not to stall when you throw it in.*

throw into

1. To put someone or something suddenly or forcefully into some condition, position, or activity: *The funny movie threw him into a fit of laughter.*
2. To devote, apply, or direct someone or something to someone or something: *The committee threw all of its resources into the fundraiser. The students threw themselves into their homework.*

throw off

1. To hurl or fling someone or something off with great force or speed: *The horse threw the cowboy off. The running back threw off the tackle.*
2. To remove some clothing hastily or carelessly: *I entered my apartment and threw my coat off. We threw off our jackets in the hallway.*
3. To cast something out; rid oneself of something: *I threw off all the unpleasant memories of my childhood. We threw our grudges off in order to move on.*
4. To give something off; emit something: *The exhaust pipes threw off fumes. The chimney throws soot off.*
5. To distract, divert, or mislead someone or something: *The scent threw off the dogs. A wrong measurement threw her estimate off.*
6. To do, finish, or accomplish something in a casual or offhand way; toss something off: *I threw off a quick response to the letter I'd received.*
7. To stop the operation, activity, or flow of something controlled by a flip switch: *After the meeting, I told them to throw off the lights. You can throw the current off the back porch with this switch.*

throw on

1. To hurl or fling someone or something on someone or something with great force or speed: *The campers threw some wood on the bonfire. The children threw themselves on the trampoline.*
2. To force something or someone on some unwilling or improper recipient: *The new administrator threw the responsibility on us.*
3. To commit someone to someone or something, especially for leniency or support: *The prisoners threw themselves on the mercy of the court.*
4. To put on some clothing hastily or carelessly: *I threw on a suit. We*

threw our shoes on and ran outside.

5. To start the operation, activity, or flow of something by or as if by flipping a switch: *When the meeting ended, we threw on the light. The party ended and we threw the lights on.*

throw open

To make more accessible, especially suddenly or dramatically: *The director threw open the door and walked in. After years of meeting with the city council in private, the mayor threw the meetings open to the public.*

throw out

1. To give something off; emit something: *The searchlights threw out powerful beams. The torch threw lots of light out.*
2. To reject or discard something: *The committee threw out our proposal. My boss threw my ideas out.*
3. To get rid of something as useless: *The crew threw out the garbage. The workers threw the trash out.*
4. To offer something, as a suggestion or plan: *They threw out names of people they might want to invite to the party. I threw the suggestion out just to see how people would respond to it.*
5. To force someone to leave a place or position, especially in an abrupt or unexpected manner; expel someone: *The convicted judge was thrown out of office. The headwaiter threw the disorderly guest out. The child was thrown out of school for unruly behavior.*
6. To disengage something, such as a clutch: *The racecar driver threw out the clutch and stepped on the gas. The driver threw the clutch out and sped down the road.*
7. To put some part of the body out of alignment: *After working out, she threw her back out. He threw out his shoulder trying to lift that heavy box.*
8. BASEBALL To cause some base runner to be tagged out by throwing the ball to the player guarding the base to which the base runner is moving: *The new player threw the runner out at third base. The pitcher threw out the runner at second base.*
9. BASEBALL To start a game by throwing some pitch: *The retired coach threw out the first pitch. The celebrity threw the first pitch out to great applause.*

throw over

1. To overturn someone or something forcefully: *The kids threw the cart over. A strong gust of wind threw over the sailboat.*
2. To abandon someone or something: *She threw over her boyfriend of four years. He threw over the company he founded and moved to a ranch.*
3. To reject someone or something: *She threw over our idea, calling it ridiculous. They wanted us to*

ă	pat	är	car	ī	bite	ô	paw	o͝o	took	ûr	urge
ā	pay	ĕ	pet	îr	pier	ôr	core	o͝or	lure	zh	vision
âr	care	ē	be	ŏ	pot	oi	boy	o͞o	boot	ə	about,
ä	father	ĭ	pit	ō	toe	ou	out	ŭ	cut		item

implement the new policy, but we threw it over.

throw together

1. To assemble or arrange someone or something hurriedly or haphazardly: *The cook threw together some supper. I threw together an outfit. We threw the trip together in a week.*
2. To force some people into relation or proximity with one another. Used chiefly in the passive: *The survivors were thrown together by the tragic shipwreck.*

throw up

1. To propel or discharge something into the air: *He threw the ball up and it landed on the roof. The lawn mower threw up a rock.*
2. SPORTS To execute some type of throw or a throw with some outcome: *The quarterback threw up an interception.*
3. To raise something quickly: *They threw up their hands in exasperation. The color guard threw up the flag.*
4. To eject some contents of the stomach by vomiting: *The baby threw up her dinner. He threw the medicine up.*
5. To vomit: *The passenger threw up over the side of the boat.*
6. To abandon something; relinquish something: *She threw up her campaign for mayor. He threw the idea up because there was no support for it.*
7. To construct or erect something hurriedly: *The city threw the building up in under a year. The new apartment complex was thrown up in just a few months.*
8. To refer to something repeatedly: *She threw up his past to him whenever they argued. She wanted to forget the argument, but he kept throwing it up.*
9. To project, play, or otherwise display some slide, videotape, or other recorded image: *My cousin threw the tape of vacation highlights up on the screen. The teacher threw up the slides of the operation.*
10. To post something: *The team threw up five goals. The coach threw the results up on a bulletin board.*
11. To put something forth for consideration or discussion: *The accident threw up many questions. The elections threw many surprises up.*

◆ **thrust** (thrŭst)

thrust (thrŭst), **thrusting** (thrŭs′tĭng), **thrusts** (thrŭsts)

thrust aside

1. To displace someone or something forcefully: *The board of directors thrust the president of the company aside. The officer thrust aside the security guard.*
2. To reject or refuse someone or something: *My teacher thrust aside the request for an extension. The jury thrust the defendant's pleas for mercy aside.*

thrust on *or* **thrust upon**

To force something or someone on some unwilling or improper recipient: *When they went away on vacation, they thrust all their responsibilities on us. Fame was thrust upon the reclusive author.*

◆ **thumb** (thŭm)

thumbed (thŭmd), **thumbing** (thŭm′ĭng), **thumbs** (thŭmz)

thumb through

To go through some reading material quickly or superficially, turning from page to page with or as if with the thumb: *I thumbed through the directory for my dentist's phone number.*

◆ **tick** (tĭk)

ticked (tĭkt), **ticking** (tĭk′ĭng), **ticks** (tĭks)

tick away

1. To function characteristically or well: *That old car is still ticking away.*
2. To be gradually depleted. Used of an interval of time: *The final seconds ticked away.*

tick by

To pass. Used of time: *As the minutes ticked by, we became worried that we would miss the train.*

tick off

1. To make someone angry or annoyed: *Constant delays ticked me off. The arrogant actor ticked off the director.*
2. To mark some item on a list with a check or tick: *The teacher ticked off each name as the roll was called. As the guests arrived, we ticked them off the list.*

tick over

1. To be recorded on some mechanical counting device: *When the second quarter of the game ticked over, the home team was leading by two points.*
2. To record something. Used of a mechanical counting device: *The clock ticked over the ninetieth minute, and the game ended in a tie. As the car's odometer ticked the fifth mile over, we began looking for the turn.*
3. To function characteristically or well. Used chiefly in the progressive: *Because everyone works hard, the business is really ticking over.*

◆ **tide** (tīd)

tided (tī′dĭd), **tiding** (tī′dĭng), **tides** (tīdz)

tide over

To sustain or support someone or something through a period of deficiency or absence: *A $100 loan would tide me over till payday.*

◆ **tidy** (tī′dē)

tidied (tī′dēd), **tidying** (tī′dē-ĭng), **tidies** (tī′dēz)

tidy up

1. To put something in order; clean something: *We should tidy up the house. We need to tidy this report up before we can submit it.*
2. To make things orderly and neat in appearance or procedure: *We should tidy up before the guests arrive. I need to tidy up; my hair is a mess.*

◆ **tie** (tī)

tied (tīd), **tying** (tī′ĭng), **ties** (tīz)

ă	pat	är	car	ī	bite	ô	paw	o͝o	took	ûr	urge
ā	pay	ĕ	pet	îr	pier	ôr	core	o͝or	lure	zh	vision
âr	care	ē	be	ŏ	pot	oi	boy	o͞o	boot	ə	about,
ä	father	ĭ	pit	ō	toe	ou	out	ŭ	cut		item

tie back

To draw something backward and fasten it: *I gathered my hair and tied it back in a ponytail. We tied back the curtains so that they wouldn't blow around in the breeze.*

tie down

1. To fix or hold someone or something in place with a cord, rope, or strap: *We tied down the deck chairs so they wouldn't blow away. I tied the luggage down so that it wouldn't fall off the roof of the car.*
2. To restrict someone or something in movement: *Our new baby has really tied us down—we haven't eaten out for dinner in months. The rebels have tied down the government troops in the mountains, leaving the capital vulnerable to attack. I'd like to travel more, but unfortunately, I'm tied down with a job.*

tie in

1. To bring something into a close or effective relation with something: *The college tied its fundraising campaign in with the alumni reunion. The pattern on the carpet ties in all the different fabrics in the room. In this paragraph, the author reviews the main points and ties them in.*
2. To have a close or effective relation with something: *The music should tie in with the holiday theme. If you make a remark during the lecture, the professor will discuss it as long as it ties in.*

tie into

1. To attach and anchor someone or something to someone or something with a knot: *They tied the boat into the dock.*
2. To connect something with something: *This pipe ties the housing development into the city's sewer system.*
3. To be connected with something: *All the library computer systems tie into the main branch.*

tie off

1. To attach and anchor someone or something with a knot: *We tied off the rowboat and went ashore. I passed the rope through the metal ring and tied it off with a taut-line hitch.*
2. To close or seal something with a knot: *We tied off the legs of the scarecrow's pants and filled them up with hay. The clown inflated the balloon and tied it off.*

tie over

To support someone through a period of difficulty or scarcity: *Dinner is not for three hours, but this apple should tie me over.*

tie up

1. To fasten, secure, or bind someone or something with or as if with a cord, rope, or strap: *I tied up the package with twine and sent it off. The robbers tied the bank tellers up and locked them in the vault.*
2. To secure something, such as a vessel, to a shore or pier; dock something: *Did you remember to tie the boat up? I tied the canoe up at the end of the dock. The captain pulled the ship alongside the pier, and the crew tied up.*
3. To be secured to a shore or pier; dock: *The ship tied up at the end of the pier.*

4. To keep someone or something occupied; engage someone or something: *The kids have tied up the phone all evening, talking to their friends. A project this large will tie our resources up for months. The senator is tied up in a meeting and won't be able to take your call.*
5. To place some funds so as to make them inaccessible for other uses: *Don't tie up all your cash in long-term investments. The bank has tied the money up in bad loans.*
6. To equal an opponent's score in some contest: *We tied up the game with minutes remaining. A touchdown will tie the game up. The game is all tied up at 10 points apiece.*

◆ **tighten** (tīt′n)

tightened (tīt′nd), **tightening** (tīt′n-ĭng), **tightens** (tīt′nz)

tighten up

1. To make something tight or tighter: *I pulled on the ends of the string to tighten up the knot. The mechanic tightened the bolts up with a rachet. This exercise will tighten up your stomach muscles. Tighten your belt up so your pants don't fall down.*
2. To become tight or tighter: *I knew I had a fish when the line suddenly tightened up. After the run, I walked around the track so my muscles wouldn't tighten up. I tightened up on the handlebars as I went over the bump.*
3. To make something more strict or secure: *The government is trying to tighten up the tax code. The country has tightened its borders up to prevent drug smuggling.*
4. To become more strict or secure: *Airline security has tightened up, and now all luggage must be scanned.*
5. To make something more disciplined: *The company is tightening up their management in an effort to reduce wasteful spending. The author has tightened the story up by deleting irrelevant details.*
6. To become more disciplined: *The team has tightened up under the leadership of the new coach.*

◆ **tilt** (tĭlt)

tilted (tĭl′tĭd), **tilting** (tĭl′tĭng), **tilts** (tĭlts)

tilt at

1. To charge or thrust at someone or something with lance or sword: *The knight tilted at his opponent.*
2. To fight against someone or something: *The protesters were tilting at social injustices.*

◆ **time** (tīm)

timed (tīmd), **timing** (tī′mĭng), **times** (tīmz)

time out

Computer Science To cease functioning after a period of idle time has elapsed: *The server connection times out after 15 minutes.*

ă	pat		är	car		ī	bite		ô	paw		o͝o	took		ûr	urge
ā	pay		ĕ	pet		îr	pier		ôr	core		o͝or	lure		zh	vision
âr	care		ē	be		ŏ	pot		oi	boy		o͞o	boot		ə	about,
ä	father		ĭ	pit		ō	toe		ou	out		ŭ	cut			item

◆ **tinker** (tĭng′kər)

tinkered (tĭng′kərd), **tinkering** (tĭng′kə-rĭng), **tinkers** (tĭng′kərz)

tinker around

To make unskilled or experimental efforts at repair or improvement: *I tinkered around with the toaster to see if I could fix it. On the weekends, they like to tinker around in the garage.*

tinker with

To make unskilled or experimental efforts at repairing or improving something: *I tinkered with the engine, hoping to discover the trouble.*

◆ **tip** (tĭp)

tipped (tĭpt), **tipping** (tĭp′ĭng), **tips** (tĭps)

tip off

1. To provide someone or something with a piece of confidential, advance, or inside information: *A betrayed gang member tipped off the police. Someone must have tipped the press off about the company's financial troubles.*
2. To begin with a jump ball. Used of a basketball game, tournament, or season: *The basketball game tips off at 8:00.*

tip out

1. To distribute some portion of one's tips to support staff. Used of restaurant servers: *The wait staff tips out 15 percent to the kitchen staff.*
2. To distribute a portion of one's tips to someone. Used of restaurant servers: *The servers tip out all the people who work below them. The bartender forgot to tip me out last night.*

tip over

1. To totter and fall; overturn: *The vase tipped over and water poured out across the table.*
2. To cause something to totter and fall; cause something to overturn: *The wind tipped over the sailboat. Don't stand up in the canoe, or you will tip it over.*

◆ **tire** (tīr)

tired (tīrd), **tiring** (tī′rĭng), **tires** (tīrz)

tire of

To have one's interest or patience exhausted by something or someone: *Soon after the semester started, I tired of the boring morning lectures. My parents never tired of giving me unwanted advice.*

tire out

To deplete the strength or energy of someone or something; fatigue someone or something: *Traveling always tires me out. The long ride tired out the horses.*

◆ **toe** (tō)

toed (tōd), **toeing** (tō′ĭng), **toes** (tōz)

toe in

To set or adjust something at an oblique angle: *They toed in the front speakers to direct the sound towards the center of the room. We toed the chairs in so that we could share the footrest.*

◆ **tone** (tōn)

toned (tōnd), **toning** (tō′nĭng), **tones** (tōnz)

tone down

To make something less vivid, harsh, or violent; moderate something: *We toned down our comedy routine so as not to offend our audience. The decorator suggested a beige material to tone the room down.*

tone in

To match or harmonize with something: *The sofa was a strange color, but it toned in well after we painted the walls. That new house doesn't tone in with the rest of the neighborhood.*

tone up

1. To make something firmer or stronger: *Walking to work has toned up my legs. I toned my stomach up by doing sit-ups every day.*
2. To become firmer or stronger: *My body has really toned up since I started this exercise program.*

◆ **tool** (to͞ol)

tooled (to͞old), **tooling** (to͞o′lĭng), **tools** (to͞olz)

tool up

1. To equip oneself with tools or machinery needed for a particular job: *The company tooled up to produce the new product.*
2. To equip someone or something with tools or machinery needed for a particular job: *The company still hasn't tooled up all of its new factories. The supplier travels to every workshop each week to tool them up.*
3. To supply or equip oneself with weaponry; arm. Used chiefly in the passive: *The gang was tooled up and ready for a fight.*

◆ **top** (tŏp)

topped (tŏpt), **topping** (tŏp′ĭng), **tops** (tŏps)

top off

1. To fill some container completely, especially when it is almost full to begin with: *Before we returned the rental car, we topped off the gas tank. Every time I took a sip of my water, the server would come back and top it off.*
2. To finish something appropriately: *The couple topped off the romantic evening with a walk along the river.*

top out

1. To put the framework for the top story on some building: *Workers topped out the tower with the last few beams. The contractor will top the building out at a ceremony on Tuesday.*
2. To fill something, such as a ship, until it is full: *The crew topped out the ship with cargo. We topped the rest of the box out with foam padding.*

ă	pat	är	car	ī	bite	ô	paw	o͝o	took	ûr	urge
ā	pay	ĕ	pet	îr	pier	ôr	core	o͝or	lure	zh	vision
âr	care	ē	be	ŏ	pot	oi	boy	o͞o	boot	ə	about,
ä	father	ĭ	pit	ō	toe	ou	out	ŭ	cut		item

3. To cease rising; reach the highest point or degree: *Interest rates topped out at 16 percent. The balloon rose for a while but finally topped out.*

top up

CHIEFLY BRITISH

1. To fill some container completely, especially when it is almost full to begin with: *Can I top up your coffee? I topped the fish tank up with fresh water.*
2. To supplement some income: *She tops up her salary with odd jobs on the side. He relies on book royalties to top his salary up.*

◆ **toss** (tôs)

tossed (tôst), **tossing** (tô′sĭng), **tosses** (tô′sĭz)

toss around *or* **toss about**

1. To throw something back and forth casually: *We went to the park and tossed around a football. Bring the baseball to the park so we can toss it around.*
2. To change one's position restlessly while lying in bed: *The patient tossed about in her sleep. I tossed around all night and didn't get any sleep.*
3. To discuss something informally; bandy something about: *We've been tossing around the idea of moving to a warmer climate. They tossed the proposal about at the meeting, but no one was interested.*
4. To move about restlessly; twist and turn: *The ship tossed about in the high seas.*
5. To throw, fling, or heave someone or something continuously about; pitch someone or something to and fro: *The violent storm tossed the ship about. The luggage got tossed around in the trunk of the car.*

toss aside

To discard or reject someone or something: *She opened the letter and tossed the envelope aside. Once she became famous, she tossed aside her old friends.*

toss away

To get rid of something as useless: *Don't toss this opportunity away without thinking about it. Our neighbors tossed away a perfectly good sofa.*

toss back

1. To return something with a toss: *The children on the other side of the fence asked me to toss back the baseball. The catcher tossed the ball back to the pitcher.*
2. To fling something, such as a body part, backward: *She tossed back her head and laughed. The child tossed his arms back and ran down the hill.*
3. To return some fish to the water after catching it: *As sport fishermen, we toss back most of the fish we catch. The fish was too small, so I had to toss it back.*
4. SLANG To drink something quickly, especially in one draft by suddenly tilting: *The bartender tossed back a shot of whiskey. I tossed my coffee back and left the restaurant.*

toss down

SLANG

To drink something quickly, especially in one draft by suddenly tilting: *We went to a bar and tossed down a couple of beers. I poured the medicine into a small cup and tossed it down.*

toss for

To compete for something by flipping a coin to determine the winner: *There's one window seat, so let's toss for it. The candidates tossed for the chance to speak first at the debate.*

toss off

1. To remove clothing quickly or carelessly: *We tossed off our mittens and sat down to eat. I tossed my clothes off and threw on a swimsuit.*
2. To do or finish something effortlessly or casually: *The author tossed the book off in under a month. I tossed off an article and submitted it to the magazine.*
3. VULGAR SLANG To masturbate. Used of males.

toss out

1. To reject or discard something: *The court tossed out the case when the prosecution failed to produce any evidence. We've tossed our old methods out and adopted a more modern approach.*
2. To get rid of something as useless: *We should toss out some of these old newspapers. I tossed the milk out because it was starting to turn sour.*
3. To offer something casually, as a suggestion or plan: *I tossed out a couple of ideas in the meeting, but nobody seemed to like them. We tossed the proposal out to see if there was any support among the committee.*
4. To force someone to leave a place or position, especially in an abrupt or unexpected manner; expel someone: *The official tossed the player out of the game for fighting. The club's bouncer tossed out the drunken sailors.*
5. BASEBALL To start a game by throwing some pitch: *The mayor tossed out the first pitch of the season. The pitcher tossed the ball out to start the game.*

toss up

1. To throw something into the air: *The graduates tossed up their hats in celebration. The referee tossed the ball up for the tip-off.*
2. SPORTS To execute some type of throw or a throw with some outcome: *The quarterback tossed up a Hail Mary pass. The basketball player tossed a three-pointer up.*
3. To flip a coin to decide an issue: *Let's toss up to see who goes first.*

◆ **tot** (tŏt)

totted (tŏt′ĭd), **totting** (tŏt′ĭng), **tots** (tŏts)

tot up

To calculate something, especially by addition: *If you tot up all the costs, you'll realize this project is too expensive.*

ă	pat	är	car	ī	bite	ô	paw	o͝o	took	ûr	urge
ā	pay	ĕ	pet	îr	pier	ôr	core	o͝or	lure	zh	vision
âr	care	ē	be	ŏ	pot	oi	boy	o͞o	boot	ə	about,
ä	father	ĭ	pit	ō	toe	ou	out	ŭ	cut		item

◆ **total** (tō′təl)

totaled *or* **totalled** (tō′təld), **totaling** *or* **totalling** (tō′tə-lĭng), **totals** (tō′təlz)

total up

To calculate something, especially by addition: *At the end of the game, the judge totaled the points up and declared the winner. We totaled up all the items in our shopping cart to make sure we had enough money.*

◆ **touch** (tŭch)

touched (tŭcht), **touching** (tŭch′ĭng), **touches** (tŭch′ĭz)

touch down

To make contact with the ground; land: *The tornado touched down in a remote area.*

touch off

1. To cause something to explode or rapidly ignite: *The spark touched off the puddle of fuel. A cigarette from a passing motorist touched the dry grass off and started a forest fire.*
2. To trigger something; initiate something: *Investigators wondered what could have touched the fire off. The news of the scandal touched off a public uproar.*

touch on *or* **touch upon**

1. To deal with some topic in passing: *The speech touched on all the important issues but never really discussed them.*
2. To relate to someone or something; concern someone or something: *The problem of poverty touches on every level of society.*
3. To approach the nature or condition of something; come close to something: *The fan's excitement touched on clinical insanity.*

touch up

To improve something by making minor corrections, changes, or additions: *I touched up the nicks in the paint to prevent the metal from rusting. The author touched an old essay up and submitted it for publication.*

◆ **tough** (tŭf)

toughed (tŭft), **toughing** (tŭf′ĭng), **toughs** (tŭfs)

tough out

To endure something despite hardship; get through something: *The researchers toughed out another winter in the Arctic. I wanted to leave the military academy as soon as possible, but I decided to tough it out until the end of the semester.*

◆ **tout** (tout)

touted (tou′tĭd), **touting** (tou′tĭng), **touts** (touts)

tout as

To promote or praise someone or something by comparing them to some ideal: *The press is touting the young basketball player as the next Michael Jordan.*

tout for

To seek to obtain something by persuasion, entreaty, or formal application; solicit something: *We could hear the street vendors touting for business.*

◆ **towel** (tou′əl)

toweled *or* **towelled** (tou′əld), **toweling** *or* **towelling** (tou′ə-lĭng), **towels** (tou′əlz)

towel off

1. To dry oneself with a towel: *The swimmer got out of the pool and toweled off.*
2. To dry someone or something with a towel: *I toweled off my wet feet before putting my socks on. We hosed the car down and toweled it off.*

◆ **tower** (tou′ər)

towered (tou′ərd), **towering** (tou′ə-rĭng), **towers** (tou′ərz)

tower above *or* **tower over**

1. To appear at or rise to a conspicuous height above someone or something: *The oak towered above the rest of the trees. The skyscrapers tower over the horizon.*
2. To demonstrate great superiority over someone or something: *In terms of performance, our record towers above that of any other company in this city. Her report stated that the legacy of Alexander's empire towers over all other nations of the ancient world.*

◆ **toy** (toi)

toyed (toid), **toying** (toi′ĭng), **toys** (toiz)

toy with

1. To amuse oneself idly by manipulating someone or something; trifle with someone or something: *The cat toyed with the ball in its paws.*
2. To treat something casually or without seriousness: *I had toyed with the idea of going back to college, but I never actually applied.*

◆ **trace** (trās)

traced (trāst), **tracing** (trā′sĭng), **traces** (trā′sĭz)

trace back

1. To ascertain the successive stages in the development or progress of something by reasoning backward from an effect to a cause: *We traced our family history back 200 years. Skepticism as a philosophical movement can be traced back to Sextus Empiricus.*
2. To derive from something or someone: *The counterfeit drugs traced back to an American expatriate. Many English words trace back to Greek or Latin.*

trace out

1. To sketch or delineate something: *I laid out the map and traced out the path to the park.*
2. To delineate some pattern or development over time: *The results traced out an interesting pattern of sudden fluctuations every three months. The biographer traced out the politician's rise to power.*
3. To ascertain something by reconstructing a series of events: *The police traced out the Internet cafe as the place where the virus was launched. The motive for the*

ă	pat	är	car	ī	bite	ô	paw	o͝o	took	ûr	urge
ā	pay	ĕ	pet	îr	pier	ôr	core	o͝or	lure	zh	vision
âr	care	ē	be	ŏ	pot	oi	boy	o͞o	boot	ə	about,
ä	father	ĭ	pit	ō	toe	ou	out	ŭ	cut		item

crime was so unusual that no one could trace it out.

◆ **track** (trăk)

tracked (trăkt), **tracking** (trăk′ĭng), **tracks** (trăks)

track down

To pursue someone or something until found or captured: *I tracked down the book I was looking for. The fugitives were missing for a month before the police tracked them down.*

track up

1. To cover some surface or area with tracks: *The kids tracked up the carpet with mud. In the morning, the newly fallen snow lay prettily, but by the afternoon, people had tracked it up.*
2. To move north along some path or geographical feature. Used of storms: *The storm tracked up the coast.*

◆ **trade** (trād)

traded (trā′dĭd), **trading** (trā′dĭng), **trades** (trādz)

trade down

To trade something for something else of lower value or price: *My SUV used a lot of gas, so I traded it down for a smaller, more economical car. My parents traded down their house for a condominium in Arizona.*

trade in

1. To engage in the buying and selling of some product or commodity: *Our firm trades in gold and silver.*
2. To use something as payment or partial payment for a new purchase: *You could trade in all your old records for some new CDs. We traded our little car in for a bigger model.*

trade off

To take turns: *My roommate and I trade off washing the dishes.*

trade on *or* **trade upon**

To put something to calculated and often unscrupulous advantage; exploit something: *The children of celebrities sometimes trade on their family names to receive special treatment. People expect me to trade upon my height and join the basketball team, but I play badly.*

trade up

To trade something for something else of greater value or price: *The value of our house soared, which allowed us to trade up to a larger place.*

◆ **traffic** (trăf′ĭk)

trafficked (trăf′ĭkt), **trafficking** (trăf′ĭ-kĭng), **traffics** (trăf′ĭks)

traffic in

To engage in the buying and selling of some illegal or improper product or commodity: *The police arrested the criminals who trafficked in stolen diamonds.*

◆ **trail** (trāl)

trailed (trāld), **trailing** (trā′lĭng), **trails** (trālz)

trail off

To become gradually fainter; dwindle: *The writer's prolific output trailed off as the years went by.*

◆ **train** (trān)

trained (trānd), **training** (trā′nĭng), **trains** (trānz)

train on

To focus or aim something at some goal, mark, or target; direct something at someone or something: *The guards trained their rifles on us as we approached the gate.*

◆ **trample** (trăm′pəl)

trampled (trăm′pəld), **trampling** (trăm′pə-lĭng), **tramples** (trăm′pəlz)

trample on

1. To tread heavily or destructively on something: *The children trampled on the flowers.*
2. To inflict injury on something as if by treading heavily: *Why do you trample on the feelings of those around you?*

◆ **treat** (trēt)

treated (trē′tĭd), **treating** (trē′tĭng), **treats** (trēts)

treat as

To regard and handle someone or something in some way: *The king had received warnings of an uprising, but treated them as a joke. I refuse to be treated as a second-class citizen.*

treat of

To deal with some subject or topic in writing or speech: *The essay treats of courtly love.*

treat to

To provide someone with some food, entertainment, or gifts at one's own expense: *She treated her brother to dinner and a movie. I treat myself to a day in the country once in a while.*

treat with

To engage in negotiations with someone so as to reach a settlement or agree on terms: *If they are unwilling to treat with us, we will be forced to attack.*

◆ **trespass** (trĕs′pəs, trĕs′păs′)

trespassed (trĕs′pəst, trĕs′păst′), **trespassing** (trĕs′pə-sĭng, trĕs′păs′ĭng), **trespasses** (trĕs′pə-sĭz, trĕs′păs′ĭz)

trespass on

1. To enter wrongfully onto some land that belongs to another: *We don't tolerate hunters who trespass on our property.*
2. To infringe on something, such as another's privacy, time, or attention: *Do not trespass on their patience by pursuing this matter any further.*

◆ **trick** (trĭk)

tricked (trĭkt), **tricking** (trĭk′ĭng), **tricks** (trĭks)

trick into

To cause someone to do or believe something by deceptive or fraudulent means: *The con artist tricked*

ă	pat	är	car	ī	bite	ô	paw	o͝o	took	ûr	urge
ā	pay	ĕ	pet	îr	pier	ôr	core	o͝or	lure	zh	vision
âr	care	ē	be	ŏ	pot	oi	boy	o͞o	boot	ə	about, item
ä	father	ĭ	pit	ō	toe	ou	out	ŭ	cut		

me into believing that I had won a lottery.

trick out *or* **trick up**

To ornament or adorn someone or something, often garishly: *I tricked out my car with some shiny new rims and neon lights. We tricked the bedroom out with velvet and leopard print. The dancers were all tricked out in beads and fringe.*

◆ **trickle** (trĭk′əl)

trickled (trĭk′əld), **trickling** (trĭk′lĭng), **trickles** (trĭk′əlz)

trickle down

To diffuse downward through some hierarchical structure: *The sociology professor believed that money rarely trickles down from the owners of capital to the workers who toil in the factories.*

◆ **trifle** (trī′fəl)

trifled (trī′fəld), **trifling** (trī′flĭng), **trifles** (trī′fəlz)

trifle with

To play or toy with someone or something: *Don't trifle with my affections. My strict boss is not someone to be trifled with.*

◆ **trim** (trĭm)

trimmed (trĭmd), **trimming** (trĭm′ĭng), **trims** (trĭmz)

trim down

1. To reduce something by or as if by cutting away the excess: *The company is trimming down its budget this year. The editor trimmed the long manuscript down to 200 pages.*
2. To lose weight, as by dieting or exercise: *The doctor advised me to trim down.*

trim off

To remove some excess by or as if by cutting: *I trimmed off the rotten wood. The barber will trim my bangs off.*

◆ **trip** (trĭp)

tripped (trĭpt), **tripping** (trĭp′ĭng), **trips** (trĭps)

trip on

1. To stumble or fall on account of hitting or catching the foot on something: *I tripped on the curb and fell down on the sidewalk.*
2. Slang To be under the influence of some hallucinogenic drug: *He tried to write an essay while he was tripping on acid, and it made no sense at all.*

trip up

1. To stumble or fall: *I tripped up walking upstairs and hurt my ankle.*
2. To cause someone to stumble or fall: *The soccer player tripped up her opponent with a slide tackle. The broken stair tripped him up.*
3. To make a mistake: *I would have done better on the test if I hadn't tripped up on the last section.*
4. To cause someone to make a mistake: *His inability to focus on his work trips him up every time. The unclear phrasing of the question tripped her up.*

◆ **triumph** (trī′əmf)

triumphed (trī′əmft), **triumphing** (trī′əm-fĭng), **triumphs** (trī′əmfs)

triumph over

To defeat someone or something, especially in a noteworthy contest: *By the end of the movie, good triumphs over evil and everybody is happy.*

◆ **trot** (trŏt)

trotted (trŏt′ĭd), **trotting** (trŏt′ĭng), **trots** (trŏts)

trot off

To proceed briskly: *I left work at noon and trotted off to the gym.*

trot out

To bring out and show something or someone for inspection or admiration: *The company trotted out a celebrity to endorse their product. Once politicians discover a topic the public responds to, they trot it out every election year.*

◆ **truckle** (trŭk′əl)

truckled (trŭk′əld), **truckling** (trŭk′lĭng), **truckles** (trŭk′əlz)

truckle to

To be servile or submissive to someone or something: *All the peasants in the fields truckled to the king.*

◆ **trump** (trŭmp)

trumped (trŭmpt), **trumping** (trŭm′pĭng), **trumps** (trŭmps)

trump up

To devise something fraudulently: *The corrupt cop trumped up a charge of conspiracy against the people under arrest.*

◆ **truss** (trŭs)

trussed (trŭst), **trussing** (trŭs′ĭng), **trusses** (trŭs′ĭz)

truss up

1. To tie up or bind someone or something tightly: *The bank robbers trussed up the employees and fled with the money. The costume designer trussed us up in elaborate gowns.*
2. To bind or skewer the wings or legs of some bird before cooking: *The chef trussed up the fowl. I trussed the duck up and put it into the oven.*
3. To support or brace something with a truss: *I sprained my ankle, and the coach trussed it up. The doctor trussed up the patient's arm.*

◆ **trust** (trŭst)

trusted (trŭs′tĭd), **trusting** (trŭs′tĭng), **trusts** (trŭsts)

trust in

To depend on someone or something: *The preacher told the congregation to trust in God.*

trust to

To depend on something: *I'd rather plan my financial future than trust to luck.*

trust with

To grant discretion to someone confidently: *Can you trust them with your credit card information?*

ă	pat	är	car	ī	bite	ô	paw	o͝o	took	ûr	urge
ā	pay	ĕ	pet	îr	pier	ôr	core	o͝or	lure	zh	vision
âr	care	ē	be	ŏ	pot	oi	boy	o͞o	boot	ə	about,
ä	father	ĭ	pit	ō	toe	ou	out	ŭ	cut		item

◆ **try** (trī)

tried (trīd), **trying** (trī′ĭng), **tries** (trīz)

try back

1. To call or visit a location again as the continuation of an attempt to make contact with a person or place: *The office is now closed, but you can try back during business hours.*
2. To call or visit someone again as the continuation of an attempt to make contact: *If I'm not around when you call, try me back tomorrow night.*

try on

To put some garment on in order to determine if it fits: *She went to the dressing room to try on the sweater. He tried the shoes on and said they were too tight.*

try out

1. To undergo a competitive qualifying test, as for a job or athletic team: *Thirty students tried out for the soccer team, but only twenty were chosen.*
2. To test or use something experimentally: *Have you tried out the new automated banking system yet? I tried a new brand of toothpaste out, and I really like it.*

◆ **tuck** (tŭk)

tucked (tŭkt), **tucking** (tŭk′ĭng), **tucks** (tŭks)

tuck away

1. To put something in an out-of-the-way, snug place: *She tucked away her wallet under all of the socks. He tucked the files away in the back of the filing cabinet. The cabin is tucked away in the mountains.*
2. To store something in a safe spot; save something: *The child tucked away some candy. I'll bet my neighbors have tucked millions of dollars away.*
3. SLANG To consume some food heartily: *The hungry farmer tucked away three steaks. The food left over from lunch was gone by dinnertime, since I tucked it all away during the afternoon.*

tuck in

1. To gather something up and fold, thrust, or turn in so as to secure or confine it: *The teacher told the boys to tuck in their shirts. I threw the sheet over the bed and tucked it in at the corners.*
2. To make someone secure in bed for sleep, especially by tucking bedclothes into the bed: *I tucked in my daughter and said good night. The babysitter tucked the little boy in.*
3. To draw in some body part; contract something: *She tucked in her arms and shook her head. The turtle tucked in its head.*
4. SLANG To begin to eat heartily: *Dinner was served, and we tucked in.*

tuck into

1. To gather something up and fold or thrust it into something so as to secure or confine it: *I wrote the number on a piece of paper and tucked it into my pocket.*
2. To make someone secure in some bed for sleep, especially by tucking bedclothes into the bed: *After the children put on their pajamas, I tucked them into bed.*

3. SLANG To begin to eat something heartily: *We tucked into a stack of pancakes.*

tuck up

1. To put someone or something in a snug spot: *The babysitter tucked the children up soundly in bed. I tucked up the horses in the barn.*
2. To put something in an out-of-the-way, snug place: *The cabin was tucked up among the pines. I tucked my hair up under a wool cap.*
3. To draw up some body part into a tuck position: *The diver tucked up her legs for a somersault. The gymnast tucked his knees up to his chest during the dismount.*
4. To assume a tuck position: *The flight attendants advised the passengers to tuck up for a rough landing.*

◆ **tucker** (tŭk′ər)

tuckered (tŭk′ərd), **tuckering** (tŭk′ə-rĭng), **tuckers** (tŭk′ərz)

tucker out

To make someone weary; exhaust someone: *Hiking all day tuckered me out. The long bus ride tuckered out the travelers.*

◆ **tumble** (tŭm′bəl)

tumbled (tŭm′bəld), **tumbling** (tŭm′blĭng), **tumbles** (tŭm′bəlz)

tumble down

1. To topple, as from power or a high position; fall: *That horse started out the race in the lead, but tumbled down to fifth place.*
2. To collapse: *The wall tumbled down when I leaned on it.*

tumble on *or* **tumble upon**

To come upon something accidentally; happen on something: *We tumbled on a nice restaurant while walking downtown.*

tumble to

SLANG

To come to some sudden understanding; catch on to something: *I tumbled to the reality that the other card players were cheating.*

◆ **tune** (to͞on)

tuned (to͞ond), **tuning** (to͞o′nĭng), **tunes** (to͞onz)

tune in

1. To connect to or start receiving a particular broadcast station or program: *Millions of viewers tuned in at 6:00 for the football game.*
2. To become aware of or responsive to someone or something: *It wasn't until after the disaster that I really tuned in to what was happening overseas.*
3. To cause someone to become aware of or responsive to someone or something: *One of my classmates tuned me in to politics.*

tune into

1. To watch or listen to a particular broadcast station or program: *I*

ă	pat	är	car	ī	bite	ô	paw	o͝o	took	ûr	urge
ā	pay	ĕ	pet	îr	pier	ôr	core	o͝or	lure	zh	vision
âr	care	ē	be	ŏ	pot	oi	boy	o͞o	boot	ə	about,
ä	father	ĭ	pit	ō	toe	ou	out	ŭ	cut		item

tuned into the baseball game last night.

2. To cause someone to be in a harmonious or responsive relationship with someone or something. Often used in the passive: *My therapist is tuned into my feelings. Her report tuned me into the importance of smoke detectors.*

tune out

1. To disconnect from or stop receiving a particular broadcast station or program: *I had to tune out halfway through the game last night, so I don't know how it ended.*
2. SLANG To disassociate oneself from one's environment: *When faced with so much advertising, most people just tune out.*
3. SLANG To become unresponsive to someone or something; ignore someone or something: *She tried to tune out the children's laughter so she could study. He tunes me out every time I ask him about the money that he owes me.*

tune up

1. To adjust some musical instrument to a desired pitch or key: *She tunes up the violin for the students. He tuned his cello up before practicing. The orchestra tuned up before the concert.*
2. To adjust some machine so as to put it into proper condition: *The mechanic tuned up the car. I tune the motor up every few months.*
3. To prepare oneself for some activity: *The team tuned up for the match with a scrimmage.*

◆ **turn** (tûrn)

turned (tûrnd), **turning** (tûr′nĭng), **turns** (tûrnz)

turn against

1. To change one's actions or attitudes to be against someone or something; become hostile or antagonistic toward someone or something: *The peasants turned against the cruel ruler.*
2. To cause someone or something to act or go against someone or something; make someone or something antagonistic toward someone or something: *The scandal turned public opinion against the candidate. They turned my family against me.*

turn around

1. To cause something to reverse direction or course: *The driver turned the car around. The child turned around the bike.*
2. To reverse one's way, course, or direction: *We turned around and headed back home.*
3. To reverse a decline in performance, value, or health: *The stock turned around.*
4. To cause something to reverse a decline in performance, value, or health: *The new owner turned around the company. The counselor turned our marriage around.*
5. To receive, process, and send something out: *If you drop off your dry cleaning today, we can turn it around by Monday. The bank will turn around the check quickly.*
6. To distort the purpose, intention, or content of something: *Stop turning my words around! They turned around my ideas so that I didn't even recognize them.*

turn aside

1. To deflect something: cause something to turn or deviate: *The goalie*

turned aside six of the seven shots. The manager turned all of the allegations aside.

2. To reject or refuse someone or something: *The office turned aside my request. The company turned my complaints aside.*
3. To deviate from a certain way, course, or direction: *I turned aside from the career path that my father had taken.*
4. **turn aside from** To cause someone to turn or deviate from a certain way, course, or direction: *My rowdy friends turned me aside from my studies.*

turn away

1. To rotate and face another direction; avert one's eyes: *I tried to speak to my friends, but they just turned away. Turn away while I get dressed.*
2. To send someone or something away; dismiss someone or something: *We turned away the people who were looking for a job. The new boss turns all criticism away.*
3. To repel someone or something: *The poor location of the house turned away prospective buyers. The horrible smell turned the police officer away.*
4. **turn away from** To abandon or forsake someone or something: *The volunteers turned away from the agency because they felt unappreciated.*
5. **turn away from** To cause someone or something to abandon or forsake someone or something: *Their college life turned our children away from our traditional values.*

turn back

1. To abandon one's way, course, or direction and return: *The road became too muddy, and we had to turn back. Once you sign the contract, you cannot turn back.*
2. To force someone or something to stop and go back: *Our surprise attack turned back the advancing army. The police turned us back at the border because we forgot our passports.*
3. To fold something down: *Turn back the page's corner to save your place in the book. The tailor turned the edge of the fabric back and made a hem.*

turn down

1. To diminish the speed, volume, intensity, or flow of something by or as if by turning a dial: *Turn down the radio, please. He turned down the TV so his roommate could study.*
2. To reject or refuse someone or something: *I turned down the invitation. We turned them down because their offer was too low.*
3. To fold something downward: *I turned my collar down. She turned down the flaps on her hat to protect her ears from the cold.*
4. To prepare some bed by folding the outer covering down: *The hotel maid came in and turned down the bed.*

ă	pat	är	car	ī	bite	ô	paw	o͝o	took	ûr	urge
ā	pay	ĕ	pet	îr	pier	ôr	core	o͝or	lure	zh	vision
âr	care	ē	be	ŏ	pot	oi	boy	o͞o	boot	ə	about,
ä	father	ĭ	pit	ō	toe	ou	out	ŭ	cut		item

turn in

1. To deliver or submit some assignment or work: *I turned my application in before the deadline. That actor turns in a consistent performance every show.*
2. To inform on or deliver someone or something to an authority: *I turned in the wallet that I found to the police. The criminals turned themselves in.*
3. To go to bed: *I turned in early last night.*

turn into

1. To direct one's way or course into something: *The truck turned into the gas station.*
2. To cause someone or something to take on some character, nature, identity, or appearance; change or transform someone or something into someone or something: *The designer turned a rundown house into a show place. We turned the spare room into a nursery.*
3. To change into something or someone; become transformed into something or someone: *The night turned into day. In the story, straw turns into gold.*
4. To convert something into something: *The singers turned their talent into extra money.*
5. To pour, let fall, or otherwise release something into some receptacle: *The chef turned the soup into the dish.*

turn off

1. To leave some course or direction: *Turn off at the next exit.*
2. To stop the operation, activity, or flow of something: *She turned off the television. He turned the radio off.*
3. SLANG To affect someone with dislike, displeasure, or revulsion: *That song really turns me off. The editorial turned off many readers.*
4. SLANG To affect someone with boredom: *The boring lecture turned off the class. The movie turned the audience off.*
5. SLANG **turn off to** To lose interest in something: *My family turned off to boating once we started swimming more.*
6. SLANG **turn off to** To cause someone to lose interest in something: *Breaking my leg turned me off to skiing. I looked forward to going to the beach, but after seeing all the drunk college students there, I got really turned off.*
7. SLANG To cease paying attention: *Whenever you don't like what I say, you just turn off.*
8. SLANG To cause someone to lose sexual interest: *Pickup lines turn me off. His rude behavior turned off everyone he tried to pick up.*

turn on

1. To suddenly aim or focus something on someone or something: *She turned the camera on the speaker. He turned the gun on himself.*
2. To attack someone or something suddenly and violently with no apparent motive: *The lion turned on the animal trainer.*
3. To become disloyal toward someone that one was once loyal to: *After years as an assistant, I turned on my boss and told the authorities about his tax evasion.*
4. To depend on someone or something for success or failure: *The campaign turns on attracting swing voters.*

5. To start the operation, activity, or flow of something by or as if by turning a switch: *Turn on the light bulb. Turn the generator on.*
6. To begin instantly to display, employ, or exude some affectation: *She turned on the charm. He turns a fake accent on when he doesn't want to be recognized.*
7. SLANG To take a mind-altering drug, especially for the first time: *They turned on and passed out at the party.*
8. SLANG **turn on to** To cause to become interested, pleasurably excited, or stimulated by something: *My aunt turned me on to jazz.*
9. SLANG **turn on to** To be interested, pleasurably excited, or stimulated by something: *She turned on to surfing this summer.*
10. VULGAR SLANG To excite someone sexually.

turn out

1. To turn some light off: *We turned out the lights. I turned the light out.*
2. To arrive or assemble, as for a public event or entertainment: *Many protesters have turned out for the rally.*
3. To produce something, as by a manufacturing process; make something: *The assembly line turns out 100 cars every hour. The artist turns a new painting out every week.*
4. To be found to be something, as after experience or trial: *The rookie turned out to be the team's best hitter. It turns out that he knew about the crime all along.*
5. To end up; result: *The cake turned out beautifully.*
6. To equip someone or something; outfit someone or something. Used chiefly in the passive: *The troops were turned out lavishly. They were turned out in brilliant colors.*
7. To get out of bed: *We turned out before the sun was up.*
8. To get someone out of bed: *The babysitter turned the children out at 8:00.*
9. To evict someone; expel someone: *The landlord turned out the tenants. The hotel turned the rowdy guests out.*

turn over

1. To bring the bottom of something to the top or vice versa; invert something: *The farmer turned over the soil with a plow. The angry mob attacked the police car and turned it over.*
2. To shift the position of, as by rolling from one side to the other: *I turned over the box to read the instructions on the back. You have to turn the page over to read the rest of the story.*
3. To shift one's position by rolling from one side to the other: *The puppy turned over and lay on its back.*
4. To rotate; cycle: *The engine turned over but wouldn't start.*
5. To think about something; consider something: *I spent all night turning over what you said yesterday.*

She turned the problem over in her mind.

6. To transfer possession or control of someone or something to another; surrender someone or something: *The CEO turned over the company to her son when she retired. If you find any evidence connected to a crime, you should turn it over to the authorities.*
7. SPORTS To lose possession of something, such as a ball: *Our quarterback turned over the ball five times in one game. The visiting team turned the ball over on their first play.*
8. To do business to the extent or amount of something: *The company turns over $1 million each year.*
9. To seem to lurch or heave convulsively: *My stomach turned over when the roller coaster started moving.*
10. To search someplace thoroughly: *The police turned over the house looking for evidence. The burglars had turned the place over but couldn't find the jewels they were looking for.*

turn to

1. To change the setting of something, such as a mechanical device, to some other setting by or as if by turning a dial: *Please turn the iron to a lower setting so you don't burn the shirt. That night, everyone had their TVs turned to channel 5 to watch the news.*
2. To progress through pages so as to arrive at some place: *I turned to the next page to read the rest of the story. Please turn your textbooks to page 31.*
3. To direct one's gaze to something by rotating or pivoting: *The spectators turned to the sky as the jet flew overhead.*
4. To devote or apply someone or something to someone or something: *We turned our efforts to charity and community education.*
5. To devote or apply oneself to someone or something: *I wasn't very good in math, so I turned to biology.*
6. To channel one's attention, interest, or thought to something: *In the spring, we turn to thoughts of love.*
7. To convert to some religion: *He recently turned to Buddhism.*
8. To switch one's loyalty to some other side or party: *Many disillusioned voters have turned to third parties.*
9. To have recourse to someone or something for help, support, or information: *Whom will you turn to when you are in need?*
10. To cause someone or something to take on some nature or appearance; change or transform someone or something to something: *The low temperature has turned the river to ice.*
11. To take on some nature or appearance: *The tree's leaves turned to brown in the fall.*

turn up

1. To rotate something so as to expose the underside: *We turned up the soil in the garden to prepare it for planting. I turned the log up and found hundreds of bugs underneath.*
2. To bring something that is underneath to the surface: *The plow had*

turned up a number of rocks, and we collected them for use in the wall. The children turned the shells up while they were digging in the sand.

3. To come to the surface: *A large rock turned up during the excavation.*
4. To increase the speed, volume, intensity, or flow of something by or as if by turning a dial: *I think we should turn up the temperature in the oven. Turn the radio up so we can hear it outside.*
5. To be found, especially without searching: *Don't worry about losing your keys—I'm sure they'll turn up somewhere.*
6. To make an appearance; arrive: *Many old friends turned up at the reunion.*
7. To fold something upward or so that the inside is exposed: *I turned the cuffs of my pants up and walked through the puddle. We turned up our collars and headed out into the rain.*
8. To happen unexpectedly: *Something turned up at the office, and we had to stay later than usual.*
9. To be evident or easily encountered: *That sculptor's name turns up in the art community.*

◆ **type** (tīp)

typed (tīpt), **typing** (tī′pĭng), **types** (tīps)

type in

To input something into a computer or similar device by typing: *You can type in your query when the prompt appears on the screen. Type your name in and click the button to access your account.*

type out

1. To produce something by typing: *I typed out an angry letter to the editor. It took the writer one month to type a manuscript out.*
2. To express something in typewritten form: *The lawyer typed out the client's statement. I typed the message out and posted it on the bulletin board for all to see.*
3. To display something in full or expanded form by typing: *You must type out your complete address on the credit card application. The editor was instructed to type each abbreviation out.*

type up

1. To compose a finished document from some set of notes by typing: *I hired an assistant to type up my handwritten letters. The secretary typed the handwritten notes up.*
2. To draft some kind of document by typing: *We sat up all night typing up a charter for the organization. Do you have time to type a few letters up for me?*

ă	pat	är	car	ī	bite	ô	paw	o͝o	took	ûr	urge
ā	pay	ĕ	pet	îr	pier	ôr	core	o͝or	lure	zh	vision
âr	care	ē	be	ŏ	pot	oi	boy	o͞o	boot	ə	about,
ä	father	ĭ	pit	ō	toe	ou	out	ŭ	cut		item

U

◆ **unite** (yo͞o-nīt′)

united (yo͞o-nī′tĭd), **uniting** (yo͞o-nī′tĭng), **unites** (yo͞o-nīts′)

unite with

To have or demonstrate something in combination with something else: *The new government initiative unites common sense with vision.*

◆ **urge** (ûrj)

urged (ûrjd), **urging** (ûr′jĭng), **urges** (ûr′jĭz)

urge on

To move or impel someone or something to action, effort, or speed: *The orator urged on the excited crowd to applaud even more loudly. The travelers were tired of walking, but the thought of a hot meal and warm bed urged them on.*

◆ **use** (yo͞oz)

used (yo͞ozd), **using** (yo͞o′zĭng), **uses** (yo͞o′zĭz)

use up

To consume something completely: *We used up all our money on repairs for the house. We used all the gas up before we reached the gas station.*

◆ **usher** (ŭsh′ər)

ushered (ŭsh′ərd), **ushering** (ŭsh′ə-rĭng), **ushers** (ŭsh′ərz)

usher in

1. To lead, escort, or conduct someone or something in: *The butler ushered in the guests. I ushered the bride's mother in.*
2. To precede and introduce something; inaugurate something: *The armistice ushered in a new era of peace. We ushered in the new year with a celebration.*

usher out

1. To lead, escort, or conduct someone or something out: *Bodyguards ushered the politician out of the room. The police ushered out the protesters from the ballpark. The protesters were ushered out of the meeting room.*
2. To follow or supersede someone or something: *The ability to record sound on film ushered out the era of silent movies. The partygoers ushered the old year out with a champagne toast.*

V

◆ **vaccinate** (văk′sə-nāt′)

vaccinated (văk′sə-nā′tĭd), **vaccinating** (văk′sə-nā′tĭng), **vaccinates** (văk′sə-nāts′)

vaccinate against *or* **vaccinate for**

To give someone a vaccination to produce immunity to some infectious disease: *The doctor vaccinated the child against measles. The dog has been vaccinated for rabies.*

◆ **vamp** (vămp)

vamped (vămpt), **vamping** (văm′pĭng), **vamps** (vămps)

vamp up

1. To refurbish, improve, or embellish something: *The designers vamped up the website using contemporary colors. I bought an old bookshelf and vamped it up with a new coat of paint.*
2. To put something together; fabricate or improvise something: *With no hard news available about the summit meeting, the reporters vamped up questions based only on rumor. When my turn came to tell a story, I vamped one up from tales I had heard as a child.*

◆ **vanish** (văn′ĭsh)

vanished (văn′ĭsht), **vanishing** (văn′ĭ-shĭng), **vanishes** (văn′ĭ-shĭz)

vanish away

To disappear gradually but completely: *I had to wash the shirt five times before the grass stain vanished away.*

◆ **vary** (vâr′ē)

varied (vâr′ēd), **varying** (vâr′ē-ĭng), **varies** (vâr′ēz)

vary from

To be different than something or someone; deviate from something or someone: *The researchers determined that the behavior of children who took the medicine varied from normal patterns of behavior.*

vary up

To change the variables associated with something: *The cafeteria varied up its menu with a new kind of sandwich. You've worn the same blue sweater all week—why not vary it up and wear something new?*

◆ **vault** (vôlt)

vaulted (vôl′tĭd), **vaulting** (vôl′tĭng), **vaults** (vôlts)

vault into

To attain some position as if by leaping suddenly or vigorously:

ă	pat	är	car	ī	bite	ô	paw	o͝o	took	ûr	urge
ā	pay	ĕ	pet	îr	pier	ôr	core	o͝or	lure	zh	vision
âr	care	ē	be	ŏ	pot	oi	boy	o͞o	boot	ə	about,
ä	father	ĭ	pit	ō	toe	ou	out	ŭ	cut		item

With the sale of the company, the founders vaulted into a position of wealth.

◆ **veer** (vîr)

veered (vîrd), **veering** (vîr′ĭng), **veers** (vîrz)

veer off

To turn aside suddenly and leave some course, direction, or purpose: *The tire blew out, and the car veered off the road. The road veers off to the right, so stay alert. The teacher veered off the topic and left the students bewildered.*

◆ **veg** (vĕj)

vegged (vĕjd), **vegging** (vĕj′ĭng), **veges** *or* **vegges** (vĕj′ĭz)

veg out

SLANG

To engage in relaxing or passive activities: *After work, I went home and vegged out in front of the TV.*

◆ **vent** (vĕnt)

vented (vĕn′tĭd), **venting** (vĕn′tĭng), **vents** (vĕnts)

vent on

To release some strong emotion by taking action against someone or something: *The frustrated travelers vented their anger on the employees of the airline.*

◆ **venture** (vĕn′chər)

ventured (vĕn′chərd), **venturing** (vĕn′chə-rĭng), **ventures** (vĕn′chərz)

venture forth

To proceed despite possible danger or risk: *After the storm subsided, we ventured forth to assess the damage.*

venture into

To proceed into something despite possible danger or risk: *The explorers ventured into the dark cave.*

venture on *or* **venture upon**

To come upon something by chance or fortune: *The travelers ventured on a charming country inn. The explorers ventured upon a hidden cache of gold.*

◆ **verge** (vûrj)

verged (vûrjd), **verging** (vûr′jĭng), **verges** (vûr′jĭz)

verge on

1. To be on the edge or border of something: *The park verges on the neighboring town.*
2. To approach the nature or condition of something; come close to something: *Their confidence verges on arrogance.*

◆ **verse** (vûrs)

versed (vûrst), **versing** (vûr′sĭng), **verses** (vûr′sĭz)

verse in

To familiarize someone with something by study or experience. Used chiefly in the passive or with a reflexive: *She is versed in physics. He has versed himself in the art of fencing. The music teacher will verse the students in keeping time to a beat.*

◆ **vest** (vĕst)

vested (vĕs′tĭd), **vesting** (vĕs′tĭng), **vests** (vĕsts)

vest in

To place something, such as authority, property, or rights, in the control of someone or some group: *I vested my estate in my son. The judge is very conscientious about the duties and responsibilities that are vested in her.*

vest with

To invest or endow someone or some group with something, such as power or rights: *The company vests its employees with full pension rights after five years of service. The council is vested with broad powers.*

◆ **vie** (vī)

vied (vīd), **vying** (vī′ĭng), **vies** (vīz)

vie for

To contend with another or others to attain some goal, such as a victory in a contest: *The top three students in the class vied for the title of valedictorian.*

vie with

To contend with someone to attain a goal, such as a victory in a contest: *The champion sprinter will vie with the new young athlete in the final round of competition.*

◆ **visit** (vĭz′ĭt)

visited (vĭz′ĭ-tĭd), **visiting** (vĭz′ĭ-tĭng), **visits** (vĭz′ĭts)

visit on *or* **visit upon**

To inflict something punishing or burdensome on someone or something. Used chiefly in the passive: *A plague was visited on the village.*

visit with

To converse or chat with someone: *Come over and visit with me for a while.*

◆ **vomit** (vŏm′ĭt)

vomited (vŏm′ĭ-tĭd), **vomiting** (vŏm′ĭ-tĭng), **vomits** (vŏm′ĭts)

vomit forth

1. To be discharged forcefully and abundantly; spew or gush: *The dam burst, and the floodwaters vomited forth.*
2. To eject or discharge something in a gush; spew something out: *The volcano vomited forth lava and ash. The belly of the ship opened and vomited the cargo forth.*

vomit up

To eject some contents of the stomach through the mouth: *I vomited up my dinner. The bird vomited the worm up for its young.*

◆ **vote** (vōt)

voted (vō′tĭd), **voting** (vō′tĭng), **votes** (vōts)

vote down

To reject or defeat something by vote: *Parliament voted down the amendment. Should we approve this budget plan or vote it down?*

ă	pat	är	car	ī	bite	ô	paw	o͝o	took	ûr	urge
ā	pay	ĕ	pet	îr	pier	ôr	core	o͝or	lure	zh	vision
âr	care	ē	be	ŏ	pot	oi	boy	o͞o	boot	ə	about,
ä	father	ĭ	pit	ō	toe	ou	out	ŭ	cut		item

vote in

To select someone or something by vote for an office or for membership; elect someone or something: *The members of the club voted in a new slate of officers. The president has been accused of turning her back on the public that voted her in.*

vote into

1. To select someone or something by vote for some office or for membership; elect someone or something to something: *You must meet certain requirements in order to be voted into the club. We voted her into office by a landslide majority.*
2. To ratify or reject some legislation, so as to bring it into some state of existence: *Californians must decide whether to vote these propositions into law.*

vote on

To hold a vote or referendum in order to decide the disposition of something: *The committee will vote on the proposal next week.*

vote out

To remove someone or some group from office or power by vote; depose someone or some group: *Advocacy groups are urging the public to vote out the governor. The townspeople voted the mayor out after two terms in office.*

vote through

To sanction, ratify, or approve something by voting: *The Senate unanimously voted through the reforms. Legislators are voting through a bill banning smoking in most public spaces.*

◆ **vouch** (vouch)

vouched (voucht), **vouching** (vou′chĭng), **vouches** (vou′chĭz)

vouch for

1. To give personal assurances of something or someone; give a guarantee of something or someone: *I can't vouch for that company's reliability because I've never dealt with them.*
2. To constitute supporting evidence for something; give substantiation for something: *The candidate's strong record vouches for her ability.*

W

◆ **wad** (wăd)

wadded (wăd′ĭd), **wadding** (wăd′ĭng), **wads** (wădz)

wad up

To crumple or compress something into a wad: *I wadded up the piece of paper and threw it in the trash. The janitor wadded the tissues up and threw them away.*

◆ **wade** (wād)

waded (wā′dĭd), **wading** (wā′dĭng), **wades** (wādz)

wade in

1. To walk into a substance, such as water, that hinders normal movement: *Unable to reach the buoy from the shore, I waded in toward it.*
2. To join or intervene in an ongoing conflict, debate, or controversy: *The government waded in to settle the contract dispute.*

wade into

1. To walk into something, such as water, that impedes normal movement: *The child waded into the ocean.*
2. To join or intervene in some ongoing conflict, debate, or controversy: *The government waded into the dispute and forced a resolution. The mayor waded into the debate to elaborate on a few points.*
3. To become increasingly involved in some effort: *The committee waded into the task.*
4. To attack someone or something verbally or physically: *The supervisor waded into me with a vehement attack.*

wade through

1. To walk through something, such as water, that hinders normal movement: *We waded through the water.*
2. To proceed through something with great difficulty or effort: *I waded through a boring report.*

◆ **wager** (wā′jər)

wagered (wā′jərd), **wagering** (wā′jə-rĭng), **wagers** (wā′jərz)

wager on

1. To place a wager of some amount on some event: *I wagered $10 on the first race of the evening.*
2. To place a wager of some amount on some participant in an event: *I wagered $10 on the Detroit Tigers.*
3. To place a wager or bet on some event: *I wagered on the last race of the evening but lost.*

ă	pat	är	car	ī	bite	ô	paw	o͝o	took	ûr	urge
ā	pay	ĕ	pet	îr	pier	ôr	core	o͝or	lure	zh	vision
âr	care	ē	be	ŏ	pot	oi	boy	o͞o	boot	ə	about,
ä	father	ĭ	pit	ō	toe	ou	out	ŭ	cut		item

4. To place a wager or bet on some participant in an event: *I wagered on the Chicago Bears and doubled my money.*
5. To expect or feel sure that something will happen: *You can wager on Chris being late to the meeting.*

◆ **wait** (wāt)

waited (wā′tĭd), **waiting** (wā′tĭng), **waits** (wāts)

wait around

To remain near a location in expectation: *I don't want to wait around at home until you call. We waited around for them, but they never came.*

wait for

To await someone or something; remain in expectation for someone or something: *I waited for my date in the lobby.*

wait on *or* **wait upon**

1. To serve the needs of someone or something; be in attendance on someone or something: *The clerk waited on a customer.*
2. To await someone or something: *They're waiting on my decision.*
3. To make a formal call on someone; visit someone: *We waited on the mourning widow to pay our respects.*

wait out

To delay until the termination of something: *I waited out the war in the countryside. The baseball team waited the storm out and resumed playing an hour later.*

wait up

1. To postpone going to bed in expectation: *We will be out late tonight, so don't wait up. The children waited up for their parents to come home.*
2. To stop or pause so that another can catch up: *The leader of the hike waited up for the stragglers.*

◆ **wake** (wāk)

woke (wōk) *or* **waked** (wākt), **waked** *or* **woken** (wō′kən), **waking** (wā′kĭng), **wakes** (wāks)

wake up

1. To rouse someone or something from sleep; awaken someone or something: *Be quiet, or you will wake up the baby. The alarm woke me up.*
2. To become awake; waken: *I plan to wake up early tomorrow.*
3. To make someone alert or cognizant: *The coffee woke me up. The shocking revelations finally woke up the citizens.*
4. **wake up to** To become alert or cognizant of something: *We suddenly woke up to the fact that the family business was failing.*

◆ **walk** (wôk)

walked (wôkt), **walking** (wô′kĭng), **walks** (wôks)

walk away

1. To leave by or as if by walking: *When she saw me, she quickly walked away.*
2. To emerge from a dangerous situation without serious injury or penalty: *You were lucky to walk away from such a bad car accident. The students could have been expelled for such an offense, but somehow they walked away with only a warning.*

3. To leave freely and without obligation: *The two sides walked away from the deal when they failed to reach a compromise. With no evidence to hold them on, the officers let the suspects walk away.*
4. **walk away with** To win some prize or award easily or unexpectedly: *The film walked away with ten awards.*
5. **walk away with** To steal something: *The robbers walked away with $1 million in jewels.*

walk in

1. To enter something by walking: *The door was open, so we walked in and took our seats.*
2. To enter casually, easily, or unawares: *That new student walked in off the street and became the starting quarterback. I don't think you can simply walk in and take over the responsibilities of this new job.*
3. **walk in on** To walk in and see some private situation or someone in a private situation: *They were embarrassed when I walked in on them making a mess in the kitchen. The guard walked in on a robbery.*

walk into

1. To enter something by walking: *The family walked into the restaurant and sat down.*
2. To bump into something by walking: *He wasn't looking where he was going, and he walked into a lamppost.*
3. To enter something casually, easily, or unawares: *With her connections, she can walk into any job she wants. I walked into the trap they had set out for me.*

walk off

1. To leave abruptly by walking: *My friend got angry and walked off in the middle of our conversation.*
2. To reduce or eliminate some pain or stiffness by walking: *I pulled my leg muscle a little bit, but I walked it off. The athlete walked off the muscle cramp before the game.*
3. To lose some amount of weight by walking: *She walked off ten pounds. He walked five pounds off.*
4. To shed the weight gained by consuming something: *You'll have to walk off all that chocolate cake. If I eat this doughnut, I'll walk it off this afternoon.*
5. **walk off with** To win some prize or award easily or unexpectedly: *My student walked off with first prize.*
6. **walk off with** To steal something: *Someone walked off with my wallet.*

walk out

1. To abandon or forsake one's family or other personal relationship: *After ten years of marriage, she walked out. He walked out on his family and moved to California.*
2. To leave suddenly, often as a signal of disapproval: *Offended by the*

ă	pat	är	car	ī	bite	ô	paw	ŏŏ	took	ûr	urge
ā	pay	ĕ	pet	îr	pier	ôr	core	ŏŏr	lure	zh	vision
âr	care	ē	be	ŏ	pot	oi	boy	ōō	boot	ə	about,
ä	father	ĭ	pit	ō	toe	ou	out	ŭ	cut		item

testimony, the senator walked out of the hearing.

3. To go on strike: *The contract negotiations stalled, so the union walked out.*

walk over

1. To move over something by walking: *We walked over the hot coals.*
2. To treat someone badly or contemptuously: *Teachers must be assertive or children will walk all over them.*
3. To gain an easy or uncontested victory over: *In the final football game of the year, Harvard walked over Yale 35 to 7.*

walk through

1. To perform something in a perfunctory fashion, as at a first rehearsal: *We walked through the dance routine to make sure everyone understood the moves.*
2. To guide someone through some process: *My counselor walked me through the application procedures.*

◆ **wall** (wôl)

walled (wôld), **walling** (wô′lĭng), **walls** (wôlz)

wall in

To enclose, surround, or fortify something with or as if with a wall: *We walled in the back stairway so that it couldn't be seen. The soldiers walled the fort in with logs. The valley was walled in by mountains.*

wall off

To divide or separate something with or as if with a wall: *We walled off part of the room. The school walled the students off from the outside world.*

wall up

1. To block or close something, such as an opening or passage, with or as if with a wall: *The safety inspector walled up the old mine shaft. The contractor walled the abandoned building up.*
2. To confine or seal someone or something behind or as if behind a wall: *The contractors walled up the wiring. In the fairy tale, a witch walled Rapunzel up in a tower.*
3. To form a steep vertical surface. Used of an ocean wave: *The wave walled up perfectly, and I dropped in.*

◆ **wallow** (wŏl′ō)

wallowed (wŏl′ōd), **wallowing** (wŏl′ō-ĭng), **wallows** (wŏl′ōz)

wallow in

1. To roll the body lazily or clumsily in some medium or substance: *The pig wallowed in the mud.*
2. To revel in some condition or behavior; take pleasure in some condition or behavior: *The celebrity wallowed in his fame.*
3. To be plentifully supplied: *The heirs wallowed in money.*

◆ **waltz** (wôlts)

waltzed (wôltst), **waltzing** (wôlt′sĭng), **waltzes** (wôlt′sĭz)

waltz in

To enter briskly, without hesitation, and with self-confidence: *He waltzes in every morning at 9:30 and doesn't care what his boss thinks.*

waltz into

1. To move briskly, without hesitation, and with self-confidence into some place: *I hate how she always waltzes into the office 30 minutes late.*
2. To lead or force someone to move briskly and purposefully into some place: *The teacher waltzed the troublemakers into the principal's office.*

waltz through

To accomplish a task, chore, or assignment with little effort: *Because I had studied so much, I waltzed through the exams.*

◆ **wank** (wăngk)

wanked (wăngkt), **wanking** (wăng′kĭng), **wanks** (wăngks)

wank off

VULGAR SLANG

To masturbate. Used of males.

◆ **want** (wŏnt)

wanted (wŏn′tĭd), **wanting** (wŏn′tĭng), **wants** (wŏnts)

want for

1. To desire something for the benefit of someone: *I want only the best for you.*
2. To have need of something: *Those kids will never want for money. After many hours, the stranded tourists were wanting for food.*

want in

SLANG

1. To desire entrance: *The dog wants in.*
2. To wish to join a project, business, or other undertaking: *Ever since they've seen our success, they all want in. I want in on the deal.*
3. To desire that someone join a project, business, or other undertaking: *Do you want me in on this project or not?*

want out

SLANG

1. To desire to leave: *The cat wants out. I want out of this city.*
2. To desire to leave a project, business, or other undertaking: *The recruit wanted out after realizing how risky the venture was. I want out of this program.*
3. To desire that someone or something leave a project, business, or other undertaking: *The boss wanted those employees out after they messed up the project.*

◆ **ward** (wôrd)

warded (wôr′dĭd), **warding** (wôr′dĭng), **wards** (wôrdz)

ward off

1. To try to prevent; avert: *You should take vitamins to ward off infections.*
2. To turn something aside; repel: *The champion boxer warded off the opponent's blows. The flies were annoying me, but I warded them off.*

ă	pat	är	car	ī	bite	ô	paw	ŏŏ	took	ûr	urge
ā	pay	ĕ	pet	îr	pier	ôr	core	ŏŏr	lure	zh	vision
âr	care	ē	be	ŏ	pot	oi	boy	ōō	boot	ə	about,
ä	father	ĭ	pit	ō	toe	ou	out	ŭ	cut		item

◆ **warm** (wôrm)

warmed (wôrmd), **warming** (wôr′mĭng), **warms** (wôrmz)

warm over

1. To reheat something, especially food: *Let's warm over the soup from last night. I warmed the biscuits over for you.*
2. To modify something old for reuse, especially out of laziness or lack of inspiration: *You can't take your old novel, warm it over, and expect people to like it. The writers merely warmed over the plot of their first film for the sequel.*

warm to

1. To become more kindly or favorably disposed to someone or something: *I think they are warming to my idea.*
2. To make someone or something more kindly or favorably disposed to someone or something: *We're trying to warm the committee to our new proposal.*
3. To make someone more appealing to someone or something: *The new administration is very responsive, which has warmed them to many people.*

warm up

1. To reach a comfortable and agreeable degree of heat; warm completely: *I finally warmed up by sitting next to the fire.*
2. To bring something or someone to a comfortable and agreeable degree of heat; warm something or someone completely: *The furnace warmed up the house. The fire warmed me up.*
3. To reheat some food: *Can I warm up your coffee for you? I'll just warm these leftovers up when I get home.*
4. To prepare for an athletic event by exercising, stretching, or practicing for a short time beforehand: *We warmed up for 15 minutes before starting the match. We warmed up with a few short rallies.*
5. To make someone or something ready for an event or operation: *I'll go out and warm up the car so that it won't stall. The conductor warmed the orchestra up before the concert.*
6. To become ready for an event or operation: *How long does it take the printer to warm up? The musicians warmed up before the concert.*
7. To become enthusiastic, excited, or lively: *The bar doesn't warm up until about 11:00. I warmed up to the subject after I switched teachers.*
8. To make someone or something enthusiastic, excited, or lively: *The emcee warmed up the crowd before the band came out. It took a bit of persuading, but we finally warmed them up to the idea.*
9. To become kindly disposed or friendly: *The group warmed up once the business was out of the way. I didn't warm up to them until we had gone out a few times.*
10. To fill someone with pleasant emotions: *It warms me up to know that you are on my side.*

◆ **warn** (wôrn)

warned (wôrnd), **warning** (wôr′nĭng), **warns** (wôrnz)

warn about

1. To make someone aware of the actual or potential harm, danger, or

evil associated with something: *I warned the kids about riding their bikes in the street.*

2. To make aware in advance of some actual or potential harm, danger, or evil: *The report warned about a possible attack.*

warn against

To advise someone that something is dangerous or problematic and should be avoided: *I warned them against driving without seatbelts. The doctor warns against smoking.*

warn away

To notify someone to go or stay away: *The guide warned the tourists away from the edge of the cliff. The sign warned away trespassers.*

warn of

To make someone aware in advance of some actual or potential harm, danger, or evil: *The doctor warned them of the flu epidemic. The employees were warned of the company's impending bankruptcy.*

warn off

To notify someone to go or stay away: *The sheriff warned them off the private property.*

◆ **wash** (wŏsh)

washed (wŏsht), **washing** (wŏsh′ĭng), **washes** (wŏsh′ĭz)

wash away

1. To carry away or remove something by the action of moving water: *The waves washed away the debris on the beach. Heavy rains washed the topsoil away.*
2. To be carried away or removed by the action of water: *Our boat washed away in the storm.*
3. To eliminate some corruption or guilt: *He tried to wash away his regret by getting drunk. She hoped to wash her guilt away by confessing to the crime.*

wash down

1. To cleanse the surface of something using water or other liquid: *We washed down the walls. My neighbor washed the car down.*
2. To cause something to be carried or drawn down by the action of water or similar liquid: *We tried to wash the grease down, but it stuck to the sides. I washed the tar down with the hose.*
3. To follow the ingestion of something, such as food, with the ingestion of a liquid: *After the party, we washed the cake down with coffee. I washed down the medicine with some juice.*

wash off

1. To remove something by washing: *I washed the dirt off. The cook washed off the grease.*
2. To be removed by washing: *The stain won't wash off. The dirt washed off easily.*

ă	pat	är	car	ī	bite	ô	paw	o͝o	took	ûr	urge
ā	pay	ĕ	pet	îr	pier	ôr	core	o͝or	lure	zh	vision
âr	care	ē	be	ŏ	pot	oi	boy	o͞o	boot	ə	about,
ä	father	ĭ	pit	ō	toe	ou	out	ŭ	cut		item

3. To cleanse something by using water or other liquid to remove what is on it: *Wash off the equipment before you put it away. I washed the dishes off and set them in the rack.*
4. To cleanse oneself by using water or other liquid to remove what is on one's body: *I need to wash off before dinner.*

wash out

1. To cleanse something by using water or other liquid to remove what is inside it: *Wash out the cup before you use it. I washed out my hair. The trash can smelled, so I washed it out.*
2. To remove something by washing: *She washed out the stain. He applied the conditioner, waited 30 seconds, and then washed it out.*
3. To be removed by washing: *The grease washed out without a problem.*
4. To cause something to fade by laundering: *Bleach might wash out the color. Repeated launderings washed my jeans out.*
5. To cause something to fade or appear faded: *The moonlight washed out the stars. That suit really washed him out.*
6. To carry or wear something away by the action of moving water: *The river rose and washed out the dam. A large wave washed our picnic basket out to sea.*
7. To be carried or worn away by the action of moving water: *The bridge has washed out, so we'll need to take another route.*
8. To deplete someone of vitality: *The long rehearsal washed out the cast. The long day in the sun washed us out. By evening, I was washed out from overwork.*
9. To eliminate as unsatisfactory: *The captain washed out everyone responsible for the mistake. Several employees weren't any good, and the manager washed them out.*
10. To be eliminated as unsatisfactory: *The officer candidate washed out after one month.*
11. To force the cancellation or postponement of some event because of rain: *The storm washed out the parade. Team practice was washed out yesterday.*

wash up

1. To carry something ashore by the action of water: *The current washed up some cargo from the sunken ship. The tide washed some seaweed up on shore.*
2. To be carried ashore by the action of water: *This piece of driftwood washed up onto the beach.*
3. To wash one's hands: *Please wash up before dinner.*
4. To wash dishes after a meal: *Whose turn is it to wash up?*

◆ **waste** (wāst)

wasted (wās′tĭd), **wasting** (wās′tĭng), **wastes** (wāsts)

waste away

1. To lose energy, strength, weight, or vigor; become weak or enfeebled: *The patient wasted away from cancer.*
2. To spend some time idly or wastefully: *They are wasting their lives away playing video games. The idle rich waste away their days.*

◆ **watch** (wŏch)

watched (wŏcht), **watching** (wŏch′ĭng), **watches** (wŏ′chĭz)

watch for

1. To look or observe attentively or carefully in order to spot someone or something: *The hikers watched for birds.*
2. To look and wait expectantly or in anticipation for someone or something: *I was watching for an opportunity to sell the stock.*

watch out

1. To be careful or on the alert; take care: *If you don't watch out, you'll fall on the ice.*
2. **watch out for** To be careful of some danger: *Watch out for falling rocks!*

watch over

To monitor and tend to someone or something: *The nurses watched over the patient.*

◆ **water** (wô′tər, wŏt′ər)

watered (wô′tərd, wŏt′ərd), **watering** (wô′tə-rĭng, wŏt′ə-rĭng), **waters** (wô′tərz, wŏt′ərz)

water down

1. To dilute or weaken something by adding water: *The dishonest bartender watered down the liquor. The cook watered the sauce down.*
2. To decrease the value of a share of stock, or the value of some group of shares, by increasing the number of shares available for sale: *Investors are concerned that stock option grants will water down their holdings. I hope that decision doesn't water the stock values down.*
3. To reduce the strength or effectiveness of something: *In the end, the legislation was watered down by multiple amendments. The speaker watered his message down with lots of boring stories.*
4. To wet the surface of something entirely: *The fire department watered down the houses near the brush fire. The road crew watered the dusty road down.*

◆ **wave** (wāv)

waved (wāvd), **waving** (wā′vĭng), **waves** (wāvz)

wave aside

1. To direct someone or something to stand aside by or as if by waving the hand or arm: *The police waved aside the crowd. I waved my friends aside.*
2. To ignore or dismiss someone or something: *This review waves aside the actors' performances. The supervisor waved the new assistant aside.*

wave down

To signal and cause someone or something to stop by waving the hand or arm: *I waved down a cab. The stranded motorist waved a police car down.*

ă	pat	är	car	ī	bite	ô	paw	o͝o	took	ûr	urge
ā	pay	ĕ	pet	îr	pier	ôr	core	o͝or	lure	zh	vision
âr	care	ē	be	ŏ	pot	oi	boy	o͞o	boot	ə	about,
ä	father	ĭ	pit	ō	toe	ou	out	ŭ	cut		item

wave off

1. To dismiss or refuse something or someone by waving the hand or arm: *The celebrity waved off our invitation to join our group. The bus driver waved us off and refused to stop.*
2. SPORTS To cancel or nullify something by waving the arms, usually from a crossed position: *The official waved off the goal because time had run out. The referee waved the penalty off after reviewing the play.*
3. To acknowledge someone's departure by waving the hand or arm: *We went down to the train station to wave off the politician. We waved our guests off at the airport.*

wave on

To encourage or signal someone or something to proceed by or as if by waving the hand or arm: *The police officer waved the pedestrians on. The crowd waved on the runners.*

wave through

To direct or allow someone or something to pass through by or as if by waving the hand or arm: *We slowed down at the gate, but the guard waved us through. The customs officials waved through the passengers who had no luggage.*

◆ **wean** (wēn)

weaned (wēnd), **weaning** (wē′nĭng), **weans** (wēnz)

wean from *or* **wean off**

1. To accustom some young mammal to nourishment other than something, as the mother's milk, obtained by suckling: *The mother weaned the child from breast milk. The child was weaned from the breast.*
2. To detach someone from something to which one is strongly habituated or devoted: *I finally weaned myself from cigarettes. They were weaned from their drug habits at the rehabilitation center.*

wean on

1. To accustom some infant mammal to take nourishment other than by suckling: *The mother weaned the child on formula.*
2. SLANG To accustom someone to something from an early age. Used chiefly in the passive: *Moviegoers who were weaned on the TV series will find the film to their liking.*

◆ **wear** (wâr)

wore (wôr), **wearing** (wâr′ĭng), **wears** (wârz)

wear away

1. To erode or consume something by long or hard use, attrition, or exposure: *The sea is wearing away the rocks. Repeated washings have worn the fabric away. The tough climate wears away at the roof.*
2. To be gradually eroded or consumed by long or hard use, attrition, or exposure: *The paint on the house is wearing away.*

wear down

1. To damage, diminish, erode, or consume something by long or hard use, attrition, or exposure: *The weather wore the shingles down. The heavy crowds wore down the carpets.*

2. To be gradually damaged, diminished, eroded, or consumed by long or hard use, attrition, or exposure: *The water pipes have been in use for more than 100 years and are starting to wear down.*
3. To fatigue, weary, or exhaust someone or something: *The race wore me down. The new employee is wearing down my patience.*
4. To become fatigued, weary, or exhausted: *I was beginning to wear down, so I took a bus home instead of walking.*
5. To cause someone to submit by relentless pressure or resistance: *By holding out, we finally wore them down. Management finally wore down the union, and the strike was ended.*

wear in

To loosen or soften some new clothing by wearing it: *That sweater will feel better after you wear it in.*

wear off

1. To diminish gradually in effect until gone: *The drug wore off after eight hours.*
2. To be gradually removed by long or hard use, attrition, or exposure: *So many people touched the picture that its luster finally wore off.*
3. To gradually remove something by long or hard use, attrition, or exposure: *The inclement weather wore off the awning on my porch. The snow wore the shine off my car.*

wear on

To pass gradually or tediously: *The hours wore on as we completed our chores. As the day wore on, I became more and more tired.*

wear out

1. To become unusable through long or heavy use: *The tent wore out after last summer's trip.*
2. To make something unusable through long or heavy use: *The tough job wore out my saw. Miles of hiking wore my shoes out.*
3. To make someone weary; exhaust someone: *The children wore me out. The class wore out the substitute teacher.*
4. CHIEFLY SOUTHERN US To punish by spanking: *If you don't behave, I'm going to have to wear you out.*

wear through

1. To consume something by long or hard use; go through something: *The car wore through two sets of brake pads. I wore through two pairs of boots hiking the Appalachian Trail.*
2. To put some hole or gap in something by long or hard use or attrition: *I wore a hole through the toes of my socks.*
3. To penetrate or sever something by attrition: *The sharp corner eventually wore through the fabric. The nail wore my sock through.*
4. To become severed or perforated by long or hard use, attrition, or exposure: *The strap wore through.*

ă	pat	är	car	ī	bite	ô	paw	o͝o	took	ûr	urge
ā	pay	ĕ	pet	îr	pier	ôr	core	o͝or	lure	zh	vision
âr	care	ē	be	ŏ	pot	oi	boy	o͞o	boot	ə	about,
ä	father	ĭ	pit	ō	toe	ou	out	ŭ	cut		item

The cable wore through to the metal.

◆ **weary** (wîr′ē)

wearied (wîr′ēd), **wearying** (wîr′ē-ĭng), **wearies** (wîr′ēz)

weary of

To lose patience with or interest in something or someone: *I soon wearied of their constant bickering.*

◆ **weasel** (wē′zəl)

weaseled *or* **weaselled** (wē′zəld), **weaseling** *or* **weaselling** (wē′zə-lĭng), **weasels** (wē′zəlz)

weasel out

SLANG

1. To back out of some situation or commitment in a selfish or sly manner: *The party was boring—you were smart to weasel out early. My cousins weaseled out of contributing to the gift.*
2. **weasel out of** To elicit something from someone by artful or devious means: *At first, they wouldn't admit that they were to blame, but I weaseled the truth out of them.*

◆ **weather** (wĕ*th*′ər)

weathered (wĕ*th*′ərd), **weathering** (wĕ*th*′ə-rĭng), **weathers** (wĕ*th*′ərz)

weather in

1. To cause something to be inoperable, inaccessible, or unable to move safely due to adverse weather: *This storm will weather the fleet in. The storm could weather in the climbers for days. The squadron is weathered in because of dense fog.*
2. To cause something to remain inside due to adverse weather: *A northeaster weathered us in for most of our vacation. Bring a book to read in case we get weathered in.*

weather out

1. To spend, endure, or survive some storm: *We weathered out the storm in a shelter. I'm not sure if we will evacuate the area or stay here and weather the storm out.*
2. To force the cancellation or postponement of some event because of adverse weather: *Our flight was scheduled for 6:00, but the storm weathered it out. The picnic was weathered out.*
3. To spend, endure, or survive something: *I weathered out five tours in Vietnam. The first weeks of school are difficult, but you'll weather them out.*
4. To become exposed by the erosion of surrounding material: *Some of the dinosaur bones remain embedded in the rock, while others are lying on the surface where they weathered out. We found many geodes that had weathered out and were lying in the sand.*
5. **weather out of** To become separated from some surrounding material by the erosive effects of weather: *The holes are where hematite has weathered out of the sandstone. We found gold that had weathered out of a vein upstream.*

◆ **wed** (wĕd)

wedded (wĕd′ĭd), **wed** (wĕd) *or* **wedded** (wĕd′ĭd), **wedding** (wĕd′ĭng), **weds** (wĕdz)

wed to

1. To join someone to someone else in matrimony: *The chaplain wedded the bride to the groom.*
2. To cause someone to adhere devotedly or stubbornly to something. Used chiefly in the passive: *The group was wedded to the idea of building a new school.*

◆ **wedge** (wĕj)

wedged (wĕjd), **wedging** (wĕj′ĭng), **wedges** (wĕj′ĭz)

wedge in

To lodge or jam something or someone in some location: *I accidently wedged my hat in the flue. The box was wedged in the crawl space.*

◆ **weed** (wēd)

weeded (wē′dĭd), **weeding** (wē′dĭng), **weeds** (wēdz)

weed out

1. To remove some weeds: *We weeded out the clover. The gardener weeded the dandelions out.*
2. To separate or get rid of some unfit or undesirable part; eliminate someone or something: *The interviewers weeded out most of the applicants. The coach weeded the weaker players out.*

◆ **weigh** (wā)

weighed (wād), **weighing** (wā′ĭng), **weighs** (wāz)

weigh against

1. To compare something to something else in order to make a decision: *When we weighed our decision against the alternatives, it was clearly the wrong choice.*
2. To affect someone or something adversely in an evaluation: *My poor test scores will weigh against me.*

weigh down

1. To hold or bend something down by applying weight: *I weighed the trail map down on the ground with stones. The vines were weighed down by their heavy grapes.*
2. To burden or oppress someone or something: *Heavy backpacks weighed down the hikers. The responsibilities of the new job weighed me down.*

weigh in

1. To be weighed at an official weigh-in for an athletic competition: *The boxer weighed in before the fight. The fighter weighed in at 250 pounds.*
2. To weigh something officially, as for travel on an airplane: *The ticket agent weighed our bags in. After the agent weighed in my suitcase, I went to the gate.*
3. To join an ongoing discussion, debate, or competition: *The president still hasn't weighed in on the issue. After striking out twice, the player finally weighed in with a base hit.*

weigh on *or* **weigh upon**

1. To cause to sink or bend heavily by or as if by added weight: *The bad news weighed on the prices of oil stocks. A coating of ice weighed upon the slender branches.*
2. To preoccupy someone with a feeling of guilt or blame: *The consequences of their mistake weighed on them. Heavy guilt weighed upon the thief.*

weigh out

1. To measure or apportion some specific quantity by or as if by weight: *The clerk weighed out a pound of cheese.*
2. To weigh or otherwise evaluate something: *We weighed out the hamburger and found we needed another pound. I wasn't sure that they gave us the correct amount, so I weighed it out.*
3. To determine the relative value of some set of things: *The council listened to our requests and carefully weighed them out.*

weigh with

To be of importance to someone when making a decision: *The issue of taxes will weigh heavily with the voters.*

◆ **weight** (wāt)

weighted (wā′tĭd), **weighting** (wā′tĭng), **weights** (wāts)

weight against

To cause something to have a slant or bias against someone or something: *They weighted the rules against the visiting team.*

weight down

1. To fix or hold something in place with added weight: *I weighted down the papers so they wouldn't blow away. The campers weighted the tarp down with rocks.*
2. To impair the performance of someone or something by or as if by adding weight: *The project weighted the company down with too much debt to survive in this competitive market. The team was weighted down by its inexperience.*

◆ **weird** (wîrd)

weirded (wîr′dĭd), **weirding** (wîr′dĭng), **weirds** (wîrdz)

weird out

SLANG

1. To cause someone to experience an odd, unusual, and sometimes uneasy sensation: *I thought we were friends, so that argument really weirded me out. I weirded out that gas station attendant when I asked for the nearest gun store.*
2. To experience an odd, unusual, and sometimes uneasy sensation: *I weirded out when I noticed their resemblance to each other.*

◆ **well** (wĕl)

welled (wĕld), **welling** (wĕl′ĭng), **wells** (wĕlz)

well over

1. To build up and overflow the boundaries of a container: *I left the tap on, and the water in the bathtub welled over and spilled onto the floor. Tears welled over and ran down my cheeks. My anger welled over, and I yelled out.*
2. To become filled and overflow: *My eyes welled over with tears. My heart welled over with joy.*

well up

To rise to the edge of a container, ready to flow: *Lava welled up in the crater. Tears welled up in my eyes, but I did not cry. I could feel anger well up in me.*

◆ **wet** (wĕt)

wet (wĕt) *or* **wetted** (wĕt′ĭd), **wetting** (wĕt′ĭng), **wets** (wĕts)

wet back

To cause something to lie flat by making it wet and brushing it back: *Now that I have short hair, I have to wet it back or it stands on end. I washed my face and wet back my hair.*

wet down

1. To wet the surface of something entirely: *The painter wet down the canvas. We wet the car down before applying the soap.*
2. To cause something to bend down or lie flat by making it wet: *I wet down my hair so that it wouldn't stick up. The heavy dew wet the grass down flat.*

◆ **whack** (wăk, hwăk)

whacked (wăkt, hwăkt), **whacking** (wăk′ĭng, hwăk′ĭng), **whacks** (wăks, hwăks)

whack off

VULGAR SLANG

To masturbate. Used of males.

◆ **whale** (wāl, hwāl)

whaled (wāld, hwāld), **whaling** (wā′lĭng, hwā′lĭng), **whales** (wālz, hwālz)

whale into

To strike or attack something or someone forcefully: *The batter whaled into the baseball. The politician whaled into the press for their inaccurate reporting.*

whale on

1. To strike or hit someone or something repeatedly and forcefully; thrash someone or something: *The street gangs whaled on each other until someone called the police.*
2. To criticize someone vehemently: *Our boss whaled on all of us for missing the deadline.*

◆ **wheedle** (wēd′l, hwēd′l)

wheedled (wēd′ld, hwēd′ld), **wheedling** (wēd′l-ĭng, hwēd′l-ĭng), **wheedles** (wēd′lz, hwēd′lz)

wheedle out of

1. To obtain something from some person through the use of flattery or guile: *The swindler wheedled my life savings out of me.*
2. To defraud someone of something through the use of flattery or guile: *The swindler wheedled me out of my life savings.*

◆ **wheel** (wēl, hwēl)

wheeled (wēld, hwēld), **wheeling** (wē′lĭng, hwē′lĭng), **wheels** (wēlz, hwēlz)

wheel around

1. To turn around or as if around a central axis; rotate or revolve: *The merry-go-round wheeled around.*

ă	pat		är	car		ī	bite		ô	paw		o͝o	took		ûr	urge
ā	pay		ĕ	pet		îr	pier		ôr	core		o͝or	lure		zh	vision
âr	care		ē	be		ŏ	pot		oi	boy		o͞o	boot		ə	about,
ä	father		ĭ	pit		ō	toe		ou	out		ŭ	cut			item

2. To turn rapidly to face the opposite direction: *I wheeled around to face the attacker.*
3. To cause something to turn rapidly to face the opposite direction: *The principal grabbed my shoulder and wheeled me around.*

wheel out

To present someone or something, by or as if by wheeling them into view: *The coach wheeled the star quarterback out for an interview. The company wheeled out charts supporting its claims.*

◆ **while** (wīl, hwīl)

whiled (wīld, hwīld), **whiling** (wī′lĭng, hwī′lĭng), **whiles** (wīlz, hwīlz)

while away

To spend some duration of time idly or pleasantly: *The campers whiled the hours away by singing songs. We whiled away the summer.*

◆ **whip** (wĭp, hwĭp)

whipped (wĭpt, hwĭpt), **whipping** (wĭp′ĭng, hwĭp′ĭng), **whips** (wĭps, hwĭps)

whip by

1. To pass quickly, as of a gust of wind or an interval of time: *As I got older, the years whipped by.*
2. To pass someone or something quickly: *The runner in second place whipped by the leader.*

whip into

1. To manipulate something into some particular condition, by mixing it rapidly with a utensil so as to introduce air: *The chef whipped the cream into a froth.*
2. To excite or provoke someone or something into some mental state: *The speaker whipped the crowd into a frenzy.*
3. To force or compel someone or something into some state of conformity by or as if by flogging or lashing: *The musher whipped the dogs into line. The drill sergeant whipped the soldiers into shape.*

whip off

1. To snatch, pull, or remove something in a sudden manner: *The worker whipped off his cap. The storm whipped the shingles off.*
2. To snatch, pull, or remove something from something in a sudden manner: *The storm whipped the roof off the house.*
3. To make or produce something quickly: *The guitarist whipped off a chord. I whipped the letter to the editor off in 10 minutes.*

whip out

1. To take out or present something suddenly or quickly, often with a flourish: *I whipped out my new credit card to pay for dinner. We didn't know the police had warrants until they whipped them out.*
2. To make or produce something quickly: *The new assembly line can whip out 30 cases an hour. The novelist whipped ten pages out each day.*

whip through

1. To move rapidly through something or some place, as of a gust of wind or violent storm: *The wind whipped through the canyon.*

2. To accomplish or proceed with something swiftly: *The students whipped through the easy homework assignment.*
3. To read something quickly: *I whipped through a magazine while I waited for my appointment.*
4. To beat and froth up some liquid thoroughly: *You must first whip the batter through before adding the sugar.*

whip up

1. To churn or agitate something into a state of turbulence: *The storm whipped up the sea, endangering the ships. The wind whipped the fire up so that it raged out of control. The car whipped up the leaves along the road.*
2. To cause something to form by churning or agitating: *The storm whipped up massive waves in the normally calm sea. The hurricane whipped several tornados up in its wake.*
3. To rouse the emotions of some group of people; excite some group of people: *The candidate whipped up the mob with talk of reform. The finale whipped the audience up into a frenzy.*
4. To summon some collective emotion or sentiment by exciting a group of people: *The promoters whipped up enthusiasm for the new film. We'll need a lot of hype to sell this product, and our marketers can whip it up.*
5. To prepare something quickly or easily: *We whipped up a light lunch before setting out. I whipped some oatmeal up in just a few minutes.*
6. **whip up on** To defeat someone decisively; outdo someone: *The home team whipped up on its rival last weekend.*

◆ **whisk** (wĭsk, hwĭsk)

whisked (wĭskt, hwĭskt), **whisking** (wĭs′kĭng, hwĭs′kĭng), **whisks** (wĭsks, hwĭsks)

whisk away

1. To remove something with quick light sweeping motions: *The waiter whisked the crumbs away. My girlfriend whisked away the check before I could see it.*
2. To escort, conduct, or carry someone or something swiftly and quietly away: *The bodyguards whisked away the politician after the speech. The ambulance whisked the accident victim away to the hospital.*
3. To indulge someone's fancy by conducting or transporting them away: *I was whisked away from my boring life after I accepted the job offer. My boyfriend whisked me away to Paris.*

whisk off

1. To remove something from the surface of someone or something with quick light sweeping motions: *My friend whisked the crumbs off the table.*

ă	pat	är	car	ī	bite	ô	paw	o͝o	took	ûr	urge
ā	pay	ĕ	pet	îr	pier	ôr	core	o͝or	lure	zh	vision
âr	care	ē	be	ŏ	pot	oi	boy	o͞o	boot	ə	about,
ä	father	ĭ	pit	ō	toe	ou	out	ŭ	cut		item

2. To remove something or someone from something swiftly and quietly: *The waiter whisked the dish off the table. They whisked the actor off the stage.*
3. To escort, conduct, or carry someone or something swiftly and quietly away: *The bodyguards whisked off the politician after the speech. My parents whisked us off. The victim was whisked off to the hospital.*
4. To depart on an errand swiftly and quietly: *The salesperson whisked off and returned with the perfect gift.*
5. To indulge someone's fancy by conducting or transporting them away: *My partner whisked me off to New York. The butler whisked off the guests to the dining room.*

◆ **whistle** (wĭs′əl, hwĭs′əl)

whistled (wĭs′əld, hwĭs′əld), **whistling** (wĭs′ə-lĭng, hwĭs′ə-lĭng), **whistles** (wĭs′əlz, hwĭs′əlz)

whistle at

1. To express admiration or desire for someone or something by whistling: *The construction crew whistled at passersby.*
2. To express approval or disapproval of someone or something by whistling: *The audience whistled at the performers.*

whistle for

To summon someone or something by whistling: *I whistled for my dog.*

◆ **white** (wīt, hwīt)

whited (wī′tĭd, hwī′tĭd), **whiting** (wī′tĭng, hwī′tĭng), **whites** (wīts, hwīts)

white out

1. To erase or cover something so that it cannot be seen or read: *I whited out the information on my computer screen. Some of the words in the passage were whited out, and the students had to fill them in.*
2. To cause something or someone to be rendered incapable of seeing the surrounding area because of falling or blowing snow: *The drivers were completely whited out during the blizzard.*

◆ **whiten** (wīt′n, hwīt′n)

whitened (wīt′nd, hwīt′nd), **whitening** (wīt′n-ĭng, hwīt′n-ĭng), **whitens** (wīt′nz, hwīt′nz)

whiten up

1. To become whiter: *The towels whitened up when I washed them with bleach.*
2. To cause something to become whiter: *The dentist whitened up my coffee-stained teeth. This polish will whiten your golf shoes up.*

◆ **whittle** (wĭt′l, hwĭt′l)

whittled (wĭt′ld, hwĭt′ld), **whittling** (wĭt′l-ĭng, hwĭt′l-ĭng), **whittles** (wĭt′lz, hwĭt′lz)

whittle away

1. To undermine, reduce, or weaken something by small increments until completely gone or useless: *The long climb up the mountain whittled away his strength. We whittled their lead away with a series of small gains.*
2. To weaken or be gradually reduced by small increments: *My courage whittled away with each step forward I took.*

3. To eliminate something by whittling it: *The carpenter whittled the excess wood away. The sculptor whittled away the clay until a perfect form emerged.*
4. To whittle continuously: *They whittled away until they had finished carving their sticks into spoons.*

whittle down

1. To reduce the size of some piece of wood by cutting small bits or paring shavings: *I whittled down the pencil's tip to expose more lead. I bit nervously on my pencil until I had whittled it down to nothing.*
2. To reduce something gradually, as if by whittling with a knife: *The couple whittled down their debt by making small payments. We whittled the other team's lead down to one point with a series of small gains.*

◆ **whiz** *or* **whizz** (wĭz, hwĭz)

whizzed (wĭzd, hwĭzd), **whizzing** (wĭz′ĭng, hwĭz′ĭng), **whizzes** (wĭz′ĭz, hwĭz′ĭz)

whiz by *or* **whizz by**

1. To pass quickly, as of a moving object or an interval of time: *I looked out the window of the train and watched the faces whiz by.*
2. To pass someone or something quickly: *The motorcycle whizzed by us on the freeway.*

whiz through *or* **whizz through**

1. To accomplish or proceed with something swiftly and energetically: *My smart friend whizzed through the math homework.*
2. To move rapidly through something: *The football whizzed through the receiver's hands.*

◆ **whore** (hôr)

whored (hôrd), **whoring** (hôr′ĭng), **whores** (hôrz)

whore out

1. SLANG To make someone's services available in a way that compromises one's principles for personal gain: *In order to earn money, the Shakespearean actor whored himself out to amusement parks. The literary agency whored out its talent to ghostwrite books.*
2. VULGAR SLANG To make someone's body available for sexual relations in exchange for payment.

◆ **wig** (wĭg)

wigged (wĭgd), **wigging** (wĭg′ĭng), **wigs** (wĭgz)

wig out

SLANG

1. To lose control of one's emotions: *I wigged out when I saw the lion. My parents wigged out on me when I took the car without asking.*
2. To cause someone to lose control of his or her emotions: *Their new song totally wigs me out. That*

ă	pat	är	car	ī	bite	ô	paw	ŏŏ	took	ûr	urge
ā	pay	ĕ	pet	îr	pier	ôr	core	ŏŏr	lure	zh	vision
âr	care	ē	be	ŏ	pot	oi	boy	ōō	boot	ə	about,
ä	father	ĭ	pit	ō	toe	ou	out	ŭ	cut		item

haunted house wigged out the little kids.

◆ **wiggle** (wĭg′əl)

wiggled (wĭg′əld), **wiggling** (wĭg′ə-lĭng), **wiggles** (wĭg′əlz)

wiggle out

1. To free oneself from something by turning or twisting the body with sinuous writhing motions: *I wiggled out of the tight sweater.*
2. To extricate oneself by sly or subtle means from some situation; worm one's way out of some situation: *I wiggled out of taking the exam by pretending I had a headache.*

◆ **will** (wĭl)

willed (wĭld), **willing** (wĭl′ĭng), **wills** (wĭlz)

will to

To grant something to someone in a legal will: *My grandfather willed all of his land to me.*

◆ **wimp** (wĭmp)

wimped (wĭmpt), **wimping** (wĭm′pĭng), **wimps** (wĭmps)

wimp out

SLANG

To withdraw from a commitment or course of action because of cowardice or insecurity: *I don't want to stand in line for the roller coaster if you're going to wimp out at the last minute.*

◆ **win** (wĭn)

won (wŭn), **winning** (wĭn′ĭng), **wins** (wĭnz)

win at

To achieve victory in some activity or event: *I usually win at chess. I used to be good at poker, but now I can't win at any card games at all.*

win back

To regain, through effort or contest, something or someone that one has lost or no longer has: *My friend is at the casino, trying to win back what he lost last night. Her boyfriend left her, but she's sure she will win him back.*

win out

To succeed or prevail: *After a two-year battle in the courts, she eventually won out.*

win over

To succeed in gaining the favor or support of someone; prevail on someone: *The politician spent a long time trying to win over the undecided voters. At first they didn't want to join us for dinner, but we finally won them over.*

win through

CHIEFLY BRITISH To overcome difficulties and attain a desired goal or end: *The soccer team won through to the finals.*

◆ **wince** (wĭns)

winced (wĭnst), **wincing** (wĭn′sĭng), **winces** (wĭn′sĭz)

wince at

To shrink or tense up involuntarily in response to something that causes pain, distress, or discomfort: *I winced at this month's phone bill.*

◆ **wind** (wīnd)

wound (wound), **winding** (wīn′dĭng), **winds** (wīndz)

wind back

To set some clock or counter to an earlier reading: *Don't forget to wind your clock back for standard time. When he sold the car, he wound back the odometer to make the car seem newer.*

wind down

1. To diminish gradually in energy, intensity, or scope: *The party wound down as guests began to leave.*
2. To cause something to diminish in energy, intensity, or scope: *We should wind down this meeting and go home. The discussions have been interesting, but now it's time to wind them down and go home.*

wind up

1. To coil the spring of some mechanism completely by turning a stem or cord, for example: *I wound up my alarm clock. If you wind this toy soldier up, it will march across the floor.*
2. To coil something completely, as onto a spool or into a ball: *He wound the excess string up into a ball. She wound up the cable around the rod.*
3. To come to a finish; end: *The meeting wound up at 9:00.*
4. To bring something to a finish; end something: *We need to wind up this project before January. This card game is fun, but let's wind it up before dinner.*
5. To put something in order; settle something: *She wound up her affairs before leaving the country.*
6. To arrive in some place or situation after or because of a course of action: *I took a long walk and wound up at the edge of town. If you spend too much money now, you'll wind up in debt.*
7. To distress or perturb someone or something mentally or emotionally: *Seeing those awful newspaper headlines really winds me up. The students are getting wound up about all the homework they have.*
8. To twist the body in preparation to throw or hit: *The soccer player wound up and shot the ball into the net.*

◆ **wink** (wĭngk)

winked (wĭngkt), **winking** (wĭng′kĭng), **winks** (wĭngks)

wink at

1. To close and open the eyelid of one eye deliberately in order to convey a message, signal, or suggestion to someone: *I knew she liked me when she winked at me.*
2. To pretend not to see something; ignore something: *The monarchy winked at corruption in the ministry.*

wink out

To become quickly extinguished, especially following a weak burst

ă	pat	är	car	ī	bite	ô	paw	o͝o	took	ûr	urge
ā	pay	ĕ	pet	îr	pier	ôr	core	o͝or	lure	zh	vision
âr	care	ē	be	ŏ	pot	oi	boy	o͞o	boot	ə	about,
ä	father	ĭ	pit	ō	toe	ou	out	ŭ	cut		item

of activity: *The candle flickered and winked out. The street lamps winked out one by one.*

◆ **winnow** (wĭn′ō)

winnowed (wĭn′ōd), **winnowing** (wĭn′ō-ĭng), **winnows** (wĭn′ōz)

winnow away

1. To remove some material, such as chaff, from grain by means of a current of air: *Modern machines can winnow away all the chaff very efficiently. The farmers winnow the chaff away by flinging the grain into the air with a large blanket.*
2. To get rid of some unfit or undesirable part; eliminate something or someone: *The process will winnow away the weakest candidates. The editor winnowed most of the errors away.*
3. To reduce some group by separating or eliminating the unfit or undesirable part: *The process winnowed away the field of candidates.*
4. To remove some material from a mixture by means of a current of air or water: *The wind has winnowed away the sand from the soil. Water currents pick up mud from the riverbank and winnow it away, exposing the rock.*

winnow out

1. To separate some material, such as chaff, from grain by means of a current of air: *The farmer winnows out the chaff with a machine. There is always some debris in the harvest, but we winnow it out.*
2. To separate or get rid of some unfit or undesirable part; eliminate something or someone: *The lions tend to winnow out the sick antelope. The political process will winnow the weakest candidates out.*
3. To sort or select some fit or desirable part; extract someone or something: *We winnowed out the top candidates from the rest and interviewed them. There are only a few good pieces of wood in this shipment, and it will take a long time to winnow them out.*
4. To rid some group of unfit or undesirable members: *The test winnowed out the applicant pool.*

◆ **winter** (wĭn′tər)

wintered (wĭn′tərd), **wintering** (wĭn′tə-rĭng), **winters** (wĭn′tərz)

winter on

1. To feed on something during winter: *The deer winter on tree bark.*
2. To feed some animal something during the winter: *We wintered the cows on cornstalks.*

winter over

To spend, endure, or survive a winter: *The scientist wintered over at the South Pole. My plant has wintered over successfully for three years.*

◆ **wipe** (wīp)

wiped (wīpt), **wiping** (wī′pĭng), **wipes** (wīps)

wipe away

1. To remove or eliminate something by wiping: *I wiped away the child's tears. Dust had settled on the table, so I wiped it away.*

2. To destroy or eliminate something as if by wiping: *A strong hurricane wiped away the entire village. Mudslides wiped our home away.*

3. To reduce something to zero; invalidate something: *Business was so bad this year that it wiped away all our savings. I had a big lead in the bicycle race, but a sudden burst of speed by my opponent wiped it away.*

wipe down

To wash or dry the surface of something by wiping: *I wiped down the deck chairs after it rained. Wipe the counters down after you finish cooking.*

wipe off

1. To remove something from the surface of something or someone by wiping: *Between the games, I wiped the sweat off my forehead and had a drink of water. I wiped the fog off my glasses.*

2. To remove something, especially a liquid, by wiping: *I tried to wipe off the water, but the seat was still damp. I scrubbed so hard that I wiped the paint off. I wiped off the sweat from my forehead.*

3. To clean or dry the surface of something or someone by wiping: *Wipe off your feet before you enter the house. I washed the dishes and wiped them off.*

4. To eliminate something from or as if from some surface: *A nuclear war could wipe us all off the earth. Wipe that smile off your face! The tornado wiped the village off the map.*

wipe out

1. To destroy something completely; obliterate something: *A mudslide wiped out the road to the village. Another strong wind could wipe the damaged building out completely.*

2. To kill someone or something, especially a group or part of a group: *The invaders wiped out the entire population of the countryside. This disease could wipe many of the villagers out.*

3. To exhaust the strength or energy of someone; wear someone out: *The hike up the mountain wiped us out. The long practice wiped out the whole football team.*

4. To reduce some value or amount to zero or nothing: *The reckless spending wiped out the budget surplus. The company's renewed sales wiped their debts out completely.*

5. To reduce someone to poverty or bankruptcy: *A bad harvest wiped out the remaining farms. My travel expenses are going to wipe me out.*

6. To invalidate or nullify something: *A grand slam wiped out six innings of flawless pitching. A silly remark wiped the politician's reputation out completely.*

7. To erase data from some computer storage device: *The program wipes out the old data before writing the*

ă	pat	är	car	ī	bite	ô	paw	o͝o	took	ûr	urge
ā	pay	ĕ	pet	îr	pier	ôr	core	o͝or	lure	zh	vision
âr	care	ē	be	ŏ	pot	oi	boy	o͞o	boot	ə	about,
ä	father	ĭ	pit	ō	toe	ou	out	ŭ	cut		item

new data. Reformatting a disk will wipe it out.

8. To lose one's balance and fall, as when skiing or surfing: *At the top of the hill, I wiped out and nearly hit another skier.*

wipe up

1. To remove something completely, especially a liquid, from a surface by wiping: *Please wipe up the milk you spilled. There was a puddle by the door, so I wiped it up.*
2. To clean or dry something or someone by wiping: *Please wipe up those vases before putting them on the table. I wiped the baby up with a washcloth after feeding time.*
3. To succeed in winning all of something: *The team wiped up all the blue ribbons in the tournament that afternoon.*

◆ **wire** (wīr)

wired (wīrd), **wiring** (wīr′ĭng), **wires** (wīrz)

wire in

1. To install or connect something or someone with wires: *If we wire in the VCR, we won't be able to unplug it easily. I wired the television in with our stereo. You can't take the radio out of this circuit; it's wired in.*
2. To implement some computer functionality directly through electronic circuitry rather than through programming. Used chiefly in the passive: *The computer can perform mathematical operations quickly because they are wired in.*
3. To determine or put something into effect by some physiological or neurological mechanism. Used chiefly in the passive: *Many basic reflexes, such as breathing and the beating of the heart, are wired in.*
4. To connect to a communication network by radio: *The taxi was stuck in traffic, so the driver wired in to say they would be late.*

wire into

1. To connect something or someone to something or someone by wires: *I wired a battery-powered amplifier into the microphone.*
2. To implement some capability through logic circuitry that is permanently connected within some computer or calculator and therefore not subject to change by programming: *The engineers wired the video card directly into the computer so it would run faster.*
3. To determine or put something into effect by some physiological or neurological mechanism. Used chiefly in the passive: *The ability to distinguish colors is wired into the anatomy of the eye.*

wire up

1. To connect, equip, or install something with or as if with wires: *The technician wired the computer up. When I first wired up the VCR, it didn't work properly.*
2. To equip something with power or Internet access: *They wired up the library so the students could access online journals. We took the big spare room and wired it up for use as a recording studio.*
3. To secure something with wires: *We wired up the flagpole so that it wouldn't blow over. A surgeon had to wire my jaw up after the accident.*

4. To cause someone to become stimulated, excited, or alert, as from a stimulant or a rush of adrenaline: *That cup of coffee really wired me up. Too much soda has wired up the kids, and they're getting out of control.*

◆ **wise** (wīz)

wised (wīzd), **wising** (wī′zĭng), **wises** (wī′zĭz)

wise up

SLANG

1. To become aware, informed, or sophisticated: *After staying with my old job for too long, I wised up and found a job I really enjoyed.*
2. To make someone aware, informed, or sophisticated: *The expensive medical treatment wised me up to the importance of having extra money in my savings account. If you think you know something about cars, read this book—it will wise you up!*

◆ **wish** (wĭsh)

wished (wĭsht), **wishing** (wĭsh′ĭng), **wishes** (wĭsh′ĭz)

wish away

To eliminate some problem by merely desiring or pretending that it did not exist: *They tried to wish away the war by gathering support without taking any action. Do you think you can wish your troubles away? Poverty cannot be wished away.*

wish for

1. To express a desire for something or someone: *The child tossed a penny in the well and wished for a new bicycle.*
2. To have or feel a desire for something or someone: *For weeks I've been wishing for a big snowstorm so I could go skiing.*

wish on *or* **wish upon**

1. To impose or force something on someone; foist something on someone: *Her enemies wished a hard life on her. I would never wish such a cruel punishment upon anyone.*
2. To call on some charm or omen to grant a wish: *Some people wish on falling stars. If I find a four-leaf clover, I'll wish upon it for a successful time in school.*

◆ **wolf** (wo͝olf)

wolfed (wo͝olft), **wolfing** (wo͝ol′fĭng), **wolfs** (wo͝olfs)

wolf down

To eat something greedily, ravenously, or voraciously; gorge: *How did you wolf down that pizza so quickly? I grabbed the hamburger and wolfed it down in 30 seconds.*

◆ **wonder** (wŭn′dər)

wondered (wŭn′dərd), **wondering** (wŭn′də-rĭng), **wonders** (wŭn′dərz)

wonder about

To be filled with curiosity or doubt about something or someone: *I*

ă	pat	är	car	ī	bite	ô	paw	o͝o	took	ûr	urge
ā	pay	ĕ	pet	îr	pier	ôr	core	o͝or	lure	zh	vision
âr	care	ē	be	ŏ	pot	oi	boy	o͞o	boot	ə	about, item
ä	father	ĭ	pit	ō	toe	ou	out	ŭ	cut		

often wonder about the condition of the world. Do you ever wonder about the decision you made to quit school?

wonder at

1. To be surprised or puzzled by something or someone: *I wonder at your willingness to follow your boss's strange orders.*
2. To be awed or astonished by something or someone; marvel at something: *The children wondered at the colorful fish in the aquarium.*

◆ **work** (wûrk)
worked (wûrkt), **working** (wûr′kĭng), **works** (wûrks)

work against

1. To move or act contrary to something or someone: *The new ideas work against the way we do things now.*
2. To move or act in opposition or resistance to someone or something: *Your meticulous attention to detail sometimes works against you.*
3. To be successful at countering something or someone: *The soccer team must find a strategy that works against the opponent's defense.*

work around

1. To wrap or pass something around something by repeated, continuous, or applied effort: *The knitter worked some decorative stitching around the edge of the sleeve.*
2. To achieve a goal in such a way as to avoid some difficulty: *Can we work around the problem, or do we have to solve it?*

work as

1. To serve the purpose of something: *The pegs on the wall work as coat hangers.*
2. To do the work associated with someone or something: *At night, I work as a waiter.*

work at

1. To exert force on something repeatedly or continuously: *The plumber worked at the clog with a plunger.*
2. To direct persistent or diligent effort toward something: *You must keep working at your piano exercises if you want to improve.*
3. To do work in some particular place: *I'm working at home today. I'm working at my desk.*
4. To hold a job at some place: *I used to work at the hospital before I got a job at the bank.*

work away

1. To labor continuously with zealousness or diligence: *I've been working away on the problem all night. I worked away at the problem until I solved it. We must work away until we are finished.*
2. To remove or eliminate something from something by repeated, continuous, or applied effort: *I worked away the rough spots with sandpaper. I worked the metal burrs away with a rasp.*
3. To damage, diminish, erode, or consume by long or hard use, attrition, or exposure: *Years of exposure to rain and snow finally worked away the paint. You can see where the hinges have worked the wood away.*

work for

1. To be employed by or work on behalf of someone or some

organization: *I've worked for the government for the past ten years. I started my own company, so now I work for myself.*

2. To provide labor in exchange for something: *The traveler didn't want any money; he said he would work for food.*
3. To work on behalf of some cause: *Our organization works for the humane treatment of animals.*
4. To function or operate correctly when used by someone: *The VCR always seems to work for me, but whenever someone else tries it, it freezes up. They should stick with the same strategy, because it worked for them last year.*
5. To function or operate correctly when used for some purpose: *The bug spray only works for mosquitoes.*
6. To meet the requirements of someone; fit someone: *Unless it has three bedrooms, I don't think the house will work for us. Can we find a restaurant that works for all of us?*
7. To be appropriate for someone; befit someone: *I'm not sure that color works for you.*

work in

1. To cause something to be inserted by repeated or continuous effort: *Hold the cloth in one hand and work in the thread using a needle. The dough won't absorb the extra flour unless you work it in by kneading.*
2. To insert or make space for something: *When I wrote the report, I worked in a request for money. It's an unusual proposal, but I think I can work it in.*
3. To make time available for something or someone in an otherwise busy or filled schedule: *I know you don't have an appointment, but the doctor will try to work you in.*
4. To share equipment at a gymnasium or fitness center with a person who is already using it: *He had been using the weight machine for 30 minutes, so I asked if I could work in.*

work into

1. To insert or introduce someone or something into something by repeated, continuous, or applied effort: *The thief worked the pick into the lock. The chef slowly worked the flour into the batter. The speaker worked a mention of her latest book into her speech.*
2. To make time available for something or someone in something, such as a busy schedule: *The student worked a few field trips into the semester's calendar.*
3. To manipulate something into some particular condition through repeated, continuous, or applied effort: *I rubbed my hands together and worked the soap into a lather.*
4. To excite or provoke someone or something into some mental state: *Their constant shouting slowly worked me into a fuming rage.*

ă	pat	är	car	ī	bite	ô	paw	ŏŏ	took	ûr	urge
ā	pay	ĕ	pet	îr	pier	ôr	core	ŏŏr	lure	zh	vision
âr	care	ē	be	ŏ	pot	oi	boy	ōō	boot	ə	about, item
ä	father	ĭ	pit	ō	toe	ou	out	ŭ	cut		

work off

1. To get rid of something through effort or work: *I started to run two miles a day in order to work off some weight. I owed them a large debt, but I worked it off by painting their house.*
2. To use something or someone as a foundation or source of energy to perform work: *This laptop works off batteries. I worked off my strengths as a writer to convince the newspaper to hire me.*

work on

1. To exert oneself physically or mentally in order to do, make, or accomplish something: *The author is working on a new set of short stories.*
2. To practice something in order to acquire or polish a skill: *You need to work on your handwriting.*
3. To effect a desired result on something: *The medicine works on coughs. This joke never fails to work on him.*
4. To exert an influence on someone: *Her friends worked on her to join the group.*

work out

1. To remove or eliminate something from something by repeated, continuous, or applied effort: *We tried for hours to work the stain out of the shirt. No matter how hard we tried, we couldn't work the knot out of the rope. I worked out the tangles with a comb.*
2. To solve or resolve something by work or effort: *The mathematician worked out the answer over several days. We have our disagreements, but we always work them out.*
3. To formulate or develop something: *The lawyers worked out a strategy for the trial. We have no plans yet; we still need to work them out.*
4. To discharge or arrange to discharge some obligation or debt: *I worked out my high phone bill with the creditors.*
5. To prove successful, effective, or satisfactory: *The new strategy may not work out.*
6. To have some specified result: *The ratio works out to an odd number. It worked out that everyone left on the same train.*
7. To engage in strenuous exercise for physical conditioning: *You look very trim and fit; have you been working out? I work out at the gym twice a week.*
8. To subject some part of the body to exertion for physical conditioning: *Sit-ups work out the abdominal muscles.*
9. To exhaust or deplete something. Used chiefly in the passive: *After a hundred years in operation, the mine was worked out.*
10. **work out of** To have some place as a central office or work location: *I work out of my house.*

work over

1. To do something for a second time; rework something: *The studio requested that we work the film over and give it a happy ending.*
2. To dominate one's opponent in a contest, conflict, or competition: *Our team really worked their team over in the final game of the season. We need to get more defensive, or they'll work us over.*
3. To criticize, scold, or ridicule someone harshly: *The sergeant will*

work you over if you don't stand at attention.

4. SLANG To inflict severe physical damage on someone or something; beat up someone or something: *If you don't do what the gang leader tells you to do, he'll work you over.*

work through

1. To succeed in resolving something through effort: *I worked through the problems I was having with my teacher, and now I'm doing better in class.*
2. To move something or someone slowly and laboriously through something: *The bodyguards worked the politician through the crowd.*
3. To proceed or progress slowly and laboriously through something: *The explorers worked through the underbrush. The fender of the car was scraping against the tire and slowly worked through the rubber.*

work to

1. To follow some plan or schedule: *They worked to a timetable.*
2. To cause something or someone to reach some level through repeated, continuous, or applied effort: *The rock singer worked the audience to a frenzy.*
3. To reach some level through repeated, continuous, or applied effort: *The baseball team worked to a three-run lead.*

work toward

1. To exert oneself in order to achieve some goal: *I enrolled in college last year and I am working toward a degree in medicine.*
2. To move something or someone in the direction of something or someone by exerting effort: *I caught a large fish on my line and slowly worked it toward the boat.*

work up

1. To arouse the emotions of someone or something; excite someone or something: *The skillful politician worked up the crowd. What I read in the newspaper today really worked me up.*
2. To increase one's skill, responsibility, efficiency, or status to some level through work: *I'm increasing my exercise routine and am slowly working up to 30 sit-ups a day.*
3. **work up to** To intensify gradually to some state: *The film works up to a thrilling climax.*
4. To develop or produce something by mental or physical effort: *I worked up my appetite while mowing the lawn. The doctors worked up a patient profile before making their diagnosis.*

◆ **worm** (wûrm)

wormed (wûrmd), **worming** (wûr′mĭng), **worms** (wûrmz)

worm into

1. To introduce or insert oneself into some position or condition by subtle or artful means: *He wormed into the role of director by trickery and guile.*

ă	pat	är	car	ī	bite	ô	paw	ŏŏ	took	ûr	urge
ā	pay	ĕ	pet	îr	pier	ôr	core	ŏŏr	lure	zh	vision
âr	care	ē	be	ŏ	pot	oi	boy	ōō	boot	ə	about,
ä	father	ĭ	pit	ō	toe	ou	out	ŭ	cut		item

2. To introduce or insert someone or something into some position or condition by subtle or artful means: *She wormed her sister into the department without anyone realizing it. I wormed the controversial statement into the article without any of the other editors knowing about it.*

worm out of

1. To elicit something from someone by artful or devious means: *The clever police officers wormed a confession out of the suspect.*
2. To extricate oneself from some situation by artful or devious means: *You can't worm out of this situation, so don't even try.*

◆ **wrangle** (răng′gəl)
wrangled (răng′gəld), **wrangling** (răng′gə-lĭng), **wrangles** (răng′gəlz)

wrangle with

1. To be strenuously engaged with some problem, task, or undertaking: *I have been wrangling with this problem for days and still cannot solve it.*
2. To quarrel noisily or angrily with someone: *I couldn't sleep because my brothers were wrangling with each other all night. John is wrangling with his roommate over the phone bill.*

◆ **wrap** (răp)
wrapped (răpt), **wrapping** (răp′ĭng), **wraps** (răps)

wrap around

1. To clasp, fold, or coil something about someone or something: *She wrapped her arms around his neck and hugged him.*
2. To coil or twist about something or someone: *The flag wrapped around the pole.*
3. To continue automatically to be entered on a new line of text if there is too much text to fit on one line. Used of word-processing texts: *The input to early computer text editors did not wrap around, so you had to hit a carriage return at the end of every line.*

wrap in

1. To cover, envelop, or encase something or someone by folding or coiling something about: *I wrapped myself in a blanket and sat by the fire.*
2. To enclose and secure something in some material: *We wrapped the package in newspaper and bound it with string.*

wrap up

1. To cover, envelop, or encase something or someone, as by folding or coiling about: *I wrapped the baby up in a blanket. The nurse wrapped up my ankle with a bandage.*
2. To enclose something, especially in paper, and fasten it: *We wrapped the birthday presents up. I wrapped up the sandwich and took it with me.*
3. To put warm clothing on someone: *My mother wrapped me up in a parka and snow pants. The nanny wrapped up the children and sent them to the park.*
4. To bring something to a conclusion; settle something finally or successfully: *The two executives met and wrapped up the deal. Let's wrap this meeting up before dinner.*

5. To summarize something; recapitulate something: *He wrapped the proposal up in the final paragraph. That statement wraps up our sentiments.*
6. To come to a conclusion; finish: *As soon as this project wraps up, I'm going on vacation.*
7. **wrap up in** To immerse or absorb someone completely in something. Used chiefly in the passive: *I tried to talk to her after the meeting, but she was wrapped up in a conversation.*
8. **wrap up in** To involve someone in something. Used chiefly in the passive: *We were shocked when we learned that our neighbors were wrapped up in criminal activities.*
9. Sports To pin or tackle someone or something: *The wrestler wrapped his opponent up. The lineman wrapped up the punter for a 15-yard loss.*

◆ **wrest** (rĕst)

wrested (rĕs′tĭd), **wresting** (rĕs′tĭng), **wrests** (rĕsts)

wrest from

1. To obtain something from someone or something by pulling with violent twisting movements: *I wrested the hammer from his fist.*
2. To usurp or obtain possession of something forcefully from someone or something: *The duke wrested power from the monarchy.*
3. To extract something from someone or something by or as if by force, twisting, or persistent effort: *In class I struggled to wrest the meaning from an obscure poem.*

wrest off

To obtain or remove something from someone or something by pulling with violent twisting movements: *The thief wrested off the hood ornament from the car. I wrested the car keys off him.*

wrest out

1. To obtain something from someone or something by pulling with violent twisting movements: *The farmer dug into the soil and wrested out a fresh turnip. The bullies wrested the book out of the little boy's hands and ran off with it.*
2. To extract something from someone or something by or as if by force, twisting, or persistent effort: *I was finally able to wrest out some meaning from the jumbled essay. The police wrested a confession out of the suspect.*
3. To escape from something by pulling with violent twisting movements: *The cat wrested out of my arms and jumped to the floor.*

◆ **wrestle** (rĕs′əl)

wrestled (rĕs′əld), **wrestling** (rĕs′lĭng), **wrestles** (rĕs′əlz)

wrestle with

1. To contend with someone by grappling and attempting to throw or immobilize one's opponent: *I*

ă	pat	är	car	ī	bite	ô	paw	o͝o	took	ûr	urge
ā	pay	ĕ	pet	îr	pier	ôr	core	o͝or	lure	zh	vision
âr	care	ē	be	ŏ	pot	oi	boy	o͞o	boot	ə	about,
ä	father	ĭ	pit	ō	toe	ou	out	ŭ	cut		item

wrestled with my cousin in the living room until my mom ordered us to go outside.

2. To contend or struggle with something or someone: *The students wrestled with the math problem all afternoon.*
3. To strive in an effort to master something: *The thieves must wrestle with the guilt that weighs on them.*

◆ **wriggle** (rĭg′əl)

wriggled (rĭg′əld), **wriggling** (rĭg′ə-lĭng), **wriggles** (rĭg′əlz)

wriggle out

1. To free oneself from something by turning or twisting the body with sinuous writhing motions: *I tried to pick up the cat, but it wriggled out of my grasp and ran away.*
2. To extricate oneself by sly or subtle means from some situation; worm one's way out of some situation: *He always wriggles out of trouble by placing the blame on someone else.*

◆ **wring** (rĭng)

wrung (rŭng), **wringing** (rĭng′ĭng), **wrings** (rĭngz)

wring from

1. To extract some liquid by twisting and compressing something: *I wrung the water from the cloth and laid it out to dry.*
2. To obtain or extract some information by applying force or pressure to someone: *My mother finally wrung the truth from us, and we told her everything.*

wring out

1. To twist, squeeze, or compress something, especially so as to extract liquid: *I wrung out the wet towel. Wring the clothes out before you hang them on the line.*
2. To extract some liquid by twisting or compressing something: *Wring out the suds from the dishcloth when you're done washing the dishes. She twisted her hair to wring the rain out of it.*
3. To obtain or extract some information by applying force or pressure to someone; extort something from someone: *We can wring out the story from him if we question him long enough. The prosecutor wrung the truth out of the reluctant witness.*

◆ **write** (rīt)

wrote (rōt), **written** (rĭt′n), **writing** (rī′tĭng), **writes** (rīts)

write away

To send a written request: *I wrote away for a replacement part when my vacuum cleaner broke down.*

write down

1. To set something down in writing: *I wrote down all my thoughts in a journal. If you remember the address, write it down before you forget it again!*
2. To reduce something in rank, value, or price: *The store is writing down all obsolete inventory. When the tickets didn't sell, we wrote them down to half price.*
3. To disparage something in writing. Used chiefly in the passive: *The movie was written down in all the newspapers.*
4. To write in a conspicuously simple or condescending style: *The author wrote down to the unsophisticated audience.*

write in

1. To cast a vote by inserting some name not listed on a ballot: *The members of the minority party wrote in their candidate's name on their ballots. Write me in for mayor in the next election!*
2. To insert something in a text or document: *I wrote in a disclaimer at the end of the article. You forgot to cite your sources for the paper, so I wrote them in for you.*
3. To insert a character or scene into a narrative work: *The editor insisted that the author write in a happy ending to the story. I revised the play and wrote some new characters in.*
4. To communicate with some organization by mail: *Please write in with a completed entry form.*

write off

1. To cancel something from accounts as a loss: *The bank has written off the account balance as an unrecoverable debt. After efforts to collect the payment failed, we decided to write it off. We wrote the trip off as a business expense.*
2. To consider something a loss or failure: *We wrote off the first day of our vacation because it rained all day. The doctors wrote him off when a treatment couldn't be found for his illness.*
3. To deem someone or something inconsequential and disregard them: *I wouldn't write off the option of going to nursing school. Critics wrote the singer off as a novelty act.*
4. To send a written request: *I wrote off to the university for an application.*

write out

1. To express or compose something in writing: *I wrote out a check for $70. It's easier to learn new words if you write them out and memorize them.*
2. To write something in full or expanded form: *The teacher wrote out the Latin abbreviations on the board and explained their meanings. The secretary took the shorthand notes and wrote them out.*
3. To delete or exclude something or someone from a narrative work or record: *In the revised version of the script, the playwright wrote out the character of the detective. The author wrote the scene out of the novel. Radical thinkers tend to be written out of history books.*

write up

1. To write a report or description of something, as for publication: *The scientist wrote up her discovery in a medical journal. I wrote the arts festival up for a local newspaper.*
2. To compose a finished document from some set of notes: *The clerk wrote up the minutes of the meeting. The professor wrote her lectures up into a book.*
3. To draft some type of document: *My lawyer wrote up a contract spelling out my rights and respon-*

ă	pat	är	car	ī	bite	ô	paw	o͝o	took	ûr	urge
ā	pay	ĕ	pet	îr	pier	ôr	core	o͝or	lure	zh	vision
âr	care	ē	be	ŏ	pot	oi	boy	o͞o	boot	ə	about,
ä	father	ĭ	pit	ō	toe	ou	out	ŭ	cut		item

sibilities. I forgot to write the questionnaire up before the interviews.

4. To write something to completion, especially quickly or easily: *This morning after breakfast I was inspired and wrote up a little story about dragons. Once our script idea was approved, we went back to the office and wrote it up.*

5. To report someone in writing, as for breaking the law: *The police officer wrote me up for speeding. The cop wrote up the pedestrian for jaywalking.*

6. To overstate the value of assets: *The company wrote up its real estate assets in order to avoid a long-term loss of resources. The new accountant looked at the figures in the ledger and realized that the previous accountant had written them up.*

7. To bring something, as a journal, up to date: *The bookkeeper came in once a month to write up the account books. Once you update an invoice to the ledger, the computer automatically writes it up in the sales journal.*

◆ **wuss** (wŏŏs)

wussed (wŏŏst), **wussing** (wŏŏs′ĭng), **wusses** (wŏŏs′ĭz)

wuss out

SLANG

To withdraw from a commitment or course of action because of cowardice or insecurity: *I was going to go into the haunted house, but then I wussed out and stayed in the car.*

XYZ

◆ **x** (ĕks)

x'ed (ĕkst), **x'ing** (ĕk′sĭng), **x's** (ĕk′sĭz)

x out

1. To make X-shaped marks on something to indicate that it should be deleted, canceled, or ignored: *The editor will x out any offensive lines in your letter before publishing it. I wrote my number on the sheet and then, thinking again, I x'ed it out.*
2. To remove someone or something from a list or record: *Many details of the Spanish civil war have been x'ed out of the history books to make room for more recent events. My name should be on the admissions list unless they have decided to x me out.*

◆ **yak** *or* **yack** (yăk)

yakked *or* **yacked** (yăkt), **yakking** *or* **yacking** (yăk′ĭng), **yaks** *or* **yacks** (yăks)

yak at *or* **yack at**

SLANG

1. To talk at length to someone without regard for his or her interest: *My neighbors yakked at me about their new dog for over an hour.*
2. To nag someone noisily or peevishly: *Her parents yakked at her for getting home so late.*

yak up *or* **yack up**

SLANG

To eject some contents of the stomach by vomiting: *He was so sick today that he yakked up his lunch. The dog ate some leather and then yakked it up.*

◆ **yap** (yăp)

yapped (yăpt), **yapping** (yăp′ĭng), **yaps** (yăps)

yap at

SLANG

1. To bark sharply or shrilly at someone or something: *The sheepdog yapped at the stray sheep.*
2. To make a sharp, often hostile or scolding remark to someone: *The batter yapped at the pitcher after he was hit by a pitch.*

◆ **yearn** (yûrn)

yearned (yûrnd), **yearning** (yûr′nĭng), **yearns** (yûrnz)

yearn for

To have a strong, often melancholy desire for someone or something: *The sailors out at sea yearned for their families.*

yearn over

To feel deep pity, sympathy, or tenderness for someone or something:

ă	pat	är	car	ī	bite	ô	paw	ŏŏ	took	ûr	urge
ā	pay	ĕ	pet	îr	pier	ôr	core	ŏŏr	lure	zh	vision
âr	care	ē	be	ŏ	pot	oi	boy	ōō	boot	ə	about,
ä	father	ĭ	pit	ō	toe	ou	out	ŭ	cut		item

The entire nation yearned over the lives lost in the accident.

◆ **yell** (yĕl)

yelled (yĕld), **yelling** (yĕl′ĭng), **yells** (yĕlz)

yell at

To shout at someone or something in anger, often at length: *The coach yelled at the team after they lost the game.*

yell out

1. To shout something loudly and generally; announce something: *Audience members yelled out song requests for the band to play. If you know the answer to the question, yell it out.*
2. To utter a loud strong cry: *I yelled out when I stubbed my toe.*

◆ **yield** (yēld)

yielded (yēl′dĭd), **yielding** (yēl′dĭng), **yields** (yēldz)

yield to

1. To give oneself up to someone, as in defeat: *The platoon chose to fight to the end and would not yield to the enemy.*
2. To give way to some pressure or force: *The door yielded to a gentle push.*
3. To give way to some argument, persuasion, influence, or entreaty: *I'm dieting, but I sometimes yield to temptation and eat a cookie.*
4. To give up one's place, as to one that is superior: *The moderator opened the conference and then yielded to the chairperson.*

yield up

To sacrifice or concede something: *The civilians yielded their town up to the invaders without a fight. I sometimes dream of yielding up the comfort of modern society to live in a remote cabin deep in the woods. The boxer held the heavyweight title for three years and then yielded it up to a young contender.*

◆ **zero** (zîr′ō)

zeroed (zîr′ōd), **zeroing** (zîr′ō-ĭng), **zeroes** (zîr′ōz)

zero in

1. To aim or focus something, such as a weapon or telescope, toward a specific target or location: *The enemy spotted the approaching aircraft and zeroed in their missiles. Zero the telescopes in on the watchtower.*
2. To identify with increasing accuracy a property of something, especially its location: *We are finally zeroing in on the location of the smuggling ring.*
3. To adjust the aim or sight of a weapon by repeated firings: *The soldiers fired a few rounds in order to zero in their rifles. I zeroed the gun in at 100 yards.*
4. **zero in on** To direct one's gaze or attention to something: *The children zeroed in on the display of toys in the store window.*

zero out

1. To reset something, such as a counter or clock, to zero: *The timekeeper forgot to zero out the stopwatch in between sprints. I zeroed the odometer out and measured the length of the road.*
2. To reduce some quantity to zero: *This final payment will zero out your balance on the loan. I called*

the bank and zeroed out my account.

3. To cut off the funding for something, such as a government program: *The new administration is planning to zero out subsidies and benefits for illegal aliens. Our social assistance program had funding until the government zeroed it out of the budget.*

◆ **zip** (zĭp)

zipped (zĭpt), **zipping** (zĭp′ĭng), **zips** (zĭps)

zip by

1. To pass quickly, as of a moving object or an interval of time: *The summer zipped by so fast that we didn't get the chance to do half of the things we planned to.*
2. To pass someone or something quickly: *The cars zipped by the people on the side of the road.*
3. To pay a brief visit: *My friends zipped by for a quick lunch.*

zip through

1. To accomplish or proceed with something swiftly and energetically: *She zipped through college in just three years.*
2. To read something quickly and with ease: *I zipped through five chapters of* Great Expectations *in less than an hour.*
3. To move rapidly through something: *The bird zipped through the air to its nest.*

◆ **zone** (zōn)

zoned (zōnd), **zoning** (zō′nĭng), **zones** (zōnz)

zone for

To restrict some section of an area or territory to some specific use: *That area used to be farmland until the city zoned it for industrial use. That entire block is zoned for residences, so you can't open a business there.*

zone off

To restrict or reserve a section of some area or territory: *The city zoned off these blocks for commercial use. The police zoned the town hall off from vehicular traffic.*

zone out

SLANG

1. To lose concentration or become inattentive: *I sensed the class was zoning out, so I started talking louder.*
2. To lose awareness of one's surroundings: *An hour after I took the cough syrup, I lay back in bed and zoned out.*
3. To refuse to pay attention to someone or something; ignore someone or something: *The athlete zoned out the jeering crowd and made the free-throw shot. Every time I try to give you advice, you zone out everything I say.*
4. To cause someone or something to lose awareness of one's

ă	pat	är	car	ī	bite	ô	paw	o͝o	took	ûr	urge
ā	pay	ĕ	pet	îr	pier	ôr	core	o͝or	lure	zh	vision
âr	care	ē	be	ŏ	pot	oi	boy	o͞o	boot	ə	about,
ä	father	ĭ	pit	ō	toe	ou	out	ŭ	cut		item

surroundings: *The medication that I take zones me out.*

5. To exclude someone or something by restricting a section of an area or territory: *Farmers complain that the government has zoned them out of the best farmland. The city zoned out adult entertainment companies.*

◆ **zonk** (zŏngk)
zonked (zŏngkt), **zonking** (zŏng′kĭng), **zonks** (zŏngks)

zonk out
SLANG
1. To go to sleep, especially due to exhaustion; conk out: *I was so tired that I zonked out without even taking off my shoes.*
2. To lose consciousness or awareness: *The driver zonked out behind the wheel and ran off the road.*
3. To cause someone or something to lose consciousness or awareness: *Even a small dose of this cough syrup can zonk you out.*

◆ **zoom** (zo͞om)
zoomed (zo͞omd), **zooming** (zo͞om′ĭng), **zooms** (zo͞omz)

zoom by
1. To pass quickly, as of a moving object or an interval of time: *The hours zoom by when you're doing a job you enjoy.*
2. To pass someone or something quickly: *He zoomed by us in a car and didn't even stop to see if we needed a ride!*

zoom in
1. To simulate movement toward an object with or as if with a zoom lens: *The director zoomed in on a face in the crowd. The shot zooms in through a window to a family sitting at a table.*
2. To increase the apparent size of part of an image of something in order to view it more closely, as when using a magnifying lens: *The camera can't zoom in far enough to capture their expressions. Zoom in on this part of the document too see whether the text lines up with the illustration.*
3. To enter rapidly: *The firefighting helicopter zoomed in to pick up more water.*
4. **zoom in on** To narrow and intensify the examination of someone or something: *In our presentation we zoomed in on the financial problems facing the company.*

zoom off
To leave or drive off rapidly: *They just zoomed off without saying goodbye. I zoomed off in my sports car.*

zoom out
1. To simulate movement away from an object with or as if with a zoom lens: *The camera zoomed out from the house to reveal the vast landscape.*
2. To decrease the apparent size of part of an image of something, especially to view it as if from a greater distance or from a wider perspective: *This computer software allows you to zoom out of the document to see the entire page.*
3. To exit rapidly: *We got dressed and zoomed out to the party.*